# Pioneer Families

of

# Orange County

# New York

Compiled by

## Martha and Bill

## Reamy

HERITAGE BOOKS
2007

**HERITAGE BOOKS**
*AN IMPRINT OF HERITAGE BOOKS, INC.*


**Books, CDs, and more—Worldwide**

For our listing of thousands of titles see our website
at
www.HeritageBooks.com



Published 2007 by
HERITAGE BOOKS, INC.
Publishing Division
65 East Main Street
Westminster, Maryland 21157-5026

International Standard Book Number: 978-1-58549-601-4

# TABLE OF CONTENTS

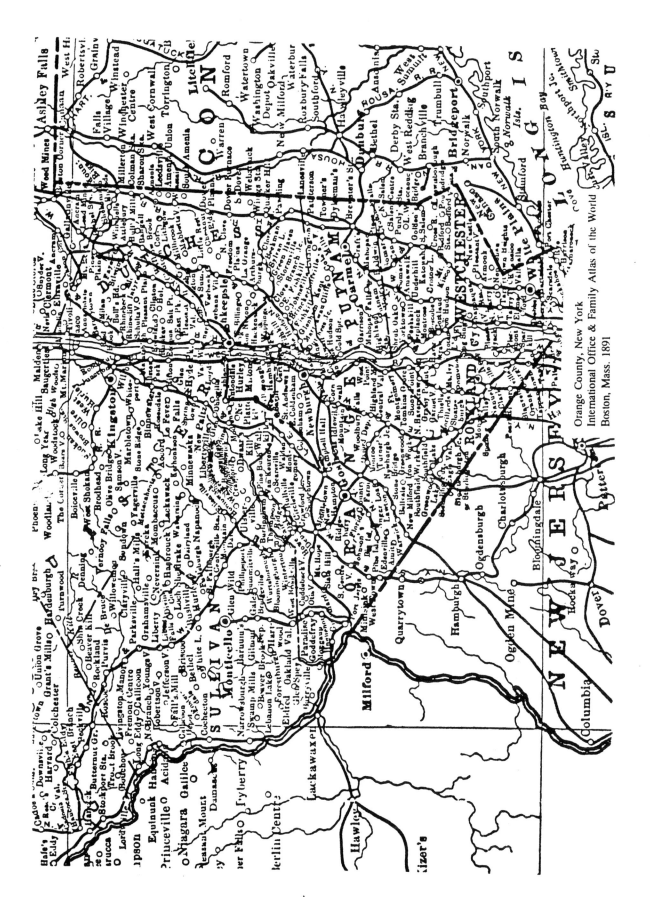

Orange County, New York
International Office & Family Atlas of the World
Boston, Mass. 1891

# PREFACE

This volume is intended to be the first of a series on early settlers of New York counties. The project was undertaken with the intention of bringing some order to the genealogical research chaos found in the state of New York. Fellow researchers have frequently confided to me their dread of searching a New York ancestor after finding lines in the orderly records of New England. The manner of record keeping, with few published town records compared to New England, leads to frustration.

I have long been fascinated with turn-of-the-century local histories--sometimes referred to as mugbooks. Their wealth of genealogical information, undocumented and unindexed tomes, they are available in limited editions, and frustrating for researchers to use.

In this volume I have taken a number of such sources and combined the lineages found therein. It is by no means complete, nor does it cover every such volume ever published regarding Orange County, New York. In cases where information found disagrees among volumes, conflicting data has been added in brackets [].

Families are presented in alphabetical order by surname. Each family is preceded by at least one family member's name printed in bold type. Each person listed in bold type is the subject of a biography in one of the local histories cited. [P] designates a portrait of that person will be found accompanying his or her biography. Also at the head of each family entry is the reference and page number where the data was found. Within the body of each family writeup, each individual whose line is carried beyond their first appearance, their name appears in all capital letters.

The lineages presented here are for the most part from undocumented sources and should be checked against primary records. This information should be used as clues for further investigation, but in some cases they may be the only surviving references available. No attempt was made to correct the spelling of names; all are as they were found.

Many of the books used in this work, a list of which follows, can be obtained through the Latter Day Saints local Family History Libraries, through rentals of books from various genealogical rental and society libraries, can be found reprinted, or can be ordered on microfiche through University Microforms Inc. in Ann Arbor, Michigan.

Persons researching the area of Orange County, New York are encouraged to subscribe to the excellent newsletter published by the Orange County Historical Society in Goshen, New York.

# REFERENCES

A - *History of Orange County, New York: With Illustrations & Biographical Sketches of Many of its Pioneers and Prominent Men*, Edward Manning Ruttenber & L. H. Clark, et al. (Philadelphia: Everts & Peck, 1881)

AA - *American Ancestry, Giving the Name & Descent, in the Male Line, of Americans Whose Ancestors Settled in the United States Previous to the Declaration of Independence, A. D. 1776*, originally published, Joel Munsell's Sons, reprinted Baltimore, Genealogical Publishing Co., 1968.

C - *The Early Records of the First Presbyterian Church at Goshen, New York, from 1767 to 1885*, Charles C. Coleman, Goshen, NY, 1934.

D - *The American Descendants of Chretien DuBois of Wicres, France*, William Heidgerd for the DuBois Family Association, Huguenot Historical Society, New Paltz, NY, 1968.

E - *An Outline History of Orange County, with an Enumeration of the Names of its Towns, Villages, Rivers, Creeks, . . .*, Samuel W. Eager, Newburgh: S. T. Callahan, 1846-7.

GFM - *Inscriptions of German Reformed Cemetery at Montgomery, Orange County, New York* copied & compiled by Lila James Roney, 1925.

H - *The History of Orange County New York*, edited by Russell Headley, Van Dusen & Elns, Middletown, NY, 1908.

LDS Ancestral File - Lineages contributed to the Latter Day Saints Church and found as computerized CD-ROM records in local Family History Libraries.

N - *Newburgh, Her Institutions, Industries and Leading Citizens* by John J. Nutt, Newburgh: Ritchie & Hull, Proprietors *Newburgh Journal*, 1891.

NC - *Centennial Chronicle: 100 Years of the Newburgh Story, With Illustrations & Historical Sketches, 1865-1965*, edited by Helen Ver Nooy Gearn (Newburgh, NY, 1965)

NH - *Orange County New York, A Narrative History*, Almet S. Moffatt, Washingtonville, NY, 1928.

SW - *The Swartwout Chronicles 1338-1889 & the Ketelhuyn Chronicles 1451-1899*, Arthur James Weise, New York, 1899.

T - *History of the Minisink Country*, Horace E. Twichell of Port Jervis, NY, 1912.

TN - *History of the Town of Newburgh*, E. M. Ruttenber, Newburgh: E. M. Ruttenber & Co., Printers, 1859.

U - *Ulster County, New York Probate Records in the Office of the Surrogate, at Kingston, N.Y. . . .*, Two Volumes, Gustave Anjou, New York, 1906.

W - *Walden and Its Environs With Pen and Camera*, Wallkill Valley Publishing Association, Walden, NY, 1914.

# ABBREVIATIONS USED

atty. = attorney
b. = born
c. = circa
Co. = county/company
d. = died
D.A. = District Attorney
d/o = daughter of
grad. = graduated
inf. = infantry
j.p. = justice of the peace
L.I. = Long Island
m. = married
prop. = proprietor
Ref. = Reformed
regt. = regiment
res. = resident/residence
Rev. = Reverend/Revolutionary War
s/o = son of
twp. = township
Univ. = university
unm. = unmarried

Standard US Postal abbreviations were used for states.

**ABRAHAM, JOHN**                                    U2-40-1
house carpenter of Newburgh.

In his will, dated 15 Aug. 1785, **JOHN ABRAHAM** names his
    wife Anna and children:
Andrew.
Major, a minor in 1785.
Susannah.
Henry.
James.

George Merriett, beloved friend, appointed executor. Will
proved 11 July 1789, Lewis Donnovan of Newburgh, Schoolmaster, Amasa Sprague, Henery [sic] Evens & Lewis Donnovan.

**ACKLEY, JOHN T. [P]**                             A-562-3
of Goshen.                                           & C-47

DANIEL ACKLEY[1] m. Miss --- Grovesnor of an English fami-
    ly, and had:
1799, AUGUSTUS A.
Hiram, of IL.
George.
Catharine, m. Robert Collins.
Jane.
Hannah, m. Thomas Bellamy.

AUGUSTUS A. ACKLEY[2], s/o Daniel, b. 1799 VT; to Orange
    Co. as young man; m. c. 1821 Maria d/o Edward Mapes, b.
    1801, d. c. 1863. Mapes family were early Goshen settlers.
    AUGUSTUS was a tailor, farmer & merchant; res. Sugar-
    Loaf & d. there 12 April 1866, also res. Chester. Children:
William P. of Goshen.
James H., dec'd.
1825 April 3, JOHN T.
Joanna, m. Hayden Wheeler of Middletown, NY.
Daniel E.
Wycliffe W.
Hannah, m. J. W. Riker
Augustus.
Henry.
Thomas.
Mary.

JOHN T. ACKLEY[3], s/o Augustus[2], b. Sugar Loaf; clerked in
    Newburgh and Chester; 1845 to NY, bookkeeper, 1849 to
    San Francisco, CA and owned hardware business. 1865 to
    Goshen; m. 23 June 1858, Sarah J., d/o Cornelius Westervelt
    of NY City whose ancestors were early NY settlers, and had:
Minnie A., m. 18 Oct. 1883, James Demarest of NY City. Res.
    Goshen.
Edward H.
Jennie M.
Edith.
John.

**ADAMS, LEWIS D.**                                 H-771

LEWIS D. ADAMS, b. Sussex, NJ, 15 June 1839; farmer
until age 18 and took up tinner's trade. 1862 enlisted in 124th
Regt., Co. F, NY Vol. Inf. In business in Warwick at end of the
war, 6 years later to Florida, Orange Co., operated hardware
store until 1898. He m. Marietta Ackerman of Warwick 28
Sept. 1870. She d. 24 Dec. 1900.

**ADERTON, THOMAS J.**                              H-771

THOMAS ADERTON[1], sailor, from NY City to Orange Co.
1828. His son, Capt. L. Aderton[2] m. Isabella Swain. He was a
sailor & farmer. They had a son:
    THOMAS J. ADERTON[3], merchant, postmaster, town clerk
& farmer at Savilton, town of Newburgh, where he was b. on
the homestead in 1847. He m. Mary Lockwood & had 2
children, one a son A.L., clerk at Newbergh Post Office, and a
dau. (unnamed).

**ADOLPH, JOSEPH H.**                               H-771-?

JOSEPH H. ADOLPH, b. in Highland Falls, 1857; in meat
business there since 1886. Res. 2 years in Milwaukee & 6 years
in CT, returned to Highland Falls. Catholic. He m. Mary
Champion of Hartford, CT & has 2 sons & 1 dau.

**AHRENS, JOHN [P]**                                W-87

JOHN AHERNS, b. Giehle, Province of Hanover, Germany 23
    Oct. 1865, was s/o John & Kathryne Ahrens. To America
    1884 in wholesale grocery business with an uncle. He runs
    the feed, coal & lumber business formerly owned by James
    Todd since 1892. In 1890 he m. Ida F. Ahrens of Jersey
    City, and had:
Kathryne.
Elvena.
Mary Elizabeth.

**ALEXANDER, GEORGE B.**                            H-772
of Newburgh.                                         CN-15

Duncan Alexander, brother of William, "familiarly known in
the history of the Revolution as Lord Stirling," was an early
settler & listed in the Newburgh Town Directory for 1750.

HARVEY ALEXANDER[1] m. Amanda Kernaghan and had:
1843, Nov. 5, GEORGE B.
Joseph K., sheriff of Orange Co.

GEORGE B. ALEXANDER[2], s/o Harvey, b. village of Corn-
    wall, Orange Co. Moved with parents to Little Britain in
    1844. Learned carpenter's trade with father, 1886 to CA,
    sheriff of Orange Co. on his return after 1891. 1895 m.
    Elvira S. Scott, d/o William J. & Maria (Newkirk) Scott, and
    niece of David A. Scott & moved to Campbell Hall, where
    **GEORGE** was associated with brother Joseph in general

store, postmaster. **GEORGE** & Elvira have one son, Harvey, age 10.

---

**ALLEN, DAVID**                                    A-661

of Minisink, well known as a cancer doctor; had children:
James.
Samuel.
Lathrop.
Anna.
Maria.
Gabriel.
Irena.
William.
Joseph.
Phebe.
Henry B., newspaper correspondent of Westtown.

---

**ALSOP, JOHN**                                    A-214

**JOHN ALSOP**[1] settled in New Windsor with his brother-in-law, Joseph Sackett Jr. in 1724/25. He purchased land of Peter Matthews. **JOHN**, father of John Jr.[2] of "Revolutionary War history."

---

**ANDREWS, SAMUEL**                                H-772

**SAMUEL ANDREWS**[2], of the Walden Knife Works, b. England 1858, s/o William Andrews[1] & Sarah Harrison, who came to America when **SAMUEL** was an infant. **SAMUEL**[2] m. (1st) Clara Ashbury & had Ethel & Alice. He m. (2d) Alfa Mussey.

---

**ANTHONY, WALTER CASE**                           H-772

of Newburgh.

THEODORE VAN WYCK ANTHONY m. Mary H. Case and had **WALTER CASE ANTHONY**, b. Fishkill, NY, 24 Aug. 1842. He grad. Union College 1864, read law in office of David F. Gedney & later Stephen W. Fullerton. D.A. 1877 & 1880.

---

**ARKILLS, CHARLES W.**                            H-773

DARWIN ARKILLS[1], b. Scotchtown, Orange Co. m. Minerva Gray of Thompsonville, and had:
Laura N.
Fred J.
1867, Oct. 4, **CHARLES W.**

**CHARLES W. ARKILLS**[2], s/o Darwin[1], b. Fallsburgh, Sullivan Co.; decorator & painter, with Ontario & Western RR in Newburgh; later at Kilmes Wire Works, Newburgh. Member Ref. Dutch Church at Grahamsville; now res. near Campbell Hall with his father. He m. Julietta Rose of Grahamsville, Sullivan Co., 20 June 1888, and had:
Laura.
Lelia.

Sadie L.
Viola K.
John I. C.

---

**ARMSTRONG, SAMUEL**                              H-773

--- ARMSTRONG[1], farmer, m. Elizabeth J. Shafer, both of Crawford, Orange Co. Their son:
   **SAMUEL ARMSTRONG**[2], b. Thompson's Ridge, Orange Co. 14 May 1878, pharmacist; m. Emma Faith McNeal of Mongtomery, Orange Co.

---

**ASHLEY, DR. MAURICE CAVILEER**                   H-773-74

**DR. ASHLEY**, superintendent of the Middletown State Homeopathic Hospital since 1902; b. Port Republic, NJ, 3 July 1863; 1884 attendant in the asylum in Trenton, NJ & after 2 years to Middletown.
   Studied at Hahnemann Medical College at Philadelphia, grad. 1892. He m. 30 Aug. 1888, Harriet Meade of Johnson, Orange Co. & has two daus. in early teens. **DR. ASHLEY** served in the medical dept. of the National Guard for 12 years & as surgeon of the 1st NY Regt. (1907).

---

**AU, CHARLES**                                    H-774

CHARLES AU[1] (dec'd.), carpenter on J. Pierpont Morgan farm, m. Ellen McGrisken, and had:
CHARLES AU[2], b. 1877 on Morgan farm in town of Highland. Trained as a barber & employed at US Cadet Barracks, West Point. Catholic. He m. Katherine Powers & has 2 sons & 1 dau.

---

**AYRES, CLARENCE**                                H-774, CN-34

**CLARENCE'S** father was a sailor on a whaling vessel and served during the Civil War.
   **CLARENCE** b. Town & village of Mt. Hope, 27 Nov. 1875, with family to Middletown at age 9. Printer, age 17 telephone lineman at Middletown 6 years; Newburgh 2 years; 1904 to Warwick. He m. Anna Coolton of Goshen. Congregational Church members. They have one dau., Frances, b. Dec. 1889.

An EBENEZER B. AYRES was a worker in clocks & watches early in Newburgh.

---

**BAILEY, FRED**                                   H-775

merchant of Otisville.

FRED b. 4 June 1854. Studied at Ellicottville, Cattaraugus Co. & was employed there by the American Express Co. for 9 years. Dec. 1892 to Otisville, Orange Co., to Newburgh 1894 in wholesale grocery business 1 year, returned to Otisville.
   4 Sept. 1876 **FRED** m. Chloe Mary Vaughan of Ellicottville. Members of Otisville Presbyterian Church; he served Tenth Separate Co., National Guard. No living children.

**BAILEY, JONATHAN**  A-679-80
**C-13-14, 22, 53, 64, 100, 102, 110, 112-14**  LDS Anc. File

**JONATHAN BAILEY**[1] was b. 28 June 1745, Southhold L.I.; to Orange Co. during the Rev. War, when he served with Gen. Washington. After the war he went to Goshen and 1777 to Ridgebury; m. 11 Sept. 1783, Keturah Dunning [Conkling], (widow of Jacob Dunning), nee Jackson. Keturah, b. 1749, d. 29 March 1832. **JONATHAN** had another wife, Phoebe Horton, he d. at Ridgebury, Orange Co., NY 17 Feb. 1814. They had:

1784, Aug. 29, JONATHAN JR.
1787, May 27, Christine, m. Nathan Parrott, d. 3 Nov. 1865.
1789, May 24, Lavine (Laverna), m. Braddock Decker; d. 27 March 1863.
1792, Sept. 3, Phoebe, m. Samuel Parrot; d. 2 Aug. 1852.

**JONATHAN BAILEY JR.**[2], s/o Jonathan[1], b. Goshen, served in the War of 1812. He m. Catherine Stewart in 1806; she b. 7 April 1783, d. 5 Sept. 1866, bur. Old Ridgebury Methodist Cemetery. Jonathan d. 5 March 1860. They had:

1814, March 15, Benjamin Franklin, now res. on old homestead. [LDS Anc. file gives another Benjamin Franklin Bailey who d. 25 Feb. 1814.]
Eliza, m. Gilbert F. Monden.
Charlotte, m. Richard A. Elmer.
Julia, m. James T. Coulter.

**JONATHAN BAILEY SR.**[1] had a brother, NATHANIEL, who also came to Orange Co. and settled at Wawayanda. He m. Margaret Wickham 29 March 1782, & had:

1780, Sept. 10, Nathaniel (Nathan). Is probably the Nathaniel Bailey who m. 9 Sept. 1798, Bathia Tryon. Bathia widow of Nathaniel was a church member at Goshen 27 April 1818.
1783, April 25, Benjamin.
1784, Aug., Abigail.
1788, Feb. 11, Israel Wickham.
1789, June 28, Columbus.
1791, Feb. 8, Barcas.
Wickham W.

Goshen church records indicate that there was more than one Nathaniel Bailey family in the parish in this time period. It is noted in the membership roll that Abigail, wife of Nathaniel Bailey, dec'd. as of 30 March 1827 and a Mary, d/o Nathaniel Bailey & Mary Peck was b. 8 Nov. 1776.

## BAIRD FAMILY OF WARWICK  H-775-6

The Bairds of Avondale were of the ancient Berg Scots Clan as long ago as the days of Robert Bruce (1309) & were on the side of the Lord of Lorne against the victorious Bruce. The spelling Byard (Norman-French) was changed to Baird. Family from Scotland to France at an early date.

**FRANCIS BAIRD**[1], of town of Warwick before 1766, of . Scotch-Irish desc., d. in Warwick 1799/1800. He or his father sailed from Bally Castle, Co. Antrim, Ireland. His children:
WILLIAM EAGLES.
Samuel.
John.
Abia Francis.
Anna.
Margaret, m. Joseph Walling of Walling family of Warwick.

**WILLIAM EAGLES BAIRD**[2], s/o Francis[1], m. Sarah DeKay, d/o Thomas, and had:
NATHANIEL WHEELER.
Abia Francis.
Fanny, m. --- Blain.
Mary (Polly), m. Thomas Hathorn Burt.
Jane.
Sally, m. Nathaniel Pelton.
Christine, m. David Barclay.

**NATHANIEL WHEELER BAIRD**[3], s/o William Eagles[2], r Abigail Denton & their descendants res. in Town of Warwick & are named as:
John Baird, m. Mary DeKay.
Julia Baird, m. Thomas E. DeKay.
Samuel Denton Baird, m. Sarah Parks; have son who lives wi. his mother on the homestead, William Parks Baird.
Mary Baird, m. Ogden Howell.
Frances Amelia Baird, m. George W. Sanford, 1847.
Sarah Baird, m. Thomas J. Taylor.
William Henry Baird, m. Mary ---.
Charles Roe Baird, m. Anna M. Jayne.

**BAKER, FRED**  H-776
of Newburgh.

**FRED BAKER**[1], manager of Newburgh branch of Swift & Co., b. Germany 1834, to America 1853. He has one son, FRED[2], who has a farm at Marlboro. FRED[2] has two sons:
William, meat market in Newburgh.
John J., meat market in Newburgh.

**BARBER, PATRICK**  A-380-1, U2-75-6

**PATRICK BARBER**[1], settled in Montgomery c. 1764. In his will dated 22 Sept. 1791 he names his wife Jane. Their children.
Margaret m. John Davison.
FRANCIS.
John.
William.
Joseph.
Archable, d. young.
Jane, d. young.
Samuel, d. young.

COL. FRANCIS BARBER[2] d. at Fishkill 7 Feb. 1783. His obituary: Killed in Camp on Jan. 11 by a tree being felled, he was son of Patrick Barber of Neelytown. Buried in Goodwill Cemetery. His children are mentioned in his father's will, but not named.

---

**BARCLAY, P[eter] MOIR [P]**      A-178A & H-776
physician of Newburgh.

Dr. ALEXANDER BARCLAY[1], physician, b. Scotland; practiced in Newburgh, NY; emigrated with family Nov. 1835. Owned drugstore in Newburgh. He m. Mrs. Mary J. Fraser Watt, of Watt family of Scotland, and had:

1834, 9 [20] April, **P[eter] MOIR BARCLAY[2]**, b. Aberdeen Scotland, practicing physician of Newburgh; surgeon 19th Regt. Inf. of NY; 19 June 1872, m. Hattie [Harriet] E., eldest d/o the late Capt. C. B. Armstrong of Newburgh. Had dau., Maude, who m. John B. Rose, brick manufacturer of Newburgh.

---

**BARNES FAMILY**      H-777

EDGAR BARNES, b. Orange County, 16 July 1834, at age 7 to NY City with parents. Worked at Pine Bush (1851-54) then to Newburgh & worked at William K. Mailler & Co. as shipping clerk. 1874 formed partnership with James H. Matheos; retired 1898. VP of local bank. He m. (1st) Theresa Pack of NY, who d. leaving 4 children, 3 living:
Anna.
Minnie.
Arthur, member of firm Barnes & Atkins, meat smokers & packers.

EDGAR m. (2d) 1870, Sophie H. Parsons of Newburgh.

---

**BARNES, GEORGE T. [P]**      H-778

GORDON BARNES[1] m. Esther A. Tate, and had:
GEORGE T.[2], b. Montgomery, Orange Co., 1881; apprenticed to tinsmith & plumber, served 7 years employment at Middletown where he was employed by the late George A. Swalm. Has res. Newburgh since 1889. Started plumbing business in 1892. 1895 m. Miss Cory of R.I. They have one dau.

---

**BARNES, J. MILTON**      H-778
of Central Valley.

MATTHEW BARNES[1] m. Mary Van Duser, and had:
J. MILTON[2], b. Cornwall, Orange Co., 1844; apprenticed to carpenter, located in Central Valley in 1876, in mercantile business with Alfred Cooper. Postmaster 1885 & 1892. 1884 m. Hannah, d/o the late Hon. Morgan Shuit.

---

**BARN[E]S FAMILY OF NEWBURGH**      H-779-80

**BARNES, NATHANIEL [P]**      A-368C
physician of Newburgh.

ISAAC BARNES[1], after 1782 to Cobbleskill, Schoharie Co., and after 10 years to "wilds of Otsego, Co;" m. ---, his son:
NATHANIEL BARNES[2], b. 1782 Litchfield, CT, d. 17 Sept. 1879.; to Ulster Co. before age 30, contractor to build turnpike roads; to Newburgh c. 1822, then he m. and settled at Middlehope. Blinded by accident at age 70. Mar. 3 Jan. 1828, Effie d/o Dr. William Dusinberre of the town of Plattekill, Ulster Co.; Effie b. 3 April 1796, d. 5 Aug. 1880, and had:

1828, Oct. 16, WILLIAM D.
1831, Feb. 20, NATHANIEL.
1833, DANIEL D.
Mary E.

WILLIAM D. BARN[E]S[3], s/o Nathaniel[2], fruit grower & agriculturalist of Mt. Hope; 1860 m. Elizabeth A. Carpenter. William d. Oct. 1904. Children:
Edwin W.
Mary.
George D.
John S.
Nathaniel H., dec'd.

NATHANIEL BARN[E]S[3], s/o Nathaniel[2], agriculturalist & fruit grower of Newburgh, b. Middle Hope. Teacher, 1st town supervisor (1866); at age 23 m. Martha Waring & had 4 sons & 1 dau. Those still living:
James, dry goods merchant, Newburgh.
Charles, produce business in NY.

DANIEL D. BARN[E]S[3], s/o Nathaniel[2], b. Middle Hope, now retired on the farm of his birth. Breeder of trotting horses. 1857 m. Hester D., d/o Capt. L. S. Carpenter of Marlboro. Children:
3 daus.
1863, Nathaniel C., b. Middle Hope, manager of father's farm, j.p., m. Mary E., d/o Dr. Kidd of Newburgh. She d. 1889, leaving one dau., Natalie C.

---

**BARNETT, ROBERT HIRAM**      H-778-9
of Newburgh.

Family desc. of English ancestor who commanded in the Battle of Barnett.
ALFRED A. BARNETT[1], b. London, England, to America in early 1860's, m. Bessie Rowell, a Mayflower desc. connected to the families of Fields & Morse. Their son:
ROBERT HIRAM[2], b. Gloversville, Fulton Co., NY, 13 June 1870, (Warren Rowell, NY inventor is his maternal uncle). Read law with Andrew J. Nellis of Johnstown & later studied at NY Law School, grad. 1895. Practiced at Johnstown, removed to Mechanicsville, NY for 3 years, to Newburgh in 1901.

---

**BARTRAM, CHARLES W.**      H-780-1
of Newburgh.

He is general superintendant of Sweet, Orr & Co., b. Dutchess Co. Teacher & associated with the clothing industry at Ossing, NY 9 years; m. Hannah E. Willsea of Tarrytown, and had:

Dr. William C.

Nellie E.

_____

**BATE, DAVID W.**                                    A-147
attorney.

JAMES BATE[1], A.Q.G. of the Army of the Revolution; m. ---, had son:

**DAVID W. BATE[2]**, b. Shawangunk, Ulster Co.; served in War of 1812, county judge, m. (1st) Harriet M. Isaacs; (2d) Mrs. Polhamus, who survived him. No issue.

_____

**BEAL, WILLIAM R.**                                  H-781

JOSEPH REYNOLDS BEAL[1] m. Elizabeth Austen, from England to America c. 1830. Their son:

**WILLIAM R. BEAL[2]**, b. Newark, NJ, 1838, was orphaned at an early age. Employed at Newark Gas Light Co. & later with gas co. at Elizabeth. 1855 to Yonkers, 1866 to 23d Ward NY City. Also involved in real estate & building operations. Presently pres. of Newburgh Light, Heat & Power Co. Warden at Holy Trinity Churcy, NY City & a "Grand Army Man." 1863 m. Eleanor Louise Bell; living children:

Reynolds, artist.

Gifford, artist.

Thaddeus R., manager Poughkeepsie Light, Heat & Power Co.

Albert R., manager gas dept. of Poughkeepsie L, H & P.

Mrs. Charles E. Acker.

Mary Reynolds Beal.

_____

**BEATTIE, JAMES R. W. [P]**                          A-411
farmer of Montgomery.

ROBERT BEATTIE[1], b. Ireland, to America, settled in Ulster Co., m. ---; only child:

ROBERT BEATTIE[2], 1794 to Montgomery; m. --- Crowell, of Irish parentage, and had:

John.

Thomas.

William.

Robert.

1786, Oct. 14, JAMES R.

Smith.

Hannah.

Mary.

JAMES R. BEATTIE[3] son of Robert[2], b. 14 Oct. 1786, d. 29 March 1871; Montgomery; tanner & currier; m. 6 Feb. 1810, Charlotte d/o David Belknap of Newburgh (since 1769), who d. 26 Dec. 1874, age 86, and had:

1811, Elizabeth Frances.

1815, Catharine Isabella.

1817, Hannah Jane.

1819, Justus C. McLeod.

1823, Maria O. B.

1825, June 12, **JAMES R. W.**

1829, Sarah M.

1831, Matilda G.

**JAMES R. W. BEATTIE[4]**, son of James[3], b. Montgomery; dairy & grain farmer, member of Reformed Presbyterian Church, "Covenanters" at Coldenham. 22 March 1854, m. Elizabeth d/o William and Elizabeth Martin Flemming; family of Co. Antrim, Ireland, to America 1832, settled twp. of Newburgh, and had:

1854, Nov. 14, William James.

1856, April 6, Charlotte Elizabeth.

1857, Sept. 20, Samuel Oliver.

1861, May 9, Maria Esther.

1864, Nov. 21, Frederick Martin; now dec'd.

1867, Sept. 13, Maggie J.

_____

"Dr. Beattie came to us (Town of Crawford) and died among us in his eightieth year." [H-172]

_____

**BELCHER, OSCAR W.**                                 H-78?

**MR. BELCHER** recently purchased the Lee farm (1907), town of Cornwall; has res. in Orange Co. nearly 50 years. Born in Passaic Co., NY, since 1859 farmer of what is now Town of Tuxedo.

_____

**BELKNAP FAMILY**     H-782-3, TN-267-72, E-82, 146, 161,
                       U2-177-8, LDS Anc. File, C-18, C-20

The name Belknap (Belknoppe) is of Norman origin & literally means "people of the beautiful hill." ABRAHAM BELKNAP[1], b. 10 March 1589, Sawbridgeworth, England, s/o Bennet Belknap (Beltoft) & Grace Adam. ABRAHAM m. 28 Oct. 1817, Latton, Essex, England Mary Stallion, d/o Thomas & Mary (Dalton) Stallion of Latton, Essex, England. To Lynn, MA 1637. Later removed to Salem, where he d. in 1643. He left 4 sons & 1 dau. Abraham's children:

Abraham.

Jeremy.

1627, March 16, SAMUEL.

1633, May 12, JOSEPH.

Hannah.

SAMUEL BELKNAP[2], s/o Abraham[1], b. North Weald, Essex, England; m. 1652, probably at Hingham, MA, Sarah Jones, d/o Robert & Elizabeth (Soane) Jones. Robert of Reading, England & Hingham, MA. SAMUEL d. 11 Nov. 1701, Haverhill, Essex, MA. Sarah d. at the same place 18 April 1689; she was b. 1629 in Reading, Berks, England. They had:

ABRAHAM BELKNAP[3], b. 4 June 1660, Salem, MA; m. 14 Jan. 1690/1, MA, Elizabeth Ayer, b. 19 Aug. 1674, at Haverhill. They had, b. Framingham, MA.:

1695, Abraham.
1704, Jeremiah.

JOSEPH BELKNAP[2], s/o Abraham[1], b. Strawbridgeworth,
England & settled in Boston, MA, where he was admitted
freeman 1653; a founder of "Old South Church" 1668;
dismissed to Hatfield, where he lived 1682-96. Returned to
Boston & d. there 14 Nov. 1712, aged 82. He married 3
times; (1) Ruth ---, and had:
1658, Jan. 26, Joseph.
1660, Sept. 25, Mary.
1663, Aug. 13, Nathaniel.
1665, July 1, Elizabeth.

JOSEPH m. (2) Lydia ---, and had:
1668, Nov. 27, Ruth.

JOSEPH m. (3) Hannah Meakins, b. 13 March 1647, Roxbury,
MA; d. 26 Dec. 1688; they had:
1673, June 8 [29 June 1670], THOMAS.
1676, March 17, Ruth.
1678, June 27, Abigail.
1681, April 26, Abraham.
Samuel.

THOMAS BELKNAP[3], s/o Joseph[2] & 3d wife Hannah, was b.
in Boston. He m. 5 March 1694, at Cambridge, Jane, b. 5
June 1667, d/o Thomas Cheney & Jane Atkinson, of Cambridge, MA & settled in Woburn in 1698. Their children:
THOMAS.
1699, Nov. 4, Jane.
1702, 3 May, BENJAMIN.
1704, May 18, Hannah.
1707, May 24, SAMUEL.
JOSEPH, clerk of the Newburgh precinct 1763.

Thomas, Benjamin and Samuel all removed to Newburgh
between 1749 & 1763. Samuel settled first in 1749 & purchased
tract known as "Baird Patent" which was divided among his sons
Isaac & David & his brother Thomas on his death. Benjamin
later settled in New Windsor.

THOMAS BELKNAP[4], s/o Thomas[3] & Jane, m. Sarah Hill 14
Dec. 1726, and had:
Thomas.
Sarah.
Joseph.
John.
Jonathan.

BENJAMIN BELKNAP[4], s/o Thomas[3] & Jane Cheney Belknap,
m. Hannah Richardson and had:
Abraham.
Ruth.
Isaac.
Hannah.
Jeduthan.
Sarah.

Olive.

SAMUEL BELKNAP[4], s/o Thomas[3], b. Billerica, MA, m. Lydia
Sterns 13 Nov. 1729 at Billerica, d/o Isaac & Mary (Merriam) Sterns. To Newburgh 1749, where he d. 1 Jan. 1771;
Lydia d. 8 May 1784. They had:
1730, MAY 27, WILLIAM.
1731, Nov. 11, Ruth, d. 1734.
1733, 14 Dec., ISAAC.
1735, 18 Oct., Samuel.
1737, Feb. 28, Lydia, m. Edward Riggs 25 Nov. 1782 & settled
in NY & later in Newburgh where she died. She was a
school teacher.
1739, Jan. 13, ABEL.
1739/40, Jan. 9, Mary, d. 15 July 1820.
1742, May 14, Ruth; d. 6 May 1745.
1744, Jan. 14, DAVID.
1745, April 17, ABIGAIL.
1748, Sept. 7, Jonathan; d. unm., 9 May 1774.
1751, April 5, Olive; d. unm. 14 March 1770.

WILLIAM BELKNAP[5], s/o Samuel[4] & Lydia Stearns Belknap,
m. (1) Hannah Flagg & had:
WILLIAM.
Hannah.
Abel.
SAMUEL.
Josiah, dec'd.
Josiah.
Lydia.
Gershom & a twin dau.

WILLIAM m. (2) Mary Flagg & had:
Cyrus.
Mary.

WILLIAM BELKNAP[6], s/o William[5] & Hannah Flagg Belknap,
settled in Newburgh & m. Martha Carscadden 20 July 1785,
& had:
William.
Lydia, m. Edmund Sanxay.
Hannah.
Stephen.
Robert.
George.
Nancy.
Susannah.

SAMUEL BELKNAP[6], s/o William[5] & Hannah Flagg Belknap,
before the Revolution res. Woburn, MA, occupying his
father's homestead. He served in the war & afterward was
elected to the MA Legislature; later removed to Newburgh
& died there, 31 March 1821. By his first wife, Mrs.
Abigail Lewis, Samuel had:
Abigail.
Timothy.
Ruth.

Samuel m. (2) Abigail Flagg & had:
Raphael.
1763, Dec. 10, SAMUEL.
Olive.
Elizabeth.
Lydia.
Seth.
Charles.

SAMUEL BELKNAP$^7$, s/o Samuel$^6$ & Abigail Flagg Belknap, m. Mary Goldsmith 6 April 1790. Samuel d. 19 May 1845; their children.
Lucinda.
Ira.
1794, Sept. 7, WILLIAM GOLDSMITH.
Samuel.
Fanny.

WILLIAM GOLDSMITH BELKNAP$^8$, s/o Samuel$^7$ & Mary, served in the War of 1812 & the War with Mexico. He d. near Ft. Washita in Chickasaw Nation 10 Nov. 1851. He m. Ann Clark, d/o Joseph of Newburgh, and had:
Anna Mary.
Clara.
William Worth.
Frederick Augustus.

ISAAC BELKNAP$^5$, s/o Samuel$^4$, b. Woburn, MA, d. 29 April 1815 at Newburgh; m. (1) Bridget Richardson of Woburn MA, who was b. 30 Sept. 1737 & d. 8 Aug. 1777. She was d/o Stephen & Mary (Sawyer) Richardson. Before the Rev. War, Isaac ran a freighting business Newburgh to NY City & beyond. He was apptd. Capt. of Rangers in the Rev. War. He d. 29 April 1815, aged 82. His adventures recounted in TN-269. Children of his first marriage:
Bridget.
1751, 3 Oct., ISAAC JR.
Mary, m. Derick Amerman.
1755, April 26, Elizabeth, m. John Warren, b. 25 Dec. 1755, Framingham, MA. Both d. Saratoga, NY, he 24 Dec. 1824, she 21 June 1837.
Olive.
Bridget, m. Leonard Carpenter.
Richardson.
Abel.
William.
Olive.

ISAAC m. (2) Mrs. Deborah Coffin, widow of Capt. Caleb Coffin & d/o Col. Briggs Alden of Duxbury, MA & a lineal desc. of John Alden of the Mayflower. They m. 10 Sept. 1778. Isaac is named as an early businessman of Newburgh, along with his father. He had:
Amelia, m. Charles Birdsall.
Alden.
Briggs.
Judah.
Lydia.

Deborah.

ISAAC BELKNAP JR.$^6$, s/o Isaac$^5$ & first wife Bridget Richardson, is described as a man of great personal wealth and high moral character. Member of the state legislature, judge of co. courts, member Newburgh Dutch Reformed Church. He d. intestate & administration of his estate was granted 30 Aug. 1788 to Elizabeth Belknap of New Winsor, his widow. He m. (1) Elizabeth Coleman who d. 9 Jan. 1816. She was a d/o Joseph of Newburgh, formerly of Sherburn, Nantucket Island. Their children:
Elizabeth.
Richardson.
Fanny C., m. David Crawford.

ISAAC JR.$^6$ m. (2) Mrs. Susan Smith, widow of William H. Smith. No issue recorded here.

ABEL BELKNAP$^5$, s/o Samuel$^4$ & Lydia Stearns Belknap, d. 1 Nov. 1804, aged 66. Served as chairman of committee of safety for Newburgh during Rev. War; engaged in soap manufacture that has lasted four generations. He m. (1) Molly Richardson 4 Oct. 1765, and had:
1766, Aug. 4, STEPHEN.
Chancey.
Sarah.
Molly.

ABEL$^5$ m. (2) Hannah Williams of Huntington, L.I. 6 June 1776 & had:
Rachel Fleet.

ABEL$^5$ m. (3) Hannah Williams of Sharon, CT, and had:
1785, Dec. 30, Abel.
1787, Sept. 23, MOSES HIGHBY [P].
1789, July 20, AARON.
Margaret.
Edwin Starr.
Julia Ann.

STEPHEN$^6$, s/o Abel$^5$ & 1st wife Molly, d. 28 Oct. 1848; m. Mrs. Sarah Mace & had:
Dr. Savilian, d. unm. at Mobile.
Mary C., m. Aaron B. Gardiner.
1768, March 13, CHAUNCEY F.
Rufus R.

CHAUNCEY F. BELKNAP$^7$, s/o Stephen$^6$ & Sarah, d. June 1840; served in military. He m. (1) 9 July 1788, Sarah, d/o Jonathan Belknap, & had:
Mary, d. unm.
Stephen, d. in infancy.
Sarah, m. (1) James Black, (2) David Brown.
Rebecca, d. unm.

CHAUNCEY$^7$ m. (2d) Mercy, also a d/o Jonathan Belknap & had:
1797, Dec. 9, Rufus R.

Thomas, d. in infancy.
Clarissa.
Mercy.
Cornelia, m. Alsop Stewart & had Lydia.
Clementine.
Rachel.
Chancey.
Jane Ann, m. David E. Fowler.

MOSES HIGHBY BELKNAP[6], s/o Abel[5] & 3d wife Hannah Williams of CT, engaged in family soap business, he d. 4 Jan. 1855; m. (1) Margaret, d/o Samuel O. Gregory who d. 27 Feb. 1724, & had:
Ruletta, d. 11 Aug. 1850.
Abel W., d. 26 June 1847, m. Sarah, d/o Capt. Samuel Johnson & left son Abel W.

MOSES HIGHBY BELKNAP[6] m. (2) Ruth P. Cook, who d. 23 Oct. 1833, leaving son MOSES COOK BELKNAP, b. 2 Feb. 1832.

MOSES COOK BELKNAP[7], s/o Moses Higby[6], b. Newburgh, carried on family business under name of Belknap & McCann. Bank cashier, member First Presbyterian Church, d. at Newburgh, 3 Oct. 1892. He m. (1st) 1857, Mary H. Mailler, d/o William K., she d. 31 May 1858. He m. (2d) 1862, Marietta McCamly, d/o David of Warwick, NY, she d. 1873 and left 3 sons [see WILLIAM COOK BELKNAP[8] below] & 1 dau. MOSES COOK[7] m. (3d) 1875, Evelina, d/o Dr. Nathaniel Deyo; they have 1 son & 1 dau. living.

WILLIAM COOK BELKNAP[8], s/o Moses Cook[7] & Marietta McCamly, was b. Newburgh 15 July 1864. He was educated in East Hampton, MA; m. Helen, d/o George W. & Margaret (Brown) Kerr, 15 Dec. 1890. William Cook carried on the family soap business. Vestryman at St. George's Church. Children:
1897, Dec. 10, William Kerr.
1899, April 8, Helen Kerr.

AARON BELKNAP[6], s/o Abel[5] & 3d wife Hannah Williams of CT, m. Mary Josepha L. S., d/o Samuel Belknap (s/o Samuel & Lydia Stearns Belknap). [Another source states that this Aaron m. (1) Mary, d/o Samuel O. Gregory, who d. 19 Jan. 1833; no issue. He m. (2) Sally D. Munn, who d. 1855; no issue.] His children from 1st source:
Ethelbert B., d. young.
Samuel M., d. in infancy.
1794, Dec. 11, Aaron Betts, res. NY, atty., m. Rachel T. Price & settled in NY.

DAVID BELKNAP[5], s/o Samuel[4] & Lydia Stearns Belknap, b. 14 Jan. 1744, d. 11 March 1831; m. Sarah Case & had:
Olive.
David.
Daniel C.
1781, July 26, Hezekiah; grad. Princeton College 1805; studied law; d. 23 May 1814.

Sarah.
Justin.
Fanny.
Charlotte.
Oliver.

ABIGAIL BELKNAP[5], d/o Samuel[4] & Lydia Sterns Belknap, b. 17 April 1745, res. Newburgh & after her marriage to Josiah Talcott removed to Hancock, MA where she & husband united with Society of Shakers. She d. May 1793. They had the following children [TALCOTTS]:
Lydia.
Josiah.
Jeffery.
Samuel.
Olive.
Jonathan.
David.
Abigail.

JOSEPH BELKNAP[4], s/o Thomas[3] & Jane Cheney Belknap, m. Margaret Russell of Watertown, MA, 9 April 1754, and had:
Thomas.
JOSEPH.
Phebe.
Lydia.
Daniel.
James.

JOSEPH BELKNAP[5], s/o Joseph[4] & Margaret, m. Sarah Clement at Goshen 11 Sept. 1792, & had:
1793, March 24, JAMES.
Harriet.
Ann Eliza.
Sarah.
Elsie.
Thomas.
Amanda.

JAMES BELKNAP[6], s/o Joseph[5] & Sarah Clement Belknap, b. Town of Crawford, m. Clarissa Ring, d/o Samuel of Cornwall in June 1816 & settled in Newburgh. He served in the militia in War of 1812; public offices including port master.

**BELKNAP, BENJAMIN**                                    U2-92
of New Windsor, yeoman.

In his will dated 16 Feb. 1792, **BENJAMIN BELKNAP** is identified as the s/o Isaac Belknap Sr. & wife Sarah. He mentions Isaac Hamilton, eldest child of his sister Sarah Hamilton. Will was proved 2 June 1792 by John Belknap of Newburgh, yeoman; Enos Chandler & William Hollan. Administration was granted to Mathew Dubois.

**BELKNAP, ISAAC**　　　　　　　　　　　　**U2-16**
yeoman of New Windsor.

**ISAAC BELKNAP SR.** in his will dated 27 Sept. 1787, names
his wife Sarah and children:
Isaac.
Benjamin [see above entry].
Olive.
Prudence.
Sarah, m. James Hamilton.

_____

**BELL, JAMES B. [P]**　　　　**A-500-01, C-15, C-112-13**
of Wallkill

JOHN BELL[1], b. Co. Down, Ireland of Scotch Ancestry, 1753;
to America 1772; soldier of the Rev. War under George
Washington; farmer; d. 23 Feb. 1834. M. (1st) 28 April
1785, Keziah Mapes, b. 1776; settled Wallkill. Keziah
Presbyterian Church member, d. 1810. John member of
Presbyterian Church at Deerpark. Children (all settled in
Orange Co. except 1st son; all reared families except Thomas
& James B.):
1786, April 22 [bapt. record says he was b. 17 Oct. 1786],
　　Benjamin; settled in OH.
1788, July 7, Alexander.
1790, June 22, Jane, m. M. L. Godfrey.
1792, May 23, John.
1794, July 13, William.
1797, April 20, Moses.
1799, March 4, Thomas.
1801, March 10, **JAMES B.**
1803, April 25, Gabriel.
1805, July 2, Lewis.
1807, June 3, George W.

JOHN[1] m. (2d) Mary Crane; no issue.

**JAMES B. BELL[2]**, last surviving child of John[1] and Keziah
(Mapes) Bell, tailor, farmer and dealer in real estate; m. (1st)
25 Oct. 1826, Harriet Tuthill, b. 1802, d. 6 May 1874.
Members of Deerpark Church, Howell Presbyerian and 2nd
Presbyterian Churches. JAMES B. m. (2d) 1875, June 10,
Harriet d/o George Pelton (s/o Peleg, b. CT, early settler of
Wallkill) and Sarah Tuthill of Wallkill. Harriet b. 16 Nov.
1816, and m. (1st) Peter H. Bell; (2d) Daniel Mapes and (3d)
**JAMES B. BELL.** She had 7 children by Peter H., one now
living: Jane m. Andrew Myres of Wantage, NJ. **JAMES B.
BELL** had no children.

_____

**BENEDICT FAMILY**　　**H-783, LDS Anc. File, AA6-110-11**

THOMAS BENEDICT[1] of Nottinghamshire, England, (1617-
1689), res. in MA Bay & later in Southhold, L.I. & Norwalk,
CT, m. Mary Bridgum and had:
JOHN BENEDICT[2], b. Southold, L.I., freeman of Norwalk
1680, deacon & assemblyman, m. Phoebe, d/o John & Sarah
Gregory of Norwalk & had:

JAMES BENEDICT[3], b. Norwalk, CT 5 Jan. 1685, d.
Ridgefield 25 Nov. 1762, one of the original settlers of Ridge-
field, CT, j.p., author; m. 1709, Sarah, d/o Thomas & Mary
Hyatt of Norwalk. JAMES separated from the church in
Ridgefield and at Warwick helped establish the First Baptist
Church. To Wyoming, PA in 1773, returned to Warwick at the
time of the Wyoming Massacre & d. there 9 Sept. 1792, aged
72. and had:
James[4]. His son, James Benedict[5], built a home in Warwick in
　　1779, which is occupied by the present owner, Capt. James
　　W. Benedict.
1714, March 20, PETER.

PETER BENEDICT[4], s/o James[3], b. Ridgefield, d. at North
Salem CT 1787; m. (2) 23 June 1737, Agnes Heaton, d/o John
Tyler of Branford, CT & widow of Rev. Samuel Heaton, and
had:
ABNER BENEDICT[5] of North Salem, Middletown, New
Lebanon and North Stamford, CT, b. at North Salem 9 Nov
1740, d. at Roxbury, NJ 19 Nov. 1818; grad. Yale 176!
chaplain in Continental army in the Rev. War. He m. Lois, d/c
Dr. Northrop of New Milford, CT, & had:
JOEL TYLER BENEDICT[6], b. Middletown, CT 6 Sept
1772, d. at Philadelphia, PA 21 Oct. 1833, Presbyterian clerg·
man; m. 1 Jan. 1795, Currance, d/o Deacon Adin Wheeler ℧
Southbury. She d. 4 June 1862, aged 90 years. They had
George Wyllys Benedict[6] res. of Burlington, VT.

DANIEL BENEDICT[1], b. 1716, Ridgefield, CT & wife
Agnes, d/o James & Mary (Hyatt) Wallace, had a son:
DANIEL BENEDICT[2], b. 2 April 1743 at Fairfield. He m.
Mary Wood 28 July 1774, she d/o Timothy Wood. DANIEL[2]
d. at Warwick, Orange Co., NY 23 Dec. 1822. They had
JAMES BENEDICT[3], b. 24 April 1791 at Warwick. JAMES m.
Elizabeth Hall & d. 14 Feb. 1844.

_____

**BENEDICT, JAMES D.**　　　　　　　　**H-783**

WILLIAM SMITH BENEDICT[1] (no relationship given to
above) purchased Wickham farm c. 1839, removed to Warwick
April 1867 & d. there 22 Sept. 1883. His son:
**JAMES D. BENEDICT[2]**, b. 1 mile from Warwick 2 Sept.
1834, farmer. To Warwick 1871 for 9 years; removed to
Wickham farm where he d. 17 Feb. 1898. He was married &
his wife provided land for "The James D. Benedict Sunshine
Rest Home" on land near Wisner.

_____

**BENEDICT, JAMES H.**　　　　　　　　**H-783-4**

JAMES H. BENEDICT b. on homestead at Stone Bridge, 13
Feb. 1854 & lived there with his father for 35 years; dairy
farmer. 14 Nov. 1888 m. Ada Pitts, and had:
1899, Oct., Laura.
1890, Dec., W. Smith.

_____

## BENEDICT, JOHN VAN DUZER                    H-784

**JOHN V. BENEDICT** is noted as 8th in desc. from Thomas & 5th in desc. from Elder James, the first of the name in Orange Co. (See above.) He was b. in Town of Warwick 1 Jan. 1837 in house now known as the "John Blain" house. He is the s/o Abner Benedict & Julia A. Van Duzer, each also descended from Thomas & The Elder. **JOHN** res. with his parents near Edenville, Orange Co.

## BENEDICT, JOHN W.                    H-784

**HENRY A. BENEDICT** (1818-3 April 1900) m. Laura T. --- (1826-still living). They had 10 children, 8 still living, among them:
**JOHN W.**, b. on homestead 16 Aug. 1855; dairy farmer on land in the family since 1817.

## BENNETT, CHARLES F.                    H-784
of Middletown.

**JOHN F. BENNETT[1]**, removed to Bloomingburgh, Sullivan Co., hotel & livery business. His son:
**CHARLES F. BENNETT[2]**, b. 15 Oct. 1869, near Middletown, was farmer & postmaster of Bloomingburgh for 2 years; livery business in Middletown (1900); recently purchased his father's homestead farm at Springside, near Middletown, in continuous possession of the family for over 100 years. He m. Kittie Bertholf, d/o Andrew T. of Howells, NY, 25 Jan. 1892. They have a son, Mortimer W. Bennett[3], a high school student.

## BIGELOW, JOHN                    H-785, AA5-126-7

**JOHN BIGELOW[1]**, b. England, emigrated early & settled at Watertown, MA. He m. 30 Oct. 1642, Mary, d/o John Warren. Their son:
**JOSHUA BIGELOW[2]** b. Watertown, MA 1745, d. at Westminster 1745; was soldier in King Philip's war. Removed to Westminster & res. on land bounty land obtained for war services. He m. 20 Oct. 1676, Elizabeth Flagg, d/o Thomas & Mary of Watertown. Their son:
**JOHN BIGELOW[3]** of Colchester, b. at Watertown, MA 30 Dec. 1681, d. Colchester 8 March 1770. Early in life to Hartford; military service. His first wife is not named, she d. 4 Nov. 1709 & he m. (2) Sarah Bigelow, (a cousin) d/o Jonathan & Rebecca (Shepherd) Bigelow of Hartford. JOHN m. (3) Abigail --- who d. 1 Aug. 1760 & he m. (4) Hannah Munn.
**DAVID BIGELOW[4]**, s/o John Bigelow[3], b. Hartford, CT, bapt. 22 Sept. 1706, d. at Marlborough 2 June 1799; m. (1) 11 Dec. 1729, Editha Day, b. 10 Sept. 1705, d. 19 Jan. 1746. DAVID m. (2) 21 Jan. 1747, Mercy Lewis, b. 30 Oct. 1709, d. 5 Jan. 1795, widow of Rev. Judah Lewis & d/o Stephen & Lydia (Belding) Kellogg of Westfield, MA. Their son:
**DAVID BIGELOW[5]** of Glastonbury & Marlborough, CT, b. Colchester 7 May 1732, d. Marlborough, 6 Oct. 1820. He m. 17 June 1762, Patience Foote, who d. at Marlborough 26

June 1791, d/o Nathaniel Foote, Jr. They had:
**ASA BIGELOW[6]**, b. Marlborough, CT 18 Jan. 1799, d. at Malden 12 Feb. 1850. He m. 18 Feb. 1802, Lucy Isham, b. Colchester, CT 22 Sept. 1780, d. Malden 14 Sept. 1853.
**JOHN BIGELOW[7]**, author, attorney, newspaper editor of the *NY Evening Post*, b. Malden, Ulster Co. NY, 25 Nov. 1817. Was consul & US minister to France; author. He m. Jane Tunis Poultney, b. Baltimore, MD 16 Jan. 1829, d. NY City 8 Feb. 1889, d/o Ivan & Jane (Tunis) Poultney.

## BINGHAM FAMILY                    A-436
of Wallkill.

**JAMES BINGHAM**, from Windham, CT, settled in northwest part of Wallkill, cooper; d. June 1844. M. Alathea Parish of CT who raised silkworms and d. Aug. 1854. Their children, all now over 70 years of age:
Anna, m. Benjamin Woodward, res. Burlington. One son, B. C. Woodward, merchant of Sullivan Co.
Abigail P., m. Lucius L. Woodward, res. Middletown.
Margaret K., unm., lives with sister in Burlington.

## BINGHAM, JOHN W.                    H-785
fruit grower of Newburgh.

**CHARLES E. BINGHAM[1]**, farmer, m. Amelia Holmes & had: 1852, JOHN W.

**JOHN W. BINGHAM[2]**, b. Marlboro, Ulster Co. Member of Marlboro Presbyterian Church; m. Mary Bloomer & has 3 children.

## BIPPUS, JOHN JACOB                    H-785
merchant of Port Jervis.

**JOHN JACOB BIPPUS**, b. Bearville, PA, with parents to Port Jervis as a child. In grocery business since 1891.

## BIRCH, CALEB                    H-785-6

**CALEB BIRCH**, boot & shoe merchant of Walden for 32 years, b. Town of Plattekill, Ulster Co., NY; m. Abbie Gale & had:
Caleb, in business with father, clerk of the Town of Montgomery.
George.
Marcus.
Leuella.

## BLAKE, JOHN JR.                    A-379
of Neeleytown.                    LDS Anc. File

**JOHN BLAKE[1]**, of English desc.; family traced back to Robert de Blakeland of Wiltshire, 1286. In 1761 JOHN purchased land in Montgomery; m. Mary Morris of Coldenham, b. Ireland, and had:
**JOHN JR.[2]**, b. Montgomery, 5 Dec. 1762; d. Jan. 1826, aged

64. Deputy sheriff of Ulster Co., res. Kingston, to Neeleytown. Congressman and other political service. M. Elsie (1761-1841), d/o William & Ann (Bull) Eager of Neeleytown, and had:

1785, Sept. 5, Mary, m. Lewis Bodine.
1787, July 13, Ann, m. David Godfrey.
1789, Nov. 19, Frances.
1792, Feb. 19, Sarah, m. John H. Milliken.
1794, Feb. 22, WILLIAM.
1797, June 4, Esther.
1799, John.
1801, Nov. 4, Elsie, m. Samuel Harvey Miller.
1808, April 16, Margaret, m. Henry Dill.

WILLIAM BLAKE[3], s/o JOHN JR.[2], m. 17 Dec. 1818, Elizabeth Jackson, b. 5 Oct. 1798, d/o William T. & Experience (Watkins) Jackson, and had:

1819, Mary E., m. Lewis Hawkins, b. 28 Dec. 1815, s/o Jonathan & Dorothy (Mills) Hawkins.
1822, Feb. 20, Francis Ann, m. Alfred Booth.
1824, April 4, Louisa R., m. Elmer Bodine.
1826, July 29, Hilah B., m. Jacob J. Shafer.
1828, May 12, John Peter Milliken, m. Frances K. Little.
1829, March 23, Elsie J.
1843, Jan. 17, William Henry Dill, m. Matilda R. Booth.

## BLANCHARD, HILAND H.                    H-786

JUSTUS BLANCHARD[1], hotel keeper, farmer, d. age 35; m. Emeline, d/o Miles Derby, b. Green Co., d. age 70. They had:
1850, Feb. 18, HILAND.

HILAND H. BLANCHARD[2], b. Acra, Greene Co., NY, supt. of saw manufacturing company of Wheeler, Madden & Clemson in Middletown; m. Sarah Biggin of Middletown & had 4 children.

## BLIVEN, ULYSSES F. P. [P]               A-504-5
of Wallkill
## BLIVEN, FRED P.                          H-786

ISAAC B. BLIVEN[1] came with two of his brothers from England to America and after he married he settled in RI and later purchased a farm in DeRuyter; to Scott, Cortland Co., to Spafford, Onondaga Co. and Auburn then to Bradford Co., PA where he d. at the age of 74. He m. Lavina Snow who d. age 64 & whose great grandfather came from France & settled in CT, where she was born. Their children:
Daniel S., res. Litchfield, PA.
Cranston V. S. of Nichols, NY.
Eliza, m. Jedediah Smith of Skaneateles, NY.
Emily Dumont, m. Elijah Miller of Auburn, NY.
Elijah F. of Steuben Co., NY.
1817, Oct. 7, ULYSSES F. PLUMMER.
Cordellia L., m. Lorenzo Sweet of Skaneateles; dec'd.

ULYSSES F. PLUMBER BLIVEN[2], s/o Isaac B.[1], learned carriage making with brother Cranston; m. (1st) 13 Dec. 1838, Clementine d/o James Haight & --- Goldsmith. Clementine d. 20 July 1860, age 48. After 1838 to Towanda to assist brother Elijah F. in carriage making; 1842 to Mechanictown, Orange Co., later to Wallkill established carriage and blacksmith shop; 1861 became involved in land sales and 1868 cattle dealer. Children of 1st m.:
Amelia Louise, widow of Harvey L. Angell of NY.
Joseph Alanson of Wallkill.

ULYSSES[2] m. (2d) 3 Oct. 1861, Caroline, widow of Harrison Harding and d/o Nathaniel Beyea and Durenda King of New Vernon, Sullivan Co. Caroline b. 13 July 1827; d. 26 June 1886 [H-786 says she d. 1880. The same source says that Ulysses & Caroline had 6 children, but only names Fred P. below.] Children:
Clementina I.
Thomas K.
Minnie C.
Ulysses F. P. Jr.
1871, Feb. 22, FRED P. BLIVEN

FRED P. BLIVEN[3], b. Michigan Corners, Orange Co farmer; m. 22 March 1897, Nettie Clara, of Middletown & have one child, Pearl who resides at home.

## BOAK FAMILY                              A-435, C-28
of Wallkill.

JAMES BOAK, b. 1772, d. May 1852; res. Keisertown, 1836 to Scotchtown, m. Achsah (d. 1860), sister of Capt. John and niece of Col. William Faulkner, and had:
1799, John; d. 1836, Scotchtown. Could be the John Boak who m. Julia Arnout, 8 Feb. 1821, at Goshen & had dau. Mary Elizabeth bapt. 18 May 1823.
Mrs. John E. Brewster; d. 1870, Scotchtown.
Lettie; d. 1825, unm.
1806, Robert, m. ---; one son living and one son d. in the late war.
Mrs. John Youngblood, near Franklin Square; d. 1877.
Melinda, unm., res. Scotchtown.
James, res. near Scotchtown, m. ---; has 2 sons.
Emily, unm., res. Scotchtown.

## BOARD FAMILY OF CHESTER                  A-615
## BOARD, JAMES [P]                   A-624, H-153
of Chester.
## BOARD, JOSEPH                             H-786
merchant & businessman of Chester.

H-153 says "James Board[1], aged 65, b. in England in 1720, came to this country with his father Cornelius, and brother David, in 1730; sent by Alexander, Lord Sterling, to discover copper mines; discovered iron ore deposits at Sterling, built there a forge in 1735, and in the year 1740 removed to Ringwood."
Another source says: "Three BOARD brothers, CORNELI-

US[1], JAMES[1], JOSEPH[1], either they or their ancestors are understood to have come over as bookkeepers for the iron-works at Ringwood, NJ."

Still another source says brothers were James, Joseph & David.

From the source that gives Cornelius as one of the immigrating brothers:
CORNELIUS BOARD[1] settled in Sugar-Loaf Valley after the Revolution and had:
John, who has son George.
Mrs. Gabriel Wisner, who has 2 daus.
Mrs. John Wood.
Mrs. Jesse Bull.
Mrs. Miles Davis.

JAMES BOARD[1], the immigrant, had sons:
JAMES.
CORNELIUS.
Philip, settled KY.

JAMES BOARD[2], s/o James[1], to Chester before 1801 with brother Cornelius, later to Goshen. James[2] d. on homestead in Ringwood Oct. 1801, leaving wife Nancy, d/o Capt. Phineas Heard of Blooming-Grove NY [see below for Nancy's 2d marriage] & children:
Polly.
Ann.
Hetty.
John H.
Eliza J.
1802, March 30, **JAMES.**

JAMES BOARD[3], b. after his father's death at Ringwood. Reared by his uncle Cornelius[2] at Chester. At age 16 tanning & currying business with Moses Ely at Washington-ville, Orange Co. He was a farmer & cattle dealer & in 1850 to Chester to manage Yelverton Estate & other businesses. Dec. 1822 m. Huldah, d/o Capt. William Hudson & Sarah Tuthhill of Blooming-Grove. Huldah b. 25 July 1801, d. 30 March 1877. Presbyterian Church members at Chester. Children:
Mary, m. John W. Roe, farmer of Chester.
Jonathan H., farmer of Chester.
Susan, m. Samuel Gillette of LeRoy, Genesee Co., NY.
Emily, m. Jesse Owen of Chemung, NY.
Nancy K., m. Joseph Durland, merchant of Chester.

Nancy (Heard) Board m. (2d) Isaac Kingsland, res. Boonton, NJ. where she d. leaving 6 children by her 2d. mar.

CORNELIUS BOARD[2], son of James[1] the immigrant, res. Chester; d. in Sugar-Loaf Valley & had:
1720, James, b. England, to America with his father in 1730.
David.

CAPT. JOSEPH BOARD[1], Rev. War soldier, had a son (GEN.)
CHARLES BOARD[2] of Boardville, NJ. Charles' son was

PETER SEELEY BOARD[3] who m. Madeline C. Conklin & had:
1842, Nov. 9, **JOSEPH.**

JOSEPH BOARD[4], b. Chester, NY, graduated Amherst College in 1867, political servant & wide traveler, member SAR. He m. (1st) 1 June 1868, Josephine Bradbury Curry; m. (2d) Hannah A. Curry. Both wives were from Tilton, NH. By his 2d m. he had:
1873, Joseph Orton.
1880, Anna Tebbetts.
1885, Josephine Clough.

———

**BODINE, HON. FREDERIC**                     A-160-1
atty. of Montgomery.

WILLIAM BODINE[1], of Huguenot ancestry who settled L.I., res. near Walden Village, Orange Co., justice of the peace & businessman, m. ---, and had:
PETER BODINE[2], m. Mary Millspaugh, res. Montgomery. Had 11 children; only ones named here:
1807, July 10, SYLVANUS[3], s/o Peter[2], d. age 71 in Steuben Co.; m. Sarah Ann d/o John Horton of Goshen, and had:
    Amasa.
    **1855, FREDERIC.**

FREDERIC BODINE[4], s/o Sylvanus[3], b. Montgomery, N.Y, Presbyterian Church of Montgomery member. He m. (1st) 5 June 1862, Mittie Graham and had one son, Theodore; m. (2d) 16 Nov. 1870, Mrs. Emma Decker of Montgomery.

———

**BONNYMAN, JAMES**                     H-787

JAMES BONNYMAN, b. 1 Sept. 1854, Batriphnie, Banffshire Co., Scotland; to America 1872, located in Philadelphia, PA for 9 years as florist. To Warwick 1880. Large grower of roses & carnations. Member Dutch Reformed Church. He m. Catherine Amelia McPeek, d/o Lewis & Sarah, 16 Sept. 1883. They have 14 living children, one d. young. Those given here:
1885, May 17, Alexander M.; grad. Columbia College of Pharmacy.
1887, May 31, Amy R.
1893, May 27, Douglass.

———

**BOOTH, FRED**                     H-787

FRED BOOTH, b. Yorkshire, England, to America 1884, secretary & general manager of the Firth Carpet Co., then located in Philadelphia; now located in Firthcliffe, Orange Co., NY.

———

**BOOTH, JESSE**                     H-787-8, C-37
of Middletown.

ALFRED BOOTH[1] of Hamptonburgh m. Dollie Watkins (Ree of Goshen, in Jan. 1843, and had:

Matilda Roe, m. W. H. D. Blake of New Paltz, NY; d. Oct. 1904.

Hanna Caroline, m. George Slaughter of Campbell Hall.

Marianna, m. Lewis H. Woolsey of New Phaltz.

Sarah Reeve, m. Samuel B. Hepburn of East Orange, NJ.

1853, May 8, **JESSE**.

**JESSE BOOTH[2]**, b. Campbell Hall, farmer on homestead owned by family for 200 years, m. Keturah Crowell of St. Andrews, NY, 7 Jan. 1885. Members of Presbyterian Church of Hamptonburgh. They had:

1885, Sept. 28, Anna Louise; d. age 16 months.

1888, Oct. 26, Dollie Watkins.

1890, Jan. 12, Pierson.

1893, Oct. 23, Alfred.

1896, Sept. 26, Wellington.

[NOTE: Goshen church records show marriages of: 24 Jan. 1789, Jesse Booth m. Dolly Watkins, and Jan. 1843, Alfred Booth of Hamptonburgh m. Dolly Reeves of Goshen, wit: James Cooper Reeve & T. T. Reeve.]

**BOOTH, VINCENT [P]**　　　　A-375, 656a, C-43
of Hamptonburgh.

CHARLES BOOTH settled at Neeleytown, Town of Montgomery, c. 1730. He had two sons, Charles & George. Charles & George each m. a d/o William & Sarah Bull. One of George's daus. m. Capt. William Jackson of the Rev. War. This could be the George below.

GEORGE BOOTH[1] from Southhold, L.I., settled in Orange Co. in 1741. His son:

BENJAMIN BOOTH[2] m. Sarah, d/o William & Sarah (Wells) Bull; farmer of Orange Co. Their son:

THOMAS BOOTH[3], farmer, d. on homestead in Hamptonburgh (formerly part of Goshen) 3 Oct. 1824, m. Jane Barker of SC. Children:

Jesse.

John, atty. of Goshen; d. IA.

1794, **VINCENT**.

Nancy, m. Washington Wood of Newburgh.

Amelia, m. Joseph Slaughter.

Louise, dec'd.

**VINCENT BOOTH[4]**, b. Hamptonburgh, farmer & miller; m. 9 Feb. 1826, Mary A., d/o William & Sarah (Booth) Conning, of early Orange Co. pioneer family. He is noted in Goshen church records as a witness at the wedding of George Gouge of Hamptonburgh & Matilda Booth of Goshen on 23 Jan. 1867. **VINCENT** spent his entire life on the homestead, where he d. 1 Nov. 1871, survived by his wife.

**BORDEN, JOHN GAIL**　　　　　　　H-788

JOHN G. BORDEN, b. Galveston, TX 4 Jan. 1844, youngest s/o Gail Borden, famous inventor. To NY at age 13 &

assisted father in establishing condensed milk business. Served in 150th NY Vols., enlisted at Poughkeepsie; later served in 47th NY Vol.

After the Civil War to Brewster, NY & in 1874 on the death of his father, succeeded him as president of Borden Condensed Milk Co. 1881 to Walkill & purchased the 'John P. Andrews' farm; retired in 1884. He d. Oct. 1891 in Ormond, FL, aged 47.

**BOURNE, CHARLES CLAYTON**　　　　H-789
of Newburgh since 1889.

CHARLES, b. Brooklyn, NY 1865, brick manufacturer at Fishkill Landing, Dutchess Co.; m. Anna, d/o James Fullager.

**BOWMAN, PHINEAS**　　　　　　A-143, TN-289
attorney of Newburgh.

PHINEAS was a captain in MA Regt. during the Rev. War: to Newburgh with Army and stayed. The second source says h[e] served as a Col. and also states that he was a great practic[al] joker who lost character & fortune during his last years by habit[s] of intemperance. "His memory is preserved only through the medium of anecdotes," which are here presented. Attorney [of] Ulster Co., 1791. His wife Mary d. 22 March 1813, age [5] Their child:

Mary m. Benjamin Anderson.

**BOYD, WILLIAM P.**　　　　　　　AA3-74-5
of Conesus, NY.

JOHN BOYD[1] of Scotland m. Dorcas Bennett. The name Boyd is derived from the Gaelic word Boidh, or Boidel, meaning fair or yellow. Their son:

EBENEZER BOYD[2] of Boyd's Corners, NY, b. Scotland c. 1735, d. at Kent, NY 29 June 1792. Probably to America 1750, was a capt. in the Rev. War. He res. in Westchester & Putnam Cos., NY, m. 1763/4 Sarah Merritt (b. New Bedford, NY 29 Oct. 1740, d. at Kent 29 June 1817), d/o Joseph & Polly (Theal) Merritt. Their son:

PHILIP BOYD[3], b. New Bedford, NY 24 May 1771, d. at Conesus, NY 31 May 1823, served in War of 1812. He m. 7 Feb. 1793, Elizabeth Barrett, b. New Bedford 6 April 1773, d. Coneus 30 Aug. 1836. They had:

Justis[4], d. on Lake Erie 16 June 1838 by the burning of the steamboat *George Washington*, from which he saved about thirty children's lives & was buried at Silver Creek, NY.

1806, Dec. 18, HIRAM.

HIRAM BOYD[5], s/o Justis[4], b. Newburgh, NY, to Conesus at age 16, farmer. He m. 6 Nov. 1836, Jane McNich, b. Richmond, NY 25 Aug. 1808, d. 17 April 1883, d/o James & Jane (Allen) McNich, pioneer settlers of Conesus who came from PA in 1806. They had:

WILLIAM P. BOYD[6], b. Conesus 26 March 1849, author & publisher. He m. 28 Sept. 1870, Mary R. Allen, b. 22 June 1850, d/o Matthew & Mary A. (Thorpe) Allen. They had one child, Victor H. Boyd, b. 21 March 1878.

**BOYNTON, EDWARD C.**                    H-789-90

MAJOR E. C. BOYNTON m. Mary J. Hubbard and had in 1864, at West Point, NY, **EDWARD C.**, who grad. 1887 Cornell University; assisted in labors of Thomas Edison 2 years, electrical engineer, held many positions in NY & MN.

**BRADLEY, THOMAS W.**                    H-790
of Walden.

**THOMAS** was for 50 years in the employ of the NY Knife Co. as president & treasurer; President of Walden National Bank & officer of other banks; political service. He m. 1867 Josephine Denniston, d/o Col. James of Little Britain. **THOMAS** served in the Union Army in the Civil War & was awarded the Congressional Medal of Honor at Chancellorsville; wounded in Gettysburg and in later battles.

**BRADNER, IRA S. [P]**        A-185-6, H-224, H-231, C
physician of Middletown, and desc. of:        **LDS Anc. File**

Rev. JOHN BRADNER[1], b. 1692 in Edinburgh, Scotland, s/o Gilbert b. 1666 in Scotland and wife Susanna ---. JOHN first Presbyterian minister of Goshen, settled there 1721; d. 1732. Served as pastor of Cold Spring Presbyterian Church, Cape May, NJ before being called to Goshen. He m. Christiana, d/o Alexander & Christian (Thompson) Coville, in Gretna Green, Scotland in 1712, over her father's wishes. Christina b. 1693, d. 1759 in Goshen. The Covill family were Huguenot refugees in Scotland. Rev. John was a graduate of the University of Edinburgh in 1712. Their children:
1719, Calvin, b. NJ [crossed out & changed to Colvill[e].]
1725, John Jr., b. NJ.
1720, Gilbert.
1721, Sarah.
Christian. According to Goshen church records Benjamin Ludlum m. Christian Bradner 27 Jan. 1783 & had a son John b. 4 July 1792, son Daniel Elsworth Ludlum 18 Nov. 1786 & son Collvil Bradner Ludlum, b. 28 Oct. 1789.
1733, Benoni (Rev.), grad. Princeton College 1755, settled in Jamaica, L.I. in 1760; 1762 to Church Nine Partners, Dutchess Co. He m. R. Bridges. A Benoni Bradner d. 29 Jan. 1806 at Chester, aged 50, pleurisy.
1734, Susanna, 1789 m. Joseph Carpenter, b. 1692, NY, s/o Samuel & Sarah Carpenter of Jamaica, NY.
1736, Mary.
1738, Elizabeth Bradner, m. John Steward I. [See Steward family.]

BENJAMIN BRADNER[1] m. Mary Wickham 16 July 1789; he d. 17 Oct. 1827, aged 57. She dec'd. by 16 Nov. 1794. They had:
1780/90?, May 16, THOMAS WICKHAM.
1791, Dec. 23, Covill; could be the Calvin Bradner m. Sarah Denton 29 Dec. 1818 in Goshen church records & had son John Denton Bradner, bapt. 1 May 1823.
Bapt. 1794, May 4, William. Could be the William Bradner

who m. Frances E. Wood, 3 Jan. 1822, at Goshen.

BENJAMIN[1]'s further children; perhaps by a second wife:
1797, Jan. 29, Frances.
Bapt. 1800, May 3, Horace.
Bapt. 1803, June 26, Maria.

THOMAS WICKHAM BRADNER[2], s/o Benjamin[1], b. Goshen, Orange Co., farmer, Presbyterian Church member at Goshen, m. Susan Smith, 6 Feb. 1816, & had:
Bapt. 1817, Aug. 2, William Fisk, farmer; dec'd.
Bapt. 1818, Oct. 31, Eliza Anderson, m. David Redfield, Goshen merchant, 22 June 1858; d. Goshen.
1820, June 2, Dr. **IRA S.**
Bapt. 1822, Nov. 2, Rev. Thomas Scott, Presbyterian Clergyman at Glen Cove, L.I. A Rev. Thomas Bradner of Milford, PA m. Agnes Wilson of Goshen 22 May 1850.
Bapt. 1824, Aug. 6, Harriet Newell; d. unm.
Harvey, farmer of Goshen; dec'd.
Susan Emily, m. Joseph Young[s] of Goshen, 6 Dec. 1865.
Caroline.
Bapt. 1827, Nov. 8, Frances Maria.
Bapt. 1830, May 1, Horace Howard.
Bapt. 1832, Aug. 4, Henry Melanclton.
Bapt. 1839, Nov. 2, Susan Emily.

Goshen church records show deaths of Frances Maria at age 5 & Horace Howard, aged 3, both of scarletina. Frances d. 17 May & Horace 5 July 1832.

**DR. IRA SMITH BRADNER[3]**, son of Thomas Wickham Bradner[2], b. Goshen; practiced in Scotchtown; 1857 to Middletown; served as surgeon 56th Regt. NYV; m. Sarah Jane d/o John G. Houston and Susan Bronson, b. 18 July 1819, and had:
Julia E., physician of Middletown.
Susan, m. Odell Hathaway of Newburgh.
1849, Oct. 6, Fred H., physician of Middletown; d. Jan. 1880.
John Fremont, attorney of Middletown.
Isabella G.

**BRADNER, JOHN B.**                    H-790-1
of Bellvale.

JOHN BRADNER, b. 1849, farmer, store clerk, postmaster, bank trustee, storekeeper at Greenwood Lake; owns orange grove in St. Petersburg, FL. He m. Clara R. Hunt in 1873 & they had 4 children, 2 living.

**BRADNER, WILLIAM A.**                    H-791

JACOB HOWE BRADNER[1], d. 1901, m. Sarah C. Vanderoort & had 6 children, 4 living:
1867, May 23, **WILLIAM A.**
John H., of Olean.
Carrie, m. S. D. Tilt of Warwick.
Samuel Blain Dolson of Bowie, AZ.

**WILLIAM A. BRADNER[2]**, b. on farm near Warwick; purchased farm of James Bell, dairy farmer.

## BRANT, JOSEPH                              T-52, 96

JOSEPH BRANT was the name of a Mohawk Chief; a description of him by Capt. Jeremiah Snyder, who was taken prisoner near Saugerties with his son Elias, is found in this reference, along with a drawing of Brant. Joseph was b. in OH c. 1742, d. 24 Nov. 1807, a Shawnee by birth & a Mohawk by adoption. It has been said that he is a son of Sir William Johnson.

## BREWSTER, EUGENE A.                        A-157, 220
atty. of Newburgh; lineal desc. of Elder Brewster of Plymouth Pilgrims.

SAMUEL BREWSTER, desc. of Elder Brewster of Plymouth, of New Windsor in Rev. War era, an immediate ancestor of:
EUGENE, b. 13 April 1827, NY; to Newburgh with parents at age 3; m. Anna W., d/o Rev. John Brown, D.D., 1859.

A Samuel Brewster was an early settler at Orangeville, Town of New Windsor; built sawmill & dewlling house with forge in 1755.

## BREWSTER, GEORGE RICHARD                   H-791
attorney of Newburgh.

This family traced through Brewsters of L.I. & CT to Nathaniel, member of Harvard grad. class of 1642, his father Francis to America from London, England & settled in New Haven, CT.
**GEORGE RICHARD**, b. Newburgh 17 Nov. 1873, grad. Yale 1894, Vestryman St. George's Church; m. 18 Jan. 1899, Margaret Conley Orr, d/o the late James of Newburgh.

## BREWSER, NATHANIEL R.                      H-791-2

WILLIAM BREWSTER, who came over in the *Mayflower*, the progenitor of the Brewsters in America.

NATHANIEL R. BREWSTER[3], farmer of East Coldenham, town of Newburgh is a descendant. His father was William C.[2] and grandfather Nathaniel[1], who originally cultivated the homestead in Coldenham. **NATHANIEL** near his home unearthed the skeleton of a mastoden, which is now in the NY Museum of Natural History. **MR. BREWSTER** established here a school for nervous & backward children in 1896.

## BREWSTER, WALTER H.                        H-792

**WALTER H. BREWSTER[2]** is descended from an old Orange Co. family. He is supervisor of Town of Blooming-Grove & the s/o Henry S.[1] Brewster & Harriet Halsey. **WALTER** was b. on the family farm in Blooming-Grove in 1869, farmer; m. Elizabeth, d/o Rev. Warren Hathaway. They have one

son, Henry.

## GEORGE E. BRINK                           H-792
RR agent, Chester.

GEORGE E. BRINK[1] of Franklin, NY m. Lucretia Trundell of Vernon, NJ and had:
**GEORGE E.[2]**, b. 7 Dec. 1879 at Franklin Furnace, NJ; with mother to Warwick, NY at age 3.

## BRINK, LEANDER                            H-792

JAMES BRINK[1], b. Town of Wallkill, Orange Co., 1804, of Dutch ancestry. His son,
**LEANDER BRINK[2]**, b. Town of Shawangunk, Ulster Co., NY 30 Jan. 1833; with parents at age 2 to Schuyler Co.; 1854 to Middletown & clerked with uncle Hiram Brink, furniture dealer until Oct. 1857 when he was taken in as partner. 1864 to Saginaw, MI, manufacturer of salt. Retired to Middletown, N.Y. 1867. He m. Mary Horton, d/o Hiram of Wallkill Twp., 1857.

## BRINSON FAMILY OF WALLKILL                 A-433

THOMAS and SAMUEL BRINSON, brothers, settled in the north part of Wallkill. Thomas[1] sold his farm to son-in-law Abner Bull who m. Thomas' dau. Maria[2]. Abner d. 1857. Children of Maria & Abner (BULL):
Mrs. Charles Mills of Millsburgh.
Mrs. William D. Hurtin of Circleville.
Sarah, d. unm. 1860.
Mrs. William Gale of Rahway, NJ.
Thomas, d. 1871.

## BROCK, T. HUNT                            H-792-3

T. HUNT BROCK, b. Scranton PA 1870. Started in hotel business in 1881 at Hotel Windsor at Scranton, remained 10 years & then removed to Port Jervis in 1901 & purchased the Erie Hotel.

## BROOKS, CHAUNCY                           H-793
builder of Montgomery.

CHAUNCY BROOKS, b. at Eagle Valley in what was then Town of Monroe. His father to what is now called Tuxedo.
CHAUNCY m. 1889 Martha, d/o Thomas & Mary (Mould) Wait, and had:
Charles W., civil engineer, res. DC in employ of the War & Navy Dept.
Alida W., attended Univ. of NY; teacher.
Minnie M., res. Montgomery, music instructor.

CHAUNCY has been a teacher, architect & builder contractor & has a brother, Malcom, res. Monroe.

## BROOKS, GEORGE H.                    H-793-4

GEORGE H. was b. at Mountainville in 1875; to Turners, NY,
   blacksmith; 1879 to Chester, Town of Sugar Loaf & back to
   Chester 1791; buggy manufacturer. Methodist. He m. Sept.
   1885 Eliza Litchult, and had:
Dora L.
Lena C.
Elsie.
Helen.
Merry.
Clarence.
Phoebe J.

   GEORGE'S father [not named here] is still living at Little
Britain, in Town of New Windsor, aged 90.

## BROWN, CHICHESTER              A-165-6, TN-303
physician of Newburgh

JOHN BROWN[1] of Monaghan, Ireland, was dealer in hardware,
   books & stationary there.   To America 1798 settled in
   Newburgh, followed by his wife & family in 1800.   He
   established a "Universal Store" there [like a dept. store
   today--for copy of a newspaper ad for this store, see CN-34]
   & d. 1 Oct. 1825, aged 67.   His wife was Alice Chichester,
   of Scotch parentage; she d. 14 Sept. 1829.   Their children:
1783, Jan. 20, CHICHESTER.
John, m. Eliza Case of Goshen; he d. 1852, no issue.
JAMES S.
Isabella, m. Robert Wilson; d. 1821.
Anna Jane, m. John Forsyth; d. 1852.
Edward, d. 1820.

CHICHESTER BROWN[2], s/o John[1], d. 8 Aug. 1849; m.
   Catherine d/o Dr. George Graham of Shawangunk, and had:
John James, m. Mary R. Van Arsdale, who d. 5 March 1855,
   leaving one son, Chichester. [Another source gives John &
   James as two separate persons.]
Dr. George, m. Jeanet, d/o George Bruce of NY; has Bruce B.

JAMES S. BROWN[2], s/o John[1], m. Sarah Haines, and had:
Hannah Jane.
Ann Eliza.
Sarah.
John C.
Isabella.
Achsah.

## BROWN, C. FRANK                      A-160
attorney of Newburgh.

   C. FRANK BROWN, s/o Hon. JOHN W., b. 12 Sept. 1844;
m. 27 June 1876, Hattie E. Shaffer of Poughkeepsie.

## BROWN, DAVID                         H-794
express business in NY City.

DAVID BROWN m. Mary J. Baxter and has one dau.,
Genevieve.  He has a country place at Newburgh, purchased in
1903.

## BROWN, EBER L.                       H-794

   EBER L. BROWN, of Town of Minisink, large landowner
in Orange Co., was b. Sussex Co., NJ in 1828.  Worked in NY
City & in 1848 to CA in mining.  His father was b. in Unionville.  EBER is a silk manufacturer, has a wholesale grocery
business & is a bank director.  He was m. twice: (1st) to Sarah
E. Lewis & (2d) to Caroline M. Lain.  By his 2d m. they have
12 children, 5 living.

## BROWN, EDWARD ALLEN                 H-794-5
prop. Brown Hotel, Middletown.

   MR. BROWN was b. Town of Greenville, Orange Co., 7
Dec. 1840; to Middletown 1888.  Had hotel business in NY
City, New Orleans LA, Logansport IN & Port Jervis NY.  He
was Orange Co. sheriff 2 years.

## BROWN, REV. JOHN, D.D.          A-302a-03, C-18
Protestant-Episcopal minister of Newburgh.

REV. JOHN BROWN, b. 19 May 1791, NY City; ordained at
   St. Paul's P.E. Church NY City 1812; served at Fishkill,
   Newburgh, New Windsor, Monticello, Middletown, Cornwall
   and Marlborough; m. 1819, Nov. 15, at St. George's Church,
   Frances Elizabeth, d/o Robert Ludlow, who d. 18 April 1872,
   and had:
Mary m. Daniel T. Rogers.  [Goshen church records show
   wedding of Mary Brown & Robert Rogers, 15 Dec. 1789.]
Margaret T. L. m. George W. Kerr, banker of Newburgh.
Augusta P. m. Moses Ely.
Helen.
Anna W. m. Eugene A. Brewster, Newburgh lawyer.
John Hobart.
Charles L.

## BROWN, JOHN K.                       W-92

JOHN K. BROWN, b. Coldenham, NY 1854, farmer, now
   occupies farm in Wallkill Valley.  He was the eldest s/o John
   J. Brown & Sarah Laird; m. Virginia Reade of Brooklyn, NY
   3 April 1878, and had:
John Taylor.
Susie L.
Annie C.
Thornton Knox.
Laura V.
Leonard Wilson.

## BROWN, JOHN W.                       A-149

Attorney, b. Dundee, Scotland, 11 Oct. 1876.  Brought by father
in 1801 to Putnam Co., NY and then to West Newburgh where

he conducted a fulling-mill. He has served as a j.p. and Congressman (1832 & 34); m. Eliza d/o Selah Reeve.

## BROWN, R. T.           H-795

MR. BROWN, of Brown & Whitten, merchants at Pine Bush, was b. NY City & m. Elizabeth Decker; they have 13 children.

## BROWN, U. GRANT           H-795

U. GRANT BROWN[2] is of Welsh descent. His ancestors from Wales to America 1650 & settled at L.I., Oyster Bonds (now Glen Port).

DANIEL T. BROWN[1] m. Lucretia --- & had 5 children, two living.
1863, July 28, U. GRANT.
Linus W., res. New Orleans, LA.

U. GRANT BROWN[2], b. at Burnside, Orange Co., farmer. He m. Anna Sinsabaugh of Cornwall, NY 27 March 1889, and had:
Edna.
Josephine.
Helen.

## BROWN, WILLIAM S. [P]        A-783-4
of Cornwall.

The first BROWN[1] emigrated from England to Cromwell before the Rev. War. His children:
JOHN.
William.
Thomas.
Nathaniel.
Frank.
Amelia m. Martin Hallock of Monroe.
Ann m. Edward Coffee of Cornwall.

JOHN BROWN[2], b. Cromwell, farmer; m. Hannah Cronk and had 16 children, those who survived childhood:
Ann, m. E.B. St. John of Cornwall.
1809, Aug. 3, WILLIAM S.
Henry.
Edward.
John.
Hedges.
James.
Elliot.
Louisa, m. John Requa of NY.
Esther, m. Baldwin Fox of Brooklyn.

WILLIAM S. BROWN[3], b. town of Cornwall; apprenticed to John Golow to learn trade of dressing deer hides for buckskin in Vail's Gate (town of New Windsor, now known as Tooker's Gate). Removed to NY worked as carter and lime

burner. Removed to Rockland, ME & returned to NY, where in 1857 he purchased land in Cornwall, where he has served as town officer. 20 March 1830, m. Martha, d/o John & Ann Rose of Flatbush, L.I. Martha b. 10 April 1807; d. 23 May 1876. Children:
Louisa Ann, d. in childhood.
George Ogden, d. 1856, Aug. 20.
John Ross, businessman of NY.
Hannah M., m. Alphea Phillips of Blooming-Grove.
Charles, d. 1881.
Hezekiah P., businessman of NY City.
Harriet F., m. Robert S. Talbot of Blooming-Grove.

## BRYSON, ALLEN [P]          W-86

ALLEN BRYSON resides at Saratoga Farm (Montgomery) on forks of the Goshen & Middletown Rd. 18 Nov. 1869 he m. Emma F., d/o John & Emily Mould, and had:
Alice, m. George Bell of Reading, PA.
Carrie, dec'd.
Josepha, at home.

## BUCKBEE, WILLIAM WISNER      H-79

MR. BUCKBEE is the grandson of Capt. John Wisner. He wa. b. 12 July 1861 at Wisner, Orange Co. at a home that has been in his family for 140 years. He was a farmer, coal & feed dealer & postmaster at Wisner; d. 12 July 1861. His wife was H. Elizabeth Wisner & they m. 7 Oct. 1885, and had:
Emma.
Albert.
Anna.
William.
Francis.
Henry.
Louise.

## BULL FAMILY OF SOUTH CAROLINA    H-798-9

STEPHEN BULL & BARNABY BULL, s/o Josiah Bull of Kingshurst Hall, emigrated to SC in 1670 in the ship *Carolina*. They were the uncles of WILLIAM BULL who emigrated in 1715, settling at Hamptonburgh, Orange Co., NY.

STEPHEN was deputy proprietor for Lord Ashley 1674-1682 and is buried at his seat, Ashley Hall. Stephen's son, Hon. WILLIAM BULL, res. Charleston, SC, the 1st American to graduate in medicine at Lyden in 1734; he. d. in London in 1791, was an officer in both the early Indian Wars; served as lt. gov. 1738 to 1744. William's son, Stephen, resided at Sheldon & had a son, Gen. STEPHEN BULL of the Revolution.

## BULL FAMILY OF WALKILL        A-433
## BULL, ALBERT [P]       A-493, C-80
of Wallkill.
## BULL, CHARLES R.          H-796
## BULL, DANIEL [P]          A-428a

of Crawford.

**BULL, DANIEL H. [P]**          A-654a
of Hamptonburgh.          C-22
**BULL, EBENEZER**          H-796
**BULL, HARRISON**          A-504
of Wallkill
**BULL, HORACE [P]**          A-428
of Crawford.
**BULL, IRA [P]**          A-625-6
bank dir. & farmer of Chester.
**BULL, IRVING CRAWFORD**
chemist.          H-797
**BULL, JAMES M. [P]**          A-563
of Goshen.
**BULL, JESSE [P]**          A-648-9
**BULL, JOHN S. [P]**          A-244-5, H-795-6
**BULL, RICHARD**          H-797-8
**BULL, STEPHEN**          H-798
wholesale grocer of Newburgh.
**BULL, WILLIAM [P]**          A-651-3, H-252a, 250-1,
          H-254-5, C-16, LDS Anc. File

BULL, WILLIAM[1], b. Wolverhampton, England, Feb. 1689, was an early settler of Orange Co. Church record at Wolverhampton shows the records of the family back to 900 A.D. His father was b. in Ireland & William was also raised in Ireland. [H-250: family left for Dublin in Feb. 1689 & gives William's father as John, and his grandfather as Josias of Kingshurst Hall.] William was apprenticed in England as a mason; emigrated 1715, built first house on Wawayanda Patent; m. Sarah Wells in 1718. Sarah was an orphan brought up by Christopher Denn(e) & his wife Elizabeth. William d. Feb. 1755, age 66; Sarah b. in NJ, opposite Staten Island 6 April 1694, d. 21 April 1796, age 102 years & 15 days & was bur. in the family graveyard at Hamptonburgh, leaving 355 living descendants. [For the story of Sarah's settlement see T- 32.] Their children, all b. Hamptonburgh:

1721, May 3, JOHN.

1723, March 13, WILLIAM.

1725, Sept. 1, Sarah, m. Charles [George] Booth of Hamptonburgh.

1727, Dec. 27, THOMAS.

1729, Nov. 17, ISAAC.

1731, May 29, Esther, m. 1750, John Miller of Montgomery, b. 1724.

1733, Feb. 3, Mary, m. Benjamin Booth of Hamptonburgh, b. 1728.

1736, May 1, Margaret, m. 1757, Silas Horton of Goshen, b. 1729.

1738, May [March] 24, Catharine, m. James Faulkner of Wallkill, b. 1731.

1740, Nov. 4 [3], Ann, m. William Eager of Neelytown, b. 10 Nov. 1728.

1743, May 29, Richard, m. Jemima Budd of Goshen, b. c. 1743.

1745, March 4, Eleanor, m. Henry [Wilhelmus] Weller of Montgomery, b. 1745.

Sarah (Wells) Bull m. (2d) Johannes Miller, early settler of Montgomery. He d. 1782.

JOHN BULL[2], s/o William[1], b. on homestead at Hamptonburgh, m. 9 Aug. 1807, Hannah Holly of Goshen, b. 1728, and had:

Ebenezer.

Sarah, m. Richard Earl.

Elizabeth, m. Peter Earl.

Mary, m. John Tuthill.

William.

1758, Nov. 12, SAMUEL.

John.

1762, 25 Oct., RICHARD.

DANIEL.

Esther, m. William Brush.

Crisse (Chrisie). Goshen church records show that Elizabeth, wife of Chrisse Bull d. 8 June 1809, aged 41; consumption.

1772, Feb. 15, ISAAC.

SAMUEL BULL[3], s/o John[2], b. 12 Nov. 1758, res. Circleville, blacksmith & farmer; served in Revolutionary War; m. 15 April 1787, Margaret Gale, b. 28 March 1762; both bur. at Hamptonburgh, and had: (boys were all stone masons)

Benjamin.

Sarah Margaret.

William.

1793, Nov. 28, SAMUEL JR.

Phebe.

George.

Oscar.

SAMUEL BULL JR.[4], s/o Samuel, m. Mary Osborne, b. 1795, d. 4 May 1875. Samuel Jr. was a drummer in the War of 1812, a Master Mason, owned farm in Circleville and gave land for the Presbyterian church. He d. 13 April 1857. Children:

John, merchant at Circleville.

William H., farmer at Circleville.

Mary, m. Charles H. Stringham of City Island, NY.

Daniel, merchant at Burlington, Sullivan Co.

Robert, farmer and stone mason of Circleville.

1832, Jan. 20, **HARRISON.**

Catharine, m. James H. VanFleet of Jersey City; dec'd.

Elizabeth, m. George M. Beakes, M.D. of Bloomingburgh, NY.

HARRISON BULL[5], s/o Samuel Jr., b. Circleville; 1856 with brother Daniel merchant at Circleville until 1874. Postmaster of Circleville (1856); j.p. (1870) and now serving 4th term. 5 Jan. 1858, m. Nancy, d/o Bartlett D. and Sarah C. (Sample) Bennett of NY, and had:

Georgianna.

Irene C.

RICHARD BULL[3], b. Hamptonburgh, m. 12 April 1800, Lena [Goshen church records give her name as Sarah], d/o Benjamin Harlow of Phillipsburgh, & settled in Chester in the Sugar Loaf Valley; farmer & miller, d. 5 Jan. 1845. Lena/Sarah b. 19 June 1772, d. 2 March 1854; Presbyterian Church members. Their children, all b. Chester:

18

1801, Feb. Hannah, m. Joseph Ray of Warwick; she now dec'd.
1802, Dec. 27, **JESSE.**
1805, Jan. 15, James H., res. Monroe.
Harvey.
1806, Dec. 11, **DANIEL H.**
1809, Dec. 27, IRA.
Charles W., d. 11 Oct. 1865, age 53.

**JESSE BULL**[4] s/o Richard[3], b. Chester, m. 15 Feb. 1827, Caroline, d/o Cornelius & Annas Board of Chester. **JESSE** was a farmer & d. 5 Jan. 1878. Their children:
Susan, d. young.
Phebe Ann, m. Isaac V. Wheeler of Warwick.
John J., d. young.
1832, Aug. 1, Hannah; d. 4 May 1851.
1834, July 18, Mary Elizabeth; d. 26 Nov. 1849.
Susan Caroline, res. on homestead.
1838, CHARLES RICHARD.
Emma Lena, m. Nathaniel B. Zambriskie of Hackensack, NJ.

**CHARLES RICHARD BULL**[5], s/o Jesse[4], res. near Oxford Depot, was b. Blooming Grove; farmer, co. commissioner, bank director & other business. He m. Harriet, d/o Jesse Roe of Chester & had:
Jesse, at home.
Caroline, m. Clarence S. Knight.
Mary, m. S. B. Patterson.

**BULL, DANIEL H.**[4], s/o Richard[3] b. on homestead; m. 8 Jan. 1840, Mary Ann, d/o Nathaniel & Mary (Kingsland) Board of NJ. Children:
Harriet; d. 27 Aug. 1865, age 24.
Mary B., m. John W. Harlow, farmer of Wallkill.
Sarah; d. 6 Aug. 1865, age 21.
Anna L., at home.
Charles W.; d. 23 Aug. 1865, age 19.
**RICHARD.**

**RICHARD BULL**[5], b. at Campbell Hall, s/o Daniel Harlow Bull[4] & Mary Ann Board, is a descendant of William Bull & Sarah Wells; a 6th generation descendant on his father's side & a 7th generation descendant on his mother's. He m. Annie Wells of Newburgh whose mother was d/o Mehetable Bull & Capt. William Bull, officer of the Revolution. They have one son, Charles Wells Bull, a jeweler in NY City.

**BULL, IRA**[4], s/o Richard[3], m. 10 Dec. 1845, Phebe, d/o Ira Hawkins & granddau. of Moses Hawkins [see below.] Their children:
Hannah Lena m. Erastus W. Hawkins of Brooklyn.
Mary Adaline.
1850, Aug. 21, Jesse James; d. infancy.
Phebe Ann.
Sarah Wells m. Thomas W. Houston of Goshen.
1857, Dec. 2, Iretta Hawkins; d. 16 Oct. 1871.
Charles Ira.
1864, Oct. 24, Frank M.; d. 16 Oct. 1871.

IRA HAWKINS m. Hannah, d/o Gen. Abram Vail of East Division, Goshen and had 3 sons & 3 daus. Only one named:
1825, Nov. 28, Phebe m. **IRA BULL.**

DANIEL[3] BULL, s/o John[2] b. on the homestead at Hamptonburgh; settled in town of Chester, large land owner & Quaker, d. age 84; m. Lena Harlow of Hamptonburgh, who d. c. age 45, and had:
Stephen, lived & d. on homestead at Chester.
Ebenezer, lived & d. on original Bull homestead at Hamptonburgh.
Phebe m. Joseph Booth of Hamptonburgh.
1798, March 25, JOHN MILTON.

JOHN MILTON BULL[4] s/o Daniel[3] & Sarah, m. Martha d/o Joseph and granddaughter of Charles Durland who came from L.I. in 1756. Charles served in the French & Indian War and later settled in Chester at place now owned by his grandson James Durland. Martha b. 1800, May, now oldest living member of the Chester Presbyterian Church (1881). JOHN MILTON BULL settled on farm in Little Long Pond in Monroe, farmer; d. 29 Nov. 1879, and had:
Sarah, d. young.
Ebenezer res. Westchester Co.
Mary Ann, d. age 42.
1830, April 3, **JAMES M.**
Samuel, res. on homestead of father in Monroe.
Elizabeth, m. Joseph W. Young; d. at Oxford 1858, **Nov.**
Emily, became 2d wife of Joseph W. Young.

**JAMES M. BULL**[5], b. Monroe, dairy farmer, m. 25 Jan. 1859, Ann Elizabeth d/o George S. Conkling and Mary Seeley and grandau. of Joshua Conkling who came from L.I. and was an early settler of Goshen. Mary Seeley (b. 8 June 1835) was d/o Thaddeus Seeley, s/o Thaddeus an old resident of Chester. Children of **JAMES M.** & Ann Elizabeth Bull:
George Seeley, drowned young.
Albert C.
Cornelia.
John Milton, d. young.
Whitfield H.

BULL, ISAAC[3], s/o John[2] b. 15 Feb. 1772, farmer in town of Monroe; d. 16 Oct. 1846; m. (1st) Hannah Mapes who d. 16 March 1812, age 36, and had:
1795, March 6, Maria; d. 21 June 1818.
1797, March 11, Franklin; d. 1855.
1798, Nov. 30, Sarah, m. Francis Bowman.
1800, Oct. 11, David; d. Dec. 1880.
1802, Feb. 7, Hiram W.; d. 26 July 1863.
1805, Aug. 23, Daniel; d. 14 Sept. 1813.
1808, Feb. 25, Elizabeth, m. Francis Bowman [sic]; d. 12 **Aug.** 1873.
1809, Nov. 26, **JOHN SPRINGSTEAD.**
Infant, d. unnamed.

Isaac m. (2d) Rachel Marvin who d. without issue 27 Jan. 1829, age 55.

JOHN SPRINGSTEAD BULL[4], b. Monroe, s/o Isaac[3] and 1st wife Hannah Mapes, b. Slattery, town of Monroe; d. 17 Nov. 1876. Clerk at Hamptonburgh at age 14; emp. of brother-in-law, David H. Moffatt at Washingtonville at age 17 and purchased the business in 1832. Old Clinton farm town of New Windsor of Walter Halsey and farmed until his death. Member of Blooming-Grove Congregational Church. 22 Nov. 1832, m. (1st) Melissa d/o James and Mary (Chandler) Gregg of Bethlehem, Orange Co., who d. with no issue 12 March 1833.

JOHN S.[4] m. (2d) 11 Nov. 1835, Currence B. d/o Samuel & Bethiah (Reeder) Moffatt of Blooming-Grove, who was b. 8 Oct. 1815, and had:
Sarah Frances.
Melissa, m. Thomas H. Moffatt of NY City.
Josephine.
1844, July 14, STEPHEN M.
Isaac J., res. Washingtonville.
Anna B., m. Andrew Weyant of Orange Co.
1855, Austin C., farmer on homestead.
Emma L.
[Three daus. and one son reside at home.]

STEPHEN M. BULL[5], s/o John S.[4], b. on the Clinton homestead in Little Britain, in 1864 to Newburgh; m.26 May 1869 Martha, d/o Samuel Oakley, & had:
Emily Grace.
John Springstead.

WILLIAM BULL[2], s/o William[1] the emigrant, m. Anne Booth of Hamptonburg, b. 1731, & had:
1753, June 20, MOSES[3], d. 23 Dec. 1844; and he had one son:
1773, June 19, MOSES JR.[4]

MOSES BULL JR.[4], b. Scotchtown in the town of Wallkill; d. 16 May 1848. 28 July 1795, m. Dolly Moore, b. 17 June 1771, d. 14 May 1855. Members of the Presbyterian Church; both bur. in Scotchtown Cemetery. Soon after their marriage they settled on farm in eastern Wallkill & had:
Sophia, m. Thomas Bell of Geneva, NY.
Arietta, m. John Patterson of NY; d. 1866.
1801, Jan. 16, Elijah (twin); d. 1870.
1801, Jan. 16, ELISHA (twin). [NOTE: Another source gives birth dates of the twins as 1817.]
Rev. Ralph, Presbyterian clergyman at Westtown, Orange Co. 21 years.
Marianne, widow of the late Daniel Cousins [Cougens] of Middletown.
Caroline (twin), m. (1st) Andrew McWilliams; m. (2d) Harvey [Charles] McMonagle of Wallkill.
Catherine (twin); d. 1829 aged 21.
Mehitabel, m. Moses McMonagle of Wallkill.
Rhoda, m. Hezekiah Conner of Wallkill; d. 1836.
Emma, m. Charles B. Conner of Wallkill; d. 1880.
Julia, m. Harvey J. H. [John H.] McWilliams of Circleville.
[One source gives a second Ralph, d. 1877.]

ELISHA BULL[5], s/o Moses Jr.[4], b. Wallkill; d. 22 June 1870, in MO while visiting his son. Farmer of the town of Warwick, member of Presbyterian Church of Amity; m. (1st) 4 March 1828, Harriet d/o Walter and Abigail (Cowin) Everett of Wallkill, b. 1806, d. 3 Sept. 1836, and had:
1829, April 16, ALBERT.
Walter.
Harriett, m. Henry Howe of Warwick.

Elisha m. (2d) Susan Dusenberre and had:
Sidney.
Harrison.
Charles.
Henry.
John P.

Elisha m. (3d) Mary Nichols; no issue.

ALBERT BULL[6], s/o Elisha[5], b. Wallkill, res. Western NY, Chester and Middletown, Orange Co.; drug business with Dr. Harvey Everett in Middletown; m. 20 June 1867, Ella B. d/o Leander and Nancy (Barkley) Crawford, b. Jan, 1845, and had:
Anna M.
Frank.
1879, Jan. 24, IRVING CRAWFORD.

IRVING C. BULL[7], s/o Albert Bull[6] & Ella B. Crawford, b. Middletown, Orange Co. In Oct. 1903 he formed Bull & Roberts, consultant chemists & metallurgists in NY City. 20 April 1904 he m. Mabel Dorothy Horton, youngest d/o James of Middletown & 7 July 1905 they had son Irving Horton Bull.

THOMAS BULL[2], s/o the emigrant William[1], m. (1) Mary Kerr of Florida, Orange Co., b. c. 1727, & settled in twp. of Crawford; he m. (2) Sarah Gale, b. c.1727. His son:
1761, DANIEL[3], farmer, 1780 m. Catherine Miller who d. 1 Oct. 1841, age 77. DANIEL d. 14 Nov. 1849; and had:
Thomas, m. Sarah Mills.
Hannah, m. Alexander Thompson.
Abner, m. Maria Brinson.
David C., m. Maria Barkley.
Keturah, m. William Bull.
Catharine, m. James H. Crawford.
Mary, m. Rev. John Johnson.
1787, March 21, HENRY.
Milton, m. Esther Crawford.
Sarah, m. Denton Mills.
Miller.
Daniel, m. Sarah Thompson.
John, d. young.

HENRY BULL[4], s/o Daniel[3] m. 4 Jan. 1810, Jane Stitt. Henry was a farmer and Presbyterian; he d. 1 Dec. 1863. Jane d. 1 Nov. 1857. Children:
1810, Oct. 17, Horace.
Celia, m. Johanis M. Hunter.
John S., dec'd.

Elmer W., dec'd.
Alpheus.
Catharine A.
Angeline, widow of John A. Stitt.
Esther, m. Charles M. Miller.
Mary E., m. S. C. Duryea.
William H., dec'd.
Daniel K.
Sarah L., dec'd.
Albert, dec'd.
Charles.

In 1821 the record shows that Daniel & Catherine had 52 grandchildren, all living except two had died in infancy.

ISAAC BULL[2], s/o William [1], m. Sarah Mulliner [Milliner], of Little Britain, b. 1724, and had:
1767, Peace, m. John Waldo, b. c. 1758, Windham, CT. They had Paulina Waldo, b. 1791, Harrison WV, who m. Berkely Barlett.

Below are supposed members of the above Bull family, which cannot be definitely placed.

## BULL, EBENEZER                                    H-796

**EBENEZER BULL** was the son of Ebenezer & Jane Bull who had 13 children. He was b. 3 March 1846 at Hamptonburgh, Orange Co., the 5th generation in direct descent to those who built the house in 1722. He is a dairy farmer & m. Anna, d/o Byard Walling of Middletown, 17 Oct. 1894.

## BULL, HARRY                                        H-796-7

**HARRY BULL** is the s/o William & Phoebe Bull of Stony Ford, Orange Co., where he was b. 25 May 1872, one of 8 children, 5 still living. He is a farmer & attended the Ag. College at Cornell University, Ithaca. He m. Lucille Pierson of Hamptonburgh, d/o W. H. & Elizabeth, and had:
Keturah, aged 7.
Henry, aged 6.

## BULL, SAMUEL SR.                                   A-432
of Wallkill, blacksmith; res. NY during the Rev. War, and had:
Samuel, res. Circleville.
Benjamin, moved to OH.
Oscar, on homestead.
Phebe, d. unm.

This Samuel could be Samuel[3], s/o John[2], but it cannot be confirmed from the records consulted for this work.

## BULL, WILLIAM                                       H-799

**WILLIAM BULL**, b. 25 July 1830 on the family homestead farm near Stony Ford, Orange Co. He is the 5th of his generation of this name to occupy the homestead, which house was built by the 3d William Bull, who served with Washington at Valley Forge & the Battle of Monmouth. **WILLIAM** graduated Princeton in 1851, was j.p. & postmaster of Stoney Ford, farmer. He m. Phoebe Bull, one of 8 d/o Ebenezer Bull of Hamptonburgh, 22 Nov. 1859. Their children:
Ebenezer Henry.
Bartow W.

Members of First Presbyterian Church of Campbell Hall.

## BULL, WILLIAM EDGAR                                 H-791
of Charleston, SC.

**WILLIAM E. BULL**, nephew of Stephen & Barnaby Bull progenitors of the Bull family in SC, & s/o Edmund Llewellyn & Mary Evelina (Bruen) Bull. Edmund Llewellyn is a descendant of William, who emigrated from Kingshurst Hall, Wolverhampton, England in 1715 & settled in Orange Co. **WILLIAM E.** was b. in Orange Co. 1817, removed to Charleston in 1832 & d. there in 1892. He m. Evelina Bruen in March 1844 & had 15 children.
The line of descent is:
William Bull m. Sarah Wells & had,
John Bull m. Hannah Holley & had,
Chrisie [probably s/o John Bull[2] & Hannah Holly above, but cannot be confirmed from records consulted for this work] Bull m. Elizabeth Case & had,
James D. Bull m. Nancy Rogers & had,
**WILLIAM EDGAR BULL.**

The information found on **WILLIAM E.** in this source does not agree with other information found & previously given.

## BUNN, ISAIAH                                        H-799-800

OBADIAH BUNN[1] m. Hanna I. Wilson & had 6 children, all living. Among them:
22 July, 1858, ISAIAH.

**ISAIAH BUNN[2]**, b. North Church, NJ, res. NY City & Hamburgh, bottling business. To Warwick 1887; m. Minnie Vanderhoff of Warwick & had:
Minnie, at home.
Howard, at home.

## BURNET, ROBERT [P]                                  A-241-2
of New Windsor.

ROBERT BURNET[1], from near Edinburgh, Scotland to America 1725, 1st settled at Raritan, NJ; tailor; 1729 to Little Britain [now Town of New Windsor] accompanied by brother who later returned to NJ [unnamed]. Presbyterian, d. 1774 in 73rd year; m. Ann Reid d/o John, and had:
JAMES.
John.
Robert.

Thomas.
Patrick.
Sarah.
Mary.

JAMES[2] had son, **ROBERT BURNET**[3], b. 22 Feb. 1762, Little Britain; soldier of the Rev. War and stationed at West Point; m. 9 June 1784, Rachel DeWitt who d. 4 June 1830, at age 68. She was a sister of Moses DeWitt and a niece of Mrs. Gen. James Clinton. **ROBERT** acquired land in New Windsor area, served in various political offices, including j.p. and was a businessman and at the time of his death was the last surviving original member of the Society of the Cincinnati and last surviving officer of the Army of the Rev. He d. 24 Nov. 1854, age 93. His children:

Alexander C.
Charles.
Jane.
Moses DeWitt, sheriff of Orange Co., had one son, John Barber Burnet, res. Syracuse.
Mary DeWitt.
Robert Jr.

----

**BURROUGHS, E. R.**      H-800
metal worker.

**E. R. BURROUGHS** is president & manager of the Abendroth & Root Mfg. Co. & has resided in Newburgh since 1901; from Greenpoint, NY.

----

**BURROWS, W. J.**      H-800

ALEXANDER BURROWS[1] m. Jennette Todd & had:
1856, W. J.

**W. J. BURROWS**[2], b. NY City, at age 2 with parents to Newburgh. Farmed with Fenton Cosman 8 years & purchased his present fruit farm. He m. Nancy E. Morrow & they have 5 children. Members Marlborough Presbyterian Church.

----

**BURT, A. J.** [P]      A-610
of Warwick.
**BURT, JAMES** [P]      A-607-8
of Warwick.

This English family settled early in CT.

DANIEL BURT[1] from CT to NY in 1746, settled on wild land in Warwick, Orange Co.; returned to CT and back to Orange Co. in 1760, where hamlet of Bellvale is now located, erected flour and saw mills; m. Hannah --- in 1760 & had 10 children, among them:
JAMES BURT[2], b. 1760, Oct. 25. Served in the Legislature (1797-1826) & other political officer on a local & national level; member Baptist Church of Warwick. 15 Aug. 1803 m. Abigail, d/o Benjamin Coe, and had:

Mary.
Benjamin.
1791, Nov. 28, STEPHEN A.
Phebe.
1798, March 9, **JAMES.**
Thomas M.

STEPHEN A. BURT[3], s/o James[2], m. 27 May 1818, Paulina, d/o Jeremiah Fairfield, and had:
Caroline.
Edward Fairfield.
1826, Oct. 27, **AUGUSTUS J.**
Abigail Jane.
Abigail Jane (2d).
Anna Scott.
John.

AUGUSTUS J. BURT[4], s/o Stephen A.[3], last adult male res. in Bellvale, was b. there. From 1845 "custodian" of post office, bank officer & businessman; m. 19 Aug. 1853, Ann E. Wilson of Bellvale, and had 9 children, those surviving:
James W.
Augustus.
Mary.
Gertrude E.
Maud.

JAMES BURT[3], s/o James[2] & Abigail, res. Warwick, farmer & member of Baptist Church; j.p., town supervisor & bank pres. 25 Dec. 1828, m. Mrs. Mary Harding, d/o Charles Gillett, and had:
Peter, dec'd.
Sarah.
Abigail.
Thomas, dec'd.
Lydia.

Mary (Gillett) Burt d. 16 July 1865.

----

**BURT, GRINNELL**      H-800-2
of Warrick.

James Burt was the grandfather of **GRINNELL BURT** who was b. in Bellvale, Orange Co. on 7 Nov. 1822 & d. 3 Aug. 1901. **GRINNELL** was orphaned at age 14. He read law and helped organize the Warwick Valley Railroad in 1859, was a founder of Christ Church. In 1849 he m. Jane S. VanDuzer (d. 1870), d/o Isaac of Warwick. Their children:
Frank Howard, d. in infancy.
Kate V. D., m. Charles Caldwell of Newburgh.
Lily, m. Frederick Halstead of Brooklyn.
Jane, d. 1903.
Mary Herrick, resides on homestead.

In 1886, **GRINNELL** m. (2d) Louise Pierson, d/o Samuel V. of Middletown and had Grinnell, Jr. and Howard, twins.

----

## BURT, THOMAS        H-802-03
of Warwick.

**THOMAS BURT**, b. 5 Jan. 1821; both parents died when he was c. age 15 and he went to live with his uncle, Thomas M. Burt, in Albany. He worked in OH and returned to his father's farm & sawmill which he operated until 1868, when he removed to Warwick, where he how lives. He operated a lumber & coal business and was an organizer of the Warwick Savings Bank. In 1846 he m. Hannah Sayer. They had children:
Elizabeth.
Lydia.
Annie.
Mrs. Vernon B. Carroll.

_____

## BUSH, GILMORE O.        H-803
of Town of Tuxedo.

**GILMORE O. BUSH** is the s/o James S. and Eliza J. (Minerly) Bush. He was b. in Arden, Orange Co., 1863. He spent 5 years in CT & in 1886 removed to Tuxedo Park to join police force. Deputy sheriff since 1886; postmaster since 1899.

_____

## BUSH, HORACE G.        H-803-4
of Monroe.
## BUSH, PETER B. [P]        A-808
of Monroe.C-15

This family originally from Holland.

HENRY BUSH[1], b. Orange Co., had:
Samuel.
John.
1783, Nov. 11, PETER H.
Henry.
William.
Martha.
Rebecca.
Rachel.
Margaret.

PETER H. BUSH[2], s/o Henry[1], b. Northern NJ; d. 4 May 1836. Res. Ramapo, Rockland Co., NY; millwright. He m. (1st) Mary, d/o James Smith of Monroe & had:
Matilda.
Mary Ann.
Henry.
James.
Margaret.

PETER H.[2] m. (2d) Abigail Smith, sister of his 1st wife, and had:
Elizabeth.
Samuel J.
1830, June 8, **PETER B.**
Nathaniel D.

Rachel.
Sarah.
Eleanor.
Cornelius.
Arminda.
Phebe.
Hudson.

**PETER B. BUSH**[3], s/o Peter H.[2] & Abigail, b. Orange Co., with family to vicinity of Greenwood Iron Works; 1862 to Monroe; m. 1858, Harriet, d/o David Ford of Monroe, and had:
Minnie H.
Greeley.
Samuel.
1863, March 13, **HORACE.**

**HORACE G.**[4], s/o Peter B.[3] & Harriet (Ford) Bush, b. Town of Monroe, on farm on which he has always resided. He m. Mary F. Smith and had:
Peter.
Horace S.

Goshen church records show a Henry Bush m. Esther Wilkison 6 April 1785.

_____

## BUTTERFIELD, DANIEL        U2-101
of Wal Kil.

In his will dated 7 March 1792, **DANIEL BUTTERFIELD** names nephews James McVey & Thomas Watkins & sisters Elenor Terry, Esther Everet & Anne Tuttle. He mentions a wife, but does not name her.

_____

## CALDWELL FAMILY OF MT. HOPE        A-506

ASHBEL CALDWELL[1] m. Sylva Stevens, who escaped from Wyoming [PA] at the time of the massacre and went through the forest on foot to CT. She m. (2d) John Seybolt.
Ashbel & Sylva's son Elisha[2] had a son, Harvey R.[3], res. Otisville.

_____

## CALDWELL, JOHN R. [P]     A-239-40, H-804, E-147
of New Windsor.

Caldwells were early family of Antrim, Ireland nobility.
JOHN CALDWELL[1] operated bleachery in Co. Antrim at the outbreak of the Irish rebellion; his sons:
John.
Andrew.
RICHARD.

RICHARD CALDWELL[2], convicted of high treason and sentenced to be executed, saved by Lord Cornwallis and sent to America. Settled at Salisbury Mills, Orange Co. and operated flaxseed oil mill; m. Maria d/o John Chandler (d. 1815), early merchant and patriot of Blooming-Grove. Richard's father and brother John also emigrated to America.

Richard served in the 25th Regt. of Infantry in the War of 1812, d. of exposure during military operations in Northern NY 22 Nov. 1812, age 35; bur. at village of Champlain, NY. Maria d. 23 Jan. 1877, age 88 years, 6 months. Their children:

1810, July 12; **JOHN R.**

Mary, m. Dr. Marcus Sears of Blooming-Grove and is now dec'd.

**JOHN R. CALDWELL[3]**, s/o Richard[2], b. Salisbury Mills; lived with grandfather John Chandler. Studied at St. John's College, Annapolis, MD where his uncle, Rev. Dr. Rafferty was president. Age 16 entered counting house of uncle John Caldwell, merchant of NY; age 18 to Blooming-Grove and farmed old Chandler homestead; 1831 to town of New Windsor, dairy farmer. Member of 1st Presbyterian Church of Newburgh; m. 13 Sept. 1831, Ruth d/o John Nicoll of New Windsor, and had:

William, farmer of New Windsor.
John N., farmer of New Windsor.
1839, CHARLES.

**CHARLES CALDWELL[4]**, b. Town of New Windsor; d. 8 May 1902. He was a surveyor in business in Newburgh by 1863; bank trustee, railroad chief engineer of Lehigh & Hudson River Railroad. In 1874 he m. Kate Van Duzer Burt, d/o Grinnell Burt of Warwick, NY.

## CAMPBELL FAMILY OF CAMP-BELL HALL (HAMP-TONBURGH)     A-654-5

**CAPT. LACHLIN CAMPBELL**, Scotsman of isle of Isley, Northern Britain to NY, transported 83 Protestant families from Scotland to NY (1738-40). Purchased farm in Orange Co. (at that time Ulster Co.). 1745 returned to Scotland to volunteer under Duke of Cumberland; returned to Campbell Hall in NY and shortly thereafter died there. His children:

Donald, b. at the Hall in NY; apprenticed to merchant in NY; 1775 served in the military for the British; later served the American cause.
George.
James.
Rose m. --- Graham.
Lily m. --- Murray.
Margaret m. Dr. --- Eustace and had a son, Gen. J. J. Eustice.

## CAMPBELL, FRANK H.     H-805
farmer of Warwick.

**FRANK H. CAMPBELL** was the only s/o William & Grace (Hamlinton) Campbell. He was b. Vernon, NY 9 Feb. 1850. He m. Emma Jayne, only d/o Lewis of Florida, Orange Co. FRANK in wholesale milk business & bank director & sportsman. Their children:
Lewis, served in Philippines in US Army.
Grace Hamlinton.
Frances Edith.

## CARPENTER FAMILY OF CHESTER & GOSHEN     A-614     C-99, 101, 103

There are many Carpenter families documented as resident in Goshen, Orange Co., NY in the book, *A Genealogical History of the Rehoboth Branch of the Carpenter Family in America* by Amos B. Carpenter (Amherst, MA, 1898). Unfortunately, none match data found on the the Carpenter families of Orange Co. given below.

COVILL CARPENTER m. Sarah --- & had:
1771, Sept. 15, COVILL.
1774, Jan. 28, Elizabeth
1776, April 3, Phebe.

The Covill above could be the same as: COLVILL CARPENTER settled in Chester and had sons:
Daniel.
Jesse, res. Chester

C-103 gives James & Jesse, s/o Covill Carpenter & Sarah Hall his wife, b. 4 June 1778 in their Goshen baptismal record.

## CARPENTER FAMILY OF WALLKILL     A-434, C-9, 79

WILLIAM CARPENTER from Goshen to farm near Van Burenville; "was in the war;" children:
William, d. 1875.
Benjamin, res. WI.
Mrs. Jacob Mills, res. near Westtown.
Mrs. Ebenezer Mapes; d. Middletown, 1869.
Eleanor, unm.
William, had 12 children, including Joel [only one named.]

The WILLIAM CARPENTER above could be the same William Carpenter who appears in Goshen church records who m. Hannah Vail 2 March 1777. Same records show a Hannah Carpenter d. 28 July 1807, aged 23 of phrinitis.

## CARPENTER, BENJAMIN [P] A-354-5, TN-293-4, E-161-2
businessman of Newburgh.

**BENJAMIN CARPENTER[1]**, b. England 1730; emigrated to America at an early age and settled on L.I., then to Latintown, now in the town of Marlborough, Ulster Co., where he died; m. 1764, Jane d/o Rev. Mr. Leonard of Goshen. They had 6 children, only ones named:
Jacob, ship builder.
LEONARD.

**LEONARD CARPENTER[2]**, s/o Benjamin[1], was a ship builder & owner of the Newburgh ferry, among other enterprises; m. Bridget d/o Isaac Belknap and had:
1793, Feb. 14, **BENJAMIN.**
1812, April 2, ELIZABETH.
Isaac R. of Newburgh. unm.
Jane Belknap, unm., res. Newburgh.

ALEXANDER.

Sarah Lydia Stearns, res. Newburgh, unm.

Cynthia Warren m. Francis Crawford of Newburgh; res. Detroit, MI.

BENJAMIN CARPENTER[3], s/o Leonard[2], was one of the founders of the Bethel Mission and member of the 1st Presbyterian Church; d. 31 Jan. 1871; m. Caroline S. d/o John Warren of Saratoga Springs who d. 5 April 1856, and had:

Mary F., widow of late Lewis M. Strong of Northampton, MA.
John W., d. infancy.
Warren, attorney; d. young, 1849.
Alida Josepha, m. Horatio B. Reed.

ELIZABETH CARPENTER[3], d/o Leonard[1], m. William Thayer 2 April 1812. William b. Brooklyn, Windham Co., CT 21 Sept. 1784. They settled in Newburgh c. 1800, accompanied by William's brother John, and William d. there 9 April 1855. Children of Elizabeth & William (THAYER):

William L.
John S., m. Catharine d/o Jira A. Stearns, formerly of Pittsfield, MA.
Elijah C., m. Mary J., d/o Hamilton Morrison of Montgomery
George A.
Charles F., m. Anna F., d/o Lewis Miller of New Windsor.
Anna B., m. Henry W. Dolson.
Caroline M.
Elizabeth C.

ALEXANDER L. CARPENTER[2], s/o Leonard[1], m. Elizabeth Lawrence of Fishkill; he d. at his res. in OH 1 Oct. 1848. Their children:

Sarah L.
Isaac L.
Lawrence F.

Early marriage records at Albany record issuance of licenses to 7 persons named Benjamin Carpenter.

———

CARPENTER, S. G. [P]                    A-173
physician.

Capt. SOLOMON CARPENTER[1] of Jamaica, L.I. (will 1763), one of the first land owners in town of Goshen, formerly known as Wawayanda; Presbyterian. In 1715 sold land in Goshen to John Carpenter of Jamaica, L.I. (probably his father), who in turn sold it to his son John in 1779. Capt. Solomon's children:

Solomon
1798, March 2, NEHEMIAH.

NEHEMIAH CARPENTER[2], s/o Solomon[1], farmer of Goshen, Mt. Hope and Chester; Presbyterian, d. 20 April 1858; m. 5 Jan. 1824, Elizabeth d/o Caleb Goldsmith of Scotchtown, b. 17 April 1800, and had:

1825, Jan. 6, DR. SOLOMON G.

1834, Nov. 12, Mary E., m. Jehiel G. Clark, merchant at Chester.

DR. SOLOMON G. CARPENTER[3], drugstore with father at Chester (1848-50); m. Mary S. d/o Jacob Feagles of Amity, Orange Co., 12 Nov. 1857; Mary d. 7 June 1865, age 37, and had:

Lizzie.
Mary S.
Clara.

———

CARPENTER, OLIVER R. [P]        A-691, C-25, 102, 105
of Wawayanda.                              H-805, C-110

JESSE C. CARPENTER[1], of English parentage, settled L.I.; 1732 to Goshen, Orange Co., where he m. a d/o John & Susan (Colville) Bradner. John res. Edinburgh, Scotland; to Goshen 1721, d. 1732, preacher. Their child:

BENJAMIN CARPENTER[2], b. 1754; d. 28 Sept. 1820. Served in the Rev. at Ft. Montgomery; m. Lydia Chandler of Craigville, Orange Co., and had:

1777, May 2, NATHANIEL.
1780, Aug., James (Jemmy).
1786, April 1, Samuel & Hannah, assumed twins as Goshen church records show birth date the same day.

NATHANIEL CARPENTER[3], s/o Benjamin[2], b. East Division of Town of Goshen, d. 3 July 1846. Mason at Washingtonville, farmer of Hamptonburgh; m. 10 Feb. [5 April] 1809, Pilotta [Phila], d/o Joel Coleman, Rev. War soldier. Pilotta d. 20 Oct. 1840. Their children:

1810, John C.
1813, June 30, OLIVER R.
1817, Julia Ann.
1819, Mary C.
1824, William H.

OLIVER R. CARPENTER[4], s/o Nathaniel[3], b. Town of Goshen; dairy farmer of Hamptonburgh, member Congregational Church of Middletown. 1851 purchased farm in Wawayonda Twp. 14 Nov. 1850, m. Ph[o]ebe Jane, d/o Joshua McNish of Middletown, and had:

1852, GEORGE W.
1853, John W.
1858, Charles Oliver.
1860, Mary Ida; dec'd.
1863, Lillie Dale.
1865, Maggie Jane; dec'd.
1868, Nathaniel Bradner; dec'd.

GEORGE WICKHAM CARPENTER[5], eldest s/o Oliver R.[4] & Ph[o]ebe J. Carpenter, b. 15 Jan. 1847, resides on homestead farm which has been in his family since 1764. He m. Hattie Bennett of Middletown in 1882. Members of the First Congregational Church of Middletown.

———

## CARPENTER, GILBERT                                H-805-6

of Monroe.

**GILBERT CARPENTER**, s/o Dr. Ethan B. Carpenter, who served in the Assembly 1850, b. Monroe in 1850. Member of the grain, feed & coal firm of Carpenter, Webb & Co. & bank director. He m. Irene, d/o John K. Roe, and had 3 sons & one dau., one son being Lewis R., a bank cashier.

It is noted that **GILBERT** had a brother, William, who d. 1877.

------

## THE CARTER FAMILY OF NEWBURGH          TH-297-300

ENOCH CARTER[1], b. Philadelphia, PA was a Quaker of English ancestry. He had one brother, Joseph, an officer in the English Navy who d. unm., and one sister, Mary Carter, who was the 2d wife of Adloph DeGrove. Enoch removed to NY before the Rev., tanner & currier. During the war he was forced to relocate near Ft. Montgomery, returned to NY after the war & d. there 1792. He m. Sarah Rivers, a widowed d/o Adolph DeGrove by his first wife, and had:
1772, Nov. 2, JONATHAN.
ADOLPH.
MARGARET.
MARY.
Enoch, d. age 20, no issue.
Rebecca, m. Mr. --- Rose & has descs. res. in Town of Cornwall.

JONATHAN CARTER[2], s/o Enoch[1], d. 30 May 1820; to Newburgh 1798. He m. (1) Elizabeth, d/o John Anderson, who d. 1799 of yellow fever at age of 17, no issue. Jonathan m. (2) Bridget, d/o Benjamin Smith, who d. 1803, leaving one child:
Elizabeth Carter who m. Ward M. Gazlay.

Jonathan[2] m. (3) Jane Linderman, who d. Nov. 1830 & left children:
Enoch [P], res. Newburgh.
Margaret, m. Levi D. Woolsey.
Catharine, m. Henry Ryder.
Charles.

ADOLPH CARTER[2], s/o Enoch[1], m. Ann McDowell of NY, and had:
George.
Joseph.
Sarah.
Ann.
Mary.
Margaret, m. Samuel Reeve.
Richard.
Elizabeth.

MARGARET CARTER[2], d/o Enoch[1], m. R. Henry Richards & had:
Henry, d. age 13.

James, d. age 31 & left issue, Sarah, now widow of Dr. Charles Peck & Henry W. [Carter], both of NY.

MARY CARTER[2], d/o Enoch[1], m. Benjamin Halstead, eldest brother of the late Capt. Charles Halstead of Newburgh. Mary d. in her 29th year & left one child:
Margaret R. Halstead, m. Samuel Callanan of NY.

------

## CASE FAMILY OF GREENVILLE              H-242-43

JOHN CASE[1] of New England m. Mary Mead, d/o Ebenezer of near Waterloo Mills in Minisink. John d. on homestead west of Westtown in 1844; Mary d. 1847. Their children:
James M., j.p. 1850-74 in Minisink, unm.
E. INMAN.
JOHN B.
STEPHEN.

E. INMAN CASE[2], son of John[1], d. 1888 & had:
John, Jr.
Joseph.
Ira L., res. Middletown, school commissioner.
Jefferson.
Anson.
Amelia.

JOHN B. CASE[2], s/o John[1], clergyman, d. 1886, and had:
John B., Jr.
Stephen J.
Joseph M.
Tisdale.
Joshua L.
Sarah.
Flora.

STEPHEN CASE[2], s/o John[1], grad. Madison Univ. 1840, served 6 years as pastor of Broadway Baptist Church near Wykertown, Wantage Twp., NJ. May 1848 pastor of Mt. Salem & Greenville churches (Baptist) where he served until his death in 1895. His children:
John E.
Joshua, Jr., auctioneer of Unionville.
Joseph M.

------

## CASE, ADELBERT L.                              H-807

DELL & Sarah J. CASE[1], hotel owners, had:
Pearl.
1877, Feb. 3, **ADELBERT L.**

ADELBERT L. CASE[2], b. Plattsburg, Erie Co., NY, worked in restaurant business in Greenville, PA. 1904 landlord at Burnside Inn near Burnside, Orange Co. He m. at East Sidney, Delaware Co., 28 Feb. 1803, Jennie A. Floyd & they have one son, Howard L., age 2. He is Methodist; wife is Episcopal.

------

## CASE, WALTER      A-145-46
Attorney of Newburgh.

**WALTER** is the s/o Rev. Wheeler Case of Duchess County. Was a member of Congress (1819-21); Newburgh to Fishkill & d. there. Mar. Sarah d/o Jonathan Hasbrouck (2) of Newburgh. Their grandson is Walter C. Anthony of Newburgh, County D.A.

## CASH FAMILY OF WAWAYANDA      A-680, T-29-30
## CASH, MERITT H.      A-170
physician.

DANIEL CASH[1], b. New England, to Pittston, PA and then to Wyoming Valley, to Millsburgh in town of Minisink; he and wife d. in 1789; their children:
Isaac.
Nathan.
1768, Jan. 23, REUBEN.
Mehitable.
Ziphorah.
Polly.
Betsey.
Millicent.

REUBEN CASH[2], himself & his mother survivors of the Wyoming Massacre of 1778 [for their story see T-29-30], m. Millicent (d. 3 Sept. 1838, aged 63), a d/o John Howell, Sr. and had:
Sally.
Hannah.
1803, **DR. MERITT H.**
Capt. John M.
James M.
Solomon V. R.
Phebe M.
Fanny.
Selah J.

The daus. were wives of Roswell Mead, Samuel Vail Sr., John E. S. Gardiner, and Parmenas Horton; although which dau. m. which is not given.

**DR. MERITT H. CASH**[3], b. Rutger's Place near Ridgebury, town of Minisink; m. late in life Hannah d/o Hon. Joseph Davis. Dr. Merritt d. 26 April 1861.

## CASSEDY, ABRAM S. [P]      A-159
attorney of Newburgh.

ARCHIBALD CASSEDY[1] emig. to Rockland Co. from the north of Ireland around the time of the Revolutionary War. He was of Scotch Irish desc. His son:
CASSEDY, ARCHIBALD[2], b. Rockland Co., farmer & merchant; m. Lydia d/o Judge Gurnee of Rockland Co., who emigrated from Paris during the Revolutionary War. Their child:
CASSEDY, ABRAM S.[3], b. Ramapo, Rockland Co., 29 Nov.

1833; student in Clarkstown, NY 1855; county clerk of Orange County 1857, clerk Board of Supervisors 1858-62; 1859 to Newburgh; 1862 County D.A. & other public service including mayor of Newburgh in 1880; bank director. Mar. 1861, Margaret J. d/o the late Dr. Charles Drake of Newburgh.

## CASSEDY, WILLIAM F.      H-807-8
attorney of Newburgh.

**WILLIAM F. CASSEDY**, b. Newburgh 4 Oct. 1862, studied law with A. S. Cassedy. 1897 joined with Hon. Charles F. Brown; farmer & bank director. He m. Frances M., d/o James A. Townsend and has two children:
J. Townsend.
William F. Jr.

## CASTERLIN, CHARLES E.      H-808

RICHARD CASTERLIN[1], b. Rockport, NJ 10 Aug. 1828, had wagon shop at Unionville, Orange Co., NY; 1874 opened Minisink Hotel, which he still operates. He m. Mahala Rogers, b. Rockport 7 June 1830. They had 5 children, 2 living:
1854, May 25, **CHARLES E.**
Fred, operates hotel in Butler, NJ.

**CHARLES E. CASTERLIN**[2], b. Rockport, Sussex Co., NJ. About 1857 to Middletown to dry goods store of B. C. Woodward & Co. Removed to Little Falls, Passaic Co., NJ, 1888 returned to Unionville; 1893 purchased Aspell Hotel in Florida, Orange Co., which he now operates. 14 Jan. 1880 he m. Mary E. Kellogg of Little Falls & had 3 children, one living:
1887, Oct. 15, Harold M.

## CHADEAYNE FAMILY OF CRAWFORD      H-172

John Chadeayne, settled in Crawford as early as 1820. His son, Henry F. was the father of the present town supervisor.

## CHADWICK, JOSEPH      H-808-9
manufacturer & bank president of Newburgh, NY.

**JOSEPH CHADWICK** was the s/o of a cotton spinning mill owner at Rockdale, England. He was b. Heywood, Lancashire, England 24 Oct. 1841; to America 1865, settled Rutherford, NJ. 1878 to Newburgh. He m. Margaret, d/o William Smith of Manchester, England a dyer, bleacher & finisher of cotton goods. They have 4 sons & 1 daughter.

## CHANDLER, NATHANIEL      U2-23
carpenter.

NATHANIEL CHANDLER, in his will dated 30 Aug. 1784, named his children:
Joseph.

John.
Sarah Brewster.
Hannah Moffet.
Phebe Clements.
Mary Greag.
Abigail Moffat.
Lydia Carpenter.
Experience Nicholson.
Enos.

Will proved 26 Dec. 1787 by John Denniston of New Windsor, yeoman, who appeared with Thomas Fulton & Joseph Chandler.

---

## CHARLTON, REV. RICHARD      TN-323
of Newburgh.

From his obituary: **REV. RICHARD CHARLTON** first missionary of Newburgh & New Windsor "on Tuesday last, departed this life, at his home in Staten Island, aged 72 years." (From *Gaines' Mercury* of Oct. 11, 1777.) He was b. Ireland, to America at New Windsor on Hudson & then NY City, asst. minister of Trinity Church. He was then apptd. missionary of Staten Island in 1747.

---

## CHRISTIE, GEORGE W.      H-809

**GEORGE W. CHRISTIE** was one of 11 children born to Samuel Christie & Jane Elston. He was b. on a farm near Unionville, Orange Co., 17 Oct. 1836. He ran a summer hotel at Rutherford, NJ & later managed creameries at Unionville, Slate Hill & New Milford. In 1885 he purchased farm at Pine Island, where he d. 19 April 1907. Was a member of the Presbyterian Church of Amity. He m. Elizabeth Kelley of Port Jervis 15 Nov. 1865, and had:
1872, Aug. 19, Sarah Adele.
1874, March 20, Samuel Hayne, atty.

---

## CLARK FAMILY OF WALLKILL      A-434, C-17, 37

VINSON CLARK from L.I. to Orange Co. before 1800; store & tavern, raised hemp and flax and other businesses; d. 1839. [He could be the same as the <u>VINCENT</u> CLARK who m. Patience Stringham 21 Jan. 1788 as recorded in Goshen church records.] Children:
William; d. 1832.
John; d. 1872. [Could be the same John Clark of Goshen who m. Jane Hammond 3 May 1843.]
Patience, m. three times, now res. of WI and widow of Rev. Mr. Clark.
Oliver; d. 1845 leaving two sons: William & Daniel.
Mrs. Lewis Bell of Bull Hack; d. 1871.
Thomas; dec'd.
Vinson J.; d. Waymark, PA.
Hector; d. Oct. 1832; 1st person bur. family yard on farm.
James S.; dec'd.

---

## CLARK BROTHERS.      H-809
merchants at Thompson's Ridge, Town of Crawford.

IRA CLARK m. Eliza Barkley and had Joseph H. Clark who m. Mary Hunter. Joseph H. was town clerk & j.p. at Crawford and d. in 1883, aged 86. He was a school teacher at Searsville for 15 years. His sons are the Clark brothers in the heading:
Theodore G.
George H.

The brothers purchased their business from J. Erskine Ward in 1897.

---

## CLARK, HON. GEORGE [P]      A-362-3
of Newburgh.

WILLIAM CLARK[1] of north of Ireland to Newburgh, m. Mary --- and had:
1817, Aug. 6, GEORGE.
Anna E. m. ex-Mayor Judge Copeland of Brooklyn and is "only survivor of family of 10 children."

**CLARK, GEORGE**[2], b. Newburgh, at age 16 apprenticed to Daniel Farrington & Benjamin Lander of Newburgh to learn trade of painter. 27 June 1840 m. Augusta d/o Jason W. and Martha (Griffith) Rogers of town of Montgomery and removed to NY City and carried on painting business 15 years; returned to Newburgh 1856 and did political service as the 1st Mayor of Newburgh (1866-70); succeeded by brother in law Robert Sterling. George belonged to Presbyterian Church on 23rd Street NY City and 1st Presbyterian Church of Newburgh. He d. 3 June 1871, and had:
Mary Augusta m. T. Powell Townsend of Newburgh.
George H., atty. of Newburgh.
Martha Louisa m. Jonas Williams of Newburgh 1876, 8 Nov.; d. 1877, July 15.
Robert Sterling, grad. Princeton 1874; d. 20 Aug. 1876.

---

## CLARK, HON. HULET [P]      A-674, H-287

Family locally noted by reason of so many falling victims to the dysentery in 1825; 6 dying within 16 days. A son, William W. Clark, member of Assembly 1880-1881.

DAVID CLARK[1], of English desc., res. and d. in Westchester Co., NY. His son:
CALEB CLARK[2], b. 1760, Westchester Co., m. Jemima Kniffen. To Otisville, Orange Co., c. 1796 and later to Minisink, where he d., 1840. Children:
1790, March 26, HULET.
Wallace m. Sarah Smith.
Jerusha m. Moses Durland, res. Greenville.
David m. (1st) Nancy Slauson; (2d) Betsy Manning.
Phebe m. Lewis Seybolt.
James F. m. Abbie Hallock, res. Greenville.

CLARK, HULET[3], s/o David, b. Bedford, Westchester Co., NY, 1812 m. (1) Mary d/o Zebulon Hallock of Greenville. Served 148th NY Regt. of Militia, j.p. & judge. After his marriage, a farmer in Greenville; 1 April 1828, bought farm in Minisink, where he d. March 31, 1857. Mary d. 2 Sept. 1825. All of their children except Chauncey d. in August 1825:

Chauncey H. m. (1st) Angeline Slauson; m. (2d) Mary Corwin, res. Wawayanda.
Alfred.
Bertha.
Samuel J.
James Monroe.
Henry Hallock.
Zebulon H.

Judge **HULET CLARK** m. (2d) Emeline, widow of John Greenleaf and d/o Ephraim & Amy Forbes of New London, CT, and had:

Bertha, res. on homestead.
William Harvey m. Emily, d/o Robert Robertson of Wawayanda, res. Minisink; public servant. Emily d. 1907. They had one son, Robert H., present town superintendant, res. on homestead.
Caleb m. Phebe A., d/o Henry Decker of Minisink; physician who served in 92d NY Regt. in Civil War; farmer of Minisink.
Elizabeth C. m. Gilbert W. Roe, res. Oshkosh, WI.
George Dallas, res. on homestead, farmer.

Emeline d. 2 June 1876.

Harvey H., Alfred, W.L. & W. W. Clark are named as desc. of David Clark of town of Minisink. [H-241]

Hulet D. Clark, farmer & businessman of Minisink, b. 1835 Sussex Co., NJ; d. 2 April 1897. In 1860 purchased farm in Mt. Hope; 1866 purchased farm Town of Minisink, near Westtown, where he d. 2 April 1897; m. Margaret, d/o Roeloff Swartwout from Holland & settled at Kingston, NY 1655. Hulet D. & Margaret had 3 children, one, Clarence G., in 1885 owned flour & feed store, m. Mary d/o H. Reeves Horton & had Julet D. & Julia K. H-810.

---

## CLARK, JAMES ALONZO — H-810

**JAMES A. CLARK**, b. 26 March 1845 at Middletown, clerked for Alexander Wilson; in 1862 clerked for hardware store of Scott Brothers & became partner of the firm in 1879; m. Mrs. Emma (Cole) Dunning in 1887 & had 23 Oct. 1888, Mildred Murray Clark.

---

## CLARK, ROBERT H. — H-810-11

**ROBERT H.** was s/o Hon. William Harvey and Emily A. (Robertson) Clark. William H. b. 1829, d. 1907, held public office. Son **ROBERT** was b. near Westtown, farmer & postmaster.

---

## CLARK, WILLARD M. — H-811

town superintendent, Wallkill.

**WILLARD M.** is s/o William L. Clark of Greenville. He was b. 23 Aug. 1861 in Salem, NJ & moved with his parents to Greenville, Orange Co., NY. He has been a teacher, school commissioner, farmer & removed from Greenville to Middletown in 1890. He m. Mamie Clark of Greenville & has a daughter, Ethel.

---

## CLAUSON, HENRY P. — H-811

dairy & fruit farmer of Newburgh.

**HENRY** was b. in NJ in 1842; to Newburgh in 1868. He has served as town superintendent & sheriff; m. Mary E. Monell and had:

John.
Charlotte, m. V. J. Kohl.
Harry.

---

## CLINTON, CHARLES — A-214, 238-9, C-32, AA6-52-3
## CLINTON, GEORGE [P] — A-142, U2-160

**CHARLES[1]** b. Sept. 1690 in Ireland, of English & Scotch desc., s/o James C. of Corbay, Co. Longford, who was s/o William of England, a grandson of Henry Clinton, 2d Earl of Lincoln. **CHARLES**, with company of relatives & neighbors from Co. Longford, Ireland to America May 1729, settled in Little Britain [Town of New Windsor/precinct of Highlands, founded & named by him.] 1731. He was a surveyor, judge, served in French & Indian War; d. Little Britain 19 Nov. 1773, age 83. **CHARLES** m. Elizabeth Dennison (1704-1779), d/o Alexander of Longford, Ireland sailed for Philadelphia 20 May 1729 in *George & Ann*. Children:

Catharine, b. Ireland, m. Col. James McClaughry.
James; d. at sea.
Mary; d. at sea, "on the passage."
1732, April 28, ALEXANDER, physician.
Charles, physician & surgeon, d. 1781, aged 56.
1736, Aug. 9 [18] or Sept. 18, JAMES.
1739, July 26, **GEORGE**.

ALEXANDER CLINTON[2], s/o Charles[1], in his will dated 19 Feb. 1757, mentions his brother George and Jane McClaugry (no relationship mentioned). Witnesses: John McClaghry & John Davis. ALEXANDER m. Mary Kane in Nov. 1757. He was surgeon apothecary in the College of NJ & d. 11 May 1758.

JAMES CLINTON[2], s/o Charles[1], served in the French & Indian War under his father, Maj.-Gen. during the Rev.; farmer & surveyor after the war. He m. (1) in 1765 [1764], Mary, d/o Egbert DeWitt & sister of Simeon DeWitt, who claimed desc. from Jan DeWitt, grand pensionary of Holland. JAMES m. (2) Mrs. Mary Gray. He died age 75, Little Britain, 22 Dec. 1812. His 3rd son:

DEWITT CLINTON[3], b. 2 March 1769, Little Britain, Governor of NY and office holder in many other capacities. He d. at

Albany 11 Feb. 1828. He m. (1) 1795, Maria, d/o Walter Franklin, wealthy Quaker merchant of NY City, d. 1818; he m. (2) Catharine, d/o Dr. Thomas Jones of NY. They had George W. Clinton of Buffalo & Albany, b. Newtown, L.I., 13 April 1807.

**GEORGE CLINTON[2]**, s/o Charles[1], b. Little Britain [what is now Town of New Windsor, & then in Ulster Co.], was first governor of the state under the Constitution of 1777; d. while Vice President of the US; served in US Army in 1776. He m. Cornelia Tappen, only d/o Petres & Tyante Tappen of Kingston, 7 Feb. 1770. Res. in New Windsor until 1777, to Little Britian & later to Poughkeespie. Children:
1774, June 29, Cornelia T., b. New Windsor.
1778, Oct. 18, George W., b. Poughkeepsie.
1780, July 16, Elizabeth, b. Poughkeepsie.
1783, Oct. 14, Martha, b. Poughkeepsie.
1785, Oct. 6, Maria, b. NY.

---

**COCHRAN, ISAAC**                                   H-811-12
farmer of Newburgh.

ISAAC, s/o Alexander & Margaret (Greery) Cochran, b. town of Newburgh 29 Oct. 1823; in 1839 with parents to NY City & engaged in grocery & tea business with father until 1860, when he began the manufacture of carriages. In 1866 he retired to Newburgh to farm. In 1850 he m. Rachel Sommerville, who d. 1891. They had 7 children. Members Reformed Presbyterian Church since 1868.

---

**COCKS, CHARLES C.**                                   H-812
of Cornwall.

CHARLES E. COCKS[1] m. Margaret Campbell, both b. Monroe, Orange Co. Established grocery business at Cornwall Landing in 1850. Their children:
CHARLES C.
Isaac M.

CHARLES C. COCKS[2], b. Cornwall, NY & has always resided there. Member of grocery firm of C. E. Cocks & Son.

---

**CODDINGTON, WILLIAM HENRY**                           H-812

WILLIAM HENRY CODDINGTON, fifth s/o William Henry & Susan Coddington, b. Ulsterville, Ulster Co., NY 15 June 1872; farmer & blacksmith; in 1893 affiliated with the now Bordon Condensed Milk Co. He m. Della Louise Bennett of South Centerville 26 June 1901, and had:
Frank M.
Florence Elizabeth.
Ralph B.

Mrs. Coddington member Presbyterian Church of South Centerville.

---

**COLDEN FAMILY OF MONTGOMERY**  A-295, W-11-12
TN-264-5

Dr. CADWALLADER COLDEN, Surveyor General of the province, settled in what is now Coldenham in 1728 on a patent of 3,000 acres where he res. until his death. He gave his son, Cadwallader Jr., on his marriage, 500 acres of land where the son built what is known as the Colden house, on the Montgomery & Newburgh State Road at Coldenham in 1765. Cadwallader Jr. built the Thomas Colden mansion for one of his sons; it is situated at Colden Hill, a mile north of Coldenham. On the decease of Thomas it was occupied by Cadwallader C. Colden & more recently by Messers. John and Joseph Kelly.

ALEXANDER COLDEN, of Town of Newburgh, eldest s/o Gov. Colden. He removed with his father in 1728 to Coldenham. Apptd. Ranger of Ulster Co. 1737 & soon removed to Parish of Quassick, where he purchased lands & a wharf now known as Powell's Dock. He also built a flour mill later known as "Hasbrouck's Mill." Owned lands that were known as "Town of Newburgh Plot." He built what was known as "Old Newburgh House," Colden & Water Sts. in Newburgh. He res. with family until 1762 when he removed to NY with his father & apptd. Joint-Surveyor Gencarl & later postmaster of NY City. He petitioned in 1742 to operate a ferry between Newburgh & Fishkill. ALEXANDER d. 1775, aged 50. He had 4 daus. & 2 sons who removed to England during the American Revolution; his branch of the family is extinct in America.

---

**COLDWELL, THOMAS**                           H-812-14, C-27

THOMAS d. 1905, was the oldest manufacturer of lawn mowers in America. He was b. Staleybridge, Lancashire, England 1838; to America at an early age. Worked in NY City & Fishkill; invented lawn mower that resulted in formation of Chadborn & Coldwell Mfg. Co. at Newburgh. His children:
William H., in father's business.
Harry T., in father's business
A daughter, Mrs. E. C. Ross.

---

**COLEMAN, EDSON**                         A-561-2, 562e
of Goshen.                               & T-33, C-25, 27, 42
**COLEMAN, N. C. [P]**                          A-562e

WILLIAM COLEMAN[1], b. England, one of the first settlers on L.I. This family's story of early settlement & Indian capture of Mrs. Coleman found T-33. Children:
THOMAS.
John.
George.

THOMAS COLEMAN[2], s/o William[1], had:
Curtis.
1732, July 2, THOMAS.
Deborah m. Jacob Brown.

THOMAS COLEMAN³, s/o Thomas², m. Elizabeth Roe, b. 1730, and had 4 sons & 2 daus., among them:

THOMAS COLEMAN⁴, b. 27 April 1767, d. 21 Feb. 1822. Farmed on banks of the Hudson in Town of Cornwall, the first of the family to settle in Orange Co., m. (1st) Mary Galloway, b. 28 April 1767, and had:

Elizabeth m. Obadiah Smith.

Ann m. Morris B. Pilgrim.

Charlotte m. Morris Stephens.

1792, March 19, WILLIAM.

Roe.

Thomas.

Children by THOMAS's 2d m., wife not named:

Samuel.

Emery.

Henry.

All children above res. Monroe, Orange Co.

WILLIAM COLEMAN⁵, s/o Thomas⁴, apprenticed to painter; m. Ann d/o Nathaniel & Margaret (Bradner) Conkling of Goshen, who was b. 19 Oct. 1793 & d. 29 April 1876. Until 1794 res. at Hackettstown, NJ & then purchased carding mill in the Town of Warwick, near Florida; owned for 30 years. Members Presbyterian Church at Florida. Children:

1815, Dec. 9, NATHANIEL C.

1817, Aug. 28, Thomas J., NY merchant; d. 8 May 1878.

1819, July 28, John C., farmer at Milwaukee, WI.

1822, Mary E. m. P. P. Demarest of Goshen; d. 20 April 1876.

1823, Nov. 23, Cornelia A. m. A. L. Beyea of Rye, Westchester Co.

1825, July 18, Harriet Eveline, 'present wife' of P. P. Demarest.

1828, Aug. 21, George C., res. CO.

1831, June 6, Caroline, was wife of Henry D. Welty of Auburn, NY; d. 1877, Jan. 8.

1834, Jan. 26, Margaret A.; d. 9 July 1868, unm.

NATHANIEL C. COLEMAN⁶, eldest child, worked in father's mill & farm, dairy farmer; m. 17 Nov. 1840, Fanny Maria d/o John & Eunice (Smith) Knapp & great-granddau. of William Knapp, progenitor of Knapp family in Orange Co., to Town of Goshen from Horseneck, CT. Fanny b. 21 June 1817. Member of Methodist Church at Goshen. Children:

1841, June 5, Mary E.; d. 31 Aug. 1863.

Harriet Eliza, d. infancy.

Anna A. m. Robert Osborn of Goshen 14 Nov. 1865.

Fannie E. m. Giles E. Goodrich of Goshen.

Nathaniel C.; d. age 5, 5 Aug. 1858.

Addie W.

JOEL COLEMAN¹, "a desc. of William," b. Goshen, res. Hamptonburgh, farmer & soldier of the Rev.; d. Scotchtown in Wallkill, 24 Oct. 1840, age 84. Children by his first wife [not named]:

Rumsey, d. on homestead.

Joel, d. on homestead; could be the Joel Coleman who m. Sally Harlow 12 Sept. 1815.

Philena [Phila], m. 5 April 1809, Nathaniel Carpenter.

Keziah, m. James Manning.

1740, Sept. 12, HULL.

Oliver.

Rachel m. John Brown.

JOEL¹ m. (2d) Mrs. Mary Owen, d/o Hiram Dunning, who d. 1845, age 84. They had one child, Alfred, farmer of Wallkill, now age 76 & res. Middletown, NY.

[ H-814: Alfred [may be the Alfred above] and Catherine Coleman had a son, Galen, b. near Mt. Hope, Orange Co., 31 Dec. 1859. To Middletown to learn machinist's trade; m. Mary Alice Coleman, b. 19 March 1852, of Wantage, NJ. They m. at Spartanburg, SC 7 Jan. 1880 & had one child, Frank Edson Coleman, b. 29 Aug. 1882, m. Eva M. Birtwistle of Middletown 5 June 1907.]

HULL COLEMAN², s/o Joel¹, m. 1810, Lois, d/o Mrs. Mary Owen. Lois d. 3 July 1857. Hull was a farmer of Warwick, later removed to Florida Village. Member Presbyterian Church; d. 28 Aug. 1865. Children:

1811, Dec. 24, Eliza, m. Thomas S. Nanny of Amity, Town of Warwick; d. 14 Jan. 1866.

1815, March 3, EDSON.

1817, May 23, Almeda, m. William H. Waterbury of Warwick.

1819, March 14, Frances M., m. (1st) John M. Ferrier; (2d) Louis M. Jayne of Warwick.

EDSON COLEMAN³, b. on homestead in Warwick. 26 Aug. 1838 m. Hannah Elizabeth, b. 2 March 1818, d/o Hon. John W. Wisner of Elmira, NY, atty. & judge of Chemung Co. & his wife Elizabeth, d/o Richard Ryerson, whose ancestors from Amsterdam to America. The Ryersons settled in L.I. and 1701 to Bergen Co., NJ; later to Sussex Co., NJ. EDSON 1839 to Goshen, farmer, member Presbyterian Church at Amity.

JEFFREY WISNER, grandfather of Mrs. Coleman & father of John W. Wisner, was a cousin of Henry G. Wisner of Goshen (d. 1824).

————

**COLEMAN, JOSEPH**          U2-205-6
Yeoman of Newburgh.

JOSEPH COLEMAN d. intestate & named are Eunice, his widow & administrators Isaac Bellknap & Daniel Birdsall Jr. of Newburgh. Inventory done 9 April 1791.

————

**COLFAX, ROBERT W. [P]**          A-626-7
of Chester.

ROBERT COLFAX¹, res. Pompton, Passiac Co., NJ. He & his brother Gen. WILLIAM were bodyguards of Gen. Washington; farmers & makers of iron ore. Robert was a judge & d. at Pompton leaving a large family that included:

WILLIAM R. COLFAX², b. 1791 at Pompton; m. Elizabeth, d/o Joseph Hogan. She d. c. 1868, aged 66. WILLIAM d. 1873. Res. West Milford, NJ, miller & farmer. Children:

Mary Jane; dec'd.

Sarah m. Isaac Scofield of Parsippany, NJ.
Harriet R. m. Edmund Miller of West Milford.
Deborah m. Albert Baldwin of Newark.
Eliza m. A. H. Lawrence, farmer of Blooming-Grove.
1825, Dec. 25, **ROBERT W.**
Ellen F. m. George W. Colwell of NY.
Saphronia m. G. Van Emburgh of Newark.
Joseph H., merchant of Keokuk, IA.
Hannah m. Henry Hanfield, merchant of NY.
Richard & William, twins. Richard merchant at Ridgewood, NJ;
   William res. Bloomfield, NJ.
Maria L. m. James N. Cooley of West Milford.

**ROBERT W. COLFAX**[3], s/o William R., b. West Milford, age 17 to Chester & apprenticed to J. H. & G. W. Colwell, cabinet makers; 1856 stove-tinware salesman at Chester; community service, member Presbyterian Church at Chester; m. 3 Jan. 1849, Almira d/o Major James & Susan (Drake) Holbert of Chester. Almira b. 6 March 1819. Their child:
Emily H. m. James S. Roe, farmer of Chester.

NOTE: " . . . William R. [Colfax] was the father of Robert W. Colfax, a sister of whom, Harriet, m. Jacob M. Ryerson, s/o Judge Martin Ryerson, of NJ."

"A grandson of William Colfax, ex-Vice-Pres. Colfax, is a cousin of the subject of this sketch."

**COLLARD, WILLIAM M.**                     H-814
of Warwick.

**WILLIAM M.** was s/o Jerome & Mary E. (Hallock) Collard. He was b. town of Warwick, Orange Co., 14 Aug. 1857. Carpenter; grocery business. He m. Mary E. Roberts of Bull's Mills in 1879. They own 200 acres of land near Greenwood Lake.

**COMFORT, H. D.**                     H-814-15, GFM-8

**H. D. COMFORT**, a s/o the late Daniel H. Comfort, is a manufacturer of ice cream at Newburgh since 1900. He was b. Town of Crawford; m. Mary Schaefer, d/o Jacob of Montgomery, NY. They have 2 sons and 2 daughters; one son, J. Edmund, in business with his father.

Buried at the German Reformed Cemetery at Montgomery are Daniel Comfort, d. 12 Sept. 1854, aged 83 years, 4 months, 7 days & his wife Phebe, d. 16 April 1864, aged 86 years, 11 months.

**COMINGS, DANIEL G.**                     H-815
of Middletown.

GILMAN TAYLOR COMINGS[1] m. Rhoda Worthington & had 6 children, 2 living:
18--, May 17, **DANIEL G.**
Mrs. Elvira LaForge of Metuchen, NJ.

**DANIEL G. COMINGS**[2], b. in Sussex Co., NJ, 1878 to Orange Co., millwright, ice & coal business. He m. 1884, M. Louisa Smith of Newark, NJ and had:
Mary Viola.
Bertha L.
Florence A.
William D.

Members St. Paul's Methodist Church at Middletown.

**CONKLIN, GEORGE RENSSELAER**              H-815-16
of Monroe.

**GEORGE R. CONKLIN** was b. in Monroe in 1843, s/o Rensselaer C. & Mary E. (Howzer) Conklin. To NY 1860 in business until 1865. Two years at Lake Superior iron district & 1868 back to Monroe; coal & feed business with C. T. Nott of Vernon, NJ. He m. (1st) Isabella Roberts in 1869; (2d) 1885 Mary E., d/o the late Chauncey B. Knight.

**CONKLING, NATHANIEL**              A-523, C-17, 26, 53
of Goshen.

The first Conkling of this family in America settled at L.I. In 1780/81 a Conkling res. at an early settlement that has since become known as Conklingtown in Goshen. Sgt. Nathaniel Conkling, b. c. 1740, L.I., went to Orange Co. His wife was Martha ---, his children:
Nathaniel, farmer at Goshen, m. Elizabeth Garner 1784.
1765, May 12, Samuel, to Middletown.
1767, May 3, Enos [Eneas], farmer at Goshen.
1770, Oct. 7, Joshua, on old homestead.
1772, Dec. 18, Elizabeth, d. unm.
Dau. m. Joseph Conkling.

The Goshen Presbyterian Church records show a Nathaniel Conkling m. Margaret Bradner 5 June 1788. Also that Martha, widow of Nathaniel, was dec'd. by 12 June 1785. In the same church records is another marriage of a Nathaniel Conkling, 16 Oct. 1811, to Deborah Young.

"Deliverance Conkling, who lived near Wickham's Pond, stated 'that he was 71 years old; and has known personally Lancaster Symes, one of the Wawayanda patentees' . . ." [H-152, deposition taken 1765.]

**CONNER, DR. MILTON C.**                     H-816
of Middletown, NY.

**DR. CONNER**, b. on farm near Scotchtown, Town of Wallkill, 6 Sept. 1853; teacher at Ft. Ann, NY; studied Detroit Medical College & College of Physicians & Surgeons of NY City--graduated 1883. He m. Frances Adelaide Cox of Middletown.

## COON, CHRISTOPHER                                    A-380

**CHRISTOPER** was a character of early times in Town of Montgomery; soldier of Hessian Troops, tinker & trumpeter, taken prisoner in Battle of Trenton in 1776.

## COOPER, MATTHEW GRANT                              H-816

**MATTHEW** was b. 4 Feb. 1865 at Glenwood, NJ. He is a farmer & had a meat business at Franklin Furnace, NJ; retired to Eden Station, Orange Co. in 1800; dairy farmer. He m. Clara (Van Sickle) Slaughter of Eden 14 Dec. 1904 and has:
1905, June 29, Gerald French.

## CORTWRIGHT, SANFORD H.                            H-816-17
professor of Westtown.

**SANFORD A. CORTWRIGHT**, b. 1858 in Town of Greenville, Orange Co., s/o Alfred & Margaret (Elston) Cortwright. In 1893 he m. Emma, d/o Rensselaer & Rachel (Weygant) McKelvey and has one son, Alfred.

## CORWIN FAMILY OF MT. HOPE
### A-507, H-327, LDS Anc. File

JOSHUA CORWIN[1], b. 25 March 1733/35, before the Rev. War removed from Southhold, L.I. He m. Anna Paine, b. 6 Sept. 1733. His children by 1st marriage:
1756, March 6, Joshua.
c. 1758, Peter.
c. 1760, David.
c. 1762, Abner.
c. 1764, Anna.
c. 1766, Joseph.
1769, Dec. 25, JOHN.
c. 1770, Jemima.
   Child by 2d m.:
c. 1772, Benjamin, had son William b. 1811, who m. Lydia Smith of Middletown.

JOHN CORWIN[2], s/o Joshua[1], m. Julia Vail, b. c. 1769 & had:
c. 1791, Isaac.
c. 1793, Elizabeth.
c. 1795, John.
c. 1797, Samuel.
c. 1799, Julia.
c. 1801, Abram.
1801, Oct. 23, ESTHER.
c. 1805, Benjamin H.
c. 1807, David.
1809, Jan. 28, ARCHIBALD.
c. 1811, Peter.
c. 1813, Julia.
c. 1813, William.
c. 1815, Julia.

ESTHER CORWIN[3], d/o John[2], b. Mt. Hope, m. Jacob Elston of

Minisink, b. 10 Oct. 1801 & had (ELSTON):
1826, Jan. 21, MARGARET CORWIN.
1827, May 6, SARAH.
1829, May 6, Lemuel Ellsworth.
1831, May 9, still born child.
1832, May 20, Esther Eliza, m. Aaron Putnam Truesdell, b. 18 Sept. 1833 at Owego, NY.

MARGARET CORWIN ELSTON[4], d/o Esther (Corwin) Elston[3] b. Minisink; m. (1) Richard Edsall, b. 27 May 1824, Deerpark, Soffolk & (2) James Hamlin Schofield, b. 10 Oct. 1821, Beemerville, NJ. She had by 2d m. (SCHOFIELD):
c. 1851, Hattie.
1853, Dec. 10, Richard Edsall, b. Port Jervis, m. Mary Josephine Finn, b. 25 March 1857, Port Jervis.
1856, March 31, Esther Annie.
1869, May 6, Arthur Fairchild.

SARAH ELSTON[4], d/o Esther (Corwin) Elston[3], b. Minisink, m. Henry Hubbard Phillips, b. Bellows Falls, VT 19 Aug. 1828, & had children b. in PA, NY & MO.

ARCHIBALD CORWIN[3], s/o John[2], m. Abigail Farman, b. 4 Feb. 1815 & had:
c. 1835, Harriet.
c. 1837, Theodore.
1839, Nov. 11, Mary Louise, m. Charles Emmet Corwin, b. 22 Dec. 1839.

## COTTER, JOHN ISAAC                                 H-818

JOHN H. COTTER[1], physician of Poughkeepsie had:
1881, Aug. 22, **JOHN ISAAC.**
Isaac, attending Poughkeepsie high school.
Mary, attending Poughkeepsie high school.

**JOHN I. COTTER**[2], M.D., practices medicine at Campbell Hall. He was b. Jackson's Corners, Dutchess Co., NY; to Poughkeepsie at age of 12. Graduated Albany Medical College 1904.

## COX, WILLIAM                                        U2-92
of Wall Kill.
## COX, JOSHUA                                         U2-89

**WILLIAM COX** in his will dated 13 July 1791 names his wife Elizabeth and children:
John.
Benjamin.
Mary.
Joshua.
William.
Abigail.

David Corwin & Isaiah Vail, "friends," apptd. executors. Will proved 30 Jan. 1792 by Isaiah Vail, Jr. of Wall Kill, farmer; Jonathan Swezy & William E. McNeal.

24 June 1791 **JOSHUA COX** [res. not stated] made a will, filed in Ulster Co., in which he named his brother Benjamin [perhaps the Benjamin Cox above], his sisters Mary Sealyand Abigail Gale & brothers John & William. Josiah Vail & Isaac Willen, executors.

---

**CRABTREE, WILLIAM & SONS**            H-818
manufacturers of worsted yarns.

WILLIAM CRABTREE, b. England 1846, d. England on a visit June 1903; migrated to America 1864 & located at Philadelphia. In 1867 he m. Harriet Pritchett, d/o Edmund & Elizabeth (Robertshaw) Pritchett, all b. England. Their children:
Harry.
Edmund.
John A.
William E.
Charles B.

---

**CRAIG FAMILY OF BLOOMING-GROVE**            H-139

JAMES CRAIG, from Paisley, Scotland with his family to the area in 1790. His son, HECTOR, b. in Scotland in 1775, m. a d/o John Chandler in 1796. He was a Congressman (1832-25 & 1829-30), ran a paper mill & manufactured hemp. HECTOR had a son-in-law, Barrett Ames, a cotton merchant at Mobile, who had a son-in-law, E. Peet, who erected a cotton factory.

**CRANE, JOHN SEARS, M.D. [P]**   A-560, C-29, 55, 89, 126
of Goshen.

JOHN CRANE[1] m. Abigail ---. Goshen church records note Abigail, wife of John Crane dec'd. as of 3 Nov. 1811. They also note that John Crane d. aged 59, of entiric mania, 3 Oct. 1824. They had one son:
**JOHN SEARS CRANE**[2], [bapt. record gives him the middle name of Sayre] b. Town of Goshen, 3 Aug. 1795; grad. Princeton 1818 & studied medicine in NY City under Dr. Hosack; m. 18 April 1822, Sarah Smith of Goshen and had 6 children, 3 survived to adulthood. He practiced in Milford, PA & engaged in business with brother-in-law, Benjamin Strong in Goshen. Partnership with John C. Wallace, (1837-1855); was involved in insurance & banking, member Goshen Presbyterian Church. Served 19th Brig. Inf. NY State from 12 Oct. 1825. Named children:
1769, Nov. 29, Lydia.
1776, April 30, Peggy.

---

**CRANSS, HENRY**            U2-25
farmer of Montgomery

In his will dated 15 Feb. 1787, **HENRY CRANSS** names his children:
Zekiel.
Henry.
Jonathan.

Will was proved 28 Jan. 1788 by Joseph Whelan physician of Montgomery and William Steuart.

---

**CRAWFORD FAMILY OF CRAWFORD**            A-415
                                          H-188, TN-311-12
**CRAWFORD, DAVID [P]**            A-355-56, C-79, 102
of Newburgh.

All Newburg Crawfords are of Irish origin & all are more or less remotely connected. JOHN CRAWFORD[1] came to America from Ireland 1730 [1718], settled in Little Britain, purchased land in New Windsor 18 Oct. 1737. His children:
DAVID.
Mary m. John Van Arsdale.
Jane m. James Dennison.
James, settled in now what is Town of Crawford.

DAVID CRAWFORD[2]; could be the David in Goshen church records as d. 7 April 1805, age 70, pleurisy. [wife not named] He had son:
FRANCIS CRAWFORD[3], of Newburgh. Remained on homestead at Little Britain until 1806, to Newburgh & entered mercantile & freight business; d. 23 April 1829, age 67. M. (1st) Eunice Watkins, who d. 1791, age 28, and had:
Samuel.
Thomas.
c. 1788, **DAVID.**
James, in business with father in Newburgh; m. Elizabeth Munson who, after his death, m. (2d) John Farnum.

FRANCIS[3] m. (2d) 1792, Dec. 1; Lydia d/o Jeduthan Belknap; he m. (3d) Fanny Denniston, wid. of Capt. Isaac, b. 20 Jan. 1780, d. 26 Feb. 1829.

**DAVID CRAWFORD**[4], b. Little Britain; 1810 deputy sheriff of Orange Co., Capt. in War of 1812; d. 23 July 1856. He m. Fanny C., d/o Isaac Belknap, 15 May 1822, and had:
Isaac R.; d. young.
Mary Elizabeth m. Sands McCalmy 6 Aug. 1844; d. 8 July 1845, leaving dau. Mary E. C. McCalmy.
James Thomas; d. young.
Anna m. Richard A. Southwick 11 Oct. 1849 & had: Fanny C., Anna C. & Florence; Anna dec'd.

**CRAWFORD, LEANDER [P]**            A-426-27
of Crawford.

JAMES CRAWFORD[1] m. Mary Wilkin, members of congregation of Golen, Ireland in 1718 & among the earliest settlers of Town of Crawford, which town was named for them. Their children, all b. in America:
1719, Dec. 15, John.
1722, Jan. 21, James.
1724, March 3, Jane.
1729, Aug. 11, David.
1732, June 9, SAMUEL.
1734, Feb. 21, Joseph.

SAMUEL CRAWFORD[2], s/o James[1], had a son:

JOHN[3], who was a Rev. War veteran; member Presbyterian Church at Hopewell, farmer, m. Sarah Barkley and had:

ROBERT I.

Andrew, tanner & currier of Mt. Hope.

George.

Nancy, unm.

Sally m. Daniel G. Shaver [Shafer] of Crawford.

John B., res. Crawford; d. Havana, NY.

Israel, farmer of Crawford, m. & had Israel & Leartus.

Eleanor m. Nathan Crawford of Chemung Co., NY.

Julia m. Jonathan C. Gillespie, res. Pine Bush.

Keturah m. Harvey [Hill] Harris of Bloomingburgh.

Julia is the only survivor of this generation, now age 80 [1881].

ROBERT I. CRAWFORD[3], s/o Samuel[2], res. near the old Hopewell Church, m. Deborah, d/o Benjamin Dickerson of Crawford, formerly of L.I. Deborah d. several years before ROBERT, who d. 1861, age 77. Their children:

Emeline Millicent, d. unm. [Another source says Emeline & Millicent are 2 people.]

1810, Oct. 2, LEANDER.

John Addison, farmer of Crawford.

Albert, farmer of Crawford; dec'd., d. Orange Lake, where he had removed.

George of Middletown.

Sally Ellen m. N. H. Harris of Montgomery; d. 1880.

Esther, d. unm.

Robert, farmer of Crawford.

Theron, res. Crawford.

Angeline m. Stansbury Gillespie of Crawford.

LEANDER CRAWFORD[4], eldest s/o Robert[3], m. 23 Jan. 1838, Nancy A., b. 9 Jan. 1808, d/o Samuel Barclay & Agnes McCurdy of Crawford & granddau. of Robert McCurdy who d. 15 Sept. 1807, age 85. Samuel a Rev. War soldier, d. 17 April 1814 age 76; Agnes d. 20 Sept. 1844, age 80. The McCurdys & Crawfords were members of Good-Will Presbyterian Church. Leander was a farmer at Searsville and later at Collabar in Crawford; 1858 removed to Middletown, member Hopewell Presbyterian Church & 2d Presbyterian Church of Middletown. Their children:

1838, Nov. 2, James B., lumber merchant of Chicago, d. 24 Oct. 1866.

Anna m. Alsop Purdy, merchant of Middletown.

Ellen B. m. Albert Bull, druggist of Middletown.

"The names of James, John, William & Samuel [CRAWFORD] appear upon the old military roll of 1738 for 'Wall-a-kill,' . . ."

_____

**CRAWFORD, SAMUEL M.**                         **A-171-2**
physician.

Family of Scotch extraction, early to North of Ireland & later settled in Montgomery (now Crawford) NY, birth & death place of:

SAMUEL CRAWFORD[1], farmer, m. --- McCurdy of the same place, and had:

Archibald.

1777, MOSES.

Robert.

Jonathan.

4 daus.

MOSES CRAWFORD[2], farmer of Crawford, m. Elenor d/o Alexander Thompson of Montgomery & had:

Alexander.

1810, Feb. 5, **SAMUEL M.**

Jonathan.

Matilda m. N. P. Hill.

Isabella; d. young.

Jane T. m. William B. Crawford.

Mary.

SAMUEL M. CRAWFORD[3], s/o Moses, b. Twp. of Montgomery; studied at Schenectady, res. Montgomery; April 1836 m. Eliza A., d/o John C. Niemyer of VA. Members of Presbyterian Church in Montgomery. Had 8 children, surviving:

Matilda m. J. C. Wilbur.

Susan V.

Henry V.

Mattie m. C. H. Hinckley.

_____

**CRIST FAMILY OF MONTGOMERY A-372, GFM-15, 36**

HENRY CRIST was a pioneer settler of Orange Co. He had one son, JACOB, who had:

William, dec'd, no issue.

Jacob, drowned in the Hudson coming back from NY, where he had gone to get his wedding clothes.

Henry.

Buried at the German Reformed Cemetery in Montgomery are Henry D. Crist, d. 12 April 1829, aged 42 years, 2 months, 9 days, & his wife, Charity, d. 30 March 1864, aged 71 years, 10 months, 18 days. Also a Henry Crist who d. 14 Jan. 1845, aged 84 years, 11 months.

STEVANUS CRIST is named as a pioneer settler. His children are given as:

Christian.

Jonathan.

Simeon.

David.

_____

**CRIST, GEORGE W.**                         **H-818-19**

NELSON CRIST was a s/o Philip who engaged in early stage coach business between Goshen & Kingston. Nelson was also great-grandfather of **GEORGE W.**[2]

THEODORE J. CRIST[1], b. on the family farm 22 April 1844, m. Cecelie Mapes and had:
1875, Dec., Grant.
Clara, resides at home.
1875, Feb. 22, **GEORGE W.**
Abigail B., resides at home.
Frank M., m. Emily Mortimer of Brooklyn, NY.
Mary Belle (?), m. Frank Cox of Middletown; d. July 1898.

GEORGE W. CRIST[2], b. on homestead farm in the Town of Hamptonburgh.

_____

**CROFTS, CHARLES E.**                                    **H-819**

CHARLES E. CROFTS, superintendent of the NY Knife Co. of Walden since 1876, b. in Sheffield, England; 1872 to America & located at Walden. He m. Emma Marsden & had 12 children, 3 living. Among them:
Arthur, in business in NY City.
Emma L., student.

_____

**CROMWELL, JOHN [P]**                                    **A-244a**

"It is assumed" that the Cromwell ancestor to America was Col. John Cromwell[1], 3rd son of Richard Cromwell and a brother of Protector, Oliver of England. This Col. John had a son:
JOHN CROMWELL[2], emigrated from Holland to New Netherlands and res. 1686 at Long Neck, Westchester Co., later known as Cromwell's Neck; m. and left 2 sons:
John.
1696, JAMES.

JAMES CROMWELL[3], s/o Col. John[2], d. 1780; m. Esther Godfrey and had:
172 7, Dec. 5, JOHN.
James.
William.

JOHN CROMWELL[4], s/o James[3], res. Harrison, Westchester Co; m. Anna Hopkins of L.I. who was b. 12 Jan. 1730. John was a patriot during the Rev. & d. 1805. Their children:
1752, Nov. 6, JAMES.
Daniel.
John.
Joseph.
William.
Naomi m. Rev. Mr. Halstead.
Esther m. John Griffin Jr., of North Castle.
Hannah m. William Field of Cortlandt Manor.

JAMES CROMWELL[5] m. 15 May 1782, Charlotte, d/o Aaron Hunt of Greenwich, CT, b. 18 Nov. 1762, d. Jan. 1830. James farmed at Morrisania; grocer in NY City, to Sufferns, Rockland Co., farmer & blacksmith. Purchased farm in Monroe, Orange Co. (then known as Southfield); Quaker, d. 23 Dec. 1828. Children:
Hannah m. David Griffin of Westchester Co.

Rebecca m. George Fritts of Monroe.
Daniel, carpenter & builder, res. & d. in NY City.
James, farmer on family homestead, Monroe.
Oliver, res. Cornwall.
Ann m. John Haviland of Westchester Co.
David, res. & d. Cornwall.
Aaron.
William & Mary, twins; d. young.
William, NY merchant; d. at old homestead.
1803, July 26, **JOHN.**

JOHN CROMWELL[6], s/o James[5], in business in NY until 1847 when he purchased farm of Leonard Nicoll, Town of New Windsor; home near Moodna. He was a Quaker. He m. (1) 12 Oct. 1826, Letitia, d/o Abijah & Patience Haviland of White Plains, Westchester Co. Letitia d. 1861. Their children:
1827, Nov. 4, Walter, res. CA.
1829, March 24, James, res. Bedford, Westchester Co.
1831, July 24, Oliver, res. New Windsor.
1838, May 25, David, res. White Plains, Westchester Co.

JOHN[6] m. (2d) 25 June 1863, Elizabeth, d/o Charles & Ann (Conklin) Cox of Town of Newburgh.

_____

**CRONK, HARRY A.**                                    **H-819**

HARRY A. CRONK, b. 20 May 1877 at Binghamton, NY; 1902 with Borden Milk Co. He m. Ora J. Whitlock of Ithaca, NY, 24 March 1897. They have one daughter, Camilla Eleanor, age 4.

_____

**CROSBY, INCREASE [P]**                                    **A-164-5**
physician.

Four Crosby brothers from Scotland to America. They settled in PA, MA & in the South.
INCREASE CROSBY[1] studied medicine in New England, to Orange Co. from MA in the late 1700's & m. Isabella Milliken of Ulster Co. and had:
1791, Nov. 12, ROBERT.
Cyrenus.
Mary m. John Jordan of Orange Co.

ROBERT CROSBY[2] farmer; m. Catherine, d/o Joseph Whalen, b. 1797, May 10, d. 17 March 1852. Robert d. 26 Aug. 1833. Their children:
Cyrenus; d. young.
Increase.
Joseph V. W.
1826, June 16, R. Melliken; 1860 m. Hannah C., d/o David C. Ball of Crawford, and had 5 children.
Dau. d. infancy.

_____

**CROWELL, ROBERT [P]**        **W-**
farmer & dairyman.

**ROBERT B. CROWELL**, s/o Robert B. & Sarah June (Burns) Crowell, was b. at St. Andrews, Orange Co., 1847; studied law with John J. Monell of Newburgh; grad. Albany law school 1868. 1870 he m. Catharine Garrison of the Town of Newburgh & located on his father's farm near Wallkill; 1882 purchased "Echo Hill Farm" at west Wallkill, where he still resides. They had 5 children.

**CUDDEBACK FAMILY OF DEERPARK A-705, T-4, 120**
**CUDDEBACK, GEORGE [P]**        **A-751-2**
Bank Director of Deerpark & Port Jervis.

The family name was originally Caudebee (Huguenots) "of Town of Caudebee in Normandy, founded in 1400." They emigrated to either England or Holland. JACOB[1], French Huguenot, to America before 1690; landed in VA & settled on the east bank of the Hudson River, north of NJ, fur trader at age 20; lived to be nearly 100 years of age. He m. Margaret Provost at Esophus or "elsewhere along the Hudson." She was d/o Benjamin Provost, trader of the 1690 settlement in valley of Neversink. They had 9 children: [one source says they had 5 sons & 11 grandsons]:

Benjamin, lived to age 80 in Deerpark; unm.
WILLIAM.
James, m. Neelje Decker, res. near Deckertown, NJ; d. age 30, left numerous desc. res. Niagara Co., NY.
Abraham, m. Esther Swartwout; in old age moved to Skaneateles, where his children had previously settled; d. c. age 80. The story of Capt. Abraham's Indian fighting adventures in early Orange Co. found T-4.
Dinah, m. Abraham Lovis of Rochester; settled in NJ.
Eleanor, m. Evert Hornbeck of Rochester; res. Deerpark.
Elsie, m. Flarmanus Van Gordon, res. at the Flat Rocks in NJ.
Morice, m. George Westfall, res. NJ.
Naomi, m. Lodewyck Hornbeck of Rochester.

**WILLIAM CUDDEBACK[2]**, s/o Jacob[1], m. Jemima Elting of Old Paltz, settled on homestead & had:
James.
Abram.
BENJAMIN.
Roolif.
Sarah.

**BENJAMIN CUDDEBACK[3]**, m. Catharine VanFliet. He is the only one who had descs. in the area in 1890. He d. intestate & administration of his estate was granted 7 March 1788 to his widow. They had 7 children, one of which was:
HENRY CUDDEBACK[4], b. 23 March 1771, m. Esther Gumaer, b. 23 Sept. 1774, and had:
Catherine.
Elizabeth.
Simeon.
Jacob G.

Huldah.
Cynthia.
Benjamin.
1815, Aug. 10, GEORGE.

**GEORGE CUDDEBACK[5]**, s/o Henry[4], m. 21 Dec. 1848, Margaret, d/o John D. Carpenter of Carpenter's Point. Members Reformed Church of Port Jervis. Their children:
Henry G. m. 18 Sept. 1878, Libbie O'Riley who d. 29 Nov. 1879.
John D.; dec'd.
Mary Ellen; dec'd.
Esther; dec'd.
Margaret; dec'd.
Alice; dec'd.
Martha E.
George Jr.

**CUDDEBACK FAMILY OF DEERPARK**        **A-712-13**

Cuddeback Hotel was built by Peter Cuddeback, Postmaster.

ABRAHAM CUDDEBACK[1] had a son, WILLIAM A.[2], who had a son:
JAMES CUDDEBACK[3], res. Cuddebackville now age 85; m. a d/o Benjamin Cuddebach who d. at the age of 91.

The story of "Capt." Abraham Cuddeback's Indian fighting adventures in early Orange Co. recounted in T-4. For a description of his papers, now in possession of his descs., see T-59.

**CUDDEBACK, WILLIAM L.**        **H-820**
physician of Port Jervis

WILLIAM L. CUDDEBACK, M.D., is a descendant of French Huguenots (see above) of that name who settled in Deer Park in 1690, coming from Caudebec, France, known in ancient days as Normandy. He was one of six children of Elting and Ann Bevier (Elting) Cuddeback, born in the town of Deer Park 26 April 1854. Studied medicine in office of Dr. Solomon Van Ettan of Port Jervis, attended Bellevue Hospital Medical College, NY & grad. in 1876. Practiced at Port Jervis in 1892 with Dr. H. B. Swartwout. He m. Alice D. Malven 16 Oct. 1880, d/o George & Philenda (St. John) Malven of Port Jervis, and had:
Frank E.
Edgar C.
Elizabeth M.
Alice M.
Philenda.

**CULBERT, WILLIAM A. M. [P]**        **A-184-5**
physician.

CULBERT, WILLIAM A.M., b. 4 Nov. 1822, in NY City; practiced in Brooklyn; to Newburgh with A. Gerald Hull,

M.D. (1847); m. 12 Oct. 1852, Henrietta d/o Robert & Louisa A. Powell, granddau. of Thomas Powell.

## CURTICE, BENAJAH                    U2-152
yeoman of Wallkill.

In his will dated 12 Feb. 1745, **BENAJAH CURTICE** names his wife as Mary and mentions his children and his aged father, but no names are given. Mary Curtice of Otterkill, in her will dated 20 March 1764, mentions her youngest son, Jeremiah, and other sons Noah, Benajah & Thomas.

## CUSHING, THOMAS P.                  H-820

**THOMAS P.**, s/o James Cushing, b. NY City 31 Dec. 1863. James moved to Orange Co. in 1871, ran general store at Vale's Gate, d. 1903. **THOMAS** has served as clerk in Town of New Windsor, postmaster at Vail's Gate, j.p. & Erie Railroad agent.

## CUSHMAN, CHARLES U.           A-194, TN-319-20
newspaperman.

**CHARLES U. CUSHMAN**, a desc. of ROBERT CUSH-MAN, "one of the original company of Pilgrims who sailed for the New World, 1620, Aug. 5, O.S."

**CUSHMAN, CHARLES**, b. Hartford, Washington Co., NY, 20 March 1802; res. Rutland VT, Boston MA & Newburgh NY. He was raised by his grandfather & after his death res. with his father in Bennington. At age 17 he was apprenticed to a book-store & printing office at Rutland, VT; at age 19 to Boston & later NY. To Newburgh & purchased *Political Index* & established the *Orange Telegraph* (later the *Newburgh Telegraph*) in 1829. He was customs officer & merchant of NY city; retired in 1852; 1853 elected member of Assembly. In 1858 he removed to Rhinebeck, Dutchess Co., where he d. 1 June 1857, after an illness of only a few hours. He was nearly 6 feet tall, clear complexion, blue eyes, rather fleshy & well formed. He m. 4 June 1832, Mary, d/o Capt. Charles Birdsall & granddau. of Isaac Belknap; d. without issue in Rhinebeck, NY 1 June 1859.

## DALES, JOHN                          H-820-21
real estate & insurance man of Newburgh.

JOHN DALES[1] m. Sarah Calvin & had son:
JOHN[2], b. Delaware Co., 1820; d. 26 March 1908. 1839 to Newburgh in employ of Crawford Mailler; worked at Memphis TN, NY City & Jordan NY--flour miller. 1865 retired to Newburgh in partnership with W. O. Mailler, wholesale grocer & freight business. Member Calvary Presbyterian Church. In 1845 he m. Susan, d/o Jacob Oakley, who d. 24 Nov. 1890. They had:
William M., d. 1 Nov. 1883; left one daughter, Helen M.
Mary Belknap, m. Charles D. Robinson and had a daughter, Julia. Mary d. 14 Jan. 1900.

## DANA, HERBERT S.                     H-821
Erie Railroad agent at Craigsville, NY.

**HERBERT** was b. Gardner, ME; to Orange Co. 1893, telegraph operator in the office of PA Coal Co. at Newburgh. Postmaster 1907. He m. Nellie Robinson of CT and had:
George.
Stephen.
Frederick.

## DARBY FAMILY OF WALLKILL             A-434

**DANIEL DARBY**, b. Newburgh, 1799, May; to Wallkill 1823; m. Julia d/o William Carpenter & res. Van Burenville.

## DARLINGTON, THOMAS                   H-822-4

PETER DARLINGTON[1] m. Maria Wilde. He was one of the first paper manufacturers in the US. He d. 21 Jan 1851; she d. 20 Aug. 1900, aged over 100 years. They had:
1826, Aug. 29, **THOMAS**.

**THOMAS DARLINGTON**[2], b. Salisbury Mills, Orange Co., d. 15 May 1903 & buried at the same place as he was married, University Place Presbyterian Church, NY City. Through his mother's line he is a descendant of Gov. Bishop of CT; of Daniel Rayneau, 1st freeholder of the Huguenot Colony of New Rochelle; of Richard Wilde, Esq. of Flushing, NY and of Edward Griffin of VA Colony. On his father's side he is descended from the Darlington's of Yorkshire, England and Edinburgh, Scotland.

**THOMAS** studied law in NY City & established the firm of Darlington, Spring & Russell & later Darlington, Irving & Hoffman. He was a Presbyterian Church member; taught Sunday School at the Mulberry Mission of the South Park Church in Newark, NJ. 1 Aug. 1850 he m. Hannah Anne, d/o James Yarrow Goodliffe, who d. in 1901 & is buried in NY City. Their children:
Alfred Ernest, dec'd.
Alice, dec'd.
James, P. E. Bishop of Harrisburg, PA.
1858, Sept. 24, THOMAS J.
Charles Francis, atty.
Gustavus C., physician.
Marion Goodliffe.
Margaret, m. --- White.

**THOMAS J. DARLINGTON**[3], s/o Thomas[2], b. Brooklyn, NY. He grad. College of Physicians & Surgeons, NY in 1880. Practiced in Newark, NJ; 1882 to Kingsbridge, NY until 1904; Commissioner of Health NY City. SAR member & many other organizations.

## DAVEY, THOMAS WESLEY                 H-824

**THOMAS**, b. Town of Greenville, NY 6 Jan. 1850; associated with factories in Middletown & spent 2 years in oil fields of PA. He m. Maria Wood of Haverstraw, NY, and had:

Irving W.

Mina May.

Lewis Jacob.

___

## DAVIS FAMILY OF WAWAYANDA   A-688, H-287, C-79

JOSHUA DAVIS SR., located in the area before 1775; driver of 1st vehicle on wheels that ever passed over the road from Goshen through Ridgebury. He could be the Joshua Davis who d. 14 Aug. 1805, age 73, of fever. Had 4 daus & 2 sons, among them:

Joshua.

James.

Dau. m. Richard Ferguson. [Three possible daus. of this Joshua are named in the Goshen church baptismal records: Levene, b. 24 Aug. 1786, Azuba, bapt. 6 Sept. 1778 & Sarah, b. 14 Nov. 1785.]

A JOSEPH DAVIS, of town of Minisink (Wawayanda), freed his slave Frank Bounty in March 1799. He gave him the use of a house & lot in Brookfield or Slate Hill, where Frank raised a large family.

A JOHN DAVIS was the first settler on McIntosh patent, Town of New Windsor in 1726.

## DECKER, ABRAHAM   U2-94
of Shawangunk, yeoman.

HENDRICK DECKER[1] m. 18 Dec. 1696, Antje Quick, and had:

Bapt. 1698, Sept. 11, Geertje.

Bapt. 1699, Oct. 29, Femmetje.

Bapt. 1702, May 10, Sara.

Bapt. 1709, Sept. 11, Sarah.

Bapt. 1712, March 9, Johannes.

HENDRICK m. (2) Annajen Kortright and had:

Bapt. 1720, June 19, **ABRAHAM**.

HENDRICK m. (3) Anna Tietsort and had:

Bapt. 1723, June 30, Elisabeth.

Bapt. 1725, Oct. 3, Neeltjen.

ABRAHAM DECKER[2], s/o Hendrick[1], m. 1747 Aug. 12, Elisabeth Schut, and had:

Bapt. 1748, June 8, at Shawangunk, Abraham.

Bapt. 1750, Oct. 28, Jacobus.

Bapt. 1753, May 17, Uriah.

Catrina, m. Everet Dekker.

Leah, m. Jacob Deeker.

Elisabeth.

ABRAHAM's will, dated 26 Sept. 1791, names his wife as Catherine, also names above children and his brother Gerret Decker, dec'd. Also states that his son Uriah now dwells on a lot that was lately purchased of Manessah Decker. Will proved 28 April 1792 by Johannes Bruyn of Shawangunk, Ellas Winfield & George Smith.

___

## DECKER, ABRAHAM LINCOLN   H-824-5

ABRAHAM LINCOLN DECKER is the son of John H. Decker (d. 1877) and Elsie Fullerton. He was b. Newburgh 16 Jan. 1865. Worked at drug store in Paterson, NJ; City Editor at the *Times* in Middletown, NY 12 years; served in 1st NY Vol. Infantry during the Spanish American War; coroner & county sheriff (1907). He m. Natalie Weygant 31 Oct. 1890 and had:

1892, Richard Stivers.

1896, John Weygant.

___

## DECKER, ISAIAH W.   H-825, W-91-2
retired farmer of Walden.

LEVI DECKER had a son William D. Decker who m. Ellen Jane Crans. They were the parents of **ISAIAH W. DECKER**.

W-91-2 mentions an Isaiah W. Decker, farmer of the Valley of Wallkill, b. Town of Montgomery. He retired & removed to Walden May 1907. His parents are not named.

___

## DECKER, JOHN E.   H-825
farmer near Middletown.

EZEKIEL & Anna DECKER are the parents of **JOHN E.**, who was b. 1 May 1860 at Dwaarkill, Ulster Co., NY. He m. Martha Jane, d/o Abraham Vernooy 2 April 1895 and had one son, Adrien Vernooy Decker, b. 11 Aug. 1897. Members First Congregational Church at Middletown.

___

## DECKER, JONATHAN   U2-52
of Montgomery.

In his will dated 23 June 1789, **JONATHAN DECKER** names his wife Mary and the following children:

Jonathan.

Eleaser.

___

## DECKER, JOSEPH H. [P]   C-21, A-409-10, H-204
farmer of Montgomery, of Dutch extraction.

JOHANN DECKER[1], b. 1741, April 16, res. Kingston, Ulster Co., and later in Blooming-Grove; m. Annatie Halbrouck of Marbletown, Ulster Co., b. 29 Dec. 1747. Their children:

Jacob.

1770, CORNELIUS.

John.

Rachel.

Ann.

Jonah.

Elsie.
Matthew.

A Johannes Decker paid the largest assessment in 1775 in Town of Goshen. A son, Johannes Jr. is also listed as a large tax payer. [H-204.]

CORNELIUS DECKER[2], s/o Johann[1], res. twp. of Montgomery; d. 1835; m. Hannah Duryea of Blooming-Grove, 30 Jan. 1796, and had:
George.
1809, May 12, JOSEPH H.
John.
Ann.
Hannah Maria.
Rachel.
Caroline.
Dolly.
Cornelius.

JOSEPH H. DECKER[3], s/o Cornelius[2], member Reformed Dutch Church of Montgomery; m. 30 Dec. 1804, Maria d/o Adam Dickerson of Montgomery, b. 25 Oct. 1804, and had:
1821, Hannah Jane, m. 7 May 1853, Hon. Hugh Barkley Bull of Crawford Twp., b. 1 Oct. 1816, of an early Orange County family, atty. They had one child, Maria P., d. 25 Feb. 1880.
1823, Harriet A.
1830, Francis C., only surviving child of Joseph H. (1880/1); teacher, farmer, 1875 to the farm res. of parents, "Saratoga Farm;" unm.
1839, Joseph H.
1842, Anna Mary.
1835 [sic], Cornelius

## DECKER, PHILIP                    H-186, GFM-38

PHILIP DECKER, whose ancestors came from Holland, res. Town of Crawford. At age 16 drove a team from Ward's Bridge to Valley Forge with a load of corn for Washington's army.
A Philip Decker is bur. at the German Reformed Cemetery at Montgomery. He d. 27 April 1832, aged 85 years.
E-270 says that a Philip Decker, an early resident of Town of Montgomery, came from Holland & was the father of Isaiah.

## DECKER, SAMUEL                    H-825-6

SAMUEL DECKER, b. 12 March 1851 near village of Amity, Orange Co., was a descendant of a Holland Dutch emigrant who settled at what is now Glenwood, NJ and later settled in central NY, but left one son at Glenwood.
His grandfather, ABRAM SMITH, was a Rev. soldier who taught school in Orange Co. for 50 years. Abram's wife was Maria.

SAMUEL to Town of Greenville, NY to purchase farm; teacher & j.p. He m. 16 Oct. 1878 Cornelia Sergeant, only d/o

Jeremiah a cattle dealer & farmer of Gardnersville. Their children:
Margaret, m. Frank Neail of Mt. Hope.
Phebe, m. Hiram Tyler of NY City.
Frank, at home.
Effa, at home.

## DECKER, WILLIAM G. [P]                    W-

WILLIAM G. DECKER, b. Ulster Co., NY 15 March 1864, farmer until 1896; entered employ of the Prudential Life Insurance Co. at Newburgh, Asst. Supt. of Walden. Member 1st Reformed Church of Walden; 1888 m. Anna MacGowan of Middletown, and had:
Edith.
Leslie.

## DEENE, CHRISTOPHER             A-650, H-223-4, 250

CHRISTOPHER DEENE (DENN), Frenchman, carpenter & res. of New York City as early as 1702, purchased land in present Town of Goshen in 1712 (a patentee of Wawayanda), although it is questionable if he ever lived there except temporarily. In 1701 he was a res. of NY City & d. there in 1722/3. His wife Elizabeth d. NY (will 29 Dec. 1730). They had no children, but brought up orphan girl Sarah Wells who m. William Bull (first marriage in town limits of Goshen) of Wolverhampton, England, & settled in Orange Co.

## DE GROVE FAMILY OF NEWBURGH        TN-295-5, 298

PETER ADOLPH DE GROVE[1], French Huguenot, settled in NY; merchant. He had:
Adolph, removed to Island of Jamaica, where he died. He res. there with his brother Peter, who returned to America & settled in Boston.
PETER.
Alfie, m. Garret Schuyler, merchant of NY.

PETER DE GROVE[2] m. Rebecca and had:
Peter, d. unm.
ADOLPH.
Rachel, m. Capt. John Anderson; has no surviving descs.
Rebecca, m. --- Albertson; has descs. in Stryker, Lawrence & Crolius families of NY.

ADOLPH DE GROVE[3], s/o Peter[2], settled in Newburgh in 1777/8 with other refugees from NY at the time of the occupation by English forces. Established a bakery & hotel in Newburgh, helped organize First Presbyterian Church; he d. 29 Nov. 1796, aged 76. He m. (1) in 1780, Miss --- Lawrence; m. (2) Mary, sister of Enoch Carter; no issue. Mary d. 20 April 1824 in her 85th year. Children of Adolph's first marriage:
ADOLPH.
WILLIAM.
John,; probably m. & left issue.

SARAH.

Mary, m. Capt. --- Smith & left issue, Benjamin & Rebecca Smith.

ADOLPH DE GROVE[4], s/o Adolph[3], Asst. Quartermaster at Newburgh (1780), m. 1780, Rhoda Coles of Queens Co., and had:

Robert C., m. Miss --- Smith & had 1 son who d. without issue.
ADOLPH L.
John, d. unm.
Coles, d. unm.
Samuel, d. unm.
Sarah, m. John Mitchell of L.I., left no surviving children.

ADOLPH L. DE GROVE[5], s/o Adolph[4], m. Catharine Gallow of Newburgh & had:

Edward W., res. NY with 2 sons: Stephen C., d. unm. & Charles H., now dec'd, left children.
Adolph L., d. unm.
Elisa, m. Dr. Wooster Beach.
Catharine, m. Noah Tompkins.
Rebecca Jane, m. William Clark.
Sarah, unm.

WILLIAM DE GROVE[4], s/o Adolph[3], had [wife not named]:
Michael, left 7 children.
Quinsey, d. Dec. 1860, left no issue.
Sarah, m. Mr. --- Sobietes.

SARAH DE GROVE[4], d/o Adolph[3], m. (1) Mr. --- Rivers and had a dau., Sarah, who m. --- Hartwich; Sarah m. (2) Enoch Carter.

---

## DE KAY, FRANK H.                                   H-826

FRANCIS M. DE KAY[1] m. Nellie Sisson and had:
Child, d. in infancy.
Lucille, m. James H. Vealey.
1866, Aug. 11, **FRANK H.**

FRANK H. DE KAY[2], b. Town of Warwick at New Milford. In furniture & undertaking business with Mr. Butt at early age. Retired 1903. He m. Margaret Pelser of Paterson, NJ 14 April 1891. Members Christ Episcopal Church, Warwick. Their children:
1893, March 5, Elwood Frank; d. 10 July 1902.
1896, June 5, Doris Pelser.

---

## DEMEREST, ABRAM [P]                      A-628c, H-163
of Chester, of Huguenot extraction.

JAMES DEMEREST[1] settled in Town of Warwick [on ridge near Sugar Loaf] from Bergen Co., NJ. He had 12 children, among them:
NICHOLAS DEMEREST[2], b. 26 Feb. 1762, m. Mary Bontan, b. 3 Jan. 1770, d. 15 Aug. 1836; Nicholas d. 10 June 1845. Their children:

1788, Sept. 16, Catharine; d. 13 May 1911.
1790, Feb. 4, Elizabeth, m. Jesse Marfee of Goshen.
1792, March 1, James S.
1794, Feb. 11, Samuel.
1796, Nov. 17, Nicholas.
1798, Sept. 27, Margaret.
1800, Sept, 14, **ABRAM.**
1802, Dec. 29, Mary, m. John Lawrence of Warwick.
1804, Sept. 17, Hannah.
1807, April 8, Jane, m. Ezra Holbert of Warwick.
1809, Feb. 3, Caroline, m. E. M. Bradner of Warwick
1811, July 13, Catherine, m. William S. Benedict of Warwick.

ABRAM DEMEREST[3] m. 27 Oct. 1842, Eliza Jane, d/o ISAAC & Mehetabel (Wells) SMITH of Chester [see below], who was b. 17 April 1808. After his marriage, **ABRAM** res. on homestead at Warwick; 1850 to West Chester; 1854 to Village of Chester. Their children:
Nicholas m. Isabella B., d/o Daniel McNeal of Montgomery, res. on home farm.
1846, Oct. 17, William; d. 18 May 1856.

ISAAC SMITH, b. 8 March 1755, Jamaica, L.I., d. 14 Oct. 1836, Town of Chester. He m. Mehetable, d/o Joshua Wells, a des. of Hon. William Wells, b. near Norwich England in 1608, to America 1635 on ship *Free Love*; attorney in England & high sheriff of New Yorkshire, L.I. Isaac & Mehetable's dau., Eliza Jane m. **ABRAM DEMEREST[3]**.

---

## DEMAREST, CORNELIUS HENRY.              H-826-7
farmer of Warwick.

DAVID DEMAREST, b. Beauchamp, Village of Picardy, France, m. Marie Soheir. With their 5 children they sailed from Amsterdam 16 April 1663 on ship *Bontekol* (Spotted Cow) for New Amsterdam. They res. 2 years on Staten Island, then to Harlem 12 1/2 years & purchased land in vicinity of Hackensack, NJ; during the Revolutionary War to Orange Co. Among family members was:
CORNELIUS C. DEMAREST[1], soldier of the Rev. under Col. John Hathorn & organizer of the Reformed Church of Warwick. He was father of **CORNELIUS HENRY[2]**, and willed his farm to his son and grandson Henry Pelton Demarest resides there today.

CORNELIUS HENRY DEMAREST[2] was b. Warwick, 25 June 1820 & d. 10 Dec. 1889. Member of the Consistory of the Reformed Church. In 1845 he m. Elizabeth A. Pelton, d/o of Henry of Warwick, and had:
1848, Feb. 5, Charles M., m. Annie E. Armstrong, d/o Rensselaer of Warwick. Charles M. d. 8 June 1905.
1852, Feb. 8, DeWitt Clinton, m. Harrie Hudson of Denver, res. Passaic, NJ.
1854, April 29, Mary Elizabeth, m. Christie Romaine of Hackensack, NJ.
1856, Oct. 25, Henry Pelton, m. Eliza J. Tolland of Florida, NY;

41

resides on family farm.
1858, May 29, Julia, unm., res. Warwick.
1860, Feb. 27, David, unm., res. Boston, MA.
1862, April 24, Anna, unm., res. Warwick.

## DEMARST, GEORGE HOUSTON          H-827
farmer.

**GEORGE H. DEMARST** was b. near Wisner 26 June 1873.
He was of the 7th generation to reside on this (dairy) farm.
He m. Edith May Stevens of Sugar Loaf on 2 Nov. 1898,
and had 4 children, 2 living:
James Henry, age 6.
Agnes Wood, age 3 months.

## DEMOTT, MICHAEL          E-87, A-200, LDS Anc. File

**MICHAEL DEMOTT**[1] lived as early as 1764 & kept a tavern.
Town meetings were occasionally held at his home in Town
of Newburgh. He had a number of children, among them:
William.
JACOB.
Isaac, who inherited the estate, which was later purchased by a
Mr. Ellis & later passed into the hands of Daniel Wilson.

**JACOB DEMOTT**[2], m. Marie Tunis & had:
1678, Martie [Marya/Maria].
1680, Matthias.
1682, Johannes [John].
1684, Dirck [Richard].
1685, Anthony.
1687, Michael.
1689, Elizabeth.
1691, Jacob.

## DENNISTON FAMILY OF TOWN OF BLOOMING-GROVE          H-137
## DENNISTON, HON. AUGUSTUS  H-827-8, LDS Anc. File

**ALEXANDER DENNISTON**[1], brother-in-law of Charles
Clinton, was a Scotch Presbyterian immigrant from Town of
Edgeworth, Co. of Longford, Ireland in 1729. He served in
Col. Ellison's New Windsor regiment, 1738 & 1755. His
sons, all of whom served in the Ulster Co. Regt. during the
Rev. War. His children:
James.
George.
ALEXANDER.
William.
JOHN.
Charles.
4 daus.

**ALEXANDER DENNISTON**[2], b. Ireland, m. Frances Little, d/o
George, & had an only son:
**JAMES DENNISTON**[3], settled in town of Blooming-Grove,
came with his father to America [1729] & settled in Town of

New Windsor. He m. Jane Crawford; d. 1805 [1825], and
had:
JAMES.
Alexander.
Abraham.
2 daus.

**JAMES DENNISTON**[4], s/o James[3], inherited father's homestead;
d. 1825, and had:
ROBERT.
4 daus.

**ROBERT DENNISTON**[5], officer of the militia, j.p., county
judge, Assemblyman (1838); state senator (1841-47), etc. His
children:
William Scott, surgeon in Army; d. of fever July 1862.
James Otis, 1st Lt. & Capt. Co. G, 124 NY State Vols., mustered out 3 Sept. 1863 on account of wounds; studied
theology.
Robert, served March to Oct. 1863 & resigned on account of
bad health; d. Aug. 1864.
Henry Martyn, US Navy Sept. 1861; served 40 years & retired
at age 62 as rear admiral.
AUGUSTUS.
6 daus.

**AUGUSTUS DENNISON**[6], b. Town of Blooming-Grove,
the youngest s/o Robert & Mary Denniston; d. 1898. He worked
in Albany; 1862 quartermaster of the 124th Regt. NY Vols.,
resigned because of illness. Political service & businessman.
Res. in old home built by his father in 1824. In milk business.

**JOHN DENNISTON**[2], s/o Alexander[1], could be the John
Denniston b. 15 Dec. 1750 at Little Britain who m. Anna
Moffatt, d/o Samuel & had:
1775, Samuel Moffatt.
1777, Jan. 23, Fannie.
1778, Dec. 14, John S.
1776, April 23, Anna Moffatt, b. New Windsor, m. Jacob
Schultz, b. 23 April 1776, New Windsor.

## DENTON FAMILY OF WAWAYANDA
          A-677, C-90, 102, 105, CN-15

**REV. RICHARD DENTON**[1], b. Yorkshire, England 1586; grad.
Cambridge 1623, minister of Coley Chapel in Halifax, Eng-
land; to Boston with Gov. Winthrop in 1630. Preached at
Watertown, MA & Wethersfield & Stamford, CT; 1644 with
part of congregation to Hempstead, L.I.; returned to England
and d. there in 1662, age 76. His sons:
Richard.
SAMUEL.
Daniel, to Jamacia, L.I. in 1656; 1670 published first history of
the colony of NY. Had a son James who appears in the
Newburgh Town Directory for 1750 & erected a grist mill at
Denton's creek & a small store.
Nathaniel, to Jamaica in 1656.

JOHN.

SAMUEL DENTON[2], s/o Rev. Richard[1], had a dau. Catharine who m. Jacob Mills, Esq. of Wallkill and had 12 children. One child, William, m. only d/o Wickham Denton of L.I.

JOHN DENTON[2], s/o Rev. Richard[1], had a son:
JAMES DENTON[3], who had:
Amos.
JOHN.
William, settled in Orange Co., returned to L.I. near Beaver Pond & d. there.
Thomas, had a dau. who m. Jason Wilkin, res. Lagrange.

JOHN DENTON[4], s/o John[3], located in village of Goshen on old Carpenter farm; had 3 wives & 14 children. He m. (1st) Jane Fisher of L.I.; (2d) Elizabeth Wisner, d/o Henry; (3d) Mary Gale, d/o Hezekiah who res. near what is now called Lagrange. Children from Goshen baptismal register:
Bapt. 10 Feb. 1778, Thomas.
Bapt. 21 Feb. 1778, Sarah.
Born 14 Sept. 1779, Mary.

From the same church register: John Denton, d. 21 July 1826, aged 65; dropsy in chest. Also recorded is the death of a Thomas W. Denton, aged 35, d. of delerium tremens 7 Aug. 1827, and marriage of a Thomas Denton to Elizabeth Sodon, 3 June 1809.

————

## DE WITT FAMILY OF DEERPARK
### A-704-5, H-204, U1-54-58, 65-6, U2-82-3, LDS Anc. File

TJERCK CLASSEN DE WITT[1], [George Nicholas] b. Groatholt in Sunderlant, Holland, s/o Nicholas of Holland, to America settled at Wiltwyck (now Kingston) in 1672. He m. at New Amsterdam 24 April 1656, Barbara Andriessen from Amsterdam. Children:
ANDRIES.
c. 1659, Taatje, b. Albany; carried off by the Indians at the burning of Kingston in 1663, later rescued. She m. 1677, Matthys Mattysen Van Kuren, s/o Matthys Jansen & Marg. Hendrickse.
Bapt. 1662, Feb. 12, Jannetje, m. Cornelis Swits (Swetts).
Bapt. 1664, Feb. 17, Klaes.
Bapt. 1666, Feb. 14, Jan, m. Wyntje Kierstede, d/o Roeloff K. & Ikee Roosa. In his will, dated 29 Oct. 1700, (U-1-123) he is identified as of Rochester & names children: Barbara m. Jan Gerritse Decker; Ikee (Agnes); Blandina, m. Jurian Westphael; Rachel, m. Isaac VanAken; & Jannetje m. Abraham VanAken.
Bapt. 1668, Oct. 15, Geertruy, m. 24 March 1688, Hendrick Hendricksen Schoonmaker.
Tjerck.
Jacob, m. before 1 March 1696, Grietje Vernooy, d/o Cornelius & Annatje Cornelis.
Rachel, m. Cornelis Bogardus, b. 1640, s/o Cornelis B. &

Helena Teller & had 1 child, Barbara. U1-65 names him as s/o Evert Bogardus originally of Woerden near Utrecht, Germany & Anneke Jans.
LUCAS.
Peek, m. (1) 2 Jan. 1698, Marytje Janse Vanderberg, of Albany, and (2) 21 Dec. 1723, Maria Teunis, widow of Jacob De-Mott.
Tjerck.
Marritje, m. (1) 3 Nov. 1700, Hendrick Hendrickson Kortright, s/o Hendrick Jansen Kortright & Catharina Hansen Webber, and (2) 6 Sept. 1702, Jan Macklin.
Bapt. 1684, Jan. 14, Aagje, m. 23 Aug. 1712, Jan Pawling, bapt. 2 Oct. 1681, s/o Henry Pawling & Neeltje Roosa (d/o Albert Heymanse R.) who removed to Philadelphia.

ANDRIES DE WITT[2], s/o Tjerick Classen De Witt[1], m. Jannetje Egbertsen on 7 March 1682. She bapt. NY 11 Jan. 1664, d. 23 Nov. 1733 & was d/o Egbert Meindertse & Jaepe Jans. Capt. Andres was accidentally killed 22 July 1710. They had:
Bapt. 1683, Jan. 12, TJERCK.
Bapt. 1684, Sept. 28, Jacob.; d. young.
1686, Aug. 22, Barbara, d. infant.
1688, April 30, Klaes, d. infant.
1689, Oct. 30, Barbara, m. 25 March 1715, Johannes Van Lewven.
1691, Dec. 30, Jacob, m. 9 May 1731, Heyltje Van Kampen, d/o Jan & Tretje (Dekker) Van Kampen.
1693, Jan. 21, Maria, m. 30 Oct. 1713, Jan Roosa Jr., s/o Jan. R. & Hilligond (Van Buren) Roosa.
1695, Dec. 7, Helena, m. 6 June 1719, Jacob Swits, s/o Cornelis.
1697, April 1, Andries; d. 2 July 1701.
1699, March 18, EGBERT, m. 4 Nov. 1726, Mary Nottingham.
Bapt. 1701, March 26, JOHANNES.
1703, Feb. 20, Andries, m. 3 Dec. 1731, Bregien Nottingham.

TJERCK DE WITT[3], s/o Andries[2], m. (1) 18 Nov. 1708, Anne Pawling, bapt. 19 June 1687, d/o Henry P. & Neeltje Roosa. Anne is noted as dec'd. in her son Henry's will, made in 1752. They had:
1710, May 7, Andries; d. 23 July 1711.
Bapt. 1711, April 22, Neeltje, m. 9 Sept. 1734, Wessel Jacobse Ten Broeck, bapt. 7 Dec. 1712, s/o Jacob T. B. & Elisabeth Wynkoop. She m. (2) Samuel Stout.
Bapt. 1714, Jan. 24, HENRY.
Bapt. 1717, Aug. 8, Johannes, m. 30 Oct. 1749 in Bermuda.
Bapt. 1722, July 15, Petrus, m. 8 June 1749, Rachel Radcliff, bapt. 14 Dec. 1723, d. 20 July 1794, d/o Joachim R. of Hyde Park, Dutchess Co. Petrus d. 3 Jan. 1790.
Bapt. 1728, March 3, Andries, m. 17 Dec. 1757, Rachel DuBois, bapt. 5 Jan. 1737, d. 24 Aug. 1829, d/o Isaac DuBois & Neeltje Roosa. Andries d. 9 June 1806. His will, dated 17 March 1800, at Ulster Co. names children Neeltje who m. Petrus Elmendorf; Tjerck & Izaack.

HENRY DE WITT[4], s/o Tjerck[3], in his will dated 30 Oct. 1752 is noted as a merchant of Kingston. He m. 10 Nov. 1738, Maria Ten Broeck, bapt. 13 June 1717, d. 19 May 1769, d/o

Jacob Ten Broeck & Elisabeth Wynkoop. Henry served as town clerk & Ulster county treasurer. He d. 17 Sept. 1753. Their children:

1739, Dec. 2, Elizabeth, m. May 1769, Edward Whitaker, bapt. 27 Sept. 1741, s/o Edward & Hilitje (Burhans) Whitaker.

1741, Sept. 9, Tjerck Claes, m. 28 Sept. 1773, Jannetje Eltinge, bapt. 16 April 1743, d/o Jacobus Eltinge & Elisabeth Hall. Tjerck d. 7 Oct. 1812.

1743, Nov. 21, Jacob, m. Nov. 1768, Martha Dean, b. Norwich CT, 27 Jan. 1748, d. Feb. 1838, d/o Jabez. Jacob d. 16 Sept. 1814 in Norwich.

Bapt. 1745, Oct. 11, John.

Bapt. 1748, March 13, Anna, m. 24 Sept. 1775, Peter Bogardus, s/o Petrus & Rebecca (DuBois) Bogardus.

1750, Sept. 8, Henry, b. Montreal, Canada, m. 10 May 1772, at Norwich, CT, Hannah, d/o Jabez Dean.

EGBERT DE WITT[3], s/o Andries[2], m. 4 Nov. 1726, Mary Nottingham, & had:

Bapt. 1727, Oct. 15, Andries, physician, lived & d. at New Paltz; m. 24 April 1748 Jannetje, d/o Johannes & Jennecke (Low) Vernooy. Had a son Simon who was surveyor-general of the state.

Bapt. 1719, April 13, JACOB RUTZEN.

1731, William, m. 30 May 1762, Susanna Chambers.

Bapt. 1733, Sept. 19, m. 26 Oct. 1765, John E., m. Catharine, d/o Cornelius Jr. & Neeltje (DuBois) Newkerk.

Bapt. 1735, Dec. 14, Stephen, m. 8 Dec. 1770, Wyntje, d/o John and Venni (Nottingham) Brodhead.

1737, Sept. 5, Mary (Polly) m. 18 Feb. 1765, Gen. James Clinton of New Windsor, s/o Charles C. & Elizabeth (Denniston) Clinton; they were parents of DeWitt Clinton.

Bapt. 1739, April 1, Egbert.

1741, May 3, Thomas, m. 18 Feb. 1783, Elsie, d/o Jacob & Maria (Hoornbeck) Hasbrouck.

Bapt. 1743, Jan. 19, Benjamin.

Bapt. 1745, Oct. 20, Napannock, Reuben, m. 11 Nov. 1772 Elisabeth, d/o Moses and Elsje (Klaarwater) Depuy.

JACOB RUTZEN DE WITT[4], s/o Andries[3], settled in the Peenpack neighborhood; m. 15 April 1756, Jennecke (Jane) Depuy, d/o Moses & Margaret (Schoonmaker) Depuy. JACOB purchased land in Sullivan Co., on Natesinck River. 1788 Jacob Rutzen DeWitt & Egbert J. DeWitt were issued a certificate of survey for Lot 145 in town of Chemung. Children:

Moses.

Egbert.

Jacob.

Margaret.

Mary.

Elesabeth.

Rachel m. Robert Burnet of New Windsor.

Janneke.

Hannah.

Esther.

In his will made 14 Dec. 1776, Jacob Rutsen DeWitt names son-in-law William Rose and his brother's son Simon DeWitt. He is identified as JACOB RUTSEN DE WITT of Mamacotting.

JOHANNES DE WITT[3], s/o Andries[2], m. 27 June 1724, Mary, d/o Charles B. & Maria (Ten Broock) Brodhead, and had:

Bapt. 1725, March 28, Ann; m. 13 May 1749, Conrad, s/o Gerrit & Grietje (Ten Eyck) Newkerk.

1727, CHARLES.

Bapt. 1728, Nov. 10, Andries; m. Blandina, d/o Abraham & Jenneke (Elmendorf) Ten Eyck.

Bapt. 1737, April 17, Maria.

CHARLES DE WITT[4], s/o Johannes[3], merchant; m. 20 Dec. 1754, Blandina, d/o Gerritt & Margaret (Elmendorf) DuBois, & had:

Bapt. 1744, Nov. 2, Johannes C.

Bapt. 1758, July 9, Margrietie; m. 10 April 1783, Johannes Bruyn.

Bapt. 1760, Oct. 12, Maria, m. 10 April 1783, Jacobus Hasbrouck.

Bapt. 1762, Aug. 15, Gerret, m. 15 Nov. 1786, Catharine Ten Eyck.

Bapt. 1764, Nov. 18, Anna, m. 16 Feb. 1786, Peter Tappen.

CHARLES[4] made a will at his house in Marbletown, NY dated 7 July 1776 because he was due to make a trip to New York City in a few days & thought he might "fall a victim to British Tyrants who are arrived in order to Invade that Metropolis" & was uncertain if he would return. This will was proved 4 Jan. 1788 by Lucas Elmendorph yeoman of Hurly, Benjamin Nukerk & Cornelius Cripsel. One of the executors appointed was his sister's son Benjamin Nukerk Jr.

LUCAS DE WITT[2], s/o Tjerck Classen[1], m. 22 Dec. 1695, Annatje Delva, d/o Anthony Delva & Jannetse Hillebranis & had:

Bapt. 1697, March 7, Jannetje, m. 19 July 1717, Cornelis Longendyk, s/o Pieter Janse Longendyk & Geertie Cornelis.

Bapt. 1699, Nov. 12, Barbara, m. 25 March 1715, Johannes Van Leuven, who m. (2) 22 May 1725, Hilligond Roosa.

Bapt. 1700, Dec. 8, Jan, m. after 26 Sept. 1731, Ariantje Osterhoudt, d/o Gysbert Osterhoudt & Maritje Bogardus, of Catskill.

Bapt. 1703, Sept. 16, Luycas, m. 17 Jan. 1729, Catherine Roosa, b. Hurley, d/o Evert Roosa & Tietje VanEtten. Luycas was commander & joint owner with his father of a sloop, *St. Barbara.*

---

**DICKERSON, ABRAHAM**          A-381, E-270

**ABRAHAM DICKERSON** settled in Montgomery just before the Rev. War. He had a saw mill on a small stream near his house in Town of Montgomery; m. Annie Mould, and had:

Mrs. Jacob Alsdorf.

Mrs. Jacob Millspaugh.

Mrs. William Soper.

Adam.

## DICKERSON, WILLIAM L.    H-828
atty. of Montgomery.

**WILLIAM L. DICKERSON** was the son of Jacob and John B. (Millspaugh) [sic] Dickerson. His ancestors settled in Orange Co. before the Rev. War. **WILLIAM L.** read law for Hon. A. S. Cassedy; admitted to the bar in 1892. Member of First Presbyterian Church.

## DICKEY, JAMES NATHANIEL    H-828-9
bank cashier of Newburgh.

**JAMES NATHANIEL DICKEY** is the s/o William & Esther (James) Dickey. He was b. 12 July 1846 in Newburgh. He clerked at the office of Judge J. J. Morrell; 1856 with Quassick National Bank. He m. 1865, Eve Brown and has 3 daughters.

## DIKEMAN, EDWIN J.    H-829
pharmacist of Goshen.

**EDWIN** was b. Goshen, NY 1876, s/o Edwin & Elizabeth (Jay) Dikeman. Edwin b. Goshen, d. 19 July 1895. **EDWIN** graduated Columbia University 1897. He m. Henrietta Coleman, d/o Hon. Roswell C. of Newburgh NY, and has a son, Edwin J. Jr. Member of the Orange Co. SAR.

## DILL, JOHN    U2-76-7
of New Windsor

In his will dated 20 Sept. 1788, **JOHN DILL** mentions his brothers Caleb and Robert. Caleb is dec'd. and his son John and daus. Jean, Deborah, Meary & Betsy are named. Robert's six sons each received money, but were not named. "To Joseph and to James 40 pounds each," but no surnames for these persons. Executors: Abraham Neely of New Windsor, yeoman; James Faulkner & David Hill.

## DOLSEN [VAN DOLSEN] FAMILY OF WAWAYANDA    A-677-8; A-681, C-128

This family is Dutch and a very old one in the state of NY. There is a tradition that the fist child born in New Amsterdam (New York) was a Dolsen (Van Dolsen). Dolsentown (Dolsen's meadow) is now in Wawayanda.

ISAAC DOLSEN[1] from Fishkill, Dutchess Co. in 1756 to what has long been known as Dolsentown. Millwright, m. Polly Huzzy of an English family in NJ; d. 1795. Children:
JAMES.
Isaac, unm.

JAMES DOLSEN[2], s/o Isaac[1], served in the Rev. He m. Phoebe Meeker and had:
James, took father's place in Rev. War; dec'd.

Asa; dec'd.
SAMUEL.
Polly; dec'd.
Abby; dec'd.

SAMUEL DOLSEN[3], only surviving child of James[2], now age 82 (1880/1). His children:
Frederick, who had a son, Theophilus.*
Mrs. Emmit Moore of Middletown.

* Goshen church records record a m. of a Theophilus Dolson to Cecelia Hathaway of Goshen 19 Nov. 1837. (C-35.)
Same records (p. 128) give the children of Theophilus and Liava Dolsen as:
1810, Aug. 28, Aaron Austin.
Ellen.
Henry Wisner.
1812, Oct. 21, Frederick.
All bapt. 10 Nov. 1814.

Bapt. on the same day, 10 Nov. 1814, in the same place are children of Frederick & Margaret Dolsen:
Emeline.
Elizabeth.
Theophilus.

## DOMINICK, DE WITT C. [P]    W-
of Walden.

**DE WITT C. DOMINICK**, b. Gallupville, Schoharie Co., NY 1851, studied at Cornell Univ. in Ithaca, grad. 1881. Ten years principal of the Walden Public School; coal, lumber & feed business of the late Taylor & Bateman, real estate, etc. He was married twice; children by his first marriage:
D. Clinton Dominick, atty. in office of Judge A.H.F. Seegar of Newburgh.
Elma C., student at Troy, NY.

## DOWNING, CHARLES [P]    A-358-60, NC-53
horticulturalist of Newburgh.

SAMUEL DOWNING[1], of English desc., b. 1761, from Cambridge to Newburgh and to Montgomery; carriage maker. Due to poor health retired to Newburgh and became nurseryman; m. Eunice ---. [N-53 says Samuel came from Lenox, MA.] Samuel d. 1 Nov. 1822; Eunice d. 29 Oct. 1838. Their children:
1801, Jan. 24, Emily, m. Sylvester Ferry; d. 11 March 1867.
1802, July 9, **CHARLES**.
1804, Feb. 22, George W.; d. 5 April 1846.
Fanny; d. infancy.
1815, Oct. 31, ANDREW J.

**CHARLES DOWNING**[2], trained with his father in nursery business & later ran with brother Andrew; m. 20 Sept. 1830, Mary, d/o Samuel Wait of Montgomery, NY. Mary d. 18 Oct. 1880. No issue.

ANDREW DOWNING[2], s/o Samuel[1], b. Newburgh. He was a landscape gardener, horticulturist, architect and author. At age 23 he bought out Charles' share of the business & m. Caroline Elizabeth de Wint of Fishkill; d. on burning steamer *Henry Clay* near Yonkers, 28 July 1852, "with members of his family and some friends."

**DRAKE, CHARLES**                              A-169-70
physician.

**CHARLES DRAKE**, b. Herkimer Co., d. 29 Jan. 1863, political servant. After graduation to Plattekill, Ulster Co., m. --- Heaton, d/o Dr. Adna Heaton and removed to Newburgh; member of Trinity Episcopal Church, Newburgh. He had a son, J. Hallock Drake of NY, atty.

**DRAKE, VICTOR M. [P]**                        A-189-90, C-91
newspaper man & farmer.

JOSEPH DRAKE[1], a lineal desc. of Sir Francis Drake of England, d. 1794 in England. His grandson:
FRANCIS DRAKE[3], of Blooming-Grove, NY m. (2d), Rebecca Clark. Francis was a British prisoner of war in 1779. They had 9 children, among them one son:
RUFUS J. DRAKE[4], m. Rhoda Pierson, d/o Rachel Bull, whose mother was a DeWitt & sister of Mary De Witt, DeWitt Clinton's mother. Rhoda d. 1866. Rufus served 2 years as a vol. in the 81st PA Regt. (War of 1812) & d. 25 March 1828 [27 Feb. 1828], aged 52, of intemperance, leaving widow & 5 children, 2 sons & 3 daus., among them:
VICTOR M. DRAKE[5], b. Milford, PA, 20 March 1813; res. Orange Co., NY & Sussex Co., NJ. At age 11 apprenticed to printer & later newspaper owner. Living at age 86 at this printing.

**DREW, BRICE L.**                              H-289
farmer of Eden.

**BRICE L. DREW**, s/o Gilbert & Elizabeth Drew, was one of 5 children. He was b. in Vernon, Sussex Co., NJ, 6 March 1866. **BRICE L.** is a fruit & dairy farmer & member of the Glenwood Methodist Church. He m. Millie Moorehouse of Amity, d/o Linn & Emily, and has children:
1892, June 24, Ernest.
1895, July 17, Emily.
1902, May 1, Albert George.

**DRURY, ERASMUS DARWIN [P]**                   A-240-1
of New Windsor.

WILLIAM DRURY[1] m. Eunice Hall; early res. of Worcester, MA, businessman & Legislator. They had:
DR. JOHN WALDO DRURY[2], b. Worcester, MA, 21 Oct. 1791; age 19 in US Army in War of 1812; 1818 to New Windsor, settled on old Parshall homestead, where he d. 8 Oct. 1847. He m. 2 Jan. 1822, Jemima, d/o Moses & Ruth (Miller) Parshall. Their children:

1823, Jan. 28, **ERASMUS DARWIN.**
1825, Nov. 26, Mary A., m. Robert Finney of New Windsor, 18 Oct. 1848; she d. 3 May 1863, and had: Moses D.; Loanna F.; Eura E. & Robert D. All res. on portion of old Parshall tract.

**ERASMUS DARWIN DRURY[3]**, s/o John Waldo[2], b. New Windsor, farmer, member Goodwill Presbyterian Church of Montgomery; d. suddenly 25 Dec. 1872. 20 Nov. 1845, m. Mary E. Finley; she d. 30 Sept. 1869. Children, all sons were farmers and all res. at family seat:
Lamira.
Charles W.; d. 12 March 1878.
John James.
George W.
Frank.

**DU BOIS FAMILY** A-554-5, U1-34-5, 41, 46-7, 51-2, 123-4, 158-62, 190, AA6-25-6, D-1, 14
**DU BOIS, ABRAHAM**       U2-116-17, 163, LDS Anc. File
of New Paltz

The DuBois family is one of the oldest of the noble houses of Cotentin, in the Duchy of Normandy.

CHRETIEN DU BOIS[1], a Huguenot of the family of DuBois Seigneurs de Beaufermez and deBourse, b. 1597, at Wicres, LaBassee, near Lille, in French Flanders now Artois, s/o Jacques, Louis Wallerund (Marquis Du Bois) & wife Madeline Renee De Croix (b. 1566, Angers, Anjou, France). He m. Jeanne Masic Brunel, b. 26 March 1599, Main-Et-Loire, Chenille-Change, St. Pierre, France. CHRETIEN (CHRISTIAN) dec'd. at the time of his son Louis' marriage in Manheim in 1655, was a res. of Wicres. Children, b. Wicres, Artois, France:
1621, Albert.
1622, Jan. 18, Albert Pierre.
1622, July [June] 17, Francoise, m. at Leyden, Pierre Billou of Normandy, France. They settled at Staten Island, NY.
1625, March 30, Annennette.
Bapt. 1625, Nov. 30, Anne.
1626, Nov. 13, JACQUES.
1627, Oct. 27, LOUIS (LOWYS).

Another source says that Chretien had four children: Francoise, Anne, Louis & Jacques; and possiblly Antoine & Isaac. [D].

JACQUES DU BOIS[2], left France & went to Leyden, where he became a manufacturer of silks. He m. Pieronne Bentyne, b. c. 1642, at Leyden, Holland, & had (all but last 2 b. in Holland, Jonathan & Pierre b. Kingston, Ulster Co., NY. Below dates may be for bapt. rather than birth.) JACQUES d. in 1676, a year after joining his brother Louis in America. One source says all his children b. in Holland. His widow m. John Pietersy.:
1664, April 2, Marie.

46

1665, March, Jacobus (Jacques), m. Susanna Legg, d/o William & Susanna (Marret) Legg, bapt. 23 Sept. 1678, Kingston, NY.

Bapt. 1666, Oct. 3, Jean Marie [Jeanne, b. 30 Oct. 1667?], m., probably at Staten Island, Hendrick Jansen Van Den Bos.

Bapt. 1667, Oct. 30, Jean Jacques, m. (?) Judith Sicard.

1669, Aug. 11, Anne, m. Joost Hite & she d. 1760. They settled at Germantown, PA. Joost d. in 1757, his will made in Frederick Co., VA 1757.

1671, July 29, Jonathan [Jehan/John].

1674, March 17/18, Pierre [Peter], m. Jannetje Burhans, b. Ulster Co., NY c. 1676, d. 1732, d/o Jan Burhans & Helena Traphagen.

1676, Christian, b. during voyage to America.

LOUIS DU BOIS[2], b. Wicres, in the province of Artois, France, 27 [28] Oct. 1626 [1627]; m. at the French Church at Manheim, Germany, 10 Oct. 1655, Catharine Blanshan (Blancon/Blanchan), b. 1727 in Manheim, d/o Matthew, a burger of the city of Manheim; 1660 with wife, and sons to America, & settled at Hurley, Ulster Co. (Shawangunk, now known as "Sky-top.") Matthew Blanshan emigrated to America 27 April 1660 with wife Madeline Jorisse & minor children: Madeline aged 12, Elizabeth aged 9 & Matthew aged 5 and another dau., Maria, & her husband, Anthony Crispell. LOUIS was elder of the French Reformed Church established in New Paltz, 1683. He was known as Louis de Wall, or Louis the Walloon. On 26 May 1677 the Esopus Indians conveyed to Louis DuBois & associates a tract of land over the Rondout Kill. Louis d. at Kingston, NY 23 June 1693. After his death, Catharine m. (2) Jean Cottin; she d. 1713. Louis made 2 wills dated 30 March 1686 & 22 Feb. 1695/6. Children:

1656, Sept. 29, Abraham, b. Manheim.

1658/9, Isaac, b. Manheim, Baden, Germany, m. June 1683, Maria Hasbrouck, b. Mowdestadt, Paltz, Germany, 8 Jan. 1644. Isaac d. 1690. Had a son Daniel who m. Mary LeFevre.

1659, Dec. 26, ABRAHAM.

Bapt. [b.] 1661, Oct. 9, JACOB.

Bapt. [b.] 1664, Sept. 14, Sarah, m. 12 Dec. 1682, Joost Jansz [Janzen] Van Meteren, of Marbletown, s/o Jan Joosten of Tiederwelt who came to America with wife Maycken (Mary) & 5 children. Sarah & Joost had Jan Jansen Van Meteren & Rebecca Van Meteren.

Bapt. 13 March 1667, David, m. 8 March 1689, Cornelia Varnoye, b. 3 April 1667, Ulster Co.

1668, Isaac.

1760, SOLOMON.

Bapt. 1671, June 18, Rebecca, d. young.

Bapt. 1675, April, Ragel [Rachel], d. young.

1677, LOUIS.

1679, Jan. 3, MATTHEW.

1680, May 12, Magda Ena [Magdalena].

**ABRAHAM DU BOIS**[3], s/o Louis[2], b. Manheim, Germany, m. 6 March 1681, Margaret Deyo (DeJou), d/o Christian, and had:

Bapt. 1682, June 20, Sarah, m. 13 June 1703, Roelof Eltinge [Etling], s/o Jan Elting & Jakomyntie Sleicht.

1685, April 17, Abraham, m. 12 Oct. 1717 Maria LaResiliere (Larzalere).

1687, Oct. 16, Leah, m. Philip Fires (Firre/Ferree), b. at Steynweiler, Bavaria, Palatinate, near Kandel, settled in Lancaster, PA.

Bapt. 1689, Oct. 13, Rachel, m. (1) 6 April 1713, Isaac DuBois, s/o Solomon DuBois, settled at Peskoine Creek, PA. She m. (2) in Philadelphia, 23 Fe. 1734, William Coats.

Mary, twin of Rachel, bapt. same day, d. young.

1693, May 21, Catherine, m. 4 Oct. 1728, William Danielsz [Donaldson], settled at Lancaster, PA.

Bapt. 1700, Feb. 18, Noah, d. young.

Bapt. 1703, June 20, Joel, d. 1734. Res. Somerset Co., NJ.

**ABRAHAM**'s will, dated 1 Oct. 1731, mentions his wife Margaret and the above children.

JACOB DU BOIS[3], s/o Louis[2], b. at Kingston, NY, d. at Hurley June 1745; m. (1) 8 March 1689, Lysbeth Varnoye & (2) Gerritje Gerritsen, d/o Gerrit, s/o Cornelius van Nieuwkirk, b. c. 1600. He had by 1st wife:

Bapt. 1690, May 25, Magdalena, m. (1) 30 Dec. 1710, Gerrit Roosa of Kingston; m. (2) in Kingston 20 Oct. 1718, Pieter Van Este of Hurley.

Children of 2d wife:

1693, May 31, Barent, b. Hurley, d. 22 Jan. 1750, Kingston; m. Jacomyntje Dubois, d/o Solomon Dubois & Tryntje Gerritsen. They were double first cousins; removed to Bucks Co., PA.

Bapt. 1695, June 9, LOUIS.

Bapt. 1697, May 13, Gieltje.

Bapt. 1700, March 29, Gerrit, d. young.

Bapt. 1702, Feb. 1, Isaac, m. (1) 1732, Neetlje Roosa, (2) 1760, Jannettje Roosa.

Bapt. 1704, Feb. 13, Gerrit, m. Margret Elmendorf. Res. Hurley.

Bapt. 1706, March 24, Catherine, m. 12 Feb. 1725, Peter Smedes, s/o Benjamin & Helena (Louw) Smeades of Kingston.

Bapt. 1708, Oct. 31, Rebecca, m. Peter Bogardus, s/o Evart Bogardus & Tjaatje Hofman.

Bapt. 1720, Nov. 10, Johannes, m. 11 Dec. 1736, Judike Wynkoop, d/o Cornelius.

Bapt. 1713, Dec. 20, Zara, m. 21 June 1734, Conrad Elmendorf Jr. of Hurley.

Bapt. 1716, May 27, Neeltjeu, m. 9 Sept. 1737, Cornelius Nieukerk of Hurley, s/o Gerrit Nieukerk & Grietjen Ten Eyck.

LOUIS DU BOIS[4], s/o Jacob[3], b. at Hurley 6 Jan. 1695, d. at Pittsgrove, NJ 1784, from Salem Co., NJ c. 1720 with brother Barent. Served in militia. He m. 22 [21] May 1720, Margaret Jansen, d/o Matthys Jansen & Anna Elmendorf. They had:

1721, Jacob.

1722, Matthew.
1724, Anna.
1726, Gerritje.
1730, Elizabeth.
1732, Cornelius.
1734, April 10, PETER.
1737, Joseph.
1739, Benjamin.

PETER DU BOIS[5], b. Pittsgrove, NJ, d. there 21 Aug. 1795, served in Rev. war; m. 1758, Amey, d/o Jeremiah & Sarah (Blackman) Greenman. Their descs. settled in PA.

SOLOMON DU BOIS[3], s/o Louis[2], b. Hurley, patentee of New Paltz. His will dated 26 June 1756, witnessed by Noah Eltinge, Lewis J. Dubois & Andris Dubois. He m. 1692, Tryntje Gerritsen, d/o Gerrit Focken & Jacomyntje Sleght, and had:
Bapt. 1691, Sept. 27, Isaac, m. Rachel DuBois, d/o Abraham. Res. Perkiomen, PA. His daus. Catharine, Margaret, Rebecca & Elizabeth named in father Solomon's will. Isaac d. Perkiomen, PA 10 Feb. 1729.
Bapt. 1693, Nov. 5, Jacomyntje, m. 23 April 1715, Barent DuBois, s/o Jacob, her double first cousin. She a widow by 1756.
Bapt. 1697, May [April] 16, Benjamin, m. Catrina Zwylant [Zuyland] of Hurley; inherited all his father's lands in Katskill, Albany Co.
Bapt. 1700, Feb. 11, Sarah, m. 17 Nov. 1720, Simon Jacobse Van Wagenen, s/o Jacob Aartsen Van Wagenen & Sara Pels of Kingston.
Bapt. 1702, Oct. 18, Catryn, d. infant. DuBois family book states that this is the Catharine who m. 9 Dec. 1722, Peter Matheus Louw of New Paltz. In this reference her death date is given as pre 1743, per her father's will.
Bapt. 1705, April 15, Magdelena, d. young.
Deborah.
1707, Dec. 9, CORNELIUS.
1710, Aug. 1, HENDRIKUS.
Bapt. 1713, Dec. 20, Magdalena [named in her father's will as Helena], m. 14 July 1734, Josiah Elting, s/o Roelof Elting & Sarah DuBois. Josiah served in Rev. War.

CORNELIUS DU BOIS[4], s/o Solomon[3], b. Esopus, m. 7 April 1729, Anna Margaret Heogthaing. His will, dated 6 Nov. 1780, identifies him as of New Paltz. In it he names his wife and children:
Bapt. 1730, March 29, Tryntjen (Catharine), m. 27 Jan. 1762, Matthew DuBois.
Bapt. 1732, Jannetie, m. Jacob Hasbrouck.
Bapt. 1734, March 31, Wilhelmus.
Bapt. 1736, Oct. 21, Josia.
Bapt. 1739, Aug. 5, Rachel, m. Col. Lewis DuBois of Marlborough. She is dec'd. by 1780 & her children are named in her father's will as Nathaniel, Wilhelmus & Polly.
Bapt. 1742, May 2, Lea, m. 28 May 1762, Cornelius D. Wynkoop. They had children Dirck & Lea. Lea is dec'd. by 1780.

Bapt. 1745, April 21, Jacomyntjen, m. Andries Bevier of Wawarsing.
Bapt. 1747, Oct. 4, Sara, m. Jacob Hasbrouck Jr. of Marbletown & had sons Cornelius Dubois, Josia & Nathaniel Dubois Hasbrouck.
Bapt. 1750, July 8, Cornelis, m. Gertrude Bruyn.

Will proved 23 April 1781 by Denie Raleya of New Paltz, yeoman & David Louw of same place, blacksmith. Cornelius was a slave owner & bequeathed several in his will.

HENDRIKUS DUBOIS[4], s/o Solomon[3], m. 6 May 1733, Jannetje Hooghteling. His will, on file in Ulster Co., describes him as yeoman of New Palz & is dated 21 June 1774. He names his wife & children:
Bapt. 1734, April 21, Philip, dec'd. by 1774. He m. 22 March 1757, Anne Hue.
Bapt. 1736, Feb. 15, Solomon, m. 25 Oct. 1762, Ariaantje Dubois.
Bapt. 1738, Feb. 12, Dina, m. 26 Nov. 1759, Abraham Eltinge. She dec'd. by 1774.
Bapt. 1740, Oct. 9, in Shawangunk, Tryntie (Catharine), m. Matheus Dubois.
Bapt. 1743, May 1, Henricus, m. Rebecca VanWagenen.
Bapt. 1745, June 30, Methusalem.
Bapt. 1747, June 28, Lea, m. Christofel Kiersteden.
Bapt. 1749, Dec. 24, Rachel, m. Johannis A. Hardenbergh.
Bapt. 1751, Oct. 27, Methusalem, m. (1) Gertrude Bruyn, (2) Catherine Bevier.

Will witnessed by Severyn T. Bruyn, Jacobus Bruyn Jr. of Shawangunk & Joh's. Bruyn.

LOUIS DUBOIS[3], s/o Louis[2], m. Rachel B. Hasbrouck, d/o Abraham, 19 Jan. 1701 & had:
Bapt. 1701, Dec. 7, Maria, d. in infancy.
Bapt. 1703, June 6, NATHANIEL.
Bapt. 1706, March 24, Maria (Mary), m. 6 Dec. 1728, Johannes Hardenbergh of Rosendale.
Bapt. 1708, June 20 Jonas.
Bapt. 1710, Dec. 31, JONATHAN.
Bapt. 1714, Oct. 31, Catrina, m. 25 Jan. 1734, Wessel Broadhead, s/o Charles Broadhead & Maria Ten Broeck.
1717, Louis, m. Charity Andrevelt & settled in Staten Island.

NATHANIEL DUBOIS[4], s/o Louis[3], b. New Paltz; d. 12 May 1763, Salisbury Mills, Town of Blooming Grove. He m. (1) Gertrude Bruyn, d/o Jacobus Bruyn & Tryntje Schoonmaker. They had:
1727, Rachel.
1728, Lewis.

Gertrude (Bruyn) DuBois d. before 1733 & Nathaniel m. (2) Gertrude Hoffman, d/o Zacharias Hoffman & Hester Bruyn of Salisbury Mills, & had:
1734, Zacharias.
1734, Hester.
Jonas.

Renaltje.
Frederick.

JONATHAN DUBOIS[4], s/o Louis[3], m. Elisabeth, d/o Andries &
Cornelia (Blanjean) LeFever of Nescatock & had:
1733, Lewis J., m. Catharine Broadhead.
Bapt. 1735, Dec. 25, Rachel, m. 17 Dec. 1757, Andries DeWitt.
Bapt. 1737, Oct. 16, Andries, m. Sarah LeFevre.
Bapt. 1739, Oct. 28, Nathaniel.
1741, Cornelia, m. Cornelis Vernooy.
Bapt. 1743, Dec. 25, Jonas.
Bapt. 1746, April 20, Maria, m. Abraham Bevier.

Jonathan[4], in his will dated 14 July 1746, is identified as of
New Paltz Precinct, yeoman. He names wife & children & his
brother Nathaniel DuBois & 2 brothers-in-law Johanes Hardenbergh & Wessel Broadhead, executors. Witnesses were Cornelius
DuBois, Evert Tervelger Jr. & J. Bruyn. Will proved 30 Aug.
1749.

MATTHEW DUBOIS[3], s/o Louis[2], b. Hurley, m. 17 Jan. 1697,
Sara Metthysen [Van Keuren/ Kuren], d/o Mattys Matthysen,
& had:
Bapt. 1697, July 18, Louis, m. (1) 16 April 1718, Jannetjen Van
Vliet, d/o Gerrit Van Vliet & Pieternella Swart; m. (2) in
Dutchess Co., Gerritje Van Voorhis, widow of Elias Van
Benschoten.
Bapt. 1698, Oct. 6, Mattheus Jr., d. c. 1774; m. (1) Sarah
Humphries; (2) Deborah Simpkins.
Bapt. 1701, Jan. 26, Hiskia, d. 1 Oct. 1757, Ulster Co. 17 June
1722, m. Anna Peersen, d/o Matthys Peers & Anna Winnen.
Bapt. 1703, May 30, Ephraim, m. 10 Nov. 1727, Anna Catrina
D'Lamateer, res. Dutchess Co.
1705, March 17, JOHANNES.
Bapt. 1707, Nov. 2, Taatje, m. 22 Sept. 1726, Johannes Tappen,
s/o Teunis Tappen & Sara Schepmoes. Res. Dutchess Co.
Bapt. 1712, Jan. 13, Jesse, m. Elizabeth Lewis, d/o Thomas
Lieuwis & Anna Maria Vanderburgh. Res. Dutchess Co.
Bapt. 1713, Oct. 4, Elias (Eleazer/Elisa), d. 1786; m. (1) 12 June
1739 Mary Van Voorhees, d/o Johannes Coert Van Voorhees
& Barbara Van Dyck of Flatlands, L.I.; m. (2) at Poughkeep-
sie, 18 Nov. 1772, Sarah (Susanna) Vanderburgh, d/o Henry
& Magdalin & widow of --- Cooper.
Bapt. 1715, Dec. 4, Catrina, m. Robert Brett, s/o Roger &
Catharine (Rombout) Brett. Res. Dutchess Co.
Bapt. 1719, Nov. 1, Gideon, m. Sarah Van Kleeck, d/o Barent
& Antoinette (Parmentier) Van Kleeck & widow of William
Van Vliet. Res. Dutchess Co.
1721, May 18, Jeremiah, b. Kingston, d. Beekman, Dutchess Co.
12 May 1796. He m. 28 June 1741 Rachel Viele, d/o Peter
& Johanna Mydertse (Van De Bogaard) Viele.

JOHANNES DUBOIS[4], res. Kingston, miller; m. 13 Nov. 1728,
Rebecca Tappen, d/o Teunis Tappen & Sara Schepmoes, &
had:
Bapt. 1727, Sept. 7, Sarah, m. 30 Nov. Petrus Masten.
Bapt. 1734, 7 April, Mattheus, m. 14 April 1768, Catrina Hoof.
Bapt. 1735, Dec. 26, Maria.

Bapt. 1737, Nov. 6, Tjaatjen (Catharine), m. Evert Bogardus.
Bapt. 1790, Feb. 10, Teunis.
Bapt. 1742, Feb. 7, Arriaentie, m. 25 Oct. 1762, Solomon
Dubois.
Bapt. 1743, Sept. 25, Taatjen [Tjatie], m. William Thompson 23
Oct. 1743.
Bapt. 1745, Dec. 25, Joshua, m. 15 April 1769, Catharine
Schepmoes.
Bapt. 1747, Jan. 17, Jeremiah, m. 18 Oct. 1770, Catreina
Matsen.
Bapt. 1750, Aug. 19, Johannes, m. 17 Dec. 1773, Marya
Oosterhout.

In his will , dated 14 Feb. 1772, Johannis[4] named grandchil-
dren Abraham & Sarah Masten, children of his dec'd. dau.
Sarah. Will proved 18 Oct. 1787 by Gerret Van Keuren of
Kingston, blacksmith & Abraham Hasbrouck & Abraham Van
Keuren, Jr.

Unplaced Du Bois family:

HENRY DU BOIS, s/o Henry, in his will dated 26 May 1784,
is identified as farmer of New Paltz. In his will he mentions
his wife, but not by name, & names children:
Philip.
Maritje.
Garret.
Jenny.
Methusalem.
Rebeckah.

Will proved 3 March 1788 by son Methusalem of New Paltz,
yeoman & James Burns of the same place, schoolmaster; also
Catherine DuBois.

CATHARINE DU BOIS, d/o Henry [sic] & granddau. of
Methusalem DuBois, m. Elting France (his mother was d/o
Peter Elting of New Paltz). They res. Ulster Co. and had a dau.,
Marian Jane who m. Adam H. Sinsabaugh, as his 4th wife.

---

**DU BOIS, EVERETT B. [P]**           **W-85**

**EVERETT DU BOIS**, b. Town of Shawangunk, 22 April 1862;
1883 purchased farm south of Galeville. Farmer until 1898,
assessor of town 13 years, postmaster at Wallkill 1898. He
m. Ida McElhone 1883 & had:
Kathryn C.
Ida Mae.

---

**DUER, JOHN**        **A-146, C-80, LDS Anc. File**

COL. WILLIAM DUER[1], Army of Rev., m. Catharine Alexander, d/o Major Gen. Alexander (Lord Stirling). They had:
William A., atty.
1782, Aug. 8, JOHN.
Alexander, who had 2 daus.: Mrs. J. V. Beane & Mrs. David F.

Gedney.

c. 1787, MARIA THEODOSIA (Theodora).

**JOHN DUER**[2], b. Albany, atty at Goshen; to NY c. 1820, Superior Court Justice (1849), legal author; d. 8 Aug. 1858. He m. Annie Bunner of NY City, sister of Rudolf Bunner (Goshen). From Goshen church records, pp. 80 & 84: A child of John Duer, Esq. d. at 3 week from pneumonia, 26 Jan. 1808. Another son of John Duer, Esq. d. at 5 months from enteritis, 15 Dec. 1816; and still another child died at 5 months of fits, 29 March 1818.

"Another brother-in-law was Morris Robinson, of Orange Co., s/o Beverly Robinson of the British Army whose father was an associate of Benedict Arnold."

**MARIA THEODOSIA DUER**[2], d/o William [1], m. Beverly Chew & had (CHEW):

c. 1815, Caroline.

c. 1817, Beverly.

c. 1819, Lucy Ann, m. William Duer.

c. 1821, John William.

c. 1823, Catherine Alexander, m. Thomas H. Kennedy.

c. 1825, Alexander Lafayette, m. Sarah Augusta Prouty.

c. 1827, Robert.

c. 1829, Mary, m. Martin Kennedy.

c. 1831, Morris Robinson, m. Theodora Kennedy.

**DUMVILLE, WALTER**                    H-829-30

farmer & dairyman.

**BENJAMIN DUMVILLE**[1], b. England, to America 1827, located in Newburgh. He m. Miriam Harris in Newburgh & was first wholesale butcher in the town. Their son:

**WALTER**[2], b. 9 May 1843, Town of Newburgh, m. 16 July 1873 Josephine, d/o John & Catherine O'Brien of NY City. Members of the Unitarian Church.

**DUNN, WILLIAM H. [P]**                    W-86

Mr. DUNN resides on the road from St. Andrews to Modena, dairy farmer & member of New Hurley Reformed Church. He has 2 children:

Anna.

Chester.

**DUNNING FAMILY OF WAWAYANDA**          A-679
                                         H-153, 830-31

JACOB DUNNING[1], one of the first settlers of Goshen, from English family, had son:

JOHN[2], who had son:

BENJAMIN DUNNING[3] to Ridgebury 1809 from Wallkill, where he was born. Noted as living in West Chester area in early 1800s.

**DUNNING FAMILY**                    H-830-1

The Dunning family is an old and well-known English family associated with Orange Co.

GEN. BENJAMIN DUNNING[1] [could be the Benjamin above] m. Isabel Wilson and had:

Virgil.

BENJAMIN FRANKLIN.

William T.

Angeline.

BENJAMIN FRANKLIN DUNNING[2], m. Ruth Seeley and had:

Isabel, m. Thomas P. Fowler.

Frank.

WILLIAM F., dec'd.

Frederick Clark, dec'd.

Alice, M., m. Allen Starr.

WILLIAM F. DUNNING[3], s/o Benjamin Franklin[2] & Ruth Dunning, law partner of Charles O'Conor; m. Ruth Seely of Orange Co. and had:

1856, May 29, WILLIAM FULLERTON.

WILLIAM FULLERTON DUNNING[3], b. City of NY, d. 1 April 1907 after a short illness. William F. studied in Dresden, Saxony & grad. Princeton 1877. In 1883 he m. Clara Frost of New Orleans, LA. He is survived by his wife and 6 daughters.

Aline Frost, dec'd.

Ruth Seeley.

Marceline Randolph.

Clara Frost.

Isabel Fowler.

Elizabeth Belcher.

Wilhelmine.

**DURLAND, DEWITT C. [P]**                    A-556f
**DURLAND, JAMES [P]**     A-623-4, C-18, LDS Anc. File
of Chester.
**DURLAND FAMILY**                    H-831-2
**DURLAND, J. SEELEY**                    H-832-3
**DURLAND FAMILY OF WAWAYANDA**     A-679, H-241

JAN GERRETSE DORLANDT[1], b. 1629 in Holland, m. c. 1650 in Brooklyn, NY, ---, who was b. & d. in Brooklyn. Their son, GERRET GERRETSE DORLANDT[2], b. 1655 in Brooklyn, m. c. 1684 Gertrude Aukes Van Nuys of Brookyn. Gerret d. after 1741. One of their children, JOHN DORLANDT[3], b. c. 1688 in Flatbush, NJ, m. c. 1713 in NY, Mary Birdsall of Brooklyn. One of their children was:

CHARLES DURLAND[4] b. Oyster Bay, L.I., NY 19 March 1731, from L.I. to Chester, Orange Co. 1756 [1754]; soldier of French & Indian War; m. (1) at Chester in 1755, Jane Swartwout (1730-1812) & settled near Village of Chester; d. c. 1800, age 67. CHARLES m. (2) 4 June 1799, Sarah Satterly. Children of 1st wife:

1756, 12 Nov., Mary, m. John [Janathan] Wood of Minisink, b. 11 Oct. 1755.

1758, 1 June, Catharine.

1760, 21 April, GERRET.

1762, March 31, JOSEPH.

1766, Jan. 16, Elizabeth, m. Vincent Wood of Goshen.

1768, May 24, CHARLES.

1772, April 16, Rosannah [Roxanna], m. Peter Holbert of Minisink on 25 Aug. 1789, at Goshen & had son Peter Jr., b. c. 1796.

1772, April 16, Susannah.

1773, Aug. 31, JOHN.

1775, Feb. 11, SAMUEL.

GERRET DURLAND[5], m. Mary Struble, b. c. 1762 in Orange Co., & had (1st 2 children b. Orange Co., the rest b. Luzerne Co., NY):

c. 1786, SAMUEL C.

c. 1795, Gerret, m. Rosella Eaton, b. 1798, Luzerne Co., NY.

c. 1797, Charles.

c. 1799, Raphael.

c. 1804, Benjamin, m. (1) --- Decker, (2) Elizabeth Remy.

c. 1806, Elmira, m. Webb Jenks.

SAMUEL C. DURLAND[6], s/o Gerret[5], m. Catherine Manning & had:

1836, Nov. 9, Martha Ann, m. Andrew Houser, of Minisink & had dau. Amelia Houser, b. 30 Jan. 1864 & m. George Jackson Hoard of Union, SD.

JOSEPH DURLAND[5], s/o Charles[4], b. Orange Co., scout at close of Rev. War; farmed on homestead. He m. Martha Board, b. 1765 [Orange Co.], of Ringwood, NJ, 28 Aug. 1828. Res. Chester, members First Presbyterian Church. Joseph d. 28 Aug. 1828; Martha d. 13 Dec. 1797. Children:

1789, April 22, James, drowned young (10 June 1802) on pond near homestead.

1791, Jan. 20, CHARLES B.

1793, March 8, Thomas; d. 10 June 1802.

1795, Sept. 12, Elizabeth m. Jonas King, 6 April 1815, at Chester. She d. 22 Oct. 1843.

John, drowned young on pond near homestead. [Another source also names a son Thomas who also drowned at a young age.]

JOSEPH[5] m. (2d) Sally, d/o Samuel Satterly, she d. May 1838, age 60. Their children:

1800, May 28, Martha, widow of John Milton Bull of Blooming-Grove.

1801, Sept. 13, Christina. [Could be the Kezia below, as she is not named in the same source where Christina appears.]

1803, Feb., JONAS.

1804, Dec. 17, SAMUEL S.

Kezia; d. young.

1807, Sept. 15, Jane.

1809, March 8, Susan m. George Mapes of Goshen; she now dec'd.

**JAMES.**

1813, Sept. 7, Thomas E., m. Mary Ellen Booth, b. IL 22 June

1817 & their children b. Hancock Co., IL. Seeley; now dec'd.

Martha, Thomas & James survive (1880/1) & res. on homestead.

CHARLES B. DURLAND[6], s/o Joseph[5], m. 24 Feb, 1814, Maria Youngs, b. 14 Sept. 1792 in Orange Co. They had, all b. Chester, NY:

1815, Jan. 30, Jane.

1816, Dec. 8, Emily, m. James M. Brown of Chester.

1818, Dec. 8, ANDREW J.

1820, Dec. 19, Benjamin F., m. Emeline C. Halstead.

1823, Jan. 7, Elizabeth.

c. 1828, EDWIN R.

1827, April 15, Jane.

1829, July 24, Julia Anna, m. Garret Post.

ANDREW DURLAND[7], s/o Charles[6], m. Elizabeth R. Barney, b. c. 1820 in NY, & had:

1841, July 26, Jane B.

1844, March 2, Charles.

1846, June 29, Thaddeus.

1848, July 21, Andrew J.

EDWIN DURLAND[7], s/o Charles[6], m. --- Roe & had:

1847, Dec. 4, Caroline Roe.

1850, April 13, Emily, m. Roswell W. Chamberlain.

1851, Nov. 23, Henry R., m. Eugenia W. Banker.

1855, Jan. 2, Benjamin.

1864, Aug. 22, William F., m. Elizabeth D. Mapes.

JONAS DURLAND[6], s/o Joseph[5] b. on the homestead, m. Abigail Little b. 1805, d. Oct. 1876. Jonas d. 1865. Their children:

c. 1822, Martha m. Edward Millspaugh, farmer of Goshen.

c. 1824, Orpha J. m. Cornelius B. Wood, farmer of Chester, & had Cyrus Foss Wood, b. c. 1855 in NY.

1825, Sept. 20, Cornelia; d. age 21.

c. 1826, OSCAR.

c. 1827, Alice, m. James Tuthill.

c. 1828, Fanny, m. John Houston.

c. 1829, Seely, m. Fanny Hunter.

1830, July, James Seeley; d. age 19.

1832, Aug. 24, NELSON.

1835, May 1, **DE WITT C.**

Sarah m. John C. Walling of Goshen; dec'd.

Louisa; d. age 10.

JONAS[6] res. Minisink until 1830, when he removed to Town of Goshen and d. there. Members of First Presbyterian Church of Florida.

OSCAR DURLAND[7], s/o Jonas[6], farmer of Chester, m. Matilda Youngs & had:

c. 1855, Alice.

c. 1857, Fanny.

c. 1858, **J. SEELY.**

**J. SEELEY DURLAND**[8], s/o Oscar[7] & Matilda C. Durland, m. Fannie R. Hunter of Monroe, 26 Oct. 1894. They had:
Anna T.
Stanley, d. 1895.

**NELSON DURLAND**[7], s/o Jonas[6], d. 1871. He m. Phoebe Kellogg & had:
c. 1855, Mary, m. W. S. Board.
c. 1856, Sarah, m. A. D. Jessup.
c. 1858, Nellie.

**DE WITT C. DURLAND**[7], s/o Jonas[6], m. (1st) 30 Dec. 1858, Marietta, d/o George S. Conkling and Mary Seeley of Chester who d. 9 Dec. 1872, age 35. Their children:
c. 1860, Jonas Howard, b. Chester, m. Carrie Knapp.
c. 1862, James Murray.
c. 1865, Bradford Conkling.
c. 15, Clara M., m. Willard H. Bull.

**DE WITT C. DURLAND**[7] m. (2d) 10 June 1875, Therese, eldest in family of 3 sons & 5 daus., of Samuel McCain & Anna Ward of Hoboken, NJ & granddau. of William McCain, res. Amity, Orange Co., ancestors earliest settlers of Warwick. William McCain's wife was Sarah Jennings. There was one child of this 2d marriage, Ella McCain Durland, perhaps the same person as "Nellie McCain" below. **DE WITT** was a trustee of the Florida Presbyterian Church. Children:
1877, Nellie McCain.
1879, Dewitt C.
1883, Dewitt C.
1886, Orpha Jane.

**SAMUEL S. DURLAND**[6], s/o Joseph[5], d. 1833. He m. Amelia Vernon, b. 1806 East Norwich, L.I., NY. [LDS Anc. File names this Samuel S. as the s/o Jonas[6] & wife Abigail Little. They also name wife Amelia Vernon as the wife of his brother James, also given as the son of Jonas[6]. Amelia could have m. 2d Samuel's brother after his death in 1833, as brother James' children are not b. until 1837. Numbers have been left as found in sources other than the LDS File.] They had:
1832, March 16, JOSEPH.
1833, Aug. 23, Sarah Letitia, m. Henry Wisner Wood, of Orange Co.
Samuel S.

**JOSEPH DURLAND**[7], s/o Samuel[6], b. on the family homestead now occupied by his brother Samuel S. JOSEPH was a partner with his stepfather, James Durland, at Chester Mills, for some time. Joseph m. 25 Feb. 1857, Nancy Kingsland Board, d/o Maj. James J. Board of Boardville, NY, who later settled at Sugar Loaf Valley, Chester, NY. Nancy b. 1 Nov. 1835. In 1855 he joined the Presbyterian church. Joseph is the great-grandson of Charles Durland, who settled in Chester in 1754, from L.I. Children of Joseph & Nancy:
1858, April 28, JAMES BOARD.
1860, March 25, FRANK.
1862, July 15, Amelia Vernon.

1865, Oct. 22, Marion; d. 23 May 1903.
1878, Feb. 14, Nettie Eugenia, m. William T. Moffatt of NY City.

**JAMES BOARD DURLAND**[8], s/o Joseph[7], m. Sarah Andrews 12 Nov. 1884. Sarah b. March 1861 in Orange Co. They had:
1885, Aug. 22, Violet.
1888, Dec. 14, Rose.
1891, Dec. 28, Joseph.
One other child.

**FRANK DURLAND**[8], s/o Joseph[7] and Nancy, b. in the Yelverton Inn in the old village of Chester, NY. He m. 22 April 1891, Mary Burt Sanford of Warwick, NY, d/o William Moore & Sarah (Burt) Sanford. Sarah was d/o James Burt. Their children:
1892, July 13, William Sanford; student.
1898, March 29, Nancy Booth; student.

**JAMES DURLAND**[6], s/o Joseph[5], merchant at Chester with brothers & dairy farmer; public service; member Chester Presbyterian Church; m. 1835, Amelia, d/o John Vernon of L.I., b. 23 Sept. 1806, d. 19 Dec. 1876. [LDS Anc. file names him as s/o Jonas[6] & wife Aigail Little. Amelia Vernon 1st m. his brother, Samuel S.] Their surviving children:
1837, May 6, Jane m. John Bartlett Tuthill of Chester; d. 1867, age 30.
1840, June 21, SAMUEL S., res. on homestead with father.
1842, March 2, Maria.
1844, Sept. 16, Martha m. Alfred B. Roe, farmer of Chester.
1846, Aug. 14, Charles.
1847, Dec. 1, John J., farmer & merchant of Rushford, MN. He m. Julia Blakely, b. c. 1845 in Orange Co. & children Sarah & James b. in WI.

**SAMUEL S. DURLAND**[7], s/o James[6], m. Margaret Seely of Chester & had:
1868, Aug. 29, Jane T.
1873, Sept. 14, Seely Tuthill.

**CHARLES DURLAND**[5], s/o Charles[4], to Wawayanda before 1800; first settled near Bushville in present town of Greenville; to near Ridgebury, where he died; kept public house. He m. Lydia Terry of Southold, L.I. & had, all b. Minisink:
1799, April 27, Thomas Terry.
1801, Sept. 24, JOHN.
1803, Dec. 14, JOSEPH.
1806, Feb. 9, CHARLES ADDISON.
1808, July 10, DANIEL TERRY.
1810, Aug. 21, Esther Jane, m. Lawrence Ferguson of Middletown.
1813, May 10, STEWART (STEWARD) TERRY.
1816, April 22, Ezra T.
1819, Sept. 29, SARAH.
1821, Nov. 28, THOMAS TERRY.

JOHN DURLAND[6], s/o Charles[5], m. Martha Hulse & had:
1830, March 11, Charles Mortimer, m. Frances Goff & had Kate Goff Durland who m. E. D. Edgerton of Orange Co.
1832, Dec. 9, Lewis Hudson, m. Sarah E. Bailey of Livonia NY & had Charles Mortimer, Frances Louise, Sarah Elizabeth & Lewis Hudson Jr., all b. Watkins, NY.

JOSEPH DURLAND[6], s/o Charles[5], m. Catharine Maria Dunning & had, all b. Binghamton, NY:
c. 1831, Lydia.
1833, Harriet, m. G. B. Perkins of Elmira & had Lucy & Frederick, both b. Binghamton.
1834, March 18, DANIEL TERRY.
c. 1836, Jacob.
1838, Charles Oscar, m. Sarah Elliott of Elmira & had Grace Elliott Durland, b. 1874, m. Frederick Westlake of Elmira.

DANIEL TERRY DURLAND[7], s/o Joseph[6], m. Susan Lovejoy, b. 16 March 1837, Binghamton, NY & had (1st child b. Orange Co., the rest b. in Elmira, NY):
1868, Feb. 3, Frederick Lovejoy.
1873, Charles Edward.
1875, April 10, Harry Courtney.
1879, Jan. 29, Louise.

CHARLES ADDISON DURLAND[6], s/o Charles[5], m. Julia Johnson of Orange Co. & had, b. at Chester:
1859, Phoebe A., m. William R. Conkling of Chester.
1863, Sept. 11, Edward Stewart.

DANIEL TERRY DURLAND[6], s/o Charles[5], m. Clarissa Jane Green, b. 20 Feb. 1817 in Orange Co. & had (all b. Middletown except Lydia Etta & Clara May, b. Greenville.):
1837, Dec. 8, Ezra Terry, m. Emma Green, b. 1847, IL.
1839, July 19, Elvira.
1841, Jan. 18, Esther Jane, m. John B. Manning.
1842, Oct. 8, Ellen Frances, m. Daniel Terry Graham, b. c. 1840 Norfolk, NE.
1844, May 24, Joseph Edwin.
1847, Feb. 8, GILBERT F.
1849, May 19, CHARLES BULL.
1851, 9 June 9, Josephine.
1853, June 7, Andrew J., m. Winnie Persis Richards, b. c. 1855 in Norfolk, NE.
1856, Oct. 23, Daniel Willis, m. Mary Irene Mapes, b. 1861, Orange Co., NY.
1860, Nov. 25, Lydia Etta.
1863, Sept. 22, Clara May, m. Burt Mapes & had Bernice & Donald Durland, both b. Norfolk, NE.

GILBERT F. DURLAND[7], s/o Daniel Terry[6], m. Mary Jane Wood, b. 5 Feb. 1857 in State Hill, NY, & had (all b. Middletown):
1878, Jan. 1, Mabel Clair.
1879, June 29, Mary Alvira.
1882, March 29, Edna Alvira.
1886, Sept. 13, Lulu Irene.
1892, April 8, Gilberta.

One other child.

CHARLES BULL DURLAND[7], s/o Daniel Terry[6], m. Lillian Mapes & had (all b. Middletown):
1879, Oct. 16, Laura Bell.
1885, Cecil.
1890, Nov. 15, Charles Alsop.
1893, March 16, Dorothy.

STEWART TERRY DURLAND[6], s/o Charles[5], m. Phoebe Lee & had:
1825, Feb. 23, Addison Charles, m. Rose L. King & had John Stewart b. 1876 & Alfred Brice b. 1879.
1843, Feb. 23, Alfred Lee.
1847, May 9, Sarah Emma, m. John R. Manning & had Jennie D. Manning.
1849, June 29, Lydia Jane, m. George E. Bennett.
1852, July 12, Ira Lee, m. (1) Lily R. Wilson & (2) Etta Carpenter, b. c. 1857 in KS. He had Bertha May, b. 14 July 1890 in KS.
1853, Aug. 13, Phoebe Ellen.

STEWART TERRY DURLAND[6] m. 2d Sarah Jane Case, b. 16 June 1825 in NY.

SARAH DURLAND[6], d/o Charles[5], m. William C. Johnson & had (JOHNSON):
1844, Charles D., m. Caroline Harding.
1846, Jacob M.

THOMAS TERRY DURLAND[6], s/o Charles[5], m. Sarah E. Jackson of Orange Co. & had (all b. Slate Hill):
1856, Charles J., m. Lena Clark & had Elizabeth, Hope, Faith & Charles J., all b. Jersey City, NJ.
1857, John B.
1860, Alice L.
1862, Etta A.
1864, George Lewis.
1866, Julia F., m. Benjamin Horton of Westtown.
c. 1868, Elizabeth, m. Louis Van Orden.
c. 1870, Jennie.

In later life THOMAS TERRY[6] purchased the former Phineas Howell farm near Slate Hill.

JOHN DURLAND[5], s/o Charles[4], m. --- Holbert & had:
1791, MOSES.
1797, JOHN HOLBERT.
c. 1809, HENRY.
1816, JAMES F.
c. 1836, Sarah, m. --- Wood of Orange Co.
c. 1839, Elizabeth, m. --- Wood.
c. 1841, Peter.

It is possible, but seems highly unlikely, that JOHN had these children in this time span, even if he had more than one wife.

MOSES DURLAND[6], s/o John[5], m. Jerusha Clark & had (all b. Minisink):
c. 1815, Clark.
c. 1817, George A., m. --- Green.
c. 1820, Maria, m. --- Green.
c. 1822, Adeline, m. --- Owen.

JOHN HOLBERT DURLAND[6], s/o John[5], m. Hannah Owen & had:
1824, Caroline, m. --- Whittock.
1832, COE.
c. 1833, Elizabeth.

JOHN HOLBERT DURLAND[6] m. (2) --- DRAKE & had:
1837, Elmeda, b. Huguenot, m. --- Cuddeback.

COE DURLAND[7], s/o John Holbert Durland[6], m. (1) Antoinette Baird of Orange Co. & had:
1855, Carrie, b. Honesdale, PA, m. John D. Wiston, b. 1879, PA.
1868, Josephine, b. PA, m. Fred B. Whitney of PA.

COE m. (2) Emma Gustin, b. 1843 in Orange Co. & had (all b. Honesdale, PA):
1871, Fannie, m. C. R. Bradley of Honesdale.
1879, Louise.
1885, Antoinette.

HENRY DURLAND[6], s/o John[5], m. --- Wood or Orange Co. & had:
c. 1830, John H.
c. 1833, Oliver E., m. --- Taylor of Orange Co.
c. 1835, Elizabeth, m. --- Mills of Orange Co.

JAMES F. DURLAND[6], s/o John[5], m. --- Drake of Orange Co. & had:
c. 1832, Nathaniel D.
c. 1834, Angeline, m. --- Van Etten of Orange Co.

SAMUEL DURLAND[5], s/o Charles[4], m. Elizabeth Cheshire, b. March 1772, L.I. & had:
1796, Feb., Mercy.
1798, April 3, Mary.
1799, Oct. 12, Matilda, m. Daniel House.
1801, Oct. 6, DANIEL.
1803, Oct. 6, ALBERT.
1805, July 17, Sophia, m. Silvanus Tupper of Orange Co.
1807, June 30, JOHN C.
1809, June 9, Elicy, m. Charles Arkell of Orange Co.
1813, June 16, COE.
1815, March 13, Elizabeth, m. Elias S. Bailey of Orange Co.

DANIEL DURLAND[6], s/o Samuel[5], m. Martha Vernon & had:
1830, WILLIAM V.
1834, May, Mary Elizabeth.
1837, Sept., George Mapes, m. (1) --- Smith & (2) Fanny McCoy & had son George.

WILLIAM V. DURLAND[7], s/o Daniel[6], m. --- Smith of Orange Co. & had:
c. 1851, Henrietta, m. (1) --- Shultz & (2) --- McCain.
c. 1853, Emma, m. Benjamin DuBois.
c. 1855, Amelia V., m. E. Wannemaker
c. 1857, Charles Winfield, m. Margaret Loss.
c. 1859, Martha.

ALBERT DURLAND[6], s/o Samuel[5], m. Phoebe Swan & had:
1826, Feb. Gabriel.
1828, Elizabeth.
1831, Feb. 23, Wilmot A.
1832, Dec. 11, Charles S.
1834, Sept. 20, Jesse L., m. Arrietta W. Youngs & had Ralph Youngs Durland, b. 1882 Oxford Depot, who m. Ellen Brophy, b. 1881 in Ireland.
1837, Aug. 14, Sarah Ann.
1839, March 5, Hannah.
1843, Jan. 5, John Milton, m. Kate Lawrence.

JOHN C. DURLAND[6], s/o Samuel[5], m. Adeline Dusenberry & had (all b. Sullivan Co.):
1834, Stephen D.
1836, Phoebe Ann.
1838, James Townsend.
1840, Oct., Samuel.
1843, Emily.
1845, Peter Dusenberry.

COE DURLAND[6], s/o Samuel[5], m. Harriet Dusenberry of Orange Co. & had:
1837, July 27, Jane.
1839, Aug., Sibyl.
1841, Abby.
1843, Nov., Thomas Edwin.
1846, Feb. Harriet Emily.

———

**DURYEA, JOHN E.**        H-833, C-100-01

JOOST DURYEA, to L.I. from Holland in 1675, a French Huguenot. Descendants:
YOST (or George) DURYEA[1] , **JOHN E.'s**[5] great-great grandfather, from Jamaica, Queens Co. to Blooming-Grove, Orange Co. He d. 1760, buried at Grey Court. His son:
GEORGE DURYEA[2] was a soldier of the Rev. & m. Hannah Hanson of Goshen. They had five sons & 4 daus., [one dau. was Hannah, b. 21 April 1776] among them:
JOHN DURYEA[3], b. 21 Feb. 1774, m. 1800 Mary, d/o Samuel & Jeanette (McCurdy) Crawford of Town of Montgomery and settled in Bloomingburg, Town of Wallkill. They had six children, the youngest was:
SAMUEL C. DURYEA[4] m. Emily Tuthill and has been a resident of Crawford since 1838. Samuel and Emily are the parents of:
**JOHN E. DURYEA**[5], b. 6 Sept. 1840, Town of Crawford, removed to Pine Bush in 1905. He m. in 1863, Jane Frances Hunter, who d. in 1883, and had:

Emily C.
Mary F.
Edna H.
Anna Z.

---

**DUSENBERRY, SAMUEL T.**        H-833
Ass't. postmaster at Tuxedo Park.

SAMUEL T. is the s/o William B. Dusenberry & S. E. Wallace. He was b. Stony Ford, Orange Co. 1873; m. Lenor Clark of Monroe, NY. They have one son, William Wallace.

---

**EAGER FAMILY**        A-374, 380, C-19, 20, 21
of Montgomery.
**EAGER, THOMAS**        U2-94-5, LDS Anc. File
of Wall Kill

WILLIAM EAGER[1], from Monaghan, Ireland c. 1728 to Westchester Co., NY with wife & 2 children, and after 13 years to Neelytown; m. Elsa McGrada in Ireland, family originally of Scotland, res. in Ireland c. 100 years. Their children:
Mary, b. Ireland, m. William Monell.
WILLIAM.
THOMAS.
Elizabeth m. James McMunn.
Ann m. John Davis.
Jane m. John Harlow.

WILLIAM EAGER[2], s/o William[1], b. on passage to America; age 13 with family to Neeleytown; m. (1st) Miriam Butler; they had one child, d. young. He m. (2d) Ann, (1740-1813) d/o William & Sarah Bull of Hamptonburgh, then Town of Goshen, and had:
1763, Nov. 17, William m. 9 Feb. 1786, Elizabeth d/o Samuel Watkins, Esq. William d. 19 Feb. 1835.
1765, Aug. 13, Thomas, m. Margaret Blake.
1768, March 2, SARAH.
1769, March 4, Ann m. Elijah McMunn of Montgomery, 31 May 1792, at Goshen.
1774, June 11, Mary Ann, m. Charles Bodine of Montgomery.
C. 1776, Esther m. Samuel Dunning of Wallkill, 29 Nov. 1796, at Goshen.
1780, Dec. 8, Eleanor m. Philip Mobray of Wallkill.
Elsie m. John Blake.
C. 1782, Anthony; d. young.

SARAH EAGER[3], d/o William[2], m. Capt. James McBride of Neeleytown, 28 Aug. 1792, at Goshen, and had:
GENERAL JOHN MC BRIDE[4], b. 20 Aug. 1797, Hamptonburgh. He m. Elizabeth Hulse, b. 1/2 July 1800, they had, all b. Hamptonburgh:
1822, George Eager, m. Phebe Church Wilbur, b. 24 Oct. 1825, Walkill.
1834, Sarah E.
1836, Jane.

THOMAS EAGER[2], s/o William[1], m. Martha McNeal. In his will, dated 24 June 1789, he names his children:
John.
Thomas.
Martha.
Leda, m. Thomas Watkins.
Meriam, m. John Bowhanon.
Jane.
William.
James.
Edward.

Thomas Watkins, executor; will proved 26 June 1792 by John McCamly of Wall Kill, yeoman; Arthur Buchannan & Edward McHenry.

---

**EAGER, SAMUEL W.**        ???

SAMUEL W. EAGER, b. Montgomery, NY; atty., postmaster, congressman & j.p., m. Catharine d/o John McAuley, Newburgh merchant, and had:
John M., atty. of Newburgh, St. Louis, NY.
Samuel W. of Racine, WI.
Frank.
One son, unnamed.

---

**EAGER, JOHN L. D.**        H-833-4

ISAAC L. EAGER[1] m. Fannie M. Bodine and had:
JOHN L. D. EAGER[2], b. Walden 1850, in hide & tallow business at Montgomery since 1875; served as j.p. He m. Emma Decker in 1876, and had:
Leonard.
Clarence.
Ray.

---

**EAGER, JOSEPH C.**        H-834

JOSEPH CASE EAGER[1], dairy farmer & j.p., d. 1903. His children were:
1859, Aug. 21, JOSEPH C.
Caroline, m. Cornelius Zabriskie of Newark, NJ.

JOSEPH C. EAGER[2], b. on a farm near Hamptonburgh, where he now resides.

---

**EAGER, WILLIAM CASE**        H-834

WILLIAM C.[1] (d. 18 April 1878) & Mary C. EAGER had one son & four daughters:
Mary L.
Jennie.
Belle.
Fannie.
1865, Dec. 9, WILLIAM CASE.

WILLIAM CASE EAGER[2], b. in Warwick & d. suddenly as the result of an accident 11 Feb. 1904. In 1899 he m. Hattie J. Aldrich, d/o Mr. & Mrs. Hiram Still of Warwick. He helped his mother with her general store, which he assumed management of until his death. He was a fireman, town collector & a sportsman. His earliest ancestor in Orange Co. lived on a farm near what is now called Neelytown, and some of his ancestors sill reside there. His great uncle was Samuel W. Eager, the first historian of the county.

---

## EASTON, THOMAS HORTON                     H-835

JAMES EASTON[1], b. 15 Jan. 1824 at Milford, PA, m. Hannah E. Corwin of New Vernon 24 Feb. 1849. James resided in Dunkirk, Howells, Saginaw (MI) (1863 & Orange Co. 1864). He had a general store. Their children:
1849, Nov. 21, Nellie R., m. Schuyler D. Grazer of Otisville.
1855, Feb. 2, Ada; d. March 1856.
1853, Jan. 25, **THOMAS HORTON.**

**THOMAS HORTON EASTON[2]**, b. on homestead farm near Otisville, worked on railroad and later as a farmer. He m. Frances N., d/o Dimmick & Sylvia A. (Cadwell) Wilkin on 14 March 1875, and had:
1877, Feb. 11, HARRIET D.
1881, June 14, NELLIE W.
1885, Sept. 10, Sylvia E.

HARRIET D. EASTON[3], d/o **THOMAS[2]**, m. Henry A. Holley of Otisville and had (HOLLEY):
1898, Aug. 26, Henry E.
1901, April 30, Elizabeth C.
1905, Sept. 20, James Easton.

NELLIE W. EASTON[3], d/o **THOMAS[2]**, m. Joseph K. Corwin and had (CORWIN):
1905, July 19, S. Gilbert.
1907, March 2, Francis Horton.

---

## EATON FAMILY OF GREENVILLE
### A-693, H-240-1, C-13

ROBERT EATON[1] settled in Greenville soon after the Rev. War at what is now known as "Eatontown," and had:
JOHN.
William.
Robert.
Samuel.

JOHN EATON[2], s/o Robert[1], had sons:
Gabriel, retired to Unionville, where he died.
Daniel H., res. near Slate Hill, Wawayanda.

ALEXANDER EATON[1] was a pioneer in the same area the same time as Robert above. He had one son, THOMAS[2] and a grandson, JAMES EATON[3], now res. at Port Jervis. An Alexander Eaton m. Esther Martin 24 Aug. 1782 in Goshen.

Also a JAMES EATON was a contemporary of Robert & res. in the area called Eatontown.

---

## ECKER (ACKER), WOLVERT                     TN-282

JAN ECKER[1], early Dutch settler of Greenburgh, Westchester Co., NY, was b. there 17 Jan. 1732, at what is now known as "Sunny Side" & previously known as "Wolfert's Roost," built by Wolfert (Wolvert) Ecker, Dutch burgher of Greenburgh. JAN's[1] name first appears as a deacon of the Dutch Church at Sleepy Hollow. By his wife Magdalentje he had:
WOLFERT.
Cornelius.

WOLFERT ECKER[2], s/o Jan[1], in his will dated 1753 names his sons:
Stephen.
SYBOUT.

SYBOUT ECKER[3], had a son:
WOLFERT ECKER[4] who in 1772 purchased a portion of the Harrison Patent & soon removed to Newburgh, whre he d. 17 Jan. 1799, aged 67 years. He was a Rev. patriot, Chairman of the Committee of Safety; miller after the war & manufactured brick. He established the landing on the Hudson now known as Hampton & also a ferry between that place & Wappinger's Falls. He d. of cancer of the face, from which he suffered many years. Wolfert's first wife is not named here & she d. without issue. His second wife was Sarah, d/o William Pugsley of Westchester Co (she m. 2d George Merritt), & they had:
Isaac, d. unm.
SUSAN.
DEBORAH.
WILLIAM.
PHEBE.
SARAH.

SUSAN ECKER[5], d/o Wolfert[4], m. (1) Joseph Williams & had (WILLIAMS):
Wolvert A.
James.
Clementine.

SUSAN[5] m. (2) Leonard Smith & had son William Smith who drowned with many others on the sloop *Neptune* in 1824.

DEBORAH ECKER[5], d/o Wolfert[4], m. Dr. John Pinckney of Dutchess Co., NY, a member of the SC branch of the family, & had:
Isaac.
Caroline.
Harriet.
Edward.
Julia.
Theodore.
Deborah.

WILLIAM ECKER[5], s/o Wolfert[4], served in the War of 1812; d. 1827, aged 48, while a member of the Legislature. He m. Sarah Badger of Poughkeepsie, NY, & had:

Theodore, res. CA.

Clara.

Phebe, m. Mr. --- Mead of St. Louis, as his second wife.

Susan, m. Mr. --- Mead of St. Louis, as his first wife.

George.

Charles, res. CA.

PHEBE ECKER[5], d/o Wolfert[4], m. Hon. John P. Jones of Sullivan Co., NY & had (JONES):

Samuel.

William.

Perthenia.

Mary.

Henrietta.

Phebe.

SARAH ECKER[5], d/o Wolfert[4], m. James Lockwood of Norwalk, CT & had (LOCKWOOD):

Catharine F.

Harriet C.

William E.

John E.

---

**EDMONSTON, THOMAS S. [P]**        A-172-3, 214

Physician.

JAMES EDMONSTON[1] with wife Margaret Smith to Orange Co. in 1720 [1727?] from Enniskillen, Co. Tyrone, Ireland. They res. 7 years at Plymouth, MA and then to New Windsor, Orange Co. Children:

WILLIAM.

Sally m. Patrick McDaniel.

WILLIAM EDMONSTON[2], s/o James[1], m. Jane, d/o David Sutherland of Canterbury, Cornwell; had 4 daus. & 3 sons, among them:

James, maj. in Rev. War; farmer near Newburgh, d. 1844.

WILLIAM HENRY.

WILLIAM HENRY EDMONSTON[3], s/o William[2], physician at Jacksonville FL, d. NY; m. Gertrude Harris of Poughkeepsie and had:

Samuel, physican of NY City.

DeWitt Clinton, physician of Newburgh.

Harris, physician of Washingtonville & later Newburgh where he died.

1804, March 13, THOMAS S.

THOMAS S. EDMONSTON[4], "next youngest of the family," b. near Newburgh. Ran drug business during medical training. Licensed Herkimer Medical Society in 1829; settled at Chester & d. there from overwork and exposure 11 March 1852. Presbyterian Church at Chester. He m. Drusilla, youngest d/o JOHN & CHRISTINA (WELLS) DECKER

[see below] & granddau. of Johannes Decker, who in 1768 owned mill & property where Walden, Town of Montgomery is now a village. Their children:

John Decker.

Cornelia Mitchell.

The DECKERS were among the earliest settlers of Esopus. 1689 BROHERSON DECKER, Huguenot settled in Ulster Co. Drusilla Decker who m. Thomas Edmonston, had a sister, Cornelia, wife of George G. Mitchell and one brother, Theodore Wells.

JOHN WELLS[1], original settler in Orange Co., had a son:

JOSHUA WELLS[2], b. Goshen 1744, m. Rhoda Booth, granddau. of William Bull & Sarah Wells. Their daughter:

CHRISTINA WELLS[3] m. John Decker, father of Drusilla (above).

SARAH WELLS was the first white woman in the Town of Goshen; lineal desc. of Hon. William Wells, atty. of England who came to America and served as high sheriff of New Yorkshire on L.I.

---

**EDSALL, ALVA WISNER**        H-835

dentist of Warwick.

ALVA WISNER EDSALL is the s/o Thomas A. & Phoebe (Miller) Edsall. He is of the 7th generation of early settlers of New Amsterdam (now NY City) in 1637, they being large owners of timber lands where Hackensack, NJ is now located. They later moved to Northern NJ and numerous branches of the family still found in the vicinity. ALVA m. 1891, Caroline Welling of Warwick, and had:

Marian, age 12.

Maurice, age 5.

---

**ELLIOTT, EDWARD R.**        H-836

physician of Montgomery.

DR. ELLIOTT, b. Dutchess Co. 1854, a s/o Rev. Joseph & Harriet (Andrews) Elliott. He graduated 1874 in medicine from the Univ. of NY & has practiced in Montgomery since 1878. He m. Lydia Wright & they have one son, Clyde.

---

**ELMER, NATHANIEL**        A-163, C11, 87, LDS Anc. File

of Florida, physician.

NATHANIEL ELMER, native of Sharon, CT, m. ---, d/o Judge William Thompson & had:

William, physician of Goshen, m. Mary Allison 29 June 1779. He is indicated as dec'd. in church records by 1804. A Mary Elmer d. aged 40 of spotted fever 30 March 1810, another Mary Elmer d. aged 57 in April 1821, fits.

Nathaniel, physician of Denton.

Jesse of Bellvale.

Mrs. Robert Armstrong.

Mrs. Smith, who later m. Joshua Conkling. By Mr. Smith she

had: John C. of Goshen & Mrs. Ira Gardner; by Mr. Conkling she had: William S. of Goshen; Enos S. of NY; George S. of Iowa; Mrs. Samuel Wilson of Bellvale & Nathaniel E., res. on Dr. Elmer homestead.

LDS Anc. File shows Nathaniel above, b. 17 Feb. 1733 in Norwalk, Fairfield Co., CT, m. 1751, Anna Thompson & d. 17 Dec. 1797. He is given as the s/o Jonathan Elmer, b. 8 May 1687 in Hartford, CT & Mary ---, b. c. 1690 in Norwalk & d. Sharon, CT 22 Jan. 1783. _____

**EVANS FAMILY et al**                    H-262-3
of Town of Highlands

Land around West Point granted to Capt. JOHN EVANS by the British crown previous to the Rev. War. 1723 lands resumed by the crown & granted to Charles Congreve; 1,463 acres. In 1747, 332 acres were granted to John Moore, who devised them to Stephen Moore, merchant of Caswell, NC. In 1790 land was sold to the US government.

Hugh McClellan, Rev. soldier, settled in small house on West Point property where he died, leaving a wife & dau. who were dispossessed by the US government in 1839. _____

**EVANS, CHARLES A.**                    H-836-7
soldier, newspaperman, rancher & farmer.

CHARLES A. EVANS, b. 11 Sept. 1845 in NY City. At age 16 enlisted in NY with the 12th Regular Infantry for the Civil War, was a drummer boy in May 1862. He has resided in South KS, Chicago & NY City. In 1888 he removed to Orange Co. He m. Jennie E. Morrill of Brandon, VT in 1867, and had:
A son, now living in Chicago.
Mrs. F. L. Andrews of Whitehall.
Frances.
Austin. _____

**EVANS, GEORGE W.**                    H-837
cattle & horse dealer of Town of Crawford.

GEORGE W. EVANS is a s/o John A. & Marie (Walker) Evans. He was b. in Walker Valley, Ulster Co. He served in the Civil War in his teens & m. Anna L. Relyea 6 Jan. 1869, a d/o Christopher & Sarah (Sprague) Relyea. _____

**EVANS, THOMAS GRIER**                    AA3-65
of NY City.

JOHN EVANS[2], b. England 21 May 1709, d. Drumore [Lancaster] PA 4 July 1798, served in French & Indian War, c. 1747 removed from Cecil Co., MD to Lancaster Co., PA. He m. 1748, Sarah Denny. JOHN was s/o James Evans[1], who came from England with wife & 4 children to settle in Cecil Co., MD. JOHN[2] & Sarah had:
JOHN EVANS[3], b. Drumore, PA 2 Nov. 1762, d. Little Britain, PA 4 July 1797. He m. 1786, Jane, d/o Thomas &

Isabella (Polk) Grubb, & their eldest son:
THOMAS GRUBB EVANS[4], M.D. of Goshen, NY, b. Chestnut Level, PA, 31 March 1789; d. at Goshen, NY 16 Aug. 1829. He m. 15 July 1813, Mary Swezy of Goshen, d/o Jonathan & Elizabeth (Seward) Swezy. Served in 19th Brigade, NYSM, 1821. THOMAS[4] & Mary had:
JAMES SIDNEY EVANS of Kingston, NY, b. Goshen 15 Feb. 1816, d. Kingston 25 Aug. 1857; banker. He m. 26 June 1850, Mary DeWitt of Kingston, d/o Jacob Hasbrouck DeWitt & Sarah A. Sleight. Jacob 5th in desc. from Tjerck Claeszen DeWitt, who settled in Kingston in 1661. Their only surviving son is **THOMAS GRIER EVANS**, b. Kingston, Ulster Co., 22 Oct. 1852. _____

**EVANS, WILLIAM**                    H-837
retired at Westtown.

WILLIAM EVANS is a s/o William & Rosetta (Corwin) Evans & was b. in Town of Minisink on the family homestead. He has resided at Middletown & NY City & has been a merchant & bank president as well as community service. He m. Julia Denton, d/o Theodore B. of Denton, NY. Their children:
A daughter, m. Albert H. Horton of Johnson, NY.
Sidney, businessman of Salt Lake City. _____

**EVERETT, HARVEY**    A-171, C-106, 111, LDS Anc. File
physician.

EPHRAIM EVERETT[1], b. 12 Dec. 1742, of English origin, from L.I. in 1762 & settled in Town of Wallkill, Orange Co., upon which he res. until his death 1834, Dec. Early member of Presbyterian Church at Scotchtown. He m. Beulah, d/o David Moore, early settler of Goshen, who d. in 1789. Children:
1769, April 26, Julia m. Obadiah Howell.
1771, Jan. 11, EPHRAIM.
1772, July 9, Walter.
1774, Feb. 4, Lydia m. David Reeve.
1775, Nov. 17, Hephzibah m. Daniel Moore.
1779, May 30, Benjamin.
1782, Oct. 25, DAVID.
1785, June 30, Freelove m. Samuel Kirk.

EPHRAIM EVERETT[2], s/o Ephraim[1], d. 4 July 1828; m. Deborah Corwin, b. 4 Dec. 1777 at Wallkill, & had:
c. 1797, Gabriel.
1801, Oliver.
1805, ADDISON.
1807, Azubah.
c. 1809, Abigail.
1810, Israel.
c. 1812, Lewis.
1813, George.
1815, Ephraim.
c. 1817, David.
c. 1819, Alonson.

c. 1821, Deborah Ann.

ADDISON EVERETT[3], s/o Ephraim[2], m. Eliza Ann Elting of
Kingston & had:
1832, Aug. 30, Ann Eliza Adelaide, b. NY City, m. John Stout
White, b. 15 Feb. 1818 in Middletown, Monmouth Co., NJ.
1835, April 4, Schuyler, b. NY City, Queens Co., m. Rachel
Sanders, b. 1838 in Wilmington, DE.

DAVID EVERETT[2], s/o Ephraim[1], farmer & town assessor; m.
Sarah, d/o Andrew Clark McNish, of Scotch desc. &
grandson of Rev. George McNish, progenitor of the family
in Orange Co. Sarah was b. in Wallkill 1789; d. 1872;
David d. 1848, their children:
1811, Dec. 19, HARVEY.
Henry L.; d. Middletown age 59.
George Whitfield; d. age 59, unm.

HARVEY EVERETT[3], physician, studied at Minisink, NY City
& Woodstock VT, grad. 1834 & settled in Middletown;
public service. He m. Jan. 1837, Sarah A., d/o Walter &
Abigail (Corwin) Everett of Wallkill, who was b. March
1811. Their surviving children:
Darwin, physician at Bellview Hospital, NY City until 1866; to
Middletown.
Genevieve m. Frank B. Denton of Middletown.

## FALLS FAMILY OF NEW WINDSOR W-

ALEXANDER FALLS, innkeeper, emigrant from Ireland, to
America with Clinton family in 1729, member of Col.
Ellison's New Windsor Regt. in 1738, known as the foot
company of military of the Precinct of Highlands. He had
6 children, 4 sons & 2 daus., those named here:
Samuel (2d son), m. Mary Denton; wounded at Ft. Montgomery
during Rev. War.
Another son, wounded & taken prisoner at Ft. Montgomery &
later died in the Old Sugar House prison in NY during Rev.
War.
Edward, succeeded his father as innkeeper at Alexander's death;
on Edward's death his widow m. Samuel Wood & the name
of the inn was changed to Woods.

## FANCHER FAMILY H-838

ELIAS FANCHER[1], b. Darien, CT, 19 Jan. 1793; to Warwick
in early boyhood with is father. Elias m. Sarah Jones, b.
Warwick 10 Sept. 1795 and had 8 children, 2 living:
1831, Dec. 15, Julia, m. Wisner Wood of Paterson, NJ.
1836, March 22, DARIUS

DARIUS FANCHER[2], farmer, m. Sarah Catharine Sayer of
Warwick, and had:
Edwin, physician of Middletown.
Sayer, wholesale grocer of Middletown.
Clinton W., dry goods store.
Frank, feed business in Goshen.

Lillie, m. William A. Bradner of Warwick.

## FARNUM, HENRY H. [P] A-738
of Deerpark.

HENRY H. FARNUM b. Litchfield (Port Jervis), CT 10
May 1808; in childhood moved to Otsego Co.,; canal engineer;
to Port Jervis 1842 and became partner with Charles St. John in
mercantile business; retired 1861. Banker of Port Jervis 1853 till
his death; member of Reformed Dutch Church. He was one of
12 children [his parents not named]. He m. (1st) Abigail Ann,
d/o the late Stephen St. John, 11 Jan. 1837; she d. May 1874; m.
(2d) "Mrs. Diana Farnum in 1879" who survives him.

## FARNUM, HENRY H. H-838
of Port Jervis.

HENRY is the s/o Peter E. & Mary R. (Conkling) Farnum.
He m. Ruth Smith of Port Jervis & they have one son, Henry H.,
Jr.

## FEAGLES, JACOB R. H-838
peach grower & dairy farmer.

JACOB was b. on the Feagles homestead 31 March 1863. He
m. (1st) Belle Hyatt of Warwick 5 Dec. 1889 & (2d) Emma
J. Vealy of Amity on 25 Oct. 1893. Children of 2d mar-
riage:
Jacob H.
George W.
Mary Elizabeth.
Henry Barney.
Emma.

## FEAGLES, NATHANIEL R. [P] A-612-13
of Warwick.

JACOB FEAGLES[1] was b. in Germany and had son:
JACOB FEAGLES[2], to America, res. Chester, Orange Co.,
blacksmith. His children:
1792, Jan., JACOB.
William.
Nathaniel.
Caroline m. Robert Stoutenburgh.

JACOB FEAGLES[3], s/o Jacob[2], m. c. 1815, Susan Roe of
Orange Co., res. Amity in the Township of Warwick, and
had:
David.
Charles.
1821, Sept. 25, NATHANIEL R.
Henry B.
William.
Mary.
Susan.
Robert.
Clariss.

**NATHANIEL R. FEAGLES**[4], b. Amity; 1850 to NY City, butcher; 1855 back to Orange Co., farmer & horse breeder; Presbyterian Church at Amity member; m. 1858 Elizabeth, d/o Peter N. Ryerson of Vernon, Sussex Co. NJ. They had 9 children, survivors:

Mary.
Susan.
Jacob [could be Jacob above, b. 1863.]
Anna.
Charles.
Nathaniel R.
Elizabeth.
Henry.

### FEBER, ISAAC                                           CN-10

**ISAAC FEBER** is found in the Newburgh Directory for 1709, the year the town was settled by immigrants from the Palatinate of the Rhine. He is listed as husbandman & viner, aged 33; his wife, Catharine, aged 30, and their son, Abram, aged 2 years.

### FIERE, DANIEL                                          CN-10

**DANIEL FIERE** is listed in the Newburgh Directory for 1709, the year the town was founded & settled by immigrants from the Palatinate of the Rhine. He was husbandman, aged 32; his wife Anna Maria, aged 30, and children:

Andrew, aged 7.
Johannes, aged 6 years.

### FINCH FAMILY OF MT. HOPE                             A-506-7

JOHN FINCH[1] from Horseneck, CT to Goshen, NY and had:
JAMES FINCH[2], b. Goshen, served in French & Indian as well as Rev. War; to site of Middleton in Town of Wallkill before Rev. War, later to vicinity of Finchville. Baptist church deacon. He m. Catharine Gale and had:
1768, July 25, JAMES JR.

JAMES FINCH JR.[3], j.p. 1798-1830; co. judge; d. 7 Dec. 1843, aged 75; Baptist church member. He m. 1794 Sarah ---, b. 23 Sept. 1772, d. 1 Dec. 1843, and had:
1795, May 20, Zophar.
1797, May 1, Catharine; d. 30 Dec. 1843.
1799, Sept., Margaret; d. 12 Feb. 1807.
1802, Feb. 28, P.G.
1804, April 30, Coe; d. 12 Sept. 1832.
1806, Nov. 20, Julia.
1809, Jan. 24, Jesse; d. 23 Nov. 1843.
1811, April 11, James M.; d. 4 Feb. 1844.
1813, June 28, John; d. 9 Dec. 1843.
1819, Aug. 9, Sarah; d. 2 Dec. 1843.

### FINLEY, JOHN                                          U2-183
yeoman of New Windsor.

**JOHN FINLEY** d. intestate & on 24 Nov. 1789 administration of his estate was granted to his widow Elisabeth, James McClaughrey Jr. of Montgomery merchant & Joseph Gasherie.

### FISCHER, JOHANNES                                     CN-10

**JOHANNES FISCHER** appears in the Newburgh Directory for 1709, the year the town was founded by immigrants from the Palatinate of the Rhine. He is listed as smith & husbandman, aged 27; his wife Maria Barbara, aged 26 & their son, Andries, aged 2 weeks.

### FISK, JONATHAN                              A-143, TN-306-7
Newburgh atty.

**ROBERT & SYBIL (GOLD) FISKE**[1], who lived at Broad Gates, Loxford, near Framlingham, Suffolk Co., England had a son, WILLIAM[2], whose eldest son was WILLIAM[3]. His grandsons were:
JOHN.
William of Wenham.

JOHN FISKE[5], grandson of William[3], to Salem, MA 1637, settled at Wenham, later removed to Chelmsford, MA, where he d. in 1676. His youngest son, Rev. MOSES FISK[6] of Braintree had Rev. SAMUEL FISK[7], who had Maj. Gen. JOHN FISK[8] of Salem.
JONATHAN FISK[9], s/o Maj. Gen. John[8], res. Williamstown, VT, legislator & judge. His son:
JONATHAN FISK[10], b. Amherst, NH 26 Sept. 1773; d. 13 July 1832; school teacher, to Ware, NH (1795) living with family of Amos Wood; 1796/7 to NY; office of Peter Hawes to study law 1799; practiced in NY counties of Orange & Ulster; to Newburgh in 1800. Congressman (1809), US Atty. Gen. So. Dist. NY state (1815). He m. in 1803/4, Sarah Van Kleek of Poughkeepsie, b. 18 March 1773; d. 6 June 1832. TN-308 is statement by him at the end of his life that indicates that he had a very unhappy family life. It is noted under "unusual incidents" (E-224) that in 1804 Jonathan Fisk, Esq. horsewhipped Jonathan Cooley, Esq. publically in the street. Children:
Theodore S.; found dead in the street in NY 1854 or 55.
James L.; d. in Pensacola, 1835.
Delaphine R. E. m. J. C. Bisbee; d. 22 July 1846.
Mary M.; d. 8 June 1822.
Son; d. age 2 months.

### FLANAGAN, JOHN H.                                     H-839
farmer of Newburgh.

**JOHN H. FLANAGAN** was b. in Ireland 1843; to America 1851. He m. Miss --- Shields & had 7 children.

### THE FLEWWELLING FAMILY                               TN-278
of Newburgh.

This family is of Welch origin & among the early settlers of

L.I.; JOHN FLEWWELLING[1] of that place to Newburgh c. 1760. He m. Elizabeth Smith & had:

John, m. Deborah Denton, had 10 children, all d. young.

Morris, m. Jane Merritt & had Elizabeth who m. William Palmer.

ABEL.

Sarah, m. Nehemiah Denton.

Mary, m. Cornelius Polhamus.

Hannah, m. George Winslow.

ABEL FLEWWELLING[2], s/o John F.[1], m. Abigail Purdy & had:

Charlotte, m. Samuel Purdy.

Elizabeth, m. William Harding.

Samuel, m. Julia Caulfield.

Clarissa, m. John Fowler.

John, m. Eunice Palmer.

Abigail, m. Thomas Fowler.

Amelia, m. Richard Taylor.

Guilford, m. Leah Harding.

Jane, m. George Harding.

The name of Flewwelling is now extinct in Newburgh, but not in Ulster Co.

**FORD, CHARLES T.**                    H-839-40
of Central Valley.

**FORD, PATRICK**                       A-790

PATRICK FORD[1] was early res. of Monroe; his son:
DAVIS FORD[2] had:

CHARLES T.

Benjamin.

John.

Townsend.

Henry.

David J.

William.

Mrs. Peter B. Bush.

Mrs. Charles Campbell.

Mrs. Milton Pemberton.

1844, CHARLES T. FORD[3], m. Martha Weggant & had:

**CHARLES T. FORD[4]**, b. Southfield; res. Southfield MI, Newburgh, Albany & Turners NY. Road builder of Orange Co.; proprietor of Turner Hotel at Turner's Station. In 1868 he m. Josephine McKelvey & had:

J. Barlow.

Bertha.

Harriet Louise.

**FORD, HENRY T.**                      H-840
postmaster of Central Valley.

**HENRY T.**, s/o Benjamin & Frances C. (Denniston) Ford, b. 1866. Store at Woodbury 6 years & in 1897 purchased grocery business of George D. Wood in Central Valley.

**FORSYTH, JOHN [P]**              A-358b, TN-310
of Newburgh.

JOHN FORSYTH b. near city of Aberdeen, Scotland 1786/7; to America 1805, intending to settle in NC or GA where some branches of his father's family were, instead to Newburgh in 1810 to visit Rev. Mr. Scrimglour of Assoc. Reformed Church, an old friend of his mother's, and remained. Builder, bank director, pres. of Newburgh Stem Mills & the Branch RR. He m. (1st) Jane, eldest d/o John Currie, who settled in Newburgh in 1802; m. (2d) Anna Jane, youngest d/o John Brown. Children by 1st wife:

Rev. John, D.D., chaplain at West Point.

Robert A.

James C.

**FOSTER, DR. JOHN L. [P]**            A-366-7
of Newburgh.

JESSE FOSTER[1] soldier of the Rev., res. Danbury, CT. His son:

DAVID FOSTER[2], cooper & farmer, b. Danbury; m. Sarah Weed; 1810 with wife & 6 children to Town of Warwick, Orange Co.; 1828 to Newburgh, where he d. 8 Aug. 1854, aged 81 years & 6 days. Sarah d. June 1848, aged c. 78. Quakers. Their children, all now dec'd., John the last to die:

William.

Alvah.

Henry.

JOHN L.

George.

Mary m. (1st) Charles Cox; (2d) Isaac N. Lester.

James.

Elizabeth.

JOHN L. FOSTER[3], teacher, medical student at Edenville NY under Dr. James P. Young; grad. Rutgers 1830; until 1836 practiced at Deckertown, NJ, then to Newburgh; farmer at Washington Wood farm at West Coldenham 14 years. After death of his father purchased family homestead near Newburgh. Member Trinity Methodist-Episcopal Church of Newburgh. He m. 17 Dec. 1834, Harriet, d/o late John Scott of Coldenham. The Scott family from L.I. to Orange Co. after Rev. Harriet was the last survivor of 10 children. JOHN d. 21 July 1840; wife d. 14 Feb. 1826. Their children:

Scott, res. NY City.

John Gray, d. 1878, 22 Jan.

David N., res. Ft. Wayne, IN; served 9th NY Militia in Civil War.

William Wisner, res. NY City.

Fanny S.; d. 8 Jan. 1868.

Albert Zabriskie, res. Terre Haute, IN.

Samuel Monell, res. Danville, IL.

Brothers Scott, David N., Albert Z. & Samuel M. ran mercantile business together at different points in the west.

**FOSTER, WILLIAM**                                    **H-840**

retired manufacturer of Newburgh.

**WILLIAM FOSTER**, b. England 1841. School teacher in England 5 years, in 1867 to America. Stroock Plush Co. & bank director. He m. Mary Ann Taylor & they had 7 children, 4 living [not named].

---

**FOWLER, ANSON J.**                                   **H-841, W-92 [P]**

atty. of Walden & Newburgh.

PETER HILL FOWLER[1] m. Anna Jansen and had:
NICHOLAS JANSEN FOWLER[2], of English & Welch descent, b. on homestead near village of Montgomery 9 May 1847. He was an associate of Fred Wiltsie in business in Newburgh-on-Hudson, NY. 1868 to Walden, NY & opened first hardware store. He m. Elizabeth Millspaugh, d/o the late Joseph G. of Walden, 29 May 1872. Nicholas has been confined to his home for several years. Children:
Joseph M., of Kingston; atty. & legislator.
1878, ANSON J.
Fred, with electric light & telephone in Walden.

**FOWLER, ANSON J.**[3], s/o Nicholas J.[2], of Wales, NY. Merchant & read law at Newburgh. Admitted to bar, 1905.

---

**FOWLER, PETER VAN BENSCHOTEN [P]**
of Newburgh.                                       **A-365-6, TN-274-5**
**FOWLER, DAVID JR.**                              **A-165**
physician.
**FOWLER, GILBERT O.**                             **A-146-7**
atty.
**FOWLER, THOMAS POWELL**       **AA3-17-18, H-841-2**
pres. NY, Ontario & Western Railroad Co.
**FOWLER, SAMUEL**                                 **U2-48, 75**
of Newburgh.

Early English family of New England. There are records in Islington, England as early as 1538, when Sir Thomas Fowler, knight & baronet dwelt in 1630.

Fowlers named with no specific relationship given: Philip, admitted Freeman of MA Colony in 1634 & settled at Ipswich. William emigrated to America 1637 and located at New Haven, CT. Supposed ancestor of CT & NY Fowlers, but no relationship proved.

WILLIAM FOWLER JR.[1] of New Haven had a son:
JOSEPH FOWLER[2], early settler near Mespat Kills, L.I. in 1665 and had a son:
1660, WILLIAM FOWLER[3], b. East Chester, NY, d. 1714. He m. Mary, d/o John Thorne of NY. [In AA3-18 WILLIAM b. 1660 at Flushing, L.I., NY is given as the 2d son of Henry Fowler of Mamaroneck, NY, b. England, d. Oct. 1704 at East Chester. This Henry m. Abigail --, & had 5 children. Henry is given as the 2d s/o William Fowler of CT, b. & m. England, and all of his children b. in England before emigration.] WILLIAM & MARY FOWLER had:

1686, JOHN.
JEREMIAH.

JOHN FOWLER[4], s/o William[3], was b. in Flushing, NY 1686; with his family to Newburgh where he d. in 1768. His wife was Abigail ---, they had 8 children, among them:
1720, **SAMUEL**.
1715, **ISAAC**.
John.
James.
Nehemiah.

**SAMUEL FOWLER**[5], s/o John[4], m. Charlotte Purdy, grandau. of Joseph & Elizabeth (Ogden) Purdy. Samuel & his brother John, having purchased a portion of the Harrison patent in 1747, removed with other members of the family, including their father John[4], to Newburgh. Samuel d. 13 Oct. 1789, age 69 years & 1 day. His will filed in Ulster Co., dated 15 Nov. 1788. Charlotte d. 30 July 1791, aged 74 years, 10 months. Charlotte's will, dated 27 July 1791, filed in Ulster Co. Will Book A. They were members of St. George's Church. Their children:
Mary, m. George Merritt, Jr.; had sons George & John. George's wife Sybal is named in grandmother Charlotte's will.
Elizabeth, m. Samuel Clark; had dau. Elizabeth.
Charlotte, m. Daniel Gidney; had 2 children, Samuel & Rebecca. Charlotte is dec'd. by 1791.
Martha, m. Reuben Tooker.
Abigail, m. Abel Flewwelling.
Glorianna, m. John Fowler, nephew of Samuel; had dau. Charlotte.
1757, SAMUEL, named as only son in his mother's will.

**SAMUEL FOWLER**[6], s/o Samuel[5], was for 40 years minister of the Methodist Episcopal Church; res. on family homestead in Newburgh. He m. (1) Rebecca Gidney & had:
Purdy, m. Charlotte Tooker & had 6 children.
Mary, m. George Wandel.
Charlotte.

**SAMUEL FOWLER**[6] m. (2) Mary Clapp and had:
Henry, m. Eliza Ann Thorne, had 1 child.
Rebecca, m. George Grove.
Electa, m. Dr. James Smith.
Samuel, m. Susan Phillips.
Charlotte, m. Henry Cox.

**ISAAC FOWLER**[5], s/o John[4], b. Flushing, L.I., d. 1787 at Newburgh. Rev. soldier, m. Margaret Theall, d/o Charles, and had:
1746, April 3 [30], ISAAC Jr.

**ISAAC FOWLER JR.**[6], only s/o Isaac[5], d. 1793 at Newburgh; m. (1st) Martha, d/o Charles Tooker of DasKammer Point; she d. March 1771 and bur. with her only child at Marlborough; m. (2d) 1773, Glorianna, d/o Caleb Merritt of Marlborough & sister of Elizabeth, wife of Dr. David Fowler. Glorianna

62

b. 7 July 1758, d. 2 May 1791. They had:
1775, Feb. 8 [5], CALEB.
Martha.
Gilbert; d. young.
Nehemiah, res. Plattefill, Ulster Co.
David, res. Genesee & Livingston Cos.
Francis, physician; d. OH.
Isaac, physician; d. OH young.

ISAAC JR. m. (3d) Mrs. Owen and had 2 children [not named.] He d. 1823.

CALEB FOWLER[7], s/o Isaac Jr.[6], d. 8 March 1826, at Newburgh; m. 28 Aug. 1798, Catharine Sebring, d/o Isaac Sebring of NY, granddau. of Catharine Sebring & Isaac Van Benschoten. Their children:
1800, Feb. 20, PETER V. B.
Caroline m. James E. Slater.
1804, April 11, Dr. Gilbert S.; d. 30 April 1832.
1806, Ann Catharine; d. 1833.
Amelia m. William D. Weygant; d. 30 Dec. 1834.
Martha B.; d. infancy.
CHARLES.
Margaret; d. young.
Matthew V.B., m. Elizabeth F. Seymour.
Jacob V.B., m. (1) Susan Jane Brinckerhoff; (2) a d/o John Currie.
1819, Elizabeth; d. 1836.
ISAAC SEBRING.

PETER V. B. FOWLER[8], s/o Caleb[7], b. Newburgh; d. 21 April 1875. 4 Oct. 1826, m. at Shawangunk, Eliza, d/o Garrett DuBois and Hannah Cooper, sister of Capt. Elias Cooper of Essex Co., NJ. Eliza b. 21 Aug. 1801 & d. 12 April 1866. Their children:
1827, July 26, HENRY D.
1830, July 17, Abram D. B.; d. 7 Oct. 1854.
1835, Oct. 27, Caleb Gilbert, farmer of Newburgh; d. 29 Jan. 1879.
1844, Peter D. B.; d. 17 Feb. 1855.

PETER[8] m. (2d) Anna, wid. of Peter H. Fowler of Montgomery, 23 June 1868. Peter passed his entire life at the home farm at Newburgh, farmer & businessman. Member of First Presbyterian Churches of Marlborough and Newburgh.

HENRY D. FOWLER[9], only surviving son of PETER[8], b. Shawangunk, farmer & bank director, res. Newburgh; m. 20 Oct. 1853, Anna, d/o M. W. DuBois of Newburgh, and had:
Eliza D.
Abram D.
William Jennings.
Charles D.
Weygart D.

CHARLES FOWLER[8], s/o Caleb[7], physician, res. & d. at Montgomery, m. (1) Sarah Hill & had 11 children, 2 sons mentioned: Dr. Charles G. & Peter H. Charles m. (2) Ann E.

McNeal.

ISAAC SEBRING FOWLER[8], s/o Caleb[7], b. Newburgh, m. 7 Sept. 1847, Mary Ludlow Powell, d/o Robert Ludlow Powell (m. Louisa Orso), s/o Thomas. They had:
1851 [52], Oct. 26, THOMAS POWELL.
1854, Jan. 5, Jacob Sebring; d. 21 Feb. 1882 in Florida, NY.

THOMAS POWELL FOWLER[9], b. Newburgh; studied for 2 years in Germany & back to NY and entered the office of Morton, Bliss & Co. (then Morton, Burns & Co.); studied law under Prof. Theo. D. Dwight at Columbia College Law School. Occupies his country place at Village of Warwick in summer months. 26 April 1876 he m. Isabelle, eldest d/o Benjamin J. [F.] Dunning a NY atty. & partner of Charles O'Connor. THOMAS POWELL had son Robert Ludlow Fowler, b. 15 April 1849; m. Julia, d/o William S. Grosbeck of Ohio.

JEREMIAH FOWLER[4], s/o William[3], d. at Rye, NY in 1776. His son:
DAVID FOWLER[5], b. 1728, d. 1806, had:
DAVID FOWLER, JR.[6], b. 28 Dec. 1755 at Crom Pond, Westchester Co., NY; d. 20 Oct. 1835. He was known as "Dr. David," studied medicine in NY City; 1786 res. Newburgh, built house now owned by David E. Fowler on road from Newburgh to Marlborough. He lived there until 1829 when he removed to Village of Newburgh. Supporter of St. George's Church. His obituary found in TN-276. David Jr. m. Elizabeth, d/o Caleb Merritt 9 Oct. 1785 & had:
1787, Jan. 18, James, d. infant.
1788, Dec. 10, GILBERT O.
1789, Dec. 27, Abigail, m. Samuel Sands Seymour; she d. 5 May 1817.
1791, May 11, Hannah; d. 20 March 1792.
1792, Dec. 11, Martha Elizabeth, m. Joseph Carpenter; she d. 10 May 1854.

GILBERT O. FOWLER[7] [P], s/o Dr. David[6], grad. Columbia Col., studied law under Solomon Sleight of Newburgh. Co. judge, member Legislature (1833), held military commission. He d. 27 Dec. 1843; m. Rachel Ann, d/o James & Ann Walker of the City of NY, 21 Dec. 1812 & had:
Ann, m. Leonard D. Nicoll & had two sons: Gilbert O. F. & Edward Nicoll.
David E., served with Gen. Sherman; m. Jane Ann, d/o Chancey Belknap & had: Isaac W., Chancey B., Edward & Annie. David is now dec'd.
Isaac Vanderbeck, unm., atty. of NY; now dec'd.
James Walker, m. Mary Frances Brown of NY & had Frederic Culbert & Frances Elizabeth.
Elizabeth, unm.

———

FRANCE, ETLING                                      A-428-9
of Crawford.

Paternal ancestors from Germany.

JOHN FRANCE[1], res. Kingston, NY, manufactured first nails in this country. He m. Sarah, only child of Peter Etting and Sarah DuPuy, 10 Oct. 1794. Peter Ettling was a large real estate & slave owner in Ulster Co. who d. 25 May 1801; Sarah DuPuy d. 26 June 1803, aged 72. JOHN d. 21 Jan. 1811. Their child:

ETLING FRANCE[2], b. 20 June 1800, built & operated sawmill, tannery & scythe factory in Town of Crawford. He m. (1st) Catherine, d/o Henry DuBois, desc. of Louis DuBois, b. Artois, France, to America 1660 & settled in Hurley, Ulster Co. ETLING m. (2d) Margaret Martin of Inwood, NJ, 17 March 1869. ETLING d. 12 May 1872.

**FULLAGER, JAMES**                                    **H-842**
contractor & builder of Newburgh.

**JAMES** was b. in England in 1828. Attended schools at Headcorn & West End of London, where with his brother he conducted an artists' lodging house. 1850 to America, settled Newburgh. 20 Dec. 1860 m. Elizabeth Hoase of New Windsor. They have 4 children, 3 living.

---

**FULLERTON FAMILY OF WAWAYANDA  A-678, C-22**

WILLIAM[1] was the first Fullerton to settle in Wawayanda, from Dublin, Ireland; d. 1786, m. Sarah Cooley. Children:
1765, March 3, WILLIAM JR.
1767, March 21, Daniel. Could be the Daniel who m. Anna Bull 25 May 1799 at Goshen.
1769, June 2, Samuel.
1771, July 5, Phineas.
1773, April 11, Sarah.
1775, Dec. 23, Jane.

WILLIAM FULLERTON JR.[2], m. Mary Whittaker, b. 20 April 1766; d. c. 1844, d/o Benjamin of Wawayanda. WILLIAM JR. d. 21 Feb. 1817. Children:
William.
Daniel
STEPHEN W.
Elizabeth.

STEPHEN W. FULLLERTON[3] s/o William Jr.[2], m. Esther Stephens, d/o Holloway, and had:
Daniel.
Elizabeth.
William, NY atty.
Mary.
Holloway S.
Stephen W., NY atty.
Peter P.
Benjamin S.
John H.
Elsay T.
Esther I.
Francis E.

---

**FULTON, THOMAS J. [P]**                              **A-242d**
of New Windsor.

THOMAS FULTON[1], b. 3 Oct. 1763; d. 26 Oct. 1814; m. Jemima Frost, b. 5 Nov. 1767, d. 26 June 1846. The Frost family were early emigrants from Dutchess Co. & located on land taken up by kinsman Robert Johnston near Bethlehem. Children of Thomas & Jemima:
1785, Dec. 5, Jane, m. Linus McCabe; d. 28 Sept. 1852.
1788, Jan. 31, Robert J.; d. 3 Sept. 1834.
1793, Aug. 26, Martha, m. William Couser; d. 1 Sept. 1876.
1804, June 10, THOMAS J.

THOMAS J. FULTON[2], b. on homestead near Bethlehem, known as "Squire Fulton," farmer, town official & judge of Orange Co.; member Bethlehem Presbyterian Church; m. 9 Nov. 1824, Mary Anna Schultz of New Windsor, b. 26 June 1807, d. Dec. 1875. Children:
Fanny E.
Mary J., wid. of Samuel M. Clemence, late of Bethlehem.
Harriet E.; d. 5 Nov. 1829.
THOMAS J. JR.
WILLIAM.

THOMAS J. FULTON JR.[3], m. Mary E., d/o Jarvis Knapp of New Windsor; d. 12 Sept. 1874. They had 3 daus.: Georgianna, Mary F. & Laura C.

WILLIAM S. FULTON[3], res. on family homestead built by his father in 1847. Member & trustee of Bethlehem Presbyterian Church, served as town clerk & assessor. He m. 10 Nov. 1859, Phebe E., d/o Sylvester M. & Annie M. Gregg of Newburgh & have:
Fanny L.
Jennie M.
Anna S.

---

**FURMAN, NICHOLAS J.**                               **H-842-3**

**NICHOLAS** was b. Spring Valley, Town of Ramapo, Rockland Co., NY 29 March 1835; d. Warwick, NY 3 April 1908. Lumber business & railroad switchman. 1860 to Port Jervis, then Newburgh, then Warwick, NY. Member of the Reformed Dutch Church. He m. (1st) Rachel A. Westervelt who d. 1872; m. (2d) Mary E. Hynard of Warwick. No children.

---

**GALLAWAY, WILLIAM T.**                              **H-843-4**

ZACHARIAH D. GALLAWAY[1], hotel operator at Scotchtown, Circleville in NY & MN, m. Catherine Thompson and had:
1826, Aug. 13, WILLIAM T.

WILLIAM T. GALLAWAY[2], b. Town of Newburgh; farmer; m. Elizabeth Fondy of Montgomery and had:
Albert, d. in infancy.
William S.
Abraham.

Mary K., m. James Hamm of Brooklyn, NY; d. 1907.

**GALLOWAY, JACOB**                          A-788-89
early res. of Monroe.

JACOB GALLOWAY[1] had a son JAMES[2], who had:
Thomas, son Timothy res. Turner's.
James Jr., removed to Elmira.
Mrs. Jacobus of NY.
Mrs. Fitch of Warwick.
Mrs. Lewis of Monroe.

A James is mentioned in town records as a path-master of dist. No. 24 in 1775.

**GARDINER, JAMES MC NAIR [P]**
physician.                          A-166-7, TN-301-2, C-44

JAMES GARDINER[1], b. Glasgow, Scotland m. --- McNair, and
    had:
1769, May 31, ROBERT.
James.
Margaret.
Cecilia.

ROBERT GARDINER[2], s/o James[1], b. Scotland; 31 May 1790
    to America, settled temporarily at Dutchess Co., NY 1795 in
    Newburgh, general store & coffee house; naturalized 1802,
    joined militia in 1812. He was a teacher, ship capt. &
    merchant. He m. (1st) Jane, d/o Benjamin Smith, 1791; she
    d. 1803; m. (2d) 19 Feb. 1804, Sybil Burr, who d. 1854.
    Robert d. 3 March 1831. Children by 1st wife:
1792, Oct. 24, JAMES M.
Robert S.; d. young.
1795, Oct. 29, Robert S. (2d).
1799, July 11, Cecilia B.

Children by 2d wife:
Jefferson V. V.
Arabella J. G. V. V.
Cicero A.; d. 24 Feb. 1875.
Demosthanes C.
Iduella T. R.
Laurence L.
Marion A.
Zelima.
Franklin M.
Lewis W., m. Frances Emily Ferry.
Baron Steuben.
Anastesia M. m. Lewis H. Stansbrough.

**DR. JAMES MC NAIR GARDINER[3]**, s/o Robert[2], b. New-
    burgh; d. 8 Dec. 1858. He m. (1st) Maria, d/o Josiah Vail
    of Wallkill, she d. 1824; m. (2d) Caroline H., d/o David
    Havens of Cornwall. Children of 1st marriage:
Robert W.
Lucy Ann Cornelia m. Dr. Daniel Wells of Newburgh.

Children of 2d marriage:
Maria A. m. Charles Smith of Newburgh; d. 2 May 1855.
James H.; d. young. Could be the James H. Garner [sic] who
    m. Mary Jane Green in Goshen 26 June 1873.
Walter Scott, poet & artist.
Caroline H.
James H. (2d); d. young.
Emma Jane m. Charles Stewart of Newburgh.
Henry C.

**GARDNER, IRA M.**                          H-844
atty.

IRA M., s/o Merit H. C. (dec'd.) & Belle (Howell) Gardner,
b. at Johnson, Orange Co., 20 Dec. 1883. He studied at
Stewarttown & Westtown, to Middletown, grad. 1903. Studied
law with Henry W. & Russell Wiggins until Oct. 1904; grad.
NY Law School 1906. Has practiced in NY City for 1 year.

**GARDNER, SILAS**                          E-203

SILAS GARDNER, an early settler of Orange Co., tradition-
ally said to be unsympathetic to the American cause, is supposed
to have while escorting a British Army wife to Canada, have
brought back to this country the seeds of the Canadian thistle, a
troublesome plant.

**GARRESS, SAMUEL H.**                          H-844
ex-pres. of village of Port Jervis.

SAMUEL, b. Sussex Co., NJ 1849; d. at his home 10 Dec.
1907. At age 19 employed by Tri-State as bookkeeper; also
partnership in livery business with Hiram Marion & grist mill in
Flatbrookeville. 1884-88 postmaster of Tri-State. 1980 to
Germantown & established grocery store. 1901 retired. Elder
of Second Reformed Church. He m. Charity Estelle Cole &
had:
Samuel Emmet, assumed his father's business on his retirement
    with S. G. Blackman.
Olive Zadie.

**GARRISON, ASAHEL B.**                          H-844
coal & farm implement dealer of Walden.

GEROW GARRISON m. Elnora Seymour of Newburgh &
had:
1884, ASAHEL B.

**GARRISON, ISAAC [P]**                          A-167
physician.

RICHARD GARRISON[1], farmer near Sing Sing, NY had son:
ISAAC GARRISON[2], farmer of Plattekill, m. Martha Denton
    and had 10 children, among them:
**DR. ISAAC GARRISON[3]**, youngest child, studied under uncle,
    Dr. Joshua Garrison of Pleasant Valley; studied in Castleton,
    VT, grad. 1823. Practiced in Newburgh until 1842 when he

removed to Brockport, Monroe Co., where he remained 17 years. June 1865 returned to Newburgh. 1827 apptd. hospital surgeon of 34th Brig. Inf., NY; member Presbyterian Church of Newburgh. He m. (1st) Matilda Miller, sister of Dr. Charles Miller; 1 child, d. infant. He m. (2d) Mary Tousley, who d. with no issue; m. (3d) Catharine A., d/o Jeremiah Scott of NY, and had:

Charles Miller, student of medicine in Newburgh.

### GAZLAY, WARD M.                              TN-315-16

From an obituary in newspaper issue of 21 April 1836: "Died Newburgh Wed. last, aged c. 54," magistrate & proprietor of the *Political Index* (1806-29). He was perhaps from PA, m. Elizabeth, d/o Jonathan & Bridget Carter & left 3 sons [not named here].

### GEDNEY, DAVID FOWLER [P]        A-156, STJ-21, 26
atty., D.A. (1856), county judge (1862).

Paternal ancestors English Quakers from England in the reign of Charles II.

ELEAZER GEDNEY, M.D.[1] of Newburgh, Orange Co. m. Charlotte Bailey of New Windsor, Orange Co., d/o Dr. Jonathan, related collaterally to the Rev. patriot Samuel Adams. Their son:

DR. DAVID FOWLER GEDNEY[2], b. Newburgh-on-Hudson, 1 Jan. 1821. His father & elder brother died before 1838 & he, his mother & an unm. sister (later Mrs. Isaac R. Van Duzer), to Goshen, Orange Co.; atty. (1845). He m. Henrietta Robinson Duer, youngest d/o Alexander, s/o Col. William Duer of Rev. Army & brother of late Judges John A. & William A. Their children:

Bapt. 1844, Alexander Duer; lost at sea off Cape Horn, 1860.
Bapt. 1852, April 11, Herbert, atty.
Child not named.

### GEE FAMILY OF HIGHLANDS                    A-812

CORNELIUS GEE res. West Point before Rev.; established ferry from Gee's Point to Constitution Island with Jacob Nelson. He had:
Jabez.
Mrs. Margaret Swim.

### GERMAN, JOSEPH                                  U2-69
of Montgomery.

JOSEPH GERMAN, in his will dated 9 Nov. 1787, named his wife Mary and children:
Henry.
Andrew.
Charity.
Elizabeth.
Mary.
Catharine.

Executors: Joannis Miller of Montgomery, William Miller & Johannis Moul.

### GEROW FAMILY                                     H-845

The Gerow family settled at Plattekill, Ulster Co. GILBERT H.[1] was the first Gerow b. in Orange Co. He m. Annie Cooley & had 7 children, the eldest was:
ELIAS GEROW[2] (b. 1813-d. age 92), m. Sarah M. Cooper. Their youngest son:
JOSEPH C. GEROW[3] of Town of Blooming-Grove, b. in the town of Hamptonburgh, Orange Co., 1854; farmer. He m. Jennie, d/o Rev. Warren Hathaway, the have 8 living children. Son Percy assists his father in business.

### GEROW, JOHN Y.                                   H-845
farmer & cattle dealer of New Windsor.

JUSTIS CODEY GEROW[1] m. Phoebe H. Young and had:
JOHN Y. GEROW[2], at age of 3 removed with parents to the farm of Thomas Pope in New Windsor.

### GIBSON, THOMAS B.                               H-845
postmaster, Village of Walden.

THOMAS GIBSON[1] m. Sarah Eager & had:
THOMAS B. GIBSON[2], b. Newburgh NY in 1859; tailor. 1883 worked for Wooster & Stoddard at Walden. Served as town clerk.

### GIDNEY, ELEAZER                              A-165, 255
physician of Newburgh.
### GIDNEY, DANIEL                  U2-68, LDS Anc. File
of Newburgh, yeoman.

ELEAZER was desc. from settlers of Gidneytown c. 1760; he d. 9 April 1830, age 72, and had:
1804, Dr. Charles S.; d. 1850.
David F. of Goshen.

In N-85 is given the earliest Gidneys of Orange Co.: Eleazer Gidney, believed of French desc., came to this country & located at the Saw Pits, and from there removed with his family to this town (Gidneytown), where he purchased 1,300 acres of land, settled four of his sons upon it, & built a house for each. After this was accomplished it is reported that this first Eleazer returned to France, where he died. Sons named here:
Joseph.
Daniel.
David.
Eleazer, had a son of the same name, who was the father of Capt. Jonathan Gidney. Eleazer was returning with his wife, one child & horse & all were drowned crossing the Hudson at New Windsor. He left two children: Eleazer & Winford.

**DANIEL GIDNEY** [could be the Daniel above], of Newburgh, yeoman, in his will dated 3 Dec. 1790 named wife Charlotta and children:

David.
Jacob.
Eleazar.
Joshua.
William, a minor in 1790.
Rebekah.
Charlotta.
Abigail.
Samuel.
Daniel, a minor in 1790.

"My friend" Eleazar Gidney named as an executor.

Another DANIEL GIDNEY family is found in the LDS Ancestral File. This Daniel (b. c. 1782) m. Sarah Wood & had a son GEORGE W. GIDNEY, b. 10 Sept. 1808 in Orange Co. GEORGE m. Caroline C. Tyler of Branford, CT in 1838 & he d. 23 Aug. 1879 in CT. Their dau. Nancy Minnie was b. in Newburgh in 1851 & m. Stephen Strong.

A JOSEPH GIDNEY purchased land in Newburgh Tract in 1760 that was settled by his sons: Joseph, Daniel, David & Eleazer; it was for him that Gidneytown was named.

**GILLESPIE, WILLIAM H.**                          H-846
farmer of Walden.

DAVID GILLESPIE[1] left Scotland with his son Samuel and they were the first settlers of Gatehouse Patent, near Pine Bush, Orange County before the Revolutionary War. His son SAMUEL[2] had son ABRAHAM[3], who had son RENWICK GILLESPIE[4] who m. Caroline Augusta Smith, b. Town of Montgomery. She d. 1904 at age 80. Renwick & Caroline were the parents of:
  WILLIAM H. GILLESPIE[5], b. 28 May 1855, now dec'd., survived by wife and 3 children.

**GILLIES, JACOB** [P]                          A-368e
of Newburgh.

JACOB GILLIES[1], early farmer of Newburgh, b. 20 April 1790; m. Martha, d/o James Waring of Newburgh, b. 30 Dec. 1796. Children:
1816, June 13, John W., res. Haverstraw.
1818, June 1, **JACOB**.
1820, Dec. 10, Wright, head of spice firm of NY, Wright Gillies & Bros.
1824, Feb. 2, Sarah W., m. Clarkson Gerow of Plattekill, Ulster Co.
1826, June 16, Martha m. David Marston.
1829, April 7, James, in spice business at NY.
1834, May 30, Charles Wesley; d. infancy.

JACOB GILLIES[2], b. on father's farm, Town of Newburgh; farmer; 22 May 1844, m. Phebe, d/o Isaac & Sabina Griggs

---

of Newburgh. Manufactured brick on old Smith proper Balmville; purchased Gardner brickyard; member Fostert ME Church. He d. 12 Feb. 1881. Had 14 children survived to adulthood:

James, in mercantile business in Newburgh.
Jacob.
Milton.
John.
Wright, in mercantile business in Newburgh.
Homer.
Ann.
Frank.
Frederick.
Martha.

---

**GLASS FAMILY**                          ⸀

The Glass family of White Lake (then Sullivan Co.), set there in early 17th century; 1806 their small son James, then 10, got lost in the woods for 10 days. His story found her⸀

---

**GOFF, JOHN** [P]                          A-
of Monroe.

Family originally from Ireland, to L.I. MICHAEL GOFF[1] Elizabeth ---, and had:
1800, Oct. 19, **JOHN**.

JOHN GOFF[2], farmer; m. 5 April 1821, Phebe, d/o Gilbei Hannah Turner. They removed to NY City where JO engaged in milk business; returned to Monroe after 14 ye He d. in Monroe, 13 Feb. 1881; she d. 24 Dec. 1878.

---

**GOLDSMITH, ALDEN** [P]                  A-648, U2-
of Blooming-Grove.                          C-15, 25, 80, 87,
**GOALDSMITH, THOMAS**              U2-26-7
of Montgomery.

THOMAS GOLDSMITH[1], one of 5 brothers to L.I. e 1700's; to Orange Co. & in 1735 took up land wl Washingtonville is now. THOMAS' will, dated 24 I 1743, names his wife as Abigail Booth (d/o Charle Abigail (Mapham) Booth) & her brother Charles as exe tors. His children:
ELISHA.
Joshua.
Richard.
THOMAS.
Abigail.

ELISHA GOLDSMITH[2], s/o Thomas[1], m. Sarah Dunnin Orange Co., 31 March 1785, at Goshen. An Elisha G smith, according to Goshen church records, d. 18 Feb. 1{ aged 79, old age. They had:
1788, July 18, HENRY.
John.

Elisha. Goshen church records show the death of an Elisha Goldsmith at age 11 from wound by scythe on 8 Aug. 1822.
Charles.
Matilda m. Peter Earle.
Sally Ann m. Peter Larary.
Dicia m. James Kelso.

HENRY GOLDSMITH[3], s/o Elisha[2], b. Blooming-Grove, farmer; m. (1st) Fayetta, d/o Peter Moore of Blooming-Grove 1815, she d. 2 Dec. 1835; m. (2d) Sarah Pelton. Children:
Adaline, res. on homestead.
Ann Eliza m. (1st) Edwin Hulse; (2d) Capt. Thomas N. Hulse of Blooming-Grove.
1820, Dec. 4, ALDEN.
Henry M., res. in the west.
Walter, res. IA.
Mary L.; d. young.
Charles H.; d. age 40.

ALDEN GOLDSMITH[4], s/o Henry[3], res. homestead, farmer & horse breeder; public service; 29 Oct. 1846, m. Catherine Cornell, d/o James & Anna Townsend of Hamptonburgh, and had:
James H.
Annie S.
John Alden.

THOMAS GO[A]LDSMITH[2], s/o Thomas[1], in his will dated 12 Sept. 1786 names his wife Catharine & children:
Joshua.
Leah.
Sarah.
Stephen.
John.
David.
Thomas.
Charles.
Phebe.
Mary.
Abigail.
Hannah Leagh.

Will proved 29 Jan. 1788 by James Barkley Jr. farmer of Montgomery, Samuel Givens & James Smith.
THOMAS GOLDSMITH m. Catharine Gale 2 Aug. 1810, at Goshen. Also give the bapt. of Elisah, child of Joshua & Deborah Goldsmith, 16 Sept. 1814.

GOTT, JOSEPH W. [P]          A-155-6, STJ-23, 25, 27
atty.

JOSEPH W. GOTT, s/o Storey Gott of Austerlitz, Columbia Co., NY, was b. 25 May 1814 in Austerlitz & raised in Red Rock, Columbia Co. 1837 to Goshen, principal of Farmer's Hall Academy; atty. (1842); d. 6 Jan. 1869. Member St. James Protestant Episcopal Church. 27 Jan. 1847 m. Charlotte Van Duzer, d/o Issac R. now dec'd. Children:

Bapt. 1848, Sept. 14, Reeve Vanduzer.
Bapt. 1851, May 29, Annie.
Bapt. 1853, Sept. 30, "infant."
Joseph W., Goshen atty.

GRAHAM, JAMES G.          156-7

JAMES G. GRAHAM, b. Shawangunk, Ulster Co., Oct. 1821; atty. of Ulster Co., political career; to Newburgh 1666. M. (1st) Mary E., d/o George G. Schofield of Walden; (2d) Margaret J., d/o Israel Knapp of Walden.

GREEN FAMILY OF MT. HOPE
          A-506, H-327, C-13, 57, 135, U2-80

Brothers, ISRAEL[1] & DANIEL GREEN came to NY. ISRAEL settled early on site of Middletown; DANIEL settled near Fitchville. ISRAEL's children:
Jonathan.
Orange, settled in MI. Orange was dismissed from the church at Goshen as of 5 Aug. 1815. He was listed as from Neeleytown. But a 17 Jan. 1822 entry gives Emeline & Mehitable, children of Orange Green & Mary his wife being baptized on that date.
NATHANIEL.
Dau.

NATHANIEL GREEN[2], s/o Israel[1], res. Otisville and later Sullivan Co.; had son Osmer B., proprietor of the hotel at Otisville.

ISRAEL GREEN'S[1] will, dated 8 Oct. 1791, names him as of Wall Kill and names wife Sarah and 3 sons listed above. Executors: Stephen Preston of Wall Kill, silversmith; Samuel Wickham & Abel Woodhull.

In Goshen church records is a m. of Israel Green & Tabithy Owen, 11 Dec. 1781.

GREGORY, NOAH [P]          A-562c, C-80, 38, 40, 42, 78
of Goshen.

The Gregory ancestors were of Scotch & French extraction. NOAH's[2] paternal grandfather an early settler of Orange Co.

SAMUEL GREGORY[1], b. Chester, Orange Co., 1763, res. Chester (then Town of Monroe), where he owned 500 acres. He m. Mary Hunter, who d. 17 Feb. 1821, age 46 years, 8 months. Gregory d. 18 Nov. 1827; both bur. in old grave-yard near Monroe. Their children, only 4 surviving in 1881:
Katy m. Joseph Stevens.
Benjamin.
Hiram.
1803, Oct. 7, NOAH.
Sylvester.
James.
Hannah m. Benjamin Van Duzer.

Elmer.
George.
John.

NOAH GREGORY[2], s/o Samuel, b. on homestead in Town of
Monroe; 1828 to Goshen, farmer; m. 23 March 1826, Sally
Maria, d/o STEPHEN & Abigail (Goldsmith) SMITH [see
below]; b. 23 May 1799; d. 7 Dec. 1879. Children:
Mary Jane, m. in Goshen 21 Jan. 1851, Joseph D. Stage of
Wallkill; now widowed. She is noted in Goshen church
records as removed as of Feb. 1850.
Stephen S.
Noah.
Goldsmith.
Harvey.
Sarah A. m. Louis Goldsmith of Walkill, 13 March 1862, at
Goshen.
1837, Aug. 11, John H., served in Civil War; d. 1863.
William H.; d. infancy.
1842, Nov. 9, Catherine E., m. Hiram T. Stage at Goshen 21
Jan. 1864; d. 1 Jan. 1880.
George Elmer.

SMITH, STEPHEN, b. 27 Feb. 1752, d. 25 July 1803; m.
ABIGAIL GOLDSMITH, b. 8 May 1757, d. 23 Dec. 1826;
had 7 children, their dau. Sally Maria m. NOAH GREGO-
RY.[2]

———

GRIER, MAJ. GEORGE M. [P]                    A-152, C-147

Scotch family, fled to Northern Ireland during persecution of
Presbyterians in Scotland. REV. --- GRIER[1], Presbyterian
minister of Wilmington, DE & Orange Co., NY had son:
REV. THOMAS GRIER[2], Presbyterian minister of Lancaster,
PA, settled as pastor Westtown, Orange Co., 1808; d. c.
1836, Cold Spring, Putnam Co., NY. His children [wife not
named]:
William.
1802, Sept. 27, GEORGE M.
Smith, merchant of Chambersburg, PA; d. c. 1870.
Hon. Thomas Evans, merchant at Pittston, PA, state legislator.
Washington Decatur, physician; d. KY.
Jane m. John Wallace of Milford, PA.
John D., merchant & connected with PA RR.

GEORGE M. GRIER[3], b. Lancaster Co., PA; age 16 settled in
Orange Co. with parents; atty., surrogate of Orange Co.
(1840). Major in old state militia, farm manager, bank
director, member of Presbyterian Church of Goshen; d. 20
Dec. 1878. He m. Frances, d/o FREEGIFT & Elizabeth
(Sweezy) TUTHILL of Goshen [see below], 7 Aug. 1833.
Frances b. 16 Jan. 1804; d. 7 Feb. 1860. Their surviving
children:
George, merchant at Goshen.
Thomas Evans, merchant at Goshen.
Mary Elizabeth.
Frances Tuthill.

All children and their mother, bapt. at Goshen 3 Aug. 1850.

JOHN TUTHILL[1], b. 16 July 1635, progenitor of family, from
England to L.I. His son JOHN[2] had son:
1698, Aug. 8, FREIGHT[3], b. L.I.; m. Abigail Goldsmith and had
3 sons & 1 dau.; to Orange Co. 1733. His son JOSHUA[4],
had:
FREIGHT TUTHILL[5], merchant of Goshen, m. Elizabeth
Sweezy and had Frances (Mrs. GEORGE M. GRIER).

Frances' mother a niece of late Judge Samuel S. Steward &
cousin of Hon. William H. Seward.

———

GRIFFITH FAMILY                              A-362-3

ROBERT GRIFFITH[1], sea captain b. Wales, m. Miss --- Peck,
d/o the "gentleman after whom 'Peck's Slip' was named."
They had:
Crissy m. Cadwallader Colden, res. Coldenham.
Robert[2], settled Orange Co. c. 1795; m. (1) Rebecca Barnes &
had 6 children, one was:
Martha[3], m. Jason W. Rogers, 1840. [See Hon. George Clark
Family.]

———

GULCH, MELCHIOR                              TN-263, CN-10

MELCHIOR GULCH, who changed his name to GILLIS,
was a carpenter from the Palatinate & settled in Newburgh on
land near Middlehope. He appears in the Newburgh Directory
in 1709 on the tax rolls of the town in 1729. At the time of his
emigration to American he was age 39 & his wife, Anna
Catharine ---, was age 43. They had a dau.:
MARGARET GULCH/GILLIS, who was aged 12 at
emigration & she m. William Ward & res. in Newburgh in 1750,
with son Heinrich Ward.
They also had a son, Heinrich, who was aged 10 years on
emigration.

———

GUMAER FAMILY OF DEERPARK          A-705, T-17-18

PETER E. GUMAER/GUIMAR[1], from France to either Holland
or England & then to MD. He finally settled in Minisink
Valley in NY with Jacob Codebec. PETER m. Esther
Hasbrouck of Kingston and had:
Hannah m. James Swartwout.
Esther m. Samuel Swartwout.
Dau. m. --- DuBois.
Rache.
PETER.

PETER GUMAER[2], s/o Peter[1] the pioneer, m. Charity DeWitt
and had:
Peter.
EZEKIEL.

EZEKIEL GUMAER[3], s/o Peter[2] & Charity, had son:
PETER E. GUMAER[4], author, teacher, farmer & surveyor, and

had:
Peter L.
Ezekiel.
Andrew Jackson.
Jacob. Could be the Jacob found in the LDS Anc. file who m. Huldah Decker, he b. 1740, she b. 1744.

## HADDEN, JOSEPH B.        W-92

JOSEPH was b. on the homestead farm, 1 mile west of the old Berea Church; cattleman. He d. 15 Feb. 1906 & buried in the family lot at Goodwill Cemetery.

## HADDEN, SAMUEL [P]        H-852
of Chester.

SAMUEL is of French Huguenot descent & was b. Rockland Co., NY 19 March 1828. His father [not named] d. of cholera in 1832. His mother m. (2d) Edward Bellamy & they removed to Florida, Orange Co. in 1839; she d. in her 81st year. His mother had 2 sons and 2 daughters by her first husband & one son and a daughter by her second; all are dead excepting SAMUEL and John.

At age 18 SAMUEL removed to Vail's Gate, Orange Co. to learn trade of carriage maker; 1852 to Sugar Loaf with James Hallock & Sons; 1854 to Chester Depot. Member of the Presbyterian Church; m. Eliza Jane McGill of Cornwall 7 May 1851; she d. 10 March 1903. Children:
Alice J.
Clara, d. age 30.
Eugene.

## HALBERT, JESSE        H-852-3
dairy farmer of Warwick.

EZRA HALBERT[1] (d. 1873) m. Phila Ann --- (d. 1844). They had six children, 2 surviving:
1842, Aug. 20, JESSE.
Albert Ruggles.

JESSE HALBERT[2], b. on farm near Lake, Orange Co., m. Emily Bates of Morristown, NJ 29 May 1878 and had:
1879, May 15, Ezra.
1881, July 25, Clarence.
1883, Jan. 13, Alfred; d. 11 Jan 1900.

## HALL, CHARLES H.        H-853
physician of Monroe.

DR. HALL's family has been in Orange Co. since before the Rev. His great-grandfather, JOHN HALL, was a Rev. soldier, and supposed a son of Lyman Hall, one of the signers of the Declaration of Independence. Stephen Hall Sr. of Warwick, brother of John, also served in the Rev. War. Both were pensiners & both were born in Peekskill, NY.

CHARLES is the s/o Alva Hall & Dermeda Hunter and was b. in Warwick, Orange Co. in 1861. He m. Tillie J. Mitchell of NY and they have 3 daughters. He has practiced medicine in Monroe since 1891.

One Hall line of descent is given as follows [no connection to above given]: Christopher Hall[1] m. Sarah --- of Groton, MA and had Christopher Hall[2] who m. Mary Homer. They had Caleb Hall[3], b. Attleboro, MA 1700, d. Peekskill 1791, m. Jane Daggart. Caleb & Jane had Reuben Hall[4], b. Attleboro 1729/30, m. Sarah Gray (?) and had Stephen[5].

## HALLIDAY, GEORGE E.        H-852
of Newburgh.

GEORGE E. HALLIDAY, b. Dutchess Co. 1874; res. in Newburgh since infancy. In business with J. M. Stoutenburgh & Sol. Cohen, shoe firm. 1907 m. Marion, d/o the late John Gail Borden of Borden Condensed Milk Co.

## HALLOCK FAMILY OF WAWAYANDA        A-677, C-45

JOHN HALLOCK[1] from England before the Rev. War, settled at Mattatuck, L.I.; served in Rev. & captured by the British. After war to Oxford, Orange Co., His brother DANIEL[1] served as his substitute in 1777. 1783 purchased land south of present village of Ridgebury. He has a son:
JOHN JR.[2], held public office in old Town of Minisink & had son:
DR. DEWITT C. HALLOCK[3], Town clerk of Minisink & later supervisor of Wawayanda, (1852-53) surveyor & physician. Was best violinist in the state. Goshen church records show the m. of DeWitt C. Hallock of Port Jervis to Jennie Lateer of Wantage, NJ 29 May 1875.

## HALLOCK, WILLIAM H. [P]        W-88

WILLIAM H. HALLOCK, b. Highland Mills in 1842; 1866 removed to Washingtonville; cattle dealer & milk producer. He has a son, Edward N.

## HALSTEAD FAMILY OF GOSHEN        A-524, C-104

RICHARD HALSTEAD[1], early settler of Goshen, later to what is now Wawayonda. His son:
MICHAEL HALSTEAD[2], d. 1830, age 73, and had:
Michael J., had 1 dau. Mrs. Charles T. Jackson.
Jesse.
Aaron.
Mrs. William Hemingway.
Mrs. Silus Hemingway.
Mrs. Alma Bailey.

Two daus. of Michael Halstead were bapt. at Goshen Church: Margaret, b. 22 Jan. 1775 & Esther, b. 15 Jan. 1779.

JOSEPH HALSTEAD[1], brother of RICHARD[1] above, also to Orange Co. at the same time. He had no children, but adopted a son.

_____

**HAND, CHARLES E.**                                    H-853-4
carpenter & farmer

EDWARD S. HAND[1] m. Charity Mailler. He was survived by his wife & 3 children, one son was:
**CHARLES E. HAND[2]**, for many years near Mountainville, Orange Co., b. town of Cornwall 1852; d. suddenly 20 Feb. 1908; m. Emma C. Smith and located in town of Woodbury.

**HANFORD, DAVID**                                    A-167-8, C-26
of Middletown.

**DAVID HANFORD**, b. 16 July 1786, Westport, Fairfield Co., CT; d. 13 Oct. 1844. 1810 to Middletown, NY; member of Presbyterian church; m. 1812, Margaret, d/o Capt. Daniel Bailey, one of the old settlers of Phillipsburgh, Orange Co. 11 June 1812, at Goshen. Surviving children:
John B., merchant of Middletown.
Caroline m. Charles Young, farmer of Hamptonburgh.

**HARER, WILLIAM**                                    H-854
of Highland Falls.

WILLIAM HARER[1] m. Miss --- Farrell of Highland Falls and had:
1852, **WILLIAM HARER[2]**, who ran billard, pool, bowling & cigar establishment in Highland Falls, which he purchased in 1906 from his uncle, Edward F. Farrell.

**HARRISON, JAMES**                                    H-854
of Newburgh.

JOSHUA HARRISON[1] m. Mary A. Emsley, both b. England, and had:
1840, **JAMES HARRISON[2]**, b. Yorkshire, England; d. 13 June 1907. At age 6 with parents to Newburgh. He m. (1st) Miss --- Lull who d. 1898; (2d) Mrs. Caroline A. Foreman (nee Ely), NY school principal. They had F. J. & James Jr.. JAMES[2] member of Harrison & Gore, silk manufactures. Mr. Gore is Mr. HARRISON's son-in-law. Members of the Methodist-Episcopal Church.

**HART, WILLIAM C.**                                    H-854-5
farmer of East Walden.

**WILLIAM C. HART**, b. town of Montgomery 18 Dec. 1843, the only child of Henry C. Hart & Hannah Jane Overheiser. To East Walden as a child, where he has since resided on the farm "Sycamore Place." 18 Nov. 1869 he m. Elizabeth Mould, youngest d/o the late Hamilton Morrison [Mould?] and had:
Henry Melvin, educator at Pueblo, CO; Butte, MT & Spokane, WA.

Robert Clarence, farmer.

Family were members of the First Reformed Church at Walden.

_____

**HASBROUCK, ABRAHAM** U1-83-9, 166-9, LDS Anc. File
**HASBROUCK, JOHN WHITBECK [P]** A-196b-c, TN-278
**HASBROUCK, GEN. HENRY C.**                           H-855
**HASBROUCK, DR. LYDIA SAYER [P]** A-196, GFM-13
newspaper editor & woman's rights advocate.
**HASBROUCK, WILLIAM C.** A-154, AA6-63-4, 142-3

This family granted nobility in the 14th century in France by Charles V.
ABRAHAM HASBROUCK[1] (Hasbrouck/Hasbroucq/Hasbroque/ Ashbrouck/Von Asbroeck) & brother Jean (John), b. near Calais, France, Wallons from Northern France to Manheim not long before the revocation of the edict of Nantes. Abraham b. c. 1649. Their father, Jean, b. c. 1616, Calais, France (wife Esther ---), had removed with 2 sons & 1 dau. into Germany. In 1673 JEAN (John) to America [see below]; Abraham followed him [1675], leaving his father & a sister who had m. one Pierre Hayaar. ABRAHAM was a follower of Peter Waldus & went from the Palatinate, landed at Boston, traveled to NY & settled in Esopus (Kingston), NY in July 1675, one of 12 New Paltz patentees & was one of a group that founded Walloon Protestant Church. ABRA-HAM m. 17 Nov. 1675, at Hurley, Mary Dego (Duyou/ Deyo/Duyon), d/o Christian Duyou (c. 1595-1687, New Paltz, NY) & wife Jeanne Verbeau/Wibau. Mary b. 1653, Mutterstadt, Rhineland, Germany. They left many desc. in Ulster Co. ABRAHAM d. 7 March 1717 of an apoplectic fit at New Paltz, Ulster Co.; Maria (Mary) d. 27 March 1741, aged 88. Their surviving children, all b. New Paltz, Ulster Co.:
1680, May 12, Rachel B., christened at New Paltz, m. Louis DuBois.
1682, Oct. 9, Anna.
Bapt. [b.] 1684, Oct. 23 [28], JOSEPH.
1686, SOLONION. [SOLOMON/ZOLOMON]
1691, Oct. 15, Jonas.
1692, June 23, DANIEL.
1696, May 31, BENJAMIN.

JOSEPH HASBROUCK[2], s/o Abraham[1], b. New Paltz, d. Guilford 28 Jan. 1723/4, aged 40 years, 3 months; m. Elsie Schoonmaker 27 [2] Oct. 1705 [6]. Elsie was bapt. 13 [12] Dec. 1685, d/o Jochem & Petronella (Sleght) Schoonmaker. Schoonmaker family to America from Hamburg, Germany in the employ of the Dutch West India Co. Elsie d. 27 July 1674, aged 78 years, 8 months, 3 days. Political servant in Ulster Co. & was described as "very affable & agreeable in company, eloquet in speech, spoke French-Dutch & very tolerable English. He was of middle stature, of fine physiog-nomy, black curled hair, fair skin, with a bloozing color, dark blue eyes." Their children:
1722, April 12, JONATHAN.

BENJAMIN.
ABRAHAM.

JONATHAN HASBROUCK³, s/o Joseph², d. 31 July 1780; m. May [June] 1751, Tryntje (Catharine), d/o Cornelius Dubois. He removed to Newburgh, where he appears in the town directory for 1750, & purchased the property now known as Washington's Head Quarters in 1753. Held local political offices & military commissions (1775). Resigned his commission in 1778 due to ill health with rank of Col. "His death proceeded from an aggravated form of gravel. He is described as a "pious worthy man, paid a good deal of reverence in hearing & reading the word of God. Good natured . . . with a great deal of forbearance . . . and knowing in common affairs of life. He was about 6'4" tall, well shaped & proportioned of body, good features, full visage of fact, but brown of complexion, dark blue eyes, black hair, with a slight curl . . . He died on Monday morning & was buried on Tuesday in the burying place on his own land, between his house & the North River, lying along side two of his sons who lay buried in the same ground." Surviving children:
Cornelius, went to Canada.
1761, Sept. 23, ISAAC. ["The descs. of Col. Hasbrouck now residing in Newburgh are through his son Isaac."]
Jonathan, d. unm.
Rachel, m. Daniel Hasbrouck, s/o Abraham³. Buried at the German Reformed Cemetery, Montgomery: Daniel Hasbrouck, d. 24 Oct. 1837, aged 77 years, 7 months, 16 days & his wife Rachel, d. 2 July 1846, aged 89 years, 2 months, 15 days. 1696, May 31, Benjamin.
Mary.

ISAAC HASBROUCK⁴, s/o Jonathan³, d. 21 Aug. 1806. He m. in 1781, Hannah Birdsall, who d. 27 Dec. 1807, aged 45 years. They had:
Jonathan, occupied the Head Quarters homestead many years.
Sarah, m. Walter Case.
Israel, d. unm.
Rachel, d. unm.
Eli, has been twice married & has Charles H., Eli Jr. & other children.
Mary.

BENJAMIN HASBROUCK³, s/o Joseph ², m. Elidia Schoonmaker and had:
Benjamin.
CORNELIUS.
Joseph.

CORNELIUS HASBROUCK⁴, s/o Benjamin³, m. Janet Kelso in 1799, and had:
1800, April 23, WILLIAM C.
Benjamin C.
Margaret, m. Capt. Eli Perry.

WILLIAM C. HASBROUCK⁵, s/o Cornelius ⁴, m. Mary E. Roe, d/o William, 28 June 1831; d. 1780, Nov. After grad. Union

College removed to Franklin, TN, principal. of academy founded by Bishop Otey. Principal at Farmer's Hall Academy, Goshen (1822); atty. (1826), assemblyman (1847). His children:
1839, Oct. 26, HENRY C.
William H., atty.
Roe.
Maria H.
Emily A.
Blandina.

HENRY C. HASBROUCK⁶, s/o William C.⁵ b. Newburgh; grad. West Point May 1861; served with 4th & 5th US Artillery & retired Jan. 1903; commandant of cadets US Military Academy at West Point; m. Laetitia Viele Warren 26 Oct. 1882 & res. Newburgh.

ABRAHAM HASBROUCK³, s/o JOSEPH² was b. at Guilford, Ulster Co., 21 Aug. 1707. He m. 5 July 1738[9], Catharine Bruyn, b. 24 June 1720, d/o Jacobus & Trynitje (Schoonmaker) Bruyn. She was of Norwegian extraction--her grandfather on her father's side having been a native of Norway & settled in Esopus while the Province was in the possession of the Dutch. ABRAHAM d. 10 Nov. 1791, at Kingston, NY. His will dated 5 Sept. 1785. Catharine d. 10 Aug. 1793. He removed to Kingston in 1735, where he commenced mercantile business. Sept. 1751 he petitioned for a patent of 2,000 acres in Evan's vacant patent, near New Paltz patent, which was granted in 1752. He was a member of the Colonial Assembly from 1739 to 1745, 1748 to 1750, 1750 to 1778; was commissioned Col. of the Ulster militia in 1757 . . . took an active part in the movements of the patriots of the Rev. Their children:
Bapt. 1740, April 4, Catherina, d. 5 Dec. 1747.
Bapt. 1742, Feb. 28, Elsie, m. 9 Nov. 1770, Abram, s/o Abram Salisbury & Rachel Ten Broeck, b. 5 Dec. 1744, d. 22 Feb. 1808; have one son, Abraham.
Bapt. 1744, March 4, Joseph, m. 25 March 1773, Elisabeth Bevier, dec. of Lawrence Bevier, one of the patentees of New Paltz. They had son Joseph, b. 25 May 1782, d. 1853, m. Jane Hasbrouck 19 Oct. 1809.
1746, Jan. 12, Geertruyd, d. 29 July 1746.
1747, Nov. 1, Geertruyd, d. 4 Dec. 1747.
1749, Jan. 15, Catherine, m. 9 Nov. 1770, Abraham Hoogteling have son Abraham.
1751, July 7, Maria, m. 25 Jan. 1778, David Bevier; had Jacobus, Abraham, Daniel, Jonathan & Joseph.
Bapt. 1753, Sept. 28, Jacobus, m. 10 April 1783, Maria DeWitt, d/o Charles.
Bapt. 1756, Feb. 8, Abraham, d. 10 June 1796, unm.
Bapt. 1758, Jan. 29, Daniel, d. 6 March 1759.
Bapt. 1760, March 9, Daniel, m. 1 June 1786, Rachel, d/o Col. Jonathan Hasbrouck of Newburgh.
Bapt. 1763, Nov. 6, Jonathan, m. 1 Oct. 1786, Catharine Wynkoop, b. 24 Oct. 1763, d/o Cornelius C. & Maria Catherine (Ruhl) Wynkoop.

SOLOMON HASBROUCK², s/o Abraham ¹, m. Sara Wagena

[Zara Jacobsz Van Wegening, b. 1 Dec. 1701, Wagondale, Ulster, NY] & had:

1722, Abraham, m. Rachel Sleight.
1725, Jacobus.
1727, Jan. 1, Jacobus, m. Dievertje Van Wagenen.
1730, Jan (John). m. Rachel Van Wageren 24 Dec. 1763. His will, dated 28 Dec. 1806, in Ulster Co., identifies him as of New Paltz. It it he names children: John E.; William Jr.; Philip; Andries; Polly & Rachel. He also names his "half brother Philip Schoonmaker" & good friends Philip Eltinge & Elias Ean.
1732, Daniel, m. Wyntje Freer.
1735, Symon.
1738, Petrus, m. Sarah Bevier.
1740, May 18, ELIAS.

ELIAS HASBROUCK[3] of Kingston, d. at Woodstock 8 Oct. 1791, served in Rev. war, m. Elizabeth Sleight, b. 9 Sept. 1737, d. 10 April 1807. They had:

1763, Oct. 20, Salomon.
1764, Oct. 8, Elisabeth, m. Abraham W. Van Gaasbeek.
1765, Dec. 31, Daniel.
1766, Dec. 18, Elias, m. Sally Carl.
1769, July 7, John Elias, m. Elizabeth Post.
1771, March 16, Sara, m. Benjamin Merkle.
1773, July 28, Daniel Elias, m. (1) Phebe Griffin; m. (2) Phoebe Salisbury.
1776, Richard Montgomery, m. Maria Jonson.
1780, July 19, Petrus Elias, m. Phoebe Freeman.

DANIEL HASBROUCK[2], s/o Abraham[1], m. Wyntje Deyo 2 April 1734, & she d. 30 Oct. 1787, aged 79 years, 11 months; Daniel d. 25 Jan. 1759. U-2-63-4 documents his will & his children are given in this source & in the LDS Anc. File:

1735, Maria.
1736, Jonas.
1739, April 29, JOSAPHAT.
1740, David.
1742, Rachel.
1746, Isaiah.
1748, Benjamin.
1749, Zacharias.

JOSAPHAT HASBROUCK[3], s/o Daniel[2], in his will dated 28 April 1811 & filed in Ulster Co., names wife Cornelia (nee DuBois, d/o Simon) & children:

Andries, m. Elisabeth Hasbrouck.
Wyntye, m. Jonas Freer.
Rachel, m. William Hasbrouck.
Daniel J.
Simon.
Zackariah.

BENJAMIN HASBROUCK[2], s/o Abraham[1], m. Jannetje De-Lange, bapt. 27 Feb. 1715, Kingston, Ulster Co., NY. They had:

c. 1722, Daniel.

c. 1724, Francis.
c. 1726, Benjamin.
c. 1728, Jacob.
c. 1730, Mary.
c. 1732, Heyltje.

CAPT. ELIAS HASBROUCK[4], soldier of the Rev. under Gen. Montgomery, was a 4th generation desc. of Abraham[1]. He res. in Kingston and had:

RICHARD MONTGOMERY HASBROUCK[5], d. age 84; m. Mary Johnson, 'nearly related to Vanderbuilt family.' They had 10 children, among them.

JOHN W. (9th child).

JOHN W. HASBROUCK[6] b. Woodstock, with father's family from Woodstock to Kingston c. 1834. Clerk, bookkeeper, res. NY, back to Kingston 1845 as journalist; 1846 purchased *Sullivan Whig* at Bloomingburgh, Ulster Co., supervisor of schools for Mamakating & postmaster at Bloomingburgh; 1851 to Middletown & published *Whig Press*; 1855 added *Hardwareman's Newspaper* & *Liberal Sentinal*. 27 July 1856, m. DR. LYDIA SAYER. Children:

Daisy; dec'd.
Sayer.
Burt.

DR. LYDIA (SAYER) HASBROUCK is the wife of John W. Hasbrouck[6]. She was b. 20 Dec. 1827, Town of Warwick, Orange Co., d/o Benjamin Sayer & Rebecca Foshee, d/o Cornelius Foshee & Elizabeth Cole. Cornelius Foshee came from France to America c. 1700; Elizabeth Cole's family from Holland to America 1625. DR. LYDIA was an advocate & wearer of the new "Camille costume, or Turkish dress known as 'Bloomer Dress.'"

JEAN HASBROUCK[1], brother of Abraham[1], came from Calais, France in 1673 with wife Anna Doyan (Deyo), and had:

Maria [Mary], bapt. Manheim, Germany, m. at Kingston, NY 1 June 1683, Isaac, s/o Louis & Catharine (Blanshan) Du Bois.
Hester, b. Manheim, m. Kingston 18 April 1692, Pierre Guimard, b. at Moise, Saintonge, France, s/o Pierre & Anne (Damour) Guimard.
Bapt. 1678, March 31 (Kingston), Abraham.
Bapt. 1685, April 4 (New Paltz), Elisabeth, m. at Kingston 2 June 1713, Louis Bevier.
Bapt. 1688, April 15 (New Paltz), Jacob, m. at Kingston 14 Dec. 1717, Esther Bevier.

JEAN[1] made out his will 26 Aug. 1712, at New Paltz, Ulster Co. It it he refers a son Isaac as dec'd., and says "if my son Abraham, who removed from this Province, should be alive and return here," he is to receive a good horse for his birth-right & the just half of all his whole real estate. He also refers to his dau. Hester as dec'd. & names her only son as Peter Guymard, under the age of 21.

———

## HASBROUCK, JONATHAN
N-84

In 1753 **JONATHAN HASBROUCK**[1], grandfather of the present Jonathan Hasbrouck, Esq.[3], who built the old stone Hasbrouck House in 1750, became owner of Lot No. 1 and 150 acres of No. 2, on the German Patent (Town of Newburgh). He erected a grist mill on the Western portion of the purchase that took in Quassaick (now Chambers') Creek. The oldest mill in this part of the country. These lands were devised by **JONATHAN** to his son Cornelius[2] & later became the property of Gen. Nathaniel Dubois.

_____

## HASBROUCK, PHILLIP
H-855, W-89
retired, of Walden, NY

**JOSEPH HASBROUCK**[1], descended from a Ulster Co. Huguenot family who settled in New Paltz before 1677 [could be the Joseph s/o Abraham above who m. Elsie Schoonmaker], m. Sarah LeFever and had:

**PHILIP**[2], who was b. New Paltz, Ulster Co., 1 April 1860; farmer. In 1882 moved with his father to farm near Walden. Lumber, coal & feed business in Walden, Hasbrouck & Sloan. He m. Mary, d/o the late George Matthews.

_____

## HASTINGS, WILLIAM GEORGE
H-855-6

**JAMES HASTINGS**[1] m. Mary J. Brown & had:

**WILLIAM GEORGE HASTINGS**[2], b. Newburgh; d. Albany 28 June 1907; m. 1891, May E. Moore of Newburgh. He was deputy postmaster, private secretary to ex-Gov. Odell, member of Assembly (1904). **WILLIAM** & May had one dau., Mildred.

_____

## HATHAWAY FAMILY OF NEWBURGH
TN-313-14

**BENJAMIN HATHAWAY (HATHEWAY)**[1], from Scotland c. 1767 & settled at Morristown, NJ, where he died. His only son, **CLEMENS HATHAWAY**[2] to Newburgh, where he d. Sept. 1801, aged 56 years, 4 months & his wife Hannah also d. there 8 June 1809, aged 56 years, 10 months. Their children:

Ebenezer.

1771, Dec. 8, JOSIAH.

**JOSIAH HATHAWAY**[3], s/o Clemens[2], was a cabinet maker & in the coasting trade & owner of the ship _Republican_ with partner George Gardiner. Josiah m. 13 Aug. 1794, Mabel, a sister of Samuel O. Gregory who d. on a sail from NY 19 July 1811. Mabel d. at Morris Plains, NJ, 13 July 1811. Children of Josiah & Mabel:

Rhoda, d. in infancy

1801, April 1, Frederick A., m. Phebe Stackhouse & had Frederick A. & Stephen Sneden.

1802, Sept. 1, ODELL SAMUEL. [P]

**ODELL SAMUEL HATHAWAY**[4], s/o Josiah[3], b. at Newburgh, was orphaned at age 7 & was taken by his uncle, Seth

Gregory of Morristown, NJ. He later returned to Newburgh & clerked for Samuel G. Sneden. He m. Helen Maria, d/o Charles Birdsall, 24 Sept. 1827 & had:

Amelia, m. Nathaniel B. Hayt.

Harriet Ann.

Josiah Augustus.

William Mott.

Sarah Sneden.

Odell Sneden.

Charles C.

Hiram F.

Helen Maria.

Edward W.

_____

## HATHAWAY, REV. WARREN
H-856

**REV. WARREN HATHAWAY** is the son of Rev. Levi Hathaway & Rhoda Miller. He was ordained in CT & served in Lebanon CT, Fall River, Medway Greene Co. NY (until 1866) & Blooming Grove Congregational Church for 46 years. He m. (1st) Cornelia Day and had 5 children, all living. He m. (2d) Elizabeth H. Miller.

_____

## HAWKINS, IRA A.
H-856-7, C-29, 30, 62, 117, 119, 120, 122, 141

**ROBERT HAWKINS**[1] & wife Mary from England on ship _Elizabeth Ann_, Capt. Cooper Master, in 1635, settled in Charlestown, MA. They had:

8 Oct. 1763, MOSES.

**MOSES HAWKINS**[2], to Orange Co., NY; m. Phebe [Catharine] Harlow & settled in East Division Town of Goshen on farm now occupied by their grand-son, Frank J. Hawkins. Children:

1791, Dec. 18, Benjamin.

1796, Jan. 31, IRA.

Samuel. Could be the Samuel Hawkins who m. in Goshen, 15 Dec. 1824, Emeline Webb.

1794, Jan. 29, Mary, m. Joshua Howell.

1800, July 4, Gilbert.

**IRA HAWKINS**[3], s/o Moses[2], m. 17 May 1821, Hannah, d/o Gen. Abram & Esther (Rockwell) Vail. Settled on farm near Chester & res. 50 years. They had:

3 June 1822, JAMES.

Mary Vail.

Phebe.

Ira.

Moses.

All children bapt. at Goshen 4 Aug. 1832.

**JAMES HAWKINS**[4], eldest s/o Ira[3], m. (1st) Adaline Green, d/o John & Julia (Roe) Green in 1844; she d. 1865. In 1845 to Hamptonburgh, where he d. 1887. Member of the First Presbyterian Church of Hamptonburgh. They had:

William Green.

James R. V.

Iraeneus, d. in infancy.

Adaline Green, m. Alfred E. Ivers of Allendale, NJ.

Charles Francis.

M. Jennie, m. James L. Price of Hamptonburgh.

1864, Aug. 4, **IRA A.**

**JAMES**[4] m. (2d) 28 Oct. 1868, Emily A., d/o George W. & Hester A. (Sanford) Price, of Hamptonburgh. By his 2d wife James had:

George W. P.

Emma Antoinette, m. John Budd Gregory.

**IRA A. HAWKINS**[5] & brother George[5] came into possession of the family farm. **IRA** kept until 1894 when he sold out to his brother & purchased C. L. Morehouse farm near Warwick; farmer, insurance man, member Dutch Reformed Church. He m. 24 Oct. 1888, Anna, d/o Valentine & Hannah (Seaman) Seaman, of Blooming Grove, who were both lineal descendants of Capt. John Seaman. Their children:

1889, 1 Dec., Valentine Seaman; d. 30 Sept. 1894.

1892, 9 March, Charles Francis, settled at L.I. in 1892.

1894, 30 Dec., Ira Allen.

1896, 20 Nov., Harold James.

---

## HAWKINS, IRWIN E.                    H-857

**IRWIN HAWKINS**, b. & reared on homestead farm near Otisville; carpenter. He m. Harriet Smith, d/o Frank & Hannah (Bell) Smith, 19 Oct. 1892. Members Otisville Methodist Church.

---

## HAWKINS, PLINY E. [P]          W-90-1, LDS Anc. File

**PLINEY** was one of 6 children of Lewis Hawkins (1815-1833) & Mary E. Blake (1819-1896) & was b. 5 June 1848. Lewis Hawkins was the s/o Jonathan & Dorothy (Mills) Hawkins. Mary was d/o William (1794-1876) & Elizabeth (Jackson) (1798-1854) Blake. **PLINY** occupied a farm 1 mile southeast of Coldenham; farmer. Member Goodwill Presbyterian Church May 1868. There is a photo of **MR. HAWKINS** with nieces Edna Twamley & Agnes B. Hawkins. He went to ND in 1885 & farmed 6 years, during which time he was a member of the First Congregational Church of Inkster. He later returned to Orange Co.

---

## HAYES, UZAL T.                     H-857

**UZAL**, b. Bloomfield, NJ, 5 Feb. 1834; 1856 in leather business in Newark, NJ. He m. Caroline A. Morris of Bloomfield in 1860; she d. 3 July 1888. They had:

Harry M.

Thomas C.

Caroline.

Mabel.

---

## HAYNE, M.S., M.D. [P]              A-675-6
of Minisink.

**FREDERICK HAYNE**[1] from Germany as young man, settled in Wantage, NJ c. 1775; m. a d/o Peter Decker of Wantage & d. there. His son:

**PETER HAYNE**[2], b. 28 May 1760, Wantage, farmer; m. Martha Lewis of Baskinridge, NJ, 5 Aug. 1784, & d. on his farm there. Children:

Frederick.

Huldah m. James Evans.

1791, Oct. 29, BENJAMIN.

Lydia m. (1st) Jacob Wilson; (2d) Manuel Coykendall.

Alva.

Lewis.

Eliza m. Evi Martin, farmer of Minisink.

**BENJAMIN HAYNE**[3], s/o Peter[2], age 17 to Morristown NJ to learn saddlery & harness making trade. 1831 moved family to farm in Wantage, NJ; 1834 traveled in the west; 1838 back to Wantage & d. there 12 Nov. 1843. M. (1st) 1815, Milly, d/o Richard Whitaker, who d. 30 Aug. 1820, aged 25. By her he had:

1816, Jan. 23, **MARCUS S.**

Peter, res. Goshen.

Milly m. Henry B. Lee, res. Chemung Co.

**BENJAMIN**[3] m. (2d) Charlotte Whitaker, sister of his first wife, who d. 7 Dec. 1869, aged 65. Children of 2d wife:

Frances m. A. W. VanFleet of Unionville.

Lewis; dec'd.

Henry; dec'd.

Caroline m. O. W. Cooke of Passaic, NJ.

Jacob.

Martha m. J. B. Hendershot of Hamburgh, NJ.

**MARCUS S. HAYNE**[4], s/o Benjamin[3], b. Bloomerville, Sussex Co., NJ; grad. Geneva Medical College Jan. 1841 & settled at Westtown, NY; 1843 m. (1st) Amelia, d/o Samuel & Belinda (Dada) Van Fleet, of Westtown. They had 2 children, both d. in infancy. Amelia d. 30 Jan. 1848. In 1844 to Mt. Salem, Sussex Co., NY until 1846, to Unionville, NY. **MARCUS S.** m. (2d) 1849, Jane, d/o Josiah & Hannah (Adams) Decker. She d. 16 July 1856. Their children:

Albert B.; d. 12 Oct. 1876, age 26.

Anna M.; dec'd.

Marcus P., atty. of Tombstone, AZ.

**MARCUS S. HAYNE**[4] m. (3d) Eliza A., d/o Samuel & Jayne (Elston) Christie of Wantage, NJ & had one son:

S. Christie, res. at home in business with his father.

**MARCUS S.** member of Presbyterian church, a physician & also operates creamery.

---

## HAZARD, SAMUEL & NATHAN
A-214, U2-176

SAMUEL & NATHAN, brothers, settled & erected a mill & laid out the Town plot under the name of Orangeville, located on Ingoldsby Patent, Town of New Windsor.

SAMUEL HAZARD [not necessarily the Samuel above], designated as yeoman, late of New Windsor, dec'd. intestate in 1788 when administration of his estate was granted to Thomas Tredwell of Smithtown, Co. Suffolk, named as his brother-in-law. His widow is named as Mary.

## HAZEN, JOHN
H-857-8

JOHN HAZEN, b. Greenwood Lake, Orange Co., 18 March 1835, d. 19 Dec. 1907. Owner of the Hotel Boulevard at Greenwood Lake & prop. of the Windermere Hotel & of the Brandon House. He m. Sarah A. Merritt of Sloatsburg who d. in 1906. They had 4 children; 2 living:
Mary, m. John VanNess.
Daisy, m. William Wright.

## HEARD, JOHN J. [P]
A-558-9, C-45
of Goshen.

JOHN HEARD[1], emigrant from England in reign of Queen Anne, settled Woodbridge, NJ, and had:
WILLIAM.
Nathaniel, served as Gen. in Rev. War; also had 2 sons who served.
Phebe m. John Taylor of Amboy.
Sarah m. James Smith of Woodbridge.
Mary m. Cyrenius Van Mater of Middletown Point.

WILLIAM HEARD[2], s/o John[1], res. Woodbridge, and had:
John.
James.
Samuel
CAPT. PHINEAS.
William.
Delia.

CAPT. PHINEAS HEARD[3], s/o William[2], soldier of the Rev.; to Blooming-Grove, Orange Co., farmer; d. c. 1812. Several children by 1st m. [wife not named] including:
Charles, large cattle dealer of Hamptonburgh.
One child by 2d m. to Hester Board [see below]:
1807, July 5, JOHN J.

JOHN J. HEARD[4], b. on homestead in Blooming-Grove, s/o Capt. Phineas[3] & 2d wife Hester, farmer, member Presbyterian Church, public service; m. 20 Aug. 1833, Mary, d/o Isaac & Keturah (Reeve) Van Duzer of Cornwall, sister of the late Isaac R. Van Duzer, atty. of Goshen. Mary was b. 12 Aug. 1812. Children:
Isaac, atty. of St. Paul, MN.
Eliza A. F.

James B., merchant of Pittsburgh, PA.
Jennie m. Newton K. Delevan of Pittsburgh, PA, 8 May 1777.
Emma.
Julia W.
Catharine m. M. A. DuBois Staats, atty. of Goshen
Fanny Benton.

Three BOARD brothers, James, David & Joseph, from England, settled in Ringwood, NJ. The eldest, James, m. Ann Schuyler and their dau., Hester Board m. Capt. Phineas Heard.
After the death of Phineas, Hester removed to Goshen & took up residence with Anthony Dobbin, who m. her sister, Ann Board. The Board children were four sons & three daus. Hester d. 17 May 1857, age 92. Ann (Board) Dobbin d. 4 March 1857, age 90.

## HELME, MANUEL GONSALES
T-68

MANUEL G. HELME, of an early family of Mamakating. His grandson, Samuel Helm, wounded in the Battle of Minisink in 1779. This reference has the story of his adventures.

## HELME, ANSLEM [P]
A-648d, LDS Anc. File
of Blooming-Grove.

THOMAS HELME[1], b. c. 1665 m. Mary Mills & had:
ANSELEM HELME[2], b. c. 1697, of Setauket, Suffolk Co., NY & d. Orange Co. He m. Ruth Brewster, b. c. 1734 & had:
ANSELM HELME[3], b. Setauket, L.I. 8 July 1750, sailor, j.p., 1776 settled Blooming-Grove on farm & m. Phoebe, d/o Sylvanus White of Blooming-Grove, 3 Feb. 1778. Phoebe d. 1833; Anselm d. 9 Dec. 1824. Their children:
1782, April 14, BREWSTER.
1785, Nathan W.
1787, Joseph W.
1789, Ruth m. Samuel Denniston.
1791, Eunice m. Samuel Strong.
1793, Phoebe m. Joseph Decker.
1795, Mary m. Apollos Halsey.
1797, Deborah m. Thomas Moffat.

BREWSTER HELME[4], s/o Anselm[3], b. Blooming-Grove, farmer; m. 1807, Experience, d/o Samuel Strong of Blooming-Grove, and had:
Elizabeth, m. William H. Thompson of Blooming-Grove; dec'd.
1817, Jan. 6, ANSELM.

ANSELM HELME[5], s/o Brewster[4], b. on homestead, attended Congregational Church at Blooming-Grove; m. 29 March 1849, Jane B., d/o Dr. Samuel Warner of Blooming-Grove, and had:
Arabella S., res. at home.
Anselm Winfield m. Anna, d/o Levi Benedict of Cornwall; res. Blooming-Grove.
Mary Ann; d. young.
Irving; d. young.
Mary E., res. at home.

## HILL FAMILY OF WALDEN        W-13, C-10
## HILL, NATHANIEL        A-381, U2-9-10

NATHANIEL HILL[1], b. Ireland 1705, d. at Dwaarskill 5 May
1780, to America 1730 & settled on the west frontier of the
Scotch-Irish settlement west of the Hudson river; member of
Capt. John Bayard's company of militia of the Wallakill
1738. He m. 1746, Susanna Armstrong, who came to
America from Caven, Ireland, c. 1730, with 2 sisters (one m.
a Mr. Hunter & the other a Mr. Gillespie) & settled in the
Dwaarskill area. Nathaniel was a farmer. His will lists his
res. as Hanover Precinct & is dated 24 April 1780 & names
his children:
James.
William.
1751, PETER.
Mary.
Catharine.
Martha. Could be the Martha who m. John McBride 26 Feb.
1778 at Goshen.
Margaret.
Susanna.
Eleanor.

PETER HILL[2], b. Dwaarskill NY, d. Montgomery 14 Oct.
1795; was a Rev. War soldier & m. Isabele Trimble 8 April
1778 & had a son:
NATHANIEL P. HILL[3], b. Montgomery 4 Feb. 1781, d.
there 12 May 1842. Was sheriff, judge & a member of Assembly & Congress, served in Capt. Peter Miliken's cavalry during
the War of 1812. He m. 24 May 1827, Matilda, d/o Moses
Crawford, for whom the town of Crawford was named. Their
son:
NATHANIEL P.[4], b. at Montgomery 18 Feb. 1832, professor
of Chemistry at Brown Univ., was a professor, manager of the
Boston & Colorado Smelting Co. in CO (1867-90), US Senator
(1879-85). He m. Alice Hale 26 July 1860. Her family early
New England settlers who res. in Newbury & Rowley.

## HILL, GEORGE S.        H-860
farmer.

WILLIAM HILL m. Ruth Augusta Hovey in 1865 in Town of
Newburgh. He purchased the Henry Miller property. One
of their children was:
1854, GEORGE S., b. at Bullville, Orange Co.; m. Sarah E.
Waugh, resided near Coldenham.

## HILTON, REUBEN        H-860-61
attorney of Newburgh.

REUBEN HILTON, s/o William H. & Mary A. (Colwell)
Hilton, b. in Newburgh in 1877. He attended Yale, graduated
NY Law School in 1901 & has since practiced at Newburgh;
port collector since 1906; m. Minnie Hawes of Washington, DC.

## HILTON, WILLIAM T.        H-861
Treasurer of Newburgh Brick Co.

WILLIAM T. HILTON, s/o John & Anna L. (Turner)
Hilton, b. 18 July 1866. Member Board of Health.

## HINCHMAN, JOHN B.        H-861

JOHN B. HINCHMAN[1], b. 5 Sept. 1820 in Paterson, NJ, is
now deceased. He operated a livery business in Sussex, NJ;
removed to Orange Co. & purchased farms of Quackenbush
& Sherwood at Neelytown. Sold both & purchased Orange
Hotel at Goshen, which he ran 6 years. He m. Eliza Hopper
of Paterson NJ & had:
JOHN JR.

JOHN B. HINCHMAN, JR[2]. m. Maggie Gray of Port Jervis, NY
in Feb. 1883. They had:
1884, Jan. 29, Catherine G.
1898, Nov. 7, Florence M.

## HINGHAM, CHARLES        H-860
hotel proprietor of Commercial Hotel.

--- HINGHAM's and his 2d wife, Elizabeth Redfield, of
Manchester, England second child was CHARLES. Mr.
Hingham was a silk manufacturer; to the US proprietor of
Wallkill House. He d. 1872 & Elizabeth managed the hotel after
his death.
CHARLES was b. Manchester, England 6 April 1867, and
to America at the age of 9 months with his parents, who settled
in Middletown.

## HOFFMAN, JOSEPH [P]        TN-300-1
of Newburgh.

JOSEPH HOFFMAN[1], b. NY c. 1773, of Swedish or Dutch
desc. His mother was a sister of the renowned Gen. Wolfe.
JOSEPH to Newburgh in 1793, employee of Adolph De
Grove & soon after with his brother, John Hoffman, purchased Mr. De Grove's bakery. 1804 he & his brother split
up & JOSEPH built his own business; John removed to the
Province of New Brunswick. JOSEPH d. 16 Nov. 1852,
aged 79. He was a Lutheran, but joined St. George's Church
in Newburgh (1805). He is described as "a man of good
common sense; had a thorough appreciation of right, &
above all he possessed a disposition that was not easily
ruffeled." He m. Maria, d/o Abraham W. Van Deusen of
NY & had:
ELIZA ANN.
Mary.
CATHARINE.
Abraham VanDeusen, d. aged 14.
Susan, d. young.
HARRIET AMELIA.
ADALINE.
CORNELIA ELLEN.

CECELIA AMANDA.
Sarah A.
Jane.

ELIZA ANN HOFFMAN[2], d/o Joseph[1], m. Robert Reeve, &
    had: (REEVE):
Fanny M.
Catharine.
Adaline H.
Henrietta H.
Robert.

ELIZA ANN HOFFMAN[2], d/o Joseph[1], m. Paddock Chapman,
    b. Putnam Co., NY, & had: (CHAPMAN):
Mary E., m. William H. Gerard.
Joseph H. H., m. Lydia W. Sanxay.
Catharine.
Susan A., m. Mr. --- Phelps.
Deborah A.
Isaac C., m. Letitia Kennedy.
Thomas P., m. Lydia Crist.
Charles F.
Caroline J.
William G.
Louisa.

CATHARINE HOFFMAN[2], d/o Joseph[1], m. William Scott as his
    2d wife. [He m. 1st Sarah, d/o John Spier & left children
    Francis & Scott.] Catharine's children: (SCOTT):
Maria.
Cornelia.
Sarah E.
Anna.

HARRIET AMELIA HOFFMAN[2], d/o Joseph[1], m. John D.
    Phillips & had: (PHILLIPS)
Maria H.
Joseph W.
John D.
Adelaide.
Clark.
Edmund.

ADALINE HOFFMAN[2], d/o Joseph[1], m. David Howell & d.
    without issue.

CORNELIA ELLEN HOFFMAN[2], d/o Joseph[1], m. Edmund S.
    Sanxay as his 2d wife. [He m. 1st, Eliza, d/o Mark McIn-
    tyre, & left one son, Edmund S.] Cornelia Ellen's children:
    (SANXAY)
Frederick D.
Charles D.
George W.

CECELIA AMANDA HOFFMAN[2], d/o Joseph[1], m. Nelson
    Haight & had (HAIGHT):
Henry Milton.
Robert W.

Joseph H.
Abraham.
Charles E.

_____

**HOFFMAN, OGDEN**                    A-148-9, STJ-10
atty., res. of Orange Co. & NY City.

OGDEN was the son of Josiah Ogden Hoffman, an atty. He
    was b. in NY City in 1793, d. 1 May 1856; midshipman in
    War of 1812, Orange Co. Dist. Atty. (1823), Legislator
    (1826-28); 1826 to NY City & had extensive political career.
    In Goshen m. Emily, d/o JONATHAN BURRELL [see
    below], and had:
Bapt. 1826, Oct. 14, George Wickham.
Ogden Jr., US Dist. Judge in CA.
Charles Burrill, res. NY City.

JONATHAN BURRELL had:
Emily m. **JOSIAH OGDEN HOFFMAN**.
Frances m. Murray Hoffman.
Caroline m. Henry Hone.
_____

**HOFFMAN, ZACHARIAS**    TN-264, U1-133-35, U2-130-1
of Newburgh/Shawangunk, yeoman.

NICHOLAS HOFFMAN[1], was s/o Martinus of Sweden who m.
    (1) in Reformed Dutch Church in Brooklyn, 22 April 1663,
    Lysbeth Hermans & (2) 16 May 1664, Emmerentje DeWitt,
    a sister of Tjerck Classen De Witt. In his will dated 12 Feb.
    1749 in Ulster Co., NICHOLAS is identified as "of the
    County of Dutchess." He m. after 30 Dec. 1704, Jannetie
    Crispel, d/o Antony, & had:
Bapt. 1706, March 17, Martin, settled in Red Hook; m. (1) 1733,
    Tryntje, d/o Robert Benson & Cornelia Roos, & (2) Alida,
    d/o Philip Livingston.
Bapt. 1709, Feb. 11, Antje.
Bapt. 1711, March 18, Anthony, settled in Kingston; m. 6 Jan.
    1738, Catharine, d/o Abraham Goasbeck Chambers.
Bapt. 1713, Dec. 6, **ZACHARIAH**, lived at Shawangunk.
Bapt. 1716, Dec. 22, Petrus.
Bapt. 1719, June 7, Hendricus.
Bapt. 1721, Dec. 3, Annetjen.
1730, Marytje.

**ZACHARIAS HOFFMAN[2]**, large landholder in Newburgh
    since 1723, one of the trustees of the Glebe until his death in
    1744. He res. in Ulster Co. before 1710. **ZACHARIAS**
    was b. at Ft. Orange & bapt. 6 Dec. 1713 [obviously as an
    adult]. 19 Oct. 1706 m. Hester Bryn (Bruyn), b. Kingston,
    of Shawangunk, who brought as dower a tract of land owned
    by the Indians. They resided in New Paltz. Their children:
Bapt. 1707, Oct. 19, Maria.
1707, Sept. 18, Gertrude, [bapt. 18 Sept. 1709] m. Nathaniel
    DuBois.
Margaret, m. Thomas Jausen.
Bapt. 1720, Feb. 7, Jacobus, m. Margretta Lefever [Fever], 6
    Dec. 1744.

Bapt. 1721, Dec. 24, Ida, m. Cornelius Bruyn, 12 Oct. 1741.
Bapt. 1724, April 6, Nicales.
Zacharias, m. Maria Terwillager 15 Jan. 1739, & had son Jacob.
Janeke, m. William Roosenkrans after 5 Sept. 1731.
Margaret, m. after 8 Aug. 1731, Thomas Jansz (Jansen) Jr.

ZACHARIAS' will, dated 25 Feb. 1743/4, names his wife & children. He was a relatively large slaveholder.

The old homestead in Shawangunk still called Hoffmantown, was divided between sons Jacobus & Zacharias, & still occupied by Zacharias.

---

### HOLBERT FAMILY OF WAWAYANDA A-679
### HOLBERT, ADRIAN [P] A-562, C-18, 44
of Goshen.

JOHN HOLBERT[1], res. Town of Chester, Orange Co.; soldier of the Rev., d. Chester, 1821, age 93; m. Mary ---, b. Holland, she d. before 1821, and had:
1768, Aug. 24, PETER.
Ebenezer.
Samuel.
John.
Mary.
Susan m. Rynard House of Chester.

PETER HOLBERT[2], b. Chester; pioneer & businessman of Minisink; Legislator (1812); m. 25 Aug. 1789, at Goshen, Rosanna b. 10 April 1770, d/o Garret Durland of Minisink. Rosanna d. 15 May 1839; PETER d. 19 Oct. 1836. Their children:
Mary, m. David Robertson; d. 1808 of spotted fever.
William; dec'd.
Martha, m. Abijah Wells.
Susan, m. Abraham Tyler.
Miriam, m. William Wells.
John.
Sarah, m. Silas C. Brown.
Harriet, m. Jacob Dunning.
Elizabeth, m. (1st) Joseph Sayer; (2d) Lynden Mulford.
1809, Aug. 11, ADRIAN.
Peter, m. a d/o William Robertson.

All children except ADRIAN[3] res. Minisink.

ADRIAN HOLBERT[3], b. Minisink, farmer; general store with brother-in-law Silas Brown at Centreville & Millsburg; farmed at Monroe; 1836 purchased Valentine farm at Goshen; 1861 to Goshen Village; 1868 to NY City; 1870 back to Goshen. 1832 m. (1st) Hannah, d/o Joshua Sayer of Minisink, b. 15 Sept. 1809; d. 20 Nov. 1843. Children:
Charles of KS.
Hannah m. George Graham of Greenville.
Mariette m. Albert W. Slater of Centralia, KS.
Sarah m. Richard Wilson; d. in Wallkill.
Jesse A.

ADRIAN HOLBERT[3] m. (2d) Harriet, d/o John Wisner of Minisink in 1845; she d. 14 Jan. 1868, & had:
Anna.
ADRIAN m. (3d) 22 Dec. 1870, Frances, d/o Joshua & Jemima (Sayer) Wells, an old family of Goshen of English desc. Frances was b. 19 Dec. 1811, m. 22 Dec. 1870.

---

### HOLBERT, FRANK H-861
of Warwick.

FRANK HOLBERT, s/o Albert Ruggles & Mary (Wisner) Holbert, b. at Lake, Warwick Twp., worked in a restaurant in NY City and in 1899 in business for himself in Park Place, NY, which was destroyed by fire. He then opened a business at 12-14 Warren St. He m. Grace Pelton 17 Dec. 1890, she the eldest d/o William W. & Alemeda (Knapp) Pelton of Warwick, and had:
1891, Oct. 26, Resnten.
1895, April 12, Albert Ruggles.
1904, June 24, Grave Pelton.

---

### HOLLENBECK, D. M. H-862
retired merchant of Turner.

D. M. HOLLENBECK, b. 1844 in Herkimer Co., NY, worked as wholesale agent in NY City; in 1872 established general store at Turners, which he continued 33 years. Postmaster, town clerk. He m. (1) Matilda Bush and had Arthur O.
D. M. m. (2d) in 1881, Elizabeth Barnes, and had:
Mary H., m. Peter H. Bush of Brewster, NY.
Cora, m. H. F. Pemberton of Central Valley.
Grace B., at home.
Alan W., at home.

---

### HOLLEY, HENRY A. H-862
of Otisville.

DAVID A. HOLLEY[1], b. 2 Feb. 1850, Ulster Co., NY, wheelwright as was his father, m. Annie Amoys of Ellenville, NY on 2 Sept. 1873, she d. Oct. 1893. They had:
1873, Oct. 7, HENRY A.
1876, July 19, Nellie B., m. Alexander Mitchell of Hopewell, NY.
1880, Feb. 22, Emma G., m. James Hawkins of Otisville, NY.

HENRY A. HOLLEY[2] m. Harriet Easton 7 Oct. 1896, and had:
1898, Aug. 26, Henry B.
1900, April 30, Elizabeth Corwin.
1905, Sept. 20, J. Easton.

---

### HORTON FAMILY OF WALLKILL
A-432, C-9, 24, 27, 53, 86

SILAS HORTON (possibly the Silas Horton whose death is recorded in Goshen church records 28 Feb. 1820, d. of old age at 90) had a son SILAS, b. in Goshen 24 Aug. 1756; m. 9 March 1777, Mary Danes; to Wallkill c. 1780. Signed pledge of independence in 1775. Their children:

Silas Danes; d. 1850.

Barnabas; d. 1867, had son Timothy. Perhaps the "Barna" Horton who m. Anna Hawkins 14 Nov. 1807 in Goshen, and/or the "Barna" Horton who m. Sarah Hawkins 5 Feb. 1814 at the same place. Anna, wife of Barna Horton is recorded as dec'd. 14 Oct. 1810.

Hiram; d. 1840.

Nelly m. Timothy Wheat.

Molly m. (1st) Israel Moore; (2d) Daniel Slauson.

Mahala m. William Wheat; only child now living in 1880.

SILAS d. 1816; his wife Mary res. with son Barnabas until her death.

_____

## HORTON, CHARLES                    H-862
of Middletown, deceased.

CHARLES HORTON, b. Colchester, Delaware Co., NY 25 Feb. 1815; tanner, the first to engage in the business in Sullivan Co., m. Betsy Grant, d/o Joseph of Sullivan Co., and had:

Lucinda.

Gurdon B.

Melvin.

Francis E.

Louise.

Florence.

_____

## HORTON, GEORGE W. [P]                A-691

GILBERT HORTON[1], of English desc., b. Goshen 23 Aug. 1782; farmer, d. 3 Feb. 1854; m. Sarah White, b. 18 Oct. 1784, and had:

Caroline; dec'd.

Eliza; dec'd.

Ocran; dec'd.

Susan; dec'd.

Chauncey.

Mary Jane.

Thomas A.

1824, March 8, GEORGE W.

Egbert J.

GEORGE W. HORTON[2], b. Goshen Twp., dairy farmer; 22 Jan. 1851, m. Henrietta, d/o George & Melicent (Ferguson) Jackson of Minisink, now Wawayanda, b. 28 Dec. 1825. Their children:

Sarah E.; dec'd.

Lawrence F. m. Harriet, d/o Vincent Robinson.

Chauncey; dec'd.

John B.

Florence W.; dec'd.

Emma J. m. Y. A. Clark; d. leaving 2 children: Henrietta & William.

_____

## HORTON, JOSEPH                    U2-37-8
of New Windsor

JOSEPH HORTON, in his will dated 13 Dec. 1785, named his wife Jane and the following children:

Courte.

Catharine.

Martha.

Polly.

Anne.

Sarah.

Will was proved 25 April 1789 by Oliver How, carpenter of New Windsor, Joshua Sears & Jeri Clark.

_____

## HORTON, SILAS R. [P]        A-648c, C-36, LDS Anc. File
of Blooming-Grove.

BARNABAS HORTON[1], b. Mousely, Leicestershire, England 1600, July 13; to America on ship *Swallow* 1635, landed at Hampton, MA. Oct. 1640 settled at Southold, L.I. & d. there July 1680. His wife was Mary Langton, b. Feb. 1606/7. His children:

Joseph.

Benjamin.

1640, Oct., CALEB.

Joshua.

1647/8, Feb. 23, JONATHAN.

Hannah.

Sarah.

Mary.

Mercy.

Abigail.

CALEB HORTON[2], s/o Barnabas[1], b. Southold, d. 3 Oct. 1702 at Cutchogue, NY. He m. Abigail Hallock, b. 3 April 1642 at Cutchogue, d/o William Peter & Margaret (Howell) Hallock. Abigail d. 7 April 1697. They had:

BARNABAS HORTON[3], b. 23 Sept. 1666 at Cutchogue. He m. April 1686 at Southold, NY, Sarah Hines of Southampton, d/o Benjamin Hines, b. 28 Aug. 1643 at Salem, Essex Co., MA & Johanna Jennings of Southampton, d/o John Jennings & Ann Young. Barnabas & Sarah had:

BARNABAS HORTON[4], b. 1690 at Southhold, res. Goshen, NY, where he d. 1782. He m. Mary Sweazy, d/o Richard, of Goshen & had:

BARNABAS HORTON[5], b. 1722 at Goshen. He m. Abigail Parshall.

JONATHAN HORTON[2], youngest son of Barnabas[1], m. Bethia Wells of Southhold, d/o William & Mary (Youngs) Wells & had (all b. Southhold):

1673, Caleb.

1674, Bethia, m. Henry Tuthill of Southhold.

1675, Barnabas, m. Elizabeth Burnette.

1677, William, m. Christina Young.

1679, Feb. 17, Mehitable, m. Daniel Tuthill.

1681, Abigail, m. --- Lyon.
1683, Dec. 23, Jonathan, m. Mary Tuthill of Oysterponds, Ny.
1687, Mary, m. David Horton.
1690, Caleb, m. Abigail Hallock.
1692, Patience.
1694, JAMES.

JAMES HORTON[3], s/o Jonathan[2], m. Anna Goldsmith of
   Southhold & had:
1718, James.
1720, Barnabas.
c. 1722, Abigail.
c. 1724, Anna.
1728, THOMAS.
1730, Dec. 25, SILAS.
1733, Dec. 25, Ezra.
c. 1735, Bethia.
c. 1740, Jonathan.

THOMAS HORTON[4], s/o James[3], m. Susanna Conklin & had
   (all b. Goshen except Thomas, b. Southhold):
1760, Samuel, m. Margaret Consalaris.
1760, Oct. 5, Thomas.
c. 1762, James.
c. 1773, Hannah.
c. 1775, Gamaliel.
c. 1777, Ezra.
c. 1779, Paul.
c. 1781, Peter.
c. 1783, Susan.
c. 1785, Bethia.

SILAS HORTON[4], s/o James[3], settled on homestead in Goshen
   Twp., 1750; m. Margaret Bull, and had:
James; d. young.
Silas; d. young.
James (2d); d. young.
1771, July 2, WILLIAM.
Anna; d. young.
Margaret; d. young.
Sarah m. David Hawkins.

WILLIAM HORTON[5], s/o Silas[4], b. on homestead, farmer; 23
   Dec. 1793 m. Phebe, d/o Phineas Rumsey of Goshen and
   had:
Sarah; d. young.
1796, May 16, WILLIAM.
1797, Oct. 4, Margaret; d. 15 Jan. 1817.
Charlotte m. Dr. James Wells, res. Goshen.

WILLIAM HORTON[6], s/o William[5], b. Goshen at homestead;
   d. 1 Dec. 1844, Goshen; physician, surgeon, botonist,
   geologist; m. 9 April 1817 Maria Ryneck of Schenectady,
   and had:
SILAS RYNECK.
Eugene m. Anna T. Haley, farmer on homestead. They had a
   son, Silas Ryneck Horton, b. 1 June 1879 at Chester, who m.
   29 July 1908 in Malone, NY Mildred Louise Hazen of

Malone.
William, physician at Craigville, NY.
Egbert; d. young.
Emily m. J. J. Dolson.
Margaret m. Samuel W. Leddel of Mendham, NJ 15 Sept. 1840.
Charlotte m. Jesse E. Moffat.
Gertrude m. Brower C. Ward.

SILAS RYNECK HORTON[7], s/o Dr. William[6], m. Sarah
Jane, d/o Jacob J. Decker of Ulster Co.
_____

HORTON, WEBB                           H-862-3, T-46
of Middletown.

ISAAC HORTON[1] built mill at Liberty Falls in 1828, made
   flour. His ancestors had settled on L.I. before the Rev. War
   & later settled in Sullivan Co. & on to Ulster Co. ISAAC
   m. Prudence Knapp in 1807 & had 10 children, one was:
1826, Feb. 24, WEBB.

WEBB HORTON[2], b. at Colchester, Delaware Co., NY was a
   wood turner & tanner; in 1854 built tannery at Narrows-
   burgh, NY. 1864 to Warren Co., PA. He m. Elizabeth A.
   Radeker of Town of Montgomery in 1855, and had:
Junius, d. 1879 while a cadet at Bisher Military Academy in
   Poughkeepsie.
Eugene, associate with US Leather Co., in NY City.
Carrie, at home.

   Members Westminster Presbyterian Church.
_____

HOUSTON FAMILY OF WALLKILL      A-434-5, C-38
HOUSTON, ROBERT H. [P]      A-488-9, LDS Anc. File
of Wallkill.

The progenitor of the Houston family emigrated from the north
   of Ireland in early 1700's to Jamestown, VA. His sons:
JOSEPH.
John, settled PA.
James, settled VA.

REV. JOSEPH HOUSTON[1], first minister of Goodwill Church
   near Montgomery, came here from VA. He m. Isabella ---,
   and had:
1726, Joseph.
JAMES.
4 daus.

JAMES HOUSTON[2], s/o Rev. Joseph[1], res. Town of Montgom-
   ery, m. Anna, b. 1736, d/o Rev. George Carr, Presbyterian
   minister of Goshen, and had:
Joseph, physician at Amity, later at Edenville, where he died.
1763, GEORGE.
Thomas.
James.
John.
Samuel.

Andrew.

Polly, m. Robert Wilken.

Jane, m. Adam Dickerson.

All children of JAMES[2] & Anna married & reared families in Orange Co.

GEORGE HOUSTON[3], settled southeast part of Wallkill, farmer; m. (1st) Jane Hunter of Dwaars Kill, d/o Robert & Ann of Montgomery, who d. 1801 aged c. 32. A founder of Scotchtown, was a Presbyterian Elder; d. Dec. 1825. Children:

Ann, m. Samuel Brown; d. near Scotchtown 1854.

John G., stayed on homestead. He m. 15 Jan. 1851, Mary W. Bradner of Goshen.

1797, JAMES.

1798, Aug., ROBERT H.

George, merchant, farmer & j.p. many years; d. Middletown.

GEORGE[3] m. (2d) Julia, wid. of Mr. Gale & d/o William Thompson of Goshen. Julia had one child by her 1st m., William Gale. Children of GEORGE & Julia:

Anthony & Jane, twins. Anthony d. Middletown & left a son D. Crawford, West Point grad. Jane m. Charles Heard; d. Hamptonburgh.

Henry, res. & d. Mechanictown.

Sally, m. Hector Van Cleft, left one son J.L., postmaster.

Samuel; d. young in 1828.

Theodore; d. young 1837.

Almira, m. Orange H. Horton, res. White Plains, Westchester Co.

Elizabeth, m. William Church, res. Orange, NJ.

Thomas; d. at Toledo, was res. of Cincinnati.

JAMES HOUSTON[4], s/o George[3], b. Scotchtown, d. Montgomery; m. Caroline S. White, b. 1807 in Montgomery, & had (all b. Montgomery):

1837, Lucinda S., m. Jonathan Miller.

1841, June 17, RUTH ANNA.

RUTH ANNA HOUSTON[5], d/o James[4], m. Francis Clark Jennings of Montgomery & had (JENNINGS, all b. Montgomery):

1860, Oct., Louisa G.

1862, Caroline W.

1864, April 20, Isaac, m. Lillie E. VanKlelck.

1867, William W.

1870, Oct. 13, George Houston, m. Emma Schwartz of NY City.

1873, Nov. 26, James Nelson Lindsay, m. Wilhelmina Hogmbraker.

1875, April, Lee Lay, m. Ruth Ella Wescott.

1878, Dec. 20, Frances Sallie.

ROBERT H. HOUSTON[4], s/o 1st m. of George[3], b. Town of Wallkill; age 16-20 learned trade of tanner & currier; 1826 to Middletown, tanner; 1831 purchased farm in area. Presbyterian Church of Middletown. He m. Mary, d/o David Dill & Elizabeth Houston, who was b. 6 April 1799 & d. 11

Sept. 1880. Elizabeth Houston was the d/o Joseph Houston, progenitor of family in Orange Co. Children of ROBERT H. & Mary:

Jane Elizabeth; d. age 18.

1833, Dec. 15, David Dill; m. 29 Aug. 1861 Catherine M., d/o John K. Moore; res. Middletown.

---

## HOUSTON, GABRIEL [P]     A-609
of Warwick.

THOMAS HOUSTON[1] settled in Middletown, NY young; member of Presbyterian Church; m. Sarah Faulkender and had:

Anna m. Henry Denton of Denton, NY.

Harriet m. Judge John Booth.

Catharine m. David Corwin.

1798, May 25, GABRIEL.

Adeline m. Rev. Gabriel Corwin, now of Cape May.

Philinda.

Jane m. Henry O. Bronson of Jackson, MI.

James F.

Franklin.

Nelson.

GABRIEL HOUSTON[2], s/o Thomas[1], b. near Middletown; m. Susan Ann Owen & moved to Glenwood, NJ on homestead of father-in-law Isaac Owen, s/o Ebenezer. Gabriel d. there 22 Jan. 1864. Their children:

Sally Ann m. Festus Vail of Warwick.

Abigail Jane.

Isaac Owen.

Thomas Erminda; d. young.

Gabriel Wisner.

Henry Owen.

Elizabeth W.; d. young.

James Nelson; d. young.

Elizabeth; d. young.

Susan; d. young.

Susan m. Thomas Pickens of Ulster Co.

Philip.

Mary O.

---

## HOUSTON, CAPT. JOHN W.     H-864
farmer of Bellvale, deceased.

CAPTAIN JOHN W., b. 20 March 1842 on the family homestead farm at Bellvale, d. 11 Jan. 1905. At age 19 enlisted in the 124th Regt. NY Vols. Made 2d Lt., was severely wounded several times. He m. Julia Baird who d. 1880. Their children:

Floyd.

George.

James.

Frank.

Clara.

12 Feb, 1892, **JOHN** m. (2d) Margaret B. Neely of Bellvale, who survived him. He is also survived by a brother, Henry W. of Bellville, & 2 sisters, Mrs. Mary Francisco of Little Falls, NJ & Mrs. J. H. Berthalf.

---

**HOUSTON, SAMUEL B.**                         **H-864**
of Warwick.

**SAMUEL**, b. 5 Dec. 1845, retail boot & shoe business & farmer; m. Salona S. Palmer of Warwick 25 Oct. 1871, and had:
Charles B., res. Brooklyn, manufacturer.
Anna G., m. Arthur Knapp of Florida, NY.
Edna K., d. 1898, age 23.

---

**HOUSTON, HON. WILLIAM H. [P]**   **A-611-12, H-863**
of Warwick.

DR. JOSEPH HOUSTON[1], res. Edenville, Warwick Twp., family of Scotch-Irish desc.; m. Nancy, d/o Gen. Henry Wisner, and had:
Henry W.; dec'd.
JOHN H.
Richard; dec'd.
George W.
Joseph A.; dec'd.
Andrew; dec'd.
Samuel; dec'd.
Harriet.
Susan; dec'd.
Jane; dec'd.

JOHN H. HOUSTON[2], s/o Dr. Joseph[1], m. 19 June 1816 Julia Ann Wheeler. John H. d. c. 1831. Children:
1817, March 27, **WILLIAM H.**
Nathaniel D.
James K.
John H.; d. young.

**WILLIAM H. HOUSTON**[3], s/o John H.[2], b. Etonville; m. 5 Jan. 1842, Ann E. Wheeler, d/o William F. of Bellvale, Orange Co. & granddau. of Isaac R. Van Duzer of Cornwall-on-Hudson. Their children, all res. Orange Co.:
William W., res. [Town of] Florida.
Julia E. m. Manson R. Brown, res. Washingtonville, NY.
John H., res. grandfather's farm.
1856, March 28, JOEL W.
Frank.
1862, Sept. 11, JAMES EDWARD.

JOEL W. HOUSTON[4], born on family homestead, 2 1/2 miles from Florida, NY, farmer; m. Anna Jessup 29 June 1881. Elder of the Presbyterian Church of Florida.

JAMES EDWARD HOUSTON[4], dairy farmer & peach grower, born on the family homestead. He purchased the farm of Thomas Jackson & m. Kissie Armstrong of Florida, NY 17 June 1884.

WILLIAM H. held local offices, was a RR officer & member Second Presbyterian Church of Florida; d. 1875, Aug. 30; Mrs. Houston d. 1879.

---

**HOWELL FAMILYS OF WAWAYANDA**        **A-680-1**

PHINEAS HOWELL settled in the area soon after the Rev.; his children:
Jason.
James.
David.

JOHN HOWELL to Wawayanda c. 1778. He had been a sailor on whaling voyages, a soldier of the Rev. & res. Sugar-Loaf before coming to Wawayanda. He d. 1790 and is bur. at the Corners, c. 2 miles below Ridgeway. His children:
Dau. m. Reuben Cash.
Dau. m. John Roberts.
Dau. m. Eliphalet Stickney.
Hephzibah, unm.
John.
Jeffrey.

BENJAMIN HOWELL, early settler of Ridgebury & Rev. soldier and his brother, Ezra of Blooming-Grove, also Rev. soldier, settled early in Wawayanda. Children of Benjamin:
James, to Steuben Co., NY.
George W., settled Goshen village.
John, Settled Goshen village & had a son, John Edward.
Daniel, removed to NY City.
Preston, res. IA.
Chauncey, res. Erie, PA.
Henry, settled IL.
Benjamin, removed to NY City.

---

**HOWELL, CLARENCE J.**                         **H-864**
dairy farmer.

CLARENCE J. is s/o Asa who d. 1897. He was b. on the family homestead, which has been in the family since 1790, located near Florida, Orange Co., NY 30 Dec. 1868 & d. 30 March 1905. **CLARENCE** m. Minnie Sinsabaugh, d/o Daniel & Ellen A. of Liberty Corners, Orange Co., 19 Nov. 1891, and had:
1892, Oct. 19, Floyd VanDuzer.
1894, Feb. 4, Clara Adams.
1895, Nov. 24, William Sinsabaugh.
1898, Dec. 3, Thomas Wheeler.
1904, May 27, Jennie Jessup.

---

**HOWELL, D. BREWSTER**                         **H-865**
farmer, Town of Newburgh near East Coldenham.

SILAS HOWELL[1], b. L.I., but to Orange Co. at an early day. He had 4 children, one was:
RENSSELAER HOWELL[2] who m. Alice Belknap and had:
David B.

Rensselaer Jr.
JOHN COLVIN.
Mary F.

JOHN COLVIN HOWELL³, s/o Rensselaer Sr., res. on family
homestead, m., & had.
**D. BREWSTER HOWELL⁴** who m. Katherine McCartney &
have 2 children: Elwood B. & Gertrude May. He ow
operates the family farm.

---

**HOWELL, DAVID H.**                    **H-864-5**
clerk of Town of Crawford.

**DAVID H.,** s/o Harvey & Emeline (Decker) Howell, was b. in
Crawford Twp. 1868. He is a tinsmith & has hardware
business in Bulville.

---

**HOWELL, EDMUND SAYRE [P]  A-647, H-141-2, H-866**
of Blooming-Grove.
**HOWELL, HEZEKIAH [P]**                **A-647, C-98**
of Blooming-Grove.
**HOWELL, NATHANIEL W.**                **H-866**

EDWARD HOWELL, from England to MA, made freeman at
Boston, 4 March 1639; settled Southampton, L.I. in 1640.
LT. HEZEKIAH HOWELL¹ is a des. in a direct line from
EDWARD the emigrant. HEZEKIAH m. Phebe, d/o Thomas
Halsey, 10 Sept. 1702, and had:
1709, May 6, HEZEKIAH.
Phebe.
Experience.
Jedediah.

HEZEKIAH HOWELL², s/o Hezekiah¹, from L.I. to Orange Co.
c. 1734, settled at Blaggs Clove [1727-37]; d. 1785. He m.
Susanna d/o Job Sayre of Orange County, 1735, and had:
Phebe.
Jane.
1741, Sept. 3, HEZEKIAH.
Stephen.
1752, Nov. 20, CHARLES.

HEZEKIAH HOWELL³, s/o Hezekiah², b. on homestead; sheriff
of Orange Co. & Continental Army officer during Rev. War;
m. Juliana, d/o Nathaniel & Sarah (Smith) Woodhull of
Mastic, L.I., and had:
1768, Aug. 21, HEZEKIAH.
Nathaniel W., res. Canandaigua NY, atty. & judge.
Susan m. Benjamin Strong of Goshen, NY.
Bapt. 9 Jan. 1774, in Goshen, Sarah Smith, m. Abraham Shultz
of New Windsor, NY.
Fanny m. Judge Nathan H. White.
Jane m. Judge Augustus Porter of Niagara.
Elizabeth m. Rev. Andrew Thompson of Rockland Co., preacher
at Nyack.

**HEZEKIAH HOWELL⁴,** s/o Hezekiah³, b. on homestead in
Blooming-Grove, farmer & businessman; d. 20 June 1855;
m. 6 Dec. 1796, Frances, d/o Maj. Tuthill of Orange Co.
Frances d. on the homestead 1830, Dec. 14. Their children:
Juliana Woodhull m. Judge Robert Denniston; d. 1825.
Hezekiah; d. unm. age 74.
NATHANIEL WOODHULL.
1805, Jan. 16, MATTHEW HENRY.
1860, Oct. 24, John W. T.; d. 1870.
Mary Brewster m. Henry F. Moffat of Blooming-Grove.
Andrew; d. young.
Gabrial.
Simeon.
Andrew.

**NATHANIEL WOODHULL HOWELL⁵,** s/o Hezekiah⁴,
grad. from Williams 1853; supervisor of Blooming Grove 1871-
72, Assembly member 1863-64. Res. on old homestead; d. in
middle life at Columbus, GA. He m. Mary Halsey, d/o Walter
& Caroline (Marvin) Halsey & had:
Joanna B.
Hezekiah.

**MATTHEW HENRY HOWELL⁵,** s/o Hezekiah⁴, farmer on
homestead; m. Julia S., d/o Daniel Brewster of Blooming-
Grove and had:
NATHANIEL W.
Charles; dec'd.
Sarah m. William Clark; res. NY.
Joanna B.; d. young.

**NATHANIEL W. HOWELL⁶,** s/o Matthew Henry⁵, res. on
homestead; assemblyman (1863-64); m. Mary, d/o Walter
Halsey, old family of Blooming-Grove, and had:
Joanna B.
Hezekiah.

CHARLES HOWELL³, s/o Hezekiah², b. Blaggs Clove; d. 1843,
Jan. on homestead. Farmer, served in the Rev. War under
Gen. George Clinton; m. (1st) 1785, a d/o Maj. Strong who
was murdered by Claudius Smith, and the same year settled
on the Howell homestead in Blooming-Grove. Their
children:
1788, March 6, Selah Strong.
1791, July 28, Clarissa, m. William Strong of Blooming-Grove.

CHARLES³ m. (2d) Elizabeth, d/o of Joseph Board, settled near
Blooming-Grove Church and had:
1803, Sept. 7, Charles Board, physician of Chester; d. 3 April
1865.
1804, Sept. 5, **EDMUND SAYRE.**
1805, Dec. 3, Joseph Henry; d. 13 Dec. 1878.

**EDMUND SAYRE HOWELL⁴,** s/o Charles³, b. Blooming-
Grove; res. 14 years in NJ then back to Blooming-Grove; m.
16 Feb. 1836, Nancy C., d/o James Bell of Warwick, and
had:
Mary E. m. Edward Fitzgerald, res. Binghamton.

Clarissa A. m. Rev. Arthur Harlow of Orange Co.

Phebe E. m. Benjamin C. Sears.

Charles H., farmer on homestead.

James B.

Caroline A. m. Dr. George H. Sears.

Harriet A.

Joseph E.

Susan E.

Effie; dec'd.

EDMUND was a member of 2d Presbyterian Church, Washingtonville.

———

## HOWELL, JAMES T.        H-865

JAMES T. HOWELL, b. on the family homestead c. 1 mile from Howells Station in Town of Mt. Hope, 25 Aug. 1845, s/o Samuel C. & Sallie Jane (Beakes) Howell. In 1869 he purchased his father's farm. He res. in NY City for 20 years in the milk business. 25 Nov. 1869 m. Ester Caroline Harding, and had:

Child, d. in infancy.

1876, Sept. 16, Lucy J., m. Maxwell R. Wright of Jersey City.

1882, Aug. 26, Charles A., at home.

———

## HOWELL, JOHN T.        H-865
physician of Newburgh.

JOHN T. HOWELL, b. Middletown, NY 23 April 1862, s/o Abraham P. & Hannah (Smith) Howell, grad. Medical Dept. of Columbia Univ., NY 1884. In 1889 he m. Sarah T., d/o Robert Steele and has 3 children.

———

## HOWELL, SAMUEL C.        H-866

SAMUEL C. HOWELL was b. Town of Wallkill 21 May, 1807, only s/o William A. & Elizabeth (Calender) Howell. Elizabeth's father was b. in VT & a lt. of the Light Horse Cavalry during the Rev. War. SAMUEL purchased a small farm in the town of Mt. Hope at the time of their marriage; railroad agent & postmaster.

———

## HOYT FAMILY OF WALLKILL        A-434, C-30

PETER HOYT, early settler, m. (2d) Mrs. Mary Vail, the mother of Mrs. William Carpenter, Jr., and had:

John.

Archibald.

Peter, now res. NJ.

Mrs. Jeremiah Cox.

Mrs. Alex Bell.

Joel; d. April 1861 & left son Samuel.

———

## HOYT, JAMES W. [P]        A-560b, C-30
of Goshen.

SIMON HOYT(E), progenitor of this family, settled in Charles-town, MA 1628. His descendant:

JOSEPH HOYT[1], res. Norodon Hill, near Stamford, CT, and had:

Joseph.

1776, April 1, HEZEKIAH.

Sarah.

Hannah.

HEZEKIAH HOYT[2], s/o Joseph[1], b. Norodon Hill; served in War of 1812; m. Esther Sellick of Stamford, CT, b. 10 Nov. 1780, d. 24 Dec. 1824. Settled Wallkill, Orange Co., c. 1800, farmer; after death of wife he res. with dau. Mrs. Miller of Middletown until he d. 17 Feb. 1835. Children:

Hezekiah. Could be the Hezekiah Hoyt who m. 19 Dec. 1824, Rachel D. Southerland.

William.

Caroline m. John Arnold; d. Luzerne Co., PA.

Harriet, wid. of Lyman B. Miller.

Maria m. Edward Steward of Arlington, NJ.

1816, April 5, JAMES W.

Henry W.; d. 1824.

Gilbert F.; d. 1824.

JAMES W. HOYT[3], 1836 storekeeper in Amity with brother Hezikiah; 1838 to Bloomingburgh, later to Burlington, Sullivan Co., constable & collector; to Middletown, merchant; to Newport on the Wallkill with brother Isaac[sic]. 1867 to Goshen, 1871 under-sheriff 1874 sheriff of the co. Served political offices. He m. 20 Sept. 1838, Loretta, d/o MAHAR W. & Rachel (Norris) HORTON of Bloomingburgh, Sullivan Co. [See below.] Children of JAMES & Loretta:

Mahar Henry.

Isaac, served 18th Regt. NY, Civil War.

Hezekiah W., 19th & 212st NY Regts., Civil War.

1848, Nov. 25, James W.; d. 1 June 1853.

Mary Louisa m. Charles W. Coleman.

1855, Nov. 12, James W. (2); d. 20 Dec. 1856.

1858, April 14, Hattie A.; d. 22 Sept. 1858.

Winfield S.

BARNABAS HORTON[1], b. L.I., early settler of Goshen in 1732; his son SILAS[2] had a son ELIHU[3], and his son:

MAHAR W. HORTON[4], b. 15 May 1787, d. 1866, Aug. 5; sheriff of Sullivan Co.; m. Rachel Norris, b. 5 April 1796, d. 26 Feb. 1859; their children:

Harman N.

1817, July 20, Loretta A., m. JAMES W. HOYT.

Harriet m. Thomas K. Beyea of Fair Oaks, Orange Co.

Napoleon.

———

## HUDSON, WILLIAM J.        H-866
bank director of Washingtonville.

WILLIAM J. HUDSON, s/o Daniel & Elizabeth (Davis) Hudson, was b. on farm on which he now resides in Town of Blooming Grove. He is the 5th generation of his family to occupy the farm. He m. Grace A. Wright and had:

Ethel.

David.

Grace.

Alma.

Clare.

William Reeves.

---

**HUGHEY, REOBERT** [sic]                                     U2-129-30

merchant of Wallkill.

In his will dated 13 Feb. 1742/3, **REOBERT** [sic] **HUGH-EY** names his wife Anna Wassall, sons James & John, and his brother James Hughey. Executors: Jacobus Bruyn Jr. & Charles Clinton, Esq. Witnesses: Johannes Miller, Johannes Newkerk & Adam Graham.

---

**HULETT, JOSEPH B.**                                         H-867

surgeon of Middletown.

**CYRUS B. HULLET[1]**, b. Waverly, NY, d. 25 Feb. 1875, m. Ruth Slawson, b. Orange Co., d. Nov. 1889. They had: 1858, Aug. 4, **JOSEPH B.**

**JOSEPH B. HULLETT[2]**, b. at Barton, Tioga Co., grad. Columbia Univ. 1887 & beginning in 1888 practiced at Middletown. He m. Lottie B. Hulse, d/o Hudson E. & Ann (Thompson) Hulse of Wallkill & has one child: J. Leslie, b. 1 April 1891.

---

**HULSE, JOHN B.** [P]                                        A-502

dairy farmer of Wallkill.

**HULSE, CAPT. THOMAS E.** [P]                                A-499-500

of Middletown.

**HULSE, CAPT. THOMAS N.** [P]                                A-645

of Blooming Grove.

**THOMAS HULSE[1]**, from England to America, soldier of the Rev., after war settled in Town of Wallkill on farm; d. age 80. His children [wife not named]:

Martin.

Phineas.

Edward.

Oliver, soldier of War of 1812.

THOMAS.

Susan m. James Mapes.

Julia m. --- Woodruff.

Abigail m. Daniel Cooley.

**THOMAS HULSE[2]**, s/o Thomas[1], res. farm outside Middletown, d. 1850, age 81; m. Phebe Emerson [Everson?] who d. 1849, age 81. Children:

Fanny.

Benjamin.

Oliver.

1796, Sept. 16, **THOMAS E.**

Julia m. Hudson Everett.

Mary m. George Cox.

---

GILBERT.

1809, March 8, **JOHN B.**

James, res. homestead farm.

**CAPT. THOMAS E. HULSE[3]**, s/o Thomas, clerked at Newburgh; 1824 to NY City in grocery business; 1828 to Kingston; later owned schooner & builder of steamboats; 1852-55 res. on farm in Wawayanda, 1855 to Middletown. Member 1st Presbyterian Church of Middletown; m. 23 Jan. 1823, Permelia A., d/o George E. Hulse & Mary Lyon of Newburgh, she b. 2 Nov. 1806. Children:

Mary A.

Charles J.; d. 1866, age 40.

Henry L., 165th Regt. NY Vol., Civil War.

Frances A. m. James V. Shenck. Both are dec'd., left dau. Mary Louise.

Harriet A. m. S. J. Curtis of NY.

Elmendore R., farmer of Wawayanda.

Eugenia C.

LaGrange W., on home farm.

Julia A.; dec'd.

**GILBERT HULSE[3]**, b. L.I., settled Wallkill, Orange Co., c. 1800. Children [wife not named]:

1770, Aug. 17, **JAMES W.**

Sarah m. Hugh Scofield.

**JAMES W. HULSE[4]**, s/o Gilbert[3], b. L.I., d. in Blooming-Grove 18 Feb. 1813; as young man to Orange Co., tanner & currier; m. Rachel Nicholson of Orange Co., her father officer in Rev. War under Arnold at Quebec. Children:

William; dec'd.

Maria; dec'd.

Gilbert W., surgeon in the Indian War under Gen. Scott; after war settled at Grand Gulf, MS, later res. in LA & moved back north during the Civil War.

1810, Oct. 31, **THOMAS N.**

Elizabeth m. Benjamin Moffat, res. IL.

**CAPT. THOMAS N. HULSE[5]**, s/o James W.[4], b. on homestead at Blooming-Grove; worked as clerk & capt. on steamboat on Hudson River; 1862 retired to homestead in Blooming-Grove. He m. (1st) Elizabeth Houton of VT, 1849, she d. 1876; m. (2d) Ann Eliza, widow of Edwin Hulse and sister of Alden Goldsmith, Esq. of Blooming-Grove.

**JOHN B. HULSE[3]**, s/o Thomas Hulse[2] & Phebe, b. 8 March 1809; m. 1834, Feb. 22, Hetta Ann, d/o Barney Horton & Anna Hawkins; Hetta Ann b. 14 Aug. 1811, d. 10 Dec. 1877. Their children:

Hudson E., farmer of Wawayanda.

Harriet Amelia m. Augustus Smith, farmer of Goshen

1838, Feb. 9, Theodore, res. NY; d. 5 April 1875.

1839, July 24, Barney H., res. NY; d. 22 Dec. 1873, leaving widow.

John Edgar, farmer of Wallkill.

1847, Sept. 16, Thomas E.; d. 18 April 1862.

Silas, res. Jersey City.

---

**HULSE, WILLIAM A.**　　　　　　　　H-867-8

JOHN H. HULSE[1] m. Mary ---, and had:
Ann, m. --- Thurston of Stoneham, MA.
1853, April 1, **WILLIAM A.**
Robert Emmet of Middletown.

**WILLIAM A. HULSE[2]**, b. Middletown, worked for Wilson H. Probost in the first milk establishment to manufacture condensed cream for the army & southern trade. He learned the plumbing trade when young at Keyport, NJ, then to Newark & to Warwick 1875 in employ of Finch & Coldwell; later opened his own plumbing & heating business. He m. Clara, d/o John L. & Julia Finch of Warwick 12 Jan. 1882, and had:
1882, Sept. 5, Elbert L.
1884, Sept. 12, Everett B.
1886, Sept. 21, Addie B.
1888, Oct. 9, William A.
1890, July 6, Janet P.

**HUMPHREY, CHARLES**　　　　　A-148, 210, 215
atty. & banker, Congresman of Ithaca.

**CHARLES HUMPHREY** served as Congressman (1825-27), Assemblyman (1834-36, 42); m. Ann Eliza, d/o Joseph & Sarah Belknap of New Windsor. His ancestor, JOHN HUMPHREY, was one of the first settlers of New Windsor. JOHN came April 1743; at his house was held the first precinct meeting of the Town of New Windsor. Another or the same JOHN HUMPHREY was the first settler in the district of Little Britain (1724-5) on the Andrew Johnston patent.

**HUNN, PETER F.**　　　　　　　　　　A-147

PEREGRIM VAN EMBAUGH m. Amelia Provost, d/o Bishop John Provost and had Catherine Van Emburgh. Catherine m. THOMAS HUNN,[1] whose ancestors came from Holland to America. THOMAS & Catherine had:

JOHN S. HUNN[2] m. Margaret FREEMAN. JOHN was cashier of Bank of Newburgh. They had:
PETER F. HUNN[3], b. 20 May 1794, Mt. Pleasant, NJ; atty. & j.p., to NY 1811 & Newburgh 1837 & d. there 31 July 1847, age 54. He m. Maria T. Griffing of Monticello, and had:
Mary.
Margaret.
Catharine.
Freneau, NY druggist.
John T.

Margaret Freeman's family desc. from Andre Fresneau (Freneau) who emigrated from France to NJ.

**HUNT, ROBERT O.**　　　　　　　　　H-868
manager of the Westtown plant of the Borden Condensed Milk Co.

**ROBERT O. HUNT**, b. Town of Minisink in 1866, s/o Robert & Catura (Osborn) Hunt, m. Lydia Winters & had 2 sons & 4 daughters.

**HUNTER, GEORGE [P]**　　　　　　　A-176
physician & surgeon.

--- HUNTER[1], farmer of Township of Montgomery, NY, had:
**GEORGE HUNTER[2]**, b. 12 July 1800; studied locally & in NY City; res. Searsville, Orange Co., d. 13 July 1870. He m. 13 Nov. 1827, Sarah, d/o Archibald Crawford & Mary Bartley; she d. 20 Jan. 1879, age 74. Children:
Mary E. m. Daniel Thompson.
Emily A.; d. young.
Samuel, Lt. Co. K, NY Vol.; d. in camp 26 Feb. 1865, age 32, of disease.
Sarah m. Theodore Merritt; dec'd.

**HUNTER, JAMES**　　　　　　U2-39-40, 181
of Wall Kill, yeoman.

In his will dated 15 May 1770, **JAMES HUNTER** names his wife Frances and children:
John.
Matthew.
James. In 1789 administration was granted to John Hunter of Montgomery on the estate of James Hunter, Jr., farmer, late of Montgomery, dec'd. intestate.
Robert.
Dau. m. Matthew Rea & has one son, James Rea.

Will proved 6 May 1789 by Alexander Kidd Jr. farmer of Montgomery, Robert Kidd & James Fulton.

**HUNTER, JOHN**　　　　　　　　　　U2-78
of Shawangunk, yeoman.

**JOHN HUNTER** in his will dated 31 March 1789, names his mother Ann, his brothers Stephen, Robert & James and his father Robert.

**HUTCHINS, JOHN NATHAN**　　TN-108, 244, 281-2
of Town of Newburgh.

**JOHN NATHAN HUTCHINS**, teacher at old Glebe School. From his obituary in the NY *Packer* issue of 18 July 1782: "He died Monday the 8th inst., aged 82, after a short illness, mathematician and astronomer." He left a widow & was bur. in Newburgh.

**HYNDMAN, WILLIAM HUGH**　　　　H-868
attorney & recorder of Newburgh.

**WILLIAM** was b. in Newburgh 131 Oct. 1861, s/o Robert (grocer of Newburgh) & Elizabeth (Gibb) Hyndman. He grad. Yale 1884 & studied law at the office of Messrs. Scott & Hirschburg. He m. Betsey Leighton Marden of Newburgh.

## INNIS FAMILY
TN-283-4

of Town of Newburgh.

JAMES INNIS[1], early settler of Bradley Patent, came to America from Ireland as an infant c. 1737 with his mother & sisters & settled in Little Britian. JAMES m. Sybil Ross of Morristown, NJ & settled in Newburgh in 1780. They had:

James, d. unm.; soldier of the Rev.

Jane, m. William Irwin & removed to OH.

Keziah, m. James Owen.

Lydia, m. Moses Hanmore.

Peter, d. unm.

Benjamin, m. Margaret Denton.

Elsie, m. Thomas Aldrich.

Sarah, m. Anthony Presler.

WILLIAM.

Aaron, m. Ruth, d/o Luff Smith & setled in Milton.

WILLIAM INNIS[2], resided on the family homestead; m. Elizabeth, d/o James Warring. She d. 18 Jan. 1846 when thrown accidentally from a wagon. They had:

Sally, m. Isaac Demarest.

Ross, m. Catharine Cook.

Rebecca, m. Richard Ward Jr.

Svgant, unm., res. WI.

William Jr., m. Catharine Jessup, res. WI.

## ISEMAN, JOHN E.
H-868-9

baker of Middletown; bank director.

JOHN E. ISEMAN, b. Wurtemburg, Germany 1835, to America 1853 & settled in NY City; operated bakery. Removed to Chester, NY & in 1861 to Middletown; m. Josephine Stoddard, d/o Ira I. & Mary Jane, and had:

Charles Wesley, in business in NY.

George H. of Middletown.

Catherine, m. W. D. Mc Queen.

Christine, at home; taught music 2 years in VA.

John E., grad. Annapolis Naval Academy, assigned to battleship *Montana*.

Members Methodist Episcopal Church.

## JACKSON FAMILY OF CHESTER
A-614

JOHN JACKSON settled in Chester & had one dau. who m. Fletcher Woodhull.

## JACKSON FAMILIES OF GOSHEN
A-524, C-9, 11-12

There were four Jackson familes mentioned in the 1775 assessment roll: William twice (assumed father & son), Henry & Richard.

RICHARD JACKSON, had a dau. who m. Thomas Wilkin and had dau. Mrs. Hoffman of Goshen.

JOHN C. JACKSON, m. Fanny, d/o William Jackson and had the late Charles T. Jackson, postmaster of Goshen and Episcopal Church Warden for more than 30 years.

CAPT. WILLIAM JACKSON, served in Rev. War, emigrated from Dublin, Ireland and had:

Mrs. John C. Jackson.

William, Rev. War patriot; d. young.

Goshen church records give the following:

Daniel Jackson m. Elizabeth McCoun 8 Nov. 1778.

Henry Jackson m. Ellinor McDougall 30 Sept. 1779.

John Jackson m. Elener Whitman 4 March 1781.

Hamilton Jackson m. Abigail Dains 26 Jan. 1777.

William Jackson m. Abigail Pearson (Pierson) 30 Jan. 1781.

## JACKSON, EZRA T.
H-869

of Chester.

EZRA T. JACKSON, b. 23 Aug. 1843 at Chester, Orange Co., NY, s/o Thomas Jefferson Jackson, who was the s/o Capt. John Jackson[1] a Rev. War veteran of the 2d NY Regt. At age 25 EZRA succeeded his father in store at Chester. He m. 15 June 1881 Margaret Douglass Davidson of Blooming Grove and had one son: William Lewis, grad. LaFayette College in 1908.

## JACQUES, JOHN
H-870

founder of Brotherhood Wine Co. at Washingtonville.

JOHN JACQUES came from NJ as a boy with his mother, locating in Washingtonville in 1812. He established the first grape vineyard in the county in 1839. His children:

John, d. 1868.

Orin, d. 1885.

Charles, sold his father's business to Mr. Emerson; has lived since in retirement on the family homestead, now aged 84. Presbyterian Church elder.

## JAGGER FAMILY OF MONTGOMERY
A-381, LDS Anc. File

DAVID JAGGER[1], b. 1731, Southampton, NY, s/o John, early Montgomery settler, m. Mary Millikin & had:

c. 1773, John.

c. 1775, Stephen.

c. 1777, David.

1779, MARY.

MARY JAGGER[2], d/o David[1], m. Andrew McWilliams, b. 5 March 1778, Galloway, Scotland & had (MC WILLIAMS, all b. Scotchtown, Orange Co.):

1806, Aug. 7, Sarah Haffy, m. James H. Dales & had: Sarah Frances, Elizabeth, Laura & Helen.

1808, Jan. 16, David Jaggar.

1809, July 14, John A., m. Susan Ann Wilkin of Montgomery & had Harriet Ann, Daniel Wilkin, Mary Elizabeth, John James,

Joseph Eugene, Abby Louise & Ralph Erskine.
1812, April 15, Mary Milligan, m. Aaron Swain & had Mary & Gideon.
1814, April 20, James Henry.
1816, Aug. 20, Elizabeth.
1818, May 27, Andrew Stansbury.
1820, July 3, Nancy Jane.
1826, Aug. 14, Isabella Ann, m. William Lyman Atwater of NY.

**JAMISON, GEORGE W.**                    H-870
publisher of *Pine Bush Herald*.

GEORGE b. Town of Crawford; teacher & insurance business at Walden; m. Julia N. Crist of Montgomery & they have one child: Hilda.

**JAYNE, DEWITT CLINTON [P]**             A-183
physician.

SAMUEL JAYNE[1], b. England, widower, m. after coming to America, had 3 sons & 1 dau., all res. on L.I. Dau. m. --- Phillips, of family that founded Phillipsburg, Town of Wallkill, Orange Co. A son settled in Florida, Orange Co. Among his children was son SAMUEL[2] who m. and had 6 sons & 6 daus., including:
STEPHEN JAYNE[3], m. Sarah, d/o Seth Marvin, Esq. of Blooming-Grove whose family served in the Rev. War. Children of Stephen & Sarah:
Amelia.
Lewis M.
Charles M. [NOTE: could be the Charles Marcus Jayne under George Frederick Jayne entry below.]
Emily.
1817, Feb. 6, DEWITT CLINTON.
Maria.
Seth.
Harriet.

DEWITT CLINTON JAYNE[4], s/o Stephen[3], b. Florida, Orange Co.; studied medicine 1834 with Dr. S. B. Barlow of Florida & grad. Yale 1839. Practiced homeopathic medicine; Presbyterian; m. 20 Dec. 1849, Mary Augusta, d/o Edwin P. Steward of Florida (brother of Hon. Wm. H. Steward, b. Florida.)

**JAYNE, GEORGE FREDERICK**               H-870
dairy farmer near Florida, NY.

CHARLES MARCUS JAYNE[1] m. Ann Eliza Thompson & had:
1843, July 25, Anna M., m. Charles R. Baird of Warwick.
1848, July 10, Sarah Augusta, m. J. A. Steward of Florida, NY.
Mary Caroline, d. 25 Dec. 1875; m. Nathaniel Seely of Hamburg, NJ.
1852, Jan., Wells Thompson, res. Brooklyn, NY.
1854, Feb. 23, GEORGE FREDERICK.

GEORGE FREDERICK JAYNE[2], b. on family homestead near Florida, NY called "View Farm." Presbyterian Church member; m. Julia E. Seward of Florida 14 Feb. 1877, and had:
1877, Nov. 10, Fred Seward.
1878, Dec. 2, Belle Clayton, m. John K. Roe of Florida.
1880, Sept. 17, Lewis Marcus, m. Nellie Waite Smith of Montgomery 18 Dec. 1907, res. at Gardiner, Ulster Co., NY.
1883, Dec. 3, Anna Mary.
1886, Feb. 17, Carrie Louise.
1890, March 19, George Vanderoef.

**JESSUP, CHARLES L.**            H-871, LDS Anc. File
dairy & peach farmer near Florida, NY.
**JESSUP, SENECA**                       H-871, C-43

The Jessup family of Orange Co., NY desc. from John Jessup of Broomhall, Yorkshire Co., England, who came to America in 1630. He resided for a time at Boston & removed to Hartford & from there to Southampton, L.I. in 1640. The Jessups came from L.I. to Orange Co. in 1784 & located in Florida, Town of Warwick.

SAMUEL JESSUP[1], b. 21 Aug. 1819, Florida, Orange Co., NY, m. Hannah Steinmetz, b. 1825 [that is according to LDS Anc. File & one other source. Still another source gives his wife as Martha ---.] Samuel's children (all b. Florida, Orange Co.):
1843, May 25, **CHARLES LEONARD.**
1844, Oct. 31, JAMES JACKSON.
1846, March 24, ANDREW JACKSON.
1847, June 11, **SENECA.**
1849, Feb. 19, Sarah Elizabeth, m. Joseph Martin & had Jennie & Bessie.
1853, May 26, Mary, m. Albert Wellington McBride & had Bertha & Julia.
1854, Oct. 10, JOHN JOHNSON.
1856, June 14, Julia.
1857, Oct. 10, Thomas.
1861, Amzi.
1865, Nov., Caroline.
1869, July 17, SAMUEL.
1872, Jan. 6, Hannah.

CHARLES LEONARD JESSUP[2], s/o Samuel[1] & Martha Jessup [LDS Anc. File gives wife of Samuel & Mother of Charles Leonard as Hannah Steinmetz, b. 1825-d. 9 Sept. 1875, Florida, Orange Co.], b. 25 May 1843 on homestead farm 2 miles from Florida, one of 13 [sic] children. At the outbreak of the Civil War he enlisted in the 91st Regt., Co. H. After the war he farmed & was elder of the Florida Presbyterian Church. He m. Sarah Jane Duryea of Craigsville, Orange Co., d/o Alfred & Mary, 18 Oct. 1865, and had:
1866, Aug. 21, Alpheus Duryea.
1868, March 12, Julia B. (Emma), m. Alton J. Vail of Middletown & had Clinton Theodore & Charles Alton.

1871, June 10, Charles Webster, m. Elizabeth Wheeler of Florida.

1886, Helene Sarah, m. Raymond Quackenbush.

JAMES JACKSON JESSUP[2], s/o Samuel[1], m. Delia Alice Van Ostrand, b. 20 Oct. 1849 in Sussex, NJ, & had (all b. Florida, Orange Co. except for last 2):

1871, Jan. 16, Elizabeth, m. William Richard Jackson & had son Richard, b. 1900 in Cheyenne, WY.

1872, March 3, Lillian, m. John Charles Fullerton of OH.

1876, May 12, Alice, m. Thomas Starforth, b. 8 April 1872, Cornsay Colliery, Lancaster, Durham, England. Their children were b. in NE.

1877, Oct. 31, Amzi Armstrong, m. Gertrude E. Johnson, b. 3 June 1888, Banner, NE.

1879, Jan. 11, James, m. Flossie Mildred Learned, b. 3 June 1886, Concordia, KS.

1885, Aug. 23, Frank Pierson, b. Palmyra, NE, m. Marie Barr, b. 25 March 1888, Lincoln, NE.

1889, June 13, Stanley, b. Lincoln, NE, m. Irma Josephine Casteel, b. 17 May 1894, Clyde, KS.

ANDREW JACKSON[2], s/o Samuel[1], m. (1) Amelia Mc Cain & (2) Zenobia Bliss. He had by 2d marriage:
Willard.
Clara.

SENECA JESSUP[2], s/o Samuel[1], b. Town of Warwick, Orange Co. He m. Jennie (Jenny) A. McCain in 1868. She was b. 27 July 1850, a d/o John Edsall & Abigail (McCamly) McCain. Her family is desc. from William McCain, soldier of the Rev. War, who came from the North of Ireland in 1728 & located in Town of Warwick. Children:
John Seward, only surviving child, res. at home.
Charles.
Maud.
Jennie.

25 Nov. 1868 a Seneca Jessup m. at Goshen, Sarah Delia McCain, of Goshen.

JOHN JOHNSON JESSUP[2], s/o Samuel[1], m. Annie Waibel, b. 1 July 1860, & had:

1885, May 26, Richard Dale, m. Mathilda Voight.

1886, Nov. 11, Bernard Leland.

c. 1888, John.

1890, July 2, Florence Myrtle, m. Arthur William Gaylord, who m. 2d Louise Waibel, b. 23 Dec. 1866.

SAMUEL JESSUP[2], s/o Samuel[1], m. Katherine Grace Waibel, b. 26 Feb. 1875 & had:

1899, Sept. 1, Ildra.

1901, Nov. 1, Samuel Jr.

JOHNSON, CHARLES J. [P]  A-560g, C-47
of Goshen.

The first Johnsons from England to America 1644, settled at Newark, NJ.

JOTHAM JOHNSON[1] res. Newark, m. Hannah Beach, and had:
Josiah.
Nathaniel.
Thomas.
James.
1793, Jan. 23, EBENEZER.
Elmira m. Henry Parkhurst.
Phebe m. Caleb Carter.

EBENEZER JOHNSON[2] m. Mary, d/o Dennis & Elizabeth Osborne of Salem, Union Co., NJ. Mary b. 1795, d. Nov. 1870. Children:
William, farmer of Essex Co., where he d. & left: Henry, d. unm.; Charles F. & Mary C.
Ebenezer, worked as mason until 1826; farmer of Clinton, Essex Co., NJ; 1870 res. Elizabeth NJ, member First Presbyterian Church of Elizabeth.
1824, March 16, CHARLES F.

CHARLES F. JOHNSON[3], s/o Ebenezer, b. Newark, NJ; m. 20 Jan. 1847, Joanna, d/o Gen. CHARLES BOARD [see below] & Joanna Seeley. Joanna b. June 1817. Farmed at Ringwood until 1859, then to Goshen, Orange Co., dairy farmer, political service. Children:
Henry P.
Charles E.
Asher, m. Kate Hawkins 20 Feb. 1884.
William.

Three Board brothers, Joseph, James & David, from Wales to Ringwood, NJ where they had charge of iron works; owned land in the Pompton Valley & many desc. became settlers in Orange Co., NJ. Joanna, Mrs. Charles F. Johnson, is a grand-dau. of Joseph.

———

JOHNSON, JOHN T. [P]  A-620, C-27, STJ-1
banker of Chester.

JAMES JOHNSON[1] [could be the James, s/o Jotham above], of Welsh desc., to Goshen as a young man, saddle & harness business; d. 25 June 1821. Member Episcopal Church of Goshen. He m. in NY City Miss --- Vantilbury, who was b. in Holland. They had:

1763, JOHN[2], b. Newark NJ; m. (1st) Miss --- Townsend and had one child:
Sarah m. Edward James, atty. of Goshen, where he d. Could be the Sarah Ann b. 29 Jan. 1796, d/o John & Margaret Johnson.

JOHN[2] m. (2d) 2 April 1814, Orpha, wid. of Timothy Little & d/o Col. John Tuthill of Blooming-Grove, Orange Co. She

was b. 11 Nov. 1781 & d. 15 June 1855; member of the Presbyterian Church. They had one child:
1815, Feb. 18, **JOHN T.**

**JOHN T. JOHNSON**[3], s/o John[2], res. with maternal grandfather Col. Tuthill one of the first settlers of Erin, Chemung Co., until age 15 when he came to Chester & clerked at store of uncle Francis Tuthill.

————

**JOHNSON, L. A.**                    H-871-2
merchant at Sparrowbush, NY.

**L. A. JOHNSON**, b. Tompkins Co., NY, m. Lillian A., d/o the late Henry F. West of Sparrowbush & Mary Stanton of Forestburg, NY who m. in 1873. **L.A.** & Lillian have 3 sons.

————

**JOHNSTON, BEVERLY K.** [P]          A-367-8

JOHN JOHNSTON[1], blacksmith of Shawangunk, Ulster Co., d. c. 1822, age 60, and had:
1818, June 21, **BEVERLY K.**

**BEVERLY K. JOHNSTON**[2], s/o John[1], b. Shawangunk; 1840 to Newburgh, emp. of John E. Goetchius, local hotel business at East Coldenham; in 1847 owner of the hotel. Served as local postmaster & other public service posts. In 1846 m. Elvira S., d/o Alexander W. Beatty & Elizabeth Moore of New Windsor. Children, all living at home:
William J.
Anna F.
John A.
Adaline L.

————

**JOHNSTON, JAMES D.** [P]           A-175
Physician of Middletown.

JAMES JOHNSTON[1], land proprietor midland counties of England had a son, JOHN B.[2], manufacturing chemist, who m. Jane Richmond and had:
John, in family business.
William, in family business.
Samuel, to America 1841, settled Newark, NJ, where he died.
1815, May 14, **JAMES D.**

**JAMES D. JOHNSTON**[3], s/o John B. & Jane, b. in Angel St., St. Martin's Le Grand, London, England; studied at St. Thomas Hospital, London; 1841 to America & settled Newark, NJ; 1842 to Middletown, Orange Co. 5 Nov. 1845, m. Deborah, d/o William Meeks & Sabrina Jaycox of Peekskill, NY. Deborah b. 4 Dec. 1825, her paternal great-grandfather English farmer of Peekskill. **JAMES** specialized in uterine surgery; was one of the first vestrymen of Grace Church, Middletown. Surviving children:
Selina Montrose, widow of Alderman William I. Underhill of Newburgh.
James Doremus.
Charles Albert.
Annie Richmond.

————

**JOHNSTON, REV. JOHN D.D.** [P]        A-306-07
Presbyterian minister of Newburgh.

**REV. JOHN's** great-great grandfather from England to Ireland with Army of King William & fought in Battle of Boyne in 1690. Later settled Co. Cavin, Ireland, where his desc. WILLIAM JOHNSTON[1] was born, the youngest of 13 children, 1 Dec. 1743; 1774 to America & settled in NY intending to return to Ireland in 7 years, but he met Jane Moncriff who came to America with her brother Charles in 1775, and they m. in 1777 & remained in America. WILLIAM was a farmer of Montgomery and had:
1778, Jan. 28, **JOHN.**

**REV. JOHN JOHNSTON**[2], b. Twp. of Montgomery, Ulster Co., (now Crawford Twp., Orange Co.). Farmer & in 1795 studied under Rev. Jonathan Freeman, pastor at Hopewell; studied various places & grad. Princeton College 1801. Served in many NY locations; m. 27 Jan. 1807, Mary, d/o Daniel Bull of Orange Co., res. Newburgh 1807, where he d. 23 Aug. 1855; Mary d. 2 March 1857. They had 10 children, 6 still living, those named here:
Mrs. Lewis D. Lockwood.
Mrs. George Lawson.

————

**JOHNSTON, WILLIAM C.**             H-872
merchant of Newburgh.

**WILLIAM C. JOHNSTON** has a harness & leather store in Newburgh. He was b. there & learned his trade with John R. Woolsey; m. Margaret L. Campbell & had 10 children. Those named here:
Robert, hardware merchant, now age 40.
W. Charles, carriage repository on Broadway.
Renwick, in livery business.

Members Westminster Reformed Church.

————

**JONES, EVAN E. & JONES FAMILIES**
hotel keeper of Hamptonburgh.      **A-214, H-872, T-45, 49**

**EVAN E. JONES**, b. Turin, Lewis Co., NY, 10 June 1856, farmer until 1902 when he came to Orange Co. to conduct Johnston Hotel. April 1906 removed to Hamptonburgh, where he is now engaged in hotel business. He m. Emma M. Peck of Turin 12 Jan. 1886, no issue.

An **EVAN JONES**, surgeon, was an early settler of Haskell Patent, Town of New Windsor; farm sold by his heirs in 1763 to Samuel Brewster.

T-45 has the story of **REUBEN JONES**, early settler taken prisoner by the Indians in Orange Co.

About 1804 two families of **JONES** bought a vast tract of land & settled in Monticello & brought in other early settlers: Platt Pelton from Putnam who started a tannery & Maj. Abraham Brownson & others from CT. T-49.

————

**JONES, CAPT. MICHAEL**     A-523 & C-33, 42, 101, 117
of Goshen.

**CAPT. MICHAEL JONES** res. on the "Drowned Lands," 3
miles from Goshen village, his <u>grandsons</u> [all Jones]:
Andrew.  Could be the Andrew Jones of Goshen who m. 28
Feb. 1866, Maggie J. Owen of the same place.  There was
also an Andrew Jones, mechanic, who m. Almeda Edsall,
seamstress of Goshen on 10 May 1832.
Anthony.
Michael.
Samuel.

A Mary, d/o Samuel Jones, was bapt. in Goshen June 1776;
and a Hannah, d/o Andrew Jones was b. 5 May 1792 & bapt. in
Goshen.

---

**JORDAN FAMILY OF CRAWFORD**     A-413, H-186

Three Jordan brothers to America from Ireland:
ROBERT.
Jonathan, settled in Bullville, 1767.
John.

**ROBERT JORDAN**, settled in Town of Wallkill 1771; m. Mary
Bull, d/o the 2d William Bull & widow of George Wilkin;
1784-5 settled at Bullville, Town of Crawford, and had:
Moses, lived & d. north part of Wallkill.
John, lived & d. north part of Wallkill.
1793, April 4, William, m. Cornelia Bull, d/o Thomas; settled
Bullville, j.p. 32 years, later res. Bloomingburgh, Sullivan
Co.

---

**KELLS, ISAAC**     H-873
farmer, Town of Montgomery.

**ISAAC KELLS** is of Scotch-Irish descent, b. in the North of
Ireland in 1833 & d. at his home 1 Oct. 1907.  He was a
member of the Goodwill Church.  He was married twice, (1)
Elizabeth Ferguson & had:
Mrs. William Whigam
Mrs. Delia Boyd, d. 1905.
[Second wife not named.]

---

**KERNOCHAN, JOHN BEATTIE [P]**     A-242-3
farmer of New Windsor.

**JOHN KERNOCHAN**[1], b. 20 Nov. 1785, d. 16 Aug. 1871; m.
7 Nov. 1815, Elsie Beattie, b. 9 Oct. 1784, d. 21 Dec. 1827.
[See below.]  Children:
Elsie J. m. Samuel McGill of New Windsor.
Sarah m. I. R. Goldsmith of New Windsor.
1821, Oct. 26, **JOHN BEATTIE.**

**JOHN BEATTIE KERNOCHAN**[2], b. New Windsor; d. 15
June 1875.  9 March 1843, m. Jane, d/o James & Prudence
Denniston of Little Britain.  Jane d. 12 April 1869.  Attended

Assoc. Reformed Church of Little Britain.  Children:
Frances M. m. Abner Mills of Wallkill; dec'd.
Adelaide, res. on homestead.
Prudence M., res. on homestead.

**JOHN BEATTIE**, of early family of New Windsor, b. 1751, d.
17 April 1840; m. Elizabeth ---, b. 1761, d. 31 March 1840.
Their dau. Elsie m. John Kernochan [above].

---

**KERR, GEORGE W.**     H-873

**GEORGE,** b. Warren Co., NJ 15 Feb. 1810.  His ancestors
came from Scotland, his father b. Freehold, NJ & removed
to Ithaca NY.  In 1831 **GEORGE** joined Bank of Newburgh,
in 1854 he was elected president of the bank to fill the
vacancy left by the death of John Chambers.  **GEORGE** d.
3 June 1890.  He had been a vestryman of St. George's
Protestant Episcopal Church for 47 years.  He was married
twice: (1) Emeline Ross, (2) Margaret T. L., d/o Rev. John
Brown.

---

**KERR, REV. NATHANIEL**     A-525, C-98

**WALTER KERR**[1], b. Scotland 1653, arrested as non-confirmist
& banished; to America, settled at Freehold, NJ, where he
became one of the founders of the famous Tennent Church
of which the brothers William & Gilbert Tennent were
successive pastors.  Walter's <u>grandson</u>:
**REV. NATHANIEL KERR**[3], d. 1804, and had:
1766, March 5, Oliver Livermore.
1767, 9 Aug., Catharine, m. Simon Hasock.
1769, Jan. 20, Hannah m. Thedorus Van Wyck.
1770, March 7, Margaret Clark.
1772, May 20, Mary.
1774, March 14, Elizabeth.

---

**KETCHUM FAMILY OF MT. HOPE**
**H-874, LDS Anc. File**

**JOHN KETCHUM**[1], b. Huntington [Southhold], L.I. 24 Jan.
1716; a lineal desc. of **EDWARD KETCHUM**, progenitor of the
family in America who settled at Ipswich, MA in 1635 &
Southwold in 1653.  Edward d. in 1655 in Stratford, CT & left
7 children.
**JOHN**[1] (of the 6th generation in America) m. Sarah Mathews
of Morristown, NJ & to Orange Co. & settled in Hamptonburgh
and later in Goshen.  In 1774 to present Town of Mt. Hope.  He
was the founder of Ketcham's Mills, near Mt. Hope Village.
John d. there 21 April 1794 & widow Sarah d. there in 1802.
Homestead passed to their son Joseph and has been continuously
occupied by family members (1774-1907).  It is now occupied
by Isaac Emmett Ketcham, a great-grandson of Joseph.
The last surviving grandson of said Joseph, bearing the
family name, was the late John L. Ketcham, s/o Joseph Jr.
(farmer, mechanic & inventor), b. 22 Feb. 1820, m. 14 Nov.
1844, Harriette Writer of Town of Mt. Hope.  She d. 30 Aug.
1870.  John L. d. 10 June 1898 & left one child: Electa J.
Ketcham Penney, res. near Finchville.

Children of JOHN KETCHAM[1] & wife Sarah Matthews:
c. 1746, Philip, m. Elizabeth Youngs.
1748, Feb. 28, John, m. Abby Hawkins.
1750, Sept. 23, JOSEPH.
1755, May 12, Elizabeth, m. John Case.
c. 1757, July 22, James, m. Rhoda Campbell.
Rhoda.
Martha.
Isaac.
Miriam, m. John Carpenter.
Ruth, m. James Tucker.
1766, Jan. 2, Mary, m. Andrew Davis.

JOSEPH KETCHAM[2], s/o John[1], b. Southhold, L.I., m. Prudence King of Suffolk Co., b. 17 Jan. 1756, & had:
1776, June 23, William.
1779, Feb. 24, Lucy, m. Daniel Downs.
1780, Aug. 7, ISAAC.
1782, June 21, JOSEPH.
1784, Dec. 1, Lydia, m. Joshua Penny.
1786, Dec. 15, Elizabeth.
1788, July 29, Rhoda, m. George Fox Reeve.
1791, May 29, Philip, m. Sarah Osburn.
1794, May 3, Prudence, m. Lemuel Wheat.
1796, Oct. 5, Sarah, m. John Penny.

ISAAC KETCHAM[3], s/o Joseph[2], b. Mount Hope, Orange Co., m. Elizabeth Beyea, b. 7 Aug. 1788, Bedford, Westchester Co., NY, & had (all b. Mt. Hope):
1807, Oct. 31, Elizabeth Youngs, m. Selah Riley Mapes, b. 11 June 1805 at Mt. Hope. They had Mary Jane, Isaac D. & James Riley Mapes.
1810, Aug. 21, Amos, m. (1) Sally Eliza Seybolt, (2) Mrs. Mgt. [sic] Seybolt.
1812, Aug. 25, Isaac Emmet, m. Abigail Seybolt.
1817, May 10, Mary Little, m. James Brown.
1819, May 4, James Lewis, m. Rebecca Corwin.
1822, Feb. 6, Joseph, m. Sarah Elizabeth Ketcham.

JOSEPH KETCHAM[3], s/o Joseph[2], m. Mary Leverick Mullock, b. 21 June 1783, & had:
1803, Jan. 21, Sarah (Sally), m. John Wallace Martin, b. 1797. They had: William, Mary Jane, Louisa Ann & Ellen Reed Martin.
1804, Sept. 17, Arminda, m. Jasper A. Writer, b. 14 Oct. 1801. They had: Lewis, George Sneeden & Mary Elizabeth Writer.
1806, Sept. 18, Lydia, m. John K. Davis & had Ira Benjamin, William Edgar & Theodore Algernon Davis.
1808, April 18, Mary Ann, m. Coe Finch.
1810, April 15, Julia Ett, m. Alexander McDowell & had Joseph Ketcham, Harriet, Mary Aveline & Oscar McDowell.
1812, Nov. 3, WILLIAM JAY.
1814, Sept. 18, CHAUNCEY LEVERICK.
1818, Jan. 12, Rebecca Jane, m. William Youngs Wilson, b. 3 March 1810, & had: Mary Elizabeth, George Marsene & Karen Adah Wilson.
1820, Feb. 22, John Logue, m. Harriet Writer.
1823, Oct. 15, Karren Newkirk, m. Ferdinand Seybolt, b. 25

Oct. 1822, & had: Marsene Merwin, William Watson & Clarence Alva Seybolt.

WILLIAM JAY KETCHAM[4], s/o Joseph[3], m. Louisa Ann Seybolt & had:
1833, Sept. 8, Lewis Youngs, m. Amanda J. Knight.
1838, Sept. 9, William Emmet, m. Mary A. Clapp.
1840, Dec. 20, Marsh Dewitt.
1841, Dec. 23, Catherine Elizabeth, m. Roscoe E. Houghton.
1844, Nov. 28, Frances Almeda, m. Roscoe E. Houghton.

CHAUNCEY LEVERICK KETCHAM[4], s/o Joseph[3], m. Sophia Wilson & had:
1840, March 5, Horace Chauncey, m. Phebe Scidmore.
1844, March 25, Eugene George.
1848, Sept. 25, Willis Wilson.
1852, Feb. 4, William Emery.
_____

**KETCHAM, B. S. [P]        A-786b, H-874, LDS Anc. File** of Cornwall.

SAMUEL KETCHAM[1] located at Mountainville before the Rev. (now known as Ketchumtown), pioneer farmer; grist mill. They were the first settlers of the town. Children, all settled Ketchamtown [wife not named]:
Samuel.
Joseph.
c. 1753, BENJAMIN.

BENJAMIN KETCHAM[2], b. Cornwall, Orange Co., soldier of the Rev., m. Mary ---, of Port Orange, who d. 5 Sept. 1832, age 82; he d. 18 May 1833, age 88. Children:
c. 1785, Abraham, lived & d. in Sussex Co., NJ.
1786, Oct. 26, CHARLES.
1787, Ann, b. Cornwall, m. Daniel C. [Daniel Powell] Carpenter. They had dau. Mary Carpenter, b. 17 April 1808, Dutchess Co., m. Hiram F. Powell of Dutchess Co.
James, res. Town of Monroe.
Joseph, res. NY City; d. on homestead.
Hannah, b. Highland, m. Martin Pempleton.

CHARLES KETCHAM[3], s/o Benjamin[2], b. on the farm; d. 1 June 1847, farmer; m. Anna Smith, b. 18 April 1876, d. 11 Aug. 1851, and had:
1813, Nov. 14, Daniel C.; d. 1854.
1819, Jan. 4, BENJAMIN S.
1823, July 13, Eliza Jane; d. 22 April 1864,.

BENJAMIN S. KETCHAM[4], farmer on family homestead; m. 26 April 1846, Mercy, d/o Nathaniel & Rebecca (Cornell) Brown, and had:
1847, CHARLES.
Theodore, farmer on homestead.
Ann E.; d. infant.
Olive A. m. James Barton of Mountainville.

CHARLES KETCHAM[5], merchant & postmaster at Mountainville, res. Town of Cornwall. He was born on the family homestead; m. Ida, d/o Capt. Jacob Smith of Cornwall. They have 2 sons & 6 daus.

---

**KIDD, JOHN [P]**          A-381, 410c, H-875, W-13
of Montgomery.

ALEXANDER KIDD[1], to America before the Rev., along with brothers Robert & Andrew. Of Scotch-Irish desc. 1736 res. in Orange Co. & is given credit for building in part the Kidd house in Town of Walden. He was an elder of the Goodwill Church; m. Jane Calderwood and had:
ROBERT.
Alexander.
James.
Anna.
Hannah.

ROBERT KIDD[2], s/o Alexander[1], m. Mary McGowan and had:
1772, June 27, ANDREW.
John.
Daniel.
Robert.
Archibald.
William.
Margaret.
Jane.
Mary.

ANDREW KIDD[3], farmer of Montgomery, d. 17 Feb. 1826; 1802 m. Margaret Kidd and had:
1803, Oct. 26, JOHN.
Anna Maria m. J. Gillespie.
Alexander.
Sidney.
Robert.
Mehetabel Jane.

JOHN KIDD[4], s/o Andrew[3], farmer of Montgomery, bank director, hwy. commissioner, attended Reformed Dutch Church of Montgomery; 16 Nov. 1826, m. Cornelia, d/o Charles Haines of Montgomery, who d. June 1876. Children:
Andrew.
Mirza.
JOHN EGBERT.
David L.
Margaret J. [A?]
Victor; dec'd.

JOHN EGBERT KIDD[5], now a retired farmer near Walden, enlisted with the Orange Blossoms, 124th NY Regt., during the Civil War. He married (1) Alice Decker & (2) Maria Adeline Decker. Children of 1st m.:
Cornelia m. George Wait.
John.

---

**KIMBER, PETER [P]**          A-674c, LDS Anc. File
of Minisink.

CASPER KIMBER[1], b. c. 1703, from England with wife Pemmetjse Williamse of Orange Co., NY, c. 1728, settled in the old Minisink patent at Pellet's Island & d. there. His children:
c. 1729, GEORGE (Joris).
c. 1745, NATHANIEL.
Ephraim.
Isaac.
Joseph.
John.
James.
Zuby.
Elizabeth.

GEORGE KIMBER[2], s/o Casper[1], after marriage purchased land at Wantage, NJ & res. there few years & later bought land in Minisink Patent c. 1750; served in Rev. War & d. a few years after. He is "of Machackemeck, Orange Co., NY." He m. Sarah Westfall, b. c. 1729, of Orange Co., their children:
Bapt. 1753, March 11, Sarah.
Bapt. 1755, Feb. 16, Margaret, m. Henry Horton of Orange Co. They had dau. Sally, b. 10 March 1785 in Minisink, who m. John Lain, b. 13 March 1781, Minisink.
1759, Aug. 26, PETER, b. Machackemeck.
c. 1765, SAMUEL.

PETER (PETRUS) KIMBER[3], s/o George[2], b. on homestead and d. there 14 March 1817; was in Minisink Massacre & served in Rev.; m. Elizabeth, d/o James Clark of Minisink and had:
Sarah.
1781, Aug. 29, GEORGE.
Catharine.
Jane.
James.

GEORGE KIMBER[4], s/o Peter[3], m. Sarah Elston, who d. 13 May 1874 in NJ. They were m. 13 April 1800, at Unionville, Orange Co. George d. 3 Nov. 1860 in Orange, Essex Co., NJ. They had:
1800, April 29, Elizabeth, m. Leonard Wintermute, farmer of Wantage; d. 28 July 1834, OH.
1802, March 14, Hannah, m. Joseph (Josiah) Bennett, farmer of Minisink; d. 4 March 1858.
1806, Aug. 20, PETER.
1816, Sept. 18, Sally Maria, m. Jacob D. Miers (Mierson), farmer of Wantage, NJ, he d. 3 Nov. 1860.

PETER KIMBER[5], s/o George[4], has always res. on homestead near Unionville, built saw & cider mills, member Baptist Church of Unionville; m. Maria (Sarah M.) Litteer (Lateer) 17 Jan. 1829; she d. 3 April 1869. Children:
Joseph E. m. Jane Shorter, res. Unionville.
Phebe Elizabeth m. George W. Rhodes, farmer of Vernon, Essex Co., NJ.
John M., res. at home.

Merilda, res. at home.
Sarah m. John L. VanGorder, farmer of Minisink.
Mary Ann, res. at home.
George Merritt, res. at home.

SAMUEL KIMBER[3], s/o George[2], m. Marie Bennett of Orange
Co., & had:
Bapt. 1784, June 13, Machackeneck, Sarah.
1791, April 2, BENJAMIN.

BENJAMIN KIMBER[4], s/o Samuel[3], m. Kezia Bennett, b. 2
Nov. 1792, Orange Co., NY. They had (all b. Unionville,
Orange Co.):
1811, Nov. 29, Susan, m. Cabel Jones, b. 31 Aug. 1813, Sussex,
NJ.
1813, Dec. 6, Charity, m. William P. Clark, b. 18 Dec. 1812,
Orange Co.
1815, Feb. 22, Phebe L., m. John N. Decker, b. 8 Jan. 1814,
Orange Co.
1816, June 10, Mary B., m. Mark Congleton, b. 17 Feb. 1814,
Hardiston, NJ.
1818, June 1, Catherine, m. John Welda of Orange Co.
1820, Sept. 13, Julia Ann, m. Erastus Elston, b. 6 June 1820,
Unionville.
1822, April 26, Abigail.
1824, Aug. 6, Sarah, m. William MacBury.
1827, Aug. 19, Jane Eliza, m. Moses Seeley, b. 5 Feb. 1823,
Orange Co.

NATHANIEL KIMBER[2], s/o Casper[1], m. --- & had:
c. 1780, ABRAM.

ABRAM KIMBER[3], s/o Nathaniel[2], m. Sally Bennett, b. 1790 at
Westtown & had:
c. 1812, Lavinia, m. (1) Silas Martin, (2) Stephen Farnham.
c. 1814, Abraham, m. Lydia Ann Van Horn of Brooklyn,
Susquehana Co., PA. Their children b. Brooklyn.
c. 1816, Millicent, m. Charles Cole.
c. 1818, Jeremiah, m. Louise Roosa.
c. 1820, David L., m. (1) Abigail Chamberlain, (2) Ruby
Chamberlain.
c. 1822, Deborah, m. George Canfield.
c. 1824, Nathaniel, m. Adelia Wood.

------

**KING FAMILY OF CHESTER**      A-614-5, II-163
**KING, JOHN [P]**             A-626
of Chester.

The first documented King served 6 years in the French &
Indian War in Canada & in 1761 res. Gray Court Meadows,
Orange Co. His children:
1757, Nov. 4, JOHN.
JOSEPH.
PETER.
Charles, went West.
Susan m. Samuel Green of Monroe.

JOHN KING[1], m. 5 Jan. 1784, Margaret Gray. After marriage
settled on Wawayanda Patent in Sugar-Loaf Valley near
Bull's Mills, Town of Chester (then Goshen); soldier of the
Rev., early member of Presbyterian Church at Chester, he d.
13 Feb. 1844. Children, all m. & settled Orange Co., except
James, Abel & Ezra:
James.
Abel.
Elizabeth m. John Woodruff; d. at Bethlehem, Orange Co.
Sarah m. Lewis H. Roe.
1793, Sept. 13, JONAS.
Ezra.
Juliana m. Anselm H. Dennison.

JONAS KING[2], res. on homestead, businessman & farmer; d. 26
Aug. 1873; m. 6 April 1815, Elizabeth, d/o Joseph Durland
(s/o Charles from L.I. to Chester 1756) & Martha Board.
Elizabeth b. 1796, d. Oct. 1843; member Presbyterian Church
at Chester. Their children:
Martha.
1817, Aug. 9, JOHN.
Lewis, res. IL.
Elizabeth m. William Masterson.
Sarah m. James W. Mapes of Cayuga Co.
Edmund.
Mary.
Phebe.
Louise m. Curtis Z. Winters.
Susan.

**JOHN KING[3]**, s/o Jonas, b. Monroe, later occupied homestead farm, farmer & some public service. 25 Sept. 1861, m.
Hannah M., d/o NICHOLAS H. CAYWOOD [see below] &
Susan Mapes of Weedsport, Cayuga Co. Members of the ME
church at Chester.

NICHOLAS H. CAYWOOD, s/o John, owned tannery & made
shoes for soldiers of the Rev., in which he served for a time
& later settled at Ovid, Seneca Co., NY, where he died 18
Feb. 1881, age 76. His wife Susan Mapes d. 11 July 1872,
age 58. Their children:
1832, Sept. 17, Hannah M. m. JOHN KING [above].
Chauncey C.
Elizabeth; d. 1860, age 23.

PETER KING[1], brother of John[1] above, had a son JAMES G.
KING[2] and he had a son, WILLIAM B. KING[3], res. Chester
Village.

JOSEPH KING[1], bother of John & Peter above, settled at
Monroe near Little Pond, Town of Chester.

------

**KIPP, GEORGE A.**              H-875-6

GEORGE A. KIPP, s/o Richard A. (3 March 1838-26 July
1897) carpenter of Goshen & Mary Ann Dailey, was one of
6 children. He was b. 31 July 1871 at Goshen; at age 15

learned carpenter's trade. He m. Clara Baker of Middletown, 26 April 1899 & had 4 children, 2 died in infancy. Living children:

1905, June 9, Alberton.
1907, Aug. 27, Dorothy.

---

**KNAPP, WILLIAM [P]**      **A-556d**
**H-876, C-20, 25, 35, 82-3, 104**

WILLIAM KNAPP[3], son of Samuel[2] and grandson of Samuel[1] (1695-1751), from Horseneck, CT to Orange Co. 1749, on 210 acre farm, part of Van Horn tract, one of the earliest settlers of Town of Goshen. Wife of Irish birth, Margaret ---. They had 9 children, those named:

1735, JAMES.
Samuel, soldier of the Rev., killed at Minisink Battle, 22 July 1779.
William.

JAMES KNAPP[4], m. Esther [Hester] Drake, b. 1741; soldier of the Rev., killed at Minisink Battle, 22 July 1779. Several of their children settled in Cortland Co., only John remained in Orange Co. Had 9 children "born between the years 1761-1779:"

1765, Aug. 24, JOHN.
Daniel.
Nathaniel.
James.
1779, March 18, Stephen.
Polly m. Stephen Crane.
Sally m. William Lucas.

JOHN KNAPP[5], d. 1 Aug. 1854; m. (1st) Elizabeth, d/o James Savage, and had:
Betsey m. Stephen Valentine, at Goshen, 24 Dec. 1807.

JOHN[5] m. (2d) at Goshen, 24 May 1794, Eunice, b. 6 Oct. 1775, d. 2 May 1853, d/o Jonathan Smith of Goshen, and had:
1795, Abigail, m. Daniel Wood, res. near Rochester, NY.
1797, Polly; d. age 16, 14 May 1815, consumption.
Fanny; d. age 16, 7 Feb. 1814, consumption.
1801, Sept. 1, John; d. March 1860.
1804, Gabriel; d. 1867.
Dolly m. Calvin [Colvin] B. Gale of Goshen, 7 Feb. 1838.
1812, April 13, **WILLIAM**.
1813, July 17, Thomas, res. Schuyler Co.
Fanny Maria m. N. C. Coleman, res. Goshen.
VIRGIL.

WILLIAM KNAPP[6], s/o John[5], m. Nov. 1857, Hannah Maria, b. Feb. 1827, d/o Robert Rutan, Esq. of Vernon Twp., Sussex Co., NJ, j.p. of Passaic Co., NJ. Children:
Isaac Thomas.
Adelia R.
William.
John.

VIRGIL KNAPP[6], had son Charles Albert Knapp[7] who m. Emma Linderman & had:
Jesse, m. Addie Crawford, in business in NY City.
Louis, m. Catherine Bull, in business in NY City.
Mabel.

[NOTE: A Nathaniel Knapp lived for a time on the Levi Geer place (Town of Chester), and a headstone with the date 1804, the initials N.K., aged 64 years, marks the place of his burial on the farm upon which Hugh Dobbin probably lived in 1738. H-163]

H-876 says that the first of the family of KNAPP in Orange Co. was Nicholas, who with his brothers William & Roger came to America from Sussex, England in 1630.

Other descendants of these brothers named here include: Isaac Knapp who was in the expedition to Canada under Sir William Phips in 1690; John Knapp (1664-1749) of Stamford, CT, captain of band train in 1716; Nathaniel of Newberry, in 2d Louisburg expedition 1758-59.

---

**KNAPP, JAMES W.**      **H-875**

JAMES W. KNAPP, b. Pine Island, Orange Co., 22 Dec. 1831, s/o William who d. at age 85. **JAMES W.** d. at age of 76. He m. a d/o PETER N. RYERSON [see below] of Glenwood, NJ on 21 Oct. 1855, and had:
Mary, m. F. E. Tither of Florida, NY.
Nicholas, of Belmont, NY.
Charles, of Goshen.
William, of Pine Island.
J. Arthur, of Florida, NY.
Elizabeth, m. Walter S. Seeley of Middletown, NY.

**JAMES W.** member of Presbyterian Church at Amity & Town Assessor.

PETER N. RYERSON was the grandson of Nicholas Ryerson who went from Amsterdam, Holland in 1801 to L.I., NY. PETER was b. at New Vernon, NJ, 9 Sept. 1814.

---

**KNEVELS, JOHN W.**      **A-149**
horticulturist, atty., newspaper editor.

DR. ADRIAN KNEVELS[1] of Santa Cruz, West Indies, with his children to NY:
JOHN W.
Isaac.
Augustus.
Granville.
Maria.

JOHN W. KNEVELS[2], to Fishkill 1737; m. Elizabeth, d/o Daniel Cromeline Verplanack & sister of Gulian C. Verplanacek.

---

**KNIFFEN, SAMUEL L.**      H-876-7, C-44
of Goshen.

**KNIFFEN, WILLIAM**      H-877
hardware merchant of Goshen.

SAMUEL LOGAN KNIFFEN, b. at Chester in 1843; 1863 to Goshen with his parents & learned tinsmith trade under his father. He m. Sarah J., 5 May 1874, at Goshen, d/o Gabriel Bennett of Goshen & they have one dau., Carrie, who m. Charles B. Coleman.

WILLIAM KNIFFEN [probably brother of SAMUEL LOGAN above], b. Chester, Orange Co., NY 1855, came to Goshen in 1863 with his father Samuel M., a tinsmith for J. W. Corwin & Co.

There is no further data on WILLIAM. He may be the son of Samuel L. above, although text states clearly he is the s/o Samuel M.

---

**KNIGHT, CHARLES T.**      H-877
of Monroe.

CHAUNCEY B. KNIGHT of Monroe m. Mary Thompson, d/o the Rev. J. J. Thompson. She d. 1908. Their son, **CHARLES T.**, in feed, coal & lumber business with his father. Also Postmaster 1897-1908 & Town Supervisor.

---

**KOCKERTHAL, JOSHUA**      TN-261-2, CN-9

JOSHUA KOCKERTHAL (Kockerthal/de Kockerthal), leader of band of emigrants, res. a short time in Newburgh, if at all. He is listed as a resident in the Newburgh Directory for 1709. He spent the last 8-9 years of his life with a company of Palatines who had settled in Columbia Co., NY in 1710. Joshua d. c. 1719. He came to America in 1708 at age 39 with his wife Sibylle, also aged 39 on emigration, & first 3 children b. Germany:

Benigna Sibylle, aged 10 in 1708; m. William Christopher Berkemmyer, Lutheran minister & settled in Albany Co.

Christian Joshua, aged 7 in 1708; apptd. superintendent of one of the Palatine settlements in Columbia Co.; d. 1731, without issue, & the family became extinct.

Susanna Sibylle, aged 3 in 1708; m. William Heurtin, goldsmith of Bergen Co., NJ.

Cathalina, b. in America; m. Peter Lynch, merchant of NY.

Louisa Abigail, b. in America; m. John Brovort, goldsmith of NY.

Joshua Kockerhal's daus. became heirs to the lands in Newburgh, which were patented to the family. They sold the property to James Smith, 13 July 1741.

---

**KOHL, GEORGE, HENRY, VALENTINE J. &**
**WILLIAM J.**      H-877-8

VALENTINE KOHL[1], b. St. Martens-on-the-Rhine, Germany; teacher & shoemaker, to America shortly after his marriage to Mary Ann Zeigler, also b. in Germany. Valentine d. 1890. He had general store at Middlehope, where their children were born:

1868, VALENTINE J.
1871, HENRY.
1874, May 17, WILLIAM J.
1876, GEORGE.

VALENTINE J. KOHL[2] m. Charlotte P. Clauson & had 2 children.

HENRY KOHL[2], attorney of Newburgh, read law in office of Judge Seeger & admittted to bar 1894.

WILLIAM J.[2], president of Newburgh City Council & former Alderman of Newburgh.

GEORGE KOHL[2] has general store & postmaster (1871 to present). Has also served as town collector.

---

**KRONKHITE FAMILY OF HIGHLANDS**      A-812-13

JOHN KRONKHITE, early settler of West Grove (Highlands), orig. of Westchester Co. His children [wife not named]:
Richard, who had son John who res. on old homestead.
Mrs. James Green.
Mrs. James Wilkins.
Mrs. Howell.

---

**LAIN, W. FRANK**      H-879, LDS Anc. File

WILLIAM LAIN[1], from L.I. in 1770 to Town of Minisink; m. Keziah, d/o Increase Mather & had, among others:
DAVID[2], b. 20 Jan. 1791, d. age 79, lived his whole life on the family farm. He m. Millicent Aber, b. 29 Aug. 1792 at Westtown, who d. 2 April 1836. Their son:
RICHARD ALLISON LAIN[3], b. 3 Feb. 1818, m. 12 Dec. 1840, Caroline Matilda Alward, b. 20 April 1820, Sussex, NJ & d. 7 July 1897. They were parents of:
1841, Emeline.
1843, Caroline Matilda.
1847, Sarah.
1849, Phebe.
1853, Dec. 16, GEORGIANA.

GEORGIANNA LAIN [LANE][4], b. at Minisink & d. 8 Dec. 1934. Georgianna m. John Werry, b. 10 July 1855 at Westtown, on 17 Oct. 1876 & had Richard Allison Werry[5], b. 25 Dec. 1881.

GIDEON LAIN[1] [no relationship to above stated] d. 1906, m. Mary Dunning & had 3 sons & 1 dau., among them. W. FRANK LAIN[2], who continues the family farm, where he was b. 1859.

---

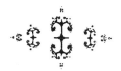

**LANDER, BENJAMIN**                    TN-323
of Newburgh.

From obituary *Journal*, 21 Sept. 1839. "Died--On Tuesday morning last, **BENJAMIN LANDER**, in the 41st year of his age. . . ."

---

**LAWRENCE, CHARLES M. [P]**            A-186
physician.

JACOB LAWRENCE[1] immigrated from Alsace, Germany at age 18, before the Rev. War, in which he served, being in the Battle of Trenton, later res. Philadelphia & Red Bank, NJ. Children [wife not named]:
Jacob.
James.
CHARLES.

CHARLES LAWRENCE[2], b. Philadelphia, d. 1845, age 56; m. Mary deFlood, d. 1826, and had:
James.
1822, July 8, **CHARLES M.**

CHARLES M. LAWRENCE[3], s/o Charles[2], b. Philadelphia, druggist in NY, res. Port Jervis. Dutch Reformed Church member; m. (1st) Margaret Holmes of Bridgeton, NJ, d. 1865, and had:
Emma m. Edgar Van Etten of Port Jervis.
Carrie J. m. D. J. Pierce of Port Jervis.
Holmes.
Charles; dec'd.

CHARLES M.[3] m. (2d) 1868, Agnes L., d/o Alexander Turner, of Scotch desc., and had:
Fred M.
Agnes Houseman.

---

**LAWRENCE, ROBERT**                    H-879
of Middletown.

ROBERT LAWRENCE, b. City of Birmingham, England in 1849, came to America with his parents in 1864; they settled in Middletown, Orange Co. He m. Amelia Thornton of Spring Glen, Ulster Co. in 1872 & had:
Howard R.
Cora B.
Ethel A.

Family members of St. Paul's Church.

---

**LAYTON, WILLIAM S.**                  H-879-80
dairy & peach farmer, Town of Warwick.

WILLIAM, b. Amity, Orange Co., 18 Jan. 1871, m. Gertrude H., d/o James H. & Catherine Miller of Florida, NY 3 Feb. 1892. Their children, all a home:
1893, June 6, Lawrence.

1895, Jan. 3, Edgar.
1896, Oct. 3, Lillian.
1898, Dec. 8, Helen.
1901, Sept. 12, William Gerald.

**WILLIAM's** father is not named, but it is stated that his father had a sister, Nellie E. Layton, m. James A. Sammis of Glenwood, NJ; she d. c. 1892.

---

**LAZEAR, WILBUR C.**                   H-880

**WILBUR C. LAZEAR**, b. 1854 on the family farm, 3 miles from Warwick, near New Milford. He was s/o Cornelius Jones Lazear & Elmira Ferrier. Cornelius in 1867 moved to Warwick & became the partner of Walter Knapp in the undertaking & furniture business. He d. 10 Jan. 1892, and son **WILBUR** continued the business. **WILBUR** m. 5 Nov. 1884, Jennie Smith, who d. 11 Feb., 1906. They had:
Cornelius S.
Belle.
Ida May.

---

**LEE, MARTIN E.**                      H-880
retired farmer of Westtown.

PAUL LEE[1], Revolutionary War veteran, had a son, DANIEL[2], who was a veteran of the War of 1812. Daniel's son LEWIS LEE[3] is the father of **MARTIN E. LEE**[4]. Lewis[3] m. Experience Teasdale, d/o ex-Judge Teasdale of Sussex, NJ. **MARTIN**[4] b. Town of Minisink in 1846, m. Alice d/o Dr. A.A. Seymour and had one daughter, Rose who m. Philip H. DuBois of New Paltz.

---

**LEE, ROBERT PERINE**                  GFM-22

**ROBERT PERINE LEE, D.D.**, b. Yorktown, Westchester Co., NY Sept. 1803; ordained Pastor of the Reformed Church at Montgomery, July 1829; d. in the 30th year of his Ministry, 30 Sept. 1858, aged 55 years. His wife was Elizabeth Wilton. Children:
John W., d. 4 April 1880, aged 46 years.
Henry W., d. 26 July 1864, aged 19.
Caroline, d. aged 1 month, 23 days.
Sarah, d. aged 10 months.

All from tombstone inscriptions at Montgomery.

---

**LEGGETT, REV. JOHN H. [P]**           A-420-1a

**REV. JOHN** b. NY City 28 May 1800; 19 May 1824 m. Mary Noel Bleecker of NY City; to Moreau, Saratoga Co., then Peekskill; Marlborough, Ulster Co.; 1833 to Hopewell Church at Crawford for 20 years; clerk of the Presbury of Hudson 20 years. In 1856 called to Middletown where he d. 31 May 1873 at the home of his youngest son, Rev. T. A. Leggett of Chester.

## LENT, ANDREW WRIGHT — H-880
atty. of Newburgh & Highland.

ABRAHAM D. LENT[1], atty., b. Clinton, Dutchess Co., NY 1850, attended Albany Law School. His son, **ANDREW LENT**[2], b. Highland, graduated Union College 1904, practicing attorney.

------

## LENT, NELSON BURTON — H-880-1

The Lent family are of Dutch ancestry & among the earliest settlers of Westchester Co., NY. NELSON was author & publisher of *History of The Lent Family in the United States from 1638-1902.*

Abraham DeRych came to America from Amsterdam, Holland to the Island of Manhattan in 1638. His son, Ryck Abrahamson, took the name of VanLent, which came from a place in Holland called "Lent."

**NELSON BURTON LENT** was b. in Town of Courtlandt, Westchester Co., 1 May 1856, s/o Nathaniel D. & Rachel (Lent) Lent. He was a compositor with the Highland *Democrat* at Peekskill NY until 1800 when with his cousin, William C. Tunstall, he established & edited the *Providence Register* at Scranton, PA. He later returned to Peekskill & later still to Newburgh, where he was employed by E. M. Ruttenber. He is a SAR member & attends the Trinity M.E. Church at Newburgh. 23 Dec. 1881 he m. Viola Frances Stone, d/o Herman & Mary of Danbury, CT., and had, all b. Newburgh:
Bertram Nelson.
Winfred Foss.
Roland Depew.
Hobart Townsend.
Sebring Round.
Mildred.

------

## LEONARD, CHAUNCEY M. & JAMES J. — H-882
of Newburgh.

**CHAUNCEY M. LEONARD**[1], b. Newburgh 1825, learned the trade of painter in NY, where he was a member of the volunteer fire dept. At age 19 he m. (1) Rebecca Smith of NY City, who d. 2 years later, leaving a dau. who m. Thomas K. Rheutan. In 1848 **CHAUNCEY** m. (2) Hope Smith, sister of his first wife & had several children. In 1850 he retired to Newburgh & resided there until his death. Public service. His son:
**JAMES J. LEONARD**[2], b. Newburgh 16 Oct. 1872, bookkeeper with house of Stephen M. Bull & later formed partnership with W. E. Doyle, wholesale grocers. Served as county clerk. He m. Mary T. Mc Quillan of Newburgh, and had:
Chauncey M.
Marion H.

------

## LESLIE, WILLIAM — TN-321
of Newburgh.

**WILLIAM LESLIE** conducted for a short time the *Newburgh Gazette*. He d. 17 Feb. 1838, of consumption. He was b. Scotland & left a large family. His son Alexander Leslie of Newburgh the only one named here.

------

## LINDERMAN FAMILY OF WALLKILL
A-435, LDS Anc. File
## LINDERMAN, HENRY S. [P] — A-504c
teacher & farmer of Wallkill.

JACOB LINDERMAN[1], of German extraction, of **Montgomery** had a son HENRY[2], b. Town of Crawford May 1764, who in 1790 settled at Wallkill; j.p. 40 years, member & deacon Hopewell Presbyterian Church. HENRY m. (1st) Sarah [one source says wife was Mary Shaw, d/o Moses, b. 1766] Shaw, who d. 1831 age 64; m. (2d) and removed to Bloomingburgh in 1842, where he d. 15 Jan. 1844, age 80; farmer. He had 10 children, 4 living:
David, farmer of Wallkill; d. 1866, Sullivan Co.
JOHN, physician of Dingman's Ferry, PA; d. PA 1875 & left 3 sons.
Willett, dist. atty. of Shawangunk Ulster Co.; dec'd.
Peter, to MI 1836 & d. there.
Elizabeth, m. Robert Thompson of NY; dec'd.
Mrs. Thomas J. Emmons, res. NY City.
Dolly, unm., res. NY City.
1807, May 28, **HENRY S.**
James O., lived & d. Kingston, Co. judge of Ulster Co. 1843-55.
Sally Jane, unm., res. NY City.

JACOB[1] m. (2d) a wid. of Col. Clark of Sullivan Co.

JOHN LINDERMAN[3], s/o Henry[2], had children:
Dr. Henry Richard, dir. of Philadelphia Mint; d. March 1879, Washington.
Garrett B., coal dealer of Mauch Chunk, PA; m. d/o Asa Packer.
Albert B., now working on project to drain Everglades of FL.
Dau. m. Asa Packer.

**HENRY S. LINDERMAN**[2], s/o Henry[2], b. on homestead at Wallkill; m. 25 Dec. 1839, Mary Ann, d/o James Martin & CATHARINE LINDERMAN [see below] of Crawford, who was b. 1810. Henry was town assessor, member of Presbyterian Church at Bullville & later at Circleville. Children:
James, farmer & Auctioneer of Wallkill.
Virginia m. Benjamin F. Van Fleet of Wallkill.
Emma m. C. Albert Knapp of Goshen.
Crotilda m. George E. Bull of Bullville.

The CATHARINE LINDERMAN above, wife of James Martin, was the d/o Jacob Linderman of Montgomery & wife Eloner ---. Jacob was s/o Johann Jacob Lindemann, b. 2 Dec. 1720, Obermoschel, Germany who m. Catharine McLean of Montgomery. Johann Jacob d. in Montgomery in 1792.

Children of Jacob Linderman[1] & Eloner:
1782, ABSALOM.
c. 1784, Henry.
1787, Sept. 15, CATHARINE.
c. 1789, Jacob.
c. 1791, John.
c. 1793, Susan.
c. 1796, Margaret.
c. 1801, Daniel.
c. 1803, Elizabeth.

ABSALOM LINDERMAN[2], s/o Jacob[1], m. Sarah --- of Crawford & had:
1813, Ann Eliza.
c. 1815, Sarah.
c. 1817, Jacob.
c. 1819, Rufus.
1821, May 6, Harriet.
c. 1822, Catharine.
c. 1824, Lucinda.
c. 1826, Margaret.
c. 1828, Charles.
c. 1830, Louisa.
1831, April 25, Theodore.

CATHARINE LINDERMAN[2], d/o Jacob[1], m. James Martin, b. 1807, of Crawford, & had (MARTIN):
1807, Nathan B., m. --- of Crawford & had Isabella.
1810, Mary Ann, m. Henry S.[2] Linderman, b. 28 May 1807 & had James, Virginia, Emma (Emily) & Crotilda.
c. 1812, Elizabeth Jane.
c. 1815, Isabella.
1817, Eli, m. Sarah M. ---, of Crawford, & had: Emily, Gaston B., & Elizabeth.

LITTELL, EDWARD G.                    H-882

EDWARD was b. Elmira, NY 5 July 1851, has res. in Rahway, NJ & Greycourt, Orange Co. Fireman on the Erie RR; later operated saw mill & general store. His great-grandfather was a Capt. Pratt Littell, Rev. War veteran who lived in Short Hills, NJ. EDWARD m. Ida Bronk Hyte of Greycourt & had:
Elizabeth A.
Edward D., of Los Angeles, CA.
William J.
Harry M.
Andrew H.
Hattie L.
Ida M.
Alfred K.

LITTLE, FRANCES                       U1-158
of Wallkill.

FRANCES LITTLE, relict of John of Stonefield, gentleman, her will dated 5 Sept. 1757, names her daus. Hannah Galatian,

Elioner McGariah & Margaret Moffat. Also mentions granddau. Frances Galatian.

———

LODGE, WILLIAM T.                     H-882-3
hotel keeper, Montgomery House.

WILLIAM was b. in Ireland 26 March 1836; to America at age 15. Farmer 1849-71 when he purchased his present hotel property. Episcopal & member of the Montgomery Church, a branch of the St. Andrew's Episcopal Church of Walden. He m. Catherine Doyle in 1863, and had, all res. Montgomery:
William T., Jr., manager of Empire House.
Marvin D., gen'ts furnishing store.
James A., horse & cattle dealer.
3 daus.

———

LOEVEN, WILLIAM             H-883, LDS Anc. File

WILLIAM was b. at Honesdale, PA 8 Sept. 1861, s/o Joseph Loeven, b. 1817 in Germany & wife Elizabeth Steffes, also b. Germany in 1827-29. Joseph & Elizabeth m. 18 May 1856 at Honesdale, Wayne Co., PA & Joseph d. there 13 Feb. 1867. Elizabeth d. 7 March 1914 in Jersey City, NJ. WILLIAM removed to Orange Co. in March 1891 & located at Middletown; removed his business to Otisville in 1906 & purchased Writer Hotel. WILLIAM m. Frances Gehrer of Honesdale, PA 16 Oct. 1889, and had, all at home:
1891 April 11, William Jr., m. Kathryn A. Sheil.
1892, June 1, Robert; he had a son Robert b. 1920 in Detroit, MI.
1894, Jan. 12, Edward.
1898, May 6, Elizabeth M.

Family are members of the Church of the Holy Name at Otisville. WILLIAM d. 14 Aug. 1942 at Otisville & Frances d. 29 Oct. 1926.

———

LOOMIS, CHARLES W.                    H-883

EPHRAIM SMITH LOOMIS[1], b. 22 May 1801, d. 27 Feb. 1869 & his wife [unnamed here] who d. 19 Nov. 1891, was b. on family homestead in Otisville that has been in his family for over 100 years. Their son:
CHARLES W. LOOMIS[2], b. Otisville, m. Phebe A. Dunlap, d/o Riley & Sarah E., 28 Nov., 1886, and had:
1887, Feb. 17, Iva Pamela, d. 19 May 1904.
1888, April 17, Antoniette Evelyn.
1890, Nov. 9, Ephraim Smith.
1894, Oct. 2, Frank Kaufmann.
1898, Feb. 19, Sarah Irene.
Family are members of the Otisville Presbyterian Church.

———

LOTT, EPHRAIM BEEMER                  H-883-4

JOHN HATHORN LOTT[1], cooper, had 10 children by his 1st wife & 9 by his 2d. One son was:

**EPHRAIM BEEMER LOTT²**, b. 25 Aug. 1862 at Sussex, NJ. He was with Warwick Valley Milk Assoc. 16 years, now foreman of the Warwick Branch of the Mutual Milk & Cream Co. Member Methodist Church of Warwick. He m. Emma Barrett of Warwick 31 Oct. 1888, and had:

Mary Lavina, at hom.

One child, d. in infancy.

_____

**LOVE, JAMES B.**                                   **H-884**

**JAMES** in 1906 purchased the Dr. Ormsber farm, between Newburgh & Village of Montgomery. He m. Maggie Urey & had:

1905, Jan., James B. Jr.

1908, March, John Robert.

_____

**LOVELAND, HENRY C.**                            **H-884**

**WILLIAM W. LOVELAND¹** m. Lucinda M. Atkins & had 12 children, 9 boys & 3 girls. Family is of English desc. & dates back in America to 1635. Child:

**HENRY C.²**, b. 13 Oct. 1853 in Chester, PA; 1872 to Middletown to learn mechanic's trade. He m. Josephine Decker 29 March 1877, and had:

**STEPHEN D.³**, m. Nellie Clark of Middletown, has one son & one dau.

Hattie, m. George C. Brundage.

_____

**LOW, JONATHAN**                                  **U2-70**
of Montgomery

In his will dated 25 Oct. 1790, **JONATHAN LOW** names wife Keertie & children:

Peter.

James.

Mary.

Catharine.

Magdelena.

Elizabeth.

Executors: Samuel Haines of Montgomery, yeoman; David Jagger & John Jagger.

_____

**LOWELL, WARREN**                                 **H-885**

**WARREN LOWELL**, b. Troy, NY, educated in Albany & NY City; 1876 to NY City with Orange Co. Milk Co., organized 1860. He m. Matilda D. Senior of NY 16 Sept. 1885.

_____

**LOZIER, OLIVER**                                 **H-885**
farmer near Savilton, Orange Co.

**OLIVER LOZIER**, b. Town of Newburgh 1837, 1868 to Savilton. Public servant. He m. Elizabeth Hanmore & had 5 children. Only one named here is Frank E., who manages the home farm & m. Mary Palmer of Ulster Co. Frank & Mary have one son, Elmore, & 1 dau.

_____

**LUDLOW, ROBERT**                                 **E-157**

**ROBERT LUDLOW**, from Warwick to Newburgh in 1796, & d. there. His children:

Mary, m. Thomas Powell.

Charles, Capt. in Navy.

1792, Augustus C., apptd. midshipman 1804 & served under his elder brother, Charles; d. in naval service.

_____

**LYDECKER, HARRY ROSS**                           **H-885**
atty. of Newburgh & Brooklyn.

**MR. LYDECKER** is the s/o Albert & Martha B. (Morrison) Lydecker & was b. in Yonkers, NY 4 March 1869. He read law in the office of Col. William Dickey, was admitted to the bar 1893. Public service. He m. 1891 Minnie A. Brown of Newburgh & has 5 children.

_____

**LYON, THOMAS J.** [P]                            **A-158**
atty. of Port Jervis.

Lyon family progenitor left Scotland before the Rev. War. We are not given his name, but his children:

Samuel, settled CT.

DAVID.

James, settled NY & later to OH.

**DAVID LYON¹**, settled Orange, Essex Co., NJ, where all his children were born:

Daniel.

Moses.

HENRY.

Sarah.

**HENRY LYON²**, farmer, distiller, manufacturer, in War of 1812; d. age 78. 1808 m. Eunice, d/o Thomas Harrison of Orange, NJ a soldier of the Rev. who d. age 98. Surviving children of 9:

Dr. S. S. of Newark, NJ.

William of Lyon's Farms, NJ.

1816, June 20, **THOMAS J.**

John W. of San Francisco, CA.

Ann m. --- Steel of Dayton, OH.

**THOMAS J. LYON³**, b. Caldwell, Essex Co., NJ; atty. for NY & Erie RR until 1867, trial lawyer, post master, legislator. 31 Dec. 1840, m. (1st) Jemima Westfall of Deerpark; survivors of 8 children born:

Sarah E.

Annie M. m. E. A. Brown of Newburgh.

John W., atty. of Port Jervis.

**THOMAS J.³** m. (2d) Miriam V. Osterhout, and had:

Thomas J. Jr.

Wallen.

Edwin F.

Mary E.

Frederick.

**MACKIN, HON. JAMES [P]**  A-361-2
of Newburgh.

JOHN MACKIN[1], carter at Newburgh & steamship line agent,
  d. c. 1829, aged 28; m. Eliza Jenkins who d. "a few years
  after her husband." Their children:
CHARLES.
1823, Dec. 25, **JAMES**.
Francis of Newark, NJ.
Mary, widow of James M. Kernochan.

CHARLES MACKIN[2], s/o John[1], merchant of Newburgh, m.
  (1st) c. 1825, Sarah J. Merritt, d/o Isaac of Hart's Village,
  Dutchess Co., niece of Charles A. Macy of NY; she d.
  before 1865. Charles to NY City & established dry goods
  firm. He m. (2d) Lizzie Hart in Paris, France.

JAMES MACKIN[2], b. Newburgh, was on his own at an early
  age; age 10 to Fishkill in employ of John Peter DeWitt,
  businessman, post master of Fishkill (1849-53), Town Supervisor (1857), legislator of Dutchess Co. & other political
  offices. He m. (1st) Sarah E. Wittsie, d/o Capt. James of
  Fishkill, she d. 1862. **JAMES** m. (2d) Sarah S., o/o ex-
  Mayor Col. James H. Britain of St. Louis, 13 Nov., 1879.

**MADDEN, HON. EDWARD M. [P]**  A-489-91

EDWARD was b. near Searsville, Town of Crawford, Orange
  Co., 1818, of Scotch-Irish, Huguenot & German ancestry.
  About age 9 his family removed to village of Walden in
  Town of Montomgery. 1839 owned & operated a tin-shop
  in Village of Middletown; 1842 in partnership operated a
  foundary; 1853 firm built saw factory & file works & later
  during Civil War manufactured steel; 1877 in partnership es-
  tablished printing co. in NY City. He also served as state
  senator. in 1843 m. Eudocia M. Robinson, d/o Rev. Phineas,
  Presbyterian clergyman. They had 6 children, 3 living:
Charles Carroll.
Edward M. Jr.
Ella.

**MAIDMENT, EDWARD**  H-890
engineer of Warwick.

Born in Shropshire, England in 1840; to America with
parents at age 6; family located in Albany, where his father, also
Edward, established a bakery & confectionary business.

EDWARD res. Chicago & since 1904 has lived in retirement on
  a farm, the Old Galloway homestead in Warwick. He m.
  Louisa Galloway, d/o Alexander H. of Warwick, who
  established a creamery business & d. 1884. Alexander was
  survived by his wife Hannah Louisa, who died 9 March
  1907, aged 90. Children of **EDWARD** & Louisa Maidment:
Alexander H. G., atty. of Hackensack, NJ.

Edward P.

**MAILER, W. H.**  H-890

W. H. MAILER, b. Cornwall in 1861, s/o Charles C. a
farmer of Mountainville. He owns meat market in partnership
with his brother George; m. Sophia J. Preston & they have 3
sons. Presbyterian Church member.

**MAILLER FAMILY OF NEWBURGH**  TN-314-15

JOHN MAILLER[1] (MILARD), from Scotland soon after the
  Rev. War & res. in NY, later in Westchester Co. & eventual-
  ly settled in Cornwall, Orange Co. His children [wife not
  named]:
James.
George.
John.
William
BARTHOLOMEW.
Jane.
Mary.
Sarah.

BARTHOLOMEW MAILLER[2], s/o John[1], m. Julia, d/o Samuel
  Ketchum of Cornwall, and had:
1805, Aug. 17, WILLIAM KETCHUM [P].

WILLIAM KETCHUM MAILLER[3], b. Town of Cornwall; at
  age 18 to Newburgh & entered service of Francis Crawford
  Co. He m. Hannah P., d/o Jacob Oakley of Coldenham on
  1 June 1830. They had 12 children, all d. in infancy except:
1831, May 26, William Oakley.
1834, Nov. 27, Mary Hannah, m. Moses Cook Belknap 16 June
  1857; she d. 31 May 1858.

**MANCE, CHARLES E.**  H-891

CHARLES is the only living child of 7 children of John S. &
  Margaret (Wilkinson) Mance. He was b. in Mance Settle-
  ment (now called Cragsmoor) in Ulster Co., 28 Nov. 1852.
  To Middletown with parents at age 14. Sign & ornamental
  painter, public servant, mayor 2 terms. 28 May 1874 m.
  Augusta, d/o Angus & Maria Taylor, and had:
Frank A., m. Belle Forrester of Providence, RI.
Mabel, m. D. H. Ackerman of Passaic, NJ.

**MANDEVILLE FAMILY**  LDS Anc. File

This family was not found in any local histories of the
county, but has been included here from LDS records that were
found when researching other Orange Co. families.

DAVID MANDEVILLE[1], b. c. 1681 in New Amersfoort, L.I.,
  NY, m. Jannetje Whoertendyk, b. c. 1687, The Bowery, NY.
  They had:
Bapt. 1709, April 6, David, bapt. NY City.

1711, Jacob, b. Pequenek, Dutchess Co., NY, m. Darah [sic] Davenport of Dutchess Co. Res. Pequenek, Putnam Co., NY.

Bapt. 1713, Feb. 18, Annetje (Anna), bapt. NY City, m. Jacobus Hennion (Henneon) of Fishkill, Orange Co.

Bapt. 1715, Sept. 18, Hendrick, bapt. NY City.

Bapt. 1717, Oct. 30, DAVID.

1720, Cornelius, m. Rachel Horton of L.I., res. Peekskill, Westchester Co., NY.

1720, Hannah, b. Flatbush, Kings Co., NY, m. Adam Vandenburgh, b. Flatbush c. 1720.

Bapt. 1724, Feb. 23, Maria, bapt. Flatbush.

Bapt. 1727, Feb. 1, Francis, m. Mary --- & all of his children bapt. in NY City except the last, dau. Frances bapt. in Orange Co., m. Henry Van Duzer of New Windsor.

Bapt. 1732, March 19, John, m. (1) Marytie Van Hoesen (Van House/Van Goese) & m. (2) Jannetje Jacobs Somerendijk Wortendyck of NY City.

DAVID MANDEVILLE[2], s/o David[1], bapt. at Hempstead, Nassau Co., NY, m. Anna Horton, b. c. 1725 at Waverly, NY & had (b. New Cornwall, Orange Co.):

c. 1745, Joseph.

1752, Jacob, m. Sarah Clark.

c. 1755, Mary, m. Samuel Westcott (Westcoat).

1757, FRANCIS.

1760, Henry B., m. Cornelia Kniffin Clark.

1762, MICHAEL.

1765, DAVID.

FRANCIS MANDEVILLE[3], s/o David[2], m. (1) Anna Weeks & had (all b. Orange Co.):

1776, DAVID.

c. 1778, Frances, m. --- Lynch.

c. 1780, Julia, m. --- Wortman & had son John b. c. 1800 in Orange Co.

c. 1782, Sarah, m. Elisha Farnum.

c. 1783, Debby Ann, m. Preston Farnum.

FRANCIS[3] m. (2) Deborah Clark & had:

c. 1785, Rachel, m. Alonzo Bently.

c. 1787, Elizabeth, m. Isaac Seely. See their children under Seely/Seeley family.

c. 1790, Thomas, m. Mercy Gilbert & had a dau. Caroline b. c. 1810 in Orange Co. who m. William Smallidge.

1793, Henry W.

c. 1795, Temperance, m. Alvah King.

MICHAEL MANDEVILLE[3], s/o David[2], m. (1) Elizabeth Clark & (2) Jane Cross. His children (b. Orange Co.):

c. 1800, Emily Jane, m. John Henry Clark of Orange Co. & had Emily Leona Clark b. c. 1820 & Mary B. Georgiana Clark, b. c. 1825.

1803, Eliza Jane, b. Newburgh, m. Thomas Hugh McGwin, b. 6 May 1788, County Armeaghe, Ireland. They moved to MI.

DAVID MANDEVILLE[3], s/o David[2], m. Sarah --- & had:

c. 1785, Daniel H.

c. 1786, Charles.

c. 1787, Jonathan.

---

## MANN, HIRAM G.                    H-891
farmer.

HIRAM was b. 11 July 1839 in Florida, Orange Co., s/o Hiram & Phoebe (Cherry) Mann; one of 11 children. 1849 family to Bellevale, Orange Co., on farm. He m. Anna Royce of Bellvale 18 March 1863 & they had 7 children. He served in the Union Army during the Civil War & is a GAR member. Their only surviving child:

Charles, res. NY, civil engineer.

---

## MANNING FAMILY OF GREENVILLE    A-693-4, H-241

JOSEPH & JOHN MANNING, brothers, settled in Orange Co. before Rev. War. JOSEPH's children:

Joseph Jr.

John.

Isaac.

Richard.

Walter.

Benjamin, had son John who res. near. village of Greenville.

Mrs. Eleazer Hulbert.

Mrs. John Fogges.

H-241 also gives another Manning, HIRAM, but does not give relationship to Joseph. It states they were all early settlers of Greenville. Joseph's sons are listed as above, but his daughters are given as: Mrs. Isaac Flint, Mrs. F. Hurlbut & Mrs. John Ferguson. HIRAM is noted as having a son HIRAM, who owned grist & cider mills at Millsburg & had a son, JOHN R., who resided in Gardnersville in Wawayanda. JOHN R., s/o HIRAM is given as having a son HIRAM JR., in business in Johnsons.

---

## MANNING, ALBERT                  H-891-2

EPHRAIM MANNING[1], b. Town of Greenville 11 Dec. 1810 on the old homestead which was purchased by his grandfather Benjamin Manning. This family is of English desc. Ephraim m. Caroline A. Rundle of Greenville 21 Nov., 1861, and had:

**ALBERT.**

Eva K., m. Abraham Wyckoff, res. NJ.

ALBERT MANNING[2], s/o Ephraim[1], b. on the homestead 2 Feb. 1864, was a teacher & manufacturer in NY City. In 1897 he returned to the homestead to manage the farm. 20 Sept. 1888 he m. Hattie E. Green, d/o Osmer B. & Harriet A. (Thorn) Green, of Otisville, NY. They have one child, Frank LeRoy Manning, b. 4 March 1898.

---

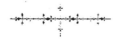

**MANNING, HULET**  H-892
farmer of Town of Greenville.

**HULET MANNING**, b. Town of Greenville 2 Aug. 1843, s/o John Manning & Mary Ann Smith, has always res. on the farm owned by his father. He m. Elizabeth M., d/o Alexander Remey of Greenville 23 Dec. 1864, and had:
Hattie, m. Clement VanEtlen, farmer of Greenville.
J. Edgar, m. Elsie Roberts of Montclair, NJ, res. NY City.
Mary A., m. Bartow W. Ball, farmer of Stony Ford, NY.
Clara D., m. Theron Shute, farmer of Greenville.

**MANY, CHARLES WILLIS, M.D.**  H-892-3

The lineage of the Many family of **CHARLES WILLIS** in America is: **BARNABAS MANY**[1], Rev. War veteran, m. Annie Everet and had:
**JOHN VICARY MANY**[2] m. Jane Howell Johnson and had:
**CHARLES MATTHEWS MANY**[3] who m. Eliza Ann Francisco and had:
**CHARLES WILLIS MANY**[4], b. 10 May 1866 at Goshen, NY. When he was age 1 his family moved to Brooklyn. He studied medicine in MA & on L.I., grad. with MD in 1894. In 1888 he m. Wilhelmina Martin of Liberty, NY whose American ancestors settled in Sullivan Co. early & later moved to Florida, NY. Their children:
Lillian Grace.
Clinton Alpheus.
Myrtle June Mary.

**CHARLES WILLIS**[4] is also said to be the great-great grandson of Thomas Horton & Susan Conklin; and the great-grandson of Peter Johnson & Bethia Horton.

**MAPES, A. W.**  H-893
of Newburgh.

**A. W.** was b. Town of Blooming-Grove, s/o the late Edward who moved to Newburgh in 1854. **A. W.** m. Sarah E., d/o the late John Parsons. The Civil War broke out shortly after their marriage & he served in the US Navy. After the war he moved to NY City & in 1883 he retired to Newburgh. Coming out of retirement in 1890 he established the Coldwell Lawn Mower Co. of Newburgh.

**MAPES, ELMER L.**  H-893-4

**ELMER**, b. on the family homestead near Middletown 27 Oct., 1885, operated a retail cigar & tobacco business. He m. Grace W. Wells of Elmira 27 June 1907 & had:
1908, June 13, Erdean Harriet.

**MAPES, GEORGE [P]**  A-561, C-10
of Goshen.

The first Mapes came to America from England and had a son, **DAVID**[1], farmer near Sugar-Loaf in Town of Goshen. The

Goshen church records the marriage of a David Mapes to Mary Cornwall 8 Feb. 1779. Children specifically noted as of his 1st marriage:
James.
c. 1770, JOHN.
Catharine m. Garret Rysdyke.
Hannah m. Isaac Bull.

Children of his 2d marriage:
Edward, killed in War of 1812.
William.

**JOHN MAPES**[2], b. Sugar-Loaf, farmer of area, d. age 62; m. Elizabeth Halleck, also of the Sugar-Loaf Valley, she d. age 84. Children:
James.
1798, Feb. 15, **GEORGE**.
Mittie m. William Roe.
John.
Hannah.
Susan m. Peter Board.

**GEORGE MAPES**[3], farmed in Wallkill; 1834 to Town of Goshen, kept public house at Mapes' Corners; m. 1828, Susan d/o Joseph & Sarah (Slatterly) Durland of Chester, who was b. 3 March 180-, d. 19 March 1870; their children:
Sarah Jane.
John.

**MAPES, NELSON B.**  H-894
Railroad station agent, Howells.

**JOHN V. MAPES**[1], farmer, m. Mary Reeves & had:
Jennette, m. Stephen Mapes of Mt. Hope, NY.
Albert, res. Middletown.
1829, March 19, **NELSON B.**

**NELSON B. MAPES**[2], j.p. of Town of Wallkill for 30 years, was b. there. He m. Lucinda Mapes in 1853 & they are members of the Congregational Church.

**MAPES, ROBERT D.**  H-894
of Howells Depot.

**ROBERT MAPES** was b. at Howells Depot, 14 Sept. 1862. In 1877 he engaged in the milk business with his father in Middletown; bought his father out in 1886 & continued the business alone until 1901. He now has a livery business. He m. Margaret Isabelle Axford of Howells in 1886. She d. 24 March 1901 & he m. (2d) 15 June 1902 Hannah Eleanor Thompson of Akron, OH.

**MAPES, SAMUEL**  A-432, C-11, H-894, LDS Anc. File
of Wallkill.

**SAMUEL MAPES**[1] settled in what is now Howell's Depot, Orange Co. from L.I. before the Rev. Family is originally from Wales & noted for the longevity of members. The LDS Ancestral File states that he was b. 14 Feb. 1735 at Southhold, L.I. & m. Mary Smith b. 8 April 1739. Their children (all b. Orange Co.):

1756, Dec. 31, Smith, m. Rachel Knight (McKnight) 10 Feb. 1779.
1759, March 13, Samuel.
1761, Jan. 7, Enos; his grandson Mr. N. B. Mapes, merchant & station master (probably Nelson B. above).
1763, Nov. 30, Samuel.
1765, May 24, SELAH.
1767, Sept. 29, Erastus.
1770, March 28, SETH.
1772, March 29, Silas (Cyrus) Haynes.
1774, April 3, William.
1780, Nov. 16, Mary; could be the dau. who is noted in one source as m. Jesse Carpenter.

SELAH MAPES[2], s/o Samuel[1], m. Rinah Riley, b. 1765, & had:
1805, June 11, SELAH RILEY.

SELAH RILEY MAPES[3], b. Mt. Hope, m. Elizabeth Youngs Ketcham, b. 31 Oct. 1807, Mt. Hope, & had:
1829, Feb. 12, Mary Jane, m. Andrew Arnold Cohill, b. 1833 Huntingdon, PA. They had: Edmund Pendleton, Haskins G., Andrew Arnold Jr., Maude, Blanch, & Thomas (all Cohill).
1834, June 12, Isaac D.
1848 [sic], July 3, James Riley.

SETH MAPES[2], s/o Samuel[1], b. Blooming-Grove, m. Julia Smith & had (b. Seneca, Ontario Co., NY, except for the last 3):
1791, Samuel, m. Hannah --- & had son George b. c. 1817.
1793, William S.
1795, April 3, Rufus, m. Abigail Allen.
1797, May 19, Calvin.
1799, Dec. 11, SOLOMAN F.
1802, Hiel Smith.
1805, Fanny.
1807, Dec. 20, John Dony.
1811, June 23, Stephen S., b. Cuyahoga Co., NY.
1813, Julia, b. Cuyahoga Co.
1817, Horace Martin, b. Cuyahoga Co.

SOLOMAN F. MAPES[3], s/o Seth[2], m. Eliza Wright, b. MI in 1802, & had:
1825, Sept. 8, Climena.
1826, Nov. 2, Oscar, b. OH, m. Mary Elizabeth Steele, b. 1829 in New Haven Co., CT. They had Harriet, Jane Elizabeth (Jennie), Frank Eugene, Warren Steele, Martha Anna (b. 1864 Burlington, IA), Truman Steele (b. 1867, MO), Abraham Lincoln, Herbert & Howard.
1828, Aug. 30, Amanda.
1830, Nov. 1, Malvina.
1832, Sept. 2, Jerusha.
1834, May 31, Artimicia.
1835, May 15, Dudley.

1841, Jan. 5, Augusta.
1842, Jan. 26, Emerene.
1846, April 9, Bianica (Blanche).
1847, George.
1849, Armenia, m. Rachel Chambers.

It is said that many family members lived frequently beyond 90 years & H-894 notes that Selah R. Corwin, of Middletown, whose mother was Priscilla Mapes, was b. 29 Dec. 1908 & is now active & can be seen upon the streets almost any clear day at this time.

At one time the family was so numerous that a portion of the town of Mt. Hope was called Mapestown, but that names has long since disappeared.

---

**MARS, JESSE DURLAND**　　　　　　　**H-895**
physician of Florida, NY.

STEPHEN MARS[1], b. Germany 1843, to America at age 27 & located in Orange Co., farmer. In 1872 he m. Annie Mary DeGraw, b. Orange Co., and had 8 children. **JESSE DURLAND MARS[2]** is their 5th child.

**JESSE[2]** was b. 7 Sept. 1880 at Bellvale & moved to Florida, NY with his parents at an early age. Stephen & Annie Mary still res. there. **JESSE** grad. Univ. of MI Medical College in 1904. He has practiced in Ann Arbor, MI (1904/5), NY City, L.I. & beginning in 1906, at Florida. He m. 10 Dec. 1907 Estelle Otis, 2d youngest d/o Josiah & Elizabeth W. Otis of Orange Co., where Estelle was b. She traces her line back to the *Mayflower*.

---

**MARTIN, JAMES G.**　　　　　　　**H-895-6**
of Middletown.

**JAMES G. MARTIN**, b. of Irish parentage in Dublin, Ireland 1 Feb. 1852, s/o John & Ann Martin. His father & grandfather were builders in Ireland & his father d. in Australia c. 1880. **JAMES** to America in 1869, settling at Middletown, builder. Nov. 1871 he m. Mary A. Cunningham of Middletown, who d. Oct. 1886. They had 5 children. He m. (2d) Mrs. Annie (Houston) Kilbride of Middletown & they have 2 children. Members St. Joseph's Catholic Church of Middletown.

---

**MARVEL, CAPT. THOMAS S.**　　　　　**H-896**
**& HARRY A. MARVEL**
shipbuilders.

**CAPT. THOMAS MARVEL[1]**, b. NY City 16 May 1834; his father moved to Newburgh in 1836 & established a shipyard. During the Civil War **THOMAS** raised Co. A, 56th NY Vols. He & John Delany were partners in the shipyard after the Civil War. In 1861 he m. Hattie, d/o John Burns of Monroe, NY & they have 2 sons & 2 daus.

One son is **HARRY A. MARVEL[2]**, superintendent of T. S. Marvel Shipbuilding Co. He was b. 1865 a Staten Island. He m. Katherine Vought of Cornwall & they have 2 children.

**MARVIN, CORTLAND S. [P]**  A-648c, C-9
of Hamptonburgh.

MATTHEW MARVIN[1], from England to America 1635, settled
at Hartford, CT & had son:
MATTHEW[2], b. England 1627, had son:
1678, Sept. 2, JOHN[3], b. CT.

JOHN MARVIN[3], s/o Matthew[2], had son:
ELIHU MARVIN[4], b. 10 Oct. 1719, d. on homestead, 11 Aug.
1803; farmer, assoc. judge, soldier of the Rev. About 1743
settled in Blooming-Grove, Orange Co.; m. Abigail, d/o John
Yelverton of Chester, and had:
Seth.
Abigail m. Sheriff Jackson.
Elihu. Could be the Elihu who m. Esther Youngs 29 Oct. 1776,
at Goshen.
John Yelverton.
Elizabeth m. John McDowell
Hannah m. John Hall.
1757, April 8, JOHN.
James.
Kezia.
Anthony.

JOHN MARVIN[5], s/o Elihu[4], b. Blooming-Grove, res. on
homestead & d. 23 June 1809. 1 May 1797, m. Fanny, d/o
Ebenezer Woodhull, she d. 7 April 1857. Children:
1800, Jan. 19, John F., m. Amelia, d/o Stephen Jayne of Florida,
NY; d. 1868, March 16.
1803, May 20, Caroline, m. Walter Halsey of Blooming-Grove;
d. 7 Feb. 1879.
1805, March 9, 1805, Van Rensselaer W., m. Juliana W., d/o
Judge Nathan White; d. 11 Feb. 1856.
1807, Dec. 11, **CORTLAND S.**

CORTLAND S. MARVIN[6], farmer, member Blooming-Grove
Congregational Church; 3 Jan. 1839, m. Melissa, d/o James
& Mary (Heard) Duryea of Blooming-Grove, and had:
WILLIAM H.

WILLIAM M. MARVIN[7], only s/o **CORTLAND S.**[6], farmer on
homestead, m. Anna M., d/o Josiah & Harriet (Tuttle) Seeley
of Blooming-Grove. Anna d. 25 Feb. 1871, age 63.

**MASON, F. N.**  H-896
businessman of Port Jervis since 1860.

F. N. MASON is in partnership with George Lea in drug
business & in 1875 entered NY College of Pharmacy; 1891
bought out Mr. Lea's interest. He has bank, telephone company,
real estate interests & has a record of public service. He m.
Phoebe C. Everett & they have one child, Mariner H.

**MATLACK FAMILY**  A-544

The American progenitor was --- MATLACK, Quaker,

emigrated from Derbyshire, England & settled in Philadelphia
around the time of William Penn. "One of his descs." TIMO-
THY MATLACK[1], was the father of Capt. WHITE MAT-
LACK[2], who m. Abby Robertson, b. Portsmouth, NH.

ROBERT ROBERTSON, b. Dalkeith, Scotland, was the
grandfather of Abby, who m. Capt. White Matlack, above.

**MATTHEWS, FLETCHER**  U2-183
of New Windsor, Esq.

FLETCHER MATTHEWS, s/o Vincent who took up land
on Evans Patent in 1720, died intestate & administration of his
estate granted on 24 Nov. 1789 to Sarah (widow), Jesse Woodhull & Seth Marvin, all of Orange Co.

**MAYER, MICHAEL**  H-896-7
manufacturer of Port Jervis.

MICHAEL MAYER, b. in French Province of Alsace-Lorraine,
came to America in 1866 & settled in Brooklyn, NY; 1895
to Port Jervis where he manufactures cut glass. In 1871 he
m. Madeline Mills, b. Alsace-Lorraine; she d. 1900. Their
children:
George, of Brooklyn.
Edward, in business with father.
Madeline, m. John W. Kelley of Port Jervis.
Josephine, m. William P. Gregg of Port Jervis.

Members of the Church of the Sacred Heart of Port Jervis.

**MC AULEY, JOHN**  E-178-80
of Newburgh.

JOHN MC AULEY came from Ireland to NY with two
elder brothers, William & Robert c. 1757. The family is Scotch
& had lived in Ireland for 100 years. JOHN had been apprenticed to a merchant in London for a time before his immigration,
where his eldest brother James resided. William & Robert
purchased JOHN's indenture & brought him to America with
them. Their parents & sister Mary remained in London. Mary
m. John Proffet Nixon & had George Nixon, late of the City of
NY, dec'd. JOHN adopted young Nixon & placed him in his
store in Newburg.
On the family's arrival in America, JOHN had been placed
in the store of William Gillerland, a wine merchant & relative.
William & Robert purchased land at Crown Point, Essex Co.,
NY. JOHN also worked in Dutchess Co. NY, Montreal, Canada
& NY City. In 1791 he m. Miss --- Sloan of Poughkeepsie &
located permanently in Newburgh. He d. 20 Nov. 1833, aged
88. Their children:
John, now dec'd.
Catherine, m. Samuel W. Eager.
Robert, now dec'd.
Mary, now dec'd.
William.

WILLIAM MC AULEY, bother of **JOHN**, res. in Essex Co. until his death. He m. Miss --- Gillerland.

ROBERT MC AULEY, **JOHN**'s other brother, located in Essex Co. until the Rev. War & then removed to Kingston, Canada; merchant. He m. Ann Kirby of Ticonderoga & had:
Robert, atty., now dec'd.
John, merchant at Kingston.
William, clergyman of the established church; studied in England & res. at Toronto.

## MC CARRELL, REV. JOSEPH, D.D. [P]    A-312-314a
of Newburgh.

**REV. JOSEPH** was b. 1795, July 9, Shippensburg, PA. His parents members of the Associated Reformed Church. He was a volunteer in the War of 1812 & witnessed the bombardment of Ft. McHenry in Baltimore. A grad. of Washington College, Washington PA 1815; taught in Bellefontaine, Greensburg & Carlisle, PA; licensed by Presbury of Big Spring, PA 1821. Served NY City, to Newburgh (1822) until his death 28 March 1864, age 69. He m. in Shippensburg, PA; his wife survived him by 11 years; survived by 4 children & 1 grandson [none named].

## MC CARTY, JOHN    H-885-6

JOHN MC CARTY[1], b. 1815 in Co. Down, Ireland, s/o Hugh, to America Feb. 1834; a mason by trade. He returned to Ireland & m. Sarah Rogers of Co. Down & returned to America & settled in Westchester Co., NY. Bridge builder & quary owner. His children:
Ellen.
**JOHN.**
Mary.
Thomas.
Sarah A.

**JOHN MC CARTY**[2], b. Westchester Co., NY, moved to Brooklyn at age 18; worked for the Board of Health, was Alderman. Later res. Goshen & Brooklyn. He m. Marguerite I. Murphy of NY City & d. 20 Oct. 1905.

## MC CLAUGHRY, JAMES    U2-13, 61-2
of Little Britain.

**JAMES MC CLAUGHRY**, in his will dated 17 July, 1790, names his wife Agnes and his brother-in-law Alexander Tilford, Alexander's wife Mary and their son & his namesake, James McClaughry Tilford. **JAMES** freed his many slaves by his will. His wife & trusty friends Thomas Moffat of Orange Co. & William Scot of Ulster Co. appointed executors.

## MC CLAGHRY, PATRICK    U2-13-14
yeoman of Little Britain.

In his will dated 28 Sept. 1774, **PATRICK MC CLAGHRY** names wife Mary and children:
Jane McCobb.
Elizabeth, m. John Finley.
Mary, m. George Denniston.
John.
James.

He also names grandsons John & Alexander McClaghry. James Barkley of Montgomery, yeoman, appeared 24 July 1787 to prove will.

## MC CLUNG, HON. BENJAMIN    H-886
atty. & mayor of Newburgh.

**BENJAMIN** was s/o Samuel McClung & Margaret Upright. He was b. New Windsor in 1867. Grad. NY City law school 1891 & the same year to Newburgh.

## MC COACH, JOHN D.    H-886-7
chief of police, city of Middletown.

**JOHN**, b. Bethel, Sullivan Co., NY in 1876, to Middletown June 1896. Drove mail wagon, later patrolman. He m. Lucy Barber of Monticello, Sullivan Co., and had:
1904, June 21, Elmer E.
1905, Oct. 10, Mildred O.

## MC CORD, JAMES [P]    A-369-70
of Newburgh.

JOHN MC CORD[1] m. Rosella Cargin, immigrants from North of Ireland of Scotch-Irish desc., to Newburgh c. 1827. John was a shoemaker, d. c. 1845, age 44; Rosella d. 4 March 1869, age 60. Children:
Jane, b. Ireland, m. William Haxby of Newburgh.
1826, July 1, **JAMES.**
William.
Eliza m. Stephen Vandewater.
Charles.

**JAMES MC CORD**[2], s/o John[1], b. Philadelphia; brush manufacturer, m. (1st) July 1848, Hester M., d/o Felix Shurter of Dutchess Co.; she d. 8 Nov. 1873. Children:
Alexander.
James Luther.
Mary Rosella.
Hester Jane.
Nellie.

**JAMES**[2] m. (2d) June 1874, Sarah A. Shurter, sister of his first wife, Hester; Sarah d. without issue 15 Jan. 1880.

## MC CREADY, ROBERT WORKMAN    H-887
contractor at Tuxedo Park, res. Sloatsburg, Rockland Co.

**ROBERT MC CREADY**, b. Belfast, Ireland in 1862, s/o James McCready & Mary McIlveen of Scottish desc. Shipbuilder & joiner, trained in Ireland; 1884 to Fall River, MA, carpenter & joiner. 1886 established business with William M. Finch building homes in Tuxedo Park. In 1889 he m. Mary, d/o John Finch of Sloatsburg and had:
Olive
Robert Halsey.

---

**MC CULLOUGH, JOHN W.**      H-887-8
tobacco business, Water St.

**JOHN W. MC CULLOUGH**, b. Newburgh 1819, d. 1892. Member First Reformed Presbyterian Church. After his decease his son, John R., continued his business until his death 31 July 1907. John R. b. 15 July 1846, was a druggist, bank director, etc.

---

**MC CURDEY, ARCHIBALD**      U2-23-4, C-17
of Wall Kill.

In his will dated 12 Nov. 1787, **ARCHIBALD MC CURDEY** names his sister Ann Wilson, wife of William, and their dau., Margrit Wilson. He mentions other children of William & Margrit, only stating that they are under the age of 18. Friends Charles Boreland, Charles Bull & Thomas Watkins apptd. executors. Will proved 11 Jan. 1788 by John McCamly yeoman of Wall Kill & Mos Polay & Milicent Vanscoy.

According to Goshen church records, an **ARCHIBALD MC CURDEY** m. Mary Libolt 30 Dec. 1788.

---

**MC DOWELL, FRED S.**      H-888
supervisor of Newburgh.

**FRED** b. Newburgh 1865, s/o James & Agnes (Frew) McDowell. Butcher. He m. Jennie Whitaker of New Windsor.

---

**MC GEOCH, RALPH L.**      H-888
physician of Goshen.

**RALPH L. MC GEOCH**, b. at Shushan, Washington Co., NY 1 Dec. 1867. Grad. NY Homeopathic College 1894 & then to Goshen. 9 June 1897 m. Sarah W. Coleman.

---

**MC GILL, WILLIAM LUSK [P]**      A-243-4
farmer of New Windsor, public servant.

HUGH MC GILL[1], b. in the North of Ireland, to NY age 17 & settled as farmer at Little Britain & later Cornwell, where he d. c. 1834; m. --- Hallock, and had:
1768, HUGH.
John, lived & d. in Cornwell.
Samuel, lived & d. in Cornwell.
Margaret m. George Vanderheiden of Troy, NY.

HUGH MC GILL[2], b. New Windsor, farmer, m. Margaret, d/o

Richard Lusk; d. 1833. Children:
James B., physician; d. 1851 Columbus, OH.
Samuel S.
1813, July 7, **WILLIAM L.**

**WILLIAM L. MC GILL[3]**, s/o Hugh[2], b. New Windsor, farmed homestead until 12 Aug. 1844, when he m. Elizabeth, d/o James & Elsie Kernochan, purchased farm of estate of Jabez Atwood. Attended Unitarian Church of Newburgh. Children:
William J.
Mary E.

---

**MC KEE, THOMAS**      U2-68
of New Windsor, yeoman.

**THOMAS MC KEE**, in his will dated 22 Aug. 1789, named his wife Margaret and children:
James.
Mary.
Margaret.
Agnes.

Executors: George Monnell of Montgomery, yeoman; James Lawrence & James Fulton.

---

**MC KINNEY, HENRY JAMES**
**& MC KINNEY, JOHN L.**      H-889

LUTHER MC KINNEY[1] m. Maria Morrison & had, among others.
1854, April 10, **HENRY JAMES.**
1856, March 6, **JOHN L.**

**HENRY JAMES MC KINNEY[2]**, third s/o the above, b. at family homestead in Town of Crawford. He d. at his residence in Pine Bush, NY 24 Sept. 1907. He farmed the family homestead until his retirement. 7 Sept. 1892 m. Kate Woodworth Rapelze. They have 3 daus.

**JOHN L. MC KINNEY[2]**, postmaster of Pine Bush, born on family homestead in Town of Crawford. He is a member of the Presbyterian Church & a merchant.

---

**MC KINNEY, WILLIAM L.**      H-889
of Montgomery.

**WILLIAM L. MC KINNEY**, b. Montgomery in 1825, s/o Benjamin W. & Hannah (Hunt) McKinney, 1854 m. Eliza Tindall. They had one child who d. in infancy. Presbyterian.

---

**MC NEAL, JOHN**      U2-40, C-11
of Wall Kill.

In his will dated 1 Aug. 1786, **JOHN MC NEAL** names his brother Edward & the following children:
Rebecca, m. Charles Borland, 28 Oct. 1779, at Goshen.

Thomas.
Daniel.
Edward.

---

**MC NISH, WICKHAM C. [P]**  A-492-3, C-11, 107-8
of Wallkill.

REV. GEORGE MC NISH[1], b. Scotland, to American 1705; licensed to preach in MD in 1706; one of the original member of the Philadelphia Presbytery; called to Presbyterian Church at Jamaica, L.I. 1710; d. 10 March 1722. He had one child:
REV. GEORGE MC NISH[2], m. d/o Joseph Smith of Jamaica & settled in Newto[w]n, NJ; later to Goshen and d. at Wallkill 1779, aged 65. George's children:
1752, Aug. 17, ANDREW CLARK.
Peggy.
Polly m. George Conkling of Goshen.

ANDREW CLARK MC NISH[3], Rev. soldier, d. 12 Feb. 1805, res. town of Middletown; in Goshen 17 Dec. 1778, m. Elizabeth Davis of L.I. b. 1752; d. 22 Feb. 1797. Children:
1779, Sept. 1, JOSHUA. [Joshua & a sister, Mary, bapt. 19 Dec. 1782, at Goshen, according to church records.]
1781, Polly.
1782, Aug. 12, Sarah, m. David Everett & had son Dr. Everett of Middletown.
1785, Sept. 21, Phebe, m. Robert Kirk.
1791, April 5, Henry, res. Mt. Hope, served in War of 1812 under Col. Faulkner; blacksmith.
1793, March 26, Andrew, carpenter & farmer of Wantage, NJ.
1795, April 24, Spicer, res. Sullivan Co. & d. there.

JOSHUA MC NISH[4], s/o Andrew Clark McNish[3], served in the War of 1812, inherited homestead; m. Mary M. Reeve, b. 4 June 1789, d/o Deacon. James of Congregational Church at Middletown, settled at Wawayanda from L.I. 1814; she d. 18 Dec. 1863. Children:
1816, Nov. 28, Andrew C.; d. age 37.
1819, Dec. 25, George; d. age 21.
1820, Jan. 17, Elizabeth.
1823, Aug. 25, WICKHAM C.

WICKHAM C. MC NISH[5], s/o Joshua[4], 1850 traveled to gold fields of CA, established jobbing & wholesale boot & shoe trade there; 1853 back east as buyer for CA business; later in tanking & producing oil in fields of PA; res. San Francisco & Boston. Lifelong member of the Congregational Church at Middletown, while res. San Francisco helped found Congregatinal Church there. 1857, Jan. m. Maritta, d/o William W. Reeve, surveyor & j.p. and Jane Ayres of Middletown. Only child:
Mary Jane.

---

**MC VOY, ROBERT J.**  H-889-90
farmer.

This family of Irish descent. **ROBERT** s/o Hugh & Martha (Glascow) McVoy, both from Ireland to America at an early date. **ROBERT** b. 12 July 1847 at Jackson's Corners (then Goshen); d. 26 April 1895. He m. Alnetta Pierson Gillespie of Montgomery 10 June 1885, & had, both at home:
1886, Aug. 21, Charles Felter.
1888, Sept. 14, Sarah Maretta.

---

**MEAD FAMILY OF WAWAYANDA**  A-679

ROSWELL MEAD from New England to Wawayanda & m. a d/o Reuben Cash & left 6 children, those named:
William H.
Reuben C.

ROSWELL held town offices in Minisink.

---

**MEAD, CHARLES [P]**  A-190-1, STJ-29
newspaperman, *Goshen Democrat.*

MATTHEW MEAD[1], colonel in Continental Army during Rev., res. Welton, Fairfield Co., CT. Had several children including:
1779, June 12, XENOPHON.

XENOPHON MEAD[2], s/o Matthew[1], b. Wilton; merchant of Newburgh, farmer of Warwick; to Mobile, AL & to OH where he d. 29 Dec. 1847. He m. Abigail, b. 3 June 1778, d. 22 Aug. 1857, d/o Moses Burr & Mabel Banks. Moses soldier in the Continental Army, of Fairfield Co., CT. Children of Xenophon & Abigail:
1802, June 20, Louisa, widow of Nathaniel Webb of Goshen.
1803, Dec. 2, Aaron Burr; removed to OH, where he d.
1808, May 17, Norman, res. in OH; d. in Goshen, NY.
1812, Dec. 17, Edwin, res. Santa Cruz, CA.
1819, Nov. 19, **CHARLES.**

CHARLES MEAD[3], s/o Xenophon[2], b. Newburgh; m. 9 May 1842, Caroline A., d/o Daniel Warden of Goshen. She b. 11 April 1821, d. 11 Nov. 1880. The Meads res. in Goshen after their marriage; children:
1851, Feb. 28, Charles Augustus.
William R.

---

**MEAD, CHARLES H. [P]**  A-786-7
builder of Cornwall.

--- MEAD[1], m. Elizabeth, d/o Gen. Nicholson of Rev. War fame, 24 July 1831, and had son:
ABRAM MEAD[2] who m. Hannah Meal, d/o Abram of Cold Spring, NY, and had:
JOSEPH N.

CAPT. JOSEPH N. MEAD[3], b. near Norwich CT; in early manhood to Cold Spring, Putnam Co., owned & ran sailing packet between Albany & NY City, later located at Garrison's Landing, Puntnam Co.; m. Phebe Garrison, d/o Judge

Henry, one of the earliest settlers of Phillipstown, of Pioneer family of L.I. Joseph d. 1841; Phebe d. Jan. 1879. Their children:

Mary Jane m. James D. Faurot of Ft. Montgomery.

Joseph Henry; dec'd.

Hannah Elizabeth of NY City, wid. of Sylvanus Coursen.

William Augustus; d. childhood.

**CHARLES HENRY.**

Sydney; d. infancy.

**CHARLES H. MEAD[4]**, s/o Capt. Joseph N.[3], b. Phillipstown, Putnam Co., NY; on death of father res. with sister at Ft. Montgomery; age 17 to Cornwall, NY, learned trade of carpenter with Daniel Taft; 1853 operated his own shop in Canterbury; later back to Cornwall. He m. June 1854, Mary E., d/o Daniel Taft of Cornwall & had 11 children, those named:

Charles S., in business with father.

Harry G., with Canada Southern RR in NY.

**MEAD, CHARLES L.**                    **H-897**
atty. of Goshen.

**CHARLES L.** is the eldest s/o William H. Mead & was b. 27 Aug. 1851 in Town of Wayanda. He studied at Princeton & Columbia Law School, grad. 1877. In 1892 County Treasurer. He m. Fannie Tuthill of Middletown 5 June 1878. **CHARLES** is a member of the S.A.R.

**MEAD, WALTER J.**                    **H-897**
pres. Montgomery & Erie RR.

**WALTER**, b. in Montgomery 16 Feb. 1824, s/o Walter & Elsie (Monnell) Mead. He married twice, & by his first wife, Laura C. Benedict, had 3 children. He m. (2d) Mrs. Ketura M. Miller, d/o Henry W. Thompson of Goshen.

**MERRIAM, HENRY [P]**          **A-555-6, C-33, 42-3, 144**

THOMAS MERRIAM[2], s/o Thomas[1], b. c. 1765, Meriden, CT; m. Hannah, eldest d/o Noah Guernsey of Litchfield CT where he was a merchant. To Schaghticoke, Rensselaer Co., NY, later purchased farm in Saratoga Co., after 10 years to the town of Harpersfield, Delaware Co., farmer, d. there 1815. His wife later m. Mr. Disbro & removed with part of the family to Cicero, Onondaga Co., where she d. age 90. Presbyterian Church members. Children:

Philomenia m. Bartholomew Andrews of Cicero.

Allen, farmer; d. Geneva, WI.

Harvey, farmer; d. Cicero.

Samuel, res. New Haven, merchant.

1802, Dec. 1, **HENRY.**

Noah, farmer; d. Cicero.

Mary m. Henry Jones of Monroe, Orange Co.

Clara, unm., res. Syracuse.

HENRY MERRIAM[3], s/o Thomas[2], b. Rensselaer Co., age 13 when his father d. & he to Litchfield for 6 years, res. with grandfather Guernsey. 1822 merchant at Elizabethtown, NJ; 1825 to Goshen NY in partnership with John J. Smith in the manufacture of tinware; 1869 retired. 2 Jan. 1833, m. Ann Eliza, d/o Isaac & Abigail (Tusten) Reeve[s] of Goshen. Ann b. 3 May 1810, member Presbyterian Church at Goshen. Children of **HENRY** & Ann Eliza:

Helen.

Henry Guernsey, hardware merchant of Waverly, NY with brother.

Charles Edward, hardware partner. 23 March 1864 Charles E. Merriam m. Jennie E. Wells, both of Goshen.

Frank Augustus, in father's business at Goshen.

Rev. Alexander R., pastor Payson Congregational Church at East Hampton, MA.

Alma E.

**MERRITT, ALEXANDER**          **H-897-8, E-200**
undertaker of Middletown.

**ALEXANDER MERRITT** was b. in Town of Blooming-Grove 30 June 1847. At age 14 to Middletown to learn carpenter's trade. 1874 engaged with his father-in-law, W. H. Knapp, as assistant to undertaking business & in 1881 partnership with W. Nelson Knapp in same. He m. May A. Knapp 3 Sept. 1873 & had:

Clarence N., m. Ella Groo, res. Paterson, NJ.

Lulu May, m. Robert Terhune, res. East Orange, NJ.

Walter K., m. Frances H. Darbee of Middletown; assists father in business.

**MERRITT, DANIEL [P]**          **A-366, TN272-4, U2-162**
of Newburgh.

JOHN MERRITT, SR.[1], b. England, settled Rye, NY, Westchester Co., NY c. 1680. His son:

GEORGE MERRITT[2], b. 1702, d. 2 Feb. 1750; m. Glorianna [Glorande] Purdy who d. 13 Sept. 1765, age 51 years, 5 months, 13 days. To Newburgh c. 1747 with Purdy & Fowler families. George's will dated 25 Jan. 1759, names him as yeoman of Highlands Precinct. It identifies lands at the White Plains given to his mother by the will of her grandfather, Umfree Underhill. Their children:

GEORGE.

Samuel, m. Phila Townsend & had several children. He d. 26 Dec. 1811, age 74.

1735, July, CALEB.

Gabriel, d. 1776, no issue.

DAVID.

JOSIAH.

1737, May 17, HUMPHRY [Umfree].

ELIZABETH.

1747, Sept. 25, Jane m. (1st) Morris Flewwalling; (2d) Elnathan Foster.

Glorianna m. Joseph Morey.

GEORGE MERRITT[3], s/o George[2], m. (1) Mary Fowler who d. 5 July 1799, age 66 years, & had:
George.
Gabriel.
Samuel.
Humphrey.
Fowler.
John.
Charlotte.
Jane.
Glorianna.
Mary.

GEORGE[3] m. (2) Sarah, widow of Wolvert Ecker.

CALEB MERRITT[3], s/o George[2], d.29 Nov. 1793, m. Martha Purdy, b. Ja. 1736, d. 24 June 1783, & had:
Abigail, m. George Weygant.
Elizabeth, m. Dr. David Fowler.
Glorianna, m. Isaac Fowler.

DAVID MERRITT[3], s/o George[2], m. Nelly Weygant & had:
Jane, m. John Hait.
Elizabeth, m. Nathaniel Harcourt.

JOSIAH MERRITT[3], s/o George[2], d. 1817. He m. (1) Anna Purdy who d. 9 Ja. 1786, aged 30, and had:
Gabriel.
Josiah.
Esther, m. Zephania Northrop.
Nancy, m. Mowbray Carpenter.
Alathea, m. John Brower.

JOSIAH[3] m. (2) Rachel Sherwood and had:
David.
Joseph.
Phebe, m. Andrew Cropsey.

HUMPHREY MERRITT[3], s/o George[2], to Middletown 1758, farmer. He purchased land on which his grandson, Daniel Merritt, now res. His children [wife not named]:
Glorianna.
Mary.
1769, Feb. 7, UNDERHILL.
Caleb.
Charles.
Moses.

UNDERHILL MERRITT[4], d. 19 Nov. 1804, run over by his wagon [details are given E-p. 88], farmer of Middletown; m. Mary --- and had:
1794, July 8, Martha, m. Gilbert Holmes, res. Newburgh; d. 14 Sept. 1848.
1796, Aug. 21, Josiah; left one son, Caleb.
1799, March 10, DANIEL & Elizabeth, twins, Elizabeth b. March 12th, m. John Goodsell; d. 28 Dec. 1824.
1801, Sept. 19, Charlotte, m. Joseph Furman, res. Plattekill; d. 24 Aug. 1824.

1804, April 21, MARIA [MARY].

DANIEL MERRITT[5], s/o Underhill[4], farmer of Newburgh, member ME Church of Middlehope, d. 1867, May 7. 22 Feb. 1826, m. Eliza Hait of Latintown, Ulster Co., b. 26 April 1805, and had:
Mary Jane m. Daniel T. MacFarlan of Yonkers, NY.
Hiram, real estate broker of NY City.
Daniel.
Theodore, druggist of Newburgh.

MARY MERRITT[5], d/o Underhill[4], m. Robert Phillips of Newburgh, & had: (PHILLIPS)
Jeanette, m. Richard Olmstead.
Mary A., m. William A. Owen.
Willard M.

ELIZABETH MERRITT[3], d/o George[2], m. Thomas Merritt, a Col. of the Cavalry in the Queen's Rangers (1780). He d. St. Catherines, Canada in May 1842, aged 82. He was a grandson of the first John Merritt.

---

**MEYNDERS, BURGER**          TN-263
of Town of Newburgh.

BURGER MEYNDERS[1], blacksmith, settled in Kingston, NY in 1686. He sold his property there to Frederick Phillipse in 1692 & in 1716 purchased from Peter Rose lands at Newburgh, where he settled. He had:
BURGER, JR.
Frederick.

BURGER MEYNDERS JR.[2], trustee of the Glebe at Newburgh 1744-1752. His land passed on to Jonathan Hasbrouck family in 1753, at which time Burger Jr. removed to Shawangunk, where he erected a mill, which was later occupied by James Bate. Mill at the mouth of the Dwaarskill.

---

**MILLER, CHARLES [P]**          A-408-09a, C-23
of Montgomery.

SAMUEL MILLER[1], emigrant at 'early date' from Ireland, of Irish & Welsh desc., to Canada & eventually settled Montgomery, Orange Co. 1764 acquired land here, militia officer (1788); d. at advanced age. Children [wife not named]:
1776, March 11, GEORGE S.
William S.
Samuel. Could be the Samuel Millar who m. Hannah Meeker 24 Aug. 1803, at Goshen.
Mary.

GEORGE S. MILLER[2], s/o Samuel[1], res. Montgomery; 1800 m. Julia, d/o Charles Young of Hamburgh; d. 5 Dec. 1828. Children, only 3 now survive:
Samuel H.
1805, Dec. 5, CHARLES.
William.

Theodore.
Sarah m. Alexander Blake.
Cornelia m. Gilbert G. Weeks.
Elizabeth m. Samuel Knapp.

**CHARLES MILLER³**, s/o George S.², b. Montgomery, member Goodwill Presbyterian Church of Montgomery; farmer, inherited father's land; m. Helen d/o John S. Young of Montgomery (now Hamptonburgh). Their children, all now dec'd.:
George S.
Julia Y.
Gilbert.
Charles A.

---

**MILLER, CHARLES S.**                    H-898
printer.

WILLIAM J. MILLER¹ m. Elizabeth E. Doty, and had:
1862, George E.
1867, Edward D.
1870, July 19, **CHARLES S.**
1874, Mary E., m. James Fintze of Newark, OH.

**CHARLES S. MILLER²**, b. near Lake Station, Orange Co., m. Minnie E. Shove of Middletown, d/o George & Julia, and had:
Victor Edward, d. age 13 months.
1895, Sept. 17, George W.

Members of the Methodist Church of Middletown.

---

**MILLER, JOHANNES**          A-376-9, C-116-16
of Montgomery.

**JOHANNES MILLER¹**, immigrated from Germany possibly as early as 1720; NY to Esopus, Ulster Co. & then to Shawangunk; weaver, Lutheran. He m. (1st) Jemima Schoonmaker, d/o Cornelius, and had a son JOHN; m. (2d) Sarah Bull, wid. of William Bull of Hamptonburgh. He later settled with neighbors in the Town of Montgomery & d. 1782, aged c. 90.

**JOHN MILLER²**, s/o Johannes¹, m. (1st) Esther Bull, eldest d/o William & Sarah and had:
Peggy.
Jemima.
1760, JOHANNES.
William, brother-in-law of Johannes E. Hendrick Van Keuren of Montgomery, commanded company of militia. Elizabeth, Margaret & Sarah, d/o William Miller & Hannah Van Currah were bapt. at Goshen 15 April 1791.

**JOHN²** m. (2d) Anne Weller, d/o Henry, and had:
JAMES W.

**JOHANNES MILLER³**, s/o John², m. Eve Mould 17 March 1779; Rev. patriot, farmer, founded turnpike companies &

school, member First Presbyterian Church of Montgomery; d. 17 Dec. 1834, age 74. Surviving children:
John m. Miss --- Oliver, d/o Judge Oliver of Marbletown, Ulster Co.
Maria m. David Hunter, Esq., of Bloomingburgh.

**JAMES W. MILLER³**, s/o John² & Anne, his children, all res. Newburgh:
John.
James W.

---

## MILLS FAMILY OF MT. HOPE          A-560, C-16

**EBENEZER MILLS** of Mill's Pond, L.I., b. 3 Aug. 1759, to Orange Co. 1786, settled near Middletown & m. 6 March 1787, at Goshen, Abigail Vail, twin sister of Isaiah Vail; farmer, d. 1829. Their children:
Isaac; had son A.J., Mt. Hope Hotel landlord (1849- ).
Henry P., settled in Miniskink, later to Onondaga Co.
Isaiah, res. Mt. Hope.
Samuel, to IN.
Sally m. J. C. Coleman of Goshen, to Allegany Co.
Phebe m. --- Wallace, res. Onondaga Co.
William, settled at Wallkill.

---

## MILLS FAMILY OF WALLKILL (MILLSBURGH)
### A-433, H-899, C-118, 120

**JACOB MILLS¹** of Little Britain to Millsburgh, his children:
Jonathan res. near Bloomingburgh.
Samuel; had son Albert.
Jacob res. Scotchtown.
Bapt. 1794, May 4, HEZEIKAH DENTON.
Bapt. 1797, Feb. 12, [William] Wickham, to L.I.
Charles, res. Millsbaugh.
Mrs. Thomas Bull, husband founded Bullville.
Mrs. Jonathan Hawkins of Hamptonburgh.
Mrs. John Gale of Milo.
Catharine, unm.
Mrs. Samuel White of Scotchtown.

**HEZEKIAH DENTON MILLS²**, only now surviving child of Jacob¹ at age 87, res. Wallkill, Capt. in War of 1812; his children:
Mrs. James White of Scotchtown.
Harrison, of Crawford.
NATHAN J., of Circleville.
Mrs. Ira Coleman of Seneca Co.
Youngest son [unnamed].

**NATHAN J. MILLS³** & wife Julia Elizabeth had 7 children, 2 d. in infancy & one d. age 14. Their surviving children:
Anna M., m. Charles E. Haight of NY City.
Lizzie J., m. Virgil K. Carpenter of Fair Oaks, NY.
Frank P., res. Bellville, Orange Co.
1867, Nov. 3, NATHAN D.

NATHAN D. MILLS[4], s/o Nathan J.[3], was b. Circleville. He m. Mary Beakes of Fair Oak, NY, d/o Howell & Anna J. on 2 March 1892. They had one son, Maurice, who d. age 2 1/2 years.

---

## MILLS, AMOS                                              A-756, C-118
res. Canterbury.

AMOS MILLS[1], j.p. 1765, had children [wife not named]:
AMOS JR.
Zachariah, went west.
Zebodiah; d. unm.
Mrs. Isaac VanDuzer.
Mrs. John Barton; Mr. Barton early Canterbury merchant.

AMOS MILLS JR.[2], had children:
Mrs. James Hawkhurst.
Mrs. Daniel Hallet of Monroe.
Mrs. Peter Neels of Troy.
Elizabeth, still living.

A Benjamin Field Mills, s/o Amos & Mary, b. 6 Oct. 1793, according to Goshen church records.

---

## MILLS, ISAAC                                             A-431
of Wallkill.

EBENEZER MILLS[1], from Mill's Pond on L.I. to Orange Co., in 1787. His son ISAAC MILLS[2], b. 5 March 1788, m. 1816 Clarissa Hulse & had a son: ANDREW J. MILLS[3], legislator (1854--5).

---

## MILLS, DR. JAMES J.                                      H-898-9

DR. JAMES MILLS, s/o Hon. Andrew J. Mills & Maria Green, is a desc. of Timothy Mills, an early settler of L.I. Timothy's son, Ebenezer, b. 1757, was first of family to settle in Orange Co. DR. MILLS is related through his maternal line on his grandmother's side to Nathan Hale & on his maternal grandfather's side to Nathaniel Green.
DR. MILLS, b. Mt. Hope, 9 May 1851, was a clerk in NY City; studied dentistry & has since 1878 practiced at Port Jervis.

---

## MILLS, PEPPER                                            H-920
farmer of Town of Montgomery.

PEPPER was s/o Elijah Mills, a farmer on the family farm for over 60 years, and wife Catura Crowell. PEPPER res. on the family homestead with his sister.

---

## MILLS, SAMUEL CRAWFORD                                   H-900
businessman of Newburgh, dec'd.

SAMUEL C. MILLS, b. Bloomingburg, Sullivan Co., NY 9 March 1839; d. at his home in Newburgh 1904. He came to Newburgh in 1857 & entered drygoods house of Stephen Hoyt & Co. In 1863 formed partnership with John Schoon-

maker & A. Y. Weller. He retired in 1885. He m. (1st) Elizabeth Vail, who d. 1868; m. (2d) Sarah McDonald, d/o Hon Stephen of Elmira, N, and had:
Stephen McDonald, dec'd.
Mary Duryea, m. 1908 Luther Winthrop Faulkner of Lowell, MA, where they reside. Mary is a member of the Quassaick Chapter DAR.

---

## MILLS, STOTT                                             H-900-01
postmaster at Warwick.

STOTT MILLS, s/o John & Sarah (Briarly) Mills [both of English extraction], b. at Paterson, NJ 26 June 1840. STOTT served in the Civil War in Co. A, 2d Regt., NJ Vols. & after the war to Port Jervis as foreman for Erie Rail Road shops for 14 years. He went West for 3 years & returned to Warwick, NY. He m. Melvina Jackson of Amity, Orange Co., 17 May 1865, and had:
Sarah.
Anna.
Isabel.
John.
Charles

Family attends the Episcopal Church at Warwick.

---

## MILLS, DR. THEODORE DENTON
### H-901-2, LDS Anc. File

This Mills family members are direct desc. of GEORGE MILLS[1], b. c. 1605, from Yorkshire England in 1665; m. Rebecca ---, d. Jamaica, L.I. 17 Oct. 1694, aged 89. George's son:
SAMUEL MILLS[2], b. 1631, d. in Jamaica, NY in 1726, and had:
JONATHAN MILLS[3], b. c. 1635 in Jamaica, m. Martha ---, & had:
1677, Jan., TIMOTHY.
Samuel.
Isaac.
Jonathan.

TIMOTHY MILLS[4], b. Jamaica, s/o Jonathan[3], settled at Mills Pond, L.I. in 1693; m. (1) c. 1693 Elizabeth ---, (2) Sarah Longbotham. He d. 30 March 1751, and had:
c. 1696, ISAAC.
1698, Miriam.
c. 1706, Deliverance, m. Josiah Miller.
1706, Elizabeth.
c. 1708, Jonas.
c. 1710, Sarah, m. Josiah Miller.
1710, JONATHAN.
1716, Oct. 5, Martha, m. Benjamin Strong.
c. 1717, Ruth, m. Eleazer Hawkins, b. Setauket, NY.
c. 1720, Mary, b. Smithtown, L.I., m. David Hawkins & had David, Timothy, Moses, Mary & Isaac.
1722, Samuel.

ISAAC MILLS[5], s/o Timothy[4], m. Hannah Miller & had (all b. NJ):
1720, Oct. 17, Hannah, b. Elizabeth, NJ, res. Orange Co., NY.
1727, Feb. 19, Isaac, m. Sarah Phillips.
1731, March 6, Joanna.
1734, Feb. 5, Sarah.
1739, William, m. Mary Reading, b. Elizabethtown, NJ, 1739.
c. 1741, Mary.

JONATHAN MILLS[5], s/o Timothy[4], b. Mills Pond, L.I., m. Ruth Rudyard, d. 1798 and had a son:
JACOB[6], b. 1746 at Mills Pond; moved to New Windsor, Orange Co. 1768/70 & later to Town of Wallkill. Jacob d. 1841. His son:
SAMUEL MILLS[7], b. 1776, d. 1860 [probably the Samuel s/o Jacob under "Mills Family of Wallkill"] had a son:
Rev. SAMUEL WICKHAM MILLS[8], b. 1820, d. 1902. Clergyman, m. Almeda June Bailey, d/o Nathaniel Bailey who was s/o Capt. Daniel Bailey, Rev. soldier. Their child:
DR. THEODORE DENTON MILLS[9], b. 9 June 1852 in Bloomsburgh, Sullivan Co., NY, studied medicine with Dr. Henry R. Baldwin of New Brunswick, NJ & Dr. Henry Hardenbergh of Port Jervis. He grad. 1876 from Columbia Univ. Medical School & practiced in Port Jervis, 1877-81, after which he removed to Middletown. He m. Christina, d/o Hon. M. D. Stivers of Middletown, and had:
1888, Nov. 10, Theodore Denton Jr., d. 14 Jan. 1889.
1892, Jan. 4, Samuel Wickham.
1890, Aug. 29, Elizabeth Stivers.

―――――

## MILLSPAUGH, HECTOR W.                       H-902

HECTOR W. MILLSPAUGH, b. 29 Jan. 1866, at Wallkill, Ulster Co., NY, was one of 5 children of Henry & Mary E. Millspaugh. HECTOR m. Rosina Stickles of Walden, d/o Steven & Hanna, on 11 March 1886, and had.
1888, April 4, Etta, at home.
1892, Sept. 21, Charles, at home.

Mrs. Millspaugh is a member of the Methodist Church at Walden.

―――――

## MIL[L]SPAUGH, STEPHEN            U2-38, GFM-14, 35
of Montgomery, yeoman.

In his will dated 19 March 1789, STEPHEN MILSPAUGH names sister Susannah and brothers Mattias & Philip. He also mentions Matthias' eldest son Jonathan & Philip's eldest son Philip. Will proved 5 May 1789 by James Sears yeoman, John Decker & John M. Hetsel.

Buried in the German Reformed Cemetery, Montgomery, are Philip Millspaugh, d. 5 Dec. 1800, aged 55 & his wife Mary Anne, d. 19 Dec. 1828, aged 78 years, 5 months, 17 days.
Also a Philip Millspaugh, d. 14 May 1834, aged 89 years, 6 days & wife Nancy, d. 10 March 1804, aged 50 years, 8 days.

―――――

## MILLSPAUGH, THERON L.                        H-902
furniture and undertaker business at Walden.     LDS Anc. File

PETER MILSPAUGH[1], possibly s/o Mathies & Anna Eva (Bosch) Milspaugh or Matthias Millspaugh & Anna Eva (Busch) Menges, was b. c. 1726 in Ulster Co., NY. PETER m. 1747 Susanah Comfort, b. 14 April 1731 at Newtown, NY, d/o Benjamin Comfort & Elizabeth Haywood. Their son:
BENJAMIN MILSPAUGH[2], b. 24 July 1750 at Montgomery, NY, m. 5 Sept. 1771 at Goodwill, Maria Mingus & had:
1775, Nov. 30, PETER BAXTER.
1784, Dec. 6, James, m. 1805 Cynthia Corwin.

PETER BAXTER MILSPAUGH[3], b., Montgomery, m. 23 Feb. 1799 at Goshen, Hiley (Hilah/Hyla) Duryea, b. 31 Aug. 1780 at Goshen, d/o Garritt & Mary. Their son:
THERON MILSPAUGH[4], could be the ancestor of the Theron in the below reference.

THERON L. MILLSPAUGH is desc. from Philip Millspaugh, soldier of the Rev. He was b. 1838, s/o Gilbert S. & Jane (Cineman) Millspaugh. At age 17 he was apprenticed to a cabinetmaker & in 1858 purchased the business from the widow of his former employer. In 1862 he m. Eleanor D., d/o Hon. David H. Smith of Town of Montgomery. They had 2 children:
Hattie C., m. Dr. J. E. Sadlier of Poughkeepsie, NY.
Gilbert S., in business with his father.

―――――

## MINTURN, JOHN CLINTON                        H-903
of Bellvale.

JOHN C. MINTURN, b. Town of Warwick in 1853, s/o James. James was a farmer & mason & desc. of Capt. John Minturn, Rev. soldier. In 1876 JOHN opened a general store in Bullville & later another at Greenwood Lake. 11 Jan. 1877 he m. Mary Ellen Hunter of Greenwood Lake, and had 3 children, 2 living:
John C., works with his father.
Mamie E.

―――――

## MITCHELL, EDGAR O., M.D.                      H-903
of Newburgh, NY.

EDGAR MITCHELL, b. in NY City in 1864; at age of 5 to Newburgh with his parents. He was s/o John James Mitchell, M.D., physician of Newburgh for 40 years. EDGAR grad. Harvard Medical College in 1892 & has practiced medicine in Newburgh since.
The family is of Puritan desc. and direct descs. of Thomas Mitchell, who settled in Block Island, R.I., 1677.

―――――

## MITCHELL, GEORGE R.                          H-903
plumber & tinsmith of Newburgh.

GEORGE MITCHELL, b. Islip, L.I. in 1859, to Newburgh in 1871 & learned his trade with J. D. Mabie. He m. Anna E.

Campbell of Newburgh & has one son [not named here].

## MOFFATT, BENJAMIN    H-903-4, C-53, 80, 90, 105, 113

SAMUEL MOFFATT[1], of Scotch-Irish desc., from Co. Antrim, Ireland, settled in Blagg's Clove, Orange Co., & d. there May 1787, aged 82. His son NATHANIEL[2] was the father of BENJAMIN.

BENJAMIN MOFFATT[3], s/o Nathaniel[2], b. Town of Blooming-Grove, Orange Co.; in 1840 to Milwaukee, WI with wife Elizabeth Hulse & 2 infant daus. He later removed to IL. Was a member of the First Congregational Church at Milwaukee & the Second Congregational Church at Rockford, IL. He d. 9 June 1857, aged 66. Their children:
Melissa.
Josephine.
Gilbert.

Goshen church records show the death of Sarah, wife of Samuel Moffatt, d. by 4 Oct. 1785 & the death of a Samuel Moffat, 6 Aug. 1808, aged 69, tumor. There is record of another death of a Sarah Moffatt, aged 77, apoplexy, 10 Feb. 1826. The same record shows the bapt. of Elizabeth, d/o Samuel Moffatt & Sarah Wilkins his wife, b. 24 Jan.; 21 Sept. 1781, dau. Mary born; and a dau. Ann b. 11 Nov. 1787.

## MOFFITT FAMILY          H-135, NH70
## [MOFFATT]                [P]

DAVID H. MOFFITT, feed miller of Blooming-Grove, m. Catherine Gregg & had:
David Halliday Moffitt, b. at Washingtonville 1839, d. NY City 18 March 1911. This David was connected with almost every important development between the Mississippi River & Rocky Mountains, particularly in the vicinity of Denver.
Also mentions Hector Moffitt & Son, coal & lumber business and John Newton Moffitt, library superintendent, of old Joseph Moffatt homestead, northwest of Washingtonville, now held by his grandsons C. R. Shons & S. L. Moffatt.

## MOFFATT FAMILY           LDS Anc. File

SAMUEL MOFFATT[1], b. 18 July 1704, Ballylig, Ireland, m. Anne Gregg, b. 12 June 1716, Sluh Hull, Fermanaugh, Ireland. Their children:
1737, William.
c. 1738, Jane.
c. 1740, Elizabeth.
1742, Thomas.
1744, Samuel, could be the Samuel under the Benjamin Moffatt entry above.
c. 1747, Margaret.
1749, John.
c. 1750, Anna, m. John Denniston, b. 15 Dec. 1750, Little Britain, NY.
c. 1752, Mary.

c.1754, Elinor.
1756, Isaac.
1758, Catherine.

## MONELL, JOHN J.                       A-155
atty. & judge of Newburgh.

SAMUEL MONELL[1] of Montgomery m. Elvira, d/o John Scott. Elvira's sister Catharine Lydia was mother of John A. C. Gray of NY. SAMUEL's child:
JOHN J. MONELL[2], res. Fishkill; m. (1st) Mary E., d/o Nathaniel Smith of CT; m. (2d) Caroline DeWitt, widow of Andrew J. Downing.

## MOORE/MC CLELLAN FAMILY OF HIGHLANDS
## A-811-12

JOHN MOORE, res. West Point, patentee, located upon his purchase c. 1725. A dau. m. Hugh McClellen before the Rev. as his 1st wife; res. West Point or West Grove neighborhood; active in support of the American cause. Hugh's children removed to NC after the war. Hugh m. (2d) a dau. of early Kronkhite family of West Grove, and had a son who d. leaving a family & a dau. m. James Denton of Newburgh; res. West Point & had [Denton's]:
John, farmer, res. below Highland Falls.
James Jr., now merchant of Highland Falls.

The Moore family were Loyalists, at opening of Rev. War went to Nova Scotia and later NC. In 1798 the US Gov't. bought West Point from Stephen Moore.

## MOORE FAMILIES OF WALLKILL    A-432, H-135, 904
## & of BLOOMING-GROVE          C-98, 100, 106, 108

DAVID MOORE was an early settler on previous place of Samuel Tryon, between Middletown & Phillipsburgh, where he settled before the Rev. He m. Mary Mapes & had:
1766, Feb. 28, William, res. Mt. Hope.
1768, Jan. 21, David Jr.; d. young.
1769, Dec. 2, Wilmot; had son Emmet who now res. Middletown.
1777, June 29, Walter of Wallkill.
Mrs. Wickham.
Mrs. Smith.
Mrs. Treadwell.
Mrs. Seeley.

Eunice, b. 20 Nov. 1771 & Mary b. 31 Aug. 1773, daus. of David More & wife Mary Mapes, bapt. Goshen. Could be any of the married daus. listed above.
Lydia More, d/o David More Jr. & Mary his wife was b. 7 April 1775; Phebe, d/o the same, b. 25 Dec. 1780, also according to Goshen church records.
Marriage record from same source: Thomas More, s/o David More & Tabitha Boreland his wife, bapt. 12 March 1783. And

William More m. Elizabeth Howell, 23 June 1782.

WALTER MOORE is mentioned as 'probably' the brother of DAVID[1], above. Walter d. 16 May 1768, aged 13 years, 6 months & 12 days. He had published religious poems at the age of 12.

Also mentioned (p. 434) is DANIEL MOORE of Wallkill who had a dau. Maria who m. Isaac B. Everett, hotel keeper of Wallkill, 1st & only postmaster of Van Burenville, 3 miles north of Howell's.

Alexander Moore & brother-in-law Albert G. Owen, the father of George A. Owen, had furniture & paint business in Blooming-Grove (1830-1850). [H-135]

Alexander Moore[1] m. Hannah Owen, and had:
1833, Dec. 25, JONATHAN OWEN.

JONATHAN OWEN MOORE[2], b. Washingtonville on the family homestead, served in the Civil War & after the war m. Helen, d/o VanRensselaer Wilbur of Albany. He removed to Washingtonville & served as j.p. & established a furniture business. He is known as "Owenie." In retirement he res. in NY City. Jonathan & Helen had one dau., Bertha, who m. O. B. Stillman of NY & has a country place at Washingtonville known as the Goldsmith homestead.

**MORLEY, JOHN W.**                    H-905
hatter & grocer.

**JOHN W. MORLEY**, s/o James & Anna (Vaught) Morley, b. Cornwall, Orange Co. in 1867. He m. Elizabeth Van Buren.

**MORRISON, DAVID A. & HAMILTON**      H-905-07

JOHN MORRISON[1], of Scotch ancestry, b. near Belfast, Ireland in 1700, to America before Rev. His son:

JOHN[2], settled before his father in America at what is now known as the Morrison homestead in Town of Montgomery, Orange Co. He m. Elizabeth Scott & had 9 children, among them:

HAMILTON MOORE[3] who m. Lydia Beemer, of Dutch descent, whose grandfather John to America bringing Lydia's father. Settled Beemersville, NJ. She lived to age 103. They had 8 children, among them:

HAMILTON MOORE[4], the "youngest but one," b. 24 Aug. 1804 at the homestead, which he inherited, farmer; d. 1881. He m. Maria Mould, d/o Jonathan & Elizabeth of Town of Montgomery, 10 Jan. 1827. This Mould family are lineal descs. of Christoffel Mould, one of the earliest Dutch settlers of the Wallkill Valley. Maria d. 26 March 1868. Hamilton & Maria had:
Jonathan M., m. Margaret Windfield; d. 1898.
**DAVID A.**
George H., unmarried, farmer on homestead. Has recently published a complete genealogical chart of the family in America.
John G., unmarried, farmer on homestead.
William H. H., m. Agnes Horton, farmer on adj. farm.
Mary J., m. Elijah Carpenter Thayer of Hamptonburgh; d. Feb. 1901.
Elizabeth M., m. William C. Hart of Walden, NY.

**DAVID A. MOORE[5]**, s/o Hamilton[4], was a teacher & in 1867 school commissioner. 1880 m. Mary R. Lipsett, a d/o the late Robert & Mary A. (Morrison) Lipsett of the Town of Montgomery. She is a grandau. of Col. William Faulkner, Rev. soldier. In 1893 the family to Newburgh, where they now res. **DAVID A.** has been County Correspondent of the US Dept. of Agriculture & Statistics Bureau of the Patent Office for 40 years. They attend Union Presbyterian Church in Newburgh. He is VP of the Historical Society of Newburgh Bay & an SAR member.

**MORRISON, JAMES W. [P]**            A-242
farmer of New Windsor.

JAMES MORRISON[1], farmer of Little Britain & hotel keeper, m. Harriet Patton, had:
William P.; dec'd.
John H.
1819, Feb. 22, **JAMES W.**
Jane H. m. Samuel Weed; dec'd.

JAMES W. MORRISON[2], s/o James[1], b. New Windsor, when he was 9 his parents died & he went to work on farm of uncle, James Patton at Washington Lake; 1842 purchased farm at Washington Square. He now attends Second Presbyterian Church of Washingtonville; he & his parents formerly worshiped at the Assoc. Reformed Church of Little Britain. He m. (1st) 16 Aug. 1843, Sarah Jane, d/o William & Nancy Stewart of New Windsor & moved to old Stewart homestead, and had:
1847, Jan. 25, William J., res. on farm with father.

Sarah Jane d. 3 April 1868 & **JAMES W.**[2] m. (2d) Jane, d/o Samuel Palmer of NY, 6 Jan. 1869; she d. 8 July 1873, no issue. He m. (3d) 15 Sept. 1874, Margaret E. Palmer, sister of 2d wife Jane; no issue.

**MOSHIER, GEORGE**                    H-907
retired contractor of Newburgh.

**GEORGE MOSHIER** is of a Newburgh family from since before the Rev. & several family members served in the Continental Army. Member Trinity Church. He m. Caroline Tilton and had:
Anna.
George Jr.
Mabel.

**MOULD, CHRISTOPHER J. [P]**  A-411, GFM-5
of Montgomery.

CHRISTOPHER MOULD[1], of German desc., settled at Montgomery at an early date. His children:
1783, Feb. 3, JOHN.
Philip. Could be the Philip Mould bur. at the German Reformed Cemetery, Montgomery, d. 12 Dec. 1866, aged 82. Also two of his wives: Elenore, d. 28 June 1837, aged 53 & Mary, d. 20 June 1881, aged 88.
Catharine.
Anna Mary.
Child, not named.

Also bur. at the German Reformed Church at Montgomery are: Christopher Mould, d. 18 April 1813, aged 65 years, 2 months, 15 days & his 2 wives: Catharine, d. 19 Jan. 1809, aged 54 years, 3 months, d days & Ruamer, d. 2 Feb. 1803, aged 49 years, 10 months, 10 days. With them is Catharine, d. 22 Feb. 1883, aged 92 years.

JOHN MOULD[2], d. March 1870; 17 June 1815, m. Mary Shafer of Montgomery, and had:
1816, May 16, CHRISTOPHER J.
Catharine.
Daniel.
Moses.
Eve.
Mary.
Martha.
Herman.
Jessie.
William.
John C.
Anna.

CHRISTOPHER J. MOULD[3], s/o John[2], member of Reformed Dutch Church, d. 24 May 1881; m. 14 Dec. 1845, Martha, d/o Milton Bull of Crawford, and had:
1846, Sept. 10, Mary Esther, m. A. M. Fulton of Monticello, NY; d. 3 Sept. 1874.
1860, July 25, Lemma.
1870, March 14, Martha.

W-92: Portrait of a John D. Mould, dairy farmer of Wallkill, not further identified.

---

**MURRAY, HON. AMBROSE [P]**  A-542-3
banker, Railroad dir., congressman of Goshen.
**MURRAY, HON. WILLIAM [P]**  A-543, C-42
businessman and after early retirement, Congressman, pres. Goshen Bank 1857.

GEORGE MURRAY[1], b. Inverness, Scotland, to America as soldier in British Army, settled at Reading, PA, where he m. Miss --- Snyder; to Orange Co., where he d. Their children:
Alexander.

John.
George.
WILLIAM.
James.
Jacob.
David.
Charles.
A dau.

WILLIAM MURRAY[2], s/o George[1], b. Orange Co., d. 1849; 1773 m. Mary Ann Beakes of Orange Co., who d. 1847, aged 72. WILLIAM was a farmer, res. Town of Wallkill, member of the Baptist Church. Children:
Archibald Y.
Sally m. William A. Sayer.
Cynthia m. Jonas Hulse.
Amanda m. Tustin Moore of Orange Co.
1803, Oct. 1, WILLIAM.
Edmund B.
AMBROSE S.
Mary Ann m. Gabriel Dunning of Wantage, Sussex Co., NJ.
Henry B.

WILLIAM MURRAY[3], s/o William[2], b. 1 Oct. 1803; merchant of NY City and later to Goshen; d. 25 Aug. 1875. 13 July 1837, m. Ellen Maria, b. 22 May 1809, a d/o Capt. WHITE and Abby (Robertson) MATLACK [see below], of NY City. Their children:
William, banker of Goshen
Maj. Henry Spencer, 7th NY State Militia, raised company for 124th Regt. Vols. & joined Army of the Potomac; d. 6 March 1874, Goshen. He m. 10 Nov. 1863, Sarah Dunning.
Robert R., enlisted in brother Henry's Co., merchant of Goshen.
Abby M.

AMBROSE S. MURRAY[3], s/o William[2], at age 17 clerked at Middletown at store of uncle, Stacey Beakes; 1831 to Goshen, clerk in bank & pres. of same in 1845. 1836 m. Frances, d/o Henry G. Wisner, atty. of Goshen, and Sarah Talman. Children:
Ellen, wid. of John V. Beam, Jr., NY City merchant.
George W., merchant of NY; 7th NY Regt., Civil War.
Wisner, Goshen Banker; d. 1876, aged 32; served 7th NY Regt.
Ambrose S., Jr., atty. of NY.

CAPT. WHITE MATLACK, a seafaring man who traded between Lisbon and Cadiz, and after there for 30 years, between NY and Liverpool in the early 1800's in sailing ships. He was b. Philadelphia, PA 16 Feb. 1778; d. 1834, NY City. He m. Abby Robertson, who d. c. 1836. Their children:
1809, May 22, Ellen, m. William Murray.
Robert V., merchant of NY City; d. in middle life in VA.

## MURRAY FAMILY OF FLORIDA, NY    LDS Anc. File

EZRA MURRAY[1], b. 11 July 1741, East Guilford, CT, s/o Jehiel & Mary (May) Murray, m. Hannah Gould, b. 4 Jan. 1744, Topsfield, MA, d/o Hubbard & Hannah (Bootman) Gould. The immigrant ancestor to this Murray family was Jonathan, b. 1665 near Edinburg, Scotland who m. Anna Bradley, b. in Guliford, CT. EZRA d. 1815 & Hannah d. in Dutchess Co., NY. Children of EZRA[1] & Hannah:

1768, Brewster, b. Cannan, NY.
1773, Aug. 30, Lucretia.
1775, Reuben.
1780/1800, ROSWELL.

ROSWELL MURRAY[2], s/o Ezra[1], m. (1) Mary Wilson & (2) c. 1798, Susannah Fitch, d/o Ebenezer & Sarah (Trumble) Fitch originally of Windham, CT. ROSWELL d. in Victor, Ontario, NY. Children (all b. Orange Co.):

1799, Sept. 7, Roswell Gould.
1802, Oct. 4, William E. m. (1) Mary Springer & (2) Helen E. Sarvis of Bloomfield, Ontario Co., NY. William d. May 1847 in Synder Co., MO.
1803, Brewster.
1804, July 2, Lucretia, m. Nathaniel Campbell.
1806, June 1, Viliate, m. Heber Chase, b. 1801 June 14, Sheldon, VT.

## MURTFELDT, EDWARD M.    H-907
funeral director of Newburgh.

EDWARD MURTFELDT was b. in Newburgh in 1853, entered employ of Peck & Van Dalfsen's furniture house in 1869; 1879 purchased undertaking and furniture business of Joseph H. Powell. The Murtfeldt family is of German desc., EDWARD was s/o Henry W. & Mary Frances (Worden) Murtfeldt & in 1872 m. Anna M. McCord. They have 6 children.

## MYERS, FRANK D.    H-907-08
physician of Slate Hill.

DANIEL MYERS[1] was the first of the name in the area and he participated in the battle of Minisink. This is one of the oldest of Orange Co. families. This Daniel had a son, Daniel Van Auker Myers[2], who had a son Daniel C. Myers[3]. Samuel S. Myers[4] was the s/o Daniel C. & he m. Mary Elizabeth Elston, and had:

FRANK D.[5], b. Town of Greenville, NY; school teacher in Town of Minisink; studied medicine at Univ. of MI, 1887. He m. Margaret Hall of Ridgebury and had:
1908, Frank D.

## NANNY, GARDNER K. [P]    A-612c
of Warwick.

JOSEPH NANNY[1], b. 7 Nov. 1785; m. 1807, Sallie Johnson, b. 13 April 1789, and had:

1808, Maria.
1810, Johnson G.
1821, Jan. 12, GARDNER K.

GARDNER K. NANNY[2], m. 16 April 1862, Adeline Arnout, d/o JOHN ARNOUT [see below] of Edenville, and had:
Frances M.
Sadie O.

GARDNER was a memer of the Methodist Episcopal Church at Edenville & d. Edenville, 7 June 1847, age 83.

Children of JOHN ARNOUT:
William H.
Samuel H.
John W.
Mary A.
Adeline m. GARDNER K. NANNY.

## NEAFIE, GEN. ALFRED    H-908-9

CORNELIUS NEAFIE[1], a member of one of the old Knickerbocker families who came to NY in 1637, built the first cotton mill in Orange Co. His son:

ALFRED NEAFIE[2], b. Walden, 8 January 1832, in 1851 began his world travels. On the death of his father he returned to Ellenville, NY; served in the 156th NY Inf. & other units during the Civil War & after the war in business in Ellenville & Goshen.

## NEARPASS, WILLIAM H. [P]    A-201
of Port Jervis, journalist.

JACOB NEARPASS[1] emigrated from Germany c. 1755, settled in Montague, Sussex Co., NJ & d. there; farmer. His children:

Baltus, d. in battle of Minisink.
JOHN.
Jacob, to Seneca Co., NY & had family.
William, settled in Montague; d. by accident.
Benjamin, settled in Montague, later to MI.
Elizabeth.
Catharine.

JOHN NEARPASS[2], s/o Jacob, m. 19 March 1785, Sarah Inkhoorn and had:
Baltus.
William.
MICHAEL.
Benjamin.
Rachel.
Mary.
Catharine.

MICHAEL NEARPASS[3], s/o John[2], inherited homestead and remained in NJ; m. (1) Jemima Cuddeback; (2) Charlotte E. Stewart, and had:

1840, May 9, **WILLIAM H.**, b. Montague, NJ.
Horace S., dec'd.
Sarah Temperance, dec'd.
Charles H.

**WILLIAM H. NEARPASS**[4], s/o Michael[3], 1856 to Port Jervis;
mercantile clerk at age 19; newspaper work in Port Jervis;
public servant; member Reformed (Dutch) Church. He m.
1867, Anna W. Newman of Brooklyn, NY, who d. 1879.
Children:
Emma E.
Charlotte A.
Anna W., dec'd.

---

**NEELEY, ROBERT**               U2-156, C-10
of Neeleytown.

In his will dated 17 Sept. 1756, **ROBERT NEELEY** names his
brothers William & John Sr., both of Neeleytown, & his wife
Isabel, and children:
Adam.
William.
David.
Matthew.
Mary.

There is the m. of a Isabella Neely to Tobias Feller on 10
Jan. 1779 in Goshen church records.

---

**NELSON FAMILY OF HIGHLANDS**
**(NELSON'S FERRY)**               A-812, H-909-10

JACOB NELSON, Sr. & Jr. desc. of colonists who settled in the
West Point area c. 1686; had ferry business from east side of
the river. Jr.'s children:
Miphiboseth; had a son, Cornelius, only member of the family
to settled on the west side of the river; to Highland Falls,
1844.
Cornelius.
Justus.
Elisha.
Mrs. Gabriel Odell.
Mrs. John Warren.
Mrs. Peter Warren.

A CORNELIUS NELSON, possibly the son of Miphiboseth
above, postmaster of Highland Falls for 30 years, real estate &
insurance business, had a son:
Moses F. Nelson, b. Highland Falls in 1867. Moses was a
real estate & insurance broker in Town of Highlands & m. Mary
Adolph in 1893, & had 3 daughters.

---

**NICOLL FAMILY OF WASHINGTONVILLE**
                                A-213, H-910

This family is of Scotch desc. Dr. JOHN NICOLL to America
in 1711 & settled in NY, d. 1743, aged 64. He purchased

Plum Point, Town of New Windsor & his son John came
into possession in 1735 & erected homestead house, which
is still standing & today owned by descs. His desc., John
Nicoll, b. Hackensack, NJ 1799, merchant of NY City, in
1844 removed to Orange Co. & m. (1) Juliana Thompson &
had a son, William who d. at age 26. He m. (2) Elizabeth
H. White, b. Blagg's Cove 1808, d. 1855. By his 2d wife he
had 8 children, all reside at Washingtonville:
Charles
Elizabeth White, m. Andrew S. Glover.
Isaac, d. in the Battle of Gettysburg in 1863; Co. G, NY State
Vols.

---

**NIVEN, DANIEL**               E-158, TN-323

**DANIEL NIVEN** emigrated from Ila, an island on the west
coast of Scotland, to NY City c. 1770. He served in the Rev.,
after war settled in Newburgh, where he purchased a farm &
mill from Mr. Belknap. He was judge of a local court, j.p. & d.
20 Nov. 1809, aged 67.

---

**NOWAK, REV. STANISLAUS J.**               H-910-11
rector of St. Joseph Roman Catholic Church, Florida, NY

**REV. NOWAK** was b. in Posen, Germany (Poland); studied
in Germany, Rome & in the US. 1895 appointed rector at
Shokan, Ulster Co. & Kingston, NY; 1892 transferred to NY
City where he organized a new Polish congregation & was later
returned to St. Joseph's, Florida. This church was established at
the request of parishioners John & Anton Dulski, Joseph Andrys-
zak, Joseph Wozniak, Ignatius Brink & John Majorowski,
appointed collectors who raised funds in 1893.

---

**OAKLEY, ISAAC K.**               A-643-4
of Blooming-Grove.

JOHN OAKLEY[1], from England to Suffolk Co., L.I. under
Dutch rule. He d. there, was a farmer. He m. --- Knickerbocker
of Brooklyn; had many children, some settled in Huntington,
L.I., others in various NY counties. His grandson:

SAMUEL OAKLEY[3] m. Sally Wood of Huntington. Samuel
was pressed into British service during the Revolution and
robbed of cattle and farm produce. Children of Samuel &
Sally:
Richard. There is a Richard Oakley bur. in the German Reformed Cemetery at Montgomery; d. 30 Jan. 1829, aged 50
years, 10 months, 28 days.
1772, Jan. 28, TIMOTHY, b. Huntington.
Jacob.
Solomon.
4 daus.

TIMOTHY OAKLEY[4], removed to New Windsor, Orange Co.
1795, merchant; 1802 to Chatham, Columbia Co.; 1813
erected one of the first cotton mills at Kinderhook; farmer &
miller. Timothy resided Cornwall-on-Hudson when he d., 26

Dec. 1844. He m. (1) Polly Brush, d/o Zophar of Hunting-ton, L.I.; (2d) Sally Ketcham, d/o Isaac of Huntington, who d. at Salisbury Mills, NY 10 April 1833; (3d) in Huntington, Prudence Mather, d. 1864. Timothy's children:

Zophar B., merchant of Huntington.

Samuel, merchant of New York.

Lewis, physician of Owego, NY.

1802, May 27, ISAAC K.

Timothy, merchant of St. Louis, MO.

Jesse, manufacturer of NY.

Mary, m. Reuben Van Alen of Chatham, Columbia Co., NY.

Sally W., m. Dr. John Vanderpoel of Kinderhook, NY.

ISAAC K. OAKLEY[5], s/o Timothy[4], at age 17 to Nassau, Rensselaer Co., tanning & leather trade in assoc. with his father and brother in milling business. After 1833 res. at the Salisbury Mills, built paper mill, flour & plaster mills. Isaac m. Christina, d/o Lucas I. & Maria (Pruyn) Van Alen of Kinderhook, 1 Feb. 1827. Christina d. at Salisbury Mills, 15 Feb. 1866. Their children:

Lucas, d. infancy.

Timothy, d. young.

Lucas, now connected with Oakley Soap Works at Newburgh with his brother John, below.

John.

Sarah Maria, d. young.

ISAAC[5] m. (2d) 9 Sept. 1873, Sarah E., d/o Thomas & Catharine (Jones) Oakley of Minisink. Sarah E. is a granddau. of John who served in the Revolution under Washington and later married and settled at Minisink.

---

## O'CONNOR, ARTHUR E.                    H-911-12

NEAL O'CONNOR[1], captain of the New Orleans Rangers in the Mexican War, had a son,

JOHN S. O'CONNOR[2], served as sgt. in the 69th Regt. NY Vol. Inf. He resided 25 years at White Mills & Hawley in PA; worked in glass factory. He m. Hannah Marrett & had 7 children, 5 living:

Anna, m. Timothy O'Connell, res. Honesdale, PA.

Mary, m. Thomas Cusick of Goshen & had 4 daughters, 2 at home & 2 dec'd.

10 March 1867, ARTHUR E.

ARTHUR E. O'CONNOR[3], s/o John S.[2] & Hanna, b. in Brooklyn, NY, ran cut glass factory at Goshen. He m. Catherine Langan of Hawley, PA 20 Feb. 1888 & had:

John, foreman at Goshen factory.

William, at school.

Arthur, at school.

Mary, bookkeeper at Goshen factory.

---

## ODELL, HON. BENJAMIN B.  H-912, NC-50-1 [P], NH-66
of Newburgh.

The ODELL family is of French & English desc. WILLIAM

ODELL[1], b. NY City, was proprietor of Bull's Head Tavern; 1835 to Orleans Co., NY & d. there over 90 years of age. His son:

ISAAC ODELL[2], b. Tarrytown, Westchester Co., NY, reared in NY City; 1820 to Orange Co., settled at DeWitt Clinton farm at Little Britain until 1830, removed to Newburgh. Isaac d. aged 65. He m. Mary A. ---, b. Westchester Co., d. NY City aged 84. They had 2 sons & 2 daughters, among them:

BENJAMIN B. ODELL[3], b. on Gov. Clinton homestead, New Windsor Town, 10 Sept. 1825, reared in Newburgh. 1843 employed by B. W. Van Nort in hotel business until 1847 when he opened his own restaurant. 1863 he purchased ice business of James R. Dixon. Other businesses & public offices of sheriff & mayor of Newburgh. Member American Reformed Church. 1850 m. Ophelia, d/o Hiram Bookstaver of Town of Montgomery, they had 11 children, those living:

1854 Jan. 14, BENJAMIN B. JR.

1856, Aug. 21, HIRAM B.

Clara, resides with father.

George C. D., professor at Columbia Univ., NY City.

BENJAMIN B. ODELL, JR.[4], b. Newburgh; sheriff & 6 terms mayor of Newburgh, Congressman & 2 times gov. of the State of NY. He d. 9 May 1926. Studied in NY & WV; m. 25 April 1877, Estelle Crist of Newburgh who d. in 1888 in a sailing accident. Their children:

Walter.

Herbert.

Bryant.

BENJAMIN B.[4] m. (2) Mrs. Linda (Crist) Traphagen, sister of his first wife in 1891.

HIRAM B. ODELL[4], s/o BENJAMIN[3], businessman & public office holder of Newburg, m. Edith Booth of Kingston.

---

## OGDEN, JAMES ALSAP                        H-913
hardware merchant of Warwick.

WILLIAM L. OGDEN[1] (d. 1902) m. Louise Baker and had (surviving children):

1861, May 28, JAMES ALSAP.

Alvertta, m. Maurice Patten.

Mary, m. Dr. S. E. Holly.

JAMES ALSAP OGDEN[2], b. Town of Mt. Hope, res. in Warwick since age of 9 months; d. 5 Dec. 1905. He m. Virginia R. Geraghty of Warwick in 1889.

---

## OLDROYD, JOSHUA                          H-913-14

JOSHUA OLDROYD, b. Yorkshire, England 29 Jan. 1838, hand loom weaver; age 18 to America & employed in the woolen mills at Mechanicstown, Orange Co. 1856-58. Later in charge of mills at Millow, Wawayanda Twp., and still later at Newton & East Granby, CT. 1857 to Newburgh & retired to Mechanicstown, Howells, Philadelphia, PA & Middletown, NY.

He m. Hannah Newsome, d/o James of Mechanicstown 6 March 1861 & had one child, d. in infancy. Attends Episcopal Church.

## O'NEAL, WILLIAM H.                    H-914

**WILLIAM H. O'NEAL**, b. Goshen 3 March 1836, at age 16 learned painting & decorating trade. He m. (1) Sarah E. Stone of Denton, NY 31 Dec. 1855; she d. 9 Feb. 1881, and had:

Sarah Louise
Henry Lincoln.
Charles Francis.

**WILLIAM** m. (2) Lydia E. Hall of Goshen 27 July 1882, she d. 1 March 1892. He worked in NY City 20 years beginning in 1856. Served in the Civil War in 84th Regt.

## ORR, JOHN [P]                         A-784-85
of Cornwall.
## ORR, WILLIAM [P]                      A-785-6
## & JOHN                                H-914-15

ROBERT ORR[1], b. Scotland, to North of Ireland c. 1700, had a son:

JOHN ORR[2], wheelwright m. Susan ORR and had a son:

DAVID ORR[3], miller of City of Armagh, Ireland, d. 1843, age c. 52. He m. (1) Elizabeth Stewart who d. 1822; (2d) Jane Stewart, a cousin of his first wife. Jane d. 1881 in Monroe, Orange Co., bur. Woodlawn Cemetery. Children by 1st wife:

David, d. young.
**JOHN.**
Jane Ann, m. Joseph S. Pruden of NY City.
Susan, m. George G. Stone of Cleveland, OH.
   Children by 2d wife:
1830, Dec. 23, **WILLIAM.**
Mary Elizabeth, m. John J. VanDuzer of Cornwall.
Sarah m. Jesse B. Birdsall of Newburgh.

**JOHN ORR[4]**, s/o David[3], to America in 1842, settled Vail's Gate and removed to Shawangunk, Ulster Co.; Oct. 1846 m. Mary, d/o Robert Fulton & Mary Cooper of New Windsor. April 1845 took up residence in Cornwall going into partnership with Robert E. Ring at the Townsend Mill, later purchased mill at Mountainville. Member Bethlehem Presbyterian Church. They had 8 children, 5 survive:

Susan A. m. Lewis A. Van Cleft of Woodbury.
Addie.
Margaret m. D. E. Sutherland of Cornwall.
Emma.
Jesse.

**WILLIAM ORR[4]**, s/o David[3], b. Armagh, Ireland; to America 11 Feb. 1847, where several sisters and brothers had already settled. Resided for one year with brother John in Cromwell; 1851 to Haverstraw and operated mill; later to Newburgh still later to Mountainville. 27 Jan. 1857, m. Margaret (Young)

Elliot, d/o William Drummond Elliot and Jean Stewart Lamb of Glasgow, Scotland. Children:

1859, March 5, **JOHN**, in business with father.
William Elliot, of NY City.
David Lincoln.
Maggie.
Mary.
Florence.
Nellie P., d. young.

**JOHN ORR[5]**, s/o William & Margaret (Elliott) Orr[4]. He was b. in Cornwall NY, in flour & coal business in Orr's Mills, Town of Cornwall. Served as Assemblyman, 1888 m. Angelique Veith of NY City, and had:

Alice.
Walter.

## OSTROM, J. W. [P]            A-183-4, C-45, 145-6
physician of Goshen.

REV. JAMES I. OSTROM[1], b. Pleasant Valley, Duchess Co., NY, 1761, Nov., Presbyterian clergyman. Served in various NY counties, d. in Marlborough Sept. 1871. He m. Eliza, d/o Col. Joshua Ward of Pleasant Valley; she d. in NY City 1842. Their surviving children:

Adelia, m. --- Huntley of Salina, NY.
1814, July 10, **DR. J. W..**
James, NY merchant.
Harriet.
John, d. in NY.

**J. W. OSTROM[2]**, b. Marlborough, NY, studied under his uncle, Rev. Mr. Kiffin of Little Falls & Dr. Arsenus Smith; grad. from medical school 1838. Practiced in Goshen (1839-49); practiced homeopathic medicine. He m. (1) 1840, Dec., Emily [Emily Charlotte in Goshen church records] L., d/o Dr. Eleazer Gedney of Newburgh. She d. 24 March 1879, aged 63. Children:

Charlotte, m. Dr. Clarence Conant, of Middletown.
Gunning B., Goshen merchant; m. 5 Nov. 1874, Susan C. Howell of Goshen.
Bapt. 3 Aug. 1850, at Goshen, Eliza Ward, m. William Van Amer, Middletown atty.
Annie m. Rev. Henry A. Dowes of Middletown.
Hiram Irwin, physician of New York City.

**DR. J. W.[2]** m. (2d), 26 April 1881, Emma Gertrude, widow of Edgar LuGar of NY and d/o Prof. L. A. Benjamin of NY City.

## OTTO, HERMAN                          H-915
farmer & businessman of Middletown.

**HERMAN OTTO**, b. Saxon, Germany 22 Feb. 1840; to America 1869 & m. Emma Wolf of New Britain, CT, and had:

Dau., d. age 7.

Emma, m. Ira Smith of Monroe, NY.
Herman, res. NY City.
Frank, of Windham, OH.
Charles, of Monroe, NY.
Anna Mae, of NY City.
Arlyne Elsie, at home.
Harry, at home.
Paul, at home.

_____

## OWEN, GEORGE A.                           H-915
merchant at Washingtonville, NY.

HON. ALBERT G. OWEN m. Phoebe M. Breed; was merchant at Washingtonville where son **GEORGE A.** was b. in 1842. **GEORGE** m. Isabelle Board in 1876 & had 6 children. Family were members of the Presbyterian Church.

_____

## OWEN, OSCAR E.                            H-915-16

JONATHAN OWEN[1] m. Elizabeth Carpenter & had:
JOHN C. OWEN[2], b. Town of Minisink 16 July 1806, d. at his daughter's home (Mrs. W. W. Hartford of Middletown). He was a merchant at Huguenot, removed to Smith's Corners. He m. Adelaine, d/o Moses Durland 16 Feb. 1833; 1838 to Ridgebury; 1847 to farm left to him by his uncle, Jesse Parshall, later to Ridgebury where he started a marble yard, until 1866 then grocery business in Middletown, which he sold to his son-in-law, George W. W. Hartford. His son:
OSCAR[3], b. 28 Feb. 1845, at Ridgebury, NY was in "monumental work" and public service. He m. Emily F. Mapledoram of Monticello, Sullivan Co., NY 28 July 1868. They had a son, Clifford A., b. 7 June 1872. Members of Universalist Church.

_____

## PADDLEFORD, ZAEL                          H-916
merchant of Monroe.

**ZAEL PADDLEFORD**, b. in Broome Co., NY in 1866, to Monroe in 1891, creamery foreman. 1894 purchased store; 1895 formed partnership with George R. Conklin. Public service. He m. Isabella S. Kinney of IA & had one son, Bruce K., in school in NY City.

_____

## PALMER, THOMAS                            U2-20
of Newburgh.

In his will dated 27 June 1787, **THOMAS PALMER** named his brother Beriah Palmer & his own wife Alenah, and children:
William.
Thomas.
Alenah.
Nancy Butler.
Sarah.
Mary Ann Dugan.
Julia.
Esther, m. Charles Hatch.

Will proved 30 Nov. 1787 by Samuel Buchanan of Newburgh yeoman, Adolphus Brower & Phineas Bowman.

_____

## PARMETER, SAMUEL                          TN-318-19
of Newburgh.

JOHN PARMETER[1], from England before 1639, settled in Sudbury, MA, his son:
JOHN PARMETER JR.[2], b. in England; a freeman of the Colony of MA 16 May 1643, had:
BENJAMIN PARMETER[3], b. c. 1646, who had:
SAMUEL PARMETER[4], b. 11 May 1722 and had:
EZRA PARMETER[5], b. 16 June 1760. Ezra's children:
1791, March 2, SAMUEL.
James.
William.
Mary.
Elizabeth, m. Col. Gardiner Thompson of Newburgh & had Ezra P., Catharine G., Gardiner G., Mary E., William P., Nancy F.,Maria T., Helen, Susan P., Charles F., George J. & Julia, all living except William & Julia.
Sarah.
Nancy, dec'd.
James.
Nancy.

SAMUEL PARMETER[6], s/o Ezra[5], b. Boston, m. 1818, Eliza, d/o Stephen Crane of Newton, MA & removed to Warwick, where they res. until 1821, when they removed to Newburgh, where he d. 29 June 1841. Eliza d. 14 Sept. 1849. They had:
1822, Charles J., d. 1826.
1830, Susan E. C., d. 1856.
1819, April 9, Stephen C., b. Warwick, m. Catharine A. McDowell, 16 Oct. 1844 & they have 5 daus.: Caroline E., Cornelia A., Alginette D., Gertrude A. & Genevieve C. & one son, Samuel J.

SAMUEL[6] was a mathematician, village surveyor, cartographer, author of "A Concise View of the United States" & other works. He was editor of the _Newburgh Gazette_ & an Episcopalian, organist of St. George's church.

## PARROT FAMILY OF GOSHEN                    LDS Anc. File

SAMUEL PARROT[1], s/o John, b. 25 July 1792, m. 1 March 1817, Phoebe Bailey, d/o Capt. Jonathan Bailey & Keturah Conkling of Southold, L.I. & Orange Co. Phoebe was b. 3 Sept. 1792 & d. 2 Aug. 1852 at Ridgebury. Samuel also d. there 10 Jan. 1835. Their children:
1819, Jan. 23, ALPHEUS.
1821, May 22, EMALINE.
1824, Oct. 28, Nancy Ann, m. Richard Van Tassel.

ALPHEUS PARROT[2], s/o Samuel[1], m. Isabel Gertrude Borland, b. 1824, Orange Co., d/o Thomas Borland & Anna McDowell of Orange Co. Alpheus d. 3 Sept. 1899 at

Bloomer, WI; Isabel d. Feb. 1824 in Orange Co. They had:

1840, July 8, Phoebe Anne, m. Volney J. Babcock, b. 1833, Gouverneur, St. Lawrence Co., NY. They lived in La Crescent, MN & later in Eau Claire, WI.

1842, Victoria, m. W. M. Perry & had (PERRY): Anne Belle, Alice, Lois & Luther.

1847, Elmira, m. --- Williams.

1848, April 2, Harriet, m. George Dallas Ackley, b. 28 Sept. 1843, Pennyan, Yates Co., NY. They removed to Eau Claire, WI.

EMALINE PARROT², d/o Samuel¹, m. Charles S. Borland of Orange Co. & had (BORLAND):

1841, Samuel.

1842, Nov. 23, Charles S., m. Mary Milligan.

1843, Mary, m. J. K. Austin.

1844, John H.

1845, James.

1849, Emma Jane, m. G. M. Seman.

c. 1851, Christina, m. T. H. Knight.

c. 1853, Ella, m. --- Wilcox.

c. 1855, Emaline, m. S. C. Brown.

c. 1857, Charlotte.

c. 1859, Alpheus P.

## PARROTT, PETER P. [P]                                    A-806-7
of Monroe.

**PETER P. PARROTT**, b. Portsmouth, NH; 1837 to Orange Co., Woodbury, town of Monroe; managed Woodbury Iron Co. 1838 to Greenwood, 1853 with brother Robert former partnership, The Parrott Iron Co. Member Protestant Episcopal Church. 1843 m. Mary Arden, d/o Richard D. of Phillipstown, Putnam Co., NY. They had 8 children (none named here).

## PARSHALL FAMILY OF GOSHEN                    LDS Anc. File

ISRAEL PARSHALL¹, b. March 1680 at Mattituck, NY, m. 4 Dec. 1702 at Southhold, Joanna Swazey, d/o Joseph Swazey & Mary Betts. Israel d. 17 April 1738 & Joanna d. 23 Feb. 1724, both at Southhold. Their son:
ISRAEL PARSHALL², m. Bethia Case 16 Nov. 1732 & had:
JAMES PARSHALL³, b. at Southhold in 1735, m. Hannah Knapp, d/o Jonathan Knapp & Elizabeth Ferris of Goshen, where Hannah was b. 1774. They had:

1755, Anna.

1757, Bethia.

1759, Catherine.

1761, Sarah.

1763, James.

1765, Elizabeth.

1767, Jonathan K.

1769, Israel.

1771, Nathaniel.

1773, Lydia.

1775, David.

## PARSHALL FAMILY OF NEW WINDSOR       A-204, H-916

ISRAEL PARSHALL¹, driven from France with Huguenots after Edict of Nantes, located at east end of L.I. at a point then called Black River and is bur. there. His son:
JONATHAN PARSHALL², purchased land in Markham Tract (Little Britain, Town of New Windsor) in 1737 & after he d. his wife removed to Pittsburgh, PA, where she died. They had two sons:
JONATHAN.
David, served in Rev. War.

JONATHAN PARSHALL³, m. Jemima Terry and had 4 sons & 1 dau. Only one named was the 3rd child, MOSES⁴, who lived & d. on the homestead in New Windsor. His dau. is Mrs. Jemima Drury⁵ [see Drury family]. Another son of Jonathan, CALEB⁴, is named (H-916).

CALEB PARSHALL⁴, born on the old homestead; later to a farm in Walden; 1870 family to Port Jervis. One of his children was:
WILLIAM A.⁵, b. 9 Dec. 1865 in Walden, attended Albany Law School & grad. Yale 1888. Back to Port Jervis in office of Hon. Lewis C. Carr; partnership with Hon. O. P. Howell & R. Ed. Schofield since 1893. Public service. 1 June 1903 m. Christine Senger, d/o Lewis C. & Florence (Corwin) Senger. They have 3 children.

---

## PATCHETT, ARTHUR                                          H-917

ARTHUR PATCHETT, b. England in 1847, d. at Montgomery, NY 30 Nov. 1901. To America 1872, located at Philadelphia, worsted manufacturer. 1880 to Montomgery, established plant with the late William Crabtree. 1874 m. Alice M. Hayes of Philadelphia & had:

Emma M., res. Montgomery.

Joseph E., in business in Kaiser, WV.

Arthur Allan, in business in Kaiser, WV.

---

## PATTERSON FAMILY OF WALLKILL                  A-433

HENRY PATTERSON of Wallkill had:

Mrs. David Linderman.

Alexander William.

Mrs. Peter Sears of Coldenham.

Mrs. John B. Cox of Middletown; d. 4 Dec. 1880, left 2 sons and 2 daus. in Middletown.

John, m. Arietta Bull of Wallkill.

Sally, unm.

James M., d. in CA.

Henry, m. Catharine Harris of Randalls' Island (owned by her grandmother), res. Harlem age 79.

---

## PATTERSON, FRANK                                          H-917
supervisor Town of Deer Park.

**FRANK PATTERSON**, with brother George H., conducts

a farm & summer boarding house known as "Eddy Farm" at Sparrowbush, where he was b. in 1865. They are the sons of J. R. & Mary E. (Doty) Patterson.

## PATTERSON, JAMES U2-67
of Newburgh, farmer.

JAMES PATTERSON, will dated 7 June 1789, names only wife Margrit & granddau. Catharine Carskadan. Robert Carskadan & Moses Lyons of Newburgh, wheelwright, named executors. Robert Irwin & William Erwin, executors.

## PATTON, WILLIAM M. H-918

WILLIAM M. PATTON, b. 30 May 1834, Town of New Windsor, d. 16 April 1907, bur. Wallkill Valley Cemetery in Walden. He was a farmer & cattle dealer who moved to Newburgh 1895; m. (1) Miss Robinson, who died "many years ago." They had one son, John R., who resides on Patton homestead near Washington Lake. WILLIAM m. (2) Anna F. Johnston, d/o the late Beverly K. businessman of East Coldham.

## PELTON, HENRY & SAMUEL H-918-20

HENRY PELTON[1] came to Warwick from Darien, CT in 1805 as a small boy with his father & settled on a farm west of the village. He was a pioneer in the Temperance Movement & d. 1873, aged 82. His son:
SAMUEL PELTON[2], d. 1906, nearly aged 80. He had:
HENRY.
James, d. 1856.
Richard, d. 1898.

HENRY PELTON[3], s/o Samuel[2], res. on family farm; teacher, engaged in business in Warwick & in NY City. Dec. 1867 m. Almeda Knapp, d/o the late John of Sugar Loaf, and had:
John.
Grace, m. Frank Holbert of NY.
Almeda.
Geraldine, m. Selah Durland.

HENRY[2] has 2 grandsons & 2 granddaughter (not named here).

## PENOYER, WILLIAM J. H-919

WILLIAM, b. Columbia County, NY, d. Jan. 1904. Ran general store for 10 years; at age 26 to Albany, bank director. He m. 1883 Anna M. Roe of Chester, Orange Co. & had a dau., Fannie, b. 1886.

## PENNY, JOSEPH A-255, E-88, TN-28, C-13

JOSEPH PENNY[1], b. in "Wales, England," schoolmaster prior to Rev. War; purchased the whole patent of Wallace [Town of Newburgh] & settled it chiefly with his children:
John. Could be the John Penny that appears in Goshen church

records as m. Sarah Simmers, 23 Sept. 1782.
1759, May 29, WILLIAM.
Robison.
Joseph.
Peter.
James.
Allen.
Nelly, never married.
Isaac.

WILLIAM PENNY[2], d. 7 Dec. 1832; m. Hannah ---, b. 20 June 1761, d. 20 Jan. 1833. Their son:
WILLIAM PENNY[3], d. 31 Jan. 1761, aged 60 years, 2 months, & 17 days; and his wife, Mercy ---, d. 4 Nov. 1857, aged 66 years.

TN-281 states that Joseph Penny's[1] eldest dau. m. Daniel Everett of Ulster Co. & that his 2d dau. m. James, s/o Robert Ross & that dau. Betsey m. William Wilson. These could be daus. of Joseph[2], s/o Joseph[1].

JOSEPH PENNY[1] sold several hundred acres to ROBERT ROSS, the father of William & Alexander Ross. Mr. Ross was a tanner & shoemaker.

There are quite a few desecs. of Joseph Penny[1] Sr. residing in Newburgh, as well as in Ulster Co. & in the city of NY.

## PETERS, GEORGE W. H-920
businessman of Newburgh; now decd.

GEORGE was s/o Charles & Phoebe (Dean) Peters. At age 16 in meat business with his father in NY City & in 1847 joined firm of Charles Peters & Son until 1863, when he moved to Newburgh. Farmer 2 1/2 years, 1889-82 meat market business with sons. Member of the Unitarian Church; d. 1907.

## PHILLIPS, ALBERT H. F. H-920

ALBERT, b. Oswego, NY in 1866, s/o John G. Phillips & Mary Fisher. Railroad foreman; m. Elizabeth Anna Heckroth of Delaware Co., NY 18 Oct. 1888 & had one dau., Clara, b. 8 April 1893. Member Congregational Church.

## PHILLIPS, JOHN EVERTSON H-920, STJ-20
of Goshen.

JOHN was s/o William & Sarah E. Phillips, b. Phillipsburgh, 20 March 1805. Grad. from Williams College in 1825; studied law with Henry G. Wisner until he d. 17 Dec. 1841. He m. 1 March 1832, Elizabeth T. Wisner, d/o Henry G. & they had 3 daus., one of which, Harriet H., still res. at home. Church records of St. James Protestant Episcopal Church in Goshen give the following children of Mrs. Elizabeth Phillips, widow, all bapt. 4 Sept. 1842. Sponsors were the mother, Mrs. Sarah Wisner and William H. Wisner:
1834, Sept. 21, Sarah Wisner.

1838, April 1, Ann Evertson.
1840, July 6, Harriet Hornbeck.

**PIERSON, JOHN**                          H-921-2
of Town of Mt. Hope.

**JOHN PIERSON,** b. on the homestead farm near Otisville in
1834, s/o Silas G. & Salome B. (Cook) Pierson. There were
4 children in the family, 2 died in infancy. **JOHN'S** sister,
Harriet N., m. Alsop W. Dodge of Otisville, she d. 20 July
1897; members of Otisville Presbyterian Church. **JOHN'S**
wife is not named, but his children are:
Silas, of Denver, CO.
John M., of Denver, CO.
Frank, at home.
Cora, at home.
Helen G., m. Eleazer Bull.
Saloma C., of Philadelphia.
Susan C., teacher at Amityville, L.I.

**PIERSON, GEORGE**                        H-921
resident of Hamptonburgh 60 years.
**PIERSON, CAPT. SILAS**      A-525, H-259-60, C-16, 118
of Goshen.

**CAPT. SILAS PIERSON**[4] was a great-grandson of JOHN
PIERSON[1], who emigrated from England c. 1650 & settled
at South Hampton, L.I. **SILAS** from L.I. 1749 to Orange
Co., res. Hamptonburgh, served in Rev. War; m. --- DeWitt,
a relative of Mrs. James Clinton, and had:
Jubal, removed to Ithaca.
Rhoda, m. Rufus J. Drake and had a son Victor M. Drake,
publisher of Goshen; res. 30 years Newtown, NJ. Rufus J.
was the s/o Francis Drake of Blooming-Grove.

H-259-60 states that Capt. Silas, early settler of Hampton-
burgh, had a son Silas, Jr. Perhaps the Silas above was the Jr.
It also mentions a George Pierson, Sr., grandson of Joshua
Pierson who in 1777 at age 16 served as a private in Col. Jesse
Woodhull's Regt.
Also mentions that the family of William Henry Pierson still
resides on the old farm. Henry m. Elizabeth Bull & had one
dau., Lucile, who m. Henry Bull of Wallkill.

There is a second Silas Pierson family in Goshen. Church
records show the marriage of this Silas to Abigail More 8 June
1785 & their children, all bapt. 3 April 1794, Matthew, Abigail,
Mary & Silas; also Elizabeth b. 27 July 1795 & a son Nathan
bapt. 17 Sept. 1797.

**GEORGE PIERSON**[5] is the great-great grandson of Silas[1].
**GEORGE,** b. 1 Jan. 1824, is eldest s/o Henry (d. 1866)
Pierson, b. Hamptonburgh & wife Mary Shaw, b. Orange
Co., d. 1853. Henry & Mary had 8 children, 4 survived to
adulthood. **GEORGE**[5] m. Mary E., d/o Oliver Thompson,
20 December 1848 & they had 4 children. Members
Hamptonburgh Presbyterian Church.

**PITTS, ELIAS**                           TN-321-2
of Newburgh.

**ELIAS PITTS,** b. Columbia Co., NY 1810, served apprenticeship in the office of the *Kinderhook Sentinel* later to Rochester & still later manager of the *Newburgh Telegraph* (1840-50).
To Poughkeepsie, editor of the *Poughkeepsie American.* 1853
apptd. to clerkship in Washington, DC. Local political leader.
He is described as a talented writer & the soul of good fellow-
ship. He was 5 feet 3 inches tall, small with a well-proportioned
body, black hair & eyes. He was m. twice, (1) Elizabeth, d/o
John Jamison of Newburgh & they had Mary E. & John M.
**ELIAS** m. (2) Margaret, d/o John White. He d. in Washington,
DC 21 July 1854 from typhoid fever, aged 44.

**PLETTEL, JOHANNES JACOB**                CN-10

**JOHANNES JACOB PLETTEL** is in the Newburgh Directory
for 1709, the year the town was founded & settled by
immigrants from the Palatinate of the Rhine. He was
husbandman & viner, aged 40 on immigration; his wife Anna
Elizabeth aged 29. Their children:
Margaret, aged 10 on immigration.
Anna Sarah, aged 8. Further along in the text Anna & Sarah
appear as two separate children.
Catharine, aged 3 years.

This source states that it appears that Johannes Jacob Plettel
d. on the passage to America & his widow m. George Lockstead.

**POST, GEORGE A.**                        H-922
builder of Port Jervis.

**GEORGE,** b. Saugerties, Ulster Co., NY, m. Hannah J. Bross
of Ten Mile River, Sullivan Co., NY, and had:
Fannie E., m. Charles Clark.
George H., mail carrier, m. Tillie Headley.
Minnie, at home.
Lillie, school teacher at Westbrookville, Orange Co.

**POWELL FAMILY**                          TN-304-6
**POWELL, THOMAS [P]**                     A-351-2
of Newburgh.

**THOMAS POWELL**[1] emigrated to America with family from
Powelton, Wales; located at Huntington L.I.; a patentee; in
Aug. 1695 he purchased "Mawmee, alias Serewanus, William
Chepy & ye rest of ye Indian proprietors the tract of land
where on the village of Bethpage is now situated" He had
[Henry below in one source is given as "either the son of or
the grandson of Thomas[1]]:
HENRY POWELL[2], b. Hempstead, 1741; d. 1781. He res. at
L.I. until the British forces obtained possession & his estate
was confiscated. He was made a prisoner & put on the
Jersey Prison Ship & later held prisoner at the Old Sugar
House. After the war he returned to L.I. & farmed on

Shelter Island until 1781, when accompanied by his son James sailing out from NY on a sail-ferry-boat, he drowned while trying to save son Joseph [other reference says son James, not Joseph], who also perished. Henry[2] m. Mary Keen in 1762, she of Irish extraction, & had:

FREELOVE.

Jacob (age 16 in 1781), d. 1823, unm.; settled NJ 1798, to Newburgh in business with brother Thomas (below). Ship builders & contractors.

THOMAS (age 12 in 1781), Quaker; d. 12 May 1856; m. Mary Ludlow, d/o Robert. Had 5 children, the youngest, Frances E. L., m. Homer Ramsdell. (See Ramsdell family.)

Joseph [James?], drowned 1781.

Martha, m. Benjamin Townsend & had: Betsey, Mary, Jacob, Nancy & Benjamin.

Eliza, m. William Seymour.


FREELOVE POWELL[3], d/o Henry[2], m. Jacob Parish & had: (PARISH)

Henry.
Mary.
James.
Nancy.
Daniel.
Thomas.
Benjamin.
Elizabeth.
Martha.


THOMAS POWELL[3], s/o Henry[2], m. Mary, d/o Robert Ludlow & had:

Henry T., d. 1834.
ROBERT L.
James A., drowned 1828.
Jacob, d. 1816.
Frances L., m. Homer Ransdall & had (RANSDALL): Mary L.; Frances J., m. Maj. George W. Rains; Thomas P.; James A. P.; Henry P.; Homer S.; Leila R.


ROBERT L. POWELL[4], s/o Thomas[3], m. Louisa A. Orso & had:
Frances E. L., now dec'd.
Mary L., m. Isaac S. Fowler.
Henrietta, m. Dr. W. A. M. Culbert.
Fanny, now dec'd.


Jacob[3] & Thomas[3] after their father's death, ran the family farm; in 1788 with their mother removed to Orange Co. & settled near Washingtonville. 1791 they removed to Marlborough, Ulster Co., where they opened a small store & erected lime kilns. Spring 1798 removed to NY. Jacob d. 1823 from a cancer of the face, aged 58; Thomas retired from business at that time & 1833 to 12 May 1856, when he died, he performed public & political service. Thomas is described as "of medium height, & in his manners he was plain & unostentious."

JAMES, b. 1 Sept. 1878, at Greycourt, Orange Co., was associated with his father John R., who d. 29 Jan. 1904, in management of hotel at Greycourt. JAMES m. 12 June 1906, Mary Gardiner of Highland Falls. His brother, Henry J., b. 27 May 1875, also in hotel business.

_____

DR. JOHN N.D.V. PRONK[1], b. Amsterdam, Holland, to America 1811, settled in Boston, MA until 1839, when on retirement to Middletown, Orange Co.; d. 1848, age 72. He m. Azubah Little, b. Orange Co., 1812. They had 11 children, those surviving:

Edwin, res. Boston.
1822, JAMES N.
Azubah L., m. Silas L. King of Bradford, PA.


JAMES N. PRONK[2], s/o Dr. John N.D.V.[1], b. Boston, MA. With parents to Orange Co.; teacher, atty. NY City (1849). Practiced at Middletown, businessman. JAMES m. 1841, Mary Ellen Mondon, d/o Gilbert F. of Port Jervis. Their surviving children:

Frances A. R.
Ferris M.
Devin N.
Ashbel C.
Louisa.
Mary, m. N. Tate of Middletown.
Nellie R.

_____

The Newburgh Purdys are descs. of FRANCIS PURDY[1] of Yorkshire, England, who removed to Fairfield, CT, where he d. 1658. His children:

FRANCIS JR.
JOSEPH.


Both FRANCIS JR. & JOSEPH were b. Yorkshire & held commissions from the crown as surveyors.


FRANCIS JR.[2] had a son, JOSEPH[3], who had a son DAVID[4] who settled in Newburgh before 1763, and had:
David.
Nathan.


Descs. of this branch of the Purdy family now res. in Ulster Co., NY.


JOSEPH[2] m. Elizabeth Ogden and had:
SAMUEL.
JOHN.
FRANCIS.
DANIEL [DAVID].
Joseph.

SAMUEL PURDY[3] s/o Joseph[2], m. Charlotte Strang & had:
Glorianna, m. George Merritt Sr.
SAMUEL.
CALEB.
GABRIEL.
Charlotte, m. Henry Fowler Sr.
HENRY.
ELIZABETH.
JOSIAH.

SAMUEL PURDY[4], s/o Samuel[3], m. Winifred Griffing & had:
Samuel.
Henry.
Jacob.
Gabriel.
Lavinia, m. Capt. Eleazer Gidney.

CALEB PURDY[4], s/o Samuel[3], m. Hannah Brown & had:
Caleb.
Samuel.
Josiah.
Andrew.
Nehemiah.
Sylvanus.
Elias.
Caroline.
Hannah.
Lavinia.
Anna.

GABRIEL PURDY[4], s/o Samuel[3], m. Bethia Miller & had:
James.
Gabriel.
Anthony.
Glorianna.
Lewis.
Henry.
Bethian.

HENRY PURDY[4], s/o Samuel[3], m. Mary Foster, granddau. of
Maj. Paulding, and had:
Elizabeth.
William.
Anna.
Henry.
1751, SAMUEL.

SAMUEL PURDY[5], s/o Henry[4], was in Yorktown & d. New-
burgh 1836. He m. Charlotte, d/o Abel Flewwelling, & had:
Henry.
Abigail.
Elizabeth.
Mary.
Anna.
Esther.
Martha.
Abel Gilford.

ELIZABETH PURDY[4], d/o Samuel[3], m. Josiah Fowler & had:
Glorianna.
Gabriel.
Esther.
Martha.

JOSIAH PURDY[4], s/o Samuel[3], m. Charity Wetmore & had:
Seth.
Alathen.
Anna.
Esther.

JOHN PURDY[3], s/o JOSEPH[2] left children:
Elisha.
Joseph.
Nathaniel.

FRANCIS PURDY[3], s/o Joseph[2], d. Newbury, 2 June 1760, age
63 years; he had:
Davis.
Abigail, m. Nehemiah Fowler.
Elizabeth, m. Arthur Smith.
Martha, m. Caleb Merritt.

DANIEL [DAVID--is called by both names in the same source]
PURDY[3], s/o Joseph[2], left children:
Isaiah.
Nathan.
David.
Gilbert.
Samuel.
Josiah.
Martha, m. Daniel Denton.
Lavinia, m. Robert Denton.

_____

**PURDY, CHARLES**                                    H-922

CHARLES b. 15 March 1842 in Sullivan Co., near New
Vernon, NY. He was one of 9 children of Ebenezer & Hettie
(Warner) Purdy, 6 still living. **CHARLES** was a farmer until
1864 when he went with the Erie Railroad as a brakeman; m.
Jessie A. Wardrop of Goshen 18 Oct. 1876. She d. 22 Dec.
1905. He is now baggage master since 1883. Member First
Presbyterian Church at Middletown.

_____

**QUAID, JOHN H.**                                    H-923
grocer of Newburgh.

JOHN QUAID[1], b. Limerick County, Ireland, to Newburgh as a
young man & began business in Oldtown. He m. ---
McGathern, of a family that settled in Blooming-Grove in
1807, and had:
William Quaid, became partner of his father in 1857. Retired in
1881.
**JOHN H.[2]**

**JOHN H. QUAID[2]**, taken in as partner in family business in 1871; m. Margaret Lord Fancher, d/o Lewis of Cornwall; she was DAR member & d. 1896. Members of St. Paul's Church.

---

## QUICK FAMILIES OF GREENVILLE & GOSHEN
### H-243, C-11

NATHANIEL REEVES QUICK, j.p. 1868-73, was a desc. of the Quick family of PA. The famous Tom Quick was a member of the same family.

A Matthias Quick m. Rhoda Carpenter 21 Sept. 1779; Peter Quick m. Phebe Sprought 28 Aug. 1806; Cornelius Quick m. Margaret Sprought 3 Sept. 1807, all at Goshen.

---

## RAINEY FAMILY OF CRAWFORD      A-416, H-189

DAVID RAINEY settled in Crawford, near Pine Bush, before the Rev. [H-189 says after the Rev.] Served under Clinton during the war, though only a boy. His children:
David, Jr.
James.
William.
Mrs. Crane.
Susan, d. young.
Jane, d. young.

"A sister of David Sr. m. James McBurney, Rev. War soldier," and had:
Mrs. John Taylor.
Mrs. John Wool.
William.
David.
Elizabeth.
Mary.
James.

---

## RAMAGE, WILLIAM B.      H-923

WILLIAM B. RAMAGE's father came from England at age of 10 to Sussex Co., NJ, where he m. Elizabeth --- & had 14 children. WILLIAM was b. in Branchville, Sussex Co., NJ 16 Jan. 1858; 1866 learned trade of carriage maker with Abraham Watts of Florida, NY & in 1871 established own business in Florida. He m. May Jane Givens of Florida, NY 3 June 1870 & had 10 children, 4 living. Methodist. Children:
Hattie, m. Charles Hall of Paterson, NJ.
Frank P., at home.
Jessie, m. M. Barry of Florida.
Leon, at home.

---

## RAMSDELL, HOMER [P]      A-352-3, H-923-4
of Newburgh, businessman & railroad builder.

JOSEPH RAMSDELL[1] was the 4th of the name in desc. from

Joseph and Martha (Bowker) Ramsdell who emigrated from England to Plymouth, MA in 1643. He m. 3 Feb. 1800, Ruth Stockbridge, a desc. of John Stockbridge who came from England in 1638. Joseph & Ruth both b. Hanover, MA, and had, all b. at Warren, Worcester Co., MA:
Joseph.
Mary.
1810, Aug. 12, **HOMER.**

HOMER RAMSDELL[2], to NY City in dry good trade (1832-40); to Newburgh & m. 16 June 1835, Frances E. L. Powell, d/o Thomas of Newburgh (his business partner), and had:
Mary L. P., d. young.
Frances J., m. Maj. George W. Rains.
Thomas P., dec'd.
James A. P.
Henry Powell.
Homer Stockbridge.
Leila R.

---

## RAMSDELL, WILLIAM CHESTER      H-924-5

WILLIAM CHESTER RAMSDELL, b. Town of Greenville, Orange Co., 29 Dec. 1858, s/o Luman S. Ramsdell, a nephew of Luman Ramsdell of Norton Hill, and Laura Ann Gedney. Family to Albany Co. when WILLIAM aged 7. WILLIAM m. Elizabeth C. Van Trump of Wilmington, DE, 1895 opened Ramsdell School in Middletown, NY.

---

## RAZEY, JAMES      H-925
dairy farmer of Florida, Orange Co.

JAMES RAZEY was b. on a farm near Harnell, Chemung Co., NY 16 Feb. 1851; res. Elmimra for 10 years, then to Chester Co., where he bought "Broadview Farm" & built Razey Cottage. His father d. 6 Aug 1864 of yellow fever [not named here] & his mother was Abigail Withey. There were four children in the family. JAMES m. (1) Susan, d/o David R. & Anna Feagles, and had:
Esther Denton, aged 23.
Danforth, aged 20.
James Lester, aged 17.

JAMES m. (2) Mrs. Phoebe J. Smith of Florida, NY 16 Oct. 1906. Member of Presbyterian Church at Chester.

---

## REDFIELD, CHARLES IRA, M.D.      H-925

DR. REDFIELD, b. Town of Wallkill, 31 Jan. 1873, s/o Foster C., who d. 6 Feb. 1875, & Sarah Louise (Fanning) Redfield. He attended Univ. of PA Medical Dept. & grad. 1894. Practice at Middletown since 1895. Member 2d Presbyterian Church. He m. Miss Ira Anna Louise Barker of Roxbury, MA 20 Oct. 1897.

---

## REED FAMILY OF WAWAYANDA      A-680

SAMUEL REED located near Slate Hill c. 1790; his sons:
Silas.
Lewis.
Alfred.

---

## REED, GEORGE W.      H-925-6

**GEORGE W. REED**, b. July 1844 at So. Centerville in what was then the Town of Minisink, but now the Town of Wawayanda. He was of Scotch parentage. Served in the Union Army during the Civil War, Co. C, 1st NY Mounted Rifles. After the war was a carpenter. Member 1st Congregational Church of Middletown.

---

## REED, HENRY WILSON      H-926

**HENRY WILSON REED**, b. Middletown, Orange Co., 3 Nov. 1875; electrical construction business. He m. Helen K. Biddlebrook, only d/o William H. Wood of Chester, NY 9 April 1901. Member 1st Congregational Church of Middletown.

---

## REEVE FAMILY OF WAWAYANDA
**A-681 & TN-286-8, CN-40-1**
**REEVE, OLIVER P. [P]**      A-496-7, LDS Anc. File
of Wallkill.

The first Reeves, brothers THOMAS & JAMES were from Wales c. 1660 & settled at Mattituck, L.I. JAMES[1], the progenitor of the Newburgh branch of the family, d. at Mattituck in 1738, aged 60. His children were:
JAMES.
SELAH.
Isaac.
Nathaniel.
Ebenezer.

(DEACON) JAMES REEVE[2] of L.I., was an early settler of Wawayanda c. 1763, res. between Middletown & New Hampton. He helped build the First Congregational Church at Middletown; m. (1st) Mary [Hephzibah?], d/o David Moore whose great-grandfather came from England in 1635 & settled at Salem, MA. Children:
JAMES JR.
Hephzibah, m. Jonas Hulse.
Polly, m. Elijah Canfield.
Child, d. young.
Mary, m. Mr. --- Canfield.

JAMES[2] m. (2d), 1770, Mary Corwin, and had:
1771, DAVID.
Daniel.
Joshua, res. MI.
Lydia.
Annie [Anna], m. Mr. -- Keene; res. at Beach Woods, PA.
Keturah.

Deborah.
Isaac.
Sarah, d. unm.
Mary.
Amutal.
Jerusha
Elijah, d. young.
Dorothy.
Julia, only child now living at age c. 85, res. Bloomingburgh, Sullivan Co., NY.

JAMES REEVE JR.[3], s/o Deacon James[2], wounded in Battle of Minisink; 1779, later settled near Slate Hill where his grandson, Hon. John H. Reeve now res. James Jr. m. Eunice Manning, b. 28 Sept. 1795, Hartford, NJ, d. 4 March 1863, Cameron, IL. Eunice d/o Isreal Manning. [Members of this branch also are found with the surname spelled 'Reeves.'] They had:
1817/18, Sept. 28, Anna Eliza, b. Hartland, NJ, d. 7 Jan. 1857, North Ogden, UT. Mar. Joseph Godfrey, b. 1 March 1774, Bristol, England, d. 18 Dec. 1880, UT.
1820, Aug. 6, Mary, b. West Newark, NJ, m. 1840, Niagara Falls, NY, George Coleman, b. 2 March 1817 Norfolk, England. She d. 1 March 1885 Park Valley, UT; he d. 18 Dec. 1846, near Santa Fe, NM.
1821, April 11, Matilda, b. Hartland, NY, m. 15 Nov. 1847 at Winter Quarters, NE, Ormus Ephraim Bates, b. 25 March 1815, Henderson, Jefferson Co., NY. She d. 1882 at Toole, UT; he d. 4 Aug. 1873 at the same place.
1822, Sealy.
1825, March 16, George, b. West Newark, NJ, m. 9 April 1846, Margaret Waldron. George d. 29 Aug. 1895.
1830, Lydia.
1832, John.
1834, Reuben.

DAVID REEVE[3], s/o Deacon James[2] & 2d wife Mary (Corwin) was a farmer of Wallkill & member of the Congregational Church at Middletown. He m. Esther (1780-1848), d/o William Wickham in 1797. David d. 1848. Their children:
Mary, m. George V. Mapes of Orange Co.
Rosetta, m. Sylvester Cooper of Mattituck, L.I.
William W. of Middletown.
James, res. Tompkins Co.
Hosea, res. Jackson Co., MI.
Arminda, wid. of Dr. Hedges of Chester, NJ.
Fanny Jane, d. age 10.
Louisa, wid. of B. W. Shaw of Middletown.
David Rose, d. Orange Co.
Benjamin Franklin, d. Philadelphia.
1822, March 10, **OLIVER P.**
Harriet, m. Rev. L. I. Stoughtenbury of Morris Co., NJ.

**OLIVER P. REEVE[4]**, s/o David[3], b. on homestead in Town of Wallkill, res. Bullville, Orange Co., merchant; 1864 to Middletown, real estate & insurance. Member Congregational Church at Middletown; m. (1st) 1852, Charlotte Redfield, d/o David G., she d. 1856 (no issue); m. (2d) Esther E.

Shorter, d/o John of Crawford, 1858. They have one son, Theodore Lincoln Reeve.

SELAH REEVE[2], s/o James[1], settled on farm near the old homestead. Rev. War patriot; removed to CT; 1784 to Newburgh, where he d. 21 Feb. 1796, aged 55. His wife d. 21 Jan. 1829, aged 84. They had:
SELAH.
JAMES.
JOSEPH.

SELAH REEVE[3], s/o Selah[2], b. L.I., miller at Hunting Grove (now Buskirk's Mills) on the Otterkill in Town of New Windsor (1798/9); later to Newburgh, manuf. of brown earthenware with Mr. Burling; later in business with William Falld. SELAH d. 11 April 1837. He m. Elizabeth, d/o Christopher & Julia (Tusten) Van Duzer of Newburgh, 1795. Julia, Elizabeth Van Duzer's mother, was a sister of Benjamin Tusten, who was killed at the Battle of Minisink. Selah[3] & Elizabeth had:
Millicent, d. infant.
Christopher, m. Maria Hasbrouck. Merchant at Newburgh & later in lumber trade in Detroit, MI.
CHARLES F. V.
Julia Ann, m. Daniel S. Tuthill.
George, m. Catherine Ingersoll; d. 1853/4.
Eliza, m. Hon. John W. Brown.
Jane, m. Alexander Mulliner.
Nathan, m. Mary d/o Selah Reeve Hobbie of Washington. He studied law with Hon. John W. Brown [his brother-in-law], practiced at Newburgh; now in lumber trade in Detroit, MI.
Harriet M., m. Rev. Mr. William McLaren, res. Fall River, MA.
Mary E., d. infant.
Selah, m. Lilly Snow of Providence, RI; now in lumber trade in Chicago.

CHARLES F. V. REEVE[4], s/o Selah[3], m. (1) Adaline Armor of NY & (2) Julia Ann Ferguson; res. Charleston, SC & later in business with brother Christopher at Newburgh. Afterwards a miller & farmer at Shawaugunk, Ulster Co.; now res. Newburgh.

JAMES REEVE[3], s/o Selah[2], mariner; taken prisoner by the British during the War of 1812; after war injured by bursting of lime kiln & d. within a year. He never married.

JOSEPH REEVE[3], s/o Selah[2], manuf. whale bone whips, a very popular item in his day. He was a gold & silversmith & dealt in clocks & watches in Newburgh. Served in War of 1812. He d. Sept. 1828 from a head injury; m. Eunice Sayer & had:
Charles, in business with his father; m. Katura Wilson.
Decatur, m. Frances A. Horton.
Anthony D., m. Miss --- Veltma.
Caroline, m. Dr. J. D. Sloan.
John, d. unm.

REEVES, CHARLES W. [P]                          A-556c

JOSHUA REEVES[1] of L.I. came with his family to Orange County. He had a son HOWELL[2] who res. Minisink and had 11 children, among them:
CHARLES W. REEVES[3], b. Chester, Orange County, 1 Sept. 1805; d. 2 Sept. 1865. 1825 merchant at Westtown in Town of Minisink; 1842 to Goshen, merchant & bank director, one of the founders of the Methodist Episcopal Church of Goshen (1947); m. (1st) 1825, Azubah Lee, d/o Squire Lee of Goshen. She d. 1853, Jan, age 43. Their surviving children of 7:
Louisa, m. Seeley Hetzel.
Floyd H., m. 18 Feb. 1863, Christine, d/o John & Hannah (DeKay) Crowdry, and had Hattie & Clara. Res. Goshen.
Coe L., 124th Regt. NY Vol., Civil War.
Ella m. Dr. J. B. Arnold of NE.

CHARLES W.[3] m. (2d) 1858, Mrs. Catharine J. Millspaugh of Warwick and had one dau., Fannie.

REILLY, JOHN                                    H-926
assessor Town of Highlands.

JOHN REILLY, b. County Mayo, Ireland, to America 1863 on ship *France*. Employed at Poughkeepsie & Newburgh, in 1870 to West Point & joined US Cavalry. 1875 established hotel & livery; m. Jane Cook, d/o ex-supervisor Cook.

RENNAU, HEINRICH                               CN-9

HEINRICH RENNAU is listed in the Newburgh Directory for 1709, the year the town was founded and settled by immigrants from the Palatinate of the Rhine. He is listed as stocking-maker and husbandman, aged 24 on emigration; his wife Johanna aged 26, and their children:
Lorentz, aged 2 years on emigration.
Heinrich, aged 5 months.

Also with his listing are Susanna and Maria Johana Liboschain, sisters of his wife, aged respectively 15 and 10 years on emigration.

REYNOLDS, HENRY                                 T-36

HENRY REYNOLDS, clerk in store in Peekskill 1777; store burned by the British & he was forced to flee with his wife & 5 children. He next settled at Smith's Cove, Orange Co. & farmer; was a Minute Man.

RHEA, MATTHEW (the younger)                     A-381
of Montgomery.

MATTHEW RHEA, b. 6 Aug. 1719, m. Catharine Hunter, and had:
Mrs. John Barber.
Frances.

Stephen.
James.
Matthew.
John.
Martha.
Robert.
William.
David.

---

## RING, THOMAS C. [P]  A-290-1
## & RING, A. SMITH  H-927
businessman & banker of Newburgh.

BENJAMIN RING[1], Quaker, patriot of the Rev., b. Wales, emigrated to PA, where he erected mills on the Brandywine; m. Rachel James & had 8 children, among them:

NATHANIEL RING[2], b. 1767, d. 1850. To Cromwell, NJ at an early age, millwright, brickyard & sloop captain; m. Martha Clark, d/o Hon. Jeremiah of Cornwall. Jeremiah was b. Bedford, Westchester Co,. NY, 1730 & d. 30 May 1808; m. Martha Newman, 27 Nov. 1752. NATHANIEL & Martha (Clark) RING had 7 children, their 6th child was:

THOMAS C. RING[3], b. Cornwall, Orange Co., 21 Oct. 1804; age 13 clerked at West Point in employ of Oliver G. Burton for 3 years. 1821 to Newburgh under employ of Matthias G. Miller; 1825 clerk in Bank of Newburgh 2 years; 1831 clerk on steamboat *Albany*; 1834 cashier of Highland Bank of Newburgh. He m. (1st) 1832, Mary Ann Osborne, d. 28 Dec. 1833, no issue; she aged 25. He m. (2d) 1837, Catharine Spier, b. 31 July 1870 [sic], d. 6 Sept. 1869. Children by 2d wife:

1838, A. SMITH.
Anna R., dec'd.; wife of Munson G. Muir.
Clara Belknap, d. infancy.

A. SMITH RING[4], b. Newburgh, m. 5 Oct. 1881, Frances Ludlow, d/o the late George W. Kerr & had Thomas Ludlow Ring. A. Smith d. 8 July 1893.

---

## ROBERTSON, JAMES  H-928

JAMES ROBERTSON, b. 6 Dec. 1846 at Liberty, Sullivan Co., NY, s/o Bronson & Abigail (Stoddard) Robertson. Carpenter; joined Navy in 1864, after War res. in Chicago 3 years & then to Monticello, Sullivan Co. With Erie Railroad in Port Jervis 10 years. 1902 manager of the bottling dept. of the Deer Park Brewery. He m. Mary E. Kinne of Monticello 2 March 1871.

---

## ROBERTSON, SAMUEL D.  H-927
of Bullville.

SAMUEL D. ROBERTSON, b. Town of Crawford in 1849, s/o Samuel, who was b. in Westchester Co., & Margaret (Martin) Robertson. In 1870 SAMUEL D. m. Hannah Powels of Newburgh & had 7 children, 4 sons & 1 dau. living.

---

## ROBINSON, HON. CHARLES DWIGHT  H-927

CHARLES DWIGHT ROBINSON, b. Auburn, Cayuga Co., 6 Feb. 1860, a desc. of George Robinson who settled in Rehoboth, MA in 1645. On the paternal side he is desc. from Zephaniah Robinson & Philip Robinson, both served in MA Regiments in the Rev. War. William Robinson, a cousin of Philip, served in CT Regiment in the Rev.

CHARLES' father, William Philip Robinson, located in Auburn in 1844 & m. Louise E., d/o William Clark Smith & Aner Lewis. William Clark was a grandson of Anning Smith of Milton, Ulster Co. & a Rev. War officer.

Before 1883 CHARLES was cashier for Chicago Branch of D. M. Osborne Co. of Auburn. To Newburg in 1883 & entered firm of John Dales & Co. SAR member. He m. (1) Mary B. Dales 16 Feb. 1882, she d. 14 Jan. 1900 & they had one dau., Julia. CHARLES m. (2) Anna B. Colwell 30 Jan. 1902 & have son Charles D. Jr.

---

## ROBINSON, HEMAN H. [P]  A-176a

REV. JONATHAN ROBINSON[1], Presbyterian clergyman of L.I. had a son:

REV. PHINEAS ROBINSON[2], b. & d. near Franklinville, L.I., b. 24 Dec. 1798; d. April 1871, bur. Hillside Cemetery, Middletown. Was the 1st principal of Wallkill Academy, Middletown; previously of Sherburne, NY; previously of SC. He m. Eliza, d/o Jonathan & Susan Day, at Clinton NY, who was b. at Thompson, Windham Co., CT 31 May 1803, and d. at the res. of her dau., Mrs. E. M. Madden of Middletown, 9 Dec. 1868. Children of REV. PHINEAS & Eliza:

Eudocia, m. Sen. E. M. Madden of Middletown; dec'd.
Ellen, m. John Hanford of Middletown; dec'd.
Sidney B., physician, served at Ward's Island & Seaman's Retreat Hospital, Staten Island where he d. of typhus, 10 Nov. 1855, age 26.
Leander Van Ess, atty. of Haverstraw; went south for his health & d. Green Cove Springs, FL, Jan. 1869.
Edward Payson, d. 1849, age 16.
Susan Frances, widow of Dr. Jeremiah Haverns of Schoharie Co., NY.
Mary Hedges, m. Phineas R. Coleman of Goshen.
Henry M., merchant of Brooklyn.
1838, Aug. 20, HEMAN H.
Thomas Spencer, NY clothier.
Charles Lincoln, d. age 14.
Caroline, d. infancy.

HEMAN H. ROBINSON[3], s/o Rev. Phineas[2], b. Belleport, L.I.; studied at Chester & Seaman's Retreat Hospital on States Island ; 1860 to Jeffersonville, Sullivan Co. until 1870 to Goshen. April 1861, m. Maria V., d/o Lemuel L. & Mary (VerPlank) Pendell of Schoharie Co., b. 10 Aug. 1838. Surviving children:
Josephine Lamont.
Sidney Moffatt.
Kitty.

Mary.
Robert Thomas.
Heman.
Henry.
Frank Leon.
Arthur.

---

**ROCKAFELLOW, FREDERICK O.**       H-928-9
funeral director of Middletown.

**FREDERICK O. ROCKAFELLOW**, b. Middletown, 14 May
1864, in business with father, John D., in funeral business in
1861. **FREDERICK** m. Marguerite R. Oliver of Chicago,
IL, & had:
Frederick O. Jr.
John D.

Family attends Westminster Church.

---

**ROCKWELL, LEWIS N. L.**       H-929

**LEWIS N. L. ROCKWELL**, b. Narrowsburg, Sullivan Co.,
NY 12 May 1875; in 1896 bookkeeper in NY City. 1905 to
Otisville & purchased general store of Joel Northrop. He m.
Irene Bloomberg of Narrowsburg 10 Jan. 1900. **LEWIS** was
one of 13 children, still living 4 sons & 2 daus. His brother,
George W., County Clerk of Sullivan Co.

---

**ROE, REV. ALFRED COX [P]**       A-765-6
of Cornwall.
**ROE, EDWARD PAYSON [P]**       A-782-3, NH-68
of Cornwall.

JOHN ROE[1], b. 1628, from Ireland to MA 1641; to Setauket,
L.I. (now Port Jefferson); d. 1711; m. Hannah Purrer and
had:
NATHANIEL ROE[2], b. 1670, d. 1752; m. Hannah Reeve (1678-
Aug. 16, 1759), and had:
1700, NATHANIEL.
John.
Elizabeth.
Hannah.
Deborah.

NATHANIEL ROE[3], s/o Nathaniel[2], m. Elizabeth Phillips (1702-
1788), res. Chester; he d. 1789. Children:
Phillips.
1744, April 9, JAMES.
Nathaniel; had at least one son, Jesse.
William.
Hannah.
Elizabeth.
Sarah.
Deborah.

JAMES ROE[4], s/o Nathaniel[3], removed to Kingston, Ulster Co.,
NY; m. 19 Oct. 1770, Elizabeth Elting, b. 8 Jan. 1745, d. 28

Sept. 1793, of old Huguenot family of Ulster Co. JAMES
was a soldier of the Rev. & d. 31 Oct. 1815, bur. Cornwall.
Their children, all b. Kingston:
James.
Elizabeth.
John Elting.
Sylvester.
Ann.
William.
Nathaniel.
Rachel.
1789, Sept. 14, PETER.

PETER ROE[5], s/o James[4], in 1824 removed to Moodna, Orange
Co. (then known as Murder's Creek). He m. Susan Williams
of New Windsor. He was a wholesale grocer & early res. in
NY City. Farmer, settled in New Windsor, 13 Aug. 1877.
Children:
Oswald William, d. young.
1823, April 7, ALFRED COX.
James Gilbert.
Susan Elizabeth.
John Peter.
William Wilberforce.
1838, March 7, EDWARD PAYSON.
Mary Abigail.

ALFRED COX ROE[6], s/o Peter[5], b. NY City, grad. NY
University; 1844 opened school in village of Canterbury
(now Cornwall); 1853 to Cornwall-on-Hudson where he
opened a boy's school. 1863 entered gospel ministry,
ordained by Presby of North River; served Union Army as
chaplain of 83rd NY Vols. & later with 104th NY Vols.,
later 3d Div., 5th Corps. After war to NY City & preached
and worked at Lowell, MA (1870); 1871 called to 2d
Presbyterian Church of Geneva, NY; 2 years later to Clyde,
Wayne Co., NY until 1877 when he retired to Cornwall-on-
Hudson. He m. 1847, March 23, Caroline P., d/o Judge
Francis Child, of Morristown, NJ, who d. 1859 leaving 2
children:
Frank C.
Caroline.

ALFRED[6] m. 2d Emma, d/o Rev. J. D. Wickham of Manches-
ter, VT, 24 Oct. 1860. Children:
Elizabeth Merwin.
Mary Wickham.
Joseph Wickham.

REV. EDWARD PAYSON ROE[6], s/o Peter[5], b. Moodna, Town
of New Windsor; studied at Auburn Theological Seminary
and in 1862 enlisted as chaplain of the 2d NY (Harris Light
Cav.), and later appointed chaplain of the Fortress Monroe
hospital. After war served in the Presbyterian Church at
Highland Falls, NY. Writer, horticulturist; m. 24 Nov. 1863,
Anna P., d/o David Sands of NY, later of A. B. & D. Sands,
druggists of that city. Their living children:
Paula Sands.

Martha Ferris.
Elting P.
Sarah Theresa.
Lindley Murray.
Edward P. Jr., d. infancy.

**EDWARD** d. at his home near Cornwall-on-Hudson in 1888.

_____

**ROE, D. HOWELL**                                H-929
of Florida, NY.

**D. HOWELL ROE**, b. 25 Oct. 1838, at age 18 clerk in grocery store of William Vail & later in livery business in Chester, where he d. 29 Nov. 1880. Town clerk & supervisor. He m. Elizabeth Rysdyk of Chester 7 June 1854; 2 children, both d. in infancy.

_____

**ROE, JESSE [P]**                                A-622-3
of Chester &
**ROE, ALFRED B.**                                H-929

JONAS ROE[1], from Scotland to America with 2 of his brothers, and settled at Florida, Orange Co., NY, c. 1730. He had 7 sons and several daus., among them:
NATHANIEL.
William, has descs. in Orange Co.
Jonas, has descs. in Orange Co.
Benjamin, m. & reared family in Sussex Co., NJ.
George, m. & reared family in Sussex Co., NJ.

NATHANIEL ROE[2], s/o Jonas[1], res. Unionville; one of the original settlers of Chester (1751), farmer; d. 1813, age 81. His wife was Susannah, who "died within 48 hours of the time of his death," aged 83. They had at least one child:

NATHANIEL ROE[3], s/o Nathaniel[2], b. 1761, Aug. 11, d. 23 May 1833; res. on homestead; m. 4 April 1782, Mary Slattery, b. 29 March 1763; d. 8 Oct. 1840. Their children:
1787, April 24, Betsey, m. Thaddeus Seeley of Chester.
1789, May 12, Abigail, m. Garret Curry; d. Chester.
1790, Dec. 2, Lewis H.
1793, Jan. 26, Juliana, m. John Green of Chester.
1795, Feb. 18, Thomas W.
1799, Feb. 13, Nathaniel S.; d. young.
1801, March 12, William.
1804, Aug. 16, Genest M.
1806, July 2, **JESSE.**

JESSE ROE[4], s/o Nathaniel[3], m. 15 Feb. 1832, Dolly Caroline, d/o Jesse & Dolly (Watkins) Booth of Hamptonburgh, b. 18 June 1812. Presbyterian Church members at Chester. Children:
1832, Nov. 12, George; d. 27 June 1850.
Thomas H., farmer of Blooming-Grove.
Harriet, m. Charles R. Bull of Blooming-Grove.
ALFRED BOOTH.
1843, Nov. 19, Virgil; d. 9 July 1863.

Mary, m. J. Erskine Mills, druggist of Middletown, NY.
1849, Oct. 27, Matilda; d. 1 May 1867.

ALFRED BOOTH ROE[5] m. Martha Durland, b. 16 Sept. 1844 at Chester. They res. on homestead farm in possession of the Roe family for 175 years & were members of the First Presbyterian Church of Chester. Their son:
**ALFRED B. ROE[6]**, b. Chester 9 June 1880, m. Frances A. Decker of Chester 3 April 1902 and had Alfred Russell, b. 20 Jan. 1905.

_____

**ROE, NATHANIEL [P]**                            A-625
of Chester.

CAPT. NATHANIEL ROE[1], settled in Chester in 1751 and had at least one child:
CAPT. WILLIAM ROE[2], in the state militia, d. 1801; m. Mary Winans, and had:
1784, May 14, David; d. 1856, res. on homestead.
Nathaniel; d. young.
1788, WILLIAM.
Hannah, m. Henry Barney; d. Warwick.
Susan, m. Jacob Feagles at Amity, where she died.
Mary, m. Gabriel Seeley, res. Chester & d. there.
Elizabeth, d. unm.

WILLIAM ROE[3], s/o William[2], m. Mittie, d/o John Mapes of Chester, who d. 1823. William was a farmer of Black Meadows in Chester & d. 1841. Children:
1815, Nov. 11, **NATHANIEL.**
John; d. 1881, aged 63.
David; d. 1878, aged 55, left wife and son, George M.
Hannah; d. age 17.

NATHANIEL ROE[4], s/o William[3], age of 8 went to live with maternal grandfather [sic], Thaddeus Seeley and after death of Gabriel Seeley in Chester on 4 April 1843, m. Sarah, d/o Gen. Charles Board and Joanna Seeley of Ringwood, NJ, grandau. of Joseph Board, who with brothers James & David from Wales to Ringwood, NJ. Sarah b. 7 Jan. 1815. **NATHANIEL** was a farmer, public servant & member of the Presbyterian Church at Chester. Children:
Charles B., farmer of Chester.
Gabriel S., farmer of Kendall Co., IL.
Thomas Beach, farmer of Chester.
Nathaniel, farmer of Blooming-Grove.
Henry M.
Hannah E.

_____

**ROE FAMILY**                               LDS Anc. File

This branch of the Roe family has been taken exclusively from the LDS Ancestral File & included here because it probably somehow fits with the above Roe families and has so many family members res. in Orange Co.

DAVID ROE[1], b. c. 1640, of Flushing, Queens Co., NY, m. Mary Roe, also of Flushing. He d. 1707 & they had:

NATHANIEL ROE[2], b. 1670, m. Elizabeth --- who d. 1705; they both d. in Flushing, NY, & had:

1695, David.
1702, NATHANIEL.
1705, William.

NATHANIEL ROE[3], b. c. 1702, Flushing, NY, m. 1725 Mary ---. Nathaniel d. before 20 Oct. 1770 in Florida, Orange Co., NY. They had (all but first child b. Orange Co., NY):

c. 1727, JONAS, b. Flushing.
c. 1730, Elizabeth.
1733, May 2, Nathaniel. Could be the Capt. Nathaniel Roe[1] in previous entry who settled in Chester in 1751.
c. 1738, David.
c. 1739, Mary.
c. 1741, Abigail.
c. 1743, Deborah.

JONAS ROE[4], m. c. 1750 in Orange Co., Phebe ---. He d. before 12 April 1798 in Orange Co., as did Phebe. They had (all b. Orange Co.):

1751, May 5, NATHANIEL.
c. 1752, ---.
c. 1753, JONAS.
c. 1755, JOSEPH.
c. 1757, BENJAMIN.
1762, Jan. 7, TIMOTHY.
c. 1764, Phebe.
c. 1766, Elizabeth.
1771, March 25, WILLIAM.
1777, April 27, GEORGE.

NATHANIEL ROE[5], s/o Jonas[4], m. Bathsheba Dunning 13 Feb. 1772. He d. 2 Feb. 1821, she d. 28 Oct. 1797. They had:

1773, May 5, Phebe.
1775, Nathaniel.
1777, Aug. 15, Jacob Dunning.
1779, Nov. 23, Jonas.
1782, Feb. 6, John.
1784, Feb. 28, Mary.
1787, April 10, Margaret.
1791, April 26, Joseph.
1801, Oct. 2, Bathsheba Maria.

Nathaniel[5] m. (2) Mary L'Hommedieu, b. c. 1755. He d. 18 Dec. 1866.

JONAS ROE[5], s/o Jonas[4], m. c. 1753, Margaret Allison, b. 10 Oct. 1757. Jonas d. before 23 Nov. 1797 in Orange Co. & Margaret d. 27 May 1833 in Florida, NY. They had:

1778, May 23, Jonas.
c. 1780, John Delansa.
c. 1782, William Allison.
c. 1783, Elizabeth.

JOSEPH ROE[5], s/o Jonas[4], m. Mary DeKay, & had:

1779, April 9, Thomas DeKay, b. Warwick, NY.
c. 1783, Joseph.
c. 1785, William.
1789, Elizabeth Christian.
c. 1791, David Jessup.
c. 1793, Nathaniel.
c. 1795, Phebe Maria.

BENJAMIN ROE[5], s/o Jonas[4], m. Catherine Demarest & had (all b. Warwick, NY):

c. 1780, William.
c. 1782, Benjamin.
c. 1785, Phebe.
c. 1790, John.
1792, Aug. 26, Jonas.
1795, Dec. 21, Jacob Demarest.
c. 1797, Catherine.

TIMOTHY ROE[5], s/o Jonas[4], m. Martha Sayre & had (all b. Florida, Orange Co., NY):

c. 1785, Susanna.
1787, Nov. 24, John Sayre.
c. 1790, Bersheba.
c. 1792, Abigail.
c. 1795, Sarah.
1799, Jan. 19, Phoebe.
c. 1800, ---.

WILLIAM ROE[5], s/o Jonas[4], m. Phebe M. Thompson, b. 16 Feb. 1772, Orange Co. & had (all children but Sarah, who was b. Goshen, b. in Florida, Orange Co.):

1791, July 14, George, m. Martha Primrose Trotter, b. 26 July 1796, Maysville, Mason Co., KY.
1792, Aug. 4, James, m. Lillis Busey.
1797, Feb. 22, Elizabeth Maria, m. Walter Wheatley.
1799, Aug. 30, John E., m. Anna Carrel.
1801, Dec. 27, William Jr., m. Elizabeth Fouts, b. 4 Oct. 1808. Removed to New Washington, Clark Co., IN & had: Mary Ann, John Loftman, Oliver & Sarah Jane.
1804, May 24, Sarah Ann, m. Thomas Dougan, b. 3 Dec. 1795, Randolph, NC. Removed to New Washington, Clark Co., IN & had 11 children there.
1806, Oct. 28, Phebe Mahala, m. Nathaniel Middaugh.
1808, Nov. 23, Eleanor B., m. Samuel L. Adair.
1811, March 26, Michael H., m. Mary Robinson.
1814, July 17, Zedich.

GEORGE ROE[5], s/o Jonas[4], m. Margaret Struble, b. 31 Aug. 1778, Sessex, NJ. They had:

1798, June 23, Leonard, b. Orange Co., NY.
1799, July 7, Nathaniel, b. Branchville, Sussex Co., NJ.
1800, Oct. 16, Eliza Maria.
1802, April 15, Phebe Savina.
1804, Jan. 22, Timothy.
1806, June 3, Charlotte.
1808, Dec. 23, James Madison.
1810, May 18, Sarah Jane.

1812, April 23, Charles.
1814, March 16, William Harrison, b. Sparta, NJ. Mar. Eliza
Cory of Sparta.

____

## ROGERS, FRED      H-929-30
manufacturer of Middletown since 1897.

**FRED** was b. at Brewster, Putnam Co. 12 July 1859. His
father, Joseph, b. near Oxford England, d. 1907; his mother,
Penelope Wilkin, b. near Bristol, England, d. 1896. Joseph
settled at Poughkeepsie & was a manufacturer of drums &
banjo heads & later removed to Bloomingburgh, Sullivan
Co., NY. **FRED** was in business with his father; m. Harriet
Pellet Moore of Middletown 28 Nov. 1880, and had:
Penelope.
Ruth Bradner, d. 25 Nov. 1907.
Helen Hyde.
Clara Elizabeth.

**FRED'S** brother Joseph now conducts the family factory.

## ROGERS FAMILIES OF NEWBURGH      C-10-11
## ROGERS, WILLIAM H.      H-930

JAMES & Elizabeth Rogers removed to Middletown in 1859.
Their son **WILLIAM** a member of the drug firm of McMon-
agle & Rogers since 1868. He m. Amelia Chattle of Middle-
town 19 May 1869, and had:
Fred S.
Thomas C., district atty. of Orange Co.
Elizabeth, m. Wickham Wisner Young of Middletown.

Marriages at Goshen: Solomon Rogers to Ann Humphrey 3
Dec. 1738; Jonathan Rogers to Martha Smith 24 Jan. 1779; &
Samuel Rogers to Jane Agur 5 May 1779.

## ROSE, CHARLES W.      H-930

**CHARLES W. ROSE,** b. 9 Sept. 1836, at Canajoharie, NY,
was a milleer at Albany, Chicago (1850), NY City (1863) &
settled at Burnside, Orange Co., as post master & miller. He
m. Sophia Schweishelm of Hanover, Germany, and had:
A child d. by accident, age 21.
Harry.
Fredia Dorothy, at home.

Members Presbyterian Church at Campbell Hall.

## ROSE, HENRY ELKANAH      H-931

**HENRY ROSE,** 1 of 9 children of Silas & Elmira Rose, b. at
Sugar Loaf 15 Feb. 1850; wheelwright & blacksmith.
Member Sugar Loaf Methodist Church. On 23 Sept. 1878
m. Mary Fitzgerald of Warwick. Her grandmother was Mary
Booth, a granddau. of Sarah Wells, 1st white woman to
Orange Co. Their children:
1880, April 11, Nellie E., m. Henry Ames of Stanford, NY.

1883, March 10, Edith S., m. Fletcher A. Herrod of Miami, FL.
1884, Sept. 2, Floyd William Dudley, res. Maxwell, NE.

____

## ROSE, JOSEPH H.      H-931
retired brick manufacturer of Newburgh.

**JOSEPH,** b. at Hamburg, NY in 1865, s/o John C. &
Phoebe (Myers) Rose, removed with parents to Haverstraw, NY
& has res. in Newburgh since 1883, when he established the
Rose Brick Co.

____

## ROSE (LA ROSS), PETER      CN-10

**PETER ROSE** appears in the 1709 Directory of Newburgh.
This is the year the town was founded and settled by immigrants
from the Palatinate of the Rhine. He was a cloth weaver, aged
34 at emigration; and his wife Johanna, aged 37. Also listed is
his mother-in-law Mary Wierman, aged 45 and Catharine, her
child, aged 2 years. **PETER** removed to PA & transferred his
interest to "one Burger Meynders, a blacksmith."

____

## ROSE, WILLIAM C.      A-713
of Deerpark.

**WILLIAM C. ROSE** was b. Sherburne, Chenango Co., 22
April 1807, his parents both b. MA, he the 2d son. Res. of
Cuddebackville until 1866 when he moved to Port Jervis,
where he d. age 66 years, 8 months, 4 days. He was a
member of the Reformed Dutch Church of Port Jervis and
was m. in 1832 (wife not named); children:
William C., Jr., of Phillipsport, Sullivan Co.
Lyman O. of Cuddebackville.
Dau. m. Dr. George H. Fossard.
Another dau. (not named).

____

## ROSS FAMILY OF NEWBURGH      A-255, 280, E-202

ROBERT ROSS[1], Scotch, first settler of Rossville, settled on the
Wallace Patent [Town of Newburgh], tanner (1770). He had:
ALEXANDER.
William.

ALEXANDER ROSS[2], s/o Robert[1], military & civilian office
holder, d. 1826, and had:
William.
James.
Alexander.
Emeline, 1st wife of George W. Kerr, Esq. of Newburgh.
Mary, m. Anthony Houston.
Agnes, m. Thomas T. Keene, res. Oshkosh, MI.
D. C. Houston.
Theo.

____

## ROSS, EDWARD C.      H-931
treas. Coldwell Lawn Mower Co.

**EDWARD C. ROSS,** b. Newburgh, a s/o Henry & Jane

(Cleland) Ross. Formed partnership with his brother George H. to continue flour & grist mill established by father; 1903 began manufacture of lawn mowers. **EDWARD** res. in England for 2 years; m. Jennie M. Coldwell & they have 2 sons & 1 dau.

**ROSS, WILLIAM**                                    A-144
atty. & member of assembly.

ROBERT ROSS[1] of Rossville, Newburgh, had a son:
**WILLIAM**[2], m. (1st) Mary S., d/o John McLean, she d. 31 March 1812, aged 26; m. (2d) Caroline Middlebrook of CT. His eldest dau., Mary McClean Ross m. John F. Butterworth.

**ROUND, SEWARD U.**                                 H-932
atty. of Newburgh.

JOHN WESLEY ROUND[1], grad. Wesleyan Univ., Middletown, CT 1842; teacher, linguist, musician, was b. 22 July 1822 at Richfield, Orange Co. & d. at Florida, NY 5 Jan. 1862. His son:
**SEWARD U. ROUND**[2], b. Florida, NY 1856, grad. Albany Law School 1880; partnership with Eugene A. Brewster, Jr. for 2 years & then established firm of Round & Chatterton until decease of Mr. Chatterton. Member Trinity ME Church.

**ROWLAND, JOSEPH W.**                               H-932
Gen. Supt. of NY Knife Co.

**JOSEPH**, b. CT 1849, with his father Joseph to Walden in 1856; father d. 1884.

**ROYCE, WILLIAM B. [P]**                      A-473, C-43
of Wallkill.

The Royce family had resided for 5 generations at & near Mansfield, CT. SOLOMON ROYCE[1], res. near Mansfield; m. Lydia Atwood of Cape Cod, MA, a desc. of Mayflower pilgrim. They had 4 sons & 2 daus., including:
SOLOMON ROYCE[2], with family from Mansfield to Town of Thompson, Sullivan Co., NY, 1804; settled 3 miles west of present village of Monticello the year after its first settlement by John P. Jones; followed the sea, was later a surveyor; d. 1859, age 81. He m. Nancy Billings, and had:
1803, ALPHEUS B.
James F., res. MI.
Charles B.
Edward G.
Thomas T., res. MI.
Margaret A. m. Moses Bush.
Nathaniel A.
Isaac B.
Stephen W.
    All of the above, except those noted, settled in Sullivan & Orange Cos., NY.

ALPHEUS B. ROYCE[3], m. Mary A., d/o William Mangan of Sing Sing, NY, b. 1811. At the time of their marriage, Mrs.

Royce was widow of Louis Purdy by whom she had a dau., Albina, who m. Caleb W. Horton of Tarrytown, NY. ALPHEUS B. d. 1870 & was bur. Middletown, NY. Alpheus for much of his life surveyor at Monticello, also res. at North Branch, Sullivan Co.; Presbyterian. Children of Alpheus B. & Mary A.:
1841, Dec. 9, **WILLIAM B.**
Ann E., m. Daniel H. Webster, of Middletown.

WILLIAM B. ROYCE[4], s/o Alpheus B.[3], b. Town of Thompson; teacher & clerk, res. NY City, Goshen & Albany; 1866 to Middletown, studied law under James N. Pronk; admitted to Bar in Brooklyn in 1867, practiced in Middletown (1875) when elected president of 1st National Bank of Middletown. He m. Mary E., d/o William O. Roe & Catharine Sly of Goshen, 12 June 1867.  Children:
William F.
Nellie B.
Herbert B.
Edith C.

**RUDOLPH, HENRY**                                  H-932-3

**HENRY** b. in Cassel, Germany in 1853, s/o Henry & Wilhemina (Helfinch) Rudolph.  1870 to NY in business in Matteawan & in 1880 to Newburgh; bakery business.

**RUGGLES, ARCHIBALD E.**                           H-933

**ARCHIBALD E. RUGGLES**, b. at Windsor, VT, s/o Edgar & Emma S. Ruggles.  At an early age in clothing firm in Claremont, NH for 7 years, then to New Berlin, NY; 1902 to Middletown. He m. Minnie L. Ainsworth of Claremont, NH 18 Oct. 1899.

**RUMSEY FAMILY OF CHESTER**               A-615 & C-31

PHINEAS RUMSEY settled in East Division of Goshen and land was later owned by several Phineas Rumseys in succession. The original immigrant (Phoneas) with 4 brothers settled on L.I., later to towns of Monroe & Goshen.  Church records of St. James Protestant Episcopal Church in Goshen (p. 30) give bapt. of Miss Eliza Rumsey, 21 May 1857, d/o the late Phineas and Charlotte Youngs Rumsey.  Also from Goshen records a Phineas Rumsey m. Eliza Duryea, d/o Henry, 19 Jan. 1829.

NATHAN RUMSEY of Monroe had sons:
Earl.
Royal S., had 14 children, all lived to maturity except 1 dau., d. age 17.
Charles.
Nathan D.
Mrs. Lamareux & later Mrs. Halock.
Dau., d. unm.

**RUSSELL, WILLIAM T. [P]**                    **A-545**
of Goshen.

--- RUSSELL[1], of what is today New Bedford, MA, had a son,
HUMPHREY RUSSELL[2], who m. Bertha Wady, and had:
JOHN W. RUSSELL[3], settled in NY City, businessman, estab-
lished line of shipping packets; 1829 settled Goshen, Orange
Co., farmed, d. 1842. He m. Frances M., d/o Samuel
Talman, who d. 1858. Their children:
Edward C.
Phebe A., m. John D. Monell of NY.
1821, Dec. 12, **WILLIAM T.**

**WILLIAM T. RUSSELL[4]**, b. NY; 1843-57 partner with David
Redfield in dry good trade in Goshen; 1857, Cashier, Orange
County Bank, later in the Goshen Bank (president).

**RUTTENBER, EDWARD M. [P]**                    **A-194**
newspaperman & author.

**EDWARD M. RUTTENBER**, b. Bennington, VT, 17 July
1824; 1837 apprenticed to the printer's trade; 1838 to
Newburgh, purchased Newburgh *Telegraph* in 1857; res.
Albany (1863-65) engaged in Bureau of Military Records.
1846 m. Matilda A., d/o Mark McIntyre of Newburgh, and
had:
Charles B., musician of NY City.
Walker F., partner of father.

**RYERSON, JOHN [P]**          **A-560d, LDS Anc. File**

MARTIN RYERSON[1], from Amsterdam to Flatbush (NY) and
later to Wallabout, L.I. He m. Annette Rapelyie, b. 8 Feb.
1646, Wallebout, d/o Joris, & had 5 sons, including:
JORIS.
Ryer.
Francis.
These sons all to NY and c. 1701 to Bergen Co., NJ & were
first settlers of Pacquanac.

JORIS RYERSON[2], m. Sarah Schouten who d. 1743, and had:
1704, April 9, Lucas (Luykas), b. Pompton, Passic Co., NJ; m.
Jonann Van Duhoff.
John.
c. 1705, MARTIN.
George.
Lucas,
Mary.
Blanding.
Elizabeth.
Ann.

MARTIN RYERSON[3], s/o Joris[2], m. Catherine Coxe, b. c. 1735
in Bergen, NJ, & settled in Hunterdon Co., NY near Flem-
ington; surveyor & king's judge, and had 5 sons & 4 daus.
(Those named here with widowed mother removed to Sussex
Co., NJ in 1770, where each reared families:)

MARTIN.
c. 1735, JOHN WILLIAM.
William A.

MARTIN RYERSON[4], s/o Martin[3], m. Rhoda, d/o Benjamin
Hull, and had:
Jesse.
David.
Anna.
Emma.
THOMAS C.
Elizabeth, m. Robert A. Linn.

THOMAS C. RYERSON[5], s/o Martin[4], d. 1838, was judge of
supreme court of NJ at the time; children:
Martin, NJ supreme court judge.
Thomas, physician, physician of NJ.
Henry Ogden, officer in Civil War.
Dau. m. Thomas F. Anderson of Newton.

JOHN WILLIAM RYERSON[4], s/o Martin[3], had son:
NICHOLAS RYERSON[5], b. 8 April 1781, Bergen, NJ, black-
smith & farmer in Vernon and "followed droving;" d. 2 Jan.
1868; m. c. 1800 Anna Farver of Vernon, Sussex Co., NY,
b. 26 Nov. 1787, d. 15 March 1873; both bur. Amity, Orange
Co. Their children:
Elizabeth, m. Amos Munson of Wantage, NJ.
1908, March 12, **JOHN N.**
Anna, m. George W. Houston of Middletown, NY.
Peter N. of Vernon.
Della m. Peter J. Brown of Vernon.
Nicholas N. of Wantage.
Abigail, m. John T. Walling of Amity.
Catherine, m. Evi Martin of Amity.
Jane, m. Abiah F. Walling of Wawayanda.

**JOHN N. RYERSON[6]**, s/o Nicholas[5], b. Town of Vernon,
Sussex Co., NJ. In grocery trade in Paterson, NJ; 1856 to
Goshen, dairy farmer; m. (1st) Aug. 1828, Hannah, d/o
Abram Van Houton of Paterson, NJ, b. 1810-d. 1832, and
had:
Annie, m. Adam Terhune of Paterson; d. 1851.
Amos, farmer of Wawayanda.
Abram, farmer of Hamptonburgh.
Catherine, m. Joshua Holbert of Chemung Co., NY.

JOHN N.[3] m. (2d) 3 Dec. 1839, Hannah, d/o Daniel Bailey of
Glenwood, NJ, b. 20 June 1820, and had:
Hannah, m. William Holbert of Chemung Co.
Elizabeth, m. Jesse A. Holbert of Goshen.
Mary, m. Daniel Carpetner of Goshen.
Annie, m. J. B. Slawson of Jersey City.
John B.
Daniel B.
Mr. & Mrs. Ryerson attend the Presbyterian Church at
Goshen.

"One of the sons who came from Bergen Co. with their widowed mother [Mrs. Catherine (Cove) Ryerson] was grandfather of our subject [**JOHN RYERSON**], and settled in Vernon township, Sussex Co., NJ, where he died, leaving by his first marriage the following children."[1]

John, res. OH, d. IN.

Hassel, res. Vernon; killed when thrown by horse; family subsequently moved to OH.

Peter, farmer of Vernon.

1781, April 8, NICHOLAS.

Children by his 2d marriage:

Jane m. Henry Post of Orange Co.

Dolly, m. (1st) Abraham Ryerson; (2d) John Snyder of Bergen Co.

Catherine, m. George Manderville; d. Bergen Co.

### RYSDYK, WILLIAM M. [P]                    A-628b
of Chester.

**WILLIAM M. RYSDYK** m. (1st) Mahala Hall, member of the Presbyterian Church, d. 1840 age 36, and had:

William T., farmer of Goshen; d. Jan. 1879, age 45.

Elizabeth, m. David H. Roe who was b. in Warwick, merchant of Chester & member of the ME Church; d. 29 Nov. 1800, age 52.

**WILLIAM M.** m. (2d) Elvira, d/o Col. Sproull of Warwick and had several children, all dec'd.

**WILLIAM M.** was a farmer in the town of Warwick, near Florida, Orange Co.; later settled at Town of Chester & raised horses. He d. 26 April 1870, aged 61.

### ST. JOHN FAMILY OF CHESTER                A-614

HECTOR ST. JOHN, from France to Chester during Rev. War, returned to France and took one son with him. After the Revolution returned to NY. He had another son and a dau. "left in the country, sent to the East, and educated." His dau. Frances m. a Frenchman "by the name of Otto and went to France." He was made Count Otto and sent as a minister to the Court of Vienna; suffered & reduced to poverty during the French Revolution.

### ST. JOHN, HON. DANIEL B. [P]              A-357-8
of Newburgh.

An early ancestor of this family settled in Norwalk, CT, from where TIMOTHY ST. JOHN[1] removed in 1756 to Sharon [CT], where he d. 1806. His son, DANIEL[2], in 1818 from Sharon to Hartford, CT; legislator & county surveyor; d. Hartford 1846, aged 85. His son:

RUSSELL ST. JOHN[3], with father in 1818 to Hartford, farmer; had son:

HON. DANIEL B. ST. JOHN[4], b. Sharon, Litchfield Co., CT, 8 Oct. 1808. Served with uncle, Milo L. Bennett, atty. of Manchester, VT; 1824 to Monticello, Sullivan Co., NY & entered store of maternal uncle, Hiram Bennett; 1848 retired from mercantile prusuits; 1843-46 town supervisor of Thompson, Sullivan Co.; 1846 Congressman; 1856 retired & removed to Newburgh, bank president.

### SANDS FAMILY OF CORNWALL                  A-756

DAVID SANDS, Quaker preacher, res. Canterbury, his children:

Nathaniel.

Mrs. Charles Newbold.

Mrs. Elias Ring.

Marietta, d. young.

### SANDS, SAMUEL                             U2-93
of Newburgh, yeoman.

In his will dated 22 May 1792, **SAMUEL SANDS** names his wife Mersey and children:

Eleazer, has no children at the date of his father's will.

Phebe, m. --- McCambly.

Levinah, m. --- Wood.

Mersey, m. --- Purdey.

Will also mentions granddau. Elisabeth Purdy, at the time under the age of 18, and says her mother, Elizabeth [sic] is dec'd. Also mentions grandsons Samuel McCambly, Samuel Rider, Samuel Wood, Eleazar Crawford. Executors are friends: David Sands, Eleazar Gidney & son Eleazar. David Gidney of Newburgh, farmer & John Gedney & John Rider proved the will 26 June 1792.

### SANFORD [SANDFORD], EZRA [P]    A-604, H-933-4
of Warwick.                        LDS Anc. File

THOMAS de SANDFORD, companion in arms of William the Conqueror in 1066, was granted lands in Salop County, England. "At present the family are represented on English soil by Thomas Heigh Sandford, who inherited the original manor of Sandford in Stropshire, England."

THOMAS SANFORD[1] of Stropshire, England, b. 1550 had a son, THOMAS[2], b. 1631 [sic], who went from England to Dorchester, MA and had 6 children, among them SAMUEL[3], who removed from Dorchester to Milford, MA and had a son, SAMUEL JR.[4] who settled in Newtown, CT and had 12 children; among them:

Ebenezer.

1711/12, Feb. 24, DAVID.

DAVID SANFORD[5] in the LDS Ancestral File is given as the s/o Thomas, b. 2 May 1675 & wife Hannah Steevens [sic] of Fairfield, CT. Thomas is given as the s/o Ezekiell Sanford, b. Dorchester, MA 1635/37 & wife Rebecca Whelpley of Fairfield.

DAVID SANDFORD[5], m. Patience Burroughs, d/o John Burrows & Patience Hinman of CT; removed from Newtown, CT to Warwick, NY; d. 1767 and had sons:

138

David.
John.
Ephraim.
1747, EZRA.

EZRA SANDFORD[6] b. Warwick [N. Killingworth, CT], d. 1822; m. Ann Hopper, b. Newtown, Fairfield Co., CT, and had (all b. Warwick):
1773, Nov. 7, Patience, m. Daniel Smith.
1775, July 22, MATTHEW.
1777, July 8, Olive.
1779, Aug. 29, Olive (2d), m. --- Morehouse.
1781, Ann, m. Archibald Doty.
1785, Sept. 22, Esther, m. William Hause Jr. They had (all b. Wayne Co., NY) Sanford Hause, b. 1805, m. Lydia Swarthout; Elizabeth Hause, b. 1807, m. Manly Swartout; Jesse J. Hause, b. 1808, m. Sally A. Swartout; Anna Hause, b. 1811; Herman C. Hause, b. 1813, m. Elvira Bacon; Hannah Hause, b. 1815; Harris E. Hause, b. 1816, m. Lucinda Maynard; Mary Ann Hause, b. 1819, m. Horace B. Avery; Elmer C. Hause, b. 1823, m. Polly Thompson & Dorcas Hause, b. 1825.
1788, March, Hannah, m. Stephen Smith of Rockland, NY. Their children b. Seneca Co., NY.
1790, Sept. 7, Mary, m. John Thomas & had Sally Ann & John Thomas.
1793, Nov. 11, EZRA.
1798, Sept., Dorcas, m. John Hull.

MATTHEW SANFORD[7], s/o Ezra[6], m. Catherine Garrison and had:
c. 1796, ABRAM.
1798, Ezra, m. Mary Ann Crowel, b. 1807 in Newark, NJ. Their children were all b. & res. in NJ.
1804, Nov. 12, Mathew, m. Elizabeth Long of Paterson, NJ. Their children & grandchildren settled in Newhampton, Warwick, Barkerville & Cohoes, NY.
c. 1806, Garrison.
1807, April 5, Jane, m. Martin Welch. Their son Benjamin Silas Welch, b. 2 Aug. 1849 in Toledo, OH, m. Phoebe E. McCullough of Columbus, OH. Their children b. OH & NE.
c. 1809, Sally.
c. 1811, Dolly.
c. 1813, Patience.
c. 1815, Eliza.
c. 1817, Catherine.
c. 1819, Anna.

ABRAM SANFORD[8], s/o Matthew[7], m. Jane Ryerson & had:
1830, George.
1840, June 15, JOHN.
c. 1842, Hester Ann.

JOHN SANFORD[9], s/o Abram[8], b. Passiac, NJ, m. Sarah Frances Hunt, b. 21 Aug. 1843. They had (all b. Goshen, NY):
1865, April 10, Alfred Harris, m. Melvina Carey.
1867, Jan. 5, Sidney Abram, m. Hettie Wolcott, b. 20 Aug.

1875, Bloomingburgh.
1868, Oct. 19, Pierson, m. Mary Jane Wolcott.
1870, Aug. 19, Frederick C., m. Hettie Wolcott [wife of brother Sidney Abram above.]
1872, Feb. 21, Ella.
1873, Sept. 10, Clara.
1877, Sept. 9, Mary Ann, m. George Howell, b. 12 Feb. 1875 at Goshen.
1881, Sept. 10, John B.

EZRA SANFORD[7], s/o Ezra[6], b. Warwick, worked on father's farm, served in War of 1812 for which he now draws a pension; m. 29 Oct. 1814, Adeline Terry who d. 13 Aug. 1875. Children (all b. Warwick, NY):
1815, Oct. 29, URIAH TERRY.
1818, May 24, HESTER ANN.
George W.
1821, Nov. 5, GEORGE W. (2d).
1824, March 8, Mary Elizabeth.
1827, Aug. 17 [22], WILLIAM MOORE.
1830, March 27, Julia A., m. Charles Morehouse.
1832, Aug. 26, PIERSON EZRA.
1836, Nov. 5, Abigial, m. John P. Gabriel & had dau. Elizabeth A. Gabriel b. 7 Nov. 1863, Watkins, NY.
1838, Dec. 25, Emily, m. (1) Lee Cleveland & (2) Adrian Tuttle. Her children (all Tuttle) are Daniel S., Adeline & Adrian.

EZRA was a farmer, miller, bank director, railroad director & member of the Warwick Baptist Church.

URIAH TERRY SANFORD[8], s/o Ezra[7], m. Mary Ann Van Duzer & had (all b. Warwick, NY):
1847, Aug. 31, Sidney H., m. Hannah T. Wright of Bellvale, NY & had Townsend, b. 14 June 1871 at Warwick.
1850, Sept. 12, Milton Lee, m. Annie Welling, b. 18 Oct. 1857 at Warwick & had Ethel Lee & Ruth.

HESTER ANN SANFORD[8], d/o Ezra[7], m. George W. Price & had (PRICE):
1838, Oct. 16, Ann E., m. James Watkins.
1840, April 28, Emily A., m. James Hawkins, b. 2 June 1822, Goshen. They had (HAWKINS): George Price & Antoinette.
1844, May 5, George S., m. Elizabeth Seely.
1846, April 23, Mary Adeline, m. Albert R. Galloway & had (GALLOWAY): Bryon S., Julia, Ezra P. & Mary Caroline, all b. Munroe, NY.
1848, Feb. 3, Jacob M., m. Helen Fay & had Edson C. Price m. Eleanor Carpenter Colemen, res. Goshen & John Armstrong Price b. Goshen.
1849, July 9, Julia H., m. E. C. Gabriel.
1852, May 20, Eva I., m. W. R. Comer b. Goshen & had, both b. Goshen, W. Russell Comer and Anna S. Comer who m. William Grant.
1858, Feb. 23, James L. Price, m. M. Jennie Hawkins, b. 29 April 1861, Hamptonburg, NY. Their children, all b. Goshen (PRICE): Clarence H., Josephine J. & Emma A.

GEORGE W. SANFORD[8], s/o Ezra[7], m. Frances Amelia, a d/o the late Capt. Nathaniel Wheeler Baird; they celebrated golden anniversary in 1897. GEORGE d. 6 Jan. 1900 & left children:
1847, Oct. 18, Lansing Haight, m. Mary P. Cooper & his child Bessie, b. 3 July 1873, m. Edward Wheeler Everett. Lansing d. 1900.
1850, July 4, Nathaniel Baird.
1854, Nov. 9, Ezra.
1856, April 19, FERDINAND VAN DERVEER.
1858, Nov. 30, George Alden, m. (1) Sarah E. Gouldy & (2) Helen E. Gillespie.
1861, Jan. 20, Mary Elizabeth.
1864, May 13, JOHN WHEELER.
1871, Oct. 30, Francis Baird, m. Sarah M. Welling & had at least one child.

FERDINAND VAN DERVEER SANFORD[9], s/o George W.[8], b. Warwick, NY, m. Rowena Herrick, b. 22 Sept. 1856, Owego, NY. They had (all b. Warwick, NY):
1886, Jan. 30, George Herrick.
1888, March 1, Ferdinand Doan.
1890, Oct. 7, Marion Burt.
1893, Feb. 20, John Alden.
Another child, unnamed.
1904, Sept. 28, William Wendover.

JOHN WHEELER SANFORD[9] s/o George W.[8], b. at Warwick, insurance & real estate brokerage business. Member Old Dutch Reformed Church of Warwick; m. Bertha M. Furman of Warwick 6 Oct. 1897, and had:
1900, Feb. 11, Frances Isabel.
1905, Jan. 29, Bertha Elizabeth.

WILLIAM MOORE SANFORD[8] s/o Ezra[7] & Adaline, in tanning business with father until 1880 when father died & he continued business alone until his death, 17 Aug. 1887. He m. Sarah Burt in Oct. 1856, and had:
1859, Jan. 21, James Everett.
1860, Dec. 12, Charles, in family business; m. Julia N. Prior, b. 9 July 1861, Fayetteville, NC. Their children: Julia M., Faith & Raymond P.
1863, Jan. 27, Mary Burt, m. Frank Durland of Chester & had two children, one was William Sanford Durland, b. 13 July 1892 in Orange Co.
1865, Feb. 26, Ezra T., m. Anna D. Feagles of NY City. They had 5 children, two were William Nathaniel & Ezra Burt Sanford.
1867, Oct. 21, Adeline (Addie), m. William R. Welling. Another source says she was wife of A. M. Reynolds of Newark, NJ.
1868, Dec. 16, William Moore Jr., m. Julia Dent Burt, b. NY City, 11 Sept. 1873.
1870, May 21, Sarah.
1872, Sept. 17, Emily, m. Abram M. Reynolds of Newark, NJ. [See entry for sister Adeline above.]
Everett, res. at home.

PERRSON EZRA SANFORD[8], s/o Ezra[7], m. Anna Scott Burt & had (all b. Warwick):
1856, July 21, Pauline, m. (1) Fred H. Bradner of Middletown, m. (2) William Wirt Wendover of Warwick.
1857, Oct. 17, Ezra.
1865, Edward Burt.

_____

SAWYER, GEN. CALVIN G. [P]                A-499

BENJAMIN SAWYER[1], res. near Carpenter's Point, on the Delaware, innkeeper & ferryman; later to Town of Goshen, near "Drowned Lands," farmer. He m. Miss --- Wood, and had sons:
John.
Moses.
1796, May 12, CALVIN G.
Franklin.

GEN. CALVIN G. SAWYER[2], s/o Benjamin[1], b. on homestead at Carpenter's Point; res. Goshen, Middletown, Hamptonburgh, d. Middletown, 2 April 1874; served in old state militia. He m. (1st) Hannah Valentine, and had:
John.
Rev. Samuel, Presbyterian clergyman of Marion, IN.
Mary E., m. Alonzo Banks of Pine Valley, Chemung Co.
Hannah V., widow of DeWitt C. Payne, formerly of Goshen; now res. Battle Creek, MI.
Harriet.
Gabriel of Clarence, IA.
Caroline.

CALVIN[2] m. (2d) Harriet, d/o Judge Armstrong of Town of Warwick, near Florida, Orange Co., at the time of their marriage a widow Smith, and had:
Alida, m. Joel H. Coleman of Blooming-Grove.
Calvin J., atty. of Clinton, TN

CALVIN[2] m. (3d) 25 Dec. 1844, Harriet W., widow of James M. Cash, brother of Dr. Merrit H. Cash and d/o Maj. JOHN WHITE (see below) and Effa Brown of Wallkill. The 3d Mrs. Sawyer was b. 1815, Aug. 18, d. 1861, 7 May; no issue.

CALVIN[2] m. (4th) 31 Aug. 1863, Effa Ann White, a sister of his 3rd wife, b. 1809, Oct. 15, surviving in 1881.

SAMUEL WHITE, farmer of near Montgomery and later of Scotchtown had a son, MAJ. JOHN WHITE, b. 22 Dec. 1768, d. 11 Sept. 1839; one of the founders of Presbyterian Church of Scotchtown; m. Effa Brown, b. 1 Dec. 1775, d. 2 May 1847; they m. 15 March 1792, and had 11 children, Effa Ann & Harriet W. were wives of **CALVIN B. SAWYER.**

_____

SAYER, BENJAMIN [P]                A-605-6
of Warwick.
SAYER, WALTER H. [P]                A-558c
of Goshen.

Three brothers from England to America in early setttlement; two located in the Eastern States and one on L.I. The Sears [sic] of Boston belong to the former branch; those of Orange Co. were descendants of the L.I. branch. Spellings are Sayer, Sayre & Sayrs. The three brothers were: Thomas (res. 1704 Elizabethtown, NJ), JOSEPH[1] (1st of family of Orange Co.) and James were all b. in Wales and emigrated to America. Joseph's wife is not named but his children are:

1731, JAMES.
John.
Daniel.
Jonathan.

JAMES SAYER[2], s/o Joseph[1], settled in what is now Town of Goshen and d. there in 1821; m. (1st) Mary Mapes and had a dau. Mary who m. Daniel Poppino. JAMES m. (2d) Mary Goldsmith of L.I., and had:
James, soldier of War of 1812; d. unm., aged 60.
1789, Nov. 28, WILLIAM.
Ruth m. Egbert Jessup of Goshen.

WILLIAM SAYER[3], s/o James[2], farmer on homestead & cattle dealer; member Presbyterian Church at Florida, Orange Co.; d. of sunstroke June 1840. He m. 1811, Martha, d/o Richard Johnson of Goshen who was b. 12 Nov. 1789 & d. Jan. 1869. Their children:
Augusta L.
1841, Sept. 15, WALTER H.; unm., res. on homestead.
George M.
Jane S.
Mary G.
Harriet T., m. John Jessup, farmer.
Sarah E., m. William L. Vail, merchant of Warwick.
Helen A., widow of James Seely of Warwick.
William H.

DANIEL SAYER[1] (could be Daniel, s/o Joseph[1] above) removed to Warwick before the Revolution, in which he served. He m. Lydia Burt, d/o Daniel and sister of the Hon. James. The descs. of "Mrs. Daniel Burt, at the time of her death in 1810, at the age of 94 years, numbered no less than 524 persons." Lydia d. c. 1796. Daniel & Lydia's son, the youngest of 9 children (4 dau. & 5 sons):
BENJAMIN SAYER[2], b. 29 April 1791, on homestead in Warwick; d. 6 Oct. 1874. He served in the War of 1812; m. 9 Dec. 1817, Rebecca Forshee of Warwick who d. 1858. Their children:
John L.
William E.
Mary E., m. Benjamin C. Burt; dec'd.
Hannah, m. Thomas Burt.
Lydia, m. John W. Hasbrouck.
Ann Eliza.
Daniel F., dec'd.
Sarah C. m. Darius Fancher.

## SAYER, BENJAMIN B.     H-935

BENJAMIN B. SAYER, b. 11 March 1859 on the homestead farm near Warwick; same farm has been in the family since 1768 & was purchased by his great-grandfather Henry Wisner, who lived in the Town of Goshen. BENJAMIN B. was farmer & distiller, m. Annie Waggoner of Glenburnie, Ontario, Canada 15 March 1893 & had:
1893, Dec. 18, Helen Bennett.
1895, June 2, Mary Feaser.
1896, Dec. 9, Benjamin Wagoner.

-----

## SAYER, GEORGE S.     H-935
businessman & farmer of Westtown.

GEORGE SAYER[1] (1812-1884), schoolteacher; 1836 to IN; 1852 to Westtown, m. Emeline C. Evans, and had:
One child, unnamed.
JONATHAN.

JONATHAN SAYER[2], s/o GEORGE[1], m. Sarah Owen, and had:
George O., atty. in NY.
Robert E., res. Westtown on home farm, m. Frances Horton.

-----

## SAYER, WILLIAM BENJAMIN     H-935-6

The Sayer family is of English origin, mentioned as living in Poddington, England in 1309.

THOMAS SAYER, from Bedfordshire, England to Lynn, MA & 1648 at Southampton, L.I. His house said to be the oldest English house standing in NY state. The family to Orange Co. 1759.

WILLIAM BENJAMIN SAYER, desc. of Thomas above, owns & occupies a stone house on Main St., Warwick, built by Francis Baird in 1766. It was called Stone Tavern & used as one until 1830. House in Sayer family since 1858. WILLIAM was b. in this house 14 March 1866 & has always lived there with his sister, Miss M. Eva Sayer.

-----

## SCHARFF, CHRISTIAN H.     H-936-7

CHRISTIAN, b. Amsterdam, Holland 26 Feb. 1834; to America with his father & settled in Newark, NJ. Atty.; partnership with James Buchanan in NY City. He m. Frances A. Seward, b. at Florida, NY 27 Jan. 1859; she b. 16 April 1836.

-----

## SCHOFIELD, R. ED.     H-937, LDS Anc. File

JAMES HAMLIN SCHOFIELD, b. 10 Oct. 1821, Beemerville, NJ & d. 12 Dec. 1876, Port Jervis, Orange Co., NY. He m. Margaret Corwin [Cole] Elston, b. 21 Jan. 1826, Minisink, d/o Jacob Elston (s/o Joseph S. Elston & Margaret Cole) & Esther Corwin of Mt. Hope. Esther Corwin was d/o John Corwin & Julia Vail. JAMES d. Port Jervis 12 Dec. 1876. Their son:
R[ICHARD] ED[DSALL] SCHOFIELD, b. Port Jervis, 10

Dec. 1853, read law at office of Judge O. P. Howell. He m. 28 Jan. 1885, Mary Josephine Finn of Port Jervis, d/o Matthew James, and had:

1885, Nov. 28, James Hamlin, m. 18 Sept. 1912, Mary Ann Seybolt, b. 12 Oct. 1884, Matamoras, PA.

Anna C., at home.

Members Presbyterian Church.

## SCHOONMAKER, D. DE WITT        H-937

He was b. at Middletown, businessman with the Borden Condensed Milk Co. since 1902. 21 April 1897 m. Mary J. McNash of Middletown.

## SCHOONMAKER, JOHN        H-937-8
## SCHOONMAKER, SAMUEL VAIL [P]        W-84-5
## SCHOONMAKER, JOCHEM        U2-54
### U1-81, U2-114-15, LDS Anc. File

The Schoonmaker family is one of the oldest in this section of the state.

HENDRICK JOCHEMSEN SCHOONMAKER[1], b. Hamburg, Germany, to America in 1654 in the military service of the Dutch West India Co., an innholder at Ft. Orange. He m. at Albany, 1657 Eliza (Elsie) Janse(n), widow of Adriaen Petersen (Van Alcmaer). After Hendrick's death in Kingston, Ulster Co., 1681, his widow m. 26 Sept. 1684, Cornelius Barentsen Slecht. Elsie was d/o Jan Jansen Van Breestde, b. c. 1596 in Bredstedt, Prussia, & Engeltje Jans, b. New Amsterdam, NY. Children:

JOCHEM.

Egbert, b. Albany, m. 13 Oct. 1683, Aannatje, d/o Samuel Berry.

Bapt. 1663, March 18, Engeltje, m. (1) Nicholas Anthony, s/o Allerd Anthony & Henrica Wessels, (2) 30 April 1699, Stephen Gasherie from Marenna, France.

Bapt. 1665, May 17, HENDRICK.

Bapt. 1669, Oct. 20, Hillstje.

**JOCHEM SCHOONMAKER[2]**, b. Albany, m. (1) 16 Aug. 1679, Petronella Sleght, d/o Cornelis Barentse Sleght & Tryntje Bysen Bos. She d. c. 1687 & he m. (2) 28 April 1689, Anna Hussey (Horsi), bapt. 27 June 1670, d/o Frederick Hussey and wife Margaret. **JOCHEM** supervisor at Rochester (1709-1712), Capt. of a company of defense against the Indians. Children:

Bapt. 1683, Jan. 15, Cornelis, m. 25 Nov. 1711, Engeltje Roosa, bapt. 20 Sept. 1685, d/o Arie & Maria (Pels) Roosa. Cornelis d. 14 Oct. 1757.

Bapt. 17 Aug. 1681, Hendrick, m. 24 Nov. 1794, Heyltje Decker, bapt. 10 Jan. 1686, d/o Gerrit & Margaret D.

Bapt. 1684, Nov. 22, Trynje, m. 18 Nov. 1704, Jacobus Bruyn, s/o Jacobus & Gertrwyd (Yselstein) Bruyn, bapt. 12 Dec. 1685. Trynje d. 27 Aug. 1763.

Bapt. 1685, Dec. 12, Eltie, m. 27 Oct. 1706, Joseph Hasbrouck, bapt. 23 Oct. 1684, d. 28 Jan. 1724. Joseph was s/o Abraham & Margaret (Deyo) Hasbrouck. Eltie d. 27 July 1764, at new Paltz.

Bapt. 1687, April 29, Jacomyntje, m. 22 Sept. 1726, Johannes Miller.

By his second wife **JOCHEM** had:

Bapt. 1690, Aug. 24, Rebecca.

Bapt. 1692, Jan. 28, Frederick, m. (1) 1 March 1713, Anne DeWitt, bapt. 15 March 1696, d/o Jacob & Grietje (Vernooy) DeWitt. Frederick m. (2) 6 Feb. 1717, Eva Swartwout, bapt. 16 Nov. 1694, d/o Thomas & Elisabeth (Gardiner) Swartwout.

Bapt. 1694, June 3, Jan, m. 7 June 1730, Margaret Hoornbeck, bapt. 13 April 1713, d/o Lodeuyck & Maria (Vernooy) Hoornbeck.

Bapt. 1695, Dec. 15, Margriet, m. 14 Feb. 1716, Moses Depuy, bapt. 27 Sept. 1691, s/o Moses & Maria (Wynkoop) Depuy.

Bapt. 1698, May 8, Jacobus, m. 15 Oct. 1729, Maria Rosenkrans, bapt. 19 Dec. 1714, d/o Alexander & Maria (Depuy) Rosenkrans.

Bapt. 1700, Feb. 18, Elisabeth, m. 3 Sept. 1719 Benjamin Depuy, bapt. 13 Oct. 1695, s/o Moses & Maria (Wynkoop) Depuy.

Bapt. 1702, April 19, Benjamin, m. 10 May 1722, Catharine Depuy, d/o Moses Depuy & Maria Wynkoop.

Bapt. 1706, Aug. 11, Antje (Heyltije), m. 12 Oct. 1709 [sic] Cornelius Wynkoop, s/o Jacobus Wynkoop & Jannetje Bogardus.

Bapt. 1708, June 20, Sara, m. 26 Aug. 1723, Jacobus Dupey, s/o Moses Dupey & Maria Wynkoop.

Bapt. 1710, Oct. 12, Jochem, m. 11 May 1730, Lydia Rosenkrans, d/o Dirck Rosenkrans & Wyntije Kierstede, d/o Roelof.

Bapt. 1713, Feb. 22, Daniel.

**JOCHEM[2]**'s residence is given as Kingston in his will dated 9 Dec. 1729.

HENDRICK HENDRISEN SCHOONMAKR[2], s/o Hendrick Jochemsen Scoonmaker[1], m. at Kingston, NY, 24 March 1688, Gerrtury de Witt, d/o Tjerck Classen de Witt & Barbara Andriessen, both originally of Holland, & had (all bapt. Ulster Co., NY):

Bapt. 1689, April 14 [11], Elsie.

Bapt. 1689, April 14 [11], Heskia(h).

Bapt. 1691, May 26, Barbara, m. 30 Oct. 1719, Wihelmus Ploeg.

1692, April 17, Elsie, m. 13 June 1713, Nicholas DeMeyer, s/o Wilhelmus DeMeyer & Catherine Bayard.

Bapt. 1694, June 3, Hendrick, m. 16 Oct. 1724, Tryntje Oosterhoudt.

Bapt. 1695, Aug. 18, Jannetje, d. young.

c. 1695, Mariae.

Bapt. 1697, July 4, Johannes, m. 15 May 1729, Ariaentje Hoogteling.

Bapt. 1699, Jan. 22 [b. 18 Jan. 1699], TJERCK.

Bapt. 1700, Nov. 3 [b. c. 1695], Jacob.

Bapt. 1702, Oct. 4, Jannetje, m. 30 Sept. 1720, Hendrick Oosterhoudt.

Bapt. 1707, March 2, Sarah, d. young.

Bapt. 1709, Feb. 11, Catrina, m. 14 Jan. 1731, Abraham Person.

Bapt. 1710, Oct. 12, SARAH.

HENDRICK SCHOONMAKER's will dated 12 Jan. 1711/12, names wife Geertruy; sons Hendrick, Johanis, Tyrk, Jacobus, Heskiah and daus. Barbara, Else, Janitie, Sarah and Mariae. He also mentions his brother Egbert Schoonmaker and friend & neighbor Edward Whittaker. Will proved 12 April 1712, by James Whittaker, Corneles Vernoy Jr. & Peter Osterhout.

TJERCK SCHOONMAKER[3], s/o Hendrick Hendricksen[2], m. 21 Nov. 1720, Theodosia Whittaker (bapt. 7 May 1719, d. 6 March 1791), d/o Edward Whittaker & Hilitje Burhans. Children (all b. Ulster Co.):
1732, Dec. 28, Geetruy, m. Egbert Schoonmaker, b. 15 Sept. 1723 in Kingston, NY. They had Theodocia, b. 5 Jan. 1753 in Rhinebeck who m. Abraham A. Post of Ulster Co.

SARAH [ZARA] SCHOONMAKER[3], d/o Hendrick Hendricksen[2], m. 19 Aug. 1726, Cornelis Macklin, of Shawangunk. Their children (all b. Ulster Co.) spelled their name "McClean:"
Bapt. 1727, May 28, JOHN.
Bapt. 1728, Nov. 17, Geertruy.
Bapt. 1732, Aug. 6, Hendrick, m. Gertrude DeWitt of Kingston.

JOHN MC CLEAN[4], s/o Sarah (Schoonmaker) Macklin[3], m. Margaretha Christ & had (MC CLEAN, all b. Orange Co.):
1755, Oct. 9, Henry.
1758, Feb. 27, Catherine.
c. 1758, Cornelius.
Bapt. 1759, Dec. 24, Margaret, m. William Lewis. They res. Dryden, Tompkins Co., NY & later in Ulster Co.
Bapt. 1770, Aug. 11, Sarah.
1772, Oct. 4, Jonas.

There was another JOCHEM SCHOONMAKER who filed a will in Ulster Co., dated 14 July 1789. He is identified as Jochem of Rochester & names his children:
Martinus.
Daniel.
Catharine, m. Jochem Schoonmaker Jr.
Antje, m. Ephraim Depuy.
Elizabeth, m. Frederick Schoonmaker.
Wyntje, m. Thomas Schoonmaker.
Lena, m. John Wansa.
John.
Jacobus.

He also names grandsons, John Jacobus [surname?] & Henry son of his son Daniel. Jacob Coddington apptd. executor. Will proved 1 March 1790 by Lodewyck & Jochem D. Schoonmaker of Rochester, farmers & Daniel L. Schoonmaker.

Hendrick's (the immigrant) grandson, Capt. Frederick Schoonmaker was a patriot & soldier of the Rev. Descs. include:
Major Abraham Schoonmaker, served in the 4th Reg. Ulster Co., NY in the Rev. and he had a son:
JOHN A. SCHOONMAKER[1], m. Rachel, eldest d/o Gustavis

& Maria (Twerwilliger) Sammons. They had 10 children, number 10 was:
JOHN[2], teacher; in March 1852, with brother Jacob, opened general store at Tuttletown. Soon after Jacob died in *Henry Clay* disaster on the Hudson. John to Newburgh in 1853, employed by Stephen Hunt. Worked for Isaac Wood, Jr. for 3 years, & then with Mr. Parmake. 1863 with Samuel C. Mills & Y. A. Weller purchased dry goods business of Col. Wood. JOHN d. 1 Jan. 1904 at his home in Newburgh. He was a member of the First Presbyterian Church, m. 2 July 1862, Mary A. Vail, and had (all res. Newburgh):
1867, March 13, SAMUEL VAIL.
Mrs. W. Clement Scott.
Elizabeth M.

SAMUEL VAIL SCHOONMAKER[3], s/o JOHN[2], was b. at Newburgh. 1885 employed at Schoonmaker & Wells; member of First Presbyterian Church. He m. Lillian W. Wardell of Philadelphia 1 Feb. 1899, and had:
John, aged 7.
Samuel Jr., aged 5.

_____

### SCHOONMAKER, THEODORE D.                    H-939

EDWARD SCHOONMAKER[1] m. Leah Rose, both of Town of Shawangunk, Ulster Co., NY, and had:
Levi[2], m. Julia Ann, d/o Samuel Butler & wife Sarah of Goshen, and had one son:
THEODORE[3], b. Town of Crawford, 28 Dec. 1836. Farmer until 1868 when he was appointed Clerk of the Surrogate's Court by his brother-in-law, Hon. Gilbert O. Hulse. His children, [wife not named]:
Anna Frances, m. Thomas Mould of the firm of Thompson-Mould.
Theodore F., of Hartford, CT, traveling salesman.
Mary Adele, at home.
Charles B., civil engineer.

_____

### SCHRIVER, ANDREW                    H-939-40

ANDREW b. 16 Dec. 1840, at Lagrange, Dutchess Co. Served in Co. A, 144th NY Vol. in the Civil War 3 years; after war served NY Conference of the ME Church for 37 years; 6 years as presiding elder in Newburgh Dist., now retired & res. on the Oak Lane farm near Chester. He m. Alida Wiltsie of Albany Co., 24 April 1877, and had:
Hiram W.
Newman E.
Paul R.
Charlotte.
Frank.

_____

### SCHULTZ FAMILIES        A-219, TN-315-6, LDS Anc. File

ABRAHAM SCHULTZ of Town of New Windsor, established a ferry from New Windsor to Fishilll in 1800.

ISAAC SCHULTZ & son kept tavern in 1776 at New Windsor.

CHRISTIAN OTTO SCHULTZ, b. 22 Jan. 1712 at Bredenfelt in the Dukedom of Mecklenburgh, Germany. He d. 5 Nov. 1785 at Rhinebeck, NY. Wife [Christina] Margaret Sharpenstein, b. 16 April 1713 at Sagendorp, Germany. She d. 20 Oct. 1789, also at Rhinebeck. Both to America in 1735, settled at Fishkill, Dutchess Co., NY & had:

Anna.
Abraham.
1740, July 28, ISAAC.
Christopher.
Margaret.
Christian.
Frederick.
Peter.
William.
Jacob.
John.

ISAAC SCHULTZ[2], b. Rhinebeck, m. 1765, Mary Kilborne (Kilburn), who was b. 4 Dec. 1749 in CT, d/o James of Glastonbury CT. ISAAC[2] was a schoolteacher & opened store in New Windsor, at what was later known as 'Schultz's Mill.' They had:
ISAAC[3], b. New Windsor, Orange Co. 15 April 1793.

## SCHWISSER, LORENTZ                                    CN-9

**LORENTZ SCHWISSER** appears in the Newburgh Directory for 1709, the year the town was founded & settled by a group of immigrants from the Palatinate of the Rhine. He was husbandman & viner, aged 25 on immigration; his wife Anna Catharine aged 26, and their child, Johannes, aged 8 years.

## SCOTT, FRANK A.                                       H-940
architect & builder of Newburgh.

**FRANK A.**, s/o John & Jane (Gedney) Scott, b. 18 July 1830 at Newburgh. The Gedney family is of French-Huguenot origin. David Gedney from France to Newburgh 1754.
**FRANK** trained in NY City & worked in the western states & in 1872 back to Newburgh; 1852 m. Mary Banks of Ulster Co., NY, and had:
Elsie Banks.
Anna Gedney.
Trustee of Unitarian Church.

## SCOTT FAMILY                                          E-224

Under 'unusual incidents' it is reported that 24 Jan. 1804, a s/o Mr. Warren Scott, aged 14 years, was killed when torn to pieces by wolves while feeding his father's sheep.

## SCOTT, W. CLEMENT                                     H-940
sec. & treas. of the Newburgh Planing Mill.

He was b. in Newburgh in 1869, s/o the late Hon. David A. Scott. In 1897 he m. Mary L., d/o John Schoonmaker, and had:
Elizabeth M.
William C. Jr.

## SCUDDER, FRANK H.                                      H-940
treas. of Middletown.

**FRANK** was b. 19 Nov. 1871 in Otisville; telegrapher for Railroad 1888-1900. He m. Elizabeth F. Scott of Jersey City, NJ 12 Oct. 1904. Members First Presbyterian Church of Middletown.

## SEACORD, HENRY                                         H-940-1
Assemblyman of 1st Dist.

**HENRY** is desc. from French Huguenots from Rochel, France who in 1682 went to England & from there to America in 1684, and Amroise Sicard, a French Protestant refugee of LaRochelle who fled England in 1682 & to America in 1684, located at New Rochelle, Westchester Co., NY in 1692.

At an early age **HENRY** entered his father's blacksmith shop & in 1891 engaged in real estate & insurance business.

## SEACORD, WILLIAM H.                                    H-941
blacksmith.

**WILLIAM H. SEACORD**, b. at Lincolndale, Orange Co., which was formerly known as Decker's Mills, m. Charlotte E. Crans 31 May 1883, and had:
Barbara A., teacher at Lincolndale.
Andrew W., student at Cornell Univ.
H. Stanley.
Charlotte C.
Ralph B.

## SEARS, BENJAMIN                                 A-414, GFM-7
of Crawford.

**BENJAMIN SEARS**, a constable of Montgomery, then to Crawford, storekeeper. He had brothers Samuel, John, James and Elnathan, all early settlers of Montgomery and all served in the Revolutionary War.

Sears found bur. in the German Reformed Cemetery at Montgomery include: Samuel, d. 7 March 1842, aged 88 years, 9 months, 30 days & Elizabeth his wife, d. 24 May 1834, aged 73 years, 2 months, 1 day. Also a Milton F., d. 12 Jan. 1845, aged 22 years, 4 months, 5 days & Mary, d. 20 Aug. 1832, aged 8 years, 3 months, 25 days.

## SEARS, BENJAMIN CHANDLER                              H-941-2
dairy farmer & political service.

BENJAMIN SEARS[1], sheriff of Ulster Co. in 1793, had son Marcus[2], a physician, who m. the d/o Richard Caldwell, Capt.

25th US Inf. in War of 1812. Richard was s/o John who purchased the family farm in 1793. Marcus[2] removed to Blooming-Grove and had:

BENJAMIN CHANDLER SEARS[3], b. Montgomery Feb. 1836. He grad. Rutgers in 1857 & m. 1866 Phoebe E., d/o Edmund S. Howell of Blooming Grove, and had:

Marcus Caldwell Sears, grad. Rutgers, 1891.

The family are members of the 2d Presbyterian Church of Wasingtonville & later BENJAMIN was deacon at the Blooming Grove Congregational Church.

## SEELY, HOWARD DAVIS     H-943, C-10, LDS Anc. File
of Chester.

THADDEUS SEELY[1], early settler of present Town of Chester, was an early Presbyterian Church of Chester member; m. Joanna Seeley 2 April 1778, and had:
Joanna, m. Charles Board of Ringwood, NJ.
1782, Aug. 15, THADDEUS.
Peter, d. young.

THADDEUS SEELY[2], s/o Thaddeus[1], m. (1st) 1805, Dec. 15, Elizabeth, d/o Nathaniel Roe and she d. 20 Sept. 1874. Children:
Joanna, d. young.
Edward, res. IL.
Mary, m. George S. Conkling of Goshen.
George, d. age 10.
1817, June 19, CHARLES B.
Gabriel.
Thaddeus, res. on homestead.
Elizabeth, d. young.

## SEELY, CHARLES B.     A-627-8

CHARLES B. SEELY[3], s/o Thaddeus[2], m. 19 Oct. 1842, Hannah Jane, d/o Benjamin C. Coleman & Eleanor Vail of Goshen. Eleanor Vail was the d/o Gen. Abram Vail of Goshen; Benjamin was the s/o Benjamin Coleman. Hannah Jane was b. 1 Nov 1817, and a member of the Presbyterian Church. Children:
Ella.
FRED B., Chester flour mill.
Hannah C., d. 2 June 1863, aged 14.
Mary Frank, d. 25 April 1872, aged 20.
Charles A.

FRED B. SEELY[4], of Goshen; Fred d. July 1891. Fred's son, HOWARD DAVIS SEELY[5], b. near Chester, 27 Jan. 1878, m. Carrie A. Mills, d/o George of Goshen & had one child, Pauline Augusta Seely.

The LDS Ancestral File gives a Thaddeus Seeley, b. 1738 in Bedford, NY, s/o Jonathan who m. c. 1733 at Bedford, Electa ---. This Jonathan was s/o Joseph Seeley & Martha ---, and the family is traced to Stamford, CT. Could possibly be the Thaddeus above.

## SEELY, GEORGE     H-942

GEORGE SEELY, b. 27 March 1837, s/o Edward & Julia Ann (Satterly) Seely; m. Helen M. Butler of Rochester NY 17 Sept. 1868, and had one child:
1874, March 3, Gaylord B.

Members Chester Presbyterian Church. Family homestead where GEORGE was born had been purchased by his great grandfather.

## SEELY, HENRY C. [P]     A-176a, C-12, LDS Anc. File
Physician.

The Seely family is of English extraction, settled in America in CT, to L.I. & 24 of the family settled in Orange Co.

BEZALEEL SEELY[1] located at Greycourt, m. Rachel Tuthill 6 June 1780 at Goshen, and had six children, among them:
ISAAC SEELY[2], b. c. 1785, near Middletown, Orange Co., and later removed to Minisink; d. age 42. He m. Elizabeth, of Cornwall-on-the-Hudson, d/o FRANCIS MANDEVILLE [see below] & Deborah (Clark) of New Cornwall, Orange Co., and had (all b. Minisink):
1805, Hector.
1807, Francis T.
David W.
1815, March 1, HENRY C.
c. 1817, Lewis T.
c. 1820, Isaac B.

HENRY C. SEELY[3], b. near Middletown, NY, studied at Chester & Fairfield, Herkimer Co.; settled at Amity; m. 1844, Almeda, d/o Rev. William Timlow of Amity, and had (all b. Amity):
c. 1845, Whitfield T., physician.
c. 1847, William H.
c. 1852, Elizabeth F.
Ruth T.

W-86 has a photo and short writeup on Harry G. Seely, s/o Mr. & Mrs. Henry Seeley, a resident of Seely Ridge Farm.

FRANCIS MANDEVILLE, b. 1757 at New Cornwall, Orange Co., NY, m. 1784, Deborah Clark of Orange Co. Francis was s/o David Mandeville b. 30 Oct. 1717 in Hempstead, NY & wife Anna Horton b. Waverly & both d. in Orange Co. David was s/o David Davdit Mandeville & Jannetje Whoertendyk. FRANCIS' dau., Elizabeth, m. Isaac Seely above. The LDS Ancestral File on this family is extensive and traces the family to L.I. in the late 1600's.

## SLEY [SEELEY], SAMUEL     U2-49, C-10
of New Windsor, weaver.

In his will dated 28 Aug. 1786, SAMUEL SLEY names his children:

John.
Samuel.
Catharine.
William.
Elizabeth, m. --- Croos.
Mary, m. --- Croos.

Could be the Samuel Sealy who m. Mary Bartlet 4 Jan 1779 at Goshen or the Samuel Seely who m. Catherine Cox at the same place 4 Dec. 1780.

## SENIOR, GEORGE [P]                    A-410-11
of Montgomery.

WILLIAM SENIOR[1], b. 1785, with wife and 12 children from Dorsetshire, England to US in 1830, to Montgomery, where he d. 1863; wife, Sarah Harvey, d. 1880, aged 93. Their children:
William.
John.
Elizabeth.
Sarah
1814, **GEORGE.**
Thomas.
Christopher.
Ann.
Edward.
Joseph.
Louisa.
Henry.

GEORGE SENIOR[2], s/o William[1], b. Stower, Dorsetshire, England, came with parents to America. He was a Presbyterian & a farmer, settled in Duchess Co.; 1844 to Montgomery, merchant & RR dir.; m. 1842, Mary A., d/o Robert Lawson of Duchess Co. Children:
William, merchant of Montgomery.
Augustus, res. Newburgh.
Mary E., m. Cornelius D. Hawkins of Montgomery.
Sarah F., dec'd.
George Edward, merchant of Montgomery.
John L., res. KS.
James Renwick, res. NY.

## SERVIN, JOHN LANSING                    H-943

JOHN L. SERVIN, b. Spring Valley, Rockland Co., NY 6 Sept. 1835, atty. of NY City until 1865. He m. Sallie Ann Forsher of Warwick in 1864 & then removed to Warwick where he purchased the Warwick *Advertiser.* Member Reformed Dutch Church at Warwick, he d. there 8 Oct. 1881. Their children:
Abraham Forshee, atty. of Middletown.
Sara, m. Dr. Stephen W. Perry of Belchertown, MA.
John Magie of Warwick.
Walter Tinkey, d. young.

## SEWARD FAMILY OF WARWICK
## HON. WILLIAM HENRY [P]                    A-570
## & FRED W. SEWARD          H-943-4, LDS Anc. File

OBADIAH SEWARD[1] emigrated from Wales and settled on Larrington River, Somerset Co., NJ in early 1700's. [LDS Ancestral File lists him, or possibly one of his sons, as b. 1702, "probably" at Brookhaven, L.I. They give his wife as Isabel ---.] His children:
1724, Eliakim.
c. 1726, Susan, m. --- Davis.
c. 1728, Obadiah.
1728, Mehitable (Hettie), m. Nathan Cooper. They had Abraham Cooper who m. Nancy Wills; Nathan who m. Elizabeth Wills & Samuel who m. Betsey Brown.
1730, May 22, JOHN.
1732, James.
1733, Isaac, m. Phoebe ---.
1735, Lydia.
c. 1737, Samuel.
1758, Daniel, m. Ann Bishop.

JOHN SEWARD[2], s/o Obadiah[1], b. Black River, NJ, m. Mary Swezy 22 March 1751, and settled in Hardyston (Sussex Co., NJ) before 1767. John served as Col. in 2nd Sussex Regt. of militia in the Revolution. Children:
1752, Polly, m. Richard Edsall.
1754, Aug. 2, Obadiah, m. Hilah Edsall.
1756, Nancy.
1758, infant dau., unnamed.
c. 1760, Heliah, m. Josiah Hurd.
1760, April 15, Elizabeth, m. Jonathan Swezy, b. 5 March 1752. Their dau., Elizabeth Swezy m. Freegift Tuthill b. c. 1780. Other children, b. Goshen: Horace b. 1782, Virgil b. 1786, Thomas b. 1789, John Seward b. 1789 [sic] & Mary b. 1794.
1762, Hester.
1765, June 10, John, m. Mary Butler.
1768, Dec. 5, SAMUEL SWEZY.
1773, Israel, m. Elizabeth ---.

SAMUEL SWEZY SEWARD[3], s/o John[2], b. in Hardyston, m. Mary Jennings, of Irish parentage, of Goshen, in 1795. Mary b. 27 Nov. 1769. They res. in Vernon and removed to Florida, NY; physician, merchant & political office holder. Their children:
1793, Aug. 23, Benjamin Jennings, b. New Foundland, NJ & m. Marcia Armstrong, had 3 children: Rev. Augustus, Clarence, and one who d. young. [LDS Ancestral File gives their children as: Augustus b. 1820 & m. (1) Sarah Ann Finn & (2) Cornelia Seward Finn; Aurelia b. 1821; Benjamin Jenings b. 1827 & Clarence Armstrong b. 1828 who m. Caroline Steuben.
1795, Nov. 22, Elizabeth.
1799, June 21, EDWIN POLLADORE.
1801, May 16, **WILLIAM HENRY.**
1805, Oct. 29, Louisa, m. Dr. Mahlon D. Canfield of Florida, NY. Their children are (CANFIELD): Augusta b. c. 1825, Frederick Allen b. c. 1827, Caroline b. c. 1829, Cornelia b.

c. 1831 & Mary b. c. 1833.
1808, Aug. 24, George Washington, m. Tempe Wick Leddel.

EDWIN POLLADORE SEWARD[4], known as Polladore, s/o Samuel Swezy Seward[3]. He m. (1) Rachel Armstrong & (2) Mary E. Terry & had:
Mrs. Dr. Jayne.
Mrs. C. H. Schaiff.
William E.
Theodore W.
Jasper A.
1845, Aug. 27, **FREDERICK W.**

FREDERICK W. SEWARD[5], s/o Edwin P.[4], b. Goshen, studied medicine in NY City & practiced in Middletown. Traveled to NM for failing health in 1876; 1882 to Goshen, NY where he became a specialist in nerves & mental health disorders. He m. (1) Ella Armstrong of Florida, Orange Co., 27 Dec. 1866; she d. 1869 & left 2 children;
Ella.
Mattie.

DR. SEWARD[5] m. (2) 1875, Mattie Corey of Plainfield, NJ, and had:
Bertha, at home.
Edwin P., ranchman in NM.
Frederick W., Jr., M.D., in business with father.

HON. WILLIAM HENRY SEWARD[4], s/o Samuel Swezy Seward[3], was b. in Village of Florida, Orange Co.; in 1823 he res. Auburn; 1824 m. Frances Adeline, Judge Elijah Miller's (Cayuga Co.) youngest dau., b. 25 Sept. 1805. **WILLIAM H. SEWARD** served as Gov. of NY and in the Legislature of the US Senate & was appointed by Pres. Lincoln to the post of Sec. of State. He d. at Auburn 10 Oct. 1872, aged 72. Children:
Frederick A., ass't. sec. of state under his father. [Could be the Frederick William listed in LDS Files, b. 8 July 1830, m. Anna M. Wharton.]
1826, Oct. 1, Maj. [Henry] Augustus of US Army, dec'd.
1836, Aug. 25, Cornelia.
1839, June 18, William Henry of Auburn, m. Janet Mcneil Watson.
1844, Dec. 9, Frances Adeline.

SEYBOLT, JOHN L.                    H-944, C-12, 15, 16, 99
dairy farmer.

PAUL LEE SEYBOLT[1], b. 18 Aug. 1830, d. 8 July 1905, m. Antoinette ---, b. 4 July 1831, and had:
1854, July 28, **JOHN L.**
Horace G., of NY City in milk business.
Alva, atty. at Oneonta, Otsego Co.
Emma, m. J. C. Jordon of Middletown.

JOHN L. SEYBOLT[2], s/o Paul[1], b. on homestead 1 1/2 miles from Otisville; m. Alice W. Riter of Otisville 18 Dec. 1878,

she b. 13 June 1858, and had:
Violet, m. George Kaufman of Middletown.
Falter Lee, at school.

This family name appears in early Goshen church records: 2 Jan. 1787 John Saybolt m. Sarah Little. Katarena, d/o John Sailbolt & Mary Criszer his wife, was bapt. there 8 June 1774. Also 30 Dec. 1780 Francess Saybolt m. Alsup Vail & Frederick Saybolt m. Abigail Reeve 17 Jan. 1786.

SEYMOUR, WILLIAM                    TN-292-3

WILLIAM SEYMOUR[2], s/o Samuel[1], b. 13 April 1758 at Greenwich, CT, m. (1) Esther Sands of L.I., and had:
William, res. Brooklyn (1867).
Samuel Sands.
Drake, accidentally shot while hunting June 1824. A full account appears in E-225 under 'unusual events' of Town of Newburgh.
Esther.

WILLIAM[2] m. (2) Eliza, d/o Henry Powell of L.I., and had:
Margaret m. Joseph Kernochan.
Mary Powell, m. James S. Abell of the US Army.

WILLIAM to Newburgh c. 1790, merchant & ship builder. 1805 suffered an injury which rendered him unable to walk for the rest of his life. He d. 1811.

SHAFER, DANIEL                      GFM-33

DANIEL SHAFER, d. 28 Feb. 1843, aged 80 years, 11 months, 1 day. His wife was Eve Youngblood & she d. 26 Jan. 1852, aged 75 years, 8 months, 1 day. One of their children was:
Electeris (son), d. 10 Jan. 1849, aged 4 years, 11 months, 19 days.

All from tombstone inscriptions from German Reformed Church at Montgomery.

SHAFER, REV. JESSE F.      H-944-5, 373, GFM-34
of Newburgh.

REV. JESSE, b. Montgomery, 12 Oct. 1828, atty. of Goshen & Newburgh until 1857, when he formed partnership with his brother Joseph D., district atty. of Ulster Co., with offices in Kingston. 1861 enlisted in 56th NY Vol. Inf.; 1869-73 operated the Youngblood farm; 1877 was ordained Presbyterian minister & pastor of the Presbyterian Church at Audenried PA 5 years. Failure of his voice forced retirement; now chaplain of Ellis Post No. 52, GAR & the 56th Regt. Vet. Assoc. In 1892 m. Anna H. Crawford of Thompson's Ridge, she d. 10 June 1891. They have one child, Susie C., who m. Walter Carvey.

FREDERICK SHAFER was an early German setler at Town of Montgomery; first tanner in town. He had a son, Daniel, also a tanner. Buried in the German Reformed Cemetery in Montgomery is: Frederick Shafer, d. 21 July 1866, aged 79 years, 10 months, 12 days. Also Elsie his wife, d. 2 Oct. 1812, aged 22 years, 6 months & 13 days. Another wife of Frederick, Eleanore Comfort, b. 17 June 1797, d. 28 May 1880.

An earlier Frederick Schafer family is buried here: Frederick who d. 22 June 1841, aged 75 years, 7 months, 17 days & Elizabeth his wife, d. 6 Sept. 1841, aged 68 years, 4 months, 18 days.

In the same plot is buried: Nancy Maria Osburn, wife of George Shafer, d. 3 April 1846, aged 29 years, 5 months, 20 days & their dau. Elizabeth, d. 26 Aug. 1841, aged 3 years, 11 months, 18 days. Catharine A. Cavanaugh, wife of George Shafer, d. 23 May 1865, aged 47 years, 8 months, 22 days.

**SHANNON, WILLIAM H.**　　　　　　**H-945**
of Newburgh.

WILLIAM is desc. from Nathaniel Shannon, b. Londondery, Ireland in 1655; of Scottish ancestry. Nathaniel to America 1687, with Navy office of the Port of Boston & member of Old South Church. Some descs. moved to the South. One desc.:

Laydon Shannon[1] served as a Major in the War of 1812, and had a son, Charles[2]. Charles was a carpenter & m. Magdalen Gruver, both b. in Richmond, Northampton Co., PA, and had:
1840, April 22, **WILLIAM H.**

WILLIAM H. SHANNON[3], b. Richmond, PA, to Newburgh 1862 to take charge of the "slating of Vassar College" & became assoc. in business with the late John Galt. He has one son, William H., Jr., who is in roofing business with him.

**SHAW FAMILY OF MT. HOPE**　　　**A-506, H-945-6**
**SHAW, BENJAMIN WOODFORD (WOODWARD) [P]**
of Wallkill.　　　　　　　　　　　　**A-497-8**
**SHAW, ROBERT [P]**　　**A-169-70, C-86, 89, 111, 114**
physician.

This family early from Scotland to North of Ireland & from there to America. WILLIAM SHAW[1] settled at Mt. Hope before the Rev. War (1750). He came from Ireland & sent for his intended wife, Mary Waldron, who came from NY to New Windsor [sic]. WILLIAM d. 1822. Desc. include great-grandson Wickham T. Shaw[4], atty. of Middletown. William's children:
John.
1780, Oct. 30, **ROBERT.**
1782, Dec. 27, WILLIAM.
Bapt. 1786, Sept. 15, Samuel McCormick.
Alexander.
Henry. Goshen church records show the death of a Henry Shaw, Jan. 3, 1820, consumption, aged 32.
[Elizabeth?] Mrs. Benjamin Woodward.
1789, May 29, Mary.

DR. ROBERT SHAW[2], s/o William[1], b. in Mt. Hope, practiced at Westtown, Orange Co.; m. 1821, Aug. 4, Meliscent, d/o

Salmon Wheat of Wallkill. **ROBERT** d. 1848. Children:
William W. Goshen church records show the death of William W. Shaw, aged 2 years 7 months, burns.
Elizabeth W.
Mary W.
Robert Livingston.
William W. (2d)

WILLIAM SHAW[2], s/o William[1] & Mary, m. Rachel Schoonover b. 19 Dec. 1792, d. 18 Dec. 1876 & inherited the homestead, where he died, 25 March 1855. Their children:
Aaron, IL state atty., judge of the supreme court & congressman. Res. Olney, IL.
HOWARD.
1817, Feb. 3, BENJAMIN WOODWARD.
Mary Waldron, m. (1st) John Myer of NY; (2d) Edward Clapp of NY, who is now dec'd.
Catherine Wesbrook, m. William Howell of Middletown.
Peggy, m. Benjamin Beyea.
Alexander McMaken.
Susan Elizabeth, m. David Robertson of Shawangunk, Ulster Co.

HOWARD SHAW[3], s/o William[2] & Rachel, auctioneer, m. Clara A. Mapes and had:
Howard.
Charles
H. James Aaron.
Florence.
Howard is "the last male descendant in that line living."

BENJAMIN WOODWARD SHAW[3], s/o William[2], b. on homestead in Mt. Hope, d. 1881, March 29; merchant of Middletown, bank pres.; m. Louise, d/o David Reeve who came from L.I. c. 1763 and settled on a farm in Wawayanda. Louisa was b. 1814, Oct. 3. **BENJAMIN** was village trustee & member of the Presbyterian Church. Children:
Esther W., m. Irving Booth of Elmira.
Pauline D., m. T. N. Little of Middletown.
Hanford L., real estate & insurance man; d. 1881, May 20.
Netta L. (Annette), m. Wesley Bradner.

**SHAW, HARRY E.**　　　　　　　**H-946**
of Newburgh.

HARRY SHAW, b. in Newburgh in 1869, s/o the late Capt. George W. Shaw. He is with the firm of Thomas Shaw's Sons, feed business.

**SHAW, THOMAS JR. [P]**　　　　**A-360-61**
of Newburgh.

THOMAS[1] & JOHN SHAW, brothers, emigrated from Ireland in 1790 & settled in New Windsor, Orange Co., NY. THOMAS had 2 sons:
1799, June 12, **THOMAS JR.**
1803, Robert.

148

**THOMAS SHAW JR.**[2], s/o Thomas[1], was b. Clinton farm, Orange Co.; to Newburgh 1832, builder & carpenter; member Union Presbyterian Church, d. 6 Feb. 1877; m. (1st) Eleanor Burnett and had one son:
Samuel Crawford.

**THOMAS JR.**[2] m. (2d) Harriet, d/o John Walsh & grandau. of Samuel Logan. Surviving children:
1824, July 31, George W.
1827, July 29, Charles B.
1834, Dec. 27, Elkanah K.

**THOMAS JR.**[2] m. (3d) Jane, d/o John Walsh.

**SHAY, JOHN**                                              U2-91
of Newburgh.

In his will dated 6 Feb. 1792, **JOHN SHAY** mentions his wife Mary and children:
Hanna.
Mary.
Francis.

Executors: Robert, John & Francis Beatty. Will proved 10 May 1792, Isaac Hennion of Newburgh, farmer, Henry Lesear, Isaac Henion & Joseph Goldsmith.

**SHORT FAMILY OF WAWAYANDA**            A-682, C-14

JOHN SHORT, early settler at Millsbaugh had:
Son known as "Si Short."
Dau. m. John Eaton.

Goshen church records give the m. of a John Short to Margrett Oakly 14 Nov. 1782.

**SHUIT, HON. MORGAN [P]**               A-806, H-946-7
of Monroe.

ELISHA SHUIT[1], b. Eastchester, Westchester Co., NY, 12 June 1788; farmer, removed to Ridgefield, CT, having m. Sallie, d/o Joseph Mead, Esq., b. 3 April 1788. Children:
1810, Joseph M.
1812, Jan. 12, **MORGAN**.
1815, Mary Ann.
Ruth, d. infancy.

MORGAN SHUIT[2], b. Ridgefield, CT; 1833 to Orange Co.; 1837 in business at Highland Mills; 1867 to Monroe; j.p. 36 years & town supervisor. He m. (1st) Mary Ann Titus, d/o Isaac B., Esq. of Monroe, a family of Quaker desc. Mary Ann d. 1867. **MORGAN** m. (2d) Phebe B. Titus, sister of his first wife. He d. at Central Valley 29 July 1884. **MORGAN**'s children:
1847, Hannah.
1849, Mary Ann.
1851, William W.

1854, Sarah M.
1856, Elizabeth T.
1860, Harriet T.
1862, Phila M.

**SILLIMAN, COL. WILLIAM [P]**                    A-98

REV. JONATHAN SILLIMAN[1], pastor Presbyterian Church of Canterbury (still living), had one child, **COL. WILLIAM SILLIMAN**[2], b. 18 Oct. 1837, Canterbury, Orange Co., NY. **WILLIAM** is a teacher & atty., and after 1860 res. at Newburgh. During the Civil War he was a recruiter & served with Col. Morrison in the 2nd NY Cav., 124th NY Vols. of Orange Co. & 26th US Colored Troops. He d. at Beaufort, SC from the effects of a wound 18 March 1864, bur. Bloomfield, NJ. His wife was Mary L., d/o Hugh F. Randolph of Bloomfield, NJ.

**SINSABAUGH, ADAM H.**                           A-554
of Goshen.
**SINSAPAUGH, ADAM**        U2-33-4, C-38, 40, 47, 147
of Montgomery.                              GFM-10, 24

In 1730 the Sinsabaugh, Millspaugh, Bookstaver & Youngblood families left Germany & settled in the Town of Montgomery, Orange Co., NY.

JACOB SINSABAUGH[1] was naturalized at Albany in 1735. He had a son, FREDERICK[2], b. Town of Montgomery, who had the following children. All stayed in the vicinity.
**ADAM.**
Mary.
Elizabeth.
Betsy.
1758, HENRY.
Frederick.
Mrs. DeHart.
Abram.

ADAM SINSPAUGH'S[3] will, dated 1 Sept. 1785, names him as of Montgomery, mentions his wife (not named) & children:
Johannis.
David.
Mary.
Hannah.
Eve.
Elisabeth.

Will proved 16 May 1788 by Johannis Decker farmer of Montgomery, Jacob More & David Dickerson. There is an old tombstone in the German Reformed Church at Montgomery: "Charity, wife of Adam Sinsabaugh . . ." The recorder was unable to decipher the rest.

HENRY SINSABAUGH[3], m. Margaret, d/o John A. Brown of Easton, PA, who was the youngest of 14 children. Margaret d. 1842, aged 74. HENRY was a merchant at Nazareth, PA

& farmer in Sullivan Co. & Town of Montgomery, Orange Co., where he d. in 1826. He was a soldier of the Revolutionary War. Children:

Susan, m. Philip Gross.

Catharine, m. Daniel Plumley of Montgomery.

David, soldier of the Revolution.

1802, May 11, **ADAM H.**

**ADAM H. SINSABAUGH**[4], s/o Henry[3], b. Town of Montgomery; m. (1st) 23 Dec. 1824, Jemima, d/o Isaac Crissey of Montgomery, b. 22 Oct. 1799. Jemima d. 19 Feb. 1832 & is bur. at the German Reformed Cemetery at Montgomery. Left 1 child:

Elizabeth, m. 3 April 1850, William Sinsabaugh, of IA [Athens, PA], at Goshen.

**ADAM**[4] m. (2d) Jane Sinsabaugh, b. 1 Nov. 1809, d. 22 Sept. 1842. Children:

Kate, m. Goldsmith Gregory of IA, 19 Feb. 1858.

William.

James B., served 4 years in US Navy during Civil War & later in Hancock's Vet. Corps, stationed in IN, where he drowned in the White River.

**ADAM**[4] m. (3d), 1845, Elizabeth, d/o Henry Scofield of Goshen, who was b. 26 Aug. 1820 & d. 11 Jan. 1861. Their children:

George, dec'd.

Henry of Goshen. Could be the Henry Sinsabaugh of Goshen who m. Clara E. Valentine, also of Goshen, 26 July 1871.

**ADAM**[4] m. (4th) 1 Oct. 1861, Maria Jane, d/o Etting & Catharine (DuBois) France of Ulster Co., NY. Maria Jane was b. 3 Aug. 1833. Her mother Catharine was the d/o of Henry & granddau. of Methusalem DuBois, who was a lineal desc. of Louis DuBois, the progenitor of the DuBois family in Esopus. Children of 4th marriage:

Nellie J., m. Robert H. Andruss of NY City, 23 Dec. 1884.

Cora DuBois.

**ADAM**[4] served in town offices in Crawford & Goshen (1840); sheriff of Orange Co. (1843), member Presbyterian Church of Goshen.

Baptisms found in Goshen Church records: Catharine, George Washington & Henry, children of Adam H. & Mary Elizabeth Sinsebaugh, bapt. 3 Aug. 1850.

---

**SKINNER, CHARLES N.**                    H-947
physician of Port Jervis.

**DR. SKINNER**, b. at Port Jervis 9 March, 1866; at age 22 studied under Dr. W. L. Cuddeback & later grad. Bellevue, NY. He m. Mary B. Hiller of Tunkannock, PA 7 June 1892. Members Reformed Church of Port Jervis.

---

**SKINNER, NATHAN [P]**            A-752-3, C-12
of Deerpark.
**SKINNER FAMILY**                    **LDS Anc. File**

Seven brothers emigrated from England; four settled in Canada and the rest came to the US; two to NY and one to NJ.

**DANIEL SKINNER**[1] "was desc. from one of the brothers, was probably born in NJ" & during his minority removed to Orange Co., & d. there; m. Mary Smith of NY 6 April 1780, at Goshen. Children:

MOSES.

Jephtha.

Stephen.

7 daus.

**MOSES SKINNER**[2], s/o Daniel[1], b. Orange Co., to Canada in 1826; m. 17 Feb. 1807, Mary Archa, of Scottish ancestry; her parents res. at Red Hook on the Hudson. Surviving children:

Nelson.

Elisha.

1816, Sept. 7, **NATHAN.**

Julia Ann.

Moses O.

Joseph.

Salome.

Elizabeth.

Drayton R.

**NATHAN SKINNER**[3], s/o Moses[2], b. near Otisville, Orange Co.; to Canada with father and later to OH; carriage maker; to Port Jervis, NY, 1839 for 14 years; 1840 m. Aseneth, d/o John D. Carpenter whose family were early settlers at Carpenter's Point. She is a direct desc. of Maj. Johannes Decker. **NATHAN** was a supporter of the Reformed Dutch Church, farmer; retired 1853 & purchased resident on the east bank of the Neversink adj. Port Jervis. Their children:

Martha Ellen, dec'd.

1844, John N.; m. 1865, Anne M. Malven, b. Stroudsburg & later removed with her parents to IA; had two children: Charles H. & Julia, both now students.

The LDS Ancestral file contains records of another Skinner family of Orange Co. as follows.

**JOSEPH SKINNER**[1], s/o Ebenezer Skinner of Malden, MA, East Haddam & Bolton, CT & wife Sarah Lord, b. 17 Jan. 1707 at Cholchester, CT, m. Martha Kinne in CT 30 April 1729. Martha b. 20 Jan. 1712, d/o Thomas Kinne (Kuine) & Martha Cox of Preston, CT. JOSEPH d. 1755/59 near Damascus, Wayne Co., PA. They had:

1730, 13 Sept., Joseph; d. c. 1748

1731, Benjamin.

1733, Daniel.

1735, May 4, ABNER.

1737, Timothy.

1739, Huldah.

1741, Martha.

1743, Calvin.

1745, Lydia.

1747, Kezia.

1749, Joseph.

ABNER SKINNER[2], s/o Joseph[1], b. in CT, d. 4 Sept. 1806, Deerpark, NY. He m. Kesiah Gustin, b. 29 March 1738 at Glastonbury, CT. She was d/o John Gustin & wife Mary. They had:
1765, Benjah Abner.
1767, Joseph.
1769, Kesiah.
1770, Susanna.
1771, John.
1773, Mary Lydia (Polly).
1775, June 23, CYRUS.
1776, Israel.
1776, Jacob.

CYRUS SKINNER[3], b. Orange Co., NY & d. there 15 June 1865. He m. c. 1799, Mary Helms of Orange Co. where she was b. 29 Jan. 1777, d/o Thomas Helme [sic] of Suffolk Co., NY & wife Mary Youngs of Orange Co. Cyrus & Mary had:
1800, Joseph.
1802, CYRUS.
1805, Betsey.
1808, Abner Calvin.
1810, Mary H.
1812, Thomas H.
1816, William W.
1819, Elizabeth.
1822, Arminda.

CYRUS SKINNER[4], b. Orange Co. & d. there 1 Nov. 1871. He m. c. 1831, Susan Archer, b. c. 1808 in Westchester, NY. Children:
1832, Joseph.
1834, Miranda.
1835, Giles.
1836, Festus.
c. 1840, Charles Egbert, m. Matilda ---.
1844, Mary J.
1845, Reuben A.
1849, Susan A.

---

## SLAUGHTER, ALANSON [P]   A-501-2
of Wallkill.

The Slaughter family went from Wales to VA. ISAAC SLAUGHTER[1], soldier of the Revolution under Gen. Washington, after the war settled at Town of Wallkill and later to Shawangunk, Ulster Co.; 1803 back to Wallkill; 1819 to Hamptonburgh, where he d. in 1838, aged 84; farmer. He married twice and had a total of 21 children; 19 grew to adulthood. His 2d wife was Jane McBride, children named here:
Benjamin.
1794, Oct. 13, JOSEPH.
Archibald.
DeWitt.
Several daus.

All located in Orange Co.

JOSEPH SLAUGHTER[2], m. 16 Dec. 1817, Amelia, d/o Thomas Booth & Jane Barker of Hamptonburgh, b. 1798, d. 14 August 1877. JOSEPH was a member of the Presbyterian Church at Scotchtown, res. Hamptonburgh, Wallkill, j.p. & co. judge. Children:
1818, Aug. 31, ALANSON.
1826, July 5, Mary Louisa; m. John T. Coleman of Hamptonburgh.
Helen, d. young.

ALANSON SLAUGHTER[3], s/o Joseph[2], farmer of Wallkill, member of Scotchtown Presbyterian Church, banker; m. 11 Oct. 1843, Mary Ann, d/o Nathaniel Bailey (s/o Daniel from L.I.) & Jennet White of Wallkill. Mary Ann b. 15 Oct. 1817. Children:
Helen Jane, m. George W. Ackerly of Montgomery.
Jennet Bailey, m. Robert G. Young of Goshen.
Ann Amelia.

---

## SLAUGHTER, FRANK   H-947
dairy farmer.

FRANK SLAUGHTER, b. near Pine Island, NY 23 Feb. 1854, assisted his grandfather [unnamed] on the farm until he was aged 32; limestone business with the Empire Steel Co. of Castasaqua, PA. He m. Annie Lousie Wilson of Brooklyn, NY 16 Dec. 1885, and had:
1886, Sept. 20, Charles B.
1888, April 6, Clara Van Sickle, m. Grant Cooper of Pine Island.
1891, April 5, Fannie Louise, m. Russell S. Ferguson of New Milford.
1893, April 29, Jerry.
1898, Dec. 28, Lu Wilcox.
1902, Jan. 1, Audrey Wilson.

Members Presbyterian Church.

---

## SLOTT, ARTHUR   A-413, H-185-6
of Crawford.

The SLOTT family came from Holland to NY in 1670, then to Hackensack, NJ, later to Rockland Co., NY and to Montgomery on the Tinn Brock at what has been called Slott Town.
CORNELIUS SLOTT, farmer of Slott Town, served in the militia in 1777 & was taken prisoner by the British, to NY City 1785, back to Orange Co., 1790 & put up saw & grist mills on the Shawangunk Kill. His children (wife not named):
ARTHUR.
Johannes.
Cornelius.

---

## SMITH FAMILY OF BLOOMING-GROVE     A-632-3

COL. WILLIAM SMITH[1], b. England at Higham-Ferrers, Northamptonshire, 1655, Feb. 2. His descs. settled L.I. and are "denominated the Tangier Smiths, in contradistinction to Richard Smith's family, called Bull Smiths." In 1675 WILLIAM was appointed Gov. of Tangier by Charles II. He returned to England in 1683, m. Martha, d/o Henry Tunstall, Esq. of Putney, Co. Surrey, 26 Nov. 1675. They arrived NY 6 Aug. 1686, purchased land at Brookhaven, where was erected St. George's Manor. He served as a justice & d. 17 Feb. 1705. Their surviving children:
1679, Henry, b. Tangier; d. 1767, aged 88.
1690, March 13, WILLIAM HENRY.
Patty.
Gloriana.
Charles Jeffrey.

WILLIAM HENRY SMITH[2], s/o William[1], settled at Mastic; m. (1st) Miss --- Merritt of Boston and had one son:
Merritt.

WILLIAM HENRY[2] m. (2d) Hannah Cooper, and had:
1720, WILLIAM.
Caleb.
Elizabeth.
Sarah.
Martha.
Jane.
Hannah.

WILLIAM SMITH[3], s/o William Henry[2], served in public office, d. 17 March 1799; m. (1st) Mary, d/o Daniel Smith of Smithtown and had:
John, senator of Suffolk Co.
Mary.

WILLIAM[3] m. (2d) Ruth, sister of Gen. Woodhull of Suffolk, and had:
Jesse.
William.
Nathaniel Dubois.
Ruth Hester.

## SMITH FAMILY OF GOSHEN     A-525, 560c
## SMITH, STEPHEN [P]     C-40-1, 104, 115
of Goshen.

HENRY SMITH[1], b. England, settled Goshen, Orange Co., c. 1743; m. Joanna ---, and had:
Henry.
Stephen.
CALEB.
Abigail.
Phebe.
Joanna.
Elizabeth.

Hannah.

CALEB SMITH[2], s/o Henry[1], d. 1784; his children:
Henry C.
STEPHEN.
Caleb.
John.
1779, June 4, Joshua.
Abby, m. Major Tusten.

STEPHEN SMITH[3], s/o Caleb[2], b. on the homestead in Orange Co., m. 1765, Sarah, d/o Benjamin Conkling whose ancestor settled early on L.I. after a time in CT. STEPHEN was a member of the Presbyterian Church at Goshen. Sarah b. 1765, d. 27 April 1818. He d. on the homestead 1824, May 31. Children:
1786, Jan. 24, Elizabeth, m. James Van Duzer.
Abigail, m. Henry Smith.
1792, Aug. 19, Benjamin Conkling, soldier in War of 1812.
Sarah, m. Josiah Smith.
1799, June 16, STEPHEN.
Joseph R.
John A.

STEPHEN SMITH[4], s/o Stephen[3], b. on homestead, business-man, Presbyterian Church member, town assessor; m. 19 Dec. 1822, Matilda, b. 15 Dec. 1804, d. 28 Jan. 1881, d/o Timothy Wood & Dolly Carpenter. Timothy's mother one of 6 daus. of Henry Smith. Children:
Sarah E., widow of Oliver B. Vail of Middletown. They m. 23 Dec. 1857, at Goshen. There is a record of Sarah E. Smith of Goshen m. Rev. Oscar Harris 15 Nov. 1860.
Stephen Augustus, m. Harriet A., d/o John B. & Hetta A. (Horton) Hulse of Wallkill.

-----

## SMITH, ARTHUR     U2-158
of Highlands Precinct.

In his will dated 17 March 1756, ARTHUR SMITH names brother Leonard, wife Keziah and children:
Joel.
Arthur.
David.

-----

## SMITH, CHARLES PARSHALL [P]     A-173-4

ISAAC SMITH[1], b. Jamaica, L.I., 8 March 1755, d. 14 Oct. 1836; to Orange Co. with parents at age 12. Farmer at Town of Chester, m. Mehetebal, d/o Joshua Wells, who was a desc. of Hon. William Wells, atty. of England, b. near Norwich 1608; settled L.I., high sheriff of New Yorkshire. "His [William's] great grandson John, being the first settler of the family in Orange Co. & d. there 4 July 1776." Mehetebal was b. 14 March 1768 & d. 22 Nov. 1831. Children of Isaac & Mehetebal:
Parshall, dec'd.
Hezekiah, dec'd.

Joanna, m. Isaac Van Duzer; dec'd.
1800, Dec. 22, ISAAC.
Sarah, dec'd.
Julia Ann, dec'd.
1808, April 17, Eliza Jane, m. Abram Demerest, still living.

ISAAC SMITH[2], s/o Isaac[1], farmer of West Milford, NJ; later to
    Chester, NY, merchant, Presbyterian Church at West Milford,
    d. 19 April 1850. He m. (1st) Katy Maria, d/o James Smith,
    b. 7 Feb. 1803, d. 19 April 1838. Children:
Joanna, m. John Yeomans of Troy, PA.
1825, Jan. 7, Sarah, m. George W. Vreeland; d. 4 Oct. 1857.
1827, Feb. 27, CHARLES PARSHALL.
Oscar F., farmer of West Milford.
1832, Feb. 24, Phebe Jane, d. 18 Feb. 1855, unm.
1834, April 3, James M., d. 10 March 1864.
Amzil, ME clergyman.

ISAAC SMITH[2] m. (2d) Mary K. DeKamp, b. 12 Aug. 1806, d.
    14 Oct. 1855 and had:
Julia Elizabeth, m. George W. Masten of Chester.

CHARLES PARSHALL SMITH[3], s/o Isaac[2], m. (1st) Caroline,
    d/o Thomas C. Jennings of Edenville, NY, 8 June 1853; she
    d. 27 March 1854, no issue. He m. (2d) Susan, d/o Jacob
    Feagles of Amity, Orange Co., who d. 15 June 1857, no
    issue. CHARLES m. (3d) Susan, d/o John B. Randolph of
    Brooklyn, NY, 2 Nov. 1859. Susan was b. 13 March 1838.
    Their surviving children:
Mary L.
Henry B.
Charles P.
Anna N.
Joseph H.
William H.

**SMITH, GEORGE** [P]    A-519-20, H-948, C-13, 88, 97
of Mt. Hope.

This Smith family is of Dutch extraction. GEORGE SMITH[1]
    was a resident of Goshen, to Wallkill Township, where he d.;
    m. Mary Tyler 22 March 1781, and had a son IRA[2], who had
    in Sept. 1800, a son GEORGE[3] in Wallkill Township. This
    GEORGE[3] removed to Mt. Hope, farmer; m. Sallie, d/o
    Robert Crawford of Crawford Township. GEORGE d. 28
    Feb. 1899, and had:
Robert C.
Charles. Could be the same Charles featured on H-947-8, b. in
    Howells in 1861, civil engineer; m. Minnie A. Holland of
    Howells in 1890.
William H.
Gabriel S. A Gabriel Smith appears in the death records for
    Goshen church, d. 19 Jan. 1823, age 41, "Intemp." Also an
    infant of a Gabriel Smith d. 6 Sept. 1836, so clearly there
    were more than one of the name in Goshen in the time
    period. Children of a Gabriel & Sally Smith, all bapt. 23
    Feb. 1812 are: Harriet, Milton, Emeline, Eliza Jane, Oscar &

Hannah.
Mary E.
1835, Feb. 8, **GEORGE**.
Oren.
Ira.
Sarah F.

**GEORGE SMITH[4]**, s/o George[3], b. Otisville, merchant &
    public servant. He m. Cynthia Green of Otisville.

**SMITH, GILBERT** [P]    A-808-9
of Monroe.

CLARK SMITH[1], Esq., b. Cornwall-on-the Hudson, had
    children:
Joseph.
ASAHEL.
Oliver.
Clark.
Isaac.
Thomas.
Rensselaer.
Elijah.
Hannah.
2 d. infancy.

ASAHEL SMITH[2], s/o Clark[1], b. Woodbury, Township of
    Monroe, d. 1866, March at Turner's; m. Elizabeth, d/o
    Gilbert Turner, and had:
1816, Oct. 1, **GILBERT T.**
Charles.
John T.
Hannah, m. King Rider.
Stephen.

GILBERT T. SMITH[3], s/o Asahel[2], b. at Turner's; 1839 to NY
    City, carter, real estate dealer; 1875 returned to Monroe,
    Presbyterian church member; m. 8 Feb. 1842, Olive, d/o
    Matthew Graham of Blooming-Grove, and had:
Alice G., dec'd.
1846, Oct. 27, **WARREN W.** (M?).
Child, d. infancy.

WARREN W. SMITH[4] (M?), s/o GILBERT T.[3], m. 27 Oct.
    1868, Sarah, d/o William Seaman, Esq. of Monroe & had:
Edward P.
Alice G.

**SMITH, JAMES**    U2-140, TN-265-6, CN-20
of Newburgh.

In his will dated 25 Feb. 1747, **JAMES SMITH** names his wife
    as Mary, and his sons:
William.
Benjamin.
Ephraim.
James.

JAMES SMITH[1], b. England, to America c. 1735; settled temporarily in NY City & then to Newburgh, where he purchased from heirs of Joshua Kockerthal in 1741, Lot #5 in the original division of the German Patent. He is probably the James Smith cited above. In the Newburgh Directory for 1750 there were four Smiths: William, James, Henry & Thaddeus. William was a blacksmith; James Smith is described as a "plain Irish farmer." JAMES' son:

BENJAMIN SMITH[2], resided on the homestead until "after the War," when he erected the house at present occupied by Eli Hasbrouck on Liberty St. He held office in the local militia in the Rev., but was jailed in Kingston in 1777 & his property confiscated & he suspected of English sympathies. He was paroled & returned to Newburgh & brought suit against the community to receive value of his property.

BENJAMIN[2] m. 16 June 1761, Elizabeth Leonard. He d. in 1813. They had:
Betsey, m. Aaron Fairchild.
Mary, m. John Anderson.
Jane, m. Robert Gardiner.
WILLIAM.
Abigail, m. Thomas Hinds.
James, lost at sea.
Benjamin, d. unmarried.
Bridget, m. Jonathan Carter.
Catharine, m. Henry Tudor.

WILLIAM SMITH[3], farmer & merchant of Newburg, m. Maria Cole of Kingston, and had:
1803, July 30, Benjamin, m. Caroline Knox Thatcher, grandau. of Gen. Knox; res. Kingston.
1805, April 29, Catharine C., m. John E. Parmelee.
1807, Dec. 11, William P. C., m. Glorianna Butterworth.
1809, Dec. 23, John Fletcher, m. Nancy Thompson; now dec'd.
1812, Nov. 30, Gardiner, m. Jane Cole of Kingston.
1815, Feb. 24, Elizabeth, unm.
1817, Aug. 6, Cornelius C., m. Margaret DeWitt of Kingston, where he now resides.
1820, Jan., Maria C., m. Thomas H. Booth; d. 11 July 1854.
1823, Dec. 14, Richard C., unm., res. Newburgh.
Ann Eliza, d. young.

---

SMITH, JOHN J. [P]                    A-556-6, STJ-56, 64
of Goshen.

JOB SMITH[1] (b. 26 Sept. 1745, d. 6 Aug. 1776), soldier of the Revolution; d. as a result of injury in the War; m. Sarah Ogden (b. 29 March 1752, d. 11 May 1827), and had:
Mary Mitchell.
Sarah, m. Elias Darby.
1772, Oct. 27, JOHN JOB.

JOHN JOB SMITH[2], b. Elizabethtown, NJ, blacksmith; m. 22 Jan. 1797, Phebe, d/o John Jewell, b. 11 July 1774, d. 23 Nov. 1835. JOHN JOB d. 9 July 1814. Children:
1798, Aug. 20, Job; d. 10 Jan. 1800.
1800, Aug. 19, JOHN JEWELL.

1803, Aug. 27, Ogden, res. Elizabeth; d. 8 Feb. 1851.

JOHN JEWELL SMITH[3], b. Elizabeth, NJ, apprenticed to tin trade with Gould Phinney of Elizabeth; 1824 to Goshen; partnership with Henry Merriam; 1849 opened hardware store & retired 1869. Member St. James' Church at Goshen; JOHN JEWELL d. 4 June 1880. 5 Dec. 1838, m. Ellen, d/o Moses & Eleanor (Holly) Sawyer of Minisink. Moses was the s/o James & Elizabeth (Bradner) Sawyer of Goshen. Ellen b. 23 Feb. 1817, d. 23 March 1864. Children:
1839, Sept. 20, Mary Ellen; d. 1 Nov. 1858.
1843, Sept. 11, Julia; m. 27 Oct. 1869 at St. James Rectory, William D. Van Vliet, merchant of Goshen; d. 28 July 1880; two children: John Jewell & Julia Marion.
John Ogden of Goshen.

---

SMITH, SILAS                          E-109-10

Lot #5, Village of Newburgh, was sold by patentee to SILAS SMITH[1]. The land descended to his son, JAMES[2], who devised it to his son BENJAMIN SMITH[3]. BENJAMIN sold the western part of the land to Thomas Woolsey & in 1782 laid out the east part into streets & blocks under the name of Washington. On his death, the land descended to his children: William L. Smith, Catharine Tudor & Abigail Hind.

---

SMITH, SOLOMON T. [P]        A-658a, C-34-5, 81, 98
of Hamptonburgh.

DERRICK SMITH[1] from Glasgow, Scotland to Orange Co. c. 1750, where he m. Hannah Gale and had:
1757, Jan. 5, Martha.
1759, March 3, Alexander.
1761, July 9, Alletta.
1763, Nov. 1, DANIEL.
1766, Jan. 20, Abel.
1768, Oct. 20, James.
1771, March 30, Mary.

DANIEL SMITH[2] 1805 settled in Wallkill (now Hamptonburgh), farmer; m. Tabitha, d/o Solomon & Tabitha (Watkins) Tuttle. DANIEL d. 25 Aug. 1810, aged 47, pleurisy. Children: (All dec'd. except Martha & Alex.)
1788, Dec. 21, GRANT.
Derrick.
Harriet.
Nathan.
Martha, res. Western NY.
Hilia Ann.
1803, April 10, Alexander, res. Hamptonburgh.
Ichabod L.
Daniel.

GRANT SMITH[3], m. Miriam, d/o Jesse Smith, 30 Jan. 1811. Jesse, b. 17 Oct. 1758, was a soldier of the Revolution & farmer of Orange Co.; m. Elizabeth Ansely; Miriam was the 4th of their 11 children. She d. 17 Nov. 1878, aged 80.

GRANT served in the War of 1812; businessman & farmer. Children:

Sarah Jane, m. John M. Miller of Wallkill 26 Oct. 1833 in Hamptonborough; res. IN.

1815, Jan. 10, **SOLOMON T.**

William A., farmer of WI, m. Martha Watkins of Orange Co.

Elizabeth, m. Richard S. Denton of Vernon, NJ, 18 Jan. 1837.

Harriet M., m. (1st) Henry B. Smith; (2d) Nathaniel D. Smith (brothers).

**SOLOMON T. SMITH**[4], b. on homestead in Orange Co., farmer, member Goshen Presbyterian Church, m. Mary, d/o Wickham & Catharine Tuttle (Tuthill) 20 Nov. 1850, and had:

Wickham T.

Martha, dec'd.

Mary d. 7 April 1870; **SOLOMON** d. 27 Nov. 1876.

---

**SMITH, WILLIAM**                              U1-152
of Montgomery, Yeoman.

**WILLIAM SMITH**, in his will dated 14 Aug. 1784, names his wife Elizabeth, his son Henry & his granddau. Mary Bookstaver. He also names his good friend Adam Beamer, whom he appointed executor. Will proved in Jan. 1791 by John McKenstry, who was also a witness, as were Matthew Hunter & William Johnston.

---

**SMITH, WILLIAM**                              GFM-3

**WILLIAM SMITH**, d. 15 Feb. 1858, aged 69 years, 6 months, 19 days. His wife was Margaret, d. 11 March 1838, aged 46 years, 6 months, 18 days. They had:

Caroline, d. 26 Oct. 1826, aged 11 years, 5 months, 1 day.

Theodore, d. 8 Oct. 1830, aged 5 months, 19 days.

Taken from tombstone inscriptions at German Reformed Cemetery at Montgomery.

---

**SMITH, WILLIAM J.**                           H-949
dairy farmer, Hamptonburgh.

**WILLIAM** was b. 21 Jan. 1851 on homestead farm, one mile from Neelytown, s/o Foster & Sarah W. (Waite) Smith. He m. Lizzie Burns of Newburgh 7 Dec. 1876, and had:

Frank W. of Ulster Co.

Nellie, at home.

Members Presbyterian Church of Montgomery.

---

**SNODGRASS, REV. BENJAMIN & REV. W. D. [P]**
of Goshen.                                      A-535-6

**REV. BENJAMIN SNODGRASS**, b. Doylestown, PA, grandson of James Snodgrass, whose parents came from the North of Ireland c. 1700 & settled in Doylestown, Bucks Co.,

PA, where his father, also James, was b. in 1761.

**BENJAMIN**[1] was a Presbyterian minister, settled in West Hanover, Dauphin Co., PA (1784), where he d. 1846. He m. Martha Davis of Philadelphia, and had 6 children, among them:

Dau., m. --- Simonton & had Rev. Ashbel Green Simonton, missionary to Brazil, founder of the First Presbyterian Church in Rio Janeiro & d. early in life.

1796, June 30, **REV. W. D.** (youngest but one of the six children).

**REV. W. D. SNODGRASS**[2], s/o Rev. Benjamin[1], studied in Dauphin Co., PA, at Washington College (PA) where he grad. in 1815, Philadelphia & Princeton. He served in VA, NC, GA NY & NJ. 9 Dec. 1823, m. Charlotte H. Moderwell of Lancaster, PA, niece of William Kirkpatrick an elder of the Presbyterian Church in Lancaster. 1849 to Goshen at age of 85 [sic].

[NOTE: This family entry is very confusing. Dates do not add up & it is hard to distinguish whether they are speaking of Rev. W. D. or his father Benjamin.]

---

**SNYDER FAMILIES OF CRAWFORD**      H-185-6, U2-27

**JOHANNES SNYDER** started a small settlement in the vicinity of Searsville, where he built a primitive log mill, which is in the records of 1768 as Snyder's Mill. The family was Dutch & made the first settlement as early as 1740.

A **JOHANNES SNIDER** of Montgomery made a will 4 Oct. 1787, in which he names his two sons, John & Henry. The will was proved 29 Jan. 1788 by Samuel Fargeson farmer of Montgomery, Christian Rump & William Steuart. Executors named were Dr. David Galeshie, Capt. Henry Smith & John Comfor. **JOHANNES** mentions his wife, but not by name.

---

**SNYDER, MICHEL GEDNEY [P]**                   A-412
of Mongtomery.

**WILLIAM SNYDER**[1], of German desc., res. east of St. Andrews, Twp. of Montgomery, farmer, m. Elizabeth Redmond. WILLIAM d. 12 Sept. 1829, aged 76. Children:

Catharine.

John.

William.

Elizabeth.

Abram.

Jane.

1804, July 28, MICHEL.

Phebe.

**MICHEL SNYDER**[2] s/o William[1], b. Montgomery; 1824 m. Priscilla Mullenix of Newburgh; MICHEL d. 11 Jan. 1873. Children:

William, dec'd.

Henry, dec'd.

1833, Aug. 7, MICHAEL GEDNEY.
Gedney, dec'd.
Abram.
John James, dec'd.

MICHAEL GEDNEY SNYDER[3], s/o Michel[2], b. Montgomery, farmer, member Reformed Dutch Church of Walden; 8 Oct. 1861, m. Catharine Louisa, d/o John & Frederika Moadinger of NY City, wid. of Alexander Gedney. She has one dau. by her first marriage, Alice Gedney, who m. Henry Seeley.

## SPAULDING, JOHN        A-194, TN-317
newspaperman of Newburgh.

JOHN SPALDING, s/o Rev. Joshua Spalding a Presbyterian minister, b. Salem, MA Jan. 1800; to Newburgh 1815 with his father. JOHN was apprenticed to Ward M. Gazlay, then of the *Political Index*, until 1822 when he began publishing the *Newburg Gazette*; in 1833-4 sold out & started the *News Journal*, which he continued until his death, changing the name to the *Highland Courier*. He m. Elizabeth L., d/o of Rev. John Johnston of Newburgh. They had several children (unnamed here). JOHN d. 22 Aug. 1853, after an illness of 2 days.

## STANTON FAMILY        T-52
## STANTON FAMILY OF MT. HOPE
### A-506, LDS Anc. File

A Stanton family of CT spent an early winter alone in Shehawken (Hancock) area & almost starved to death. Their story in T-52.

RUFUS STANTON settled near Finchville, and had:
Joseph, now res. Finchville, aged 87.
Samuel.
Nathaniel.
Jonathan.
Mrs. Ezra Hoyt.

The LDS Ancestral File gives the following family:
SAMUEL STANTON[1], b. c. 1713, m. Rebecca Worden & had:
AMOS STANTON[2], b. 26 Feb. 1739 at Stockbridge, MA. He m. Marcy Davis, also b. Stockbridge in 1744, d/o Isaac Davis & wife Charity Hall. They had son:
RUFUS STANTON[3], b. 1788 at Maryville, Montgomery Co., NY & m. Minerva Belknap. This could be the Rufus above.

## STAUNTON, BENJAMIN        E-224

Under 'unusual incidents' & dated 25 May 1808, "On Saturday last, the boy of Mr. Benjamin Staunton, noted to have been drowned in a previous paper, was found in the Hudson River c. 1 mile above the village of Newburgh. He had been fishing with David Vance & a coroner's jury pronounced that Staunton was murdered by Vance . . ."

## STERRIT, L.S.        H-949-50

L. S. STERRIT, s/o Thomas & Jane, of Scotch-English extraction who came to America after their marriage & res. at Coldham, beside the old Presbyterian Church, where L. S. was born 17 Feb. 1852. He studied law under George H. Clark at Newburgh & later under Judge James W. Taylor. L. S. d. 4 April 1907.

## STEVENS, JOSEPH F.        H-949
postmaster of Highland Falls.

JOSEPH, b. Highland Falls 1864, was in hotel business with his father, George Stephens [sic], who built Highland Falls Hotel in 1864. JOSEPH m. Lucetta Faurot, d/o Capt. Theodore, desc. of one of the oldest families in Highland.

## STEWARD/STEWART FAMILY OF GOSHEN
### H-230-32, 950-1

Two brothers, JOHN & WALTER STEWARD from Scotland to Ireland with a nurse who said that they were the sons of a man of rank who would come for them. The boys were brought up by a guardian & never claimed. They went from Ireland to New England c. 1740.

JOHN STEWARD[1], Rev. patriot, acquired property in Boston & later settled in Goshen (1744); farmer, blacksmith; m. Elizabeth Bradner, d/o Rev. John of Goshen. They had 8 children, those named here:
JOHN II, during Rev. War forged sabres & bayonets for the Continental Army, j.p.
Nathan.
Elizabeth, m. Hanibal Hopkins, s/o Gen. Reuben.

JOHN II[2] had a son, JOHN III[3], b. Goshen, to NY City for 40 years as a dry goods merchant. His 2d son, DANIEL JACKSON STEWARD[4], b. 1816 in NY City, who grad. from Princeton & is a fellow of the National Academy of Design, musician & artist. DANIEL is desc. through the maternal line from Isaac Townsend of Oyster Bay, L.I. & Capt. John Underhill, famous Indian fighter.

WALTER STEWARD[1], brother of John I, settled in RI where he started a snuff mill. His son was Gilbert STUART[2], the noted portrait painter who changed the spelling of his name because of his admiration for Bonnie Prince Charlie & the Jacobite cause.

## STEWART FAMILY OF WAWAYANDA        A-681, C-12

JAMES STEWART[1], early settler of Wawayanda, had:
Silas.
Luther. Could be the Luther Steward m. Keziah Carpenter 2 April 1780 at Goshen.
JOHN.
William, shot at Peenpack by the Indians.

Mrs. Nathan Arnout.
Mrs. William Stewart.

JOHN STEWART[2], s/o James[1], had a son LEWIS[3], now of Ridgebury.

___

**STILL, EDWIN F.**                                            **H-951**

EDWIN was b. Catskill, Greene Co., NY 30 Aug. 1878; served in Co. E, 2d NY Vol. in war with Spain; worked in Arnold's Photographic Studios in Warwick in 1901. Member Episcopal Church; m. Matilda Carson, d/o Thomas of Warwick

___

**STILLMAN, REV. JONATHAN [P]**                   **A-770**
of Canterbury.

REV. JONATHAN STILLMAN grad. Yale Class of 1817, taught one year at Andover; preached in VA; 1835 became pastor of Canterbury Presbyterian Church, Cornwall, Orange Co., until 1862. He presently res. at Canterbury at age 88. 15 Sept. 1832 m. Anna, d/o Rev. Amzi Armstrong, for 2 years pastor of the Presbyterian Church at Mendham, NJ. Rev. Armstrong's Scotch-Irish ancestors res. Enniskillen, Ireland & settled in L.I. c. 1727 & later in Warwick. The Stillman's had one son, William, atty. who d. in the late war.

___

**STINGHAM, REAR ADM. SILAS HORTON**       **A-488**
of Wallkill.                                    [See Stringham.]

JAMES STRINGHAM[1] settled Orange Co. as early as 1734. His son DANIEL[2] res. east of the village of Bloomingburgh, Town of Wallkill, storekeeper; m. --- Horton; to Newburgh 1806. DANIEL's son:

SILAS STINGHAM[3], b. 1798, Bloomingburgh, d. 1876. Apprenticed to the Navy at age of 12; served as midshipman with Capt. Ludlow under Comm. Rogers. Was in the Navy his whole life.

___

**STIVERS, MOSES DUNNING [P]**            **A-198-99 &**
**STIVERS, MOSES A., M.D.**                     **H-951**
of Middletown, newspaperman.

RANDAL STIVERS[1], b. Middlesex Co., NJ, res. Sussex Co., Twp. of Frankford, had a son:
JOHN STIVERS[2], b. 22 March 1828, Middlesex Co., NJ. Settled on farm near Beemerville, NJ, where all his children were born; 1845 removed to Ridgebury, Orange Co. 3 Oct. 1802, m. Margaret Dunning, b. near Scotchtown, Orange Co., 1 July 1803. She is still living at the age of 87 & was the d/o Jonathan & Rachel Crans Dunning. The Dunning family to Wantage, Sussex Co., c. 1806. Jonathan soldier of War of 1812. JOHN STIVERS d. 21 Feb. 1865. Children:
1855, Swept. 26, **MOSES D.**
Randal.
Jesse Lewis, Co. B., 56th Regt. NY Vol. (10th Legion).

**MOSES DUNNING STIVERS**[3], m. 26 Feb. 1855, Mary Elizabeth Stewart, 2d dau. of Lewis of Town of Wawayanda, Orange Co. **MOSES** storekeeper at Ridgebury; 1859 to Middletown, merchant, co. clerk (1864-68); 1868 purchased Orange Co. Press, postmaster of Ridgeway, served gov't. posts (late 1860's). Children:
Mary Ellen, m. Edwin T. Hanford of Middletown.
Louis Stewart.
John Dunning.
Cristina Stewart.
1872, Nov. 14, MOSES ASHBY.

MOSES ASHBY STIVERS[4], M.D., b. Middletown, connected with the house staff at NY Hospital & the NY Cancer Hospital; m. Lillian C. Hummell of Port Jervis & they had:
Mary Van Etten.

___

**STOREY, JONAS**                          **A-144, TN-309-10**

JONAS STOREY [STORER], b. Norwich, CT, 11 July 1778, d. 22 Sept. 1848. He changed the spelling of his name from Storer to Storey; teacher of Poughkeepsie, then to Newburgh, atty. & j.p. He m. Mary, d/o Isaac Schultz of New Windsor, and had:
Henry E., m. Rebecca Cook; dec'd.
Edwin, m. Abbey Basset Clark; dec'd.
Helen E., m. Orville M. Smith; dec'd.
Mary B., m. Daniel Smith.
Nathan S., m. Harriet Smith; dec'd.

___

**STRINGHAM, DANIEL**                                    **T-35**

DANIEL STRINGHAM[1] (Capt.), who m. Abigail Horton 1794, one of the first settlers of Middletown, had a family of 10 children, all b. there. One son.
SILAS HORTON STRINGHAM[2] became a noted naval officer who served in the War of 1812, Mexican War & Civil War. He d. 1876.

___

**STRONG FAMILY OF BLOOMING-GROVE**
**H-140-1, 233-4, 952**

JOHN STRONG, from England in 1629, settled in East MA. Desc.:
NATHANIEL STRONG[1] from L.I. m. Hannah, d/o Maj. Nathaniel Woodhall; he was a Maj. in the Continental Army. Nathaniel Strong was murdered at his home by Claudius Smith, 6 Oct. 1778; their son:
SELAH STRONG[2], 1st supervisor of Blooming Grove, having been j.p. of Town of Cornwall for 10 years. His son:
SELAH E. STRONG[3], superintendent of Blooming-Grove (1875-82), sheriff of Orange Co. (1888-90), survived by his widow & one son, Sherwood Strong. The Strong family homestead, home of 7 generations of Strongs, was known as "Maple Hurst" in Town of Blooming Grove, where Selah E. was b. 1843 & he d. there July 1905. [NOTE: Selah E. Strong is given as the great-great-grandson of Nathaniel, who was

murdered in 1778, in one place, and as his grandson in another.] He. m. 1873, Stella K. Hetzel of Florida, NY, desc. from old Rev. family, and had:

H. Sherwood, of NY City.

Edith, m. A. J. Norton of Saugerites, NY.

Claudius Smith was taken prisoner at Smithtown, L.I. & was publically executed Jan. 22, 1779 in Goshen for the murder of Nathaniel Strong.

---

## STRONG, GEORGE H.                    H-951-2

**GEORGE**, b. Blooming-Grove Aug. 1867; in business with Knight & Conklin 8 years; 1891 purchased feed & grain business of H. K. Wood of Warwick & 1897 in business with W. S. Board & Co. of Vernon, NJ & others. He m. Emma, d/o Henry Mapes, 10 Oct. 1888, and had:

Stella.

Harry.

Julia.

---

## STUBLEY, INGHAM                    H-952
clerk, Bd. of Supervisors in Newburgh since 1868.

**INGHAM STUBLEY**, b. in England, 1853; bookkeeper for Haigh & Mellor, woolen manufactures for 12 years; 1880 with father, William, established rag, iron & metal business. He m. Nancy J. Dickerson of Orange Co., 1875 & had two sons, William & Charles G., both in business with their father.

---

## STULL, GEORGE C.                    H-952-3

**GEORGE** is the s/o Henry J. & Mary (Fine) Stull. He was b. 7 June 1864 at Belvidere, NJ. At age 15 started in milk business, removed to Goshen 1890, retail candy & ice cream business. Member Presbyterian Church of Goshen.

---

## STURR, GEORGE W.                    H-953
of Florida, NY.

**GEORGE** was b. Herney, Hudson Co., NJ, 26 Oct. 1845, s/o Daniel R. & Sarah Sturr, the 3rd son of 5 children. At age 7 left home & went to Brooklyn, NY until age 21. Clerk in Danbury, CT; 1881 assoc. with manufacturing company in NY City; 1894 to Florida, NY where he still res. He m. Mary Louise Gregory of Ulster Co. 1867; she d. 25 April, 1906. They had:

2 sons, dec'd.

Alberta L.

Ada Cressie.

---

## SUTHERLAND FAMILY OF CORNWALL          A-755-56

Two sons of William Sutherland[1], Alexander & David, settled early in Cornwall.

ALEXANDER[2] was buried the day Ft. Montgomery was captured (1777); m. --- Mac Gregorie. Children:

ALEXANDER.

David.

Andrew.

ALEXANDER SUTHERLAND[3], s/o Alexander[2], had:

John D.

ANDREW.

David.

Mrs. John DuBois.

ANDREW SUTHERLAND[4], had:

Daniel.

David., atty.

Both west west.

---

## SUTHERLAND, ALEXANDER C.            H-953
farmer, Supt. of the Poor for co.

**ALEXANDER C. SUTHERLAND** was b. Central Valley, 9 June 1855; m. 17 Jan. 1883, Elizabeth Cooper of Central Valley, and had (living children):

Harriet C.

Martha C.

Clara E.

Annie M.

There is a portrait of Alexander C. Sutherland, H-235.

---

## SUTTON, MINARD [P]                   A-624-5
of Chester.

The Sutton family is of Scotch extraction. JOHN SUTTON[1] was an early res. of Orange Co., his sons:

Benjamin.

Joseph.

JOHN.

Abram.

William.

JOHN SUTTON[2], s/o John[1], m. Miss Bitterage Cranse of Orange Co; he d. 10 Dec. 1856, and had:

1804, Oct. 17, **MINARD**.

William.

John.

Lewis J.

Harriet, m. S. S. Loud.

Sarah Jane, m. Thomas B. Sly.

Elizabeth, m. T. J. Hasbrook.

MINARD SUTTON[3], b. Warwick Twp., d. 20 June 1868 & is survived by widow & 2 daus. Saddle & harness maker, farmer; 1846 res. Sugar-Loaf; 1855 est. creamery at Sugar-Loaf & another at Warwick in 1863; political service, member of Old School Baptist Church, Warwick; m. 1831 Sarah A., d/o Nathaniel Knapp of Sugar-Loaf. Children:

Nathaniel K.

John W.

Cyrus J.

Son, d. infant.

Ann M., m. William B. Knapp.

Sarah E., m. John M. Knapp.

Grandchildren named, all Knapp: Nathaniel S.; Mary E., m. Frederick B. LaRue; & Libbie.

---

## SWARTWOUT FAMILY OF DEERPARK

| | |
|---|---|
| | A-705, H-204, T-54, U1-91-2, LDS Anc. File |
| SWARTOUT, PETER P. [P] | A-750-1 |
| of Deerpark & | SW, AA-8:27-8 |
| SWARTWOUT, HENRY B. M.D. | H-954, AA-3:49 |
| SWARTHOUT, RALPH | SW-624-6, C-14 |

RULOFF SWARTOUT[1], s/o Thomas of Groningen, later of New Amsterdam & wife Adrientje Symons, who m. 4 Feb. 1630. RULOFF bapt. in Amsterdam 1 June 1634, m. (1) 13 Aug. 1657, Eva Alberts[on], d/o Albert Andriessen Bratt de Noorman. She was the widow of Antoine de Googes [Hooges]. [Children by her first mar.: Marichen Anneken, Catrina, Johannes & Dleonora De Hooges.] From Holland to America in 1660, bringing farm-laborers: Cornelis Jacobz van Leeuwen, Arent Meuwens from Gelderland, & Ariaen Hyberts from Jena. RULOFF m. (2) at NY 8 Oct. 1691 [22 Nov. 1691], Mrs. Francyntije Andries, widow of Abraham Lubbertisen. Ruloff apptd. 1st sheriff at Esopus. 'Probably' some of his children (all settled Peenjack Flats in 1690):

c. 1660, THOMAS.

Hendricke (dau.), m. in Kingston 16 March 1679, Huybert Lambertsen. The LDS Ancestral file names her husband as Hendrikjen Brink, b. c. 1655 in Wageningen, Holland, d. Ulster Co., NY.

Bapt. 1662, Jan. 8, Anthony.

1663 [1664], May 11, ANTHONY.

1664, Cornelia.

Bapt. 1667, March 13, Cornelia, m. before 28 April 1689, Hendrick Klaesen Schoonhoven.

1669, Rachel, m. Jacob Kip before 9 Feb. 1696.

1671, Eva, b. Hurley, m. Jacob Dingman[s] 9 Oct. 1698. Jacob b. Kinderhook.

Bapt. 1673, April 26, Bernardus (Gerardus), res. Hurley, m. 19 May 1700, Rachel Schepmoes.

[Benjamin is names as of Poughkeepsie in one source.]

ROELOFF SWARTWOUT's will, 30 March 1714, in Ulster Co. He left bequests to the children of his son Anthony & dau. Cornelia who he says is dec'd. at the time. [No names given.]

Another source says that Anthony, Barnadus & Samuel Swarthout, brothers, settled early in Orange Co., but does not name their parent.

A Major Swartwout was forced from his land in Town of Deerpark by Jerseyites in 1730 during border disputes. [H-204]

THOMAS SWARTWOUT[2], s/o Roeloff[1], of Kingston, b Ulster Co., NY [Beverswyck, New Netherlands]; m. be 4 Feb. 1683, Lysbeth [Elizabeth] Gardenier [Gordi (Lysbeth Jacobse Hovenier), d/o Jacob Janse & Jos Gardiner. He was one of the 7 grantees of Minisink Va in 1697. THOMAS[2] d. in Maghaghkemeck, Orange C 1723. Their children, 1st 3 bapt. in Kingston, next : Hurley & last 2 b. Maghaghkemeck:

Bapt. 1683, Feb. 4, Roeloff, d. infant.

Bapt. 1686, Jan. 24, Josijna, d. infant.

Bapt. 12 Feb. 1689, Roeloff.

1692, April 17, Jacobus, m. 1714, Gilletzen Cornelisse Newk d/o Cornelius Gerits & Janitje [Knust] Newkirk.

Bapt. 1694, Nov. 16, Eva.

Bapt. 1697, March 28, Rudolphus.

Bapt. 1699, Aug. 13, Jesijntje.

1702, Jan. 22, Samuel.

ANTHONY SWARTOUT[2], s/o Ruloff[1], m. [8 May 1693] 16 Jannetje Jacobus, d/o Jacobus Coobes, who was b. Rens laerswyck. They had:

Bapt. 1695, 9 June, Roelof, b. in Kingston.

Bapt. 1696, March 29, Jacobus, b. Hurley. [same as Jar below?]

Bapt. 1697, Oct. 31, Barnadus.

Bapt. 1699, Oct. 22, ANTHONY.

Samuel, m. Esther Gumaer.

JAMES, m. Anna Gumaer.

Jane.

Anna, m. John Van Vleet.

[NOTE: *The Swartwout Chronicles* does not mention the 4 children as children of Anthony & Jannetje.]

ANTHONY SWARTOUT[3], s/o Anthony[2], b. Goshen [Kingst m. Mary Armstrong. [One version of the LDS Ancestral says that it is Anthony[3]'s son, Anthony[4] below who m. M Armstrong & they list no spouse for Anthony[3].] Tl children b. Town of Goshen & 1788 they moved to Towr Ovid, Montgomery Co. & settled on Lot 94 of the Milit Tract. He is bur. near the shore of Lake Seneca. They h

c. 1721, ANTHONY.

1764, Jan. 1, RALPH (Roeloff).

1771, Sept. 1, BARNADUS.

ANTHONY SWARTOUT[4], s/o Anthony[3], [The LDS Ances File shows 2 versions of this lineage. In one Anthony[4] is husband of Mary Armstrong. The second version sho Mary as his mother, the wife of Anthony[3].] & had:

c. 1755, Rachel, b. Goshen; m. Abraham Hendricks of Gos & they had son Anthony Hendrix. She d. after 1818 Richland, OH & Abraham d. the same place on 23 N 1818.

RALPH SWARTOUT[4], s/o Anthony[3], m. 24 Nov. 1782, Lo Halstead, b. Orange Co. 1 Oct. 1767 & d. Ovid, Seneca C NY 28 Dec. 1848. Ralph d. 11 Dec. 1843. Children (f

5 b. Goshen; others b. in Ovid, listed as in Onondaga, Cayuga & Seneca Counties. The family settled in Town of Ovid c. 1796.):

1783, Dec. 27, Mary, m. Abraham Covert & had 2 children: Ralph & Abraham.

1786, April 8, Benjamin, m. in town of Ovid, Seneca Co. 5 Feb. 1807, Margaret Stull, b. in NJ 7 Oct. 1790. He d. in Lodi, Seneca Co. 19 March 1842; she 18 May 1856.

1788, Aug. 31, James; left 2 children: Charles & Sampson.

1792, Feb. 15, William, m. (1) 8 Jan. 1817, Sarah Voorheis, b. 13 April 1798, d. 23 Aug. 1820; m. (2) 17 July 1821, Elisabeth Willett, d/o Mary Josephine Mozer, b. in Bucks Co., PA, d. 12 March 1871. William d. in Ovid, MI 4 Oct. 1874. William left NY in 1837 to become one of the first settlers of the state of MI.

1793, Jan. 14, Elisabeth, m. John Bodine 14 Jan. 1793 & had: John, Sally & George.

1796, Sept. 28, Anthony, m. in Ovid, 18 June 1816, Hannah Rose, b. Onondaga Co., 7 May 1798 & d. Saginaw, MI 22 March 1877. He d. there 5 June 1881. Anthony moved to MI & settled near Ypsilanti, where he as capt. served 6 years during hostilities with Patawatami Indians & in Black Hawk War.

1799, May 28, Martha, m. James Voorheis.

1802, Feb. 5, Lois, m. Peter Van Vliet 5 Feb. 1802 & they settled in Ridgeway, MI & had: Ezekiel B., Peter & Ralph.

1804, May 28, Sophia, m. in Ovid 11 Jan. 1821, Stephen Coshun, b. there. She d. in Rockford, IL 19 Sept. 1871.

1807, Jan. 4, Ralph, m. in Ovid 26 Jan. 1826, Catharine Ann Voorheis, b. Somerset Co., NJ 6 Nov. 1806 & d. Rockford, IL 10 March 1868; he also d. Rockford 16 Feb. 1868.

1811, April 23, Sarah Ann, m. in Ovid 29 Jan. 1829, John Knight, b. Middlesex Co., NJ 15 April 1807. He d. Lodi, Seneca Co., NY 9 June 1882 & she 16 Sept. 1894.

BARNADUS SWARTOUT[4], s/o Anthony[3], b. Goshen, 1 Sept. 1771 m. Mary Halstead, b. 25 July 1772 & d. Town of Ovid, Seneca Co., NY 25 Nov. 1835. Barnadus d. there 8 Oct. 1838. Children (all b. Seneca Co.):

James, b. Town of Ovid.

1804, Dec. 22, Coe, b. Town of Romulus.

Dorothy (Dolly), m. Jared Van Vleit of NJ.

Fanny, m. Henry Liew.

Harriet, m. Gilbert Bodine.

Mary, m. Edward Sayre.

Jane, m. George Rogers.

Deborah Ann, m. James McLaferty.

Members Romulus Baptist Church.

JAMES SWARTOUT[3], s/o Anthony[2], had a son: PHILIP[4], who m. (1st) 1751 Antje Wynkoop, also of Holland ancestry, who was among the early inhabitants of Ulster Co., she d. as the result of being taken prisoner during the border conflict between NY & NJ. In Oct. 1778 the Indian Brant crossed the wilderness from DE to the Neversink & invaded Peenpack. Many settlers were killed, including an old man named Swartwout & 4 of his sons. One son, named as James,

escaped. Children of PHILIP[4]:

Gerardus.

Cornelius.

Philip Jr.

Jacobus.

PHILIP[4] m. (2d) 24 Jan. 1788, Jane Westfall, and had:

Simeon.

PHILIP.

Sallie.

James D.

Samuel.

David.

Deborah.

PHILIP SWARTOUT[5], s/o Philip[4], m. Ester Westbrook, and had:

1817, May 25, PETER P.

Jane.

Catherine.

Henry B., dec'd.

Elizabeth.

Sarah.

See next entry on Swartwout families for conflicting data on Philip[4]'s family.

PETER P. SWARTOUT[6], s/o Philip[5], b. Sussex Co., NJ; spent early life in Deerpark; m. 10 Nov. 1842 Hannah, d/o Benjamin Cuddeback of Port Jervis. PETER served in the militia, is a bank director & supports Reformed Dutch Church. Children, 6 living, 4 res. with parents:

Catharine, m. D. S. DeWitt.

Jemima.

Jane, m. H. J. Bidwell.

Elizabeth.

Philip.

Esther.

Ellen.

Benjamin.

1861, Feb. 4, HENRY B.

HENRY B. SWARTOUT[7], s/o Peter P.[6], b. Port Jervis. He m. Carrie B. Peck, d/o George V. of Port Jervis 10 March 1886. He practiced medicine at Port Jervis with Dr. W. L. Cuddeback. HENRY'S children:

Henry Lewis, d. age 1 year.

Florence.

Charlotte.

Herbert B.

––––––––

## SWART[W]OUT FAMILIES OF ORANGE CO.    SW

Below are various Orange Co. Swartwout families from *The Swartwout Chronicles 1338-1899* . . . Although they are all tied together in the original, since only families with connections to Orange Co. have been included here, it was not possible to put in all connections.

PETER SWARTWOUT[1] m. Jannetje Westfall & had:
1790, Oct. 12, PHILIP.
1792, Oct. 1, JACOBUS.
1794, Nov. 4, SARAH.
1797, Aug. 29, SAMUEL.
1800, July 28, DAVID.

PHILIP SWARTWOUT[2], b. in Maghaghkemack, Ulster Co., m. in Town of Deerpark, Orange Co., 10 Nov. 1816, Mrs. Esther Westbrook Westfall, b. 16 March 1787. PHILIP d. 3 June 1862. Their children (1st 4 b. Montague, Sussex Co., NJ):
1817, May 25, Peter P.
1819, Sept. 6, Jane, m. 10 Oct. 1837, Benjamin Whitlock.
1821, Aug. 7, Catharine, m. 12 Dec. 1839, George Robinson.
1823, April 19, Henry Brinckerhoff.
1825, Dec. 2, Elisabeth, m. 28 Jan. 1847, Peter G. Van Inwegan.
1829, Dec. 3, Sarah, m. 18 Oct. 1849, Coe Robinson.

JACOBUS SWARTWOUT[2], b. in Maghaghkemeck, Ulster Co., NY, m. Naomi Cuddeback who d. 1855; he d. Nov. 1871. Their children, all b. in Deerpark, Orange Co.:
1817, April 1, Peter, m. Mary Shimer, had 2 children & d. in Phelps, Ontario Co., NY.
1820, Aug. 2, Cornelius, m. Eleanor Carpenter & d. 1880.
1823, Sept. 7, Sarah, m. 1842, C. S. Woodward, b. in Mt. Hope 21 Aug. 1808, he d. Aug. 1883; she d. March 1897.
1826, May 15, Abraham.
1830, Jane, m. J. R. Mathers of Elkhart, IN, had 4 children & d. 1896.
Margaret, m. H. D. Clark, settled in Westlawn, Orange Co., NY.
1836, Deborah, m. in town of Deerpark Dec. 1857, Daniel L. DeWitt of Deckertown, Sussex Co., NJ, d. Deerpark Aug. 1859.

SARAH SWARTWOUT[2], d/o Peter[1], b. in Maghaghkemeck, Ulster Co., m. in town of Deerpark, Hendrick, s/o Roeloff & Baeltje Demarest Brinckerhoff, b. 23 Sept. 1787, d. 30 April 1844. Their children, all b. in Owasco, Cayuga Co.:
1815, March 25, Peter.
1817, Maria.
1819, Feb. 26, Jane.
1820, Oct. 17, Cornelia.
1822, Dec. 5, David H.
1825, Abraham Cortright.
1827, April 8, Roeloff.
1829, April 23, Martha.

SAMUEL SWARTWOUT[2], s/o Peter[1], b. in Maghaghkemeck, Ulster Co., NY m. in Minisink, Orange Co. 19 Dec. 1818, Jemima Whitlock. They had:
Eliza, m. 11 June 1855, Abraham Cortright, s/o Henry R. & Sarah Swartwout Brinckerhoff. She d. Marshall, MI 17 Oct. 1876.

DAVID SWARTWOUT[2], s/o Peter[1], b. town of Deerpark, m. there 16 Sept. 1820, Synche Cuddeback, b. there 9 April 1801. She d. there 26 Feb. 1845 & he in Oct. 1874. Children, all b. town of Deerpark:
1821, Nov. 30, Henry.
1823, Dec. 30, Jane.
1825, Dec. 17, Hester.
1828, April 12, Philip.
1830, April 27, Peter David.
1834, Aug. 22, Margaret.

_____

## PETER SWARTWOOD [SWARTWOUT] FAMILY
SW-622

PETER SWARTWOOD/SWARTWOUT m. Elisabeth Schoonmaker and had:
Jacobus, b. Maghaghkemeck, Ulster Co., NY, m. there 15 May 1791, (1) Catharine van Etten & (2) Rachel Decker. He d. in Van Ettenville, Chemungg Co. NY 1838.
Bapt. 1771, July 1, Isaac, bapt. in Walpack Twp., Sussex Co., NJ, m. Mary Swartwout. In 1800 Isaac built the first saw-mill in the valley of Cayuta Creek, near site of Swartwood & in 1803 the first grist-mill in that locale. He d. near Owego at an advanced age.
1784, Jonathan, b. Exeter, PA; m. 1784 Elisabeth, d/o Jacobus & Catharine (Van Etten) Swartwout, b. Ulster Co., NY 6 April 1796, d. Cayuta, Tioga Co., NY 5 Nov. 1849; he at the same place 24 Oct. 1847.

_____

## SWEET, CLAYTON E.
H-954-5
of Sweet, Orr & Co., largest manufacturer of overalls in US.

CLAYTON was b. at Wappinger's Falls, NY 16 June 1834; to Newburgh in 1887. Worked in NY City & retired to Wappinger's Falls to work with his father. Member Zion Episcopal Church there. In 1860 he m. Chattie Louise, d/o Hon. James Manning of Bethany, PA, a lineal desc. of Capt. Bazaliel Tyler, soldier of the Rev. killed at Battle of Minisink.

_____

## SWIM FAMILY OF HIGHLAND
A-812

CORNELIUS SWIM[1] is considered the first permanent resident of Highland Falls. He was the s/o Albert, who also settled at Highland Falls. The family had come from England c. 1686. CORNELIUS[1] was killed by the British. He had a son, JOHN[2], who had children:
Albert.
Andrew.
John.
Cornelius Jr.
William.
Samuel.
Mrs. Cashman.
Mrs. Lewis.
Mrs. Garrison.
Mrs. Rose.
Mrs. Fitch.

Dau., moved west.

**TAFT, CAPT. THOMAS**        **H-955**
of Taft, Howell Co., Cornwall Landing, NY.

COL. THOMAS is a desc. of Robert Taft who came from England to MA in 1677. He is the eldest s/o Robert & Emeline (Smith) Taft. Emeline is desc. of PA Quakers who escaped the Wyoming Massacre & settled near Woodberry Falls, Orange Co. THOMAS, b. Town of Cornwall, 28 Sept. 1840, in building business with his father & brother-in-law, C. H. Mead. He served in Co. C, 124th Regt. NY Vols. in the Civil War, was wounded at Gettysburg & taken prisoner. In 1881 he m. Mary G., eldest d/o Dr. James E. Knapp of Marlborough, Ulster Co., and had:
Thomas Knapp.
Royal M.

**TALCOTT, SELDEN H., M.D. [P]**    **A-455-6**

SELDEN H. TALCOTT, b. Rome, NY, 7 July 1842 served 15th NY Vols., engineer. He studied medicine with Dr. E. A. Munger, Waterville, NY after the war & grad. NY Homeopathic Medical College 1872; practiced at Waterville; 1875 chief of staff of Homoeopathic Charity Hospital, Ward's Island, NY; 1877 med. supervisor of the NY Homeopathic Asylum for the Insane.

**TAYLOR, ARCHIBALD R. [P]**    **A-427-8**
of Crawford &
**TAYLOR, H[AMILTON] R.**      **H-956**

JOHN TAYLOR[1], b. Scotland, to America as British soldier, having served with the army at Quebec; served in colonists' army. After war to Ulster Co., NY, tanner of Shawangunk, m. Jane Smedes of Shawangunk, and had:
1789, JOHN.
William.
Daniel.
Rachel, m. Joseph Depeu.

JOHN TAYLOR[2], s/o John[1], b. Shawangunk & d. there 1867, tanner; m. Jane McBurney of Crawford Twp. who d. 1865. They are both bur. at the cemetery of Prospect Church. Children:
1811, March 1, ARCHIBALD R.
Ann, m. N. W. Clearwater.
Oliver.

ARCHIBALD R. TAYLOR[3], s/o John[2], b. Ulster Co., civil engineer on railroad, merchant in 1842 in Ulsterville; 1849 to Pine Bush, Crawford Twp., Presbyterian; m. 16 Feb. 1856, Mary, d/o John Colwell Rainey of Crawford, and had:
Archibald.
HAMILTON R., established lumber, building materials business in 1895.
Emily.

Anne [not listed on H-956 with others]
John C., state senator.

**TEN EYCK, GEORGE**       **H-957**

DAVID TEN EYCK[1], cooper, was desc. of the early settlers from Holland to Rockland Co., NY. He m. Mary Youmans, who d. 4 Dec. 1884, aged 90, and had:
GEORGE[2], b. Rockland Co., 8 May, 1824. When he was young his father, died & he was bound out to a farmer near Sugar Loaf until age 21. Res. Maple Grove Farm, where he was reared & where he d. 13 Dec. 1900. He m. Christien Peterson of Warwick, 11 Jan. 1850; she d. on her 70th birthday, 7 Feb. 1897. Their children:
Coe H., res. Valley House at Green Lake.
Hutson G., d. age 38, architect at Newark, NJ.
George W., carpenter & builder at Elizabeth, NJ.
Mary L., m. Francis B. Knapp, res. Middletown.
Andrew, res. Middletown.

**TENNYCK FAMILY**      **LDS Anc. File**

THOMAS TENNYCK[1], b. c. 1808, had a son, FRANCIS W. TENNYCK[2], b. at Highland Mills, Orange Co., 25 Nov. 1834. Francis m. Ester Pembleton of Highland Mills, d/o Benjamin & Elizabeth (Monell) Pembleton & had:
1860, Dec. 17, David F., m. Annie Morse. David d. 9 Jan. 1925.
1862, Harry P.
1863, Elizabeth.
1868, Francis.
1870, Hattie.

**TERRY, WILMOT C. [P] A-177-8, C-17, 56, 71, 91, 94, 96**

The Terry family were early L.I. settlers from England. CONSTANT TERRY[1] to Orange Co., farmer in Bloomsburg. Children of his 1st m.:
AUSTIN.
Havens. A Haven Terry d. 1 Oct. 1831, aged 42, liver comp.
Hephzibah.
Dorothy.
    Children of CONSTANT's 2d m.:
Youngs.
Tuttle.
Nicholas.
2 daus.

Goshen church records show a m. of Constance Terry to Hephzibah Case, 5 June 1788.

AUSTIN TERRY[2], s/o Constant[1], b. Bloomsburg, farmer; m. Sarah Myers and later to Goshen, and later still to Wallkill, where he d. Children:
Van Rensselaer.
John.
Mary.

1822, Jan. 15, **WILMOT C.**
Sarah.
William A.
2 d. infancy. One child d. at age of 14 months of "croup," 16 June 1827.

Goshen church records show in membership rolls, "Azuba Cory, now Austin Tery wife, Nov. 5, 1814." Same records show the death of "Mrs. Terry, wife of Austin Terry, Consumption," 19 Dec. 1834.

**WILMOT C. TERRY**[3], s/o Austin[2], b. Twp. of Blooming-Grove, lived in early life in Goshen; 1847-50 studied under Dr. Gabriel P. Reeves of Goshen; student in VT & NY City, practiced at Ridgebury, Orange Co., ME Church member. Was a member of First Presbyterian Church at Goshen until 1842, when he was dismissed to Centerville. He m. (1st) Sarah E., d/o Dr. J. H. Halstead of Ridgebury and had one dau., Flora Bell. Sarah d. 1857, Jan. 27.

**DR. TERRY**[3] m. (2d) Mary J., d/o Henry Decker of Wawayanda, and had:
Fannie E.
Lille Gertrude.
Wilmot A., d. infancy.

### TETHER, FLOYD E.      H-957

Children of Edward J. Tether (d. 17 July 1907) & Sarah A.:
1872, Feb. 22, **FLOYD E.**
Eva J., m. Louis B. Williams, of Florida, NY.
Harry L., farmer on family homestead.
Hannah, d. age 16.

**FLOYD E.**, s/o Edward J. Tether, b. on farm between Amity & Edenville in Orange Co. Worked with Clyde Steamship Co. of NY City & later worked at Edenville. 1894 in partnership with G. S. Everett of Florida, NY. Member Presbyterian Church; m. Mary A. Knapp of Pine Island, and had:
James E.
Clifford F.
Russell K.
Beatrice M.

### THAYER, WILLIAM      H-958-9
merchant of Newburgh.

**WILLIAM'S** ancestors came from England in 1636 to settle in MA. He came from Brooklyn, CT in 1809 to Newburgh. His brother John (d. 1861) came with him. **WILLIAM** m. 1812, Elizabeth Carpenter, d/o Leonard & Bridget (Belknap). She was grand-dau. of Capt. Isaac Belknap. Children of **WILLIAM** & Elizabeth:
William L., unmarried.
John S., m. Catherine Stearns.
ELIJAH.
Charles F., m. Anna F. Miller.

Anna B., m. Henry Dolson.
Elizabeth C., m. O. L. Sypher; she is the only now living of the siblings.
George A.
Caroline M., unmarried.

**WILLIAM'S** grandchildren named:
Children of John S., living in Los Angeles, CA;
Children of Charles F., living in Washington, DC;
The Thayer family at Burnside & Mrs. Elmer Tibbetts of Newburgh;
Children of Elijah C. & Mrs. Marsh, d/o Mrs. Sypher of East Orange, NJ.

### THEW, GARRET [P]     A-560, C-40

The progenitor of the Thew family was a sea captain, settled in Rockland Co., was of Welsh desc. His descendant, DANIEL THEW, was an atty. "here" in 1791.

JOHN THEW[1] of Rockland Co. was a soldier of the Revolution & m. (1st) Alche Cooper, b. 1720. Children:
1756, Gilbert.
1758, Garret.
1760, John; d. 1822.
1763, Tunis.

JOHN[1] m. (2d) Miss --- Blauvelt and had one son:
JAMES[2], res. Rockland Lake, Rockland Co., later to Hohokus, NJ, clothier, d. age 32 in 1804. He m. Sarah Snedeker who d. 1836, and had:
1798, Oct. 27, **GARRET**.
John, d. 1822, age 22.
James, d. young.

**GARRET THEW**[3], s/o James[2], b. Rockland Lake, farmed and apprenticed to carpenter's trade. He m. 1826, Abigail, d/o John & Hannah (Gurnee) Thew of Hamptonburgh, Orange Co. He was a farmer in Warwick, near Florida, removed to Goshen in 1849, was a soldier of the War of 1812. **GARRETT** res. with dau. Elizabeth in Goshen, was a member of the Presbyterian Churches in Florida & Goshen. He had one child:
Elizabeth T., m. 12 Nov. 1857, Dr. William P. Townsend of Goshen and had: Garret Thew, Mattie Wilder, Alice, Charles Emerson & Edith.

John Thew, father of Abigail who m. **GARRET THEW**, was a son of John and Alche Thew.

THOMPSON BROTHERS OF CRAWFORD    A-415-6
THOMPSON, AUGUSTUS [P]    A-428b &
ALEXANDER    H-959
THOMPSON, DANIEL [P]    A-426
of Crawford.
THOMPSON, J. HORTON [P]    A-808d
of Monroe.

Three brothers to America from Co. Longford, Ireland c. 1776 & settled in Crawford on what is now known as Thompson's Ridge. ALEXANDER, ANDREW & ROBERT A. THOMPSON.

ALEXANDER[1] homesteaded on the north farm now owned by the present Alexander Thompson, on a part of which Hopewell Church stands. ALEXANDER d. aged 75. He had:
ALEXANDER JR.
Dau., d. young.
Dau. m. Col. Moses Crawford near Collaburgh.

ALEXANDER THOMPSON JR.[2], s/o Alexander[1], m. Hannah, d/o Daniel Bull. ALEXANDER JR. d. aged 85. Children:
Albert, physician of Ontario Co.
AUGUSTUS.
DANIEL, railroad super. & town sup.
John Alexander, atty. of Monticello.
Mrs. Hon. Alex. C. Niven, Montichello.
Mrs. W. W. Jackson, Hamptonburgh.
Mrs. Hiram Phillips, Hamptonburgh.
Mrs. S. Sherman, Davenport, IA.
Mrs. Samuel C. Brush of NY City.
Mrs. William H. Smith of NY City.

AUGUSTUS THOMPSON[3], probably s/o Alexander Jr.[2], b. 1816 on homestead on Thompson's Ridge, d. 1874, Sept. 23. He was town sup. (Crawford) 1849-50 & j.p. in 1865. He m. (1st) Hannah, d/o Abner Bull of Wallkill; (2d) Catherine A. Hunter of Crown Point. His children:
1850, ALEXANDER.
George Hunter, newspaper editor, Middletown.
Augustus, went west.
3 daus. (unnamed)

ALEXANDER THOMPSON[4], s/o Augustus[3], b. on homestead near Thompson Ridge, d. 17 Jan. 1908. He m. Abbie Beattie & had 7 children [not named here]. Elder at Hopewell Presbyterian Church.

DANIEL THOMPSON[3] has served as commissioner of highways, pres. of the Middletown & Crawford Railroad (1871), Maj. in 91st Regt. National Guards of NY. He is the s/o Alexander & Hannah (Bull) Thompson. DANIEL m. Mary E., d/o the late Dr. Hunter of Searsville in Town of Crawford & has 2 sons & 1 dau. (not named here).

ANDREW THOMPSON's[1] homestead now occupied by Nathan T. Thompson, a great grandson. His children, all settled at Crawford:
James.
William.
Robert R.
Alexander.
GEORGE.
Mrs. Nathan Young.
Mrs. Isaac Schultz.

GEORGE THOMPSON[2] of Irish parentage, res. Blooming-Grove, Orange Co., is probably the s/o Andrew[1] above. He m. Elizabeth Gregory of Monroe & had:
Abijah W.
1792, Dec. 22, NATHANIEL.
James G.
Hannah, m. Gerret Duryea.
Susan, m. Nathaniel Racket.
Mary, m. Isaac Lee.
Eunice, m. David Case.
Nancy, m. Gen. Henry Duryea.
Elmira, m. Oliver B. Tuthill.

NATHANIEL THOMPSON[3], s/o George[2], served in War of 1812, farmer; 1820 to Monroe; m. 22 Jan. 1818, Sarah, d/o Jeremiah Horton of Blooming-Grove, and had:
1821, Jan. 13, J. HORTON.
George W., res. Monroe.

J. HORTON THOMPSON[4], s/o Nathaniel[3], b. Monroe, teacher for brief time, dairy farmer, member Presbyterian Church at Monroe; m. 20 Dec. 1854, Mary, d/o Samuel Webb of Monroe, and had:
Sarah, m. Ashel Smith.
Anna, dec'd.
Nancy.

ROBERT A. THOMPSON[1], homestead on south farm now occupied by William H. & Robert I. Thompson, his great-grandsons. ROBERT A. d. aged 90. His children:
Robert A. Jr.
Andrew, minister, d. at Mt. Hope.
Mrs. Hugh Barclay.
Isabella, d. young.

_____

THOMPSON, ALEXANDER [P]    A-807, H-959, W-91
of Monroe.    [P] C-30
THOMPSON, ISAAC H. [P]    A-808c
of Monroe.

The earliest pioneer Thompson is not named here, but "probably left Ireland for a home in the New World at a very early date, and eventually located in the township of Goshen, where he married." Among his children was WIILLIAM,[1] who m. Mittie Hudson , res. Chester, and had :
George.
Robert.
1789, July 4, PHINEAS H.

Benjamin.
Elizabeth.
Keturah.

PHINEAS H. THOMPSON[2] m. 23 Dec. 1812, Rachel, d/o
Birdseye Young, and had:
Elizabeth.
Harrison.
Charles.
Phineas.
1820, Aug. 27, ALEXANDER.
Cornelia Y.
Keturah, m. Henry Smith 11 April 1827.
1827, April 11, ISAAC H.
Virgil.
Nathan Y.
Edmund.

ALEXANDER THOMPSON[3], s/o Phineas H.[2], b. Township of
Monroe, dairy farmer, member of Presbyterian Church; to
Newburgh & became carpenter; retired to Monroe & m.
1856, Feb. 19, Eleanor, d/o Peter Bush, Esq. of Monroe.
Children:
Phineas H.
Ella B.
Alexander.
All res. with their parents.

ISAAC H. THOMPSON[3], b. 11 April 1827, Monroe; carpenter
& joiner, since 1870 dairy farmer; attended Presbyterian
Church of Monroe; m. 18 Jan. 1854, Elizabeth, d/o Elmor
Earl of Monroe, and had:
Rachel, m. W. S. Allen.
Elmor.
Eliza.
Virgil.

---

THOMPSON, CHARLES M. [P]                    A-652a
of Hamptonburgh.                     C-26, LDS Anc. File

JONATHAN THOMPSON[1] settled in Orange Co. early & m.
Hannah Brooks, and had:
John I.
Lewis.
1787 [1788], Oct., OLIVER.
Jane, m. Charles Monell of Goshen.
Benjamin F.

OLIVER THOMPSON[2], s/o Jonathan[2], b. Wallkill, farmer of
Hamptonburgh, where he d. 12 March 1863. He m. Sarah
Mathers [Matthews], 2 Jan. 1812, at Goshen, d/o an early
Revolutionary family of Orange Co., she d. 6 May 1861,
aged 65. OLIVER d. 12 March 1863. Children (all b. either
Wallkill or Hamptonburgh):
1814, Nov. 7, Alfred, m. Jane Lines, he now dec'd.
1816, Dec. 17, CHARLES M.
1819, Cornelia A., m. George W. Stevens of Susquehanna Co.,
PA; she dec'd.
1822, Jan. 18, Mary Elizabeth, m. George Pierson of Hamptonburgh.
1823, Nov., John I., now dec'd.
1825, Feb. 17, Oliver Brooks.
1827, Catharine Ann, widow of Charles W. Post of Hamptonburgh.
1829, Sarah Ann, m. George W. Beardsley of Brooklyn, L.I.;
now dec'd. [LDS Anc. File J. W. Wilkin as her 1st spouse
& Mr. Beardsley as her 2d.]
1832, June 9, DAVID HENRY.
1833, Emily Frances, m. William Brett, shipping merchant of
NY.
1835, Hannah Amelia, m. A. Ferd. Cross of NY.
1838, Aug. 11, Carrie [Caroline Augusta], m. Augustus Brett,
shipping merchant of NY.

CHARLES M. THOMPSON[3], s/o Oliver[2], b. in Wallkill (now
Hamptonburgh); 1844 partner of Jennings & Thompson of
Goshen; 1848 bought James Strong farm in Hamptonburgh
& res. there, farmer, political service, member First Presbyte-
rian Church of Hamptonburg. He m. (1) Lorinda, d/o Robert
D. Hunter of Crawford May 14, 1851. She d. 5 June 1853.
They had one son:
Robert O.

CHARLES M.[3] m. (2d) Mary A., d/o John A. Wilbur of
Wallkill, and had:
Charles M.
William M.
Mary Jennie.

DAVID HENRY THOMPSON[3], s/o Oliver[2], b. Hamptonburgh,
m. Elizabeth Sayre Watkins, b. 11 July 1838, Hamptonburgh;
children:
1858, Jan. 31, Sarah Elizabeth, b. Hamptonburgh.
1859, Oct. 27, Kate Post, b. Montgomery, m. John McBride, b.
25 July 1858. Their children, all b. Hamptonburgh (MC
BRIDE): Edith May b. 1879, Elizabeth Thompson b. 1881,
Tempy Ann Rapelye b. 1883, John David b. 1885, Alma
Kate b. 1887, Anna Raplye (twin of Alma Kate) and George
Eager b. 1891.
1863, April 23, Mary Millicent, m. John N. Luquer.
1866, Oct. 28, David Henry, m. Emma Lida Tower.
1868, April 17, Emma W.
1869, Dec. 4, Edna Cornelia.
1883 [sic], Aug. 20, Tempy A.

---

THOMPSON, JAMES                              A-216

JAMES THOMPSON, "lately of Drumeal in the County of
Longford, Ireland, but now res. in Little Britain in the Co. of
Ulster, Province of NY . . ." Deed 1738. He settled on Low &
Co.'s patent in part of Town of New Windsor.

---

**THOMPSON, JAMES RENWICK JR.**     **H-959-60**
atty. of Newburgh.

REV. J. R. THOMPSON[1], pastor Westminster Church, Newburgh, m. Mary F. Lawson. Their son:
**JAMES RENWICK THOMPSON[2]**, b. Newburgh 1874, grad. Law Dept. Cornell Univ., 1896; m. Julia, d/o James Dickey, 1906.

————

**THOMPSON, JOHN HUDSON**     **A-176-7, C-40**
physician of Goshen.

BENJAMIN THOMPSON[1] m. Maria Antoinette Owen & had:
1827, March 8, **JOHN HUDSON THOMPSON[2]**, b. near Circleville, Wallkill, Orange Co. Grad. NY City 1852; 1853 practiced at Seaman's Retreat at Staten Island; 1853 to Goshen. Surgeon of 24th Reg. NY Vols.; m. 6 Oct. 1858, Adeline L., d/o Capt. Ellis A. Post of Goshen & had a son, Wilmot P., of Goshen.

————

**THOMPSON, VIRGIL [P]**     **A-502b**
of Wallkill &     **C-24, 45**
**THOMPSON, CHARLES HUDSON**     **H-959**

This family progenitor emigrated from France to America and had:
JOHN I. THOMPSON[1], b. Orange Co., farmer & businessman; to Goshen where he d. in 1861. He had:
1806, Oct. 5, **VIRGIL[2]**, b. Montgomery, Orange Co; blacksmith apprenticed under Charles Buchanan of Montgomery; 1839 to Wallkill, farmer & businesman, member Presbyterian Church of Goshen. He m. (1st) Mary Ann, d/o Jonathan & Susanna (Youngblood) Decker of Montgomery, 1837, Jan. 11. Mary Ann d. 1855, Jan. 18.VIRGIL was a teacher & later a farmer, j.p., town supervisor & member of the Presbyterian Church of Goshen.
Children:
Virgil. Virgil Thompson Jr. was a witness at the wedding of his brother Horace D. on 25 Nov. 1874.
Anna, m. Hudson E. [K.] Hulse of Wawayanda, 25 Nov. 1863.
Mary, d. infant.
1844, 3 Dec., HORACE DECKER.

VIRGIL m. (2d) 1855, Jan. 18, Ophelia, d/o Peter A. Millspaugh of Montgomery.

HORACE D. THOMPSON[3], m. 25 Nov. 1874 [1875], Sarah M. Millspaugh, d/o Dr. G. M. & Sarah (Cameron) Millspaugh, and had:
Dr. Edward Cameron, physician of Newburgh.
1877, Nov. 11, **CHARLES HUDSON**.
Anna May, at home.
Harold, farmer at home.

**CHARLES HUDSON THOMPSON[4]**, b. 11 Nov. 1877, grad. Univ. of PA Dental School 1900. Practices in Goshen.

————

**THOMPSON, WILLIAM**     **A-523, STJ-2, T-50, 143,**
of Goshen.     **H-152**

WILLIAM THOMPSON[1] settled in the south part of present town of Goshen, c. 2 miles from Florida. He had:
**WILLIAM A.**
Dau. m. DR. NATHANIEL ELMER [see below] of Warwick.
Dau. m. Robert Armstrong.

Children of DR. NATHANIEL ELMER & --- Thompson:
Dr. William Elmer of Goshen.
Dr. Nathaniel Elmer of Denton.
Jesse Elmer of Bellvale.

**WILLIAM A. THOMPSON[2]**, settled at Thompsonville in 1795 & the town was named in his honor. In 1809 appointed 1st judge in Sullivan Co. when it was formed. State Senator (1797-1800). He had children:
Morris.
William. Could be the William Beverhaut Thompson b. 10 Nov. 1804, s/o William M. & Frances A. Thompson.
Thomas.
Dau m. Col. John Cowdrey.

A William Thompson, b. 1723, was chain bearer for Col. Clinton & usually stopped, when surveying the Cheesecock patent, at Perry's near Wickham's Pond. He had talked with the Indians & remained at times in their wigwams.

————

**WILLIAM M. THOMPSON**     **H-960**

WILLIAM was b. Hamptonburgh, 20 Sept. 1865, on what was known as the Charles M. Thompson farm. He clerk of Presbyterian Church at Campbell Hall; m. Mary H. Corwin, d/o W. S. & Cornelia Corwin of NY City. They had:
Child, d. age 4.
Ruth, age 14.
William M. Jr.
Roland Harlon.

————

**THORN, JOHN W.**     **H-960**

A. D. THORN[1], Mt. Hope farmer, m. Lucinda Moore & had:
**JOHN W. THORN[2]**, b. Mt. Hope 17 Feb. 1864, feed & coal business & creamery near Middletown, later at Westtown.

————

**THORNE, THOMAS [P]**     **A-558, C-21, 122, STJ-11, 12, 53**
of Goshen.

RICHARD THORNE[1] of Great Neck, Hempstead, L.I., served in the Revolutionary War & had:
Phebe.
Betsey.
Richard.
Henry.
Latatia.
Sarah.

Daniel. Goshen church records show the m. of Daniel Thorn to Mary Johnes [Jones], 24 Jan. 1795 & the births of their children: William Edward Thorne 15 June 1795; Sarah Ann Thorn 30 March 1798 & Richard Jones Thorn, 3 Feb. 1800. They also give the death of a Daniel Thorne, aged 48, consumption, 8 Dec. 1815.

William.

1774, March 11, **THOMAS.**

John.

All raised families except Phebe & Betsey.

**THOMAS THORNE**[2], s/o Richard[1], b. Hempstead, L.I., at age 16 to Goshen to res. with uncles Daniel & William, businessman of Goshen; d. 1860, April 2. Member St. James Church Goshen. He m. (1st) Mary Hetfield (no issue); (2d) 6 [9] April 1826, Elizabeth, b. 1790, Aug. 23, d/o Col. Thomas Waters of Goshen, slaveowner & soldier of the Revolution, sheriff of Orange Co., & his wife Betsey Matthews of Washingtonville. Elizabeth d. 1865, Nov. 6. Children:

1829, Jan. 18 [8], John Waters.

Mary Elizabeth, d. 11 Oct. 1835, age 4. [Church records show Mary Elizabeth b. 13 Sept. 1827.]

1831, Jan. 16, Sarah Thurman, m. J. Francis Matthews of Middletown; res. Goshen.

---

**THORNTON, HON. HOWARD**　　　　H-960-1
atty. of Newburgh.

MAJ. JOHN THORNTON[1] of Continental & Rev. Army m. a d/o Col. Samuel Clyde of Cherry Valley, and had:

WILLIAM A. THORNTON[2]. William's wife is not named; her ancestors were DeWitts, prominent in the Rev. period in the Hudson Valley. Their son:

**HOWARD**[3], grad. Union College 1872; with office of Eugene A. Brewster of of Newburgh & later to Albany Law School, grad. 1874.

---

**TIDD, SAMUEL V.**　　　　H-961

**SAMUEL V. TIDD,** b. 1 Feb. 1842, one of 5 children, s/o John & Hulda Tidd; served in 124th Regt., "Orange Blossoms," in Civil War, taken prison & at Andersonville Prison. He m. Harriet Reeves of Howells, NY 6 March 1866, and had:

1867, Feb. 25, Addie L.

26 Aug. 1868, Harriet E.

1870, March 17, Nettie W., m. Henry Miller of Middletown.

1872, Feb. 10, Elizabeth.

1873, Oct. 23, John S., m. Julia McWhinnie of NY City.

---

**TODD, JAMES [P]**　　　　A-410b
of Montgomery.

JOHN TODD[1], b. Scotland, to Liverpool, England, merchant; m. Elizabeth Waddell of Scotch desc., and had:

Alexander.

John.

**JAMES.**

Jane.

Mary.

Elizabeth.

**JAMES TODD**[2], s/o John[1], to America at age of 12, landed alone in Quebec, to Paterson, NJ seeking relatives; to Ulster Co., NY 1837, tanner & currier; 1848 to Montgomery, farmer & tanner; m. 1838, May 26, Mary Amanda, d/o Martin R. Williams of New Hurley, Ulster Co. She was b. 1821, March 23. JAMES was a bank director & held political offices. Children (all living):

1839, June 20, Anna E., m. Dr. T. P. Knapp.

1840, Oct. 9, Mary Jane, m. W. F. Gilchrist.

1842, Oct. 9, Margaret W., m. W. H. Coleman.

1844, Oct. 6, Josephine, m. T. D. Barker.

1846, Sept. 1, Harriet B., m. W. H. Peck.

1848, Sept. 2, James J.

1864[sic], Feb. 29, Carrie Van Nest.

---

**TOOKER FAMILY OF WAWAYANDA**　　　　A-680

SAMUEL TOOKER, early surveyor, teacher of New Windsor, Goshen & Wawayanda, m. a d/o James Finch, Sr. of Mt. Hope; d. 1811. Their child, CHARLES, settled near Brookfield and had:

James H.

Samuel S., has a dau. m. James F. Vail.

---

**TOWNSEND, NICHOLAS**　　　　A-789
of Monroe.

NICHOLAS TOWNSEND came to Monroe from L.I. before the Rev. War. His children:

Mrs. Jacob Cock.

Mrs. William Cock, who has dau. Phebe, res. Canterbury.

Mrs. James Hallock.

---

**TOWNSEND, PETER [P]**　　　　A-614, 805-6, 221, E-225
of Monroe.

This is an English family. PETER TOWNSEND[1], anchor manufacturer, forges & furnace, res. L.I.; with father-in-law to Stirling, Warwick Twp. PETER m. Hannah Hawxhurst, d/o William & d. 1783. Children:

1770, PETER.

William.

Isaac.

Ann, m. Solomon Townsend.

Sallie [Sarah], m. Dr. Anthony David [Davis] of Goshen, NY.

PETER TOWNSEND[2], succeeded to father's business, smelter of iron ores; m. Alice, d/o Comfort Cornell, "early during present century." PETER d. 1857. Children:

William H.

1803, May 13, **PETER.**

Isaac.

Robert C.

George E.

Elizabeth, m. J. H. Austin of Staten Island.

**PETER TOWNSEND**[3], s/o Peter[2], b. at the Chester homestead, served as apprentice in counting house of Jacob Barker of NY; to Canandaigua, merchant; 1827 returned to Chester in business with brother in iron manufactury. He m. 9 July 1828, Caroline, d/o Capt. Jasper Parish of Southfield. Caroline d. 20 July 1874. Children:

Elizabeth, widow of Gen. Thomas Francis Meagher.

Alice.

Mrs. S.L.M. Barlow.

Caroline, m. David Crawford.

A PETER TOWNSEND, Quassaick Valley, Town of New Windsor, established cannon foundry in 1816 on Chambers Creek, on a large scale.

_____

**TOWNSEND, THOMAS POWELL**              H-961

**THOMAS P. TOWNSEND** is the s/o Jacob P., merchant, and Mary Ann (Barrett) Townsend. He was b. at Milton, Ulster Co.,, NY 26 Nov. 1836. In 1860 he moved to Newburgh, wholesale merchant until 1876, later in wholesale grocery house of James A. Townsend & Co. **THOMAS** m. Mary Augusta, d/o Hon. George Clark. They have one daughter, Florence C., who married Charles T. Mckenzie, 22 Oct. 1890.

_____

**TOWNSEND, WILLIAM P.**              A-177

physician.

**WILLIAM P. TOWNSEND**, s/o William, b. Lancaster, Worcester Co., MA, 1818, July 26; teacher, studied Groton, MA; 1839 to NY; 1840 to Shawangunk, Ulster Co.; 1844 to Castleton, VT; 1845 to Hamptonburgh, Orange Co.; 1849 to Florida, Orange Co., d. in Goshen 1876, Dec. 25. He married twice (first wife not named), m. (2d) only dau. of Garret Thew, who survives him & res. Goshen with children.

_____

**TURNER, PETER [P]**              A-807-8

of Monroe.

GILBERT TURNER[1] m. Hannah Brewster, to Monroe 1808. They had a son, **PETER TURNER**[2], b. Putnam Co., NY, 14 March 1794; d. 16 Oct. 1875, Turner's Village. **PETER** established Hotel on the Erie Railroad; m. (1st) 16 Nov. 1816, Mary Ann, d/o James Galloway; m. (2d) Nov. 1866, Mrs. Lavinia Wiley, who survives him. His children, 1st m.:

Charles of Monroe.

James G. of Monroe.

Gilbert of Monroe.

Theron S., res. Cornwall-on-the-Hudson.

**TUSTEN FAMILY**

**A-163, 523, 556, H-234-5, C-99, 101, 103, T-76**

Col. [BENJAMIN] TUSTEN SR.[1], of Goshen, before Revolution had left his son, DR. TUSTEN, on the Denne homestead, and removed to Main St., Goshen. The father moved back to the homestead on the death of his son the doctor.

Col. BENJAMIN TUSTEN[2], s/o Col. Benjamin Sr.[1], soldier of the Revolution, killed in the Battle of Minisink, 1779; children:

1770, Feb. 18, James.

1771, Nov. 22, Thomas.

1774, Feb. 8, Catharine.

1776, May 18, Sarah.

1778, Oct. 23, Abigail, m. Isaac Reeve, res. Goshen; their dau., Anna Eliza Reeve, b. 1810, May 3, m. Henry Merriam.

From H-234-5: Benjamin Tusten settled on the banks of the Otterkill, county judge & Col. in company of militia. His son, Col. Benjamin Tusten, physician & surgeon, from Southold, L.I. in 1746 at the age of 3.

Benjamin Jr. studied medicine with Dr. Thomas Wiskham at Goshen & later studied at Newark, NJ & still later at NY City; 1769 he retired to Goshen to practice medicine. He m. Ann Brown & had 2 sons (one named James) & 3 daus. Jr. was a hero of the Battle of Minisink, where he died. The story of his death found T-76.

_____

**TUTHILL, JOHN B. [P]**              A-628,

**TUTHILL, HIRAM**              H-962, C-12

of Chester.

JOHN TUTHILL[1], s/o Nathaniel, soldier of the War of 1812, farmer in Town of Blooming-Grove, m. Milicent Seeley at Goshen 11 April 1779, and had:

Orpha, m. (1st) Timothy Little; (2d) Mr. Johnson.

E. Brewster, d. Chemung Co.

John, res. & d. Chemung Co.

Milecent, m. Dr. Townsend Seeley of Kendall, IL.

Green M., res. Chemung Co.; d. Ottawa, IL.

Elizabeth, m. John L. Smith of Elmira.

1799, Nov. 30, HIRAM.

Francis, merchant of Chester; d. Chemung Co., 1850.

1819 JOHN removed from Blooming-Grove and settled in Town of Erin, Chemung Co., where he d. c. 1845, aged 84.

HIRAM TUTHILL[2], s/o John[1], b. Orange Co.; d. 1876, Sept. 18. He m. 1799, Nov. 30, Azubah Seeley, b. May 1804 & now res. in Erin, Chemung Co. Their children, all b. Chemung Co.:

Charles S. of Greenpoint, NY, merchant.

1828, Nov. 4, **JOHN B.**

Francis G., farmer of Elmira.

William M., d. age 28, 1862.

1837, Nov. 30, **HIRAM**.

168

Sarah Milecent, d. young.
Stella Azubah, d. age 17, 1862.

**JOHN B. TUTHILL**[3], s/o Hiram[2], merchant at Chester until 1867; dairy farmer, public servant; m. (1st) 10 Dec. 1856, Martha S., d/o Francis & Elizabeth (Seeley) Tuthill, b. 30 Oct. 1835, d. 25 Sept. 1857. **JOHN B.** m. (2d), 26 Jan. 1859, Jane, d/o James Durland of Chester, b. 6 May 1837, d. 23 Sept. 1867, He m. (3d), 4 Feb. 1869, Susan, d/o John & Mary Ann (Pilgrim) Fowler of Monore. John Fowler settled in Monroe from Scotland. Susan was b. 10 Nov. 1835. Children of 4th marriage:
Stella A.
Hiram B.

**HIRAM TUTHILL**[3], s/o Hiram[2], b. Elmira, Chemung Co., NY; at age 16 to Chester, Orange & clerked for Charles S. & J. B. Tuthill. 1855 clerk at Chester Bank, after 13 years returned to Elmira, dry good business 1 year; 1869 back to Chester to purchase business of Tuthill & Jackson. Now pres. of Chester Bank. He m. Pauline W. Conklin of Elmira 24 Feb. 1869. Their only surviving child, a son, Leddra W. C. Tuthill res. NY City. Another son d. Dec. 1879 at age of 10. Pauline d. 15 March 1903.

------

**TUTHILL, JAMES**                           U2-155
yeoman of New Windsor.

In his will dated 17 March 1756, **JAMES TUTHILL** names his father James & his wife Mary & children:
Joel.
Thomas.
James.
Jemima.
Mary.

------

**TUTHILL, WILLIAM B. [P]**      A-560-1, LDS Anc. File
of Goshen.
**TUTHILL, OLIVER B. [P]**
        A-556c, C-22, 27, 28, 30, 41, 44, 95, 101, 144

HENRY TUTHILL[1], b. England 16 July 1635, m. Deliverance King & settled at New Haven, CT 1638; 1840 to Southold, L.I. & d. there 12 Oct. 1717. [From *Genealogies of Long Island Families From the NY Genealogical & Biogoraphical Record, Vol. II*, Henry Tuthill[1], s/o Henry, was of Tharston, England & Hingham MA. Henry m. in England, Bridget ---, who came with him to America & m. 2d William Wells, Gent. of Southhold. In the same reference Deliverance Kinge, d/o William & Dorothy Kinge is the wife of Henry[1]'s first son John. Torry's *New England Marriages Prior to 1700* also shows Bridget as the wife of Henry[1] and John[2] (1635-1717) m. Deliverance King (1641-1688/90).] Henry[1] had a son, NATHANIEL[2], who had a son NATHANIEL[3], who had a son:

FREEGIFT TUTHILL[4], b. 8 Aug. 1698, at Southold, L.I., tailor; m. Abigail Goldsmith, res. Brookhaven, L.I.; 1730 to Goshen where he d. June 1727. [ LDS Ancestral file says that Freegift Tuthill, b. 8 Aug. 1698, was s/o John Tuthill & Mehitable Wells, of Southhold, NY.] Children (sons all served in Revolutionary War):
Abigail.
1730, Jan. 17, NATHANIEL.
Joshua.
Freegift Jr; d. in service.

**NATHANIEL TUTHILL**[5], s/o Freegift[4], b. Brookhaven, L.I., d. 1803, Sept. 16. He m. (1st) Margaret, d/o John Herod of L.I.; res. Goshen. Margaret b. 3 Aug. 1739. Children:
Benjamin.
Mary, m. Daniel Bailey.
1768, Feb. 2, NATHANIEL.

**NATHANIEL TUTHILL**[6], s/o Nathaniel[5], m. (1st), 27 Feb. 1792, Martha, d/o Joseph Wickham of Hashamomock, L.I., b. 1768, d. 1808. Children:
1783, Feb. 7, Joseph Wickham, engaged in making cannon balls during the war of 1812; farmer.
John H., in war of 1812, farmer. Could be the John Heros Tuthill who m. Sarah Youngs 5 Jan. 1819 at Goshen.
Hector C., farmer of Sempronius, NY, where he settled in 1827; member of State Legislature (1848-9).
Daniel H., atty., practiced in Warwick & was partner of Henry G. Wisner at Goshen, surrogate of Orange Co. (1827-31). Could be the Daniel Hull Tuthill who m. Caroline Wilkin 12 Dec. 1826 at Goshen.
1805, Aug. 27, **OLIVER BAILEY.**

"All of the children of the first family are dec'd. in 1881 except **OLIVER B.**"
NATHANIEL m. (2d) Mary Bodle of Wallkill & had one son, **WILLIAM B.**

**OLIVER BAILEY TUTHILL**[7], s/o Nathaniel[6], b. on the homestead, res. with brother Hector C. from ages 14 to 20; on homestead until 1873 to village of Goshen; res. Hamptonburgh in public service. Member Presbyterian Church of Goshen, also Methodist Episcopal Church at Goshen. He m. (1st) Elmira, d/o George Thompson of Blooming-Grove, 1830, June 30. Elmira b. 1805, May 20, d. 1869, May. Children:
Ezra Fisk.
George N.
Bapt. 2 Aug. 1845, Martha Elizabeth.
Oliver.

**OLIVER BAILEY TUTHILL**[7] m. (2d) Mrs. Melinda, widow of the late John Burr of Brooklyn, NY, who by her first marriage had one dau., Caroline Stacey who m. Charles Winston; both dec'd. The Winston's had one dau., Carrie Grace.

**WILLIAM B. TUTHILL**[7] was the half-brother of Oliver B. Tuthill (see above), the son of Nathaniel[6] & 2d wife, Mary, the eldest of two children of Judge William Bodle of Hamptonburgh, Orange Co. Judge Bodle served as a j.p. & elder in the Presbyterian Church at Goshen, farmer; d. Tompkins Co. Mary Bodle was b. 6 Aug. 1771, d. 12 May 1861. She m. **NATHANIEL TUTHILL** 24 March 1810. "He was b. 1768, Feb.; d. 1846, March 28." [Note: the above birth & death dates probably refer to Judge Bodle.]

**WILLIAM B. TUTHILL**[7] b. on homestead 21 April 1811; m. 31 Jan. 1833, Mary, d/o Abimael & Mary (Harlow) Young of Blooming-Grove; Mary b. 9 Sept. 1810. **WILLIAM** was a member of the Presbyterian Church at Goshen & a public servant. Children:

Charles Bodle, m. Lizzie B. Doughty 11 Jan. 1860.

William Young.

Mary Vashti, d. young.

James, of Goshen, m. Sarah A. Doughty 28 Feb. 1872, at Goshen.

Sarah Frances, m. Jewett M. Ashman of Goshen.

Nathaniel B.

Harvey Wickham, d. young.

Several generations of Tuthills with the same given names lived in the area. Goshen church records show the birth of Freegift, s/o Joshua Tuthill, 29 April 1776. He is probably the same Freegift Tuthill who m. Elizabeth Swezy 5 Jan. 1801, at Goshen. Also recorded is the death of a Freegift Tuthill on 12 Oct. 1819, aged 44, of intemperance. The same records reveal yet another Freegift Tuthill family when on 24 Sept. 1832 is recorded the death of "child of Freegift Tuthill, 11 mo., Fit."

The LDS Ancestral File gives a Freegift Tuthill b. 8 Aug. 1698, s/o John Tuthill of Southold, NY & wife Mehitable Wells. Other children of John & Mehitable are given as: John b. 1685, Mary b. 1687, Joshua b. 1690, James b. 1692, Dorothy b. 1694, Daniel b. 1700 & Jemima (Hannah?) b. 1703.

## TWEEDLE, HARRY                    H-962

**HARRY TWEEDLE**, b. Town of Montgomery in 1868, s/o John & Phebe (Comfort) Tweedle, m. Mary E. Burch & had:

John P.

Robert K.

## TYLER, CAPT. BEZALEIL          A-523, C-98

**CAPT. TYLER** was the first man killed in Battle of Minisink, the only officer that day who had previous experience in fighting Indians. He left children:

1762, June 30, John.

1767, Aug. 30, Phebe.

1771, April 5, Elan.

1773, Sept. 4, Oliver.

Goshen church records say these children are those of Bazaleel & Abigail Calkin Tyler, of Kashetonck.

## TYMESON, GARRETT H.                H-962-3

postmaster of Otisville.

**GARRETT H. TYMESON**, b. 22 Feb. 1847 at Wayne Co., PA, was s/o Truman & Elsie Tymeson. Truman was a pioneer lumberman of PA. He was a lumberman & merchant & m. 2 May 1871, Mary Garrett Carey of Middletown, NY, and had:

Harry, d. in infancy.

1872, Sept. 6, Howard, m. Mary Dempsey; res. Paterson, NJ.

Arthur, m. Helen Clark of Middletown; d. 31 March 1905.

Elsie, m. Dr. L. A. Summers of Wheaton, KS; d. 2 Aug. 1902.

Walter, res. with father.

**GARRETT** has res. Frederick KS (1877); in 1897 to NY & located at Otisville; member Otisville Presbertian Church.

## UNDERHILL, WILLIAM I. [P]          A-369-9

of Newburgh.

**WILLIAM I. UNDERHILL** is a desc. of Capt. John Underhill who emigrated to New England from England; Indian fighter.

**SAMUEL UNDERHILL**[1], farmer of Newburgh, m. Alche --- & had 12 children, the youngest was:

**WILLIAM I. UNDERHILL**[2], b. Town of Newburgh, March 1817, Newburgh grocery business before 1840 to 1847, when he was deputy sheriff under Sheriff Welling; brick making business in New Windsor, various political services; d. 1880, Jan. 1. He m. (1st) Ann Eliza, d/o Isaac Lockwood of Gardnertown & had:

William.

Son, dec'd.

**WILLIAM I. UNDERHILL** m. (2d) 4 Jan. 1871, Miss Selina Montrose, eldest d/o Dr. James D. Johnston, Englishman, physician who settled in Middletown in 1842.

## VAIL FAMILY OF GOSHEN        A-524-5, C-80, 99, 101
etc., 504b

**VAIL, A. L. [P]**      C-9, 11, 14, 108, 116, 121, AA-6-89-90

of Wallkill.

**VAIL, HORTON [P]**                    A-498-9

of Wallkill.

**JOSIAH, SAMUEL & BENJAMIN VAIL**, brothers & pioneers of Orange Co.; all settled at Wallkill. They were s/o Benjamin Vail, and Benjamin was s/o John who settled in Rye, went to Southold c. 1700; an English emigrant from a family that settled in France in the 1500's.

**JOSIAH VAIL**[1] m. Patience Corwin & had:

**ISAIAH.**

Daniel, to Western NY.

John, res. Orange Co.

Phebe, m. cousin, William Vail.

Irene, d. unm.

ISAIAH VAIL[2], s/o Josiah[1], res. on the homestead. He was farmer of Wall Kill, proved will of Joshua Cox 30 Jan. 1792; he m. Abigail Meeker, and had:

Obadiah.
Mary.
JOSIAH.
Phebe.
Irene.
Nathaniel.
Isaiah.
Abigail.
John.
Samuel.
1776, April 17, George Washington.

JOSIAH VAIL[3], s/o Isaiah[2], m. Mary [Meriam] Smith (could be the Mrs. Mary Vail d. 1 June 1811, aged 70, at Goshen, pleursy), and had:

1783, Jan. 30, MOSES.
Luther, to Seneca Co., where he d.
1787, Aug. 30, David.
1791 [1790], June 4, Samuel S., now res. Southold, L.I. at age 90.
1797, Dec. 28, Maria [Mary], m. Dr. James M. Gardiner, physician of Newburgh.

MOSES VAIL[4], s/o Josiah[3], merchant at Slate Hill, after marriage purchased land at Wallkill, farmer, where he d. 1861, Sept. 6. He m. Miriam Hulse, b. 1784, d. 1872, Sept. 30, member of Old School Baptist Church. Children:

Gabriel, followed boating on the Hudson, d. with no family.
Silas, farmer of Wallkill.
Arminda, dec'd.
Josiah, dec'd.
Dayton, dec'd.
Luther, res. on homestead; dec'd.
Maria, m. Asa D. Dolson of Muscatine, IA.
Margaret M., res. on homestead.
1829, April 22, **ARCHIBALD L.**

**ARCHIBALD L. VAIL**[5], s/o Moses[4], b. on homestead at Wallkill, clerked at Middletown & NY City and later again at Middletown in drug and later hardware business until 1876, when he purchased Orange Co. Furnace & Machine Shops; bank director & Trustee of Second Presbyterian Church; m. 20 Oct. 1853, Ruth Ann, d/o Walter Everett & Phebe Case of Middletown, b. 10 April 1832, d. 17 Oct. 1878. Children:

Phebe Ann.
Archiena.
Moses.
James Coleman.

SAMUEL VAIL[1], s/o Benjamin, b. Southold, L.I., d. at Goshen, farmer, to Goshen 1740, where he died, was one of the 20 men who organized the town of Shelter Island, 1730, m.

Hannah Petty and had:
1740, GILBERT TOWNSEND.
Michael, moved to VT.
Phebe, m. David Horton.
Experience, m. Silas Horton.
Hannah, m. William Carpenter at Goshen 2 March 1777.

GILBERT TOWNSEND VAIL[2], s/o Samuel[1], d. at Battle of Minisink 22 July 1779, m. Hannah Arnot & had:

Julia.
SAMUEL.
Phebe.
Esther.
Hannah.
Polly.
1768, Nov., JOSEPH.

SAMUEL VAIL[3], s/o Gilbert[2], of Town of Goshen, farmer, cloth-dresser & fuller; m. Hannah Dunning 14 Oct. 1783, & had:

Deborah.
Gilbert.
1787, Sept. 23, SAMUEL.
James.
John.
Anson.
Sally. A Sally, d/o Samuel Vail, d. at Goshen aged 10, 5 Jan. 1810; cause of death spotted fever.
Phebe. Could be the Phebe noted in Goshen church records as having d. 30 March 1809, of spotted fever, aged 19.
Jacob.
Julia. Could be the Julia Ann Vail who m. Hudson L'Hommideau, 20 Sept. 1823, at Goshen.
William.
Hannah. Could be the Hannah Vail who m. Jonathan B. Dunning, 14 June 1825, at Goshen.
Horace. Could be the Horace Vail who m. Ann Joline Thompson, 12 Nov. 1828 at Goshen.

SAMUEL VAIL[4], s/o Samuel[3], farmer, wool carder & fuller, res. Minisink (Gardenville), Warwick & Pochunk, now Glenwood in Twp. of Vernon, Sussex Co., NJ until c. 1834, to Town of Warwick near Amity, where he d. 1855, April 5. He m. Sally, d/o Reuben Cash & Millicent Howell of Minisink & sister of the late Dr. Merritt H. Cash, physician of Orange County who d. 1861, Apri 26, age c. 60. Sallie was b. 1794, April 5, d. 1845, Nov. 7. Children:

Festus H., farmer near Great Bend & d. there.
Reuben C., farmer of New Milford, PA, where he d.
Samuel, farmer of New Milford, PA, where he d.
Charles M.
Lewis, with *Newark Morning Register*.
Dr. M.H.C., res. Newark.
George, res. New Milford, PA.
1834, June 27, **HORTON.**
Solomon VanRensselaer, dec'd.
John M., farmer at Havana, NY.

**HORTON VAIL[5]**, s/o Samuel[4], farmer & teacher, m. 1858, Oct. 8, Sarah France, d/o John S. & Hannah M. (France) Redfield of Goshen. They have one child, Nellie.

HORTON farmed near Goshen, 1865 to Middletown, book & stationery business; trustee Second Presbyterian Church. He is the only son of Samuel left residing in Orange County.

**JOSEPH VAIL[3]**, s/o Gilbert T.[2], b. Goshen, d. at Florida, NY 1828, weaver, Rev. soldier, m. Julia Smith & had:

JAMES VAIL[4], b. Florida 28 Apri. 1788, d. there 22 May 1833, farmer, tailor; m. (1) Dec. 1810, Elizabeth Dill of Dutch ancestry, m. (2) 3 Dec. 1828, Margaret Thompson. He had:

RICHARD M. VAIL[5], b. Florida, NY 25 Jan. 1820, d. Goshen 16 June 1882, merchant, co. treasurer (1860); m. 10 Nov. 1841, Mary, d/o William Wallace Armstrong of Warwick, s/o William, s/o William, s/o Francis who came from Ireland 1727, Scotch-Irish family. RICHARD & Mary had:

CHARLES MONTGOMERY VAIL[6], b. Goshen 5 June 1843, merchant; m. 26 Sept. 1866, Hattie Halsy Durland, d/o Benjamin Young & Emeline (Halstead) Durland of Chester. CHARLES res. Brooklyn, NY.

**BENJAMIN VAIL[1]**, s/o Benjamin, m. Miss --- Alsop & had:

William of Chester [Is probably the 'cousin' who m. Phebe above. Goshen church records say "Mary d/o William & Phebe Vail bapt. 14 Aug. 1774.]

John, settled on homestead.

Benjamin, killed at Minisink.

Mary, m. John Payne.

Lydia, d. unm.

_____

### VAIL, BENJAMIN F.                                     H-963
supervisor Town of Warwick.

BENJAMIN F. VAIL, b. 23 Oct. 1843 in Chester, Orange Co., to Honesdale, PA for 13 years; 1868 to Warwick; 1890 purchased business of R. & R. J. Wisner. He m. Jane C. Cline of Warwick 31 Dec. 1868, and had:

Cora C.

Pauline F.

_____

### VAIL, HARRY                                            H-963

HARRY VAIL, b. New Milford, Orange Co., in meat business at Amity & later bought farm at New Milford; peach grower with 9,000 trees. He m. 15 June 1899, Celia Utter, d/o of J. W. of Amity, and had:

Harry Jr.

Roy.

Emily.

_____

### VAIL, JOHN CARPENTER                                 H-963-4

JOHN C. VAIL, b. Chester, Orange Co., 13 May 1846, clerk for Dr. C. P. Smith one year & at D. H. Roe's grocery 2 years. In commission business 2 years in NY City & then

to Warwick, breeder of hunting dogs, specializing in English setters. He m. Mary Reed VanDuzer of Warwick 6 April 1864, and had:

Hazel Clark.

Christine Reed.

Robert Cornell.

_____

### VAIL, WILLETT                                         H-964

WILLETT VAIL, b. at Hughsonville, Dutchess Co., NY, now known as Fishkill-on-Hudson, 11 July 1848, one of 8 living children [parents not named.] Learned mason trade at Poughkeepsie & worked on the State Hospital at Middletown, then to Florida, NY where he resided 20 years. He m. Georgiana Eliza Thompson of Florida at age 27, and had:

Son, d. in infancy.

Harrie E., m. LeRoy Davis of NY City.

Ira V. K., now of NY City.

_____

### VAN BUREN, AYMAR                                      H-964
of New Windsor since 1851.

AYMAR VAN BUREN, b. NY City 10 Jan. 1837, is of "Holland" desc. His great-grandfather, grandfather & father, Col. John D. VanBuren, all b. NY City. In 1862 AYMAR purchased a farm of Edmund Morton, own of New Windsor. In 1863 he m. Margaret, d/o Mr. Morton. Active in public affairs; member Episcopal Church.

_____

### VAN CLEFT, JOSEPH                              H-964-5, C-31
merchant & banker of Newburgh.

JOSEPH VAN CLEFT, b. Town of New Windsor in 1836, is of a family that early settled in Minisink Valley. "His mother was a member of the Cooper family of Blooming-Grove." 1855-60 he res. in NY City, hardware merchant; 1860-62 in Kansas City, MO, returned to Newburgh 1863, member of Columbus Trust Co. & American Reformed Church. 1869 m. Edwina Storey Smith, granddau. of Judge Storey; she d. April 1891.

A Levi Van Cleft of Goshen was witness at the marriage of John D. Miller of Blooming Grove & Clarrissa Goble of Goshen, at Goshen, 4 March 1830.

_____

### VAN DUSER, JAMES HARRY                               H-967

JAMES is the s/o Isaac Van Duser & Mary Case. He was b. Town of Chester, 12 Dec. 1839. At age 18 to Warwick & later to Newburgh, hardware business. He m. Sarah A. Taylor 20 Dec. 1865, d/o Isaac Taylor & Margaret Smith, of Warwick. Their children:

Ella T., dec'd.

F. Clinton, in business with father.

Marie L., m. Thomas Welling.

_____

## VAN DUZER, HENRY           H-967

j.p. Town of Cornwall.

**HENRY** is the great-grandson of Isaac & the s/o John S. VanDuzer. He res. on farm near Cornwall Station, is a piano maker; 1860 m. Catherine Cox. They have 3 children, but only Henry J. is named here.

---

## VAN DUZER, ISAAC           H-965-7, C-12

**ISAAC VAN DUSER[1]**, the first white man to settle in the Ramapo Pass, was grandson of Abraham Pietersen Van Deursen, the original American ancestor of the family who was documented in America by 1636. Abraham was a miller of New Amsterdam in 1630 & took the English oath of allegience in 1664. **ISAAC[1]** came from Tappan & located with his family in the "Throat of the Cloff," as the narrow pass of the valley was then called. He bought 400 acres that John VanBlarcum had recently purchased of the Indians and built a home. Before 1848 **ISAAC** [Sr.] bought the Andrew Nichols patent at Cornwall and moved there with his 3 sons: Isaac Jr., Tjerck & Christopher. His farm descended from father to son & has been the home of Christopher, John, Charles Reeve & George Morehouse, the present owner & son of Christopher VanDuser. **ISAAC** was living there with a large family just at the time the present Orange Co. was being settled, principally by people from Southern Orange Co., now Rockland. As the young settlers came up through the Pass, **ISAAC** was able to supply each one with a wife until his ten daughters were all married. They were the maternal ancestors of many old Orange Co. families. **ISAAC'S** children:

Wiebeth, m. Benjamin Demarest.

Agnes, m. Samuel Sidman & res. on original homestead in the valley called Sidman's Pass during the Rev.

Marietje, m. Steven Sloat & res. on VanGelder Tract upon which they founded Sloatsburg. They had one son, John, killed in the Rev. That John had a son, John Drake Sloat, Rear Admiral of the US Navy.

Leah, m. --- Galloway & located further up the pass.

Autie, m. Major Zachariah DuBois (of Woodhull's Regt.)

Mary, m. Lt. William Roe (of Woodhull's Regt.)

Martha, m. --- Rose.

Elizabeth, m. --- LaRoy.

Catherine, m. a Polish exile nobleman, --- Obrisky.

Jane, m. --- Williams.

Tjerck, m. Catherine ---.

CHRISTOPHER.

ISAAC JR.

**CHRISTOPHER VAN DUZER[2]** s/o **ISAAC[1]**, Capt. in Col. E Woodhull's Cornwall Regt. during the Rev., m. (1) Juliana Strong; they had 1 child who married Jacob Manderville and had a dau. who m. (1) Nathaniel DuBois Woodhall & m. (2) Joseph Young. CHRISTOPHER m. (2) Juliana Tusten, sister of Lt. Col. Tustin killed at Minisink. In 1807 they moved to Warwick, and had:

Isaac, businessman of Cornwall & Warwick, where grand-dau.

Mary Burt now resides. Isaac's dau., Juliette m. Col. Wheeler; his son, Isaac Reeve VanDuser, is an atty. at Goshen. J. W. Gott of that place is his desc.

Benjamin, has no living descs.

Tusten.

William, to Chemung Co., left large family.

JOHN.

Selah, banker in NY City, left large family, one son was the late S. R. of Newburgh.

Elizabeth, m. Selah Reeve.

Ann, m. Nathan Wescott.

Mary, m. Ebenezer Crissey.

Sarah, m. John Dolson.

**JOHN VAN DUSER[3]**, s/o Christopher[2], is a member of the Legislature. His children:

Joseph Benedict of Bellvale.

Charles Reeve of Warwick.

James, has descs. living in IL.

Lanor (dau.), d. unmarried.

Harriet Fancher.

Mary LaZear.

Nancy Fish.

Julia Ann, m. Abner Benedict of Warwick.

Harriet, Mary & Nancy left descs. now res. in Dundee, NY. The names Fancher, LaZear & Fish could be their married names, but are not stated as such.

**ISAAC JR.[2]**, s/o **ISAAC[1]**, & his wife resided on the homestead in 1724 & later purchased the VanGelder tract, which joined the VanDuser land on the north. His children:

Isaac 3d, m. Letitia Mills & had one son, Alexander, of Gardiner, NY, now deceased.

Adolphus, to Sullivan Co.

Benjamin, has descs. near Cornwall.

**SHADRACK VAN DUSER**, supposed desc. of **ISAAC[1]** of Rampo, but not proved, living in Cornwall during the Rev. War, had:

Isaac, m. 23 July 1780, at Goshen, Martha Tusten, moved to Goshen; served in Capt. Van Duser's Co. Several grandchildren claim that Shadrack came from Holland when son Isaac was aged 12 in 1767.

Henry. His grandson, 'Squire Henry VanDuser' of Cornwall still living on a part of the land bought by Isaac in 1748.

---

## VAN DUZER, ISAAC R.           A-153-4, STJ-13, 14, 59, 81

atty., insurance man.

**ISAAC VAN DUZER[1]**, Dutch businessman of Cornwall m. Keturah Reeves & had:

**ISAAC R. VAN DUZER[2]**, b. Cornwall, Orange Co., 1802, May 8; to Goshen c. 1826, m. 1826, Dec. 14, Annie Eve [Eliza] Gedney, d/o Dr. Gedney of Newburgh; purchased old Hurtin homestead, where his family still resides; he d. consumption 27 Nov. 1841 & is bur. in the vault in the Episcopal Burying

Ground. Children:

1827, Oct. 28, Charlotte, wid. J. W. Gott, Esq. They m. at the home of the bride's mother 27 Jan. 1847.

1829, Jan. 11, Gertrude.

1832, June 26, George Wickham; d. in early manhood.

Kitty, m. Henry Strong, Esq., president of Bank of Green Bay, WI.

Hon. G., atty., d. 1859.

1833, Sept. 11, Isaac Reeve, NY City merchant; d. 1875.

1836, July 4, Eleazer Gidney.

1841, Sept. 11, Edward Gidney. Edward was bapt. 7 Feb. 1842, at which time his mother, Mrs. Ann E. Vanduzer, is listed in church records as the relict of "J." R. VanDuzer.

**ISAAC R. VAN DUZER**[2] served as District Attorney until 1835; insurance company, bank director, vestryman at St. James Episcopal Church.

---

**VAN ETTEN, LEVI [P]**                    A-753, LDS Anc. File
of Deerpark.

**VAN ETTEN, SOLOMON [P]**              A-174-5, H-968
physician & surgeon.

ANTHONY VAN ETTEN[1] to Valley of Neversink 1743, killed by Tories in 1778. Among his children was LEVI[2], served in the 3rd Orange Co. Regt. in the Rev., d. 7 June 1865, age 75. He had:

LEVI VAN ETTEN[3], of Rochester, Ulster Co., settled in Valley of Neversink c. 1743, blacksmith. He m. Eleanor Carpenter, d/o Benjamin Carpenter & Margaret Decker & had:

Margaret, m. Simeon Westfall.

John Jr., political service; dec'd.

Jacob.

Benjamin.

1822, April 12, LEVI.

Ann Eliza.

SOLOMON.

Alva.

Ellen.

LEVI VAN ETTEN[4], s/o Levi[3], res. on homestead, farmer; 1876 m. Mrs. Mary E. Green, d/o Silas Chapman of Orange Co. The Chapman family at an early day from England to Saybrook, CT, later to Orange Co., & later still to OH. LEVI is a supporter of the Reformed Dutch Church, his wife is a member.

SOLOMON VAN ETTEN[4], s/o Levi[3] b. 30 July 1829, Deerpark, Orange Co., grad. Albany Medical College, June 1855. He settled at Port Jervis, served in 56th Reg. NY Vol. in Civil War & later in 3rd Div. of the 18th Army Corps; m. (1st) 1856, Feb. 21, Harriet, d/o Col. Levi Westbrook of Waverly, NY, who d. 1857; m. (2d) 7 Sept. 1865, Mrs. Maria B. Sawyer, d/o Hon. Nathan Bristol of Waverly, and had:

Nathan B., physician of NY City.

Nellie B., res. with mother at Port Jervis.

SOLOMON[4] d. at Port Jervis 7 July 1894 from a concussion of the brain that resulted from a fall. His great-great grandfather, Johannes Decker, served in the Rev. War & his wife's name was Margaret.

The LDS Ancestral File shows a Van Etten family of Ulster Co. that has similar names to the family above, but no definite connections. An early member of this family is JAN VAN ETTEN[1], b. 3 Jan. 1666 in Kingston, m. 30 Nov. 1702 Jannetje Roosa, d/o Arien Heymanse Roosa & Maria Pels, also of Kingston. Their son:

JACOB VAN ETTEN[2], b. Hurley 25 Dec. 1696, m. Anna Westbrook who was b. Kingston 1700 & d. Namenock, NJ 1779. Anna was d/o Johannes Westbrook b. Albany 1662-67 & m. at Kingston in 1687, Maddelen Decker. Their son:

ANTHONY VAN ETTEN[3], b. at Knightsfield 12 June 1726, m. Hannah Decker of Ulster Co., d/o Thomas & had:

LEVI VAN ETTEN[4], b. Dutchess Co. 12 Feb. 1758 & m. Grannetje Westbrook.

---

**VAN INWEGEN FAMILY OF DEERPARK**        A-705

HARMANUS VAN INWEGEN m. --- Swartwout and had at least 2 children:

Gerardus.

Hannah, m. Thomas Decker.

---

**VAN INWEGEN, CHARAC J.**                    H-968-9

CHARAC J. VAN INWEGEN was b. 14 April 1851 in the Town of Deer Park; merchant in Huguenot which his father [not named] established, also branch in Port Jervis in connection with his brother John C. **CHARAC** m. (1) Catherine, d/o Isaac & Catherine (Rose) Cuddeback & had:

Willard.

He m. (2) Ellen S., d/o Peter P. Swartwout, and had:

Lyman C.

Harold B.

Allen J.

Ralph S.

Members of the Reformed Church.

---

**VAN INWEGEN, ELI [P]**                    A-739
of Deerpark.

BENJAMIN VAN INWEGEN[1] m. Charity Cole, d/o Cornelius W. Cole & Hannah Gumaer, both of Deerpark. Their youngest child:

ELI VAN INWEGEN[2], b. Town of Deerpark, 23 April 1816, farmer until 1860 when he retired. 1870 became affiliated with the Port Jervis Savings Bank; attended services of the Dutch Reformed Church. He m. 1841, Dec. 30, Elizabeth, d/o Crissy Bull of Pike Co., PA. Children:

Julia.

Cornelius.

1849, Charles F., only surviving child; grad. Rutgers College 1871; cashier at First National Bank, Port Jervis.

## VAN INWEGEN, MOSES [P]  A-751
of Deerpark.

CORNELIUS VAN INWEGEN[1], farmer, b. 1772, m. Deborah ---, b. 1774, Oct. 9, and his eldest child:
MOSES VAN INWEGEN[2], b. 1796, Dec. 6, m. (1st) 1823, Jan. 9, Susan Mapes and had 8 children, 5 now living; m. (2d) 1850, July 6, Eliza, d/o Abraham Shimer & had 6 children, all surviving. [No children named here.] He attended Reformed Church & d. 22 April 1863, at the homestead.

## VAN KEUREN, BENJAMIN  U2-39
of Shawangunk, yeoman.

BENJAMIN VAN KEUREN, bapt. 15 Nov. 1713, s/o Tjerck Matthysen Van Keuren, m. (1) 13 July 1735, Zara Swart and had:
Bapt. 1735, Nov. 9, Tjerck.
Bapt. 1738, May 21, Hendricus.

BENJAMIN m. (2) Feb. 1753, Maria Bunschoten, widow of Johannes Schepmoes, and had:
Sarah, m. Solomon Brink.
Mary, m. Abraham Westbrook.

BENJAMIN's will, dated 14 Oct. 1786, also names a son Levy.

## VAN KEUREN, HENRY NEWTON  H-969, W-13
businessman Town of Crawford.

HENRY NEWTON VAN KEUREN is the s/o Henry L. & Eleanor (Crawford) VanKeuren, b. Town of Shawangunk, Ulster Co., NY, 1842. He was a world traveler & d. in Germany in 1907. He m. (1) 1869, Helen, only d/o John Hill, Jr.; she d. 1870 & he m. (2) in 1873, Catherine Ronk of Crawford, who d. in Newburgh in 1888.
The family were from Holland & early settlers in NY. The VanKeuren Stone house, now generally known as the Downs House, c. a mile west of Goodwill Church, on the road to Montgomery, was built in part by Hendricus VanKeuren in 1768. The house is in excellent condition (1914).

## VAN KLEECK, BALTUS L.  A-165
physician.

BALTUS VAN KLEECK to Orange Co. from Duchess; his sister was wife of Judge Jonathan Fisk. He m. a d/o Robert Boyd of New Windsor & had a son, Rev. ROBERT BOYD VAN KLEECK, of the Episcopal Church who recently died. BALTUS d. 1843, aged 69.

## VANAMEE, WILLIAM [P]  A-160
atty. of Middletown.

Descended from one of three brothers from Holland who settled early in NY. Two settled on L.I. & the other on the Hudson. WILLIAM b. Albany 9 Jan. 1847, to Middletown at age 19. Sept. 1871 m. Lida (named as Eliza in Dr. J. W.'s sketch), d/o Dr. J. W. Ostrom of Goshen.

## VAN NESS, CLARENCE  H-969

CLARENCE VAN NESS, b. Edenville, Orange Co., 28 March 1869, s/o John J. (who d. 1891, aged 73) & Anna A. (Barrett) VanNess. John was hotel man in Edenville 27 years; Anna d. 1904, aged 63. CLARENCE in meat business, then milk business; breeds horses.
Another child of John J. & Anna was Mamie E. VanNess who m. John F. Knapp of Newark, NJ.

## VAN NESS, JOHN W.  H-969-70

JOHN, b. Bellvale, Orange Co., 29 Oct. 1852; s/o Peter, wheelwright who d. 1885. JOHN continued his father's business & established others. On 9 Dec. 1880 he m. Mary A. Hazen of Greenwood Lake. They have one dau., Maud, b. 23 Sept. 23 1881; she is at home.

## VAN NESS, WILLIAM  H-970-1, C-16

WILLIAM VAN NESS, b. 26 April 1836 at Pompton, NJ, s/o Peter S. & Eliza Jane (Brown) VanNess, was one of 12 children. He was a butcher for 32 years; 1900 to Goshen & purchased the Orange Hotel. He m. Jane Stidworthy of Warwick; she of English birth & to America with her parents at age 3. Their children:
Emma B., m. Harry J. Bogart of Passaic, NJ.
Sarah Ann, m. Burt Edsall of Goshen.

The record of a wedding between Peter Vaness & Hannah Fort, at Washington Co., NY, 4 June 1787, is found in Goshen church records.

## VAN VLIET, SAMUEL C. JR.  H-970, STJ-45, 64

SAMUEL, b. Town of Blooming-Grove 29 Dec. 1833. General store of Seaman & Van Vliet in Monroe. 1861 to Oxford Depot, merchant. 20 Dec. 1858 m. Euphenia Jenkins of Monroe, youngest d/o Ira & Millie (Smith) Jenkins. They had:
Elsie J., m. M. S. G. Lent & have Helen Grace who m. William H. Smith of Chester, NY.
Effie, m. Fred L. Conklin of Chester.

The VanVliet family is of Holland origins. SAMUEL is elder of Presbyterian Church of Monroe.

St. James Church in Goshen records the m. of William D. VanVliet to Julia Smith 27 Oct. 1869. She is d/o John I. Smith. Their son John Jewell VanVliet, b. 15 Sept. 1871 & bapt. 17 Dec. 1871.

---

## VARCOE, EDWIN R.                    H-970-1
dentist of Goshen.

SAMUEL VARCOE[1], English gentleman of County of Cornwell, had:

R., b. England, to America, ME Church pastor of PA, now dec'd.

FRANCIS, b. England.

FRANCIS VARCOE[2], s/o Samuel[1], m. (1) Mary Hocken [see below]. Both Francis & Mary were b. England, where they married in 1846. To America on their wedding tour & settled in Honesdale, PA. He was a farmer & d. 1895; she d. 1865. Members of the ME Church, they had 8 children: 3 sons & 5 daus.:

Lavenia, m. Isaiah Scudder of Middletown, NY; d. 27 May 1908.

Sophia, widow of Ira S. Baxter of Wallingford, CT.

4 Nov. 1850, EDWIN R.

Elizabeth, m. Frank Sagendorph of Jersey City; d. 22 Feb. 1896.

Selina.

Mrs. T. Edson Harding of Howells, NY.

William F., physician of NY City.

Carrie, m. Herman Groffell of Jersey City.

Charles W., dentist of Walden, NY.

FRANCIS m. (2) 1875, Mrs. Elizabeth (Onger) Glenn, and had:

Kittie, m. Charles Webb of Bethany, PA.

FRANCIS was a member of the ME Church & d. 1895, aged 80 years, near Honesdale, PA.

EDWIN R. VARCOE[3], s/o Francis[2], b. near Honesdale, PA, at age 27 studied dentistry under Dr. J. W. Kesler of Honesdale; 1880 grad. Philadelphia Dental College & established practice in Goshen. Member Presbyterian Church of Goshen.

REV. EDWARD HOCHEN, father of Mrs. Mary (Francis) Varcoe, was minister of the Church of England. Mary was 1 of 7 children. Another child, Edward Jr., was clergyman under John Wesley in the Methodist Church early in the movement. On the maternal side she is the granddau. of Rev. Charles Hicks, and the great granddau. of Rev. William Geake, both also Church of England.

---

## VELTMAN, HENRY O.                    H-971-2
of town of Mt. Hope.

HENRY O. VELTMAN, b. 31 Dec. 1847, Town of Wallkill, s/o Albert Moson & Eunice (Howell) Veltman, one of 10 children, 7 daus. & 3 sons. In milk business in Jersey City, NJ 3 years & then returned to homestead farm. He m. Helen

Kennedy of Howells, Orange Co., she of Scotch desc., to America age 17. Members Otisville Methodist Church.

---

## VERNON, MONTGOMERY H.          H-972, LDS Anc. File

MONTGOMERY H. VERNON, b. 7 April 1846, Town of Monroe, s/o Elvin & Catherine Vernon, 9th of 10 children. Farmer, clerked for D. H. Roe of Chester 1 year & Burchard & Smith nearly 3 years; meat business. At Washingtonville with W. H. Hallock, brick manufacturer; onion shipper. He m. 20 Dec. 1870, Mary A. Goble of Florida, NY who d. 27 April 1906. They had 6 children, 2 d. in infancy:

Russell M., atty. of Middletown.

Emma A., m. Robert W. Anderson.

Sarah H., m. Richard M. Ferries, atty. of NY City.

George Herbert, res. at home.

The LDS Ancestral file gives a brief record of a Vernon family of Orange Co. CHARLES THOMAS VERNON, b. 19 March 1850 in Monroe, m. Emma Conkling, b. 25 April 1861, d/o William R. Conkling & Rachel Southerland of Monroe. They had one dau., Ruth, b. Feb. 1892 in Monroe.

---

## VOLCK, ANDRIES                         CN-9

ANDRIES VOLCK appears in the Newburgh Directory for 1709, the year the town was settled by immigrants from the Palatinate of the Rhine. He was husbandman & viner, aged 30 at immigration; his wife Anna Catharine, aged 27. Their children:

Maria Barbara, aged 5 at immigration.

George & Hieronemus, aged 4.

Anna Gertrude, aged 1 year.

---

## WADE, ANDREW K.                        H-972
stove & tinware establishment at Walden.

ANDREW, b. 1845 at Montgomery, a s/o Jabez P. & Susan (Millspaugh) Wade. His business was established by his brother, Joseph G. Wade, who d. in 1862. ANDREW has served as j.p. & police justice. 1879 m. Sarah Frances McVey and they have one dau. living: Frances Willard Wade.

---

## WAIT, GEORGE W.                        H-972-3
## WAIT, WESLEY [P]
surgeon dentist of Newburgh since 1885.
## WAIT, CHARLES D.                H-972, [P] W-87, C-47
businessman of Montgomery.

SAMUEL WAIT[1], from Somersetshire, England in 1821 to farm in Orange Co., NY with wife Mary Welch, who he m. in England. They had 9 children, the 5th son was:

THOMAS WAIT[2] m. Mary Mould and had:

1853, GEORGE W.

1861, May 15, WESLEY.

CHARLES D.

GEORGE W. WAIT[3], s/o Thomas[2], b. at homestead in Town of Montgomery (same property purchased by his grandfather Samuel). He m. Cornelia, d/o J. Egbert Kidd of Orange Co. family, and had:
Charles D. Jr., d. age 5.
Helen Marguerite.

WESLEY WAIT[3], s/o Thomas[2], also b. on homestead near Village of Montgomery, m. (1) 10 June 1885, at Goshen, Emily S., d/o Gen. John A. Prawlins [Rawing/ Goshen church records show her name as Emily S. Rawlins]. She d. 25 March 1898 & left one dau., Lucille R. who m. John Springstead Bull. WESLEY m. (2) Annie E. Knapp, dau. of Samuel T. of NY City. "Their mansion is located at Grand Ave. & North St., overlooking the Hudson." He has invented several dental applicances.

CHARLES D. WAIT[3] was youngest s/o Thomas[2] & Mary (Mould) Wait, b. at the homestead in Town of Montgomery; dealer in coal, lumber, cattle, etc. for NY City markets; bank director. Member Dutch Reformed Church. [W-86 says member of the Goodwill Presbyterian Church.] He m. Eliza Seymour in June 1897, she of Walden, only d/o James.

## WALLACE, GEORGE [P]                    A-504e, C-40, 97

WILLIAM WALLACE[1], of Scotch-Irish extraction, from the North of Ireland with his wife & 4 sons and two daus. at the close of the Revolutionary War & settled in MD, where he d. Children:
John, settled in Goshen, NY, teacher, merchant & Co. Treasurer; he d. there.
1777, WILLIAM.
James, farmer of Milford, PA, where he died.
Robert, lumber merchant in Philadelphia, where he died.
Jane, m. Robert Loghead of Wallkill.
Mary, m. Robert A. Thompson of Hopewell.

WILLIAM WALLACE[2], s/o William[1], to Crawford, Orange Co.; m. c. 1806, Kezia MacDowell; 1809 purchased land near Scotchtown in the Town of Wallkill; deacon of the Presbyterian Church at Scotchtown; res. Middletown & died on the homestead of his son GEORGE. Kezia d. 1842, aged 52; their children:
John C., merchant at Goshen, Co. Clerk (1843-46 & 1876-79). Could be the John C. Wallace who was a witness at the wedding of John Wallace & Mary Strong, both of Goshen, 21 Sept. 1858. A John Wallace m. Elizabeth Denton 11 April 1823, at Goshen.
William, carriage maker, res. Bullville; d. 1863 at Middletown.
Mary W., widow of Theron Libolt, res. Scotchtown.
Rebecca, widow of Walter B. Sears of Montgomery.
Robert, merchant at Goshen, d. there aged 27, consumption, 9 Aug. 1839.
Andrew T., farmer of Crawford.
Harvey, merchant of Goshen.
Martha Jane, m. John E. Corwin of Scotchtown; dec'd.
1823, July 17, GEORGE.

Alfred, d. age 13.
Matilda.
Theodore, d. age 18, 1846.
Elizabeth.
James, d. young.
James (2d), d. young.

GEORGE WALLACE[3], s/o William[2], age 14 learned trade of wagon making with brother-in-law, Walter B. Sears, in Montgomery; 11 Nov. 1846, m. Susan C., d/o OLIVER BAILEY [see below] & Susan Millspaugh of Goshen, former res. near Scotchtown. Susan b. 29 July 1825. 1848 GEORGE settled on old Baldwin homestead in Wallkill, stock raiser; 1873 manufactured bricks at Middltown. Children:
Georgiana; d. age 6, 21 March 1855.
Susan Alice, m. John W. Clark of Goshen.
Theodore.
Carrie H.

OLIVER BAILEY, s/o Capt. David Bailey was b. on L.I. & settled near Phillipsburgh in Town of Wallkill. He d. 20 Dec. 1867, aged 78. He m. Susan Millspaugh who d. 5 July 1873, age 80. Members of the Presbyterian Church at Scotchtown.

## WALLACE, REV. ROBERT H., D.D. [P]        A-231-2
of New Windsor.

REV. ROBERT H. WALLACE, Presbyterian minister, was b. Town of Montgomery, Orange Co., 12 Nov. 1796. His parents were natives of Northern Ireland, members of the Reformed Presbyterian Church. He served at Neelytown, Newburgh and Little Britain, where he d. 9 Feb. 1868, and was bur. at the churchyard at Little Britain. On his tombstone it states that he was the 4th pastor of the Presbyterian Church of Little Britain.
ROBERT had one son, Rev. R. HOWARD WALLACE, A.M., acting associate with his father, & later pastor. R. HOWARD was b. 20 Dec. 1828, Little Britain & served as army chaplain in the 168th NY Vols.

## WALLING, JOHN C. [P]                      A-558b
of Goshen.

JOHN T. WALLING[1], b. Ireland, to America as a young man, settled Vernon Twp., Sussex Co., NJ, where he d. in middle age. He m. Miss --- Baird & had:
Sarah, d. age 6.
c. 1786, FRANCIS.
Joseph.

FRANCIS WALLING[2], s/o John T.[1], tanner & currier, res. Warwick, later Cincinnati; m. (1st) Margaret Perry in Amity, Orange Co., and had:
1809, JOSEPH.
Catharine, m. Nathan Campbell.
Sally, m. Robert T. Martin.

Vincen [sic] P.
Hester.
John T.
Hannah, m. Frederick Gulick.
Abiah F.
Brice P.
William.

FRANCIS m. (2d) Mrs. --- VanCourt, sister of Gov. John
   Wilcox, and had:
Julia.
Harriet.
Mary, m. Alfred Carling.
Almeda, m. --- Chauncey of Millpaugh.
Henry C.

JOSEPH WALLING[3], b. Amity, s/o Francis[2], tanner; after mar.
   res. Hamburg, NY, then farmer in Vernon Twp., Sussex Co.,
   NJ until 1852 when he removed to Goshen. He m. Margaret,
   d/o John Campbell & Hannah Tompkins of Vernon &
   granddau. of William Campbell of Monmouth Co., NJ of
   Scotch desc. Margaret b. 1810, d. Oct. 1880. They had one
   child:
1830, April 10, **JOHN C.**

**JOHN C. WALLING[4]**, b. Hamburg, NY, to Orange Co. with
   father 1852; dairy farmer & businessman; m. (1st) 22 Oct.
   1851, Sarah, d/o William & Catherine (Lyons) Thompson of
   Vernon Twp., NJ. Sarah b. 1829, d. Jan. 1858. Children:
George T.
Albert.

**JOHN C.** m. (2d) Sarah, d/o Jonas & Abby Durland of Goshen,
   21 Dec. 1859. Sarah was b. 6 April 1837, d. 28 March
   1868, no issue. He m. (3d) 1 Jan. 1867, Anna, d/o Samuel
   T. & Phebe P. (Pearsall) Seaman of Cornwall, NY, b. 22
   April 1837. Children:
Joseph.
Maggie C.
Carrie T.
John.

---

## WALSH, HUGH                          A-221, T-297-6

The Walsh family is of English origin. **HUGH** emigrated from
   the area of Belfast, Ireland in 1764 & settled in Philadelphia.
   He later moved to NY, where he m. 1775, Catharine, d/o
   Mrs. Jane Armstrong. 1789 to New Windsor & in 1790
   purchased tract of land from Gov. Clinton on south side of
   Quassaick Creek. 1791 to Newburgh, built a dock & store-
   house now occupied by Mr. Mailler; in 1792 with James
   Craig erected the paper mill later known & run by his son
   John N. Walsh, now by grandson J. DeWitt Walsh. **HUGH**
   d. 1817, aged 72. Children:
Jane.
Mary Ann.
Eliza, m. Solomon Sleight, no issue.

Catharine, m. David Andrews of NY.
Charlotte, m. Rev. James M. Mathews, 1st Chancellor of the
   Univ. of NY.
James, m. Elizabeth d/o Alex. Robertson & settled in NY. He
   d. suddenly on a visit to Richmond, VA, leaving 5 children.
Samuel Armstrong, physician, surgeon for many years at West
   Point Military Academy; m. Hester G., d/o Pascal N. Smith
   of NY; he d. Pasaaic, NJ 1829.
John H., late of New Windsor; m. Elizabeth, d/o John DeWitt,
   formerly of Dutchess Co. Left 7 children; d. 1853.

---

## WALSH, WILLIAM [P]                     A-356-7, TN-323
## WALSH, HENRY [P]                             A-356-7
of Newburgh.
## WALSH, THOMAS [P]                               A-176a

Family of Scotch desc., settled in North of Ireland.

THOMAS WALSH[1] to America & settled in Cumberland Valley
   (PA) c. 1769, where he joined his only sister Mary, wife of
   Maj. Hawkes of Sussex Co., NJ. 1772 removed to New
   Windsor, Orange Co., settled on a farm near Washington
   Lake. He m. Margaret Brush of Rockland Co., NY, of New
   England family that settled in eastern L.I. THOMAS d. 19
   March 1819; Margaret d. 18 April 1837, aged 84. Their
   children:
1773, Oct. 4, **WILLIAM.**
John.
Thomas.
Mary.
Rachel.
1785, Dec. 24, **HENRY.**
Elizabeth.
Michael.
Harriet.
Anna.

WILLIAM WALSH[2], s/o Thomas[1], b. Town of New Windsor;
   shipbuilder at New Windsor, ran freight & passenger
   business, sloop Capt.; 1812 removed to Newburgh, dry good
   business with brother **HENRY**, gov't. service, member of
   Rev. Dr. Johnston's Church; 1827 Bank president; d. 2 Nov.
   1839 His obituary TN-323. He m. (1st) Mary, d/o Isaac
   Van Duzer of Cornwall; she d. 18 Oct. 1801. They had two
   children:
Isaac V., d. infant.
Abram, d. infant.

WILLIAM WALSH[2] m. (2d) Mary, d/o Judge Joseph Morrell
   of New Windsor, and had:
Joseph M.
Margaret.
William H.
Albert.
Charles.
Mary A.
Norman A.

John J.
Edward L.
Sarah E.

**HENRY WALSH[2]**, s/o Thomas[1], b. New Windsor, businessman at Middletown, to Newburgh 1810 in business with brother **WILLIAM**; d. 30 July 1868 after suffering stroke in 1861. Assoc. Reformed Church trustee over 50 years. 9 Sept. 1809, m. Mehetabel, d/o Capt. William Bull of Wallkill, and had:
William B.
Julia A.
James.
Abram.
1817, Oct. 11, **THOMAS**.
Mehetabel.
Henry R.
George H.
Harriet.
Augustus H.
Robert.

**THOMAS WALSH[3]**, b. Newburgh, NY, banker in Newburgh; merchant in the south with brother (not named). 1847 back to Newburgh to study medicine with Dr. Alpheus Goodman, later student in Brooklyn. Settled in Fallsburgh, Sullivan Co.; 1852 to Port Jervis.

**WARD, GEORGE N.**                                  H-973-4
dentist of Walden since 1895.
**WARD, J. ERSKINE**                                 H-974

JAMES WARD Sr.[1], b. Town of Newburgh 1797; 1826 purchased farm in Crawford Twp. His son:
JAMES WARD JR.[2] m. Elizabeth Crans, and had:
**GEORGE N.**
1864, March 4, **J. ERSKINE**.

**GEORGE N. WARD[3]**, b. Town of Crawford, Orange Co.; grad. Univ. of MD Dental School; m. Miss --- Bradnack of Middletown and had:
Elizabeth, m. George Robert Bartlett [marriage written in by hand on this copy].

**J. ERSKINE WARD[3]**, s/o James Sr.[2], b. Town of Crawford. In 1888 in feed business at Thompson's Ridge; 1898 hardware business at Pine Bush in partnership with J. L. McKinney & in 1904 established sawmill. Member SAR.

**WARREN FAMILY OF NEWBURGH**              TN-285-6

JAMES WARREN[1], of Woodbridge (now Bethany) CT, m. Abigail Thomas. JAMES d. during the Rev. War "at the North," probably at Ticonderoga, where he had gone to take care of his son Edward, then a soldier & sick. James & Abigail had:
Jason.

Sarah.
Rachel.
Abigail.
1755, Jan. 15, NATHANIEL.
Jemima.
Edward.
Richardson, killed during the Rev. on board the American frigate *Trumbull* by a cannon ball that passed through both thighs.

**NATHANIEL WARREN[2]**, s/o James[1], m. Susanna, d/o Isaac Johnson of Seymour, CT, & had:
Betsey.
Charles.
Marshall.
1787, Dec. 23, ISAAC.
1790, July 4, MILES.
Susan.

**ISAAC WARREN[3]**, s/o Nathaniel[2], b. Bethany, CT, m. 12 Sept. 1812, Leonora, d/o Israel Perkins & had:
Israel P.
WILLIAM E.
Susan H.
Isaac W.
Harris F.
Cornelia A.
George F.

**WILLIAM E. WARREN[4]**, s/o Isaac[3], to Newburgh in 1836 & clerked at Crawford & Co. until 1841; later merchant of Newburgh & NY City. He retired in 1851, after which he worked as auditor of RRs & political appointments. He m. 25 March 1840, Lydia Riggs, d/o Charles & Amelia (Birdsall) Riggs. They had one dau., Mary Cushman Warren.

**MILES WARREN[3]**, s/o Nathaniel[2], b. Bethany, CT, m. (1) Sally Coe in 1810; she d. 13 April 1855. Their children:
George T.
William S.
Edward M.; dec'd.
Edward R. M.; dec'd.
Sarah A. H.; dec'd.
John W.

**MILES[3]** m. (2) 1856, Ruth, d/o James Miller, formerly of Crawford, Orange Co., & had:
1858, May 13, Anson Miles.

**WARREN FAMILY OF NEWBURGH**              TN-284-5
**WARREN, WILLIAM L. F. [P]**                 A-288-9
banker of Newburgh.

Family of Norman desc., settled early in New England. JOHN WARREN[1] to America c. 1630, settled at Watertown, MA. His children, all probably b. in England:
John.
Mary.

DANIEL.
Elizabeth.

DANIEL WARREN[2], s/o John[1], m. 10 Dec. 1650, Mary Baron & had 9 children. Their 7th child was:
JOHN WARREN[3], b. 5 March 1665, m. Mary Brown & had 3 children, one of which was:
JOHN WARREN[4], b. 15 March 1684/5. He had:
1714/15 JOSIAH.
1725, Aug. 23, Beulah, m. John Hobbs of Brookfield.

JOSIAH WARREN[5] m. Hepzibah Hobbs & had 10 children, one of which was JOHN[6].

Presbyterian Church record at Newburgh: "JOHN WARREN[6] of MA m. Elizabeth Belknap of Newburgh, 28 July 1783." He was left an orphan as an infant & raised by his Aunt Beulah, wife of John Hobbs of Brookfield, MA. At the age of 19 he fought in the Rev., after the war res. Newburgh, Troy & Saratoga Springs, where he d. 25 Dec. 1823. Elizabeth d. 21 June 1837. Children:
1786, JOHN H.
1788, Aug. 2, Cynthia M., m. Miles Beach of Saratoga Springs.
1790, Nov., Stephen R.
1793, Feb. 4, WILLIAM L. F.
1795, Elizabeth B., m. Dr. R. R. Davis of Syracuse.
1798, Caroline S., m. Benjamin Carpenter of Newburgh.
1800, Mary A., m. James H. Darrow of Saratoga Springs.

JOHN H. WARREN[7], s/o John[6], m. Fanny Kellogg; d. 1823, Montezuma, NY. His only son:
1811, July 3, WILLIAM L. F.

WILLIAM L. F. WARREN[8], s/o John H.[7], b. Marcellus, NY, clerked at Newburgh in employ of uncle Benjamin Carpenter; director of National Bank of Newburgh & of the Warwick Valley RR; m. Catharine, d/o John H. Walsh. WILLIAM L. F. d. 22 Oct. 1879.

## WATERBURY, HON. JAMES E. [P]                A-612
of Warwick.

Family from England to Stamford, CT. JAMES WATERBURY[1], soldier of the Revolution, b. 28 Nov. 1754, m. Elizabeth Mead, and had:
Betsey.
Charles.
Catherine.
Henry.
1789, June 29, WILLIAM.
Warren.
Rufus.
Ann. (Only child now surviving.)

WILLIAM WATERBURY[2], s/o James[1], m. Nancy Weeks, d/o Col. Henry, soldier of the Rev., of Stamford CT, 24 Oct. 1811, and had:

William H.
1824, Sept. 2, JAMES E.
Eliphalet Price.

JAMES E. WATERBURY[3], s/o William[2], b. Poughkeepsie, NY, to Orange Co. with family in 1828; farmer, political office holder, businessman, Presbyterian Church; m. 29 Nov. 1848, Sarah, d/o John Wilcox, Esq. of Merritt's Island, Warwick. They have 4 children, all living (not named).

## WATERS, MAJ. THOMAS                A-524, STJ-53
of Goshen.

THOMAS WATERS lived just beyond the milestone on the Florida Rd.; early sheriff of Orange Co., children:
Thomas.
Henry.
Elizabeth, m. Thomas Thorn at Goshen 6 Aprili 1826.
Mrs. Robert Seeley.

## WATKINS, WILLIAM SAYER                H-974-5

WILLIAM S. WATKINS, b. on homestead farm, Town of Hamptonburgh 3 Aug. 1820; d. 7 Nov. 1884. Farmer; m. Emma Monell of Hamptonburgh 15 Sept. 1859, and had:
1860, July 12, Juliana B., m. B. Seward Carr of Chicago.
1866, Nov. 7, William Sayer, res. on homestead.
1867, Dec. 25, John Evans, m. Anna Eliza Blake 9 March 1905 & had 2 children: Elizabeth, b. 2 Jan. 1906 & Emma Adeline, b. 1 Oct. 1907.

## WEBB, WILLIAM B. [P]                A-503-4
of Wallkill.
## & OTHER WEBBS

SAMUEL WEBB[1], farmer of Wallkill, m. Mary Bennett & had:
1799, Dec. 13, HIRAM B.
Cynthia, m. Cornelius Van Scoy.
Esther, m. William Shaw.
Abby Maria, m. Solomon Crane.
Hannah Jane, m. BAILEY CRANE. [see below]

HIRAM B. WEBB[2], s/o Samuel[1], until 1866 farmer on the Bloomingburgh plank road, 1 mile out of Middletown; 1866 to Middletown & d. there 10 Dec. 1869. Member Old-School Baptist Society at Middletown; m. 23 Jan. 1838, Hephzibah, b. 5 Oct. 1803, d/o JONAS HULSE [see below] & Hephzibah (Reeve). Children:
Mary, m. David Murray.
James R.
Martha, m. John Anderson
Effa.
Jonas.
Isaiah.
Silas.
Hephzibah.
Israel.

Ambrose.

Lewis.

William.

BAILEY CRANE[1] m. Hannah Jane Webb, d/o Samuel, and had:

JEHIAL CRANE[2], eldest s/o Bailey, farmer of Wallkill, d. Ellenville, Ulster Co. Children (wife not named):

William B., sheriff of Ulster Co.

Harriet, m. Edwin Bartholf of Warwick.

Ira.

Mary, m. Harvey Brodhead of Ellenville.

[NOTE: This is a very obscure entry and the above are deduced as children of Bailey Crane & Hannah Jane Webb because there is simply no other family to place them in.]

SILAS HULSE[1], b. L.I., March 1726; d. 18 June 1770, fought in French & Indian War; m. Charity Smith b. 9 May 1734, d. 30 Oct. 1814. Their son, JONAS HULSE[2], b. 29 Nov. 1759, d. 23 March 1845, made spinning wheels, later was a farmer near Middletown.

JONAS HULSE[2] m. Hephzibah, d/o Deacon James Reeve who settled in Wawayanda from L.I. & was a founder of the Congregational Church at Middletown. Deacon James Reeve m. Mary (b. 25 Nov. 1713), d/o David Moore, first settler of Minisink. Mary d. 18 June 1789.

**WEBB, NATHANIEL [P]**   A-532-3, C-17

teacher, newspaper editor of Goshen.

BENJAMIN WEBB[1] had a son, BENJAMIN[2], who had a son, NATHANIEL[3], b. 16 Aug. 1798, on old homestead farm near Middletown. He d. 20 April 1855. May 1827 m. Louisa, d/o Xenophon & Abigail (Burr) Mead of Wilton, CT & sister of Charles Mead of Goshen. After marriage **NATHANIEL** opened school at Middletown; later in Montgomery & still later opened private female boarding school in Goshen. Member Presbyterian Church of Goshen.

Goshen church records show the marriage of Benjamin Webb & Sarah Vail 4 May 1788.

**WEBBER, JACOB**   CN-10

**JACOB WEBBER** is found in the Newburg Directory for the year 1709, the year the town was founded by immigrants from the Palatinate of the Rhine. He is listed as husbandman and viner, aged 30 on immigration; his wife, Anna Elizabeth, aged 25 and children:

Eve Maria, aged 5 on immigration.

Eve Elizabeth, aged 1 year.

**WEYGANT FAMILY OF MONROE**   A-789, H-983

ROBERT F. WEYGANT, d. 3 Sept. 1902, established carriage factory at Central Valley in 1867, and had (all 3 formerly of R. F. Weygant's Sons at Central Valley):

Fred.

William.

Frank E.

The first town meeting (1799) of Monroe was held at the home of JOHN WEYGANT[1], where TOBIAS WEYGANT was chosen a town officer. JOHN C.[2], s/o JOHN[1], had:

Mrs. Charles F. Ford.

Mrs. Abram Weygant.

Mrs. Alfred Cooper.

Mrs. Rachel McKelsey.

Henry.

Benjamin.

Frank.

**WEIGARD [WEYGAND] FAMILY OF NEWBURGH**
TN-262-3, CN-9, 10, 15, LDS Anc. File

REV. GEORGE HERMAN WEIGAND, b. c. 1634, of Neider, Germany, Lutheran minister of the Rhine Palatinate, rec'd. a grant of land from Queen Anne in 1708 in territory now in City of Newbugh. He had two sons, Michael below & Herrman, b. c. 1660. His son:

MICHAEL[1], b. 1656 in Pfaltz [Neider], Germany, m. c. 1686 Ann Catharina --- & was first of family to America. They settled in Newburgh, where he appears in City Directory in 1709, the year the town was founded. He was aged 52 at immigration & his wife was aged 54. Their children:

1695, Anna Maria, aged 13 at time of immigration.

1701, TOBIAS, aged 7 on immigration.

1703, GEORGE, aged 5 on immigration.

Martin.

TOBIAS WEIGARD[2], in 1725 chosen as trustee of the Glebe at Newburgh. In 1745 he bought land near what is now village of Highland Falls. His son Martin[3] opened the first principal tavern of Newburgh, where he d. 1792, leaving no issue.

GEORGE WEIGARD[2], left several children, including Michael[3]. Michael's son, Capt. Martin Weigard[4], was a ship builder & fisherman. He was a practical joker, good natured & honest. He d. 1834.

The original settler **MICHAEL** had a grandson, Martin Weigand, who appeared in the Newburgh Town Directory of 1750. The family is today represented in Newburgh by James Weygant & Col. Charles H. Weygant. (CN-15)

**WELCH, BENJAMIN**   H-979

of Little York.

GABRIEL WELCH[1] m. Eliza --- & had nine children; those still living:

1832, Oct. 11, **BENJAMIN**.

Susan, m. Martin V. B. Horton of Warwick.

Mary, m. Edsel Stage.

BENJAMIN WELCH[2] was a carpenter, later with Brown & Bailey Creameries of Amity & Edenville 5 years. 1 March 1871 to Pleasant Valley to manage his father's farm, which had been in the family since since 1844. Now has large dairy farm & is extensive peach grower. 9 July 1863 m. Mary E. Davenport of Warwick, and had:

1864, March 26, George, m. Mary Feagles of Pine Island 31 Dec. 1904.

1865, Oct. 8, Olive.

1867, Jan. 22, Daniel.

---

## WELLER FAMILY OF WALLKILL
### A-435-6, GFM-26, U2-57
## WELLER/ROWE FAMILY OF WALLKILL A-436, C-85

HENRY WELLER[1], b. Germany, both parents d. on voyage to America when he was c. 9 years old. He m. Elinor, youngest d/o William Bull & Sarah Wells, b. 1745. Children of HENRY & Elinor (all now dec'd.):

Henry. Could be the Henry who m. Letty Thomson 21 April 1791, at Goshen.

William.

ABSALOM.

Hiram. Could be the Hiram who d. 13 July 1818, aged 40, of liver complaint.

Esther.

Catharine.

HENRY[1]'s will was dated 20 March 1777. He is given as "Helmus Weller, of Hanover, blacksmith." In it he names his sons and Thomas Bull, executor. Will was proved 24 June 1789 by David Gallatin, of Montgomery, Physician.

ABSALOM WELLER[2] (d. Oct. 1827) m. Elizabeth Rowe, d/o Matthew, (d. April 1851). Matthew had purchased land in the north part of Wallkill in 1800, which he gave to Elizabeth. Absalom & Elizabeth are buried in the farm burial ground. Their children:

1801, Jan., Leartus M.

Milton, res. Middletown.

Mrs. Albert Dickinson, Middletown.

Mrs. William Dickinson, res. New Haven, CT; her dau. is wife of ex-Gov. Jewell of CT.

Mrs. William Conkling, Middletown.

Alpheus, twin.

Theodore, twin. A Rachel H., d/o Rev. Moses Freligh & wife of Theodore Weller, d. 23 April 1828, aged 28 years, 1 month, 23 days & is bur. at the German Reformed Cemetery, Montgomery.

Alfred, res. Crawford.

Margaret, d. 21 May 1813.

---

## WELLER, ALANSON Y. & JOSEPH H.  H-979-80

ALANSON & JOSEPH are brothers, but the names of their parents are not given.

ALANSON was b. Town of Crawford in 1857. Clerked at store of the late A. K. Chandler at Newburgh until 1863 when dry goods firm of Schoonmaker, Mills & Weller was formed. Retired 1886; 1889 he succeeded to the plaining mill business of Thomas Shaw's Sons, founded 1837. He spent much time managing the estate of his brother, Joseph H.

JOSEPH H. WELLER, b. Montgomery 1846; died at his home in NY City 14 Nov. 1886. To Newburgh at age 14 to clerk at dry goods firm of A. K. Chandler & Co.; to NY in 1868 as salesman for Wentz, Hartley & Co.; in 1879 member of Tefft, Weller & Co. in NY. 1876 m. Frances Conkright of Elizabeth, NJ; she d. 5 weeks before Joseph. He is buried in the family plot at Woodlawn Cemetery. Surviving children:

Lillian C., m. Ralph S. Tompkins of Fiskhill on Hudson, NY.

Edith M., m. Leonard M. Hills of NY City.

Alfred E., res. Newburgh.

Joseph Francis, student at Yale Univ.

---

## WELLER, GEORGE S.  H-980
coal dealer at Newburgh.

GEORGE was b. at Newburgh in July 1871, a s/o A. Y. Weller [perhaps Alanson Y. above]. Employed by J. W. Matthews & Co.; started his own business in 1890. He m. Constance, d/o Rev. J.A. Farrar.

---

## WELLER FAMILIES  GFM-1, 35-6

MOSES WELLER, b. 21 July 1789, d. June 9, 1843. His wife Esther ---, d. 24 Feb. 1871, aged 76 years, 2 days. Their children:

1820, Oct. 22, Catharine, d. 4 Nov. 1829.

1820, Oct. 22, Belinda, d. 22 Jan. 1849.

1823, Nov. 20, George, d. 1 March 1849.

GEORGE WELLER, s/o Peter & Margaret, d. 23 Feb. 1880, aged 45 years, 6 months, 27 days. Isabella, his widow, d. 8 Feb. 1918, aged 80 years, 9 months, 17 days. Child given here:

William Henry, d. 24 July 1878, aged 18 years, 9 months, 8 days.

Also bur. in same plot, Sarah Jane Weller, d. 3 May 1874, aged 54 years, 8 months, 15 days. No relationship given.

All from tombstone inscriptions, Montgomery German Reformed Church.

---

## WELLING, EDWARD [P]  A-606-7, C-14, 39, 114
of Warwick.
## WELLING, THOMAS [P]  A-611, H-981-2
of Warwick.

Family of Welsh lineage, to America, settled L.I. THOMAS WELLING[1] purchased land in 1704 on L.I.; to Orange Co., 1770. [H-981 states that the Orange Co. farm has been in the family since 1704.] His children:

1759, Feb. 9, THOMAS.

Richard. Could be the Richard who m. Mary Denton at Goshen 2 Nov. 1782 & had son John bapt. 5 July 1789.

John.

Mrs. Gen. John Hathorn.

Mrs. John Wheeler.

Mrs. Bronson.

THOMAS WELLING[2], s/o Thomas[1], m. 28 Feb. 1782, Sibble Beardsley of Sussex Co., NJ, and had:

Anna.

Charles, d. Sussex Co.

1786, July 8, THOMAS.

1788, April 23, **EDWARD L.**

John, res. Brooklyn, where he d.

Hannah.

Lois.

Elizabeth.

Lois (2d)

THOMAS WELLING[3], s/o Thomas[2] m. Anna Coleman & had:

John L. Could be the John L. of Warwick who m. Martha VanDuzer of Goshen, 22 Jan. 1857.

Samuel C.

William R.

1830, April 27, **THOMAS.**

Elizabeth, m. F. B. Brooks.

Harriet, m. J. C. Houston.

Hannah D., m. James Wisner.

Euphelia, m. Richard Wisner.

Sibble C., d. young.

Charles B., d. young.

THOMAS WELLING[4], s/o Thomas[3], b. Town of Warwick, farmer, bank director, member Reformed Dutch Church; m. 19 Dec. 1854 [1855], at Goshen, Caroline, d/o Aaron Van Duzer of Goshen, and had:

William R.

1864, April 28, **THOMAS.**

Edward L.

Martha.

Mary.

Elizabeth.

Carrie H.

Sarah McC.

THOMAS WELLING[5], b. 28 April 1864 on homes farm at Warwick which has been in the family for 154 yea he now farms the land. He was the son of Thomas of War (d. 9 Nov. 1898, bank director). THOMAS[5] m. Marie VanDuzer of Warwick 17 May 1893. She was d/o Ja Harvey & Sarah (Taylor) VanDuzer. They have one Thomas J. Welling, b. 3 April 1896.

EDWARD L. WELLING[3], s/o Thomas[2], b. Warwick; held l political office, served in military, supported Refor (Dutch) Church; d. 2 Jan. 1855.

---

WELLS, ALFRED [P]     A-557-8, H-982, W-8
of Goshen.   C-19, 22, 26, 34, 39, 40, 81, 85, 90, 97, 98, 104, 135, 145, LDS Anc.

HON. WILLIAM WELLS[1], b. Norwich, Norfolkshire Engl 1608, s/o Rev. William Wells, rector of St. Peter's Churc Norwich. To America c. 1635 on the "Free-Love" [W says "True Love"] of London. Atty. of England & sheriff of New Yorkshire on L.I. LDS Ancestral file st that William Wells, b. 10 Feb. 1604, at Norwich, d. 13 N 1671, Southhold, NY; m. (1) Bridget Burton of Norwich d. c. 1654 & (2) Mary (Marie) Youngs of Southhold, He is given as s/o William of Norwich & wife Elisabeth Children of William[1] & wife Mary (all b. Southhold):

1655, Bethia, m. Jonathan Horton of Southhold, NY.

1657, Abigail.

1658, Oct. 17, Patience.

1660, May 5, WILLIAM.

1661, Mary, m. John Youngs of Southhold.

1664, JOSHUA.

1666, Mehitable, m. John Tuthill.

1668, Anna, m. John Goldsmith.

WILLIAM WELLS[2], s/o William[1], m. Elizabeth Tuthill Southhold & had:

1683, WILLIAM.

1689, Jan. 31, John.

1690, Feb. 7, Henry.

1696, Feb. 3, Mary, m. Lt. Thomas Reeve.

WILLIAM WELLS[3], s/o William[2], m. Esther Homan & ha

1704, Elizabeth, m. Daniel Case.

1706, William, m. Hannah White & had William[4] b. 1747 m. Hannah Goldsmith & had James[4].

1708, Esther, m. Solomon Wells.

1711, Cravit, m. Sarah Reeves & had William b. 1740, Eliza b. 1759 & Deborah b. 1762.

1713, David.

1716, Phoebe.

1718, Deliverance, m. Joshua Case.

1721, Benjamin, m. (1) Hannah Wells, (20 Iravine Terry & Hannah Booth.

1724, Mehitabel.

JUSTICE JOSHUA WELLS[2], s/o William[1], m. Hannah Tu of Southhold. He d. there in 1744. They had:

1686/7, Mary.

1688/89, Hannah.
1689, JOHN.
1691, JOSHUA.
c. 1693, Deliverance.
c. 1695, Abigail.
c. 1697, Anna.
1699, SAMUEL.
1701, Daniel, m. Elizabeth Downs.
1703, Solomon, m. Esther Wines.
1705, Nathaniel, m. Mary Parshall.
1707, Bethia, m. John Goldsmith.
c. 1709, Mehitabel, m. William Horton.
1714, April 21, Freegift, m. Jule Anna Booth.
1717, Deborah, m. David Corwin.

The LDS Ancestral File makes no mention of son JOHN[3], b. in 1689. Books consulted mention only this JOHN[3].

JOHN WELLS[3], s/o Joshua[2], b. Southold, where he later died. He had a son, JOHN[4], b. Southold c. 1715, d. Orange Co., 4 July 1776. This JOHN[4] was the first settler of this family at Goshen & settled there c. 1735.

JOHN[4], s/o John[3], had a son JOSHUA WELLS[5], b. Goshen 1744, d. on the homestead 15 June 1819, dropsy. Soldier in the colonial army during the Revolutionary War. JOSHUA m. Rhoda Booth, grandau. of William Bull & Sarah Wells. Rhoda Wells d. 23 Dec. 1825, aged 87, palsy. They had:
Mary, m. George Phillips, 30 April 1791.
1773, March 10, John. Could be the John who m. Sarah Harlow 28 July 1798, at Goshen.
1777, Aug. 15, George.
1779, Sept. 6, JOSHUA JR.
Christina, m. John Decker.
Dolly, m. Edward Ely.
Sarah, m. James Tuthill, at Goshen 20 Jan. 1814.

JOSHUA SR.[5] & Rhoda were members of the Presbyterian Church at Goshen.

JOSHUA WELLS JR.[6], b. on homestead & d. there in 1867. He m. 10 Feb. 1801, (1st) Jemima (1779-1811), d/o Jonathan Sayer of Town of Goshen. Goshen church records show the death of the wife of Joshua Jr. at age 36 of pneumonia on 27 Jan. 1812, but do not name her. They had:
Adeline, m. James C. Reeve.
1805, Nov. 17, ALFRED.
Mary Jane, d. unm.
Jerome, physician of Goshen; d. there 13 Oct. 1839, of consumption. He m. 18 Nov. 1834, Charlotte Horton, at Goshen.
Francis, m. Adrien Holbert of Goshen.

JOSHUA JR.[6] m. (2d) Katy Ford who d. Oct. 1834, and had:
Julia Ford, m. John M. Ford.
Elizabeth Eunice, unm.

All of Joshua's children bapt. 9 Jan. 1822 at Goshen.

ALFRED WELLS[7], s/o Joshua[6], b. on & inherited homestead. June 1832 m. Lydia, d/o John Nyce of Wheat Plains, Pike Co., PA. Members of the Presbyterian Church at Goshen. Lydia d. Oct. 1871, aged 62. Children:
Jerome, d. Flushing, L.I., Oct. 1855.
JAMES EDWARD.
John N. of San Francisco, CA.
George W. of NY City.
Moses A., served in Civil War, res. Chicago.
Bapt. 1846, Nov. 7, Eugene Franklin, druggist of Waverly, NY.
Bapt. 1848, May 6, Lewis Arnell, d. Oct. 1870.
Mary Frances, m. Lewis E. Coleman of Deposit, PA, 3 May 1855.
Catharine R., m. 23 Oct. 1861, Samuel M. Slaughter of Wallkill.
Charlotte, m. Samuel Wickham Slaughter of Waverly, NY, 13 May 1873.
1852, CHARLES S.

JAMES EDWARD WELLS[8], s/o Alfred[7], b. at Dingman's, PA; d. suddenly at his home in Goshen 6 May 1907. Removed from farm to Village of Goshen in 1901, living in retirement there until his death. Presbyerian, connected with dairy farming as a living. He m. 18 Feb. 1858, Frances E., d/o William S. & Sarah T. (Wood) Conkling, and their surviving children:
William A. of Goshen National Bank.
Mrs. Cornelius Christie of Watertown, NY.

CHARLES S. WELLS[8], s/o Alfred[7], m. 23 Feb. 1876, Alice, eldest d/o Samuel Holden of Chester, and had:
S. Hadden, m. Edith Sinsabaugh in 1900.
Clara, m. J. J. Stage of Goshen.
John N., at home.

JOSHUA WELLS[3], s/o Joshua[2], m. Mary Brewster of Brookhaven, b. 1695, & had:
Bapt. 1716, JOSHUA.
c. 1717, Mary.
c. 1719, Timothy.
c. 1721, David.
1723, Jan. 5, Hannah.
c. 1725, Deliverance.
c. 1727, Abigail.
c. 1729, John.
c. 1731, Sarah.
c. 1736, Deborah.

JOSHUA WELLS[4], s/o Joshua[3], m. (1) Mrs. Hannah Wells, b. c. 1710 at Southhold & m. (2) Mary Reeves, b. c. 1718/20. His children:
1750, April 1, Selah, m. Mehitable Tuthill.
c. 1752, unnamed child.
c. 1754, Mary.
c. 1755, Hannah.
1756, Deborah.
1758, Oct. 29, Sarah.

SAMUEL WELLS[3], s/o Joshua[2], b. Southhold, L.I., m. Bethia Goldsmith [also possibly Martha Goldsmith as 2d wife] & had:

1724, Aug. 17, Youngs, m. Abigail Paine & had: Youngs b. 1745; Joseph b. 1746, m. (1) Ellice Conkling & (2) Martha Corey; Samuel b. c. 1748 & an unnamed child b. 1750.
1726, Samuel.
1728, Joshua.
1733, Aug. 5, John.
1735, Matthew.
1737, Zacheus.

---

## WELLES, FRANKLIN JOSEPH      H-981

**FRANKLIN JOSEPH WELLES** is an artist & resident of Greenwood Lake for 26 years. He m. Annie Estelle, d/o Prof. HENRI APPY.

HENRI APPY was s/o Jean Appy, conductor of the King's orchestra in Holland. Henri was a distinguished violinist & teacher who gave concert tours; conductor of the Philharmonic Society at Rochester, NY, where he d. 16 Nov. 1903, aged 73. He m. Annie Paine, a singer at Grace Church, NY, and had:

Annie E., wife of **MR. WELLES** above.
Ernest Frederic, professor of music at Newark, OH.

---

## WENZEL, FREDERICK WILLIAM      H-982

**FREDERICK** is s/o George C. & Elizabeth A. Wenzel & was b. in Newburgh 28 Sept. 1871. He is assistant postmaster at Newburgh. In 1895 succeeded his father in his manufacture of boxes. Member St. George's Church.

---

## WERRY, PETER [P]      A-674b, LDS Anc. File
of Minisink.

PETER WERRY[1], b. & d. (1818) in Cornwall, England, farmer; m. Susan Ead who d. 1827. Children:
Susan, dec'd.
Mary, m. Edward Hill, res. Devonshire Co., England.
Rebecca, m. William Smithem & after his death (1856) to America with her children, William & Rebecca. She d. at Wawayanda 10 Oct. 1874.
Betsey, m. Richard Gilbert; dec'd. Their children: Susan, Elizabeth & Mary.
1811, March 5, **PETER.**
John, to America with wife in 1840; res. Sullivan Co., NY.

PETER WERRY[2], s/o Peter[1], to US in 1834; worked at canal construction & farmer; member ME Church at Westtown. 5 Jan. 1839, m. Drusilla, d/o **WILLIAM H.** & Sarah (Gibson) CLARK [see below] of Warwick. After their marriage they res. Big Island, Goshen Twp., farmer & large landowner. Children:
Mary, m. Robert Osborn, res. Minisink.

Harriet Adelia, m. George Kerwick of Sussex Co. & d. in Wawayanda 1 June 1876, aged 33.
Drusilla, res. on homestead.
Margaret, m. Floyd Baird of Greenville; d. 11 June 1878, aged 30.
Charles P., d. 5 Sept. 1872, aged 23.
Sarah Elizabeth, res. on homestead.
1855, July 10, JOHN J.

JOHN WERRY[3], s/o Peter[2], m. Georgianna L., d/o Richard Allison Lane [Lain] & Caroline Matilda Alward. They res. on homestead & had:
1877, Emma.
1879, Charles Peter.
1881, Dec. 25, Richard Allison.

WILLIAM H. CLARK d. 21 April 1867, aged 77; his wife Sarah (Gibson) d. 1 March 1877, aged 87; they had 10 daus. & 2 sons.

---

## WEYGANT, COL. CHARLES H.      H-982-3

**CHARLES WEYGANT** was b. in Cornwall 8 July 1839. 1862 Sr. Capt. of the 124th Regt. NY State Vols., commanding Co. A. Made Lt-Col. after the Battle of Gettysburg; 1870 elected sheriff of Orange Co.; 1878-80 mayor of City of Newburgh. In 1886 developed with Henry T. McCoun, the property known as Washington Heights in Newburgh. Trustee of Trinity ME Church. He m. Charlotte Sackett in 1861 & they have one dau.

---

## WHALEN, JOSEPH [P]      A-163-4
physician of Montgomery.

JOSEPH WHALEN, b. Ireland, to America at the close of the Rev. War to what is now Town of Crawford in 1788 & to Village of Montgomery soon after. Sgt. of militia of Orange Co. 1862). Catholic. His brother, REV. CHARLES WHALEN, Irish Franciscian, 1st Catholic priest stationed in NY. **JOSEPH** m. early in life Mary Byrne, and had:
Joseph V., atty. of Montgomery; dec'd.
Mrs. McWilliams of Montgomery.
Mrs. Dennis McCool of Newburgh.
  It is believed that there were other children as well.

At the end of the sketch it names the children of **JOSEPH** & Mary as:
Elizabeth.
Mary.
Martha.
Catherine, m. Robert Crosby, grandson of Benjamin Crosby, b. 31 Dec. 1821; member of Presbyterian Church at Hopewell.
Joseph Virgil.
John Horace.

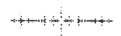

## WHEELER, ANNIAS B.       H-983

**ANNIAS B.**, s/o William (b. 1815, NY City), contractor & wife Sarah Braffett (1827-1890), b. Craigville, Town of Blooming-Grove 31 Aug. 1846. Worked as cotton spinner, farmer & with Erie Railroad. Tried to enlist 6 times & was rejected 5 times on account of his small size & light weight. Mustered in 22 Aug. 1864 in Co. C, 56th NY Inf. at weight of 90 lbs. Served until wounded in Dec. 1864; discharged May 1865. Many occupations after Civil War. He m. Hanna Oldfield of Amity, Town of Warwick, 30 May 1869 & had 12 children: 2 boys & 3 girls surviving:

Joel B. of Middletown.

Harrison W., with Middletown Fire Dept.

Melissa, m. D. H. Jones of Rutherford, NJ.

Emma E., m. John E. T. Cleghorn of Willsburg, NY.

Francis E., res. with brother Joel.

## WHEELER, ELISHA PEARL [P]       A-494-5
of Wallkill.

JOHN WHEELER[1] had a son, LEMUEL WHEELER[2], b. Pomfret, CT, 20 April 1782; carpenter & builder; merchant of Springfield, MA; also res. Red Hook, Duchess Co. & Saugerties, Ulster Co. LEMUEL m. (1st) 25 Jan. 1806, Hannah, d/o Philip Pearl & sister of Hon. Philip Pearl, b. 14 Aug. 1785, and had:

1807, Feb. 5, **ELISHA PEARL.**

Emeline, m. Charles Sandford; d. Newburgh.

LEMUEL m. (2d) Orinda Goodell, and had:

Lydia Angelina, widow of James G. Swezey.

Cordelia, res. Middletown.

**ELISHA PEARL WHEELER[3]**, s/o Lemuel[2], b. Hampton, Windham Co., CT, 5 Feb. 1807; res. Saugerties, Rhinebeck, Catskill; 1830 to Montgomery, Orange Co., stove & tin business; to Middletown 1843. Saw-works, steel working & rolling mills, etc. Member Grace Episcopal Church. 1834, in Montgomery, m. Phebe Sears of that place, b. 13 Oct. 1813, d. 3 Dec. 1878, and had:

Emeline, m. Henry S. Moshier.

James, atty. of Brooklyn & San Francisco, CA.

Hannah, m. Charles H. Horton.

Lemuel, d. 1873.

## WHEELER, ISAAC V. [P]       A-609-10, H-983-4
of Warwick.
## WHEELER, MAJ. JAMES [P]       A-608-9
businessman of Warwick.

Nine brothers [H-983 says 11 brothers] & 3 sisters, of English lineage, early res. of L.I., all later removed to Orange Co. One brother, JOEL[1] m. twice & had 5 children, among them:

WILLIAM F. WHEELER[2], b. Warwick, 2 Sept. 1791, served in War of 1812; m. Juliet, d/o Isaac Van Duzer, and had:

Dinah E.

Robert.

Ann E.

1823, March 4, **ISAAC V.**

Joel.

William W.

Milton V.

**ISAAC V. WHEELER[3]**, s/o William F.[2], b. Warwick, farmer; m. 21 June 1853, Phebe, d/o Jesse Bull. ISAAC d. 9 April 1876, last survivor of his generation of the family & inherited ancestral home of family. He was a supporter of the Reformed (Dutch) Church. His children:

Juliet V.

Carrie [Caroline] B.

1859, May 22, **WILLIAM F.**

Jesse C., d. 7 Oct. 1881.

Anna M., m. William A. Hayward; d. 16 Sept. 1899, left 2 children: Alice W. & William H.

Frank A., d. infant.

Alice.

**WILLIAM F. WHEELER[4]**, s/o ISAAC V.[3] & Phoebe, m. 22 May 1882, Tillie A. Wisner of Chester, Orange Co., and had:

William F. Jr.

Charles V.

Jesse I.

Mary A.

Roe W.

Ralph.

Ph[o]ebe Wheeler, widow of **ISAAC V.[3]**, at his death moved from the farm to the house in Warwick Village now known as "The Columns," which she purchased 1883; at her death on 21 Jan. 1904, house to her daughters Juliet & Caroline. Member Reformed Church.

Phoebe's maternal ancestors include Cornelius Board of Sussex, England who came to America in 1730; on her father's side she is desc. from William Bull & Sarah Wells.

Wheeler brothers: JOHN, Joel, Gilbert, from RI to Orange Co. JOHN[1] m. & had 2 daus. and one son, **JAMES[2]**, b. 1783 in Warwick Twp., d. 11 Sept. 1852 on homestead in Warwick. 1810 he m. (1st) Ann, d/o Martin Ryerson of NJ, and had:

Sophronia, m. --- Bevier of Grand Rapids, MI.

Anne, dec'd.

Sarah Catharine, dec'd.

**JAMES[2]** m. (2d) 1 Dec. 1829 Cornelia V. E. Hunn, d/o John S., late president of the Bank of Newburgh, and had:

Mary Elizabeth, dec'd.

John J., Lt. Col. of 156th NY Vols. during the Civil War.

DeWitt Clinton, police commissiner of NY City 15 years.

Franklin, res. MI.

Edward, collector of internal revenue for state of AR, res. Little Rock; served in 156th Reg. NY Vol.

## WHITAKER, BENJAMIN        T-, C-10, 14

**BENJAMIN WHITAKER,** wounded at the battle of Minisink in 1779, later lived & d. in Deposit. His brother John also in battle & received 9 bullet holes in his hat & clothes, but escaped unharmed.

A Benjamin Whitaker m. Abigail Pellett, 13 April 1783, at Goshen.

A Mary Whitaker m. Duncan McConnely at Goshen 20 May 1778.

---

## WHITE, HON. NATHAN HERRICK [P]
teacher, judge, j.p., farmer.      **A-646-7, LDS Anc. File**

EBENEZER WHITE[1], early settler of L.I., had a son:
SYLVANUS WHITE[2], (1704-22 Oct. 1782), Presbyterian divine who m. Phoebe Howell; lived & d. on L.I. Their son, SYLVANUS JR.[3], b. Southampton, L.I., farmer; 19 July 1730, m. Eunice Herrick 10 Oct. 1754; settled at Blagg's Clove, Orange Co. & d. 2 March 1881 [sic, should be 1818], aged 88. Eunice d. 24 Feb. 1818, aged 85. They were married 64 years. Children of SYLVANUS JR. & Eunice:
Phoebe, m. Anselm Helme.
Euphemia, d. infant.
Sylvanus, d. unm. aged 33.
Eunice, m. Daniel Poppino.
1770, June 14, **NATHAN H.**

NATHAN H. WHITE[4], s/o Sylvanus Jr.[3], b. on homestead at Blaggs Clove; d. 10 April 1855. 8 Dec. 1802, m. Frances, d/o Hezekiah & Juliana (Woodhull) Howell, and had:
1803, Oct. 24, Albert S., to IN c. 1825; m. Miss Randolph of VA. Congressman & senator of IN, district judge; d. Aug. 1864.
Nathaniel, d. infant.
1806, March 17, Morgan L., res. Orange Co.
1808, Jan. 8, Elizabeth Howell, m. (1st) Harvey Denniston & had H. A. Denniston, res. Blooming-Grove; m. (2d) John Nicoll of NY; d. 21 Dec. 1855.
1810, Dec. 10, Eunice Herrick; d. 25 June 1874.
Juliana W., m. VanRensselaer Martin of Blooming-Grove.
Abram A., res. IN.
Isaac S., res. IL.

---

## WHITEHEAD, EDWARD       H-984-5
pres. Walden Knife Co.

**EDWARD** was b. in Halifax, Yorkshire, England, s/o John & Sarah (Hill) Whitehead. To America with parents as a child.

Walden Knife Co. organized in 1870, incorporated in 1874, elected William G. Gowdy president & **EDWARD WHITEHEAD**, vice president. He became president in 1891. School trustee, member of board of education, director of local banks.

---

## WHITEHILL, ROBERT [P]       A-369
of Newburgh.

HUGH WHITEHILL[1], b. Glasgow, Scotland, m. Jeanette Murray, b. Ayshire; to America 1847, settled at Wappinger's Falls, Duchess Co.; millworker, later to Newburgh where he d. 1857. They had at least one son:
**ROBERT WHITEHILL[2]**, b. Glasgow, 1 June 1845; bookkeeper in NY City c. 1859, shipworker; USN, 2nd Ass't. Engineer, retired from Navy, to Newburgh, machinery manufacturer.

---

## WHITFORD, HENRY L.       H-985
creamery business at Johnson.

**HENRY** was b. in CT; machinist, now connected with Borden Co. To Orange Co. 1891; m. Clara Root & has 3 sons & 2 daus.

---

## WHITTEN, JOEL       H-985
of Pine Bush.

**JOEL WHITTEN,** b. Town of Crawford 8 Oct. 1818, d. at his res. in Pine Bush 29 April 1904. He was a s/o John & Mary (Moore) Whitten & m. (1) Miss M. Halstead Moore of NY City who d. in 1872. He m. (2) 14 Sept. 1881, A. Emily McGowen of Pine Bush, d/o Benjamin & Prudence (Faulkner) McGowan.

**JOEL** in business for a time in NY City & also at Burlingham with brother Isaac until he established his Pine Bush store. Retired 1880. Postmaster, member New Prospect Church (1844).

---

## WHITTEN, SAMUEL       H-985-6

**SAMUEL** is s/o Francis & Ophelia (Rainey) Whitten, b. Town of Crawford in 1863. He ran a general store for 11 years; lumber business & managed farm. In partnership with R. T. Brown at Pine Bush.

---

## WICKHAM, ISRAEL H. [P]       A-502c
of Wallkill.
## WICKHAM, SAMUEL S. [P]       A-491-2
of Wallkill.
## WICKHAM FAMILY OF WALLKILL       A-432
         C-9, 12, 20, 104, 108, 110-11, 113

JOSEPH WICKHAM[1] of L.I. m. Sarah --- and had JOSEPH JR.[2] of L.I. until 1720 (will 1734). Children included:
SAMUEL.
William.

SAMUEL[3], m. 1738, Abigail Howell & settled Town of Goshen, Orange Co., 1740; tailor. Their children:
SAMUEL.
1741, ISRAEL.
William, had a dau., Mrs. David Reeve, who had, O. P. Reeve & Mrs. B. W. Shaw.

MATTHEW.

Jerusha, m. --- Wells.

Elizabeth, m. --- Jackson.

Abigail, m. --- Smith.

Margaret, m. Nathaniel Bailey; Goshen bapt. records show b. of Israel Wickham Baily, b. 11 Feb. 1788.

Mary, m. Eli Corwin, at Goshen, 10 Dec. 1783.

Julia, m. (1st) Kadmiel Moore, at Goshen, 11 Sept. 1781; (2d) --- Gale.

SAMUEL WICKHAM[4], s/o Samuel[3], m. Mary Irwin and had:

Jerusha, m. Eliad Tyron.

1786, Feb. 28, JESSE HALL.

1788, Aug. 28, Elizabeth, m. John H. Corwin.

JESSE HALL WICKHAM[5], s/o Samuel, inherited homestead, farmer in Minisink Angle, now site of Village of Middletown. He m. (1st) Laura, d/o Samuel Benedict of Middletown, who d. 31 Aug. 1823, aged 30. JESSE H. d. 3 Oct. 1841. Children:

Temperance Ann.

Harriet Maria, m. Isaac Van Duzer.

1821, Aug. 20, SAMUEL S.

Henry Lewis, d. young.

JESSE H.[5] m. (2d) Frances Ludlum who d. 1857, and had:

Theodore.

George.

Israel.

SAMUEL S. WICKHAM[6], s/o Jesse H.[5], b. on homestead; clerk, 1846 quarry owner & other businesses; m. (1st) Ellen Adelia, d/o Frederick Dolson of Wawayanda, who d. 1868. Children:

Cecelia J.

Oscar.

Almeda D.

Samuel S.

Laura B.

SAMUEL S.[6] m. (2d) 1870, Marilla, d/o Madison Raplee of Yates Co., NY, and had:

Willis R.

ISRAEL H. WICKHAM[4], s/o Samuel[3], tailor, served in the French & Indian War; d. 1817. He m. Elizabeth, d/o Joseph Carpenter of Goshen & grandau. of Rev. John Bradner, 1st settled Presbyterian minister at Goshen who came from Scotland. Family to Middletown c. 1791. Children:

Abigail, d. unm.

1773, ISRAEL J.

ISRAEL J. WICKHAM[5], s/o Israel[4], m. 2 July 1793, at Goshen, Mary, d/o David Moore; farmer at Middletown until 1813, to father's homestead where he d. March 1821. Children:

Benjamin C., settled in the West & d. there.

1804, May 25, ISRAEL H.

Joseph, d. young.

George, d. young.

Abigail, m. (1st) Oscar Welch of MI; (2d) --- Kilpatrick.

ISRAEL H. WICKHAM[6], m. 4 March 1828, Sally, d/o Henry B. Wisner, b. 2 April 1803. She d. 26 Aug. 1868. ISRAEL farmed until 1863 when he removed to Middletown; served as j.p., d. 12 March 1868. Both Sally & ISRAEL d. of being poisoned by eating contaminated flour. Their children:

Maria, m. (1st) John N. Dunning; (2d) Herman B. Young.

George, m. Mary A., d/o Col. Morgan L. & Juliette (Conkling) Sproat of Middletown.

MATTHEW WICKHAM[4], s/o Samuel[3], m. Anna Horton 17 Aug. 1777 & had:

1782, Sept. 21, Eunice.

1784, Sept. 12 Matthew.

1799, July 14, Anna. In the two sources in which Anna is named, her birth year is given as 1799. In the Goshen church records, she is noted as baptized on 10 May 1780.

And perhaps other children.

Goshen church records show the marriage of an Isreal Wickham to Abigail Knap, 28 Sept. 1777.

---

## WIGGINS FAMILY OF MT. HOPE
### A-507, LDS Anc. File

JACOB WIGGINS[1] at Mt. Home soon after the Revolution, homestead 2 miles south of Otisville. His son,

William[2], stayed on homestead (1810-12). His "descendant" John, res. Otisville today.

JACOB WIGGINS[1] [no relationship given to Jacob above], merchant of what is now Otisville; had a son Abraham B.[2], res. near Unionville, NJ. & had:

Benjamin, went West.

Mrs. David Slauson of Minisink.

Mrs. Zachery Young of Mt. Hope.

Mrs. William Young of Mt. Hope.

The LDS Ancestral File shows a Jacob Wiggins, s/o John & wife Polly Nichols, b. 1760 in Newburgh. This Jacob m. Freelove Woodworth & d. 30 Sept. 1839 at Westernville, Oneida Co., NY. In this source the line is not continued beyond Jacob, but his siblings are given as: Anning (Ansing) b. 1767, George b. 1769, Cadwell b. 1773, Hannah b. c. 1775, John b. 1775, Mary (Polly) b. c. 1777, Nancy b. c. 1779, Betsey b. c. 1781.

---

## WILCOX, GAVIN R. M.                    H-986
manuf. of Newburgh.

GAVIN WILCOX, b. at Newtown Stewart, Whitonshire, Scotland 16 May 1849, of English & Scotch ancestry. He was s/o John & Jessie (McGregor) Wilcox, who came to America 1866 & settled at Newburgh. GAVIN employed at Washington Iron Works & learned trade of pattern maker. Worked at other local industries & held public offices. In 1872 m. Alice E., d/o Henry O. VanDuzer & had 5 children.

## WILCOX, HORATIO R. [P]                A-504d
of Wallkill.

NATHANIEL WILCOX[1], of English extraction, b. Dutchess Co., d. Canaan, Columbia Co. at res. of son John. NATHANIEL's children:

Jehial.
Jesse.
NATHANIEL.
Aaron.
Polly.
Lois.

NATHANIEL WILCOX[2], s/o Nathaniel[1], b. Town of Dover Plains, NY, farmer; m. Anna McGonigle of Scotch parentage and b. Hinsdale, Columbia Co. After their mariage to Lexington, Greene Co., NY. Both d. 1836; children, all b. Lexington:

Henry.
1795, May 8, OLIVER.
Joseph.
Jehiel.
John.
Thomas.
Margaret.
Anna.
Sarah.

OLIVER WILCOX[3], s/o Nathaniel[2], at age 16 to Austerlitz, Columbia Co., learned trade of hatter; m. Cynthia Beebe, d/o ROSWELL BEEBE [see below], 18 March 1818, and had:
1819, Sept. HORATIO R.
1837, June 30, Franklin A., b. Windham, Greene Co.; m. Anna, d/o Enoch Armitage of NY City.

HORATIO R. WILCOX[4], b. Chatham, NY, early years spent at Pittsfield, MA, 1853 to Middletown, manufacturer of hats, public service; res. in NY City, Ashland, Greene Co.; Presbyterian; m. 20 Aug. 1845, Sarah M., d/o Hon. Henry Kinsley of Ashland, and had:
Henry K., m. Frances, d/o Hon. George D. Wheeler of Deposit, NY.
Olivia, m. John W. Slawson.

## WILCOX, WALTER C.                H-986

WALTER was b. at Wurtsboro, Sullivan Co., NY, one of 7 children of Abraham & Mauguerite (Lybolt) Wilcox. One brother also named, Charles, res. Middletown. WALTER removed to Middletown, worked at Newark, NJ for a time, 1893 back to Middletown, grocer. He m. Jennie Cameron of Ellenville, NY 2 July 1890; she direct desc. of the Cameron family of Scotland. Their son is:
1891, March 31, Alonzo Potter; with father in business.

This biography mentions the following names, with no surname & no relationships to the others in the article, assumed Wilcoxes: Henry, of Port Jervis; Anna, wife of A. Dedrick, of Port Jervis; Ella, wife of Harry Miller of Jersey City; Ada, wife of James Monagham, of Jersey City.

## WILDER, VICTOR AUDERBON                H-986-7

VICTOR is the only s/o Mariner Ayers Wilder & Mary P. Smith. He was b. in Dennysville, ME 8 July 1844, also the birthplace of his father. With parents at early age to Boston, MA & res. there until outbreak of Civil War. VICTOR in 4th Regt., MA Vols. Parent moved to Brooklyn, NY during the war & he joined them there after the war. To Warwick in 1891. In 1875 he m. Lilian Macdonald & had one son: Donald, b. 1888. Members of Reformed Church of Warwick.

## WILEY, ADAM                W-92

JAMES WILEY (d. c. 1863) m. Rebecca Ritchie, and had:

ADAM WILEY was b. at Croton Falls, Westchester Co., NY 9 May 1849; res. early at Mill Plains, CT. Farmer, veterinary in employment of Borden family. 8 Nov. 1873 m. Rebecca Sweetman of Brewster, Putnam Co., NY & had 4 sons & 2 daus.; 3 sons & 1 dau. still living.

## WILKEN, SAMUEL                H-987
[Also see WILKIN]

SAMUEL, b. Monahan, Ireland 4 Feb. 1844, to America with his mother and 7 children, his father having died. Settled on Staten Island. SAMUEL to Chester, Orange Co., 11 May 1866; 1867 m. Anna S. Salisbury, and had:
Fred W.
Albert E.
Melvin R.

SAMUEL partner of Charles Christ 16 years & later started blacksmith shop. Town officer.

## WILKES, JAMES [P]                A-809
of Monroe.

GEORGE WILKES[1] res. Westport, County Mayo, Ireland; to America 1800, settled Warwick, Orange Co.; instructor, supervisor of Greenwood Furnace, d. 4 July 1847. He m. (1st) 14 Sept. 1779, Katherine Gannon, and had:
John.
Susan.
Mary Ann.

GEORGE[1] m. (2d) 1807, Sept. 22, Mrs. Mary G. Dyer who d. 4 May 1863, and had:
1808, Thomas.
1810, George.
1812, Catherine.

1815, March 21, **JAMES**.
1817, Elizabeth.
1820, Francis.

**JAMES WILKES**[2], s/o George[1], m. 19 June 1846, Abbie A., d/o Samuel Rumsey of Monroe, and had:
Mary.
Katie.
George.
James.

---

WILKIN, JUDGE JOHN G.                          A-151
WILKIN, JOSEPH M.  A-152-3, H-987, C-117, 122-24, etc.
[Also see WILKEN]

**JOHN WILKIN**[1], b. Ireland 1688/89, was s/o JOHN. John m. Elizabeth Crawford, b. 1701 & he d. in Shawangunk, Ulster Co., NY. Their son:
**WILLIAM WILKIN**[2], b. 20 Jan. 1720, at Enniskillen, Ireland, d. 1787 at Wallkill, Orange Co., NY. He m. Elizabeth Rogers of Rye, NY & had:
c. 1746, Sarah, m. Samuel Moffat.
c. 1748, Daniel.
1750, John, m. Hannah Weller.
1753, March 22, WILLIAM.
c. 1755, Jean.
c. 1757, George.
c. 1759, James W.
c. 1761, Robert.
c. 1763, Joseph.
c. 1765, Elizabeth.

**WILLIAM WILKIN**[3] settled in Wallkill, now Hamptonburgh, farmer, d. 28 Feb. 1823. Served in Revolutionary War; m. 8 April 1779, Sarah Crans, of Huguenot stock, ancs. from Holland to Ulster Co. Sarah was d/o Johannes Crans, b. 18 Feb. 1713 at West Camp, NY & wife Anna Christina Millspaugh. Anna Christina was d/o Matthias & wife Anna Eva (Busch) Menges, both b. Germany. William & Sarah bur. old graveyard Neelytown, church members. Children (all b. Hamptonburg):
1780, May 10, John.
1781, Sept. 24, Joseph, m. Mary Millspaugh.
1783, Aug. 10, Mary, m. Gawn Mackinson, b. 1768 in Ireland.
1785, Oct. 3, Adam, m. Mary Weller.
1785 [1788, Feb. 2], DANIEL.
1789, Dec. 31, Sarah (Sally), m. Adam Shafer.
1792, March 27, ESTHER.
1794, July 8, Susan, m. Luther Hornbeck.
1797, March 16, Marshall, m. Jane Dusenberry.
1799, May 15, Eliza, m. --- McKinney.

**DANIEL WILKIN**[4], s/o William[3], soldier of War of 1812; for 5 years after his marriage res. Shawangunk, Ulster Co., farmer. He & wife members of Assoc. Reformed Church at Neeleytown & later of the Covenanter Church at Coldenham. He m. 2 Oct. 1794, Harriet, d/o John B. Haines of Coldenham,

Orange Co., formerly of CT & afterward of L.I., of English anc. Harriet d. 1780, aged 76. Children:
1813, Nov. 6, SUSAN ANN.
1816, Aug. 19, Abby, m. Cornelius Hornbeck of Ulster Co.; dec'd.
1818, Oct. 22, **JOHN G**.
1821, Nov. 30, Moses B.
1824, Dec. 21, Daniel Flavel, b. Neelytown, atty. of Nashville, TN.
1828, April 18, **JOSEPH MARSHALL**.

**SUSAN ANN WILKIN**[5], d/o Daniel[4], m. John A. McWilliams & is referred as to a widow of Elmira, NY. Their children (MC WILLIAMS):
1835, April 16, Harriet Ann, b. Searsburg, m. Judson Aspinwall, b. 24 Feb. 1833, Northville, NY.
1837, May 29, Daniel Wilkin, m. Helen F. Marquand.
1840, March 25, Mary Elizabeth, m. Stephen Rose.
1842, June 16, John James, m. Esther Keeler.
1845, Feb. 6, Joseph Eugene, m. Louisa G. Benham.
1850, Feb. 13, Abby Louisa, m. Spencer S. Kingsley.
1854, June 14, Ralph Erskine, m. Mary Rachel Hubbell.

**JUDGE JOHN G. WILKIN**[5], s/o Daniel[4], teacher Monticello (1838); atty. Middletown, NY; served in state militia, bank director; m. 20 Feb. 1850, Louisa, d/o Nathaniel Cooley of Middletown, and had:
John, atty. of Middletown.
Dr. Charles H., NY City surgeon.

**JOSEPH MARSHALL WILKIN**[5], s/o Daniel[4], b. in Hamptonburgh; teacher at Kinsley School, Westpoint, atty. Newburgh; Oct. 1854 to Nashville TN. He m. Montgomery, NY, 6 Nov. 1861, Catherine, d/o Harvey D. Copley of Montgomery, and had:
Louise C.
John Flavel.
Harriet.
1878, JOSEPH M.

**JOSEPH M. WILKIN**[6], s/o of **JOSEPH M.**[5], b. town of Montgomery. Entered law office of Senator John C. R. Taylor, Middletown for 3 years.

**ESTHER WILKINS**, d/o William[3], m. Benjamin Hornbeek, b. 26 July 1787 at Gardiner Twp., Ulster Co., NY. Their children (all b. Ulster Co., HORNBEEK):
1816, Aug. 27, William.
1817, May 21, Susan.
1820, April 5, Cornelius, m. Mariah Dunn b. 18 Jan. 1823, New Paltz. They had: William b. 1845, m. Elizabeth B. Schoonmaker; George b. 1847, m. (1) Mary Cynthia Halsey of Washingtonville, (2) Abbey Wilkins & (3) Mary G. Traphagen.
1822, May 21, Simon.
1824, May 3, Jeremiah.
1825, Feb. 15, James Wilkins.

1826, May 30, Esther, m. Walter Dunn.
1832, April 24, Emeline. _____

## WILKIN, SAMUEL JONES [P]  A-148-51, C-17, 27, 30, 120

JOHN WILKIN[1], b. Wales, settled near Enniskillen, Ireland after 1680; 1728, with wife & 3 children, to Shawangunk, Ulster Co., NY, now Montgomery, Orange Co., NY, & d. there. Their children, b. after their arrival in America:
1720, Jan. 20, WILLIAM.
John.
George.
Joseph.
Jason.
Jane.
Elizabeth.
Lydia.
Mary.
Susan.

WILLIAM WILKIN[2], eldest s/o John[1], m. Elizabeth, d/o John Rogers & --- Ogden, who came from Rye, Westchester Co., NY to Wallkill when Elizabeth was young. The Wilkins settled in Wallkill & were early members of the Creecer Church at Neelytown. Their children, almost all of whom lived to old age:
Sarah.
John.
William.
Jane.
Daniel. Could be the Daniel Wilkin who m. Mary Stott at Goshen, 19 March 1788.
George, prisoner during the Revolution; d. at Ft. Montgomery, NY during war.
JAMES W.
Robert.
Joseph.
Elizabeth. Could be the Elizabeth Wilkins who m. Daniel G. Rogers 1 Jan. 1784 at Goshen.

GEN. JAMES W. WILKIN[3], s/o William[2], atty., military & political career; m. Hannah, d/o Roger Townsend of Goshen, and had:
Bapt. 1792, June 24, William Scott, pvt. secretary of NY gov. Church records also note another son, Samuel, bapt. the same day.
James W.
Bapt. 1797, June 11, Eliza Maria, m. Wheeler Case, Goshen atty. Noted in Goshen church records, baptism of George Whitfield Case, adopted child & grandchild of James W. & Hannah Wilkin, 5 Feb. 1823.
Bapt. 1797, June 11, Sally, d. unm.
Caroline, m. (1st) 12 Dec., 1826, [Daniel] Hull Tuthill; (2d) John W. A. Brewster of ME who d. leaving only son, Rev. Charles A. Brewster of Newark, NJ.
1793, Dec. 17, SAMUEL J.

1802, Sept. 1, Frances Matilda, m. John Thompson of Goshen who has one son, Rev. J. J. Thompson.
Bapt. 1804, June 24, James Alexander.

SAMUEL J. WILKIN[4], s/o James W.[3], b. Goshen, d. 11 March 1866, Goshen; m. 18 July 1816, Sarah G., d/o Col. David W. Westcott, early Goshen journalist, b. 29 May 1796. Children:
1817, Oct. 14, Mary, m. Joseph G. Ellis of Mobile AL; she d. shortly after her marriage on 10 Oct. 1842.
1819, Dec. 1, Col. Alexander, atty.; Capt. in Mexican War, 1849 to St. Paul, MN; killed while in Union service, 14 July 1864, Tupelo, MS.
1822, Jan. 9, Charles, killed in hunting accident, 22 Oct. [Aug.] 1839.
1842, Wescott, judge, res. MN.
1826, March 20, William; d. 12 May 1839.
Samuel Jones, d. young.
1829, July 23, Hannah Gale; d. 22 May 1839.
1838, Jan. 2, Sarah Wescott, m. Roswell C. Coleman, Goshen atty. _____

## WILKINSON FAMILY OF WARWICK  A-437, 575
## WILKINSON, HIRAM S. [P]  A-502-3

JONATHAN WILKINSON SR.[1], miller, from Rahway, NJ in 1791, to Bloomingburgh, NY & later to Town of Wallkill, near Circleville where he d. He & wife, Phebe Barber, members of the Hopewell Presbyterian Church. Children:
Sally, d. young.
Edward, d. young.
Samuel, d. at sea on his way to the West Indies, of yellow fever; cooper.
Mrs. Robert Osborn [Polly] of Wallkill; res. Circleville.
Mrs. John Winfield [Katy/Katie] of WI.
Phebe, m. Samuel Wisner of Circleville. [Another source gives Polly as wife of Robert O. Stone, m. before 1791.]
Mrs. Peter Redner [Betsey], Peekskill. She d. Cold Spring, NY.
Richard, unm.
1783, July 20, JONATHAN.
Mrs. John Douglass & afterwards Mrs. Buck [Sally] of Western NY.

JONATHAN WILKINSON[2], b. Rahway, NJ (or Bellvale, Warwick) m. 1806, Hannah, d/o John Puff of Wallkill who d. 1 March 1866, aged 72. JONATHAN was a cooper, served in War of 1812, res. at Circleville after his marriage until 1831; res. 2 years at Goshen, also in Shawangunk, Ulster Co., retired to Circleville, where he d. 9 Feb. 1872, aged 89. Members of the Scotchtown Presbyterian Church & later of the ME Church. Children:
Samuel, mechanic of Wallkill.
John P., cooper, res. Brooklyn, NY.
Fanny Jane, m. James Wooden; d. 1843.
Hannah P., m. George A. Foster of Circleville.
James B., cooper, res. near Towanda, PA.
1816, April 27, HIRAM S.

Washington, carpenter of Newburgh.

Matthew M., d. in TN, mason by trade.

Zaccheus, swallowed by a whale at sea, 1844.

Margaret M., widow of John S. Mance of Middletown.

Phebe, m. William Maultby of PA.

Walter W., res. Bridgeport, CT.

**HIRAM S. WILKINSON**[3], s/o Jonathan[2], apprenticed to mason, took up carpenter's trade; 1856 manufactured churning-powers, well-curbs, iron post fences, etc. Member Old-School Baptist Church at Middletown. He m. 24 Oct. 1840, Clarissa, d/o Ebenezer Mowrey & Chloe Merchant, who was b. 30 Jan. 1816. Chloe was d/o John Merchant, one of Washington's Life Guard & Tabitha Hamilton, a cousin of Alexander Hamilton. Ebenezer Mowrey was b. R.I., res. Sullivan Co., NY. Children of **HIRAM S.** & Clarissa Mowrey:

Sarah E., teacher.

Cornelia A.

------

**WILLCOX, JOHN [P]**                    **A-610**

New England family, settled early on L.I. AMOS WILLCOX[1], from L.I. to Orange Co., had 3 sons & 3 daus., among them, JOSEPH[2], m. (1st) Margaret, d/o S. Scinonson of Vernon (family from Staten Island), and had:

1800, July 28, **JOHN.**

William.

Mary.

Susan.

Sallie.

Harriet.

JOSEPH m. (2d) Nancy Stagg, and had:

Charles.

David.

Phebe.

JOSEPH d. at the age of 88.

**JOHN WILLCOX**[3], b. Amity, m. 1823, Hannah, d/o Roger Howell, res. near Amity, and had (surviving children):

Lewis.

Joseph.

William H. J. Wickham.

Margaret.

Mary.

Sarah.

Harriet.

Prudence.

Eunice Amelia.

In 1836 **JOHN** purchased of George D. Wickham property in Warwick Twp. known as Merrit's Island. Supporter of Presbyterian Church at Amity, where Mrs. Willcox is a member. Commissioner of the Drowned Lands of the Wallkill & has reclaimed much of this marshy territory.

------

**WILLIAMS, GILBERT [P]**                    **A-368d**

farmer of Newburgh.

STEPHEN WILLIAMS[1], of Westchester Co., NY, had son FREDERICK[2], also of Westchester Co. who went to Nova Scotia. FREDERICK's son, BENJAMIN WILLIAMS[3] m. Sarah Lewis (her family in Westchester Co. before the Revolution); 1808 to Newburgh, farmer. Their son:

**GILBERT WILLIAMS**[4], b. Westchester Co., 5 March 1796; served apprenticeship with Samuel Corwin, blacksmith; age 16 to Nova Scotia to take care of grandfather Frederick's affairs; after death of grandfather returned to Newburgh where he purchased his father's farm. Served Capt. Daniel Tooker's Co. of militia; member Methodist Church at Middlehope. He m. 1832, Jemima, d/o Samuel Corwin, Town of Newburgh. No issue.

------

**WILLKIN, WILLIAM**                    **U2-34-5**

of Wallkill.

In **WILLIAM WILLKIN**'s will, dated 29 Aug. 1787, he names his wife Elizabeth Rogers, d/o Israel, and the following children:

Sarah Moffat.

John.

Robert.

Daniel.

James W.

William.

George.

Elizabeth.

Jean, m. --- Rea & has one son, William Rae, a minor in 1787.

**WILLIAM** also names his brothers John & Joseph Willkin. His will was proved 17 Sept. 1788 by Andrew McCord, yeoman of Wall Kill, Eben Clark & Moses Bull. Administration was granted to John Willkin of Montgomery & James W. Willkin of Goshen.

------

**WILSON, JONATHAN D. JR.**  H-987-8
asst. d.a. Orange Co. since 1907.

**JONATHAN JR.,** s/o of ex-Mayor J. D. Wilson, was b. Newburgh 1875; grad. Columbia Univ. 1898; attended NY Law School, grad. 1900. Practiced at Newburgh. He m. Edith Van Buren.

---

**WILTSIE, JOHN RAPELYE [P]**  A-291-2
businessman of Newburgh.

HENRICK MARTENSEN WILTSEE[1], emigrated from Copenhagen, Denmark to America in early 16th century [sic]. Served in Esopus War 1663, settled on a farm at Hell Gate, L.I., m. 1660 (wife not named) & had:
MARTIN.
Hendrick.
Myndert.

MARTIN WILTSIE[2]: "From Martin, 4th in degree from Hendrick Murtensen Wiltsee and his wife, Jane Suydam, whom he married in 1733, are descended the Fishkill Landing Wiltsies, . . . having emigrated from L.I. in 1734, lacating at the Landing & at Sylvan Lake . . ." [Duchess Co.]

JOHANNES WILTSIE (relationship not given) is mentioned as serving in the militia from Duchess Co. in 1773.

JOHN RAPELYE WILTSIE, b. Sylvan Lake, East Fishkill, Duchess Co., 5 June 1814, s/o John C. Wiltsie who d. 1820 at age 38, farmer & j.p., & Lavina Rapelye, b. L.I. of family early expelled from France & were first settlers of L.I. At age 15 JOHN apprenticed to B. F. Buckingham of Newburgh to trade of saddle & harness making; 1835 opened his own business in Newburgh until 1861. He m. (1st) 17 Oct. 1837, Elmira, d/o Robert Lawson, Esq., who d. Jan. 1843. They had one son:
G. Frederick.

JOHN m. (2d) Mary Susan, d/o Rev. Luke A. Spafford of MA, sister of Judge Henry M. Spafford of LA & of A. R. Spafford of Library of Congress. Her father was a lineal desc. of Israel Putnam. Children:
Arthur V.
Elmira, m. James T. Joslin of Newburgh.
Henry, d. young.
Harriet M.
Charlotte E.
Laura S.

---

**WINFIELD, DAVID [P]**  A-168
of Crawford.

DANIEL WINFIELD[1] of Shawangunk had a son, CHARLES[2], b. Shawangunk, 15 June 1789, a physician who practiced at Crawford where he died (1858 or 59), member of Reformed Dutch Church, res. on farm adj. village of Pine Bush; he m.

Margaret Crawford and had:
Charles, district atty. (1850) & Congressman (1863, 65)
1817, Nov. 19, **DAVID C.**

DAVID C. WINFIELD[3], eldest s/o Charles, physician & bank director, to Middletown, 1841; d. 23 May 1878. 26 Nov. 1845, m. Jane, d/o the late Henry Whitney S. Beakes, s/o Stacy Beakes, early merchant of Middletown. Children of DAVID C. & Jane:
Charles H., merchant of Middletown.
David C.

---

**WINFIELD, WARD**  H-988
editor & prop. of Walden *Herald*

**WARD WINFIELD**, b. Montgomery 1868, s/o Lester, who conducted the Montgomery *Republican* 1864-1890. **WARD** m. Catherine Condon of Wales. They had 3 children, only one named here is Francis Lester who works with his father.

---

**WINTER, WINFIELD WRIGHT**  H-988
businessman of Middletown

WINFIELD, b. Winterton, Sullivan Co., NY 22 Jan. 1862; merchant at that place several years. 1896 real estate & insurance business with his brother Clarence G.; 1901 to Middletown. He m. Flora A. Harding of Winterton and had 4 children, 2 living:
Harry, at Middletown, railroad bookkeeper.
Jay W., creamery manager at Winterton.

---

**WISNER FAMILY OF GOSHEN**
A-523, H-988-92, STJ-4, 8, 9,11
**WISNER, GABRIEL OF WARWICK**
C-107, 109, 118, T-62, 608
**WISNER, HENRY**  H-990-92
res. Sharon, Barber Co., KS
**WISNER, COL. JOHN C. [P]**  A-674-5
of Minisink.
**WISNER, HENRY G.**  A-144, C-100, 107, 109
**WISNER, JEFFREY [P]**  A-607
of Warwick.

JOHANNES WISNER[1] (WEASNER) was issued the first deed in Goshen. He was b. in Switzerland [one source says he came from Scotland in 1713, another says he was an officer of Swiss Contingent of the Prince of Orange against Louis XIV of France] & settled in L.I. about the time an effort was being made to settle the Wawayanda Patent. He purchased land near Mount Eve in 1714. His children:
HENDRICH.
Adam.
Catherine.
Ann.
Mary.

HENDRICH WISNER[2], s/o Johannes[1], m. Miss --- Shaw of New England; d. 1790. Children:
1720, HENRY [Heinrich].
JOHN.
Dau.

HENRY[3], s/o Hendrick[2], served in the NY Colonial Assembly (1759-1769), member of Cont. Congress (1774) & other political service. Manufactured gunpowder in his Ulster & Orange Co. plants. Senator (1777-1782) HENRY[3] d. Sept. 1790 & was bur. in the family burying ground near Phillipsburgh, in present town of Wallkill. He m. Sarah Norton of Queens, L.I. & had:
Henry Jr. Possible children of this Henry: Harriet, b. 6 Feb. 1775, d/o Henry & Sarah Wisner. Also Sarah, b. 17 Sept. 1777, who is given as the d/o Henry Wisner Jr. & Sarah Barnett his wife. Also dau. Mary b. 7 May 1781, and son Gabriel, b. 14 March 1784.
GABRIEL.
Mrs. John Denton [Elizabeth].
Mrs. Phineas Holmes [Mary].
SARAH.

GABRIEL WISNER[4], s/o Henry[3], Ensign, killed at battle of Minisink, 1779. "Gabriel was a very eccentric man & years before the battle he made himself obnoxious to the British crown . . ." He m. Elizabeth Waters, & had:
1777, HENRY GALE.
Bapt. 1794, May 4, Gabriel.

HENRY GALE WISNER[5], s/o Gabriel[4], atty. of Goshen, ancestor of the Goshen branch of the family. He m. Dec. 1805, Sarah, d/o Samuel & Phebe Tallman of NY, b. 1784, d. April 1874. Children:
William H.
Elizabeth, widow of John E. Phillips.
Mary, m. George C. Miller of NY.
Samuel T., d. infant.
Frances, m. Hon. Ambrose Spencer Murray of Goshen.
1816, Oct. 25, Gabriel Henry.
1818, Oct. 15, Sally Ann [Sarah A.], m. Joseph H. Coates of NY.
Almat, d. unm.
1823, April 2, George Tallman of Goshen.
Bapt. 1827, Oct. 14, Martha.

SARAH WISNER[4], d/o Henry[3], m. Moses Phillips, had (all PHILLIPS):
1770, Dec. 30, George.
1773, May 18, Henry Wisner.
1775, June 20, Moses.
1778, Jan. 9, William.
1769, Feb. 21, Gabriel Norton,.
1785, July 11, Samuel.

JOHN WISNER[3], 2d s/o Hendrick[2], Capt. in the French & Indian War, served as a scout in 1757. Also Capt. in Rev. War under Col. Nicoll of Goshen. He res. at Mount Eve &

later near Wickham's Pond on land granted to him direct from the crown. He was soldier in the Sioux Contingent in the days of Queen Anne & d. 1778. He is the ancestor of most of the Wisner families of Warwick. His children:
JOHN.
1742, July 11, HENRY 3d.
William.
Asa.
Anna.
Charity.
Hannah.

JOHN JR.[4], s/o John[3], served as Capt. in Col. Isaac Nichols's Regt. of Minute Men in 1776, as did his father. This John d. 1811 & left a large family, among whom were:
JOHN.
WILLIAM ROE.

JOHN WISNER[5], s/o John[4], had a son, GEORGE T. WISNER[6], who was the father of:
RALPH WISNER[7], m. 22 Nov. 1883, Mary, d/o Henry Greene & had Roy Greene Wisner. Members Presbyterian Church in Warwick.

WILLIAM ROE WISNER[5] (21 March 1799-19 Nov. 1886) m. Eliza Miller (27 April 1800-16 July 1882). William was b. on family homestead & a farmer. William & Eliza m. 16 March 1819, and had:
1820, Feb. 15, John N.
1821, Nov. 27, David M.; d. 5 Aug. 1879.
1824, Aug. 20, HENRY.
1827, Jan. 8, Andrew D.; d. 24 May 1828.
1829, April 29, Albert A.; d. 29 May 1832.
1831, Oct. 4, James T.
1832, Dec. 21, Francis L.
1835, Nov. 26, Albert.
1838, July 24, Andrew H.; d. 19 June 1854.
1841, May 21, Mary Ann.

HENRY[6], s/o William Roe Wisner[5], was a teacher; to OH 1846. He m. (2) 1 March 1876, Sarah E. (Rowe) Jackson, M.D., a grad. of Hahnemann Medical College, Chicago. No issue of this marriage. By his first marriage (wife not named) he had:
Henry J. of Chicago.
Charles H. of Barber Co., KS.

The Old Wisner homestead is c. 1 mile north of Bellvale, Orange Co., built before the Rev. War by William Wisner, one of 4 sons of Capt. John Wisner, Jr. William d. in this house 1803. William Roe Wisner, father of HENRY is given as another son of this Capt. John Jr. William Roe Wisner d. on the farm at age 87.

HENRY WISNER 3d (sometimes written Jr.)[4], s/o John[3], resided on the homestead farm. He was member of the state legislature repr. counties of Dutchess, Orange & Ulster (1776-82); Capt. of the 'Pond Company' under Col. Hathorn,

1775, & later Lt.-Col. (1778); m. Susanna, d/o Richard Goldsmith. Henry[4] d. 29 May 1812 & bur. in the Warwick Cemetery by the side of his son Jeffery. Children:

Richard.

Susanna.

1779, April 20, JEFFREY.

JOHN.

Nancy.

Henry. Could be the Henry B. Wisner who m. Ruth Carpenter 5 April 1794, at Goshen.

Abigail.

1781, May 7, Mary.

William.

1784, March 14, Gabriel.

JEFFREY WISNER[5], s/o Henry[4], m. (1st) Hannah Wheeler, 28 Oct. 1792; Hannah d. 1813. Jeffrey d. 11 April 1855. He was town supervisor & j.p. Children:

1799, Henry.

1801, Sept. 10, John W.

1804, April 27 Harriet, m. Philander Gillett.

1806, Oct. 6, William.

1814, Sept. 23, Sarah A., m. Hammond Sly.

JEFFREY[5] m. (2d) 27 Jan. 1816, Elizabeth Armstrong, who d. 23 Dec. 1868, and had:

1817, March 23, JEFFREY AMHERST.

1818, Oct. 16, GABRIEL.

1820, March 2, Rensselaer J., res. Pittston, PA.

1822, March 17, James, res. Warwick.

1824, Feb. 4, RICHARD J.

1827, Oct. 18, J. Amherst, res. Brooklyn.

1830, June 3, Mary, m. William T. Van Deever.

1832, Aug. 15, Van Ness.

JEFFREY & wife were members of Calvary Baptist Church of Warwick.

JEFFERY AMHERST WISNER[6], s/o Jeffery[5] m. Mary Wheeler and had:

1856, July 30, CLINTON WHEELER.

CLINTON WHEELER WISNER[7], b. West Pittston, PA, 30 July 1856, d. in the Adirondacks 21 Aug. 1904. Merchant & public servant; favorate pastimes were shooting, sketching & driving. He m. Martha, d/o Thomas Welling & Caroline Van Duzer in Oct. 1879; he is survived by widow & children:

Mrs. Burton J. Berry.

John Welling.

Jeffery Amherst Jr.

Thomas Welling.

Clinton W. Jr.

Gladys.

GABRIEL WISNER[6], s/o Jeffrey[5], b. on homestead at Warwick Twp., farmer; d. 13 Jan. 1872; m. 2 Feb. 1843, Susan, d/o Solomon Carpenter of Amity, Orange Co., and had:

Henry C.

Rensselaer J.

Albert.

Mary E.

Susan E.

Carrie.

Ida.

James H.

RICHARD J. WISNER[6], s/o Jeffery[5] & Elizabeth, b. on homestead farm, Town of Warwick; d. 3 Jan. 1908; farmer. 1883 he moved to res. near the village, where he died. Banker & RR director. Member SAR & Reformed Church of Warwick. He m. (1) Euphelia, d/o Thomas Welling, 20 Dec. 1853, she d. 1881 & he m. (2) June 1883, Sarah Van Duzer. Children, all by 1st wife:

Charles E.

Annie E.

Mary Euphelia, res. Warwick.

CAPT. JOHN WISNER, JR.[5], s/o Henry[4], res. on homestead in Minisink (in the family since 1766), farmer; m. Elizabeth, d/o Maj. Peter Butholp on 16 May 1790. Elizabeth d. 16 Sept. 1843, JOHN JR. d. 23 April 1811. Children:

Susan, m. David Lee.

Mary, d. young.

Elizabeth, m. Richard Whitaker.

Agnes, m. Nathaniel Chandler.

Anna, d. young.

Tira Maria, d. young.

Henry, dec'd.

1803, April 6, JOHN C.

Temperance Ann, m. John Slauson.

Harriet, m. Daniel Sayre.

COL. JOHN C. WISNER[6], s/o John Jr.[5], b. on homestead, farmer; m. Mary, d/o Peter & Hannah (Fancher) Weed of Fairfield Co., CT; Mary d. 10 Feb. 1870. JOHN C. d. 11 Feb. 1878. Children:

1823, June 19, Peter; d. 5 July 1852, NY.

1825, Sept. 7, William H.; d. Nov. 1876.

1827, Feb. 13, Andrew J.; d. Australia, 24 April 1853.

1828, Nov. 11, Gabriel; d. 7 March 1866.

Harriet, m. Isaac E. Toland, res. Unionville, NY.

Lyman, went to IA as young man, banker at Eldora, Hardin Co.

Elizabeth, m. William E. Taylor of Warwick.

John, d. young man.

1840, Sept. 19, Mary, m. Isaac E. Toland; d. 1867.

Sarah, d. infancy.

———

WITSCHIEF, GRAHAM                                    H-992

atty. of Newburgh.

GRAHAM, b. Port Jervis 1875, s/o Peter & Florence (Graham) Witschief. Attended Albany Law School & read law with Hon. O. P. Howell. He m. Mary Farnum of Port Jervis.

———

**WOOD, ANDREW**                    H-992-3
station agent at Stony Ford, NY & postmaster.

ANDREW, b. at Cornwell, Canada 7 June 1850, s/o William &
Ann (Jardine) Wood. Telegraph operator, removed to NY
state in 1876, settled Willsboro. 4 Aug. 1884 to Stony Ford,
Orange Co. He m. Nancy Nickelson of Cornwall, Canada,
21 Oct. 1873; she d. 8 Nov. 1905. They had:
William A., m. Marguerite Wilbur of Stony Ford.
Joseph H., m. Magdelena B. Mould of Montgomery.

**WOOD, CORNELIUS B.**                    H-993
farmer, in dairy industry.

CORNELIUS was s/o John D. & Phebe (Board) Wood, b.
Town of Greenville, Orange Co., 24 Aug. 1820; d. at Chester,
16 Aug. 1907. At age 5 moved with his mother & younger
brother to home of maternal grandfather, Cornelius Board of
Sugar Loaf Valley. One of the founders of Methodist Church of
Chester; bank director & other businesses.

**WOOD, CYRUS**                    H-993

CYRUS, b. Chester, NY, 1 Jan. 1860. He was an only son
(parents not named) & followed his father's profession of
farmer. Member Methodist Church. He m. Fannie L. Roe
of Chester 31 May 1883, and had:
Anna R.
Orpha D.
Ruth B.
May B.

**WOOD, MAJ. JOHN**          A-523, T-67, C-10, 81, 90
of Goshen.

MAJ. WOOD engaged in the battle of Minisink & was the
only prisoner whose life was spared by the enemy when he gave
the Masonic sign; farmer & blacksmith; Capt. of the militia.
After return from captivity his wife had married another and he
married (2d) Hannah Carpenter of Goshen, sister of James &
Benjamin of Carpenter's Point. Their only son was SOLOMON
WOOD, although JOHN had desc. by his first wife. He d. of
apoplexy at age 67 on 4 Aug. 1810.
[Note: A-524 states that there were four John Wood's: Lt.
John lived at Summerville in Town of Goshen, Capt. John,
Major John & John Jr., son of Major John. A John Wood m.
Sarah Hulse 6 April 1779, according to Goshen church records.]

WIDOW CHRISTIAN WOOD (no relationship given to
above JOHN), d. in Goshen, 25 July 1825, aged '4 score & 5
years,' [29 July, aged 86] was at the battle at Wyoming &
narrowly escaped with her life, her husband & son killed in the
battle.

**WOOD, RICHARD L. [P]**                    A-562d,
of Goshen.          C-19, 29, 56, 104, 128, 143

TIMOTHY WOOD[1], b. England, early settler at Goshen, Orange
Co., had a son, RICHARD[2] who m. Miss --- Smith. Their
children (all res. & d. in Orange Co.):
Richard. Could be the Richard who m. Mary Conkling at
Goshen 2 April 1791.
Oliver.
1772, Jan. 18, Susannah.
1776, Dec. 29, TIMOTHY.
Joanna, m. Jonathan Owen, 3 Sept. 1791, at Goshen.

Timothy[1] may also have had a son Timothy Jr.[2], as in
Goshen church records is found: Susannah, b. 18 Jan. 1772 &
Abigail, b. 6 June 1774, d/o Timothy Wood, Jr. & wife Nelly.
The church register lists a Timothy Wood as dec'd. by 5 Nov.
1814.

TIMOTHY WOOD[3], s/o Richard[2], m. 19 Dec. 1801, Dolly
[Dorothy], d/o Michael Carpenter of Goshen, b. 22 Feb.
1781, d. 1864. TIMOTHY d. 1846. Members of the
Presbyterian Church at Goshen, as his father Richard had
been. Children:
1804, Dec. 15, Matilda, m. Stephen Smith of Goshen, 19 Dec.
1822; d. 28 Jan. 1881.
1806, Sept. 3, **RICHARD LEWIS.**
1810, April 27 [26], William Carpenter, farmer of Goshen; d. 12
Jan. 1840 [Goshen church records say aged 27, of consump-
tion]. He left one son, James J., silversmith of Brooklyn,
NY, who was bapt. 5 Aug. 1838 at Goshen.
1814, March 11, Sarah Jane; d. 19 Feb. 1879, unm.
1818, Nov. 27, Gabriel S., farmer; d. Town of Mt. Hope, Orange
Co., June 1886; left 2 daus. & 1 son. The son possily Joshua
Smith Wood, s/o Gabriel Wood, bapt. 3 Aug. 1850 at
Goshen.

RICHARD LEWIS WOOD[4], s/o Timothy[3] & only surviving
child in 1881, farmer, never married.

**WOODHULL, NATHANIEL D. [P]**
                    A-253, 645-6, H-141, 993-4
wholesale milk dealer of Blooming-Grove.
**WOODHULL, WILLIAM S.**                    A-632

RICHARD WOODHULL[1] (Wodhull, pronounced Odel or
Odhull), b. Thenford, Northhamptonshire, England, 13 Sept.
1620, settled Jamaica, L.I. c. 1648. He removed to Setauket,
then called Cromwell Bay, in 1656. Family said to be traced
to an individual in England from Normandy with William the
Conquerer in 1066. RICHARD d. Oct. 1690; his wife was
Deborah ---. Children:
1649, Oct. 9, RICHARD.
Nathaniel, d. no issue.
Deborah, m. John Lawrence of Newtown.

RICHARD WOODHULL[2], m. Temperance, d/o Rev. Jonah Fordham, of Southampton; d. 18 Oct. 1699, and had:
Richard.
NATHANIEL.
John.
Josiah.
Dorothy.
Temperance.

NATHANIEL WOODHULL[3], s/o Richard[2], settled Mastic; m. Sarah, d/o Richard Smith (2) of Smithtown, and had:
Hannah, m. Major Nathaniel Strong of Blooming-Grove & left numerous descs.
Temperance.
1722, Dec. 30, NATHANIEL.
Dorothy.
Sarah.
Richard, settled New Haven, CT; 'his family has become extinct.'
Ruth, m. Judge William Smith of Mastic.
1735, Feb. 10, JESSE.
Juliana, m. Hezekiah Howell of Blooming-Grove, mother of the present Hezekiah Howell of Blooming-Grove & Judge Nathaniel W. Howell of Canandaigua.
Deborah, m. Isaac Nicoll of Hackensack, NJ.
Ebenezer, settled in Blooming-Grove, m. Abagail Howell & had Fletcher Woodhull & several other sons & daus.
Nathaniel (Sr.) d. 9 March 1760.

NATHANIEL[4], s/o Nathaniel[4], res. Mastic, known as Gen. Nathaniel, was violently assaulted by a British officer near Jamaica, L.I. & d. 20 Sept. 1776.

COL. JESSE WOODHULL[4], b. Mastic, Suffolk Co., L.I., settled at Blagg's Clove, Orange Co. c. 1753; veteran of the Rev. War. He m. Hester, d/o Capt. Lewis Dubois of Orange Co., and had:
1797, Nov. 30, NATHANIEL.
RICHARD.
Sarah, m. John Floyd of Smithtown, Suffolk Co., NY.
Renelihe, m. Nathaniel Smith of Smithtown.
Hannah, m. Oliver Smith of Moriches.
Jesse, made several voyages to the East Indies; d. at Pine Grove, Amite Co., MS.
Ebenezer, settled near Utica, Oneida Co. & m. there.

Col. Jesse Woodhull d. 4 Feb. 1795. Hester d. 29 Nov. 1808, aged 74 years & 29 days.

NATHANIEL WOODHULL[5], s/o Jesse[4], b. & d. Blooming-Grove, m. Frances Mandevill, and had:
1815, Aug. 4, RICHARD WILLIAM.
Frances M.
Jacob, d. young.

[NOTE: Another source says that Frances Mandevill above was the wife of Nathaniel Dubois Woodhull, the s/o Richard, who was the 2d s/o Jesse, not the wife of Nathaniel above. Both lineages are given here as found; one is obviously incorrect.]

RICHARD WILLIAM WOODHULL[6], s/o Nathaniel[5], farmer of Blooming-Grove, now res. IA. 1837, Dec. 14, m. Ruth A. Strong, and had:
1838, Sept. 27, NATHANIEL D.
Adis E., commercial merchant of Chicago.
Joseph Y., dec'd.
Jacob M.
Richard S., dec'd.
Ruth E., m. Robert Beattie of Little Falls, NY.
Isabel L., d. young.
Laura F., d. infant.

NATHANIEL D. WOODHULL[7], b. on homestead, at age 15 with father to NY City and established milk business; 1860 bought out father with George Goude of Campbell Hall, Orange Co.; d. NY City, 19 April 1879. He m. Martha V., d/o John & Betsy Andrews of Saratoga Co., NY, 16 April 1862, and had:
EDWARD D.
George G.
Jennie V.
Mary L., d. young.
Nathaniel D. Jr., d. young.
Walter A.
Kate C.
Charles R.

EDWARD D. WOODHULL[8], son of NATHANIEL D.[7], was b. at Saratoga, NY in 1863; d. 8 March 1908. He res. at Monroe. Grad. Dartmouth Medical College in 1895 & m. Amy Truax.

RICHARD[5], s/o Jesse[4], m. Hannah, d/o Judge William Smith of L.I. & had:
WILLIAM SMITH.
NATHANIEL DU BOIS.

WILLIAM WOODHULL[6], s/o Richard[5] & Hannah, had children:
William Henry Howell.
Jessie.

NATHANIEL DU BOIS WOODHULL[6], s/o Richard[5] & Hannah had:
Richard.
Francis Mandeville.

A Nathaniel D. Woodhull, leader in the NY milk business is named as a grandson of Nathaniel DuBois, but it is not specified which he is the son of, Richard or Francis Mandeville.

Below is the lineage as given from the source that says that Frances Mandevill is the wife of Nathaniel Dubois Woodhull, s/o Richard who was the 2d s/o Col. Jesse. It will take a search to determine which lineage is correct.

NATHANIEL WOODHULL[5], s/o Jesse[4], m. Elizabeth, d/o Leonard Nicoll of New Windsor & d. leaving no issue, 12 April 1799.

RICHARD WOODHULL[5], 2d s/o Jesse[4], m. Hannah, b. 4 Oct. 1764, d/o Judge William Smith & Ruth Woodhull of Mystic, and had:
Jesse, d. 12 Oct. 1800, aged 5 years, 6 months, 12 days.
1796, Aug. 9, **WILLIAM SMITH.**
1797, Nov. 30, **NATHANIEL DUBOIS.**
1800, Nov. 30, Ruth Hester; d. unm. 1839, Oct. 8.

Hannah, widow of RICHARD, d. 1809, Jan. 6.

**WILLIAM SMITH WOODHULL[6]**, s/o Richard, res. Blagg's Clove, m. Fanny H., eldest d/o Abraham Schultz, Esq. of New Windsor, 10 Nov. 1825, and had:
1826, Nov. 21, Abraham Schultz.
1828, Nov. 4, William Henry.
1831, May 9, Sarah Jane; d. 23 June 1843.
1833, July 17, Jesse.

NATHANIEL DUBOIS WOODHULL[6], s/o Richard[5], m. Frances Mandevill, and had:
Richard William.
Francis M.
Jacob.

---

**WOODWARD FAMILY OF MT. HOPE**      **A-507, C-11**

HEZEKIAH WOODWARD SR.[1] to Mt. Hope from Stonington, CT, 1773/4. Goshen church records show that he m. Ellinor Vail 1 April 1779. They had a son BENJAMIN WOODWARD[2], b. 28 Feb. 1780, political service. BENJAMIN's son, CHARLES S.[3], also in political service.

---

**WRIGHT, ALEXANDER**      **A-553-4, H-994**
of Goshen (Newburgh).

ROBERT WRIGHT[1], b. Ireland, to America at the close of the Revolution with his father, settled in PA, where soon after the father died. ROBERT returned to Ireland & in 1793 there m. "a lady of wealth" & returned to America 1795 & settled at Newburgh, NY. He d. 1835, aged 66; wife d. 1851. Members of the Assoc. Reformed Church. Children:
1797, William, businessman of Newburgh; d. 1865, aged 68.
Jane, res. Newburgh.
Margaret, m. Robert W. Boyd, res. Hamptonburgh, both d. there.
John, leather manufacturer of Sullivan Co.
Francis.
Robert, dec'd.
James, removed to IN; d. at Cairo.
1813, June 6, **ALEXANDER.**
Susan, res. Newburgh.

**ALEXANDER WRIGHT[2]**, s/o Robert[1], res. Newburgh; at 18 clerk in the store of Judge Robert Denniston, Salisbury Mills

Town of Blooming-Grove 3 years; clerk at Highland Bank at Newburgh 1834, 1839 to Middletown to organize Middletown Bank; 1846 organized Chester Bank at Chester; 1851 organized Goshen Bank, president until he retired in 1857. He m. 1844, Jan. 10, Mary, d/o HENRY S. & Laura (Genung) BEAKES [see below], and had:
Mary.
Robert, d. at age 9 [8?], 1856.
1856, Dec., FRANK ALEXANDER.
Janie [Jennie?] Laura, d. 4 [5?] Jan. 1908.

**FRANK ALEXANDER WRIGHT[3]**, s/o **ALEXANDER[2]**, member of the Presbyterian church, res. Goshen. Attended Yale College.

**STACEY BEAKES**, early merchant of Middletown with large interests in Sullivan Co. regarding timber; was sheriff of Orange Co.; had a son HENRY S. who m. Laura Genung (above), and had:
William L.
Jane, m. late Dr. Winfield.
Cynthia, m. late Charles C. McQuoid, atty.
Mary, m. **ALEXANDER WRIGHT.**
All are of Middletown.

---

**WRIGHT, BARTOW [P]**      **A-170a**
physician.

DR. WRIGHT's ancestors from England to Flushing, NY. WILLIAM WRIGHT[1], b. Flushing 1766, removed to Duchess Co. & there he m. Jemima Haight (d. 1825, aged 86); farmer & j.p. under the crown of England. WILLIAM d. 1812, and had:
ENOS WRIGHT[2], b. April 1772, d. June 1855; m. Mary Woolsey of West Chester Co., 6 Jan. 1799; res. Fishkill, Duchess Co., farmer; d. Jan. 1822. Children:
Elizabeth, d. young.
Mary, m. William Anthony; d. 1826.
1805, Nov. 28, BARTOW.
Hannah, m. William Anthony as his 2d wife; d. 1860.
William W., retired merchant of NY City.
Josiah W., dec'd.

**BARTOW WRIGHT[3]**, s/o Enos[2], b. Fishkill; school at Fairfield, Herkimer Co.; 1830 practiced & settled at Campbell Hall, Orange Co.; practiced 50 years at Hamptonburgh & vicinity; railway director; attended Presbyterian Church; m. 1839, Mary Ann, d/o William & Keturah Bull, of Wallkill, NY. Children:
1840, Sept., William B., physician & Professor of Languages at Buffalo; m. Mary C., d/o Gen. Niven of Sullivan Co.
Bartow, m. Mary, d/o Dr. Walsh of Port Jervis, res. Goshen.
Catherine, d. June 1871, age 21.

---

**WRIGHT, WILLIAM [P]**  A-363-4
of Newburgh.

JACOB WRIGHT[1] m. Mary Drake, and had:
Mary E., m. Watson Clark.
Sarah, m. James D. Ford.
1818, May 17, **WILLIAM.**
John D., m. Catharine Brower.

**WILLIAM WRIGHT**[2], s/o Jacob[1], b. near Newark, Wayne Co., NY; took up trade of mechanic at early age; worked in repair-shops of railroad at Niagara Falls; constructed steam engines at Palmyra until 1842; to Rochester until 1845 & later to Providence RI till 1850; to Waterbury, CT then Hartford, CT: NY City until 1866 when he moved to Newburgh. He m. 1841, Elizabeth G. Taft and they have one dau.

**WRIGHT, WILLIAM B. [P]**  A-154-5
printer, atty.

SAMUEL WRIGHT[1], shipyard carpenter, m. Martha Brown & had:
**WILLIAM B. WRIGHT**[2], b. Newburgh, 16 April 1806; from Goshen in 1835 to Monticello; 1846 elected to Congress, 1861 Judge Court of Appeals until 1868 when he died. In his later years he res. at Kingston.

**WRITER FAMILY OF MT. HOPE**  A-506, H-327, 994-5
**WRITER, THEODORE [P]**  A-178b
physician.

There are 12 Writer families now res. in the Town of Mt. Hope, all descs. of:
JASPER (Casper) WRITER[1] (Reiter), b. Germany, arrived at Philadelphia still a minor & res. with family of a Mr. Deputy [Depew, at Little Britain, PA]. A sister accompanied him on the voyage & d. at sea. To Orange Co., res. first at Phillipsburgh area where 8 June 1775 he signed the so-called Revolutionary Pledge. He m. 8 Sept. 1772, Eve Kortright of Phillipsburg, who d. 31 [21?] Dec. 1830. Eve's paternal ancestors go back to Sebastian Van Kortright of Kortryk, Belgium, 1586. Jasper, with wife & 5 children, removed to present Town of Mt. Hope in 1784; raised family of 8 children there. He d. 15 Nov. 1842, age of over 100. Children:
1776, April 25, Aaron, settled on father's estate & had 14 children, among them Aaron K., father of Dr. Theodore Writer of Otisville.
Jasper Jr.
John Falter [T.], to PA & d. near Honesdale.
Margaret, m. (1st) --- Rundle; (3d) --- Wagoner.
Nancy, m. Joel Rundle of Greenville.
Elizabeth, m. John Van Tuyl of Greenville.
Rebecca, m. Daniel Van Tuyl & settled at Pond Eddy.
Eleanor, m. John McKeeby.
Nancy.

1776, April 25, AARON.

AARON WRITER[2], s/o Jasper, b. Mt. Hope, farmer; m. Elizabeth McKeeby, b. 13 Sept. 1776, and had:
Sarah.
Eve.
Catharine.
Jasper A.
Jemima.
Jane.
Margaret.
Elinor.
Matthew M.
1811, March 2, AARON KORTRIGHT.
JOHN F.
Elizabeth M.
Isaac V.
Benjamin N.

AARON KORTRIGHT WRITER[3] s/o Aaron[2], res. Twp. of Greenville where he d. 25 Sept. 1871; m. 21 March 1835, Abigail, d/o Daniel D. Penney of Mt. Hope, and had:
1837, July 17, **THEODORE.**
Daniel P.
Sarah E.
Josephine.
Louisa.

THEODORE WRITER[4], s/o Aaron K.[3], b. on homestead at Greenville, Town of Mt. Hope; grad. Bellevue Hospital Medical College, NY, 1866; practiced Otisville, NY. He m. 3 Nov. 1869, Helen A., d/o Osmer B. Green of Otisville; they have one son, Daniel D., age 9.

A JOHN F. WRITER[1] is featured on H-995. His father is not named, but he could be the s/o Aaron above. This JOHN m. Phoebe Rosencrants & d. 1892. Phoebe is now age 88. They had a son:
BENJAMIN F. WRITER[2], born on the homestead farm in Town of Mt. Hope, 19 May 1854. Benjamin m. Ella K. Dennis of Sussex, NJ 8 Nov. 1882, and had:
Coe.
Frank, with Borden Milk Co. at Otisville.
Elmo, connected with sanatorium at Otisville.
Henry, d. age 4.

**WYNCOOP FAMILY OF DEERPARK**  SW-620

Gerardus, s/o Cornelius Wynkoop, m. Sarah Swartwout, b. in town of Deerpark, c. 1791, & had:
1823, Sept. 17, Eliza, m. 1 Dec. 1842, Benjamin F. Hornbeck, b. 25 May 1820 & d. 27 Sept. 1854. Eliza m. (2) Aug. 1857, James M. Tillman. She d. 1895.
Sarah, m. Mr. --- Ingersoll.
Jane, m. Mr. --- Westbrook.

## YAGEL, FRANK X.  H-995-6

plumber, roofer & tinsmith in Village of Highland Falls.

FRANK was b. in Germany in 1872; to America 1883 & after 4 years schooling served apprenticeship with brothers, with whom he was later a partner. In business for himself since 1899. Tax collector & village trustee. He m. Francis [sic] Wolkin & they have 3 children.

## YELVERTON FAMILY OF CHESTER
### A-613-15, H-154, C-13, 100

This family originally of Wales, from England to L.I., then to Orange Co. JOHN YELVERTON[1], b. c. 1721, with 1 brother & 1 sister, 1751 purchased land in Chester. He was a carpenter & d. in Village of New Windsor, bur. at the Presbyterian Cemetery there. Children:
JOHN.
Anthony.
Thomas, had 3 children: James, William & Elizabeth.
James.
Several daus., one m. Mr. Carpenter of Goshen; one Mr. Howell of Goshen; one m. Mr. Carman.

JOHN YELVERTON[2], s/o John[1], had only one child, ABIJAH.

ABIJAH YELVERTON[3], s/o John[2], in a deed recorded 1765 conveyed 3 parcels of land in Goshen to John Yelverton in trust for parsonage, minister's house & burial ground & Presbyterian Meeting House for Goshen Presbyterian Church; Abijah was tavernkeeper at Chester Village; he had:
Anthony, m. 10 Jan. 1782, Elizabeth Duning.
William, res. at advanced age at Gray Court Station.
There was an Abijah Ketcham recorded in Goshen church records as s/o Abijah & Margaret Yelverton, b. 15 July 1775.

## YOUNG FAMILY OF WALLKILL  A-436, LDS Anc. File

The LDS Ancestral File gives the lineage of a Birdsey Young (probably the Birdsey given below) as: Joseph Yonges[1], b. c. 1604, m. Margaret Warren & had: Gideon Youngs[2], b. 1638 at Salem, MA. Gideon m. at Oyster Pond, NY, Sarah --- & had: Gideon Youngs[3], b. c. 1673 & m. c. 1697 Hannah Reeve of Southold, L.I. Their son: Henry Youngs[4], b. c. 1700 m. c. 1720 Ruth Carpenter of Suffolk Co., NY d/o Joseph & Susannah (Bradner) & had a son, Birdsey Youngs[5]. This Birdsey b. c. 1724, m. NY City 21 April 1762, Rachel Strong. Given as siblings of Birdsey are Henry b. 1722 & Ruth b. 1726.

BIRDSEY YOUNG[1] of Blooming-Grove had a son NATHAN YOUNG[2], b. 1782, d. 1855; farmer & trip-hammer shop; m. (1st) Margaret Thompson of Crawford who d. 1845, and had:
Mrs. William Cross, res. Crawford age 78.
Andrew T., res. Circleville, age 76.
Elizabeth, unm., res. Circleville.
Isaac, twin, M.D., res. NY City.
Birdsey, twin, d. 1841, age 30.

Mrs. Andrew Mills, res. Englewood, NJ.

NATHAN[2] m. (2d) Mrs. --- Tompkins, and had:
Nathan.
Orville.
Birdsey.

## YOUNG, CHARLES C.  H-996

CHARLES, b. Elizabeth, NJ 21 Jan. 1871. Connected with Singer Sewing Machine Co. at Elizabeth & later with Rising Sun Brewing Co. at Elizabeth & later at Orange Co. Brewery, which he purchased in 1893. He m. 8 Sept. 1895, Wilhelmina Schauble of Elizabeth, NJ, d/o Philip & Marie, and had:
Charles.
Paul.
William Joseph.
Marguerite Maria.

Members Middletown's St. Joseph Church.

## YOUNG, OLIVER [P]  A-158, H-996-7
teacher & atty. of Port Jervis.

This Young family is of English extraction & among the early settlers of CT in the 17th century.
SAMUEL YOUNG[1], b. CT, m. Anna Dilly (of Hessian desc.), to Mt. Hope after their marriage & had 8 children. Among them was:
OLIVER[2], b. Mt. Hope, 7 Oct. 1811; d. 3 Oct. 1871. Teacher at age 16 at Milford, PA; studied law & admitted to bar of Pike Co., PA 1835; practiced at Port Jervis, NY; also a civil engineer. He m. 19 Jan. 1848, at Port Jervis, Mrs. Lydia Frances Wentworth (nee Sinclair) of Bartlet, NH. Children:
Frank Sinclair, d. young.
Charles Oliver, atty. of Port Jervis.

## YOUNG, ROBERT [P]  A-560c
of Goshen.

STEWART YOUNG[1], b. Londonderry, Ireland 1785, linen weaver & farmer in Ireland. To America 1817 to St. John's, Newfoundland; to Boston & in 1820 to Craigville, Orange Co., where he d. aged 52. He m. Margaret, d/o Joseph Watson, b. 1795, d. aged 65. Both are bur. Grey Court Cemetery. Children:
Margaret.
1818, Dec. 25, **ROBERT**.
James of Chemung Co.
Joseph W., farmer of Steuben Co.
Frances J., m. Horace Mapes of Monroe; dec'd.
John; dec'd.
Stewart, runs creamery in Warwick.
Eliza R., widow of William Sutton of Warwick.
Matthew, farmer of Monroe
Alexander of Carson City.

ROBERT YOUNG[2], s/o Stewart[1], b. City of Boston; 1845 farmed in Sullivan Co., NY; 1848 m. Margaret, d/o ABRAM B. & Harriet (Harlow) WATKINS [see below] of Hamptonburgh, Orange Co. Margaret b. 27 May 1814. 1848 the family res. NY City; 1851 dairy farmers at Goshen, members of First Presbyterian Church of Florida, Orange Co. Children:

Margaret, m. Wm. T. Jayne, farmer Town of Goshen.

Robert G., res. on homestead; m. Nettie, d/o Alanson Slaughter & Mary Ann Bailey of Wallkill.

ABRAM B. WATKINS, s/o Benjamin of Hamptonburgh, d. 1859, age 84. He & his wife, Harriet Harlow had 6 sons & 7 daus.

---

ARTHUR YOUNGS, b. Kingston, Ulster Co., NY, 10 March 1872, s/o Addison Youngs, also b. Kingston, & Harriet E. Nestell of Newburgh. At age 17 worked with the late G. L. Monell at brass finishing & moulding trade. He now runs auto shop. Member 1st Presbyterian Church.

His great-grandfathers on both sides fought in the Rev. War & the War of 1812. His great-grandfather on his mother's side was a member of the body guard to George Washington and a member of the Society of Cincinnati.

---

## THE EARLIEST SETTLERS

The persons featured in the Families Section of this book cover relatively few of the early white inhabitants of the area of Orange County, New York. The sections following will help identify more of these early settlers and pinpoint them by geographic location and time period.

Orange County was erected February 23, 1798. It is bounded on the south by Rockland County and the State of New Jersey, on the west by the county of Sullivan and State of Pennsylvania, on the north by Ulster County & on the east by Hudson's River.

The first patent in the area was granted Sept. 27, 1694 to Jarvis Marshall & Company, his partner being William Welch. William Tietsoort, a blacksmith, settled on what later became the Swartwout Patent and in 1708 he sent a petition to the Governor & council of NY stating that he was formerly a resident of Schenectady, and that from the massacre at that place in 1689 he barely escaped with his life and that he met with a friendly group of Indians and was invited by them to take up his residence in the Minisink country. He obtained a license to purchase his land in 1698 and did so. He stated that his land was subsequently assumed to be included in a purchase by and patent to Matthew Ling, against which he asked protection. He is judged to be the first settler on the western border and his deed is recorded in Ulster records.

In 1713 he sold two parcels of land to Jan Decker, who, with his cousin, "young Jan Decker," were to occupy one of the parcels and his brother Hendrick Decker the other. At that time William Tietsoort was listed as a resident of Dutchess County, where he appears in the 1714 census with five other members of his family. [For a list of 82 patent holders & landowners' map, see A-16. For lists of who sold which portion of which patent see A-18, 19. Since many patent holders did not reside on their holdings, they have not been relisted here.]

Other very early settlers mentioned included William Thompson, Rev. John Brander, "first minister of the said precinct of Goshen," --- Cromeline, Christopher Deene, Benjamin Aske (at Warwick), William Bull and wife Sarah Wells, Johannes Weasner and family, Lawrence Decker (Warwick). "The proprietors and resident owners appearing as grantors [1721] were:

| | | |
|---|---|---|
| John Everett | Samuel Seeley | Solomon Carpenter |
| James Jackson | Hope Rhodes | John Alsop |
| Samuel Clowes | George McNish | Michael Dunning |
| Isaac Finch | John Holly | Samuel Gilston |
| John Carpenter | James Sands | Samuel Webb |
| John Bears | Charles Williamson | Cornelius Jones |
| Thomas Watson | John Knapp | |

1714-15 tax list of "freeholders, inhabitants, residents & sojourners in the county of Ulster," included:

### Precinct of Shawangonk, 1714-15
[Covered Shawangunk, Montgomery, Crawford, Wallkill
& part of Hamptonburgh]

| | | |
|---|---|---|
| Severgn Tenhout | Richard Windfield | Evert Terwillege |
| Zacharias Hoffman | Jacob Decker, Sen. | Col. Peter Matthews & Co. |
| Jacobus Bruyn | Abraham Schutt | Johannes Terwillege |
| Benjamin Smedes | Jacob Gerritsen Decker | Phillip Miller |
| John MacKlane | Leendert Cool, Jun. | |

### Neighborhood of Wagackemeck, 1714-15

| | | |
|---|---|---|
| Thomas Swartwout | Jacob Coddebecq | Jacobus Swartwout |
| Harmon Barentsen | Peter Guymard | |

## Precinct of Highlands, 1714-15

Peter Magregory *
Swever*
William Southerland*
Michael Wynant**
Burger Myndetsen**
Jacob Weber**
Peter LaRoss**

John Fisher**
Andres Volck**
George Lockste
Pieter Jansen**
Henry Rennau**
Wm. Ellsworth's widow**
Dennis Relje**

Alexander Griggs
Thomas Harris
Capt. Bond**
Melgert, the joyner
Christian Hennecke
Jacob Decker, Jr.
Cornelis Decker

\* Residents of district now in New Windsor.
\*\* Residents of district now in town & city of Newburgh.

## Freeholders of Shawengough, 1714-15

Capt. Jacobus Bruyn
James Spennik
Capt. Zagharias Hoffman
Cornelius Cool*
Benjamin Smedes
Henry Wileman (atty.)*
Abraham Schutt
John North
Jacob Decker
George Andrew
Evert ter Willige
John MacKneel*

Josua Smedes
Jeronimus Mingus*
Cornelius Schoonmaker
Thomas Mackolm
John ter Willige
Christoffel Moul*
Hendrik Decker
Samuel Neely*
Mattys Slimmer*
Israel Rogers*
Hendrick Newkerk*
John Neely*

Hendrick Krans*
John Williams
Edward Gatehouse*
Caleb Knapp, Senr. & Jr.
--- Galatie*
Alexander Neely *
Jeronimus Weller*
Johannis Decker
John Howard
Coll. Cortlandt

\* Known to have been freeholders in the present town of Montgomery, which was then and until 1743 included in the precinct of Shawangunk.

## Freeholders of Wagaghkemek, 1714-15

Harme barentse Van Emweegen
Samuel Swartwout*

Peter Gomar*
Barnardus Swarthout, Jr.*

John Van Vielt, Jr.
Jacob Kuddebeck*

\* In present town of Deerpark.

## Freeholders of the Highlands, 1714-15

William Chambers, Esq. *
John Umphry*
Phineas MacKentosh, Esq.*
Peter Long
Thomas Ellison*
David Sutherland*
James Ellsworth**
John Davis*
Jurie Quick
Melgert Gilli**
William Bond**
Henry Haskell*

Burger Mynderse**
Benjamin Ellsworth**
John Alsop, Esq.*
Nathaniel Foster**
William Ward
Francis Harrison, Esq.*
John Haskell*
James MacKneel, Jr.*
John Van Tien
James Gamwell*
George Wayagont**
Stephen Bedford**

Burger Mynderse, Jr.
Thomas Shaw*
William Sanders
Joseph Gale*
Doct. Colden, Esqr.
George Speedwell
George Ebina
John Monte
Tobias Wayagont**
Christian Chervis
Robert Kirkland

\*In present town of New Windsor.
\*\*In present town & city of Newburgh; Francis Harrison was a freeholder, but not a resident.

# TOWN RECORDS OF MONTGOMERY
## *Officers for 1768*

Major Colden, Supervisor; John Miller, Clark; Patrick Barber & James White, Assessors; Samuel McColm, Constable; George Smith, Collector; Henry Paterson, Constable & Collector.

Thomas Bull & Alexander Trimble, fence viewers for the East side of the kill.

J. Robinson & A. McCurdy, fence viewers for the West side of the kill.

C. Booth Jr. & William Coxs, Poor Masters for the east & west sides of the Wallkill.

## Road Districts & Pathmasters in 1767
## Town of Montgomery

Lt. Crans, Hans Jerry Smith, Andrew Walker & Jacob Crist for the road from Capt. Newkirk to the east side of our precinct to the corner of Major Colden.

James McCobb from George Monell's corner to Mr. Booth, then from Neelytown to Kings'.

James Reeves from the white oak bridge to the brook, to Barney Roe's bridge.

Jonathan Webb from the white oak bridge to the Minisink line.

David Current from Barney Roe's brook to Stringham's lane.

Jacob Crans from Hans Terry Tice to Lt. Crans.

James Crawford from Nathaniel Hile's to Walkill bridge.

Henrycon Terwilliger from Philip Mooul's to Nathaniel Hills.

Daniel Butler from John McNeal's mill to Cox.

James Crawford to Boorland's road.

William Munnel from the northwest line to Campbell's bridge, and from Mr. Konerel to the cross road.

Israel Rogers from John McNeal's mill to Capt. Faulkener's, and the road to Dinaps to Israel Rogers.

Miligan Segur from the Dwarskill to the Wallkill.

Francy [sic] Cane from the Precinct line to Smeedis' mill.

John Miligan from Snider's mill to Denis McPake, and from John Milligan's to Brasher's bridge.

Joseph Hathess for that quarter.

Thomas McCook from the Precinct line to the meeting house.

James Eager from the Hone Pot to Colwell's road.

John McConnery from his house to Mr. Neal's mill.

Daniel Butterfield from the fence of Edward McNeal to Cox's.

Jacob Linderman from --- to Hols Lander's road.

John Paterson from Capt. Newkirk's to James Wilkins.

Francis Newman from Debois's bridge to the road laid out.

Mr. Haold from Mr. Debois's bridge down the market road.

In 1769 Major Colden was re-elected supervisor. John McClean & David Corren, assessors; Petterus Crans & Thomas Neely, collectors; Samuel McColm & Peter Crans, constables. George Munnell, Matice Felter, John Semeral & John McNeal, fence viewers & prizers.

Following is a list of names which appear in the records of the Town of Montgomery, including Crawford, from 1768 to 1778. Some were in the present town of Walkill, which, till 1772, was a part of Montgomery. The list has been taken from early records; the spelling of the record has been preserved, erroneous as it may be.

| | | |
|---|---|---|
| Cadwallader Colden | James White | John Robinson |
| Edward McNeal | Francis Newman | James McKee |
| James McCord | Jacob Crist | Henricus VanKeuren |
| Samuel McColm | George Smith | Archibald McCudry |
| Jacob Linderman | John Dubois | Adam Newkirk |
| Matice Felter | Arthur Parks | David Crawford |
| Patrick Barber | Thomas Bull | Charles Booth Jr. |
| John Tate | John Miller | James McCobb |
| James Barkley | John Davidson | Christian Rockefeller |
| Henry Patterson | Alexander Tremble | George Booth |
| James Wilkens | Henry Newkirk | Nathaniel Wells |
| Johannes Mouis | William Watson | Henry Savage |

William Cox
William Dean
John Archy
Thomas Baty
Matthew Seely
Moses Philips
James Glatia
Ned Hopper
David Moore
Hans Jerry Smith
Benjamin Booth
John McGarrah
Andrew Walker
Samuel Watkins
Kia Gale
Jacob Crist
John McNeal
John Youngs
James McCobb
David Harmon
John Blake
George Monewll
Stevanus Crist
Nicholas Holtslander
Barney Roe
John McCreary
Hugh Milligan
Jonathan Webb
John Crans
Doct. Hill
David Current
Abraham Colwell
John Booth
Jacob Crans
Christian Mengus
Johannes Snider
James Crawford
Helemus Weller
William Barkley
Hans Jerry Tice
Nathaniel Hill
John Graham
Nathaniel Hill
Henrick Terwilliger
Joseph Crawford
Daniel Butterfield
Johannes Weller
John Wilkins
John McNeel
Robert Monel
Andrew Graham
William Faulkner
John McClean
Hanreck Smith
John Milliken
Patrus Crans
George Kimbark
Joseph Watkins

Thomas Neely
Jonathan Smith
Henry Snider
William Eager
James Eager
Benjamin Hains
John Colter
Zachariah Codington
William Neely
Thomas McKee
Marten Tice
Hendrick Newkirk
William Wilkins
William Still
James McBride
Johannes Decker
Daniel Snider
James Ward
Philip Milspach
John Gillespie
John Hill
Jonathan Low
Abraham Dickerson
Henry Crist
John Robinson
Adam Beamer
Jacob Crist
Joseph Crawford
Jacob Bodine
Jacob Milspach
Jacob Low
Coonrad Moore
Nicholas Davis
James Dunglass
Christian Crist
John Milligan
James Hunter
William Hill
Johannes W. Youngblood
Peter Bodine
John Young
Arthur McKing
Thomas Peacock
Mattia Shulp
Samuel Smith
Jacob Newkirk
James Milligan
Dr. Clinton
Yerry Kimbank
Dr. Smith
James Gillespie
Thomas Clineman
James Latta
Hans Nip
Robert Milligan
Robert Thompson
Jacob Sinseback
Philip Moul

William Simerall
Samule Miller
Peter Hill
John Comfort
William Miller
James Rainey
David Smith
William Comfort
John Lackey
Henry Neely
Aunt Grover
Robert Cross
Joseph Houston
Cobus Johnson
James Rea
James McBride
Little John Neely
Samuel White
James Graham
David Jagger
John Comfort
Peter DuBois
Georg [sic] Smith
Robert Dill
Teunis VanArsdall
William Moore
Grandy John Neely
Crommas Weller
William Mickles
William Bodine
Adam Sinseback
Samuel Rainey
William Crist
Hans Weller
James Houston
Henry Neely
Jason Wilkin
Cornelius Slott
Samuel Harris
John Constable
Jeremiah Fitzgerald
Stuffle Maul
James Monel Jr.
Andreas Trempour
Edward Burns
William Jackson
William McBurney
Hugh Milligan
Hans Sease
George Clark
James Jackson
Robert Hunter
David Mingus
Andrew Thompson
Robert Kidd
James McMunn

Officers of Town of New Burgh 1785: Benjamin Birdsall, Moderator; Daniel Birdsall, Clerk; Thomas Palmer, Supervisor; Richard Wood, Constable; John Belknap, Security; Joseph Bloomer & John Jerow, Evidences.

John Belknap, Samuel Stratton, Reuben Tooker, Joseph Coleman, Robert Ross, Assessors.

Daniel Hudson & Benjamin Birdsall, Poor-masters.

Capt. Isaac Belknap, Isaac Fowler Jr., Joseph Sherwood, WIlliam Coddington & John Fowler, Com. of Roads.

Martin Wygant, David Gue, David Belknap, Arthur Smith, Post-masters.

Martin Wygant, Abel Belknap, William Lawrence, Committee to settle with O. Poor.

John Robinson, Abel Belknap, Robert Waugh, George Gardiner, Robert Carscaling, Major Peddingle, Silas Gardiner, James Lyons, Samuel Griggs, Theophilus Mosher, Samuel Divine, William Conklin, Arthur Smith, Johannis Cosman, Johanis Snyder, John Stratton, John Thomas, William Cope, George Merrit, John Sniffen, Path-masters.

## PERSONS ASSESSED (1785)

| | | |
|---|---|---|
| George Stanton | John Graham | Albertson Smith |
| William Gidney | Robert Brockway | William Maloy |
| John Shay | Caleb Chase | Stephen Ireland |
| William Stanton | Henry Smith | Capt. Webb |
| Timothy Lockwood | Benjamin Knap | William Bullard |
| George Shay | Cornelius Hasbrouck | Daniel Gillis |
| Richard Ward | Thomas Smith | William Lawrence |
| Elisha King | John Jeffries | Daniel Gidney |
| Charles Denniston | Francis Harford | Timothy Wood |
| Nathaniel Coleman | Allen Rogers | Isaac Belknap Sen. |
| George Devoll | Samuel Coleman | William McRania |
| Thomas Hinks | Samuel Sands | David Raynolds |
| Samuel Bond | Burger Wygant | Daniel Birdsall |
| William Ward | Joseph Bond | Joseph Hollet |
| Richard Hudson | Joshua Lockwood | James Wearing |
| Joshua Burnet | Haunse Cosman | William Birdsall |
| Doct. Morrison | Samuel Gardner | David Downing |
| Henry Geralderman | Black Peter [sic] | Herman Chase |
| John Simpson | Gilbert Kniffen | Benjamin Raw |
| Richard King | Joseph Gidney Sr. | Isaac Benscoten |
| Thomas Donolly | Robert Baly | James Owens |
| William Russel | Thomas Merrit | Benjamin Birdsall |
| Cornelius Wood | Joseph Gidney Jr. | Abraham Smith |
| James Guthery | Samuel Slie | James Harris |
| Nehemiah Taylor | Isaac Merrit | John Smith |
| Derick Amerman | Charles Kniffen | Jonathan Brundage |
| William Wilson | Peter Snider | William Weer |
| Gilbert Edmonds | Hugh Steveson | Benjamin Lawrence |
| William Trumper | Daniel Kniffen | Azael Smith |
| Joseph Perry | Benjamin Burling | Henry Evens |
| Robert Pool | James Patteson | Isaac Belknap Jr. |
| George Westlake | Isaac Fowler | Henry Lockwood |
| William Albertson | John Rump | Joshua Brush |
| Jonathan Norris | Lewis Dunevon | James Denton |
| Samuel Westlick | Elias Lyons | Peter Aldridge |
| Martin Wygant | Robert Cooper | John Trumper |
| Samuel Weed | Eleazer Gidney | Nathan Tupper |
| Jeremiah Goldsmith | Thomas Ireland | Jacob Concklin |
| Elnathan Foster | Thaddeus Smith | Benjamin King |
| Martin Wygant Jr. | William Collard | Dennis Heins |
| William Belknap | John Kniffen | Abraham Stricklen |

Clement King
David Howell
Jonathan Cosman
Ebenezer Stricklen
John Anderson
Jacob Stricklen
Ruleph Cosman
Adolph Degrove
Abraham Cole
John Whitead
Benjamin Smith
Abraham Cole Jr.
Archibald Elliot
Aaron Fairchild
Henry Yenes
Nicholas Watts
John Caird
Robert Aldridge
Robert Ross
Walter Dubois
John Dolsan
Cornelius Terwilliger
John Dubois
Zebulen Raynolds
David Guion
Moses Bears
Uriah Drake
Zebulon Robinson
William Lawrence Jr.
John Camble
Joseph Penny
Capt. Cooper
Robert McCollum
Jonas Totten
L. Dodge
Nathaniel Divine
William Dunn
Richard Alberson
Solomon Dean
Caleb Lockwood
William Nichols
Stephen Case
Ebenezer Raymond
John Redman
Isaac Demott
William Penny

Old Mr. Cropsey
James Denton
Cornelius Polhamus
Rheuben Cropsey
Geo. Merritt Jr.
Jos[h]ua G. Adsmith
Edward Howell
Samuel Stratten
Enoch Coddington
Richard Wood
John Allen
John Belknap
Gusham Curren
John Garret
Jonathan Belknap
T[h]omas Dennisen
Hollet Jones
John Parshal
Daniel Hudson
Solemen Utter
Patrick Burnet
Edward Franklin
Wm. Buckingham
Samuel Hallock
Jesse Smith
William Scott
John Clark
James Martin
Gilbert Purdy
John Winnens
William Gardner
Ming Purdy
Benjamin Woodhull
Geage Howell
Henry Woolsey
David Belknap
Stephen Stilwill
William Smith
Francis Baty
William Bloomer
David Smith
William Bishop
William Palmer
Lewis Slutt
Jonathan Belknap Jr.
Isaac Brown

James Quigly
Joshua Case
Thomas Palmer
Reuben Holms
Garret Hardenburgh
Joseph Coleman
Jacob Halstead
Daniel Aldridge
John Warren
John Fitzpatrick
Frederick Hedly
Benjamin Coffin
Stephen Stephenus
Marvel Slutt
Samuel Wandel
Selah Reaves
David Redman
Thomas Ward
John Roe
Stephen Jones
Wolvert Acker
Benjamin Dean
Mathen McCollum
Thomas Cambel
Gilbert Aldridge
William Snider
Benona Lattimore
Gilbert Jones
John Snider
William Wite
Burres Holmes
Joseph Wilson
Samuel Pribble
Samuel Fowler
Isaac Fowler Sr.
Stephen Wardell
Samuel Fowler Jr.
Daniel Tooker
William Ward
Francis Smith
John Fowler
Daniel Fowler
Richard Torres
Daniel Thursten
Jacob Camis
Nathl. Drehmun

It is worth noticing, that in these three hundred and fourteen names, embracing the whole male population of the town, there is but one double name.

## TOWN RECORDS OF NEW WINDSOR

At a town meeting in 1763, the following were elected:
James Belknap, Clerk
George Harris, Supervisor

Assessors: Samuel Brewster, George Denniston & James Humphrey
Constable & Collector: Alexander Denniston,
Overseers of the Roads: Judah Harlow & Capt. James Clinton
Overseers of the Poor: David Crawford & John Nicoll
Fence Viewers: Andrew Crawford & William Lawrence.
Then adjourned to the house of Joseph Belknap.

1679. Road Districts & Road Masters: John Galloway, Overseer from William Muliner's to the precinct line westerly.
James Denniston, from William Mulliner's to the top of Snake Hill.
Theophilus Corwin, from the top of Snake Hill through New Windsor to Hudson's River, &c.
Samuel Arthur.
From 1763 to 1770 the following persons held office:

| | | |
|---|---|---|
| James Humphrey | Moses Fowler | Samuel Arthur |
| George Denniston | John Nicholson | James McClaurey |
| Samuel Brewster | Edward Falls | James Deniston |
| Alex. Denniston | Alexander Falls | Samuel Logan |
| James Clinton | Thomas King | Walter McMickle |
| Judah Harlow | Jonathan Parshall | George Clinton |
| John Nicoll | William Edmiston | James Denniston |
| Alexander Crawford | Robert Boyd | Isaac Shultz |
| David Crawford | Isaac Nicoll | William Jackson |
| Isaac Hodge | John Monell | James Faulkner |
| David Humphrey | John Ellison | Neal McArthur |
| William Lawrence | Francis Mandevill | Edward Neely |
| Ch. McCallister | James Jackson | Nathaniel Boyd |
| Leonard Nicoll | Patrick McClaughrey | Thomas Ellison |
| Hezekiah White | James Neely | William Mulliner |
| Silas Wood | Nathan Smith | James Neely Jr. |
| John Yelverton | Samuel Sly | Henry Man Neely |
| John Arthur | Arthur Beaty | William Ellison |
| Andrew Crawford | John Galloway | John Beaty |
| Robert Buchanan | Charles Clinton | |
| Robert Casrkadan | Reuben Weed | |

## TOWN RECORDS OF WARWICK

The first town meeting was held the first Tuesday in April 1789 & the following persons were elected for the year:

John Smith, Town Clerk        John Wheeler, Esq., Supervisor

Assessors:

Capt. James Post        Maj. Peter Bartholf        Maj. Jacobus Post
Capt. Henry Bartholf

Commissioners of Roads:
Nathaniel Mintborn        John Wood

Overseers of the Poor:
Zebulon Wheeler        James Benedict

Collectors:
David McCamly        James Benedict        David Miller

Constables:
John Blain Jr.        David Miller

Road Masters:

| | | |
|---|---|---|
| John Kanaday | Timothy Clark | John Benedict |
| George Vance | William Armstrong | Anthony Finn |
| Capt. Jackson | Major Jacobus Post | Joseph Wilson |
| Thomas Blain | Abraham Lazair | John Smith |
| Garret Post | Philip Burroughs | Calvin Bradner |
| Capt. Bertholf | James Hannah | John Armstrong |
| James Miller | David Miller | Timothy Beers |
| Jacob Gable | Henry Townsend | Abel Noble |
| Philip Ketchem | Moses Carpenter | David Lobdell |
| Caleb Smith | Caleb Taylor | Robert Ludlow |
| Jacobus Chase | David Nanny | Ezra Sanford |
| Israel Owens | Abraham Dolsan | Richard Johnson |
| John Sutton | Nathaniel Bailey | |

Fence Viewers:

| | | |
|---|---|---|
| Arch. Armstrong | Esq. Shepherd | Maj. P. Bartholf |
| James Miller | Philip Burroughs | |

## TOWN RECORDS OF CORNWALL

The first town meeting of freeholders & inhabitants of the precinct of Cornwall held on the first Tuesday in April 1765 at the house of John Brewster in Bloominggrove. Present: Selah Strong, Nathaniel Jayne, David Smith & Amos Mills, Esqs., Justices of the Peace. The following were elected:

John Brewster Sen., Clerk          Hezekiah Howell Sr. Supervisor

Commissioners of Highways:

John Brewster          David Smith          Zachariah Dubois

Jeremiah Coleman, Assessor          John Hudson, Collector

Overseers of the Poor:

Elihu Marvin          Samuel Moffatt

John Hudson, Constable for Bloominggrove
Hophni Smith, Constable for Smith's Clove
J. Sackett, Constable for the water side.

John Woolley, Overseer of the Road from the New Meeting House to Martin Remilies.
Buzaleel Seely, for Oxford, from Israel Seley's to Gregory's.
Joseph Hildrige, from the new road to Goshen road.
Nathaniel Seely, from James Sear's to Saterlie's mill.
Hezekiah Howell, for Blag's Clove.
Stephen Gilbert, for Goshen road, from the precinct line to the Otterkill.
Josiah Reeder, from the Otterkill to Col. Matthews'.
Joseph Chandler, from Col. Matthews' to county line.
Francis Drake, from Henry Mapes' to Thomas Mapes'.
James Halsted, from Teed's Bridge to New Road to Sterling.
Benjamin Strong, from the meeting house to Adam Collins' & to the new school house.
Thomas Smith, from John Erles' to Cave's.
Joel Tuthill, from Curtis Coleman's to Nathaniel Curtis' mill & along to the Round Hill.
Richard Goldsmith, from John Brewster's to Gilberts'.
Silas Youngs, from the end of Oxford to K. Youngs'.
Benjamin Gregory, from his house to Oxford.
David Sherod & Timothy Brewster, Overseers for the water side.
David Smith, from Gregroy's to John Earles' on the Clove road.
Juli Smith, from his house to Car's, & from his house to Dunbar's.

Elihu Mavin & Archibald Little, Fence Viewers for Oxford.
Austin Smith & John Earles for Woodberry Clove.
Joseph Wood & Jeremiah Clark for New Cornwall.
John Brewster & David Coleman for Bloominggrove.

At this time the town took in towns of Cornwall, Bloominggrove & Monroe & part of Chester. The town officers from 1765-1775, not naming the office. In this way we get the names of the old settlers in Cornwall, Bloominggrove & Monroe.

| | | |
|---|---|---|
| Selah Strong | John Coleman | Jonathan Tuttle |
| Josiah Reader | Isaac VanDuzer Jr. | Francis Smith |
| Nathaniel Satterly | John Woolly | James Keeler |
| William Moffatt | Austin Smith | William Roe |
| Nathaniel Jayne | Thomas Shaw | Ed. Tomkins |
| Joseph Chandle | Richard Williams | James McCleane |
| Henry Brewster | Bazaliel Sely | Eben. Stephens |
| Israel Rose | Archibald Little | R. Goldsmith Jr. |
| David Smith | Thomas Goldsmith | Jeremiah Clark |
| Francis Drake | John McMannus | Thomas Coleman |
| Stephen Hulse | Joseph Hildrige | William Thorn |
| Silvanus White | Joseph Wood | Silvanus Halsey |
| Amos Mills | John Brewster | Nath'l. Chandler |
| James Halsted | Philip Miller | Capt. J. Woodhull |
| Jonathan White | Nathaniel Sely | Dennis Kelly Jr. |
| Capt. F. Matthews | Reuben Clark | Stephen Howell |
| Jno. Brewster Sr. | Joseph Wilcox | Samuel Brinson |
| Benjamin Strong | Austin Smith | Alex. Gallaway |
| A. Cunningham | Hez. Howell Jr. | A. Cunningham |
| Langford Thorn | Daniel Coleman | Stephen Moore |
| B. Howell Sen. | Isaac Coley | Frederick Tobias |
| Thomas Smith | Ch. VanDuzer | Tho. Everson |
| David Mandervill | Stephen Gilbert | John W. Tuthill |
| John Bull | James Sayr | Josiah Seley |
| Zachariah Dubois | William Hudson | Samuel Mapes |
| Joel Tuthill | E. Galloway | Samuel Knights |
| Roger Barton | Edward Brewster | Bazaliel Seley Jr. |
| Capt. Silas Pierson | Elijah Carpenter | Phineas Herd |
| Jeremiah Coleman | David Gage | John Satterly |
| Richard Goldsmith | Nathaniel Sands | John Smith |
| Lemuel Sheldon | Moses Clark | Patrick O'Duddle |
| Natt. Seley | Elemuel Sheldon | Benj. Goldsmith |
| John Hudson | James Matthews | Jacob Kune |
| Silas Youngs | Daniel Jayne | Henry Dyer |
| David June | D. Sutherland Jr. | Garret Duryea |
| Naniad Curtis | Patrick McDaniel | Henry Attwood |
| Elihu Marvin | Jonathan Miller | Thos. Linch |
| Benj. Gregory Jr. | William Ayrs | Sutherland Hulet |
| Francis Smith | John Wagant | Hugh Gregg |
| William Miller Jr. | Joseph Hildreth | Obadiah Smith |
| Samuel Moffat | Eben. Woodhull | Henry Weasner |
| David Sherod | James Smith | Thomas Coleman Jr. |
| Garrett Miller | Samuel Knight | Caleb Coleman |
| Jacob Compton | Matthias Gilbert | Thomas Helms |
| Hophni Smith | Israel Seley | Oliver Devenport |
| Tim. Brewster | William Fitzjare | Amos Mills |
| Benj. Goldsmith | Jacob Gale | John Griffith Esq. |
| Michael Thomas | James Gray | Justus Hulse |
| J. Sackett | Samuel Strong | Ann H. Hay Esq. |
| John Earles | William Ketch | Stephen Wood |

| | | |
|---|---|---|
| Joseph Smith | Brier Palmer | Arthur Yeomans |
| John W. Clark | Nathan Marvin | Henry Wisner Jr. |
| Benj. Prindle | Samuel Ketcham Jr. | Joshua Corey |
| Samuel Earl | Daniel Wood | A. Townsend |
| Elijah Green | Chas. McKinney | Jonathan Brooks |
| William Hunter | Samuel Tuthill | Daniel Chambers |
| George Duryea | Isaac Brown | Stephen Smith |
| William Howard | Isaac Howell | Capt. J. Tuthill |
| Reuben Youngs | John Arles | Nathan Coley |
| Isaac Cooley | Zeph. Howell | Noah Carpenter |
| Samuel Rockwel | James Wilkins | Vincent Helmes |
| Paul Howell | Hons Smith | Lewis Donovan |
| Coleman Curtis | Z. Burchard | James Jordan |
| Tho. Chatfield | D. Lankester | Smith Clark |
| Seth Marven | Samuel Moffatt | Sander Galloway |
| John Beltcher | Samuel Slaughter | A. Sutherland |
| Jacob Galloway | Samuel Smith | Philip Roblin |
| Julius Smith | Iasiah Howel | Israel Osmon |
| David Sutherland | Thomas Hurley | P. McGlocklin |
| Joseph Chandler | Henry Halle | John Lomarex |
| John Miller Jr. | Stephen Peet | John Price |
| Matthew Ayres | Robert Armstrong | C. VanDuzer |
| William Herd | Isaac Garrison | Zepher Teed |
| Abner Thorp | Sylvanus Hally | John Wooley |
| L. Dobbin | Ebenezer Bull | |

## EARLIEST CHURCHES

The first church in the county was Lutheran. Lutheranism was brought to Newburgh by the Palatine immigrants of 1709. Joshua Kockerthal accompanied the nine families of immigrants as their minister, did not locate permanently with them, but removed to Columbia County. Justus Falconier, minister of the congregation of New York, served the people by an annual visit in 1710. When Falconer died in 1723, William Christopher Berkenmeyer became his successor. The church was erected between 1726 and 1731. The second Lutheran church was in the town of Montgomery.

The first Presbyterian church in Orange County was located at Goshen. In 1721 John Yelverton held church land in trust and certified that Rev. John Bradner had been settled and that a parsonage-house was being erected. The second Presbyterian church was known as Goodwill and erected in the town of Montgomery. By 1729 tradition says that about forty families that had emigrated from different parts of Ireland, but principally from the county of Londonderry, in their new home were called "the people of Wallkill." First church erected 1735, first pastor Rev. Joseph Houston.

Church of England. In 1731 The Rev. Richard Charlton was sent from London, "Society for the Propagation of the Gospel in Foreign Parts" to preach in the area. He was soon succeeded by the Rev. W. Kilpatrick who served until 1734. Three stations of the parish were established, one at New Windsor, one on the Otterkill, known as St. David's and one on the Wallkill known as St. Andrews. The New Windsor Station was changed to Newburgh in 1747 and later known as St. George's. During the war of the Revolution it practically ceased to exist, but was revived in 1815.

The Reformed Dutch Church was established in Orange County as early as August, 1716, the Rev. Petrus Vas, pastor of the church in Kingston, visited the settlements which had been founded on the Delaware River and were composed mainly of German, Dutch and Huguenot immigrants, who had come from Kingston and New Paltz. In 1737 were organized as the "united churches of Minisink" the Walpack Church, in the Walpack bend of the Delaware; the Minisink Church, 12 miles farther on; and 8 miles further up, in the forks of the Delaware and Neversink, the Maghaghkemek Church. Dominie Vas was succeeded by Rev. George Wilhelmus Mancius in 1732.

The Congregationalists never had large numbers of members in the county, but were among the early religious organizations, having been established the Blooming-Grove Church in 1759.

Associate & Associate Reformed Presbyterian Churches were founded by early immigrants of New Windsor and Wallkill. In 1752 Rev. John Cuthbertson of the Associate Presbytery of Scotland was sent to America.

Baptist missionaries were in the county as early as 1740, and Rev. Mr. Halstead, then pastor of the church at Fishkill, performed missionary labors in Dutchess & Ulster Counties.

Methodism was not practiced in Orange County until the 1780's.

From Canada at a very early date Roman Catholics were sent into the area to convert the local Indian tribes. Rev. Langdill and Rev. Dr. Ffrench, in 1817 and 1818, were the first Catholic missionaries in the county; 1826 erected St. Patrick's Church at Newburgh, the first Catholic church in Orange County.

The first colony of Friends, or Quakers, was erected in the old precinct of Cornwall before the Revolutionary War. Soon after the war they are found in Newburgh, Plattekill and Marlborough, in Ulster, towns which were originally covered by the precinct of Newburgh.

*Western view of the public buildings at Goshen.*

# GEOGRAPHICAL LOCATIONS

## TOWN OF NEW WINDSOR

Originally a town of Ulster County; located in the central northeastern portion of Orange County. The name of the town is from Windsor, England. The records of the town begin with the first town meeting held in 1763, when the following officers were chosen: Joseph Belknap, clerk; George Harris, supervisor; Samuel Brewster, George Denniston, James Humphrey, assessors; Alexander Denniston, constable and collector; Judah Harlow and Capt. James Clinton, overseers of the roads; David Crawford and John Nicoll, overseers of the poor; Andrew Crawford and William Lawrence, fence-viewers.

## VILLAGES OF NEW WINDSOR:

NEW WINDSOR:    Laid out in township plot in 1749. The first lot owners were Henry Brewster and Judah Harlow, September 1749. The proprietors in January, 1751-52 were James Tuthill, Henry Brewster, Samuel Brewster, Brant Schuyler, Evan Jones, John Yelverton, Hezekiah Howell, Joseph Sackett Jr., Ebenezer Seely, Vincent Matthews and John Nelson.

ORANGEVILLE OR MOODNA: First settled between 1728 and 1740 by Nathaniel and Samuel Hazard. Samuel Brewster built a saw-mill and Jonas Williams and sons erected a flour-mill. The hamlet has a post-office under the name of Moodna, which name was bestowed by N. P. Willis.

QUASSAICK VALLEY: Robert Boyd, Jr. in June 1775 erected a forge for the manufacture of guns, bayonets, etc. Gov. George Clinton erected a grist-mill and a saw-mill, which he sold to Hugh Walsh in 1790.

VAIL'S GATE OR MORTONVILLE:    A hamlet at the junction of the New Windsor and Blooming-Grove turnpike and the Snake Hill turnpike. The name is from Mr. Vail, an old resident, and for many years keeper of the turnpike gate. At one time was known as Tooker's Gate. From the occupation of the property by Maj. Charles F. Morton it got the name of Mortonville, by which name its post office is known.

LITTLE BRITAIN: Settled by John Humphrey in 1724 and by Peter Mullinder, Robert Burnet and John Reid (father-in-law of Burnet) in 1729. In 1731 Charles Clinton, Mrs. Mary McClaughry, Alexander Denniston and John Young settled. Named by Charles Clinton, of Irish birth and an exile. Majority of settlers were Scotch-Irish or English-Irish, nearly all were Presbyterians.

THE SQUARE: Sometimes called Washington Square, is part of Little Britain. During the Revolution known as Liberty Square.

RAGVILLE, ROCK TAVERN, ETC.:    Name of a hamlet about two miles west of the Little Britain church. Named for a man named Davenport, who had a store there and exchanged goods for rags. Site of the famous Morrison tavern and distillery, and further west Rock tavern, which takes its name from the rock on which it is erected. Both taverns were embraced in the road district known early as Hunting-Grove, which extended west to the Otterkill. The settlement Hunting-Grove has more recently been called Bushkirk's Mills and Burnside Post-office. Name bestowed by Nathan Smith, who established mills and a store there. Another once-famed locality now lost was Stonefield, the residence and grammar-school of Rev. John Moffat.

## TOWN & CITY OF NEWBURGH

The first settlers were fugitives from the Lower Palatinate of the Rhine who went to England in 1708 and petitioned to be sent to a plantation in America. The settlers were: Joshua de Kockerthal, minister and Sibylle Charlotte his wife, Christian Joshua, Benigna Sibylle and Susanna Sibylle, their children (Joshua died early in the settlement);
Lourentz Schwisser husbandman and Anna Catharine his wife and their son Johannes;
Heinrich Rennau stocking-maker and husbandman, Johanna his wife, Lourentz and Heinrich their sons, and Susanna and Maria Johanna Liboschain, sisters-in-law;
Andries Volck, husbandman, Anna Catharine his wife, Heironemus, Maria Barbara and Anna Gertrude, their children;
Michael Weigand, husbandman, Anna Catharine his wife, Tobias, George, and Anna Maria, their children;
Jacob Webber, husbandman, Anna Elizabeth his wife, and Eve Maria and Eve Elizabeth, their children;
Johannes Jacob Plettel, husbandman, Anna Elizabeth his wife, and Margaret, Anna Sarah and Catharine, their children (Johannes died on his passage or soon after his arrival in America and his widow married George Lockstead.);
Johannes Fischer, smith and husbandman, Maria Barbara his wife, and Andries his son;
Melchior Gulch, carpenter and joiner, Anna Catharine his wife, and Heinrich and Margaret, their children;

Isaac Turck, husbandman;

Peter Rose, cloth-weaver and Johanna his wife, Mary Wiernarm, husbandwoman and his mother-in-law, and Catharine, her child (removed to Pennsylvania and transfered his interest to "one Burger Meynders, blacksmith", previously a resident of Kingston);

Isaac Feber, husbandman, Catharine his wife, and Abram their son;

Daniel Fiere, husbandman, Anna his wife, and sons Andrew and Johannes;

Herman Schuneman, clerk.

Lourentz Schwisser, Isaac Turck, Isaac Feber, Heinrich Renneau and Daniel Fiere removed elsewhere, and Christian Henricke and Peter Johnson were added to the company. Justus Falconier served as minister to replace Rev. Kockerthal until his death in 1723.

In 1782 Benjamin Smith laid out streets and lots in his portion of the Kockerthal farm and gave it the name of "The Township of Washington," which consisted of 72 lots. Owners named on the first map are John Anderson, James Denton, Mr. Menge, E. C. Lutherloh, Jacob Reader, A. Fairchild, Hugh Walsh, William Forbes, Mr. Crosby, William Quackenbush, S. Clark, B. Palmer, William Thurston and Adolph DeGrove.

## VILLAGES OF NEWBURGH:

VILLAGE OF NEWBURGH:    Incorporated in 1800, the second incorporated village in the state. 1801 the Newburgh and Cochecton Turnpike Road was founded to construct a road from Newburgh to the Delaware River and Robert Browne, John DeWitt, William Seymour, Levi Dodge, Johannes Miller, Hugh Walsh, George Clinton Jr., Jacob Powell, John McAuley, Charles Clinton, William W. Sackett, George Gardner were appointed directors. In 1865 incorporated as the City of Newburgh.

BALMVILLE:  Small collection of houses two miles north of the city of Newburgh, first settled in 1709, named from a large tree growing there commonly called Balm of Gilead. Gilbert Williams (aged 80 in 1875) was a settler in 1808, coming from Nova Scotia. He named John Cosman and William Bloomer as other early settlers. Formerly called Hampton.

MIDDLEHOPE:  Small hamlet four miles north of city of Newburgh, formerly called Middletown. Name changed to Middlehope at the time of the erection of a post office and named by James P. Brown for the village of Hopeton in Scotland.

THE DANS KAMER, (Devils Dance Chamber):    Point of land forming the northwestern head of Newburgh Bay, named because it was believed that Indians held religious rites there.

HAMPTON:    Name given by William Acker, son of Wolvert, to the farm of his father. Wolvert established Acker's Ferry there soon after the Revolution. (See Balmville above.)

FOSTERTOWN:  Hamlet about four miles northwest of City of Newburgh. First settled by John and William Foster, Richard Ward and John Griggs in 1768.

ROSSVILLE:  Name of a section of the town about six miles northwest of city of Newburgh. Originally Wallace Patent, held by Joseph Penny who sold about 250 acres to Robert Ross and divided the remainder among his sons. Mr. Ross was the first settler and he established a tannery and built a stone house as early as 1770. The post office address is Savill, a name bestowed by Chauncey F. Belknap in honor of his son, Savill.

LUPONDALE:  A district, not a hamlet; seven miles from city of Newburgh, also called "Quaker Street." Named in honor of William Lupton, who owned this part of the old patent.

ROCKY FOREST:    District on the western part of the patent to Jacobus Kipp and Co. Adjoins Orange Lake on the east. Named for physical features. Henry W. Kipp, son of Jacobus, was the first settler and was a resident as late as 1778.

GARDNERTOWN:    Small settlement four miles northwest of city of Newburgh, named for Silas Gardner, one of the first settlers.

GIDNEYTOWN:    Originally part of the patent to John Spratt, purchased in 1760 by Eleazer Gidney, who with his sons Joseph, Daniel, David and Eleazer settled on it at that time.

DU BOIS' MILLS:  On Quassaick Creek, about one and a half miles west of its confluence with the Hudson. A mill was erected here by Alexander Colden in 1743, one of the oldest in the region. He sold parts of his property to Jonathan Hasbrouck in 1753. After the Revolutionary War Mr. Hasbrouck sold it to a Mr. Van Keuren; from him a Mr. Dickonson occupied it in 1798 and later became the property of Gen. Nathaniel DuBois who also erected a saw-mill and a fulling-mill.

**NEW MILLS:** About a mile and a quarter west of the city, Abel Belknap, and later owned by Daniel Niven, erected a grist-mill prior to the Revolution. Came to be called New Mills, which name was extended to the hamlet which grew up around it.

**POWDER MILLS:** About four miles northwest of city of Newburgh, where are located the powder-works of Lafflin & Rand. Originally occuped by Foster's saw-mill, was purchased in 1817 by Daniel Rogers.

**BELKNAP'S RIDGE:** About four miles west of city of Newburgh, named in honor of the Belknap family, who settled in the area in 1749/50.

**EAST COLDENHAM:** Name of Gov. Colden's settlement in the town of Montgomery, subsequently extended to the hamlet in the southwest part of the town of Newburgh. East Coldenham post office located here.

**ORANGE LAKE:** Body of water in the northwestern part of the town, covering about 400 acres, Indian name was Qussuk, or stony pond. Named by Rev. James Wilson, who resided in the vicinity. A coinage-mill was operated near its outlet by Capt. Thomas Machin about 1787, who named it New Grange.

## TOWN OF MONTGOMERY

Borders on Ulster County, part of the original John Evans Patent. In 1714 covered precinct of Shawangunk, in 1743 constituted a part of the precinct of Wallkill. Settled early by Germans and Scotch-Irish. Pioneer settlers were of the Crist, Bookstaver, Sinsabaugh, Youngblood, Shafer, Miller, Shulp, Smith, Rickey, Pitts, Newkirk, and Fillmore families. The Assembly of 1735 naturalized among other: Matys Milsbagh, Hendrick Christ, Stephanes Christ, Larens Christ, Philip Milsbaugh, Jacob Sinsebaugh, Jacob Booch Staber, and Johannis Jong Bloet.

The town was organized under the name of Hanover Precinct in 1772. It's territory, including Crawford, was set off from the old precinct of Wallkill. In 1782 the name was changed to Montgomery Precinct and continued until 1789 when it was changed to Town of Montgomery.

### VILLAGES OF MONTGOMERY:

**MONTGOMERY VILLAGE:** On the Wallkill, in the southern part of Town of Montgomery. Named in honor of Gen. Montgomery. Early settlers were John McFaught, David Crist, John McKinstry, Matthew Hunter, Samuel Smith, Arthur Parks and Oolis Shulp. The village was incoroprated in 1810.

**WALDEN:** Village in Town of Montgomery, on the Wallkill at the High Falls and known for many years by that name. Early settlers included James Kidd, who built a grist-mill, which later passed on to Johannes Decker and in 1789 was owned by Cadwallader Colden Jr., Francy Cane, Hugh Milligan, Jacob Bodine and sons (Charles & Lewis), Jonathan Low, Peter Bodine, Conrad Moore, William Bodine, Robert Kidd, Thomas Clineman and William Erwin. Named for Jacob T. Walden, former resident. An industrial center, incorporated in 1855.

**ST. ANDREW'S:** Hamlet in northeast part of Town of Montgomery. Name from an early Episcopal Church known as St. Andrew's, now located at Walden.

**COLDENHAM:** In southeast part of Town of Montgomery, near New Windsor. Name derived from the Colden family, early settlers.

**ALLARD'S CORNERS:** Hamlet in northwest part of Town of Montgomery, where a post office was established some years ago.

**SCOTT TOWN:** On the Newburgh and Cochecton turnpike, four miles east of village of Montgomery, where there used to be a turnpike gate kept by Samuel Monell. Mr. John Scott kept a store there.

**SCOTT'S CORNERS:** One and a half miles east of Montgomery village, named for John F. Scott, son of the above-named John Scott.

**KEISERTOWN:** Former name of settlement on southwest part of Town of Montgomery on the Wallkill, three miles from Montgomery. A Dutch settlement, name Keiser taken from Roman Ceasar.

# TOWN OF CRAWFORD

Borders on counties of Sullivan and Ulster. Part of the original John Evans Patent and taken from Town of Montgomery in 1823.

**VILLAGES OF CRAWFORD: HOPEWELL:** Village in west part of Town of Crawford and the name was taken from a Presbyterian Church which was formed there as a colony from the older congregation of Goodwill in Montgomery. Residents use the post office facilities at Thompson's Ridge.

**BULLVILLE:** Post office in the southwest part of the Town of Crawford. Thomas Bull was an early resident.

**SEARSVILLE:** Also known as Searsburgh, situated upon the Dwaars Kill, named in honor of Benjamin Sears, an early resident, mill owner and sheriff.

**THOMPSON'S RIDGE:** Near Searsville, a station on the Crawford Branch of the NY, Ontario and Western Railway. Daniel Thompson, postmaster.

**COLLABURGH:** In south part of Town of Crawford. Built up when situated on the old Cochecton turnpike, now deteriorating since the coming of the railroad.

**PINE BUSH:** Business place near the Shawangunk River, in north of Town of Crawford. Terminus of the Crawford Railroad. James Thompson settled in 1824/5. Other early settlers included Elijah Smith, Dr. Ewen and Abraham Mould tanner.

# TOWN OF WALLKILL

Located in western Orange County, took in the Minisink Angle and part of the John Evans Patent. Was settled compartively late. William Bull's sons William and Thomas were early settlers. Erected from Precinct of Wallkill, 1743, it then comprised the territory now held by the towns of Crawford, Montgomery, Willkill and portions of Mt. Hope and Hamptonburgh. In 1772 the precinct of Hanover was set off.

**VILLAGES OF WALLKILL: MIDDLETON:** In South part of Town of Wallkill and so named because it is midway between Montgomery and Mount Hope. The largest village in the town. Early settlers included John Green, Samuel Wickham, Daniel Moore, Capt. Jonathan Owen, Abel Woodhull, Daniel and Nathaniel Wells, Joseph and William Baird, Henry B. Wisner, Matthias Keene, Daniel Corwin, Isaiah Vail, Dr. Hanford, Jesse and Elisha Corwin, Gabriel and John Wells, Moses H. Corwin and Stacey Beakes. Incorporated in 1848.

**SCOTCHTOWN:** Settled by the families of McVey, McWhorter, McInnis, McLaughlin, McCord. Other early settlers included George Houston, Benjamin Simons, Robert Sterritt.

**MECHANICTOWN:** Two miles east of Middletown, this village spring up around the forge and trip-hammer works of Messrs. Otis & Miller.

**CIRCLEVILLE:** Halfway between Scotchtown and Bloomingburgh, on old turnpike from Goshen to Bloomingburgh, now a station on the Crawford Railroad with about 100 inhabitants. The Bull family were early settlers.

**PHILLIPSBURGH:** East of Middletown on the Wallkill. Across the river there is an elevation known as Hopper Hill, further east is Mount Joy. Was a place where powder was manufactured during the Revolutionary War.

**HOWELL'S DEPOT:** A station on the Erie Railroad, next northwest from Middletown. The post office was established about 1846, Samuel C. Howell, first postmaster.

**VAN BURENVILLE:** Village west of Crawford Junction. Post office established there in honor of President Martin Van Buren. Formerly a place of considerable business on the old stage route. Post office facilities were transferred to Howell's on the railroad and the town has declined.

**SAND STATION:** Stopping place on the Oswego Midland, a mill north of Middletown.

FAIR OAKS: Post office and station on the Midland Railroad (now the NY, Ontario & Western), established 1872. The local hotel was opened for business the day of the battle of Fair Oaks, Va.

CRAWFORD JUNCTION: A swamp and diverging point of meeting railroads; no town here only a switchman's hut and a milk-platform.

PURDY'S STATION: Stopping place on the NY, Ontario and Western Railway in northwest part of Town of Wallkill, near the Sullivan Co. line. Just a milk-station.

LOCKWOOD'S: Railway station only.

ROCKVILLE: South of Bull Hack in Town of Wallkill.

MILLSBURGH: Early name for neighborhood settled by Jacob Mills and others.

STONY FORD: Called so as early as 1767, a fording-place over the Wallkill from Montgomery; located one mile west of Lagrange.

BRIMSTONE HILL: North part of Town of Wallkill, named from the story of a drinking spree at the old log tavern. Being short of glasses, and extra one was brought in from another room that had been used in mixing up some brimstone. In the dark a patron drinking from the glass ran out into the street shouting "Brimstone! brimstone," and the place was so named.

MICHIGAN: Cluster of houses on Three-Mile Hill, the name still preserved in the name of the school district. Name supposedly came from a citizen who was in debt and undertook to make the people believe he had temporarily been to Michigan.

LAGRANGE: First post office in the Town of Wallkill, and given the name "Wallkill."

DAVISTOWN: Old name for neighborhood in east part of Town of Wallkill with numerous Davis family members.

HONEY-POT: Name of spring of water a mile or so from Circleville. Farm and district also known by that name. Richard Gale was an early settler.

GUINEA: Old name to settlement made by colored people, east of the Honey-Pot farm. The had been slaves of Col. McLaughry of New Windsor, and were freed by him between 1825 and 1828. The three heads of the old families were John, Thomas and William. Col. McLaughry gave them the land.

BULL HACK: Old name given to section of Town of Wallkill about a mile south of Circleville. Stony, rough land originally settled by William Bull.

PIERCE VALLEY: Parmalee estate about the time Franklin Pierce was elected President.

## TOWN OF MOUNT HOPE

Mount Hope is in the western portion of Orange and bounded on the north by Sullivan County. It was taken from the Towns of Deerpark and Wallkill and incorporated in 1825. The town was first named Calhoun in honor of John C. Calhoun, senator of South Carolina. In 1832 it was renamed Mount Hope. Early settlers included Jasper Writer, Ashbel Cadwell, Rufus Stanton, Israel and Daniel Green, William Shaw, Benjamin Woodward, Benjamin Dodge and Stephen St. John. John Fince was the frist immigrant and came from Horseneck, Connecticut and settled at Goshen.

**VILLAGES OF MOUNT HOPE:** MOUNT HOPE VILLAGE: In the southeastern part of the Town of Mount Hope, an early lumber center. Founded by Benjamin Woodward, hotel keeper, and Dr. Benjamin B. Newkirk in 1807.

OTISVILLE: Principal village in Town of Mount Hope, a station on the Erie Railway. The name is from Isaac Otis, originally of Massachusetts, who migrated to Orange County in 1816. The post office was established in 1819, and Isaac was the first postmaster.

NEW VERNON: On the north line of Town of Mount Hope and partly in Sullivan County.

FINCHVILLE: Hamlet in southwest part of Town of Mount Hope, named in honor of John Finch, the first settler in the vicinity.

**GUYMARD:** On the western slope of the Shawangunk Mountains, a station on the Erie Railroad. The name is the old French form of the family name Gumaer. Post office established in 1866, Peter L. Gumaer the first postmaster. Establishment of the Erie Lead Mine on the lands of the Gumaer brothers helped establish the village.

## TOWN OF GOSHEN

The central town of Orange county, located wholy on the territory of the Wawayanda Patent. The earliest settlers were Christopher Denne and Daniel Cromeline. Deeds recorded of village lots bear dates as early as 1714. Subsequent settlers in 1721 were John Everett, John Carpenter and John Yelverton and later John Everett and Samuel Clowes. Goshen Church was organized in 1721 and Rev. John Bradner settled as minister that year.

Tradition says that the name was selected for its scriptural associations. In 1764 the precinct of Goshen was divided by a line which was nearly that of the present west line of Monroe. The west part retained the name of Goshen, the east part was named New Cornwall. At that time the territory of Goshen covered the present towns of Warwick, Goshen, part of Chester, Wawayanda, Minisink, Greenville and south part of Deerpark, an immense district. In 1788 Goshen was reduced by formation of towns of Warwick and Minisink.

**VILLAGES OF TOWN OF GOSHEN: GOSHEN VILLAGE:** The place of public business going as far back as the earliest settlement. Incorporated in 1843.

**MAPES' CORNERS:** Village in south part of Town of Goshen, near Mount Lookout. A railway station of the Pine Island Branch Railroad, and named for the earliest family that settled here.

**COUNTY FARM:** Latest established post office in the County, 1880. Here is located the Orange County farm and the County House.

**EAST DIVISION & WEST DIVISION:** Terms found in early writings of the area. The township of Goshen originally divided into four parts, the Divisions of North, East, South and West. The names East and West have ever since been used, but North and South have not.

## TOWN OF WARWICK

In the southern part of the county, bounded on the southwest by the state of New Jersey. First named and settled in 1719. Earliest settlers included Lawrence Decker, a Stagg/Stage family, Thomas Blain, Thomas DeKay, John Vane, Daniel Burt, James Thompson, Nathaniel Roe, William Thompson, David Shepherd, Rev. Jonathan Elmer (brother of Dr. Nathaniel), the Al(li)son family, Capt. John Wisner, Henry Wisner, George Carr, Matthew Howell and Peter Clous (Clowes).

What now constitutes the Town of Warwick was part of the old precinct of Goshen until 1788.

**TOWN OF WARWICK VILLAGES: WARWICK:** Largest village in the town, settled by 1719. The land was originally bought of Benjamin Aske about 1746 by Col. Beardsley who laid out the village. There was no settlement until about 1764. Francis Baird and Daniel Burt erected the first houses. Incorporated in 1867.

**FLORIDA:** An old village in the Town of Warwick, the name from the Latin Floridus, covered or red with flowers. The name was given before the Revolutionary War. The post office was established before 1830, Samuel S. Seward was the first postmaster.

**AMITY:** Old village in Town of Warwick, six miles from Warwick, near the New Jersey line. Known by the old Indian name Pochuck.

**PINE ISLAND:** Terminus of the Warwick Valley Branch of the Erie Railway, began runing passenger trains in 1869. Post office was established in 1870.

**BLOOM'S CORNERS:** Derives name from the Bloom family, is near the southern boundary line of the state.

**NEW MILFORD:** In the valley of the Warwick Creek, in the south part of the Town of Warwick. Formerly called Jockey Hollow and it is stated by previous writers that an "etheral and elevated standard of morals" did not always prevail in the business of exchanging horses in the area. The post office was established in 1815.

**EDENVILLE:** An old name given to a collection of houses just east of Mounts Adam and Eve. Formerly called Postville in honor of Col. Jacobus Post, whose father first settled in the locality.

LIBERTY CORNERS: Hamlet in Town of Warwick at the west foot of Pochuck Mountains, nearly on the New Jersey state line. The post office was discontinued years ago.

NEWPORT: Name given to the Pochuck Bridge neighborhood, southwest of Amity.

SANDFORDVILLE: Hamlet in the valley of Warwick Creek, named for the Sanford family.

STONE BRIDGE: A station on the Warwick Valley Railroad, south of Wickham's Pond.

BIG ISLAND: Station on the Pine Island Railroad and named from Big Island of the Drowned Lands.

LAWTON: Station on the Warwick Valley Railroad north of Wickham's Pond.

DUTCH HOLLOW: Name of neighborhood southeast of the Bellvale Mountains.

BELLVALE: Three miles east of Warwick village, settled by Daniel Burt in 1760.

## TOWN OF CHESTER

An interior town of the County. The village was settled as early as 1751 by John Yelverton, who purchased his land from James Ensign, who had purchased from John Beers. Other early settlers included John King, George Board, Daniel Cromeline, Phineas Rumsey, Henry McElroy, Thomas Fitzgerald, John Clark, George David, David Mapes, Nathaniel Roe, John Kinner, the Howell family, Edmund Satterly, Joseph Drake, Oliver Smith, Peter Townsend, Able Noble, Isaac Cooley, the Jackson, Carpenter and Horton families, George Thompson, John Chandler, Nathaniel Knapp, the Holley family, Richard Jennings, Denton family, Daniel Hall, Matthias Jayne, John Springsted Whitman family, Thomas Beach, John Feagles, Tidd family, the Seeley brothers and William Vail, among others.

TOWN OF CHESTER VILLAGES: CHESTER: The village that grew up on the Yelverton estate. The "village at the depot" of Chester is on the Erie Railroad.

WEST CHESTER: About a mile from Chester, a small hamlet, distinct from the other villages.

EAST CHESTER: Name of the staton of the Warwick Valley Railway, one-half a mile from Old Chester.

GRAY COURT STATION: A railway junction.

THE SALEM NEIGHBORHOOD: A district on the east/southeast part of town, location of the Protestant Methodist Church of Chester and a school house.

SUGAR-LOAF VILLAGE: Named from the mountain and the valley, both known by that name in early settlement. Post office established about 1825, first postmaster Josiah Howell.

## TOWN OF BLOOMING-GROVE

An interior town of the county, this is a hilly and mountainous region. Vincent Matthews purchased land in 1721 and settled here and erected a grist-mill at the place now known as Salisbury. Edward Blagg settled in the area since known as Blagg's Clove and Jesse Woodhull settled in the area in 1753. Thomas Goldsmith built a house on the west bank of the Otterkill and other early settlers included the Moffatts and Lewis DuBois of New Paltz, tavernkeeper, John Brewster, George Duryea, Richard Goldsmith, Benjamin Gregory, John Hudson, Archibald Little, James Mapes, Elihu Marvin, Samuel Moffatt, Col. Vincent Matthews, Thomas Moffatt, Joseph Mapes, Josiah Reeder, Israel Seeley, Josiah Seeley, Selah Strong, Nathaniel Satterly, James Sayre, Nathaniel Strong, Silas Young, Zachariah DuBois, Hezekiah Howell, Daniel Mapes, David Coleman, Francis Drake, Nathaniel Curtis, Henry Davenport, John Carpenter, William Moffatt, Timothy and William Owens, Capt. Silas Pierson, Nathaniel Satterly, Benjamin Strong, Joel Tuthill, John Woolley, William, Hugh and Robert Gregg.

Blooming-Grove was part of Cornwall from 1764 to 1799 and before 1764 this territory was part of Goshen Precinct, the records of which are lost. It was organized as a town in 1799, its territory taken from Cornwall. In 1830 a part of Blooming-Grove was taken off in formation of Hamptonburgh and in 1845 a portion was set off to form the town of Chester. The name Blooming-Grove was that of the old village, and was adopted to distinguish it from Hunting-Grove, a locality then in New Windsor.

**VILLAGES OF TOWN OF BLOOMING-GROVE: WASHINGTONVILLE:** Principal village of the town, on the old public road from Newburgh to Goshen. A station on the Newburgh Branch of the Erie Railroad. Named in honor of Gen. Washington. Thomas Goldsmith probably the first settler in 1731.

**SALISBURY MILLS VILLAGE:** A hamlet on the public road about eight miles from Newburgh and three from Washingtonville. A station on the Erie Railroad. Settled by Andrew J. Caldwell, a manufacturer of leather, Isaac K. Oakley and Peter VanAlen. Gen. Vincent Matthews early erected a mill here.

**BLOOMING-GROVE:** Hamlet in a valley of the southern branch of the Otterkill usually known as the Schunemunk. Two miles from Washingtonville. A rural neighborhood now, but once the center of activity with a meetinghouse being built in 1759.

**CRAIGVILLE:** A manufacturing village and railroad station on Gray Court Creek, better known as the Cromeline. Named for the Craig family. At this place there was a forge and a powder-mill during the Revolution. James Craig about 1790 commenced the manufacture of paper, which was continued on his death by his son, Hon. Hector Craig, who also erected a cotton mill.

**SATTERLY'S MILLS:** About six miles south of Washingtonville. Named for the founder of the mills, the pioneer Nathaniel Satterly. Settled very early.

**OXFORD DEPOT:** On the Erie Railroad in southwest part of Town of Blooming-Grove. Post office established in 1842, first postmaster John H. Tuthill.

## TOWN OF HAMPTONBURGH

An interior town of the county, separated from Town of Wallkill by the Wallkill River. First settled by Christopher Deene, a resident of New York in 1701, and adoptive father of Sarah Wells. William Bull, a native of Wolverhampton, England, and one of the earliest settlers of the Town of Hamptonburgh married Sarah Wells.

The town was formed from Goshen, Blooming-Grove, Montgomery, New Windsor and Wallkill in 1830.

**TOWN OF HAMPTONBURGH VILLAGES: CAMPBELL HALL:** A station on the Wallkill Valley Railroad, formerly the Campbell residence. Capt. Lachlin Campbell, of the Isle of Islay in North Britain was promised land and came to New York to view the land and liked it very much. He was begged by the Indians, who were struck and delighted with his Highland dress, to settle there. A post office was established in 1869, B. F. Decker postmaster.

**HAMPTONBURGH:** South of Campbell's Hall, the site of the first settlement made by William Bull.

**NEELYTOWN:** An old neighborhood in both towns of Hamptonburgh and Montgomery.

**BURNSIDE:** Hamlet on the Otterkill near New Windsor. Has been known as Otterville, the name of Burnside given to the post office.

**KIPP'S:** On the line of Goshen, a milk station on the railroad.

**PURGATORY:** One mile east of the Heard farm, in early times a dismal swamp. Named by Peter Bull as a proper descriptive term.

**PARADISE:** The sunny slope where Peter Bull lived.

**LAGRANGE:** Formerly called Goosetown, which name originated in the fact that a large number of geese were raised in the neighborhood. Lagrange named in honor of Gen. Lafayette.

**DECKER'S:** Small settlement in Town of Hamptonburgh where Messrs. Decker erected a manufactory. The area was settled as early as 1730. Called St. David's Corners, the name of the church located there in 1770. This place now acquiring the name of Lincondale.

# TOWN OF MINISINK

In the southwest part of the county, bounded on the southeast by the Wallkill River and on the northeast by Rutger's Creek. One of the earliest settlers was George Kimber, who settled near Unionville about 1728. Other early settlers included William Stenard, Benjamin Smith (who was probably the first settler in the vicinity of the present Johnson's Station, for many years known as Smith's village), Christian Schultz, Peter Kimber, Charles E. Stickney, Oliver E. Wood, H. B. Allen, Capt. John Wisner, John and Reuben Whittaker, Hezekiah and Amos Wilcox, John Kimball, Cornelius Van Vliet, Philip Lee, Sylvanus and Eda Loree (Lowrey), William Lane, Paul Lee, Cotton and Increase Mather, David Christie, John Dunkin, Aaron and James Ferguson, Jonathan Shepherd, Jonathan Sayre, Noah Terry, Henry Tucker, Jonathan Tuthill, William Masters, William McMullen, Daniel and John Myers, John Ralphsnider, Samuel Schoonover, Samuel Ferguson, Wilhelmus Cole, William Horton, David Allen, John Beers, Jonathan Casterline, James and Abram Clark, Benjamin Cole, Ezra Corwin, John Neely, Jonathan Cooley, Freegift Tuthill, Hulet Clark, Isaac Decker and Joshua Sayre among others.

The Town of Minisink was formed in 1788 and its territory was a part of the Goshen Precinct. There was an early precinct under the name of Minisink which may have comprised some part of the present town, but the name was dropped after the settlement of the New Jersey boundary. This town in 1788 included the present towns of Minisink, Greenville, Wawayanda and part of the present town of Deerpark.

**VILLIAGES OF THE TOWN OF MINISINK: UNIONVILLE:** Said to be named as a reminiscence of the old dispute between New York and New Jersey as regards to the boundary line. A thriving village at the time of publication.

**WESTTOWN:** Only village in western part of the town at the time of settlement; a pleasant place overlooking the Rutger's Valley.

**GARDNERVILLE:** Small hamlet on east boundary of Town of Minisink. Named for Ira Gardner, an early settler and mill-owner.

**MILLSBURGH:** On north line of Town of Minisink bordering on Town of Wawayanda. Formerly known as Racine from John Racine, a preminent citizen.

**JOHNSON POST OFFICE:** On southern branch of Rutger's Creek, in the north part of Town of Minisink. Station on the NJ Midland Railroad.

**SMITH VILLAGE.** A rural neighborhood north of Gardnerville. Formerly a smart business place.

**WATERLOO MILLS:** In southwest part of Town of Minisink, not far from the NJ Midland Railroad. A point of early settlement, mills here before 1800. The Wilcox family were early settlers.

# TOWN OF WAWAYANDA

An interior town of the county, in the western part, settled during or at the close of the Revolutionary War. From an assessment list from 1775 the following names are taken:

| | | |
|---|---|---|
| --- Smith | Michael Halstead | Israel Holley |
| Joseph Oldfield | Anning Owen | Daniel David |
| Thomas Angle | William Eggers | James Tackling (free Negro) |
| Henry David | Israel Owen | Robert Thompson |
| James Dolsen | William Carroll | James Thompson |
| Edward David | John Finch | John Cravens |
| Benjamin Walworth | William Huff | James Reeve |
| Sayler David | Mary Carpenter (widow) | John Baylies |
| Henry White | William Huff Jr. | Elisha Hulse |
| Edward David Jr. | Benjamin Carpenter | John Shepherd |
| James Gardner | Solomon Huff | Silas Hulse |
| Gershom Sampeon | James Hulse | Michael Dunning |
| Isaac Dolsen | Mathew Deilling | Peter Rouse |
| Daniel Eggers | Gilbert Bradner | John Kimball |
| Abraham Harding | John Van Cleft | Squire Whittaker |
| Richard Halstead | Lena Kimball | Abraham Shepherd |
| David Cooley | Daniel Cooley | Nicholas Van Tassel |

| | | |
|---|---|---|
| George Oldfield | David Cooley Jr. | William Knapp |
| Headley Spencer | William Walworth | Joshua Davis |
| Moses Smith | Joseph Halstead | Daniel Cookely Jr. |
| Daniel Finch | John Williams | Isaac Finch |
| James Knapp | William Seeley | Samuel Cooley |
| Richard Jones | David Corwin | John Carpenter, blacksmith |
| Zevan Tracy | Benjamin Smith | William Reedy |
| Andrew Sullen | James Little & 2 sons | Elnathan Corey |

The Town of Wawayanda was formally organized in 1849.

**VILLAGES OF THE TOWN OF WAWAYANDA:** HAMPTON: Small hamlet, railroad station on the NY, Erie & Western Railway; a short distance from Denton.

MILLSBURGH: Point of early settlement. Formerly had an important woolen-factory, now abandoned.

RIDGEBURY: One of the earliest places of settlement, site of village owned in 1800 by Benjamin Dunning, Jonathan Bailey, Benjamin Howell, Isaac Decker & others. Name from that of "Whortleberry Hill," a neighboring ridge. Site of the Ridgeberry (Presbyterian) Church.

CENTREVILLE: Near Millsburgh, and the two places together consittute what is called Wells' Corners. Post office is at Centerville.

GARDNERVILLE: Is now comprised by a store run by J. M. Everett; a grist-mill run by John R. Manning and a wagon- and blacksmith-shop run by Charles Gardner.

BROOKFIELD: Named from its proximity to a brook, which almost surrounds it. Settled at an early date. Now better known as Slate Hill, the post office and railroad station both going by that name.

WAWAYANDA: A milk-station on the NJ Midland Railroad, north of Rutger's Creek.

DENTON: Originally known as "The Outlet," takes its name from the Denton family--Thaddeaus B. and Henry W., descendants of Richard. Elisha Eldridge from New England built a store and tavern there about the time of the Revolution. An earlier owner had been Richard Carpenter.

## TOWN OF DEERPARK

In the extreme western angle of the county and bounded on the north by Sullivan County and the southwest by the states of New Jersey & Pennsylvania. The area was long involved in boundary disputes between the states of New York and New Jersey. Early settlers included Harmanus Van Inwegen and Maj. Swartwout. This was an area where William Tietsort (Titsworth) fled to from Schenectady at the capture of that town by Indians in 1689. Patents were granted for land in the area beginning in 1697 to Jacob Codebec, Thomas, Anthony and Bernardus Swartwout, Jan Tys, Peter Gimar and David Jamison. These men are said to have come to this town in 1690. Tys and Jamison are not found in further records, so it is assumed they must have soon died or relocated. Freeholders in 1714 were listed as: Thomas Swartwout, Harmon Barentsen, Jacob Cuddeback, Peter Gumaer and Jacobus Swartwout; in 1728 as Harmon Barentsen Van Inwegen, Peter Gumaer, John Van Vliet Jr., Samuel Swarthout, Bernardus Swartwout Jr. and Jacob Cuddeback.

Early place names included: Penhausen's Landt, or Penhausen's Land, name of an Indian chief who formerly resided in the area. Seneyaughquan, an Indian name of the place where Maj. Swartwout resided. Sokapack: an Indian name. Lower Neighborhood: Contemporary with the children of the first settlers at Peenpack. Early settlers included the DeWitt family, Peter E. Gumaer, Jan Tyse, Barnardus Swartwout, Jacob Cuddeback, Anthony Swartwout, David Jameson, Jacob Cuddeback and Harmanus Van Inwegen.

The residents of the area of the Town of Deerpark were given power to vote in the County of Ulster in 1701. It was at one time under the districts known as of Wagachemeck, Machackemeck, Mamakating and Minisink. The Town of Deerpark was organized in 1798.

**VILLAGES OF THE TOWN OF DEERPARK:** PORT JERVIS: Dates from 1826 when the Delaware and Hudson Canal became certain. Named in honor of an engineer who supervised construction. Previous to opening of the canal in 1828 the post office for this area was at Carpenter's Point.

WESTBROOKVILLE: Small village northeast from Cuddebackville, on the canal. Named for an early tavern keeper, John Westbrook, who settled here before the Revolution.

PORT ORANGE: On the canal near Westbrookville, and really part of the same neighborhood.

CUDDEBACKVILLE: In northeastern part of Town of Deerpark, named in honor of old settler Jacob, one of the original patent owners.

ROSE POINT: The "port" at Locks No. 54 & 55 about one mile south of Cuddeback; also a station on the Monticello Railroad. Near the old fort of Jacob Rutsen DeWitt.

PORT CLINTON: Location of Lock No. 56 of the canal, the burial-place of the early Cuddeback colony of 1690-95.

GUMAER'S: Small hamlet in Village of Deerpark, north of Huguenot. Name from Gumaer families.

HUGUENOT: On the canal between Port Jervis and Gumaer's. Name from the fact that many early settlers were Huguenot emigrants who settled early in Kingston, their children settled in this valley.

CARPENTER'S POINT: Named for an early settler who established a ferry and owned land at the junction of the Neversink and Delaware Rivers. Is a short distance south of Port Jervis. Named for early Carpenter family.

SPARROWBUSH: Hamlet near Bolton Basin, west of Honesville, on the canal. Established post office in 1827 under name of Honesville, Dr. Dickinson postmaster. In 1844 the post office was closed and it reopened in 1850 under the present name, L. F. Hough, postmaster.

BUSHKILL: In west part of Town of Deerpark in neighborhood of the Baptist church, an offshoot of the Baptist Church at Port Jervis, that lasted only a few years.

QUARRY HILL: Local name of the school district in the extreme west of the Town of Deerpark. Name from extensive quarrying business.

SHIN HOLLOW: Euphonious name applied to a neighborhood on the slopes of the Shawangunk Mountains.

GERMANTOWN: Western extension of Port Jervis along the Delaware River. There is a glass manufactory and a population of 1000 or more.

HONESVILLE: Small hamlet on the canal west of Port Jervis, formerly known by the post office name of Sparrowbush.

BOLTON: On the canal in southwest of Town of Deerpark. Named for John Bolton, an original member of the canal company.

PARADISE: On the border with Sullivan County northwest of Cuddebackville. A station on the Monticello Railroad.

BROOKLYN: An extension of Port Jervis.

MATAMORAS: Across the Delaware River in Pennsylvnaia, but closely tied with Port Jervis in business and united by a "Roebling suspension" bridge.

## TOWN OF CORNWALL

Located on the Hudson River, this area was first explored by Henry Hudson in 1609. In 1685 Gov. Dongan purchased of the Indians the tract of country along the Hudson from Murder's Creek on the north to Stoney Creek on the south, and in 1694 this was patented to Capt. John Evans, being the first transfer from the crown. Prior to that time, however, Col. Patrick MacGregorie had settled at Plum Creek. David Toshuck had built a trading post on Sloop Hill with one McCollom. Another early resident was William Sutherland (Southerland). The precinct of Cornwall was formed in 1764 and comprised the territory of present day Blooming-Grove, Monroe and Highlands.

Settlers prior to the Revolutionary War are given as: Timothy Brewster, Jeremiah Clark (and other Clarks, Reuben, Smith, Ephraim, Gershom, Nehemiah, David, William & John W.), Joseph Chandler, Thomas Clark, David Mandeville, Amos Mills, David Miller, Langford and Joseph Thorn, Jonathan Brooks, A. Sutherland, Nathaniel (son of David) Sands, David Sutherland (Jr. & Sr.),

David Sherod (Sherwood?), Justus Sackett, Isaac Tobias (physician), William Roe, Isaac Van Duzer (Sr. & Jr.), Joseph Wood (and other Woods, Daniel, Stephen, John, Amos, Timothy and Ebenezer) and others.

**VILLAGES OF THE TOWN OF CORNWALL: CORNWALL:** Name belongs to original landing place on the river and village is large shipping point. The name *Cornwall* as applied to a village has scarcely any definite location. The post office Cornwall is at Canterbury, while near the Hudson is the post office Cornwall-on-the Hudson.

**CANTERBURY:** Oldest village in the Town of Cornwall, and the largest in popoulation. Name applied at an early day, and likely suggested by emigrants from England in memory of Canterbury in County of Kent. Patrick Sutherland was the earliest settler in the area.

**CORNWALL-ON-THE-HUDSON:** Post office located on the upland above the older village at the river, east of Canterbury, established in 1862. Also known as "the Corners," from the number of roads which intersect here. Also known as Willisville for N.P. Willis, whose residence was not far away.

**IDLEWILD:** Name given by the late N. P. Willis to his country-seat on the southern bank of Canterbury Creek, near the Hudson. Mr. Willis was a writer afflicted with pulmonary disease and located his home here, where he died.

**GARNERVILLE:** A cluster of buildings between Canterbury and "the Corners," erected on property formerly belonging to a colored man of that name who died some years ago.

**RIVERSIDE:** A new name given to what is "Cornwall," the landing and the village lying along the river. Also known as "the Hollow," or simply "The Landing."

**ROEVILLE:** A hamlet in the Town of Cornwall north of the Idlewild Brook. Named for James G. Roe, whose summer resort, known as Glen Ridge House, is nearby.

**THE MONTANA WOOLEN-MILLS:** Mills that have developed something of a village around them. Situated on Murderer's Creek.

**MOUNTAINVILLE:** Village in the Town of Cornwall near the southern bend of Murderer's Creek. A station on the Newburgh Branch of the Erie Railroad.

**SALISBURY MILLS:** Post office that accommodates a part of the town of Cornwall, but mostly in the Town of Blooming-Grove.

**BETHLEHEM:** In northwest part of Town of Cornwall. The name was first given to the Presbyterian church established early here.

## TOWN OF MONROE

The southeast most town in Orange County. The earliest settlers came from the Eastern States or from Long Island and families were generally of English ancestry. The Smith family was here as early as 1727. Early settlers mentioned in town records are Henry Brewster, Elijah Barton, John and Ebenezer Bull, John and Adam Belcher, Robert Brock (lived in the mountains near Braymertown), John Brooks, Abram Butler, Henry Cock, A. Cunningham, David Compton, P. Cashaday (Cassidy), Solomon Cromwell, William Conklin, Joseph Davis, Robert Armstrong, Owen Nobles, Samuel and Philip Robbins, James and W. M. McLaughlin, John and Peter Earle, William Fitzgerald, Alexander, Jacob and James Galloway, Elijah Green, Vincent Helms, Jonathan Hallock, John Hanse, Samuel Knight, Isaac and John Lamoreux, Henry Mapes (other Mapes' Benjamin, Smith and Bethuel), Daniel Miller, Joseph Patterson, Jacob Parliaman, Edward Robbins, Andrew and Luther Stewart, Capt. Austin Smith and Jonas Smith, Nathaniel Seeley (Sr. & Jr.), (other Smiths: David, Julius, Hophni and Thomas ; William Thorn, Nicholas Townsend, Tobias Weygant, James Wilkes (Sr. & Jr.) and others.

The town was organized in 1799 under the name of Chesekook, the name of the original patent. In 1863 an effort was instituted to divide the Town of Monroe into three towns: Highlands (not to be confused with present town of Highlands, erected in 1872 out of the territory of Cornwall), Monroe and Southfield. These towns were reunited into the Town of Monroe in 1865.

**VILLAGES OF TOWN OF MONROE: MONROE:** Village with same name as the town, on the head waters of the Ramapo, the outlet of Round Pond. A station of the NY, Lake Erie & Western Railway.

WOODBURY FALLS: A hamlet in north part of Town of Monroe on Woodbury Creek. Takes its name from the falls. Post office established in 1874, Lewis A. Van Cleft postmaster.

SEAMANVILLE: About one mile east of Monroe village on the Erie Railway, formerly a station. Early settled and location of the earliest Presbyterian meetinghouse.

HIGHLAND MILLS POST-OFFICE: Village that grew up around the mills established here. Near to Woodbury, this village was formerly known as Orange. The Townsend family were early settlers.

CENTRAL VALLEY: Small village of Town of Monroe located in valleys of the Ramapo and of Woodbury Creek. Post office established in 1871, Alfred Cooper, postmaster. A noted summer resort and the site of Cornell School and Boarding Building; also the Summit Lake House.

GREENWOOD LAKE: Post office established in 1876, L. Y. Jenness postmaster. A summer resort of note.

TURNER'S: A station on the Erie Railroad with a post office. Formerly known as Centreville. Present name honors Peter Turner, a local resident who established several businesses in the area.

QUEENSBOROUGH: Neighborhood in the valley of the southern branch of Poplopen's Creek. Area supports some mining and an acid manufactory by William Knight, the acid being extracted from wood for coloring purposes.

GREENWOOD IRON-WORKS: Village that has grown up in connection with the manufacturing operatons here.

SOUTHFIELD: Locality of the "Southfield Works" and the "Monroe Works," on the Rampo River and the Erie Railway. The industry was established about 1805 for the manufacture of pig iron. Early proprietors were William and Peter Townsend. A summer resort.

HELMSBURGH: Neighborhood south of Mombasha Lake and west of Southfield. A rural mountain neighborhood also known as Bramertown.

AUGUSTA: Station on the Erie Railway in the south part of Town of Monroe, the seat of the old Augusta Works founded at the close the the Revolution by Solomon Townsend of New York City to make bar-iron and anchors.

EAGLE VALLEY: Station on the Erie Railway in the extreme southwest angle of Town of Monore near the New Jersey line.

Other localities of special name not mentioned are "Wild-Cat Hollow," in the valley of the Indian Kill; "Parker Cabin Hollow," near Car Pond. There were many mines: Scott, Cook, Stirling, Bradley, Forest of Dean Mines, Dump, O'Neil, Mount Basha, Clove, Beering, Redback, Crawford, Coal Shier, etc.

*South View of Newburg.*

## MILITARY ROSTERS

*"A List of the first company of Militia of the presenk of the
Highlands under the command of Capt. Thomas Ellison"* [1738]

Capt. Thomas Ellison
Ensign John Young
Sgt. David Davids

Sgt. Moses Garitson
Sgt. P. McCloghery
Corp. Jacobus Bruyn

Corp. Jas. Stringham
Corp. Jonah Hazard
Clerk, Chas. Clinton

David Oliver
Arthur Beaty
Matthew Davis
John Nicoll Jr.
Alexander McKey
Robert Sparks
Jeuriah Quick
Thomas Quick
Jacob Gillis
John Umphrey
Joseph Gillis
Joseph Simson
Alexander Falls
James Clark
David Bedford
John Clark
William Coleman
Lodewick Miller
Joseph Sweezer
Peter Miller
Thomas Coleman
George Weygant
John McVey
William Ward
John Jones
William Ward Jr.

Patrick Broderick
John Mattys Kimberg
Joseph Shaw
William Smith Jr.
Caleb Curtis
James Edmeston
William Sutton
Tobias Weygant
Jeremiah Foster
Jerry Manse
Charles Beaty
Thomas Johnston
Amos Foster
Casparis Stymas
Alexander Foster
John Monger
James Young
James Luckey
James Nealy
Thomas Williams
Robert Feef
Johannis George
Joseph Butterton
Jeremiah Tompkins
Samuel Luckey
Isaac Tompkins

John Markham
William Watts
John Read
Josiah Ellsworth
Joseph McMikhill
James Ellsworth
David Umphrey
Anthony Preslaer
James Gamble
Jonathan Tomkins
John Gamble
Robert Banker
Cornelius McClean
Thomas Fear
John Umphrey Jr.
Frederick Painter
James Umphrey
Moses Elsworth
Peter Mulinder
John Marie
Robert Burnet
Jonathan Owens
Archibald Beaty
Andrew McDowell
Daniel Coleman

*"A List of the Company of Militia of the Wall a Kill
under the command of Capt. John Bayard."* [1738]

Capt. John Bayard
Ensign William Kelso
Lt. William Borland
Sgt. John Newkirk
Corp. John Miller
John Jones
Lendert Coll (Cole)
Joseph Knapp
Cornelius Cole
Isaiah Gale
Barnat Cole
Caleb Knapp
John Robinson
Robert McCord
James Gillespie
William Faulkner

Thomas Gillespie
Israel Rodgers
John Wilkins
Jeremiah Rodgers
William Wilkins
James Rodgers
Andrew Graham
James White
George Olloms
John Manley
John North
Francis Falls
John North Jr.
Cronamus Felter
Samuel North
Richard Gatehouse

James Young
John Boyle
Robert Young
Richard Boyle
Matthew Young
Robert Hughey
James McNeill
Robert Buchanan
John McNeill
James Eager
Andrew Borland
Thomas McCollum
John Borland
Sojornaro Her
John McNeill Jr.
John Haven

James Crawford
McKim Clineman
John Crawford
Jury Burger
Alexander Milligan
Hugh Flanigan
Nathaniel Hill
Benj. Bennet
Alexander Kidd
Patrick McPeck
Archibald Hunter
John Eldoris
James Hunter
Patrick Gillespie
John Wharry
John Lowry
John Mingus
Samuel Smith
Stephanus Crist
Joseph Theal
Jacob Bush
James Crawford

Benjamin Haines
Joseph Sutter
John McNeill Sr.
David Craig
Matthew Rhea
Edward Andrews
William Crawford
Samuel Crawford
Robert Hunter
Andrew McDowell
James Monsell
Philip Millspaugh
George Monell
Cronamas Mingus
John Moncll
Stuffel Mould
William Monell
Johannes Crane
Thomas Neils
John Young
Robert Neils
Hendrick Newkirk

John Neils
Frederick Sinsabaugh
Matthew Neils
Cornelius Wallace
Nathaniel Colter
Hendrick Crist
John Neily Jr.
Tunas Crist
Joseph Buttletown
Lawrence Crist
Thomas Coleman
Mathias Millspaugh & his son.
Joseph Shaw
Patrick Broderick
John Jamison
William Soutter
John McDonald
John Butterfield
James Davis
John McVey

From a list of officers & soldiers belonging to the Regiment of Foot Militia, 1738:

| | | |
|---|---|---|
| Vincent Mathews, Col. | Michael Jackson, Adjt. | Solomon Carpenter, Lt. Col. |
| James Thompson, Q.M. | George Remsen, Maj. | |

FIRST COMPANY:

Ram. Remsen, Capt.　　　　Corns. Smith, Lt.　　　　Ebenezer Smith, Ensign
　　Total of 63 men.

SECOND COMPANY:

Samuel Odell, Capt.　　　　Henry Cuyper, Lt.　　　　Benj. Allison, Ensign
　　Total of 68 men.

THIRD COMPANY:

John Holly, Capt.　　　　Michael Dunning, Lt.　　　　Sol. Carpenter, Jr., Ensign
　　Total of 121 men.

FOURTH COMPANY:

Jacobus Swartwout, Capt.　　　　Johannes Westbrook, Lt.　　　　Johannes Westbrook, Jr., Ensign
　　Total of 65 men.

FIFTH COMPANY:

Nathaniel DeBois, Capt.　　　　David Southerland, Lt.　　　　Isaac Hennion, Ensign
　　Total of 73 men.

SIXTH COMPANY:

Abm. Haring, Jr., Capt.　　　　Garret Beauvelt, Lt.　　　　John Haring, Ensign
　　Total of 72 men.

SEVENTH COMPANY:

Jacob Vanderbilt, Capt.　　　　Andrew Onderdonk, Lt.　　　　Aaron Smith, Ensign
　　Total of 60 men.

TROOP OF HORSE:

Henry Youngs, Capt.　　　　William Mapes, Lt.　　　　Michael Jackson, Cornet.
　　Total of 60 men

In 1756 the Ulster regiment was divided into two regiments. Kingston was included in the northern one and the southern took in the precincts of Highlands, Wallkill and Sahwangunk. These regiments took part in the French & Indian War.

In Sept. 1773 the officers of the Southern Regiment were: Col. Thomas Ellison; Lt.-Col. Charles Clinton; Major Cadwallader Calden, Jr. & Adjutant Johannes Jansen.

In 1775 a law for organizing militia developed districts in the state, and each district was to recruit about 85 men, including officers, between the ages of 16 and 50 years, to be formed into regiments. The Fourth Brigade when formed consisted of five Orange County regiments. The colonels of these were: William Allison of Goshen, Jesse Woodhull of Cornwall, John Hathorn of Warwick, A. Hawkes Hay of Orangetown and Abraham Lent of Haverstraw. The four Ulster County regiments were commanded by Johannes Hardenberg of Kingston, James Clinton of New Windsor, Lee Pawling of Marbletown and Jonathan Hasbrouck of Newburgh.

Col. Allison's regimental district consisted of Goshen and the western part of Orange County, Col. Hathorn's of Warwick and the southern section, Col. Woodhull's of Cornwall (then including Monroe and Blooming Grove), Col. Hasbrouck's of Newburgh, Marlborough and Shawangunk, and Col. Clinton's of Windsor, Montgomery, Crawford and Wallkill. The other four regiments belonged to territory now outside of the county.

## COL. ALLISON'S REGIMENT

William Allison, Col.; Benjamin Tusten, Lt. Col.

GOSHEN COMPANY, 1775: George Thompson, Capt.; Joseph Wood & Coe Gale, Lts.; Daniel Everett Jr., Ensign. In 1776 Lt. Coe & Ensign Everett were transferred to a minute company, and in their places William Thompson was appointed 2d Lt. and Phineas Case Ensign.

WAWAYANDA COMPANY, 1775: William Blair, Capt.; Thomas Wisner & Thomas Sayne [Sayre?] Jr., Lts.; Richard Johnson, Ensign.

DROWNED LANDS COMPANY, 1775: Samuel Jones Jr., Capt.; Peter Gale & Jacob Dunning, Lts.; Samuel Webb, Ensign.

CHESTER COMPANY, 1775: John Jackson, Capt.; John Wood & James Miller, Lts.; James Parshal, Ensign.

POCHUCK COMPANY, 1775: Ebenezer Owen, Capt.; Increase Holly & John Bronson, Lts.; David Rogers, Ensign. In 1776: Increase Holly, Capt.; David Rogers & James Wright, Lts.; Charles Knapp, Ensign.

WALLKILL COMPANY, 1775: Gilbert Bradner, Capt.; Joshua Davis & James Dolson, Lts.; Daniel Finch, Ensign.

MINISINK COMPANY, 1775: Moses Kortright, Capt.; John Van Tile & Johannes Decker, Lts.; Ephraim Medaugh, Ensign. In 1777 Martinus Decker became 2d Lt. vice Johannes Decker.

## COL. HATHORN'S REGIMENT

John Hathorn, Colonel.

WARWICK COMPANY, 1775: Charles Beardsley, Capt.; Richard Welling & Samuel Lobdell, Lts.; John Price, Ensign. In 1776 John Minthorn became Capt. in place of Beardsley, dec'd.; Nathaniel Ketcham & George Vance, Lts.; John Benedict, Ensign.

POND COMPANY, 1775: Henry Wisner Jr., Capt.; Abraham Dolson Jr. & Peter Bartholf, Lts.; Matthew Dolson, Ensign. In 1776: Abraham Dolson Jr., Capt.; Peter Bartholf & John Hopper, Lts.; Mathias Dolson, Ensign. In 1777: Peter Bartholf, Capt.; John DeBow & Anthony Finn, Lts.; Joseph Jewell, Ensign.

STERLING COMPANY, 1776: John Norman, Capt.; Solomon Finch & William Fitzgerald, Lts.; Elisha Bennett, Ensign. In 1777: Henry Townsend, Capt.; William Fitzgerald & Elisha Bennett, Lts.; Joseph Conkling, Ensign.

FLORIDA COMPANY, 1775: Nathaniel Elmer, Capt.; John Popino Jr. & John Sayre, Lts.; Richard Bailey, Ensign. In 1776: John Kennedy, Lt. vice Popino. In 1777: John Sayre, Capt.; John Kennedy & Richard Bailey, Lts.; John Wood, Ensign.

WANTAGE COMPANY, 1775: Daniel Rosekrans, Capt.; James Clark & Jacob Gale, Lts.; Samuel Cole, Ensign.

## COL. WOODHULL'S REGIMENT

Jesse Woodhull, Col.; Elihu Marvin, Lt.-Col.; Nathaniel Strong & Zachariah DeBois, Majors; William Moffat, Adjutant; Nathaniel Satterly, Quartermaster.

OXFORD COMPANY, 1775: Archibald Little, Capt.; Birdseye Youngs & Thomas Horton, Lts.; Nathan Marvin, Ensign. In 1777: Thomas Horton, Capt.; Josiah Seeley, First Lt.; Nathan Marvin, Second Lt.; Barnabas Horton Jr., Ensign.

CLOVE COMPANY, 1775: Jonathan Tuthill, Capt.; John Brewster Jr. & Samuel Strong, Lts.; Francis Brewster, Ensign.

BETHLEHEM COMPANY, 1775: Christopher VanDuzer, Capt.; William Roe & Obadiah Smith, Lts.; Isaac Tobias, Ensign. In 1776: Gilbert Weeks, Ensign.

UPPER CLOVE COMPANY, 1775: Garrett Miller, Capt.; Asa Buck & William Horton, Lts.; Aaron Miller, Ensign.

WOODBURY CLOVE COMPANY, 1775: Francis Smith, Capt.; Thomas Smith & Alexander Galloway, Lts.; John McManus, Ensign. In 1776: John McManus, 2d Lt.; Thomas Lammoreux, Ensign.

SOUTHWEST COMPANY, 1775: Stephen Slote, Capt.; George Galloway & John Brown, Lts.; David Rogers, Ensign.

BLOOMING GROVE COMPANY, 1775: Silas Pierson, Capt.; Joshua Brown & David Reeve, Lts.; Phineas Heard, Ensign.

LIGHT HORSE COMPANY, 1776: Ebenezer Woodhull, Capt.; James Sayre, Lt.; William Heard, Cornet; Azariah Martin, 2d Master.

# COL. HASBROUCK'S REGIMENT

Jonathan Hasbrouck, Col.; Johannes Hardenburgh Jr., Lt.-Col.; Johannes Jansen Jr. & Lewis DuBois, Majors; Abraham Schoonmaker, Adjutant; Isaac Belknap, Quartermaster.

CLARK'S NEWBURGH COMPANY, June 8, 1788: Samuel Clark, Capt.; James Denton & Martin Wygant, Lts.; Munson Ward, Ensign; William Albertson, Isaac Brown, Ebenezer Gidney & Hope Mills, Sgts.; Hugh Stevenson, Isaac Demott, John Simson & William Palmer, Corporals; Sol Buckingham, Drummer.

CONKLIN'S NEWBURGH COMPANY, May 4, 1778: Jacob Conklin, Capt.; Jacob Lawrence & David Guion, Lts.; John Crowell, Ensign; Robert Erwin, Robert Ross, John Lawrence & Abraham Strickland, Sergants; Jacob Strickland, Corp.; Abraham Smith, Drummer.

SMITH'S NEWBURGH COMPANY, April 24, 1779: Arthur Smith, Capt.; Isaac Fowler & John Foster, Lts.; William Conklin, John Kniffin, James Clark & Reuben Holmes, Sgts.; William Smith, William Michael & Samuel Griggs, Corporals.

# COL. CLINTON'S REGIMENT

James Clinton, Col.; James McClaughry, Lt.-Col.; Jacob Newkirk & Moses Phillips, Majors; George Denniston, Adjutant; Alexander Trimble, Quartermaster.

EASTERN NEW WINDSOR COMPANY, 1775: John Belknap, Capt.; Silas Wood & Edward Falls, Lts.; James Stickney, Ensign.

WESTERN NEW WINDSOR COMPANY, 1776: James Humphrey, Capt.; James Karnaghan, 2d Lt.; Richard Wood, Ensign.

NEW WINDSOR VILLAGE COMPANY, 1775: John Nicoll, Capt.; Francis Mandeville & Hezekiah White, Lts.; Leonard D. Nicoll, Ensign.

FIRST HANOVER COMPANY, 1775: Matthew Felter, Capt.; Henry Smith & Johannes Newkirk Jr., Lts.; William Crist, Ensign.

SECOND HANOVER COMPANY, 1775: William Jackson, Capt.; Arthur Parks & James McBride, Lts.; Andrew Neeley, Ensign.

THIRD HANOVER COMPANY, 1775: Cadwallader C. Colden, Capt.; James Milligan & John Hunter, Lts.; Matthew Hunter, Ensign.

FOURTH HANOVER COMPANY, 1775: John J. Graham, Capt.; Samuel Barkley & Joseph Crawford, Lts; James McCurdy, Ensign.

FIFTH HANOVER COMPANY, 1775: John Gillespie, Capt.; Jason Wilkins & Robert Hunter Jr., Lts.; Samuel Gillespie, Ensign.

FIRST WALKILL COMPANY, 1775: Samuel Watkins, Capt.; David Crawford & Stephen Harlow, Lts.; Henry Smith, Ensign.

SECOND WALLKILL COMPANY, 1775: William Faulkner Jr., Capt.; Edward McNeal & John Wilkins, Lts.; John Faulkner, Ensign.

THIRD WALLKILL COMPANY, 1775: Isaiah Velie, Capt.; Israel Wickham & John Dunning, Lts.; Jonathan Owen, Ensign.

FOURTH WALLKILL COMPANY, 1775: William Denniston, Capt.; Benjamin Velie & Joseph Gillet, Lts.; David Corwin Jr., Ensign.

Of the Hanover companies the First had been known as Capt. Newkirk's Company, the Second as Capt. Goldsmith's, the Third as Capt. Colden's, the Fourth as Capt. Crage's, & the Fifth as Capt. Galatian's.

Of Wallkill companies the First was located on the east side of the Wallkill, the Second on the west side, between the Wallkill & Little Shawangunk Kill, the Third south of the Second, between the Wallkill and the Little Shawangunk, and the Fourth northwest of Little Shawangunk Kill.

During the service of these organizations in the War of the Revolution there were many changes in the commands. They were home guards. In case of alarm, invasion or insurrection, the companies were instructed to march and oppose the enemy, and immediately send an express to the commander of the regiment or brigade, who was to control their movements.

Under a law passed by the Continental Congress in May, 1775, three companies of minute men were raised in the southern district of Ulster, with the following officers:

NEWBURGH MINUTE COMPANY: Uriah Drake, Capt.; Jacob Lawrence & William Ervin, Lts.; Thomas Dunn, Ensign.

NEW WINDSOR MINUTE COMPANY: Samuel Logan, Capt.; John Robinson, Ensign; David Mandeville & John Scofield, Sgts.

HANOVER MINUTE COMPANY: Peter Hill, Capt.; James Lotta & Nathaniel Hill, Lts.; Wililam Goodyear, Ensign.

These companies and one organized in Marlborough formed a regiment which was officered as follows:

Thomas Palmer, Col.; Thomas Johnston Jr., Lt.-Col.; Arthur Parks, 1st Major; Samuel Logan, 2d Major; Isaac Belknap, Quartermaster.

Another regiment was formed from two companies organized in Goshen & Cornwall, with the following officers:

CORNWALL MINUTE COMPANY: Thomas Moffat, Capt.; Seth Marvin & James Little, Lts.; Nathan Strong, Ensign, who was succeeded by William Bradley.

GOSHEN MINUTE COMPANY: Moses Hetfield, Capt.; Cole Gale & Daniel Everett, Lts. Later James Butler & William Barker were chosen lts. & William Carpenter Ensign.

The officers of the regiment were:

Isaac Nicoll, Col.; Gilbert Cooper, Lt.-Col.; Henry V. Verbeyck, 1st Major; Hezekiah Howell, Jr., 2d Major; Ebenezer Woodhull, adjutant; Nehemiah Carpenter, Quartermaster.

*Washington's Head-quarters, Newburg.*

# REVOLUTIONARY PLEDGE

On 29 April 1775 the inhabitants of the city of New York drew up a pledge that was intended as a direct test of every man's sentiments and patriotism respecting the decision of the colonies to defend themselves against the oppressive acts of the English Parliament. Anticipating a division of public sentiment, a man signing this pledge would make his will known and stated that the country could depend on him. If he did not sign, he would be equally known and marked.

In the precinct lists of the Orange County signers of the pledge the signatures in Goshen embraced the present towns of Goshen, Chester, Warwick, Wawayanda, Greenville, and a part of Blooming Grove; in Mamakating those of Mt. Hope and Deer Park; Cornwall and Highlands were included in Cornwall; in Monroe parts of Blooming Grove and the present county of Rockland; in Newburgh, New Windsor and Wallkill with Newburgh. The signatures by precincts were as follows:

## PRECINCT OF NEWBURGH.

| | | |
|---|---|---|
| Col. Jona. Hasbrouck | William Kencaden | William Foster |
| Henry Cropsey | Robert Waugh | John Saunders |
| Thomas Palmer | James Denton | William Wilson |
| William Harding | Wiggins Conklin | Benjamin Lawrence |
| Isaac Belknap | John Foster | Peter Donally |
| Joseph Belknap | Robert Beatty Jr. | Richard Buckingham |
| William Darling | Hope Mills | William Stillwell Jr. |
| John Stratton | Abraham Johnston | Jacob Morewise |
| Wolvert Acker | John Cosman | Charles Tooker |
| Lewis Holt | Silas Sperry | Nicholas Stephens |
| John Belknap | William Wear | Leonard Smith Jr. |
| Samuel Hallock | James Clark | Johannis Snider |
| John Robinson | Thomas Fish | Henry Smith |
| Samuel Sprague | David Mills | Benjamin Robinson |
| Samuel Clark | William Lawrence Jr. | James Wooden |
| Burroughs Holmes | Caleb Coffin | Andrew Sprague |
| Benjamin Birdsall | John Kernoghan | Thomas Smith |
| Samuel Bond | James Harris | Thomas Beaty |
| Benjamin Smith | Robert Harmer | Caleb Case |
| Thomas Campbell | Theo. Hagaman | Solo Buckingham |
| James Waugh | Robert Ross | David Green |
| James Cosman | William Dunn | William Bowdish |
| Moses Higby, M.D. | John Crowell | John Stillwell |
| Jonathan Sweet | Nehemiah Carpenter | Jona. Belknap |
| Reuben Tooker | Obadiah Weeks | Luff Smith |
| John Griggs | Leonard Smith | Jacob Tremper |
| David Belknap | Francis Harmer | John Gates |
| Samuel Smith | William Day | Abraham Smith |
| Daniel Birdsall | William Bloomer | Benj. Darby |
| Jeremiah Ward | John Wandel | Cornelius Wood |
| Robert Lockwood | Abraham Garrison | Israel Smith |
| William Ward | Abel Thrall | John Lawrence |
| Benjamin Knap | James Marston | Thads. Smith |
| William Russel | Phineas Corwin | George Hack |
| Samuel Westlake | Samuel Gardiner | Jacob Myers |
| John Tremper | Moses Hunt | John Shaw |
| Josiah Ward | Anning Smith | Samuel Concklin |
| Charles Willett | Samuel Sands | Corns. Hasbrouck |
| Silas Gardner | Richard Albertson | Isaac Brown, M.D. |
| Jeremiah Dunn | Jacob Concklin [sic] | Isaac Demott |
| Jacob Gillis | Martin Weigand | Peter Tilton |
| William Lawrence | Joseph Price | David Smith |

John Douaghy
John Stratton
Ste. Stephenson
Absalom Case
Joseph Dunn
John Weed
Daniel Morewise
Daniel Duboise
Jonathan Owen
Arthur Smith
Jehiel Clark
Isaac Fowler
Reuben Holms
Stephen Outman
Nathaniel Coleman
Saml. Stratton

George Leonard
Joseph Carpenter
Elnathan Foster
Daniel Thurstin
Neal McLean
John Fowler
William Palmer
Daniel Clark
George Westlake
Isaac Donaldson
Burger Weigand
William Concklin
Tunis Keiter
Charles Tooker
Hugh Quigly
John Smith

Daniel Darby
Isaac Fowler Jr.
Isaac Brown Jr.
William Wright
Hezekiah Wyatt
William White
William Whitehead
Daniel Kniffen
Daniel Goldsmith
Rob. Morrison, M.D.
Gabriel Travis
John Dolson
Nathaniel Weed
Leonard Smith

## PRECINCT OF NEW WINDSOR

James Clinton
William Robinson
John Nicholson
Arthur Carscadden
James McClaughny
Edward Lyal
Matthew DuBois
Henry McNeeley
Robert Cook
William Niclos
John Umphrey
Robert Boyd Jr.
James Umphrey
Nathan Smith
George Umphrey
Samuel Logan
Oliver Umphrey
James Denniston
James McDowell
Jacob Mills
Alexander Telford
Thomas Cook
Robert Smith
Daniel Clemence
Jonah Park
Robert Couhan
Scudder Newman
John Waugh
James Humphrey 2d
William Gage
John Davis
Alexander Kernahan
John Coleman
William Stinson
Joseph Young
Henry Roberson
Andrew Robinson
Benjamin Homan
William Fulton

William Miller
James Taylor
William Telford
Hugh Polley
John Burnet
Samuel Given
Joseph Beatty
Robert Burnet Jr.
John Smith
Timothy Mills
James M. Oliver
William Buchanan
William Miller 2d
Matthew Bell
Charles Byrn
Robert Thompson
Walter McMichael
Charles Nicholson
George Coleman
James Gage
Alexander Fulton
James Dunlap
James Faulknor
Robert Stuert
David Clark
Samuel Wood
Nathan Sargent
Nathaniel Garrison
Gilbert Peet
Andrew Dickson
James Docksey
George Coleman 2d
Solomon Smith
Peter John
Samuel Woodward
Samuel Lamb
Jonathan White
William Crawford
Alexander Beatty

John W. Milkan
Jonathan Parshall
Francis Mains
James Greer
James Miller
John Mills
John Morrison
Thomas Eliot
Hugh Watterson
Robert Campbell
Caleb Dill
Nathaniel Boyd
John Dill
Charles Kernaghan
Edward Miller
Eliphalet Leonard
Robert Whigham
William Nichols
John Crudge
Thomas McDowel
Robert Body, Sr.
James Crawford
Silas Wood
Joseph Belknap
Richard Wood
John Nicoll
John Johnston
Samuel Brewster
David Crawford
Samuel Sly
John Morrison 2d
Matthew McDowell
Henry McNeeley Jr.
Daniel Mills
Alexander Taylor
John Close (Rev.)
James Perry
William Moffat
Samuel Boyd

William Beatty
John Cunningham
George Harris
James Jackson Jr.
Stephen King
Isaac Stonehouse
John Murphy
John Hiffernan
Benjamin Burnam
James Smith

Austin Beardsley
William Park
Thomas Swafford
David Thompson
Timothy White
Nathaniel Liscomb
Dennis Furshay
William Mulliner
George Mavings
Isaac Belknap

Samuel Brewster Jr.
Nathaniel Boyd 2d
David Mandevill
Edward Betty
William Welling
Robert Johnston
Peter Welling
Joseph Sweezey
Hugh Turner

## PRECINCT OF MAMAKATING

John Young
Capt. John Crage
John Thompson
Johan Stufflebane Jr.
Benj. Cuddeback Jr.
William Cuddeback
T. K. Westbrook
Elias Travis
William Johnston
Eli Strickland
Johan Stufflebane
Capt. J.R. DeWitt
Abner Skinner
John McKinstry
Thomas Kytte
Harm. VanInwegen
Joseph Drake
Samuel Dupuy
Isaac VanTwill
Chas. Gillets
Joseph Westbrook
James McCivers
Daniel VanFleet Jr.
Joseph Hubbard
Jacob VanInwegen
G. VanInwegen
Corn. VanInwegen
Eliphalet Stevens
Reuben Babbett
Adam Rivenburgh
Robert Milliken
Stephen Larney
John Williams
Samuel King
William Smith
Valentine Wheeler
Jep. Fuller
John Wallis
Joseph Thomas
Jacobus Swartwout
Joseph Skinner
Geradus Swartwout
John Travis
Phil. Swarwout Jr.

John Travis Jr.
Jacobus Cuddeback
Robert Comfort
Petrus Cuddeback
Eph. Furgison
Rufus Stanton
Moses Miller
Asa Kimball
Jno. Barber
Zeh. Holcomb
John Fry
Samuel Daley
George Gillespy
Nathan Cook
Henry Kewkirk
Henry Ellsworth
Philip Swartwout Esq.
John Seybolt
William Haxton
David Wheeler
Robert Cook
Elisha Barber
William Rose
Jonathan Davis
James Williams
Gershom Simpson
James Blizzard
Jacob Stanton
Thomas Combs
John Gillaspy
Ebenezer Halcomb
Abraham Smedes
Abr. Cuddeback
Joseph Shaw
Aldert [sic] Rosa
Abraham Rosa
David Gillaspy
Jacob Rosa
Stephen Halcomb
Abrm. Cuddeback Jr.
Fred. Benaer
Moses Roberts
Jonathan Brooks
Daniel Roberts

Ebenezer Parks
Jeremiah Shaver
Petrus Gumaer
Joseph Ogden
J. DeWitt Gumaer
Elias Miller
Ezekiel Gumaer
George I. Denniston
Elias Gumaer
Moses Depuy Jr.
Jonathan Strickland
Johannes Miller
Jonathan Wheeler
John Douglass
Thomas Lake
Joseph Randall
Jacob Comfort
Thomas Gillaspy
Jonah Parks
Daniel Walling
Samuel Patterson
Matthew Neely
Joel Adams
John Harding
James Cunen
Eph. Thomas
Peter Simpson
Abm. McQuin
Benjamin Dupuy
Joseph Arthur
Daniel Decker
Nathaniel Travis
John Brooks
Ezekiel Travis
David Daley
Joseph Travis
Isaac Rosa
Daniel Walling Jr.
Matthew Terwilliger
Abr. Smith
Johannes Wash
Leonard Hefnessey
Daniel Woodworth

The following refused to join the Association, yet on the 14th of July 1775, swore to abide by the measures of the Continental Congress.

James Leonard
David Reynolds
James Denton
George Harding
Samuel Dewine
Gilbert Purdy
John Truesdill

Isaac Barton
George Merritt
Daniel Gidney
Gabriel Traverse
John Flavelling
Stephen Wood
Samuel Fowler

John Wiggins
Thomas Ireland
Jonas Totten
Abel Flavelling
Daniel Haines
Daniel Denton
Antho. Beetal Brant

## PRECINCT OF GOSHEN

### Minisink District

J. Westbrook Jr.
George Quick
Levi Decker
Levi VanEtten
Petrus Cole
Joel Westbrook
Petrus Cuykendal
Sylvester Cortright
Jacobus Vanfliet Jr.
James Carpenter
S. Cuykendal Jr.
Solomon Cuykendal
Moses Kortright
Nehemiah Pattison
Nicholas Slyter
Petrus Decker
Johannes Westbrook
Ephraim Middagh

Isaac Davis
John Prys
Jacobus Vanfliet
Reuben Jones
Benjamin Corson
John Bennett
Jacob Quick
Timothy Wood
Benjamin Wood
John VanTuyle
Isaac Uptegrove
Wilhelmus Westfill
Benjamin Boorman
G. Bradcock
Wilhelmus Cole
Albert Osterhoust
Daniel Kortright

Benjamin Cox
Jacobus Davis
Samuel Davis
Daniel Cole
A. VanEtten
A. C. VanAken
Johannes Decker Jr.
Jacobus Schoonhoven
Thomas Hart
Esee Bronson
Martinas Decker Jr.
Martinas Decker
Jacob Harraken
Arthur VanTuyle [?]
Daniel St. John
Asa Astly
Simon Westfall

### Blooming-Grove District

Alexander Smith
Jonathan Smith
John Case
Joshua Corey
William Hubbard
Daniel Pain
James Miller
Zeba Owen
Samuel Haines Smith
Daniel Tooker
Thomas Goldsmith
David Rumsey
Abraham Dalsen Jr.
David Horton
David Demarest
Cuppe Brooks
Joseph Elliot
Charles Tooker
Capt. Nathaniel Roe
Joshua Brown

Increase Wyman
Jonathan Horton
Moses Carpenter
Benjamin Harlow
John Pain
David Youngs
Hezekiah Warne
Joseph Drake
Caleb Coleman
Henry Wisner
William Lesly
Guilian Bartholf
Joseph Browne
Cornelius Decker
John King
Corns. VanOrsdale
Silas Horton
John Budd
William Horton
Joseph Dixon

Joseph Conkling
John Barker
Phineas Rumsey
John Corey
Garrett Duryea
William Warne
James Mapes
Jonathan Jayne
David Rogers
Isaiah Smith
Jacobus Bartholf
John Meeker
Isaac Dalsen Jr.
Solomon Smith
John Denton
Samuel Wickham
John Elliot
Abraham Springsteen
Lt. John Jackson
Joshua Brown Jr.

David Godfrey
John Bull
Gideon Salmon
John Minthorn
Silas Horton
Jacob Demarest
James Aspell
Elizah Doan
William Heard
Joseph Case
Obadiah Helms
Christopher Springsteen
David Jones
Samuel Bartholf
Nathaniel Minthorn
Peter Gale
Hendrick Bartholf
Thomas McCane
Solomon Carpenter
Joshua Davis
Ebenezer Beer
Philip Borroughs
Ensign Daniel Drake
John VanCleft Jr.
Joshua Wells
Joshua Weeks
Silas Stewart
Michael Carpenter
Wilas Hulse
Benjamin Dunning
Samuel Cooley
Jacob Finch
Samuel Cole
Cornelius Bartholf Jr.
Matthew Dilling
Michael Allison
Henry David
Casper Writer
William Wisner
John Boyle
Samuel Carpenter
Henry David Jr.
Jeremiah S. Conkling
Jonathan Cooley
Elijah Truman
Isaac Dolsen
Joseph McCane
Jeremiah Smith Jr.
Henry Smith
John Carvey
Robert Thompson Jr.
Amos Hubbs
Jeremiah Smith Sr.
John Kennady
Zephamiah Drake

James Markel
William Satterly
Jeremiah Butler
John Brown
Jacobus Laine
Ezra Keeler
John Bigger
John Ketchum Jr.
Zephaniah Huff
Joshua Reeve
Benjamin MacVea
Coleman Curtis
Daniel Reeve
Stephen Lewis
Robert McCane
Andrew Christy
Joseph Smith
Reuben Hall
Jacob Demming
Joshua Smith
Richard Jones
Lt. John Wood
Oliver Heady
Jonathan Owen
Nicholas VanTassel
Wright Smith
Samuel Jones
Squire Whitaker
John Owen
Benjamin Smith
Gilbert Bradner
David Kendle
William Walworth
Robert Thompson
Joseph Allison
Benjamin Whitaker
William Carpenter
John Hopper
David Linch
Daniel Carpenter
Abraham Harding
James Bell
James Thompson
Benjamin Forgesson
James Dolsen
Nathaniel Tuthill
Jacob Fegate
Caleb Goldsmith
Matthias Carvey
Moses Smith
Solomon Tracey
James Kemp
William Morris
Jeremiah Ferger
James Steward

Silas Pierson
Richard Bull
Phineas Salmon
Abraham Chandler
John Cravens
Joseph Todd
George Duryea
James Smith
Phineas Heard
William Marshall
William Forbes
Hezeiah Watkins
Francis Baird
Henry Roemer
Gamaliel Tansdell
Stephen Meeker
Peter Bartholf
Samuel Smith
Martin Myer
John Williams
Samuel Moffat
Thomas Engles
Richard Sheridan
David Cooley Jr.
Jonah Seely
Benjamin Currie
Benjamin Carpenter
Samuel Webb
Elisha Hulse
William Kimber
John Ferger
Hidley Spencer
Peter Miller
Stephen Bartholf
James Little Jr.
James Allison
Samuel Demarest
Jonas Wood
Israel Wells
Michael Coleman
Peter Arnot
Jonathan David
John Garvey
William Howard
David Moore
Reuben Smith Jr.
Joel Cross
Amos Smith
John Finch
Francis Mvanjoy
George Little
Thomas Barer
Amos Woolcocks
Joseph Wilson
John VanCleft

Joseph Steward
William Seely
Richard Allison
Sallier David
Benjamin Halsted
Jacob Cole
Solomon Finch
Christopher Myers
James Ramsey
William McCane
Michael Dunning
William Horton
Joseph Coleman
Henry Samis
Orinus Bartholf
Abel Jackson
Michael Halsted
Anthony Swartwout
Anthony West Brook
James Mosier
David Shephard
Jabez Finch
Daniel Rosegrout
Nathaniel Mathers
Moses Whitehead
John Little
Jeremiah Trickey
Jonathan Corney
Nathan Roberts
Obadiah Smith
Hezekiah Lawrence
Jacob Demarest
Caleb Smith
James McCane
Matthew Howell Jr.
Charles Webb
Elijah Egars
Mark Chambers
David Mapes
Nathan Bailey
Benjamin Hill
Samuel Satterly
John Bailey
Joseph Beckas
Peter Mann
Elihu Horton
Jacob Cole
Peter Townsend
Richard Holsted
David Howell Jr.
Silas Holley
Jabez Knap
Joshua Drake
Elias Oldfield
Daniel Myers

Israel Holley
John Feigler [?]
Peter Demerest
John Kinnett
John David
Henry Dobin
William Dill
Joseph Currie
Philip Redrick
James Clark
Martin McConnely
John Morrison
Benjamin Carpenter
William Kirby
Roolof VanBrunt
Joseph Halsted
James Parshall
Samuel Westbrook
George Howell
Benjamin Gabrelis
Samuel Reed
John Kinman
John Whitaker
David Lowren
James Gardiner
David Stephens
John Knapp
Solomon Roe
Saven Tracey
John Gerner
David Demarest
Benjamin Cole
Christopher Decker
Matthew Howell
Thomas Gale
Isaac Tracey
James Hulse
John Rhodes
Nathaniel Cooley
Joshua Wells
Zephaniah Kelly
William Kinna
James Hamilton
John Conner
Alexander Campbell
William Huff
Phineas Parshall
Daniel David
Michael Brooks
Joseph Chilsom
Samuel Harman
Daniel Holley
Peter Barlow
Stephen Jackson
Jeremiah Oakley

John Clar
Benjamin Demarest
Henry Hall
Edward David
David Miller
George Kemble
Solomon Hoff
Thomas Wood
James Masters
James McCane
James Schoonover
Philip Horton
Jonathan Coleman
Samuel Knapp
James Bartholf
Nathaniel Knapp Jr.
Gershon Owen
Benjamin Jackson
Joshua Hill
Samuel Finch
Abraham Dolsen Sr.
Benjamin Wallworth
John Davis
Increase Matthews
John Myers
James Reeves
Henry Clark
John Carpenter Smith
John Shepard
Henry Bartholf
Nathan Pemberton
William King
Peter Arnout
John Thompson
Thomas Angel
Samuel Chandler
John Miller
David Cooley
Zacheus Horton
Nathan Bailey 2d
Nathaniel Allison
William Vail
Landrine Eggers
Elias Clark
Daniel Cooley Jr.
Hugh Fenton
Edward David Jr.
John Gardiner
Joseph Oldfield
John Howell
Benjamin Dunning
Nathaniel Knap Jr.
Wait Smith
Samuel Sawyer
John Smith

Timothy Smith
William Reed
Isaas Hoadley
Anning Owen
Caleb Smith
Thomas Denton
Matthew Tyrel
William Helms
Bazaliel Seely
Gilbert Aldridge
William Hoff
John Mory
James Stewart
Cain Mehany
Joshua Howell
John Armstrong

Jonathan Rawson
Gilbert Howell
Daniel Egger
William Little
Solomon Smith
David Casen [?]
Moses Clark
Asa Vail
William Knap
John McDowell
Joshua Hallock
James Miller
Isaac Smith
Stephen Conkling
Joshua Herbert
Jonathan Hallock

Benjamin Attwood
William Egger (Eager)
Nathan Arnout
Jacob Hulse
Stephen Smith
Asa Derha
Andrew Miller
Phineas Case
Francis Gadlow
James Kinner
John Kimball
Oliver Smith
Abraham Johnston
Ebenezer Holly
Samuel Titus

## PRECINCT OF CORNWALL
### Includes Cornwall, Bloominggrove & Monroe

John Brewster Jr.
Jonathan Stevens
Thomas Clark
Isaiah Mapes
Bethuel Mapes
Solomon Little
Joseph Wilcox
Jonathan Brooks
Nehemiah Clark
Elihu Marvin Jr.
James Matthews
Isaac Brown
John McWhorter
Benjamin Lester
Abr'm. Ketchum
Silas Youngs
Archibald Little Jr.
Abimael Youngs Jr.
Samuel Knights
Jeremiah Howell
Jesse Marvin
John McCarty
Archibald Little
Samuel Smith
John Mapes
Samuel Ketchum
Benjamin Ketchum Jr.
John Marvin
James Tuthill
John Burges
Asahel Coleman
Samuel Seely
John Smith
James Little

David Stevens
Smith Clark
Smith Mapes
Benjamin Mapes
Samuel Gibson
Patrick Cassaday
Nathan Brewster
Richard Honiman
Seth Marvin
James Peters
Timothy Brewster
Joseph Smith
Benjamin Budd
John Pell Jr.
Phineas Helmes
William Hunter
Reuben Youngs
Israel Hodges
Thomas Sullivan
Isaac Corley Jr.
Josiah Seely
Joseph Wood
Thomas Moffat
Abraham Loce
Vincent Matthews
Samuel Ketchum Jr.
Stephen Youmans
Joseph Morrell
John Pecham
William Brown
Isaiah Howell
Micah Coleman
Nathaniel Seely
Timothy Little

Silas Benjamin Jr.
Daniel Mapes
Ephraim Clark
Nathan Marvin
Isaac Corley
Jesse Woodhull
Timothy Smith Jr.
Elihu Marvin
John Seely
David Beggs
William Roe
Jesse Teed
Josiah Pell
Joab Coleman
Thomas Clark Jr.
Silas Youngs Jr.
Jonas Seely
John Callay
James Sayre
George Baitman
Jeremiah Clark
John Wood
Stephen Gilbert
David Mandevil
Joseph Ketchum
Eleazer Youmans
Benjamin Ketchum
Jonathan Hallock
Brewster Helme
Patrick Odey
Samuel Sacket
Israel Seely
Gershom Clark
Thaddeus Seely

Samuel Mapes
William Nicholson
Daniel Coleman
David Clark
Isaac VanDuzer Jr.
Peter Reeder
Solomon Sheldon
Samuel Reeder
Silas Hall
Samuel Smith
Silas Howell
Justus Philby
Samuel Moffat Jr.
Gilbert Weeks
Silvanus Sayles
Robert Height
Ebenezer Woodhull
Samuel Moffat
Maurice Hearen
Luther Stuart
Silas Pierson
Silas Pierson Jr.
Francis Drake
Isaac Bower
Stephen Howell
Nassiad Curtis
Daniel Jones
Francis Tuthill
Michael Kelly
Joseph Collings
John Close (Rev.)
Benjamin Thorne
Jesse Seely
Richard Collingwood
Hezekiah Howell Jr.
Aaron Howell
Benjamin Carpenter
Silvanus Bishop
Robert Gregg
Isaac Vandusen 3d
Silas Coleman
Isaac Lightbody
Charick Vanduzen
Thomas Hulse
Zachariah Burwell
John Miller
John Reeder
Abner Thorp
Samuel Tuthill
George Whitaker
Isaac Lamoureux
Joseph VanNort
Peter Lamoureux
Neal Anderson
Philip Miller
Moses Strain

Benjamin Gregory
Silvanus White
Nathaniel Sayre Jr.
Richard Drake
Josiah Reeder
Obidah Thorn
Jacob Reeder
James Hall
Alexander Sutton
Paul Howell
Jacob White
Elijah Hudson
Frederick Tobias
Dennis Cooley
Zebulon Birchard
Isaac Brewster
Timothy Wood
Daniel Tuthill
Barnabas Many
Henry Dier Sr.
John Sayre
Richard Coleman
William King
Justus Hulse
William McLaughlin
Daniel Smith
Jonathan Tuthill
John Moffat
Francis Brewster
Lewis Donnovan
James Moore
John Parker
Hezekiah Howell
Nathaniel Satterly
John Kelley
James Davidson
William Gregg
Samuel Smith
John Faren
William Owen
Gabriel Lightbody
Francis Drake
James Lightbody
Abraham Butler
Joel Tuthill
Joseph Reeder
James Galloway
Joseph Reeder Jr.
Arche. Concham Jr.
Joshua Sandstar
Henry Brewster Jr.
William Conkling
John Brooks
Peter Lamoureux Jr.
James Overton
Elijah Carpenter

Justus Stevens
Bn. Craft
John Brewster
Christopher VanDuzer
Roger Barton
Stephen Reeder
Absalom Townsend
Francis Vantine
John W. Clark
Thomas Smith
Bazaliel Seely
Benjamin Corey
Hugh Murray
Nathan Birchard
Matthew Sweny
Daniel Thorne
Nathaniel Strong
Sylvanus Halsey
James Smith
James Sayre Jr.
Birdsey Young
Aaron Howell Jr.
Benoni Breck
Thaddeus Cooley
Stephen Sayles
Elijah Green
John Brooks
Zachariah DuBois
John Leonard
Thomas Collings
John Pride
Nathaniel Seely Jr.
Obediah Smith
Silas Benjamin
Daniel Deven
John Carpenter
Timothy Carpenter
Joseph Carpenter Jr.
Samuel Bartlett
John Lightbody
Hugh Gregg
Andrew Lightbody
Azariah Martin
Selah Satterly
Joshua Burwell
Arch. Cunningham
William Reeder
John Johnson
Benjamin Tuthill
Henry Myers
John Lamoureux
John Lamourex 2d
Luke Lamoureux
James Mitchell
John Carpenter 2d
Caleb Ashley

William Carpenter
Jonas Garrison
Thomas Poicy
Thomas Smith
John McLean
Thomas Cooper
Eleazer Taylor
Adam Belsher
Charles Howell
Timothy Corwin
Thomas Chatfield
John Tuthill
Isaac Moffat
James Stought
Jesse Brewster
William Hooge
Silas Corwin
Nathaniel Biggs
James Halsey
Nathan Strong
Peter Earll
Benjamin Earll
George Everston
Neal Anderson 2d
David Wilson
Thomas Gregg
Aaron DeGrauw
Henry Atwood
Togidah Dickens
William Miller
Francis Bourk
Hugh McDonel
Owen Noblen
Richard Wilks
Thomas Horton
John Wagent
John Wagent 2d
Thomas Smith
Nathaniel Jayne
Stephen Jayne
Joseph Hildreth
Silas Millis Jr.
David Bloomfield
Jacob Manderville
Daniel Harrison
Thomas Powell
Henry Davenport
Enos Prindle
Henry Hall
Joseph Canfield
John Canfield
John Carr
Thomas Linch
Joshua Miller
Dariah Stage
John Hall

Benjamin Chichester
Jonathan DuBois
William Bedall
Zacheus Horton
Austin Smith
Joseph Lamoureux
Abraham Sneden
Nathaniel Pease
Eleazer Luce
William Cook
Daniel Rumsey
William Moffat
William Bartlett
Thomas Lenington
James McClugin
James McGuffack
James Lewis
Stephen Halsey
Daniel Curtis
John Earll
Richard Earll
Silas Tucker
Rovert Brock
Reuben Tucker
Joseph Patterson
Elisha Smith
Andrew Stuart
John Williams
William Ayres
William Howard
Isaac Horton
Aaron Miller
Jacob Devo
Thomas Willett
John Johnson
Reuben Taber
Joseph Stevens
Joseph Davis
John Wolly
Daniel Jayne
John Boucke
Isaac Tobias
Henry Manderville
Lawrence Ferguson
Peter Reynolds
Joseph Gold
Israel Osmun
Ezekiel Osmun
Chester Adams
Samuel Lows
Jacob Lows
Cornwall Sands
David Causter
John Smith
Zophar Head
William Horton

Josiah Halstead
Samuel Robbins
Thomas Herley
Jacob Conten
Jacob Conten Jr.
William Clark
William Bradley
Stephen Hulse
E. Taylor
James Ludis
James Wilkins
William Owens
John Moffat
John Carpenter 3d
Joseph Chandler
Tobias Wygant
Henry Brewster
James Huff
Jacob Brown
Solomon Sarvis
Abraham Cooley
John Brase
Thomas Everston
Benjamin Jayne
Peter Lowrie
Jacob Vanduzer
Amons Wood
Isaac Vanduzer
Samuel Howard
Edward Robben
John Daynes
James Wilks
James Wilks Jr.
William Thompson
Hanes Bartlett
Solomon Cornwell
John W. Tuthill
Silas Reynolds
Peter Stevens
William Obadge
Adam Miller
Charles Field
Gilbert Roberts
Francis Manderville
Daniel Miller
Benjamin Pringle
Daniel Prindle
Oliver Davenport
William Cooper
Benjamin Canfield
Amos Miller
Garrett Miller
George Galloway
William Bell
Garret Willem Jr.
Benjamin Kelley

## PRECINCT OF CORNWALL

Benj. Miller
William Compten
Robert Miller
Matthias Tyson
Joseph Miller
Daniel Adams
John Arkils
John Barton
James Unels
James Arnold
Fanton Horn
Oliver Davenport
Robert Davenport
David June
Amos Wood
Benjamin Wood
Daniel Wood
John Wood
Jonas Smith
Joseph Cupper
Amos Whitmore
John J. Hammond
Zahud June
John Samson
Jeremiah Fowler
John Haman
Stephen Peet
Samuel Raymond
James Tuttle
John Florence
Thomas Gilbert
Benjamin Quackenbush
Patrick McDowell

Henry Dier
Asa Buck
Samuel Hall
Benjamin Goldsmith
L. Canfield
John Gee
Amos Mills
David Standley
James Southerland
Nathan June
Thomas Davenport
Henry Cunningham
Henry Reynolds
Uriah Wood
John Celly
John Wood 3d
Joseph Plumfield
Uriah Crawford
Amos Pains
Samuel Whitmore
Francis Welton
David Miller
Thomas Porter
Thomas Dearin
Jonathan Earll
Richard Langdon
Samuel Earll
Andrew Sherwood
William Sherwood
Thomas Oliver
Elijah Barton
William Douglas
Jacob Vanduzer

James Miller
Philips Roblin
John McKelvey
Vincent Helme
Timothy Owens
Patrick Ford
John Earll Jr.
Andrew Southerland
Alex. Southerland
David Southerland 3d
David Southerland
John Southerland
Gideon Florence
Richard Sheldon
Stephen C. Clark
Reuben Clark
James Scoldfield
Stephen Wood
Francis Plumsted
Joseph Canfield
George Everitt
Solomon Siles
Francis Smith
Micah Seaman
Martin Clark
Alexander Johnson
John Cronckhite
Thomas Lamoureux
Samuel Strong
Francis Miller
Alexander Galloway
William White

In Newburgh precinct the "Committee of Safety & Observation" appointed 27 Jan. 1775, consisted of Wolvert Acker, Jonathan Hasbrouck, Thomas Palmer, John Belknap, Joseph Coleman, Moses Higby, Samuel Sands, Stephen Case, Isaac Belknap, Benjamin Birdsall & John Robinson.

In New Windsor precinct the committee appointed May 6, 1775, consisted of Col. James Clinton, Capt. James McClaughry, John Nicoll, John Nicholson, Nathan Smith, Robert Boyd Jr., Samuel Brewster, Samuel Sly, Samuel Logan. In May 1776, the committee became Samuel Brewster, chairman; Robert Boyd Jr., Nathan Smith, Hugh Humphrey, George Denniston, John Nicholl, Col. James McClaughry, Samuel Arthur.

In the precinct of Mamakating, John Young chairman of committeee, certified that the pledge was signed by all the freeholders and inhabitants of the precinct June 26, 1775.

In the precinct of Goshen the committee appointed Sept. 14, 1 775, consisted in part of Isaac Nicoll, Benjamin Gale, Moses Hetfield, Daniel Everett, James Little, Joshua Davis, with Daniel Everett as Chairman. Later the names of John Hathorn, John Jackson, Henry Wisner, John Minthornes & Nathaniel Ketchum were chairmen at different times.

In the Cornwall precinct 1775, the committee consisted of Hezekiah Howell, Archibald Little, Elihu Marvin, Nathaniel Satterly, Nathaniel Strong, Jonathan Brooks, Stephen Gilbert, Zachariah DuBois, with Thomas Moffat as chairman.

In the precinct of Hanover no names of pledge-signers were reported, but the committee, appointed May 8, 1775, consisted of Dr. Charles Clinton, chairman; Alexander Trimble, Arthur Parks, William Jackson, Henry Smith, Jacob Newkirk, James Latta, Philip Mole, John Wilkin, James McBride, James Milliken, Samuel Barkley.

In the precinct of Wallkill there was no return of pledge-signers, but the committee, Jan. 30, 1775, consisted of Abimael Tonng, chairman; James Wilkins, Hezekiah Gale, Moses Phillips, Henry Wisner, Jr.

The county committee of Orange in 1776 had Elihu Marvin, of Cornwall, for chairman and David Pye was deputy chairman for Haverstraw.

# PERSONS KILLED IN THE BATTLE OF MINISINK
## July 22, 1779

Col. Benjamin Tusten
Gabriel Wisner
Capt. Bezaliel Tyler
Stephen Mead
Capt. Benjamin Vail
Nathaniel Terwilliger
Capt. John Duncan
Joshua Lockwood
Capt. Samuel Jones
Ephraim Ferguson
Capt. John Little
--- Talmadge
Lt. John Wood
John Carpenter
Adjt. Nathaniel Fitch

David Burney
Robert Townsend
Gamaliel Bailey
Samuel Kanpp
Moses Thomas
James Kanpp
Jonathan Haskell
Benjamin Bennett
Abram Williams
William Barker
Daniel Reed
Jacob Dunning
Jonathan Pierce
Joseph Norris
James Little

Gilbert S. Vail
Nathan Wade
Joel Decker
Simon Wait
Abram Shepherd
James Mosher
--- Shepherd
Isaac Ward
Eleazer Owens
Baltus Niepos
Adam Embler
Samuel Little
Ensign Ephraim Masten
Ensign Ephraim Middaugh

Residents of the Ramapo Valley were mostly Tories, and in this defile in that region known as the "Clove," the Tory Moody operated. Claudius Smith & his sons, Richard & James, were Torries who had their headquarters in the Clove. Claudius commenced his depredations in the interest of the British in 1776, and first appeared on public records, charged with stealing in 1777. He was said to be the friend of the poor, giving liberally to them of what he stole from the rich. Many exciting stories were told of his doings. When Gov. Clinton in Oct. 1778 offered a reward for the Smiths' arrest they fled to Long Island. They were recognized there & seized in their beds. Smith was tried in Jan. 1779 at Goshen & executed on the 22d of Jan. with five of his associates: Matthew Dolson, John Ryan, Thomas Delamar, John Gordon & Amy Angor. Another son of Claudius Smith, William, was shot in the mountains, and his son James was probably executed in Goshen soon after his father, with James Flewelling and William Cole. Silas Gardner was tried & sentenced as a Tory and was pardoned.

## WAR OF 1812

Below is a roll of a detached company in Col. Michael Smith's regiment of infantry, mustered in in Sept. 1814, which includes men from both Orange & Ulster Counties:

John Dunning, Captain

William Mullicks, 1st Lt.

Walter Moore, Ensign
Henry Dunning, 3d Sgt.
Archibald Y. Murray, 3d Corp.
Daniel Wilkin, 6th Corp.

Jeffrey Booth, 1st Sgt.
Oliver Clark, 1st Corp.
James Lewis, 4th Corp.
Samuel Brown, Drummer

John A. Crane, 2d Sgt.
Pierson Genung, 2d Corp.
Derrick Smith, 5th Corp.
Harvey Genung, Fifer

Elisha Brown
Abijah Brundage
Neal Brown
Levi Bennett
Daniel Brown
Nathaniel Beiley
John Benjamin
Thomas A. Booth
Benjamin Bedford
Stephen Cash
Stephen Clark
Benjamin Corey
James Crawford
Gabriel Caldwell
Andrew Christie
Nebat. Corwin
Joseph Corwin

Jeremiah Cox
Thompson Cox
Joseph Canfield
Stephen Decker
Michael Dunning
John Dunning Jr.
Samuel Fanning
Salem Goldsmith'
Henry Gale
Lyman Gregory
Moses Goldsmith
Samuel Gardner
Silas L. Gardner
John D. Goldsmith
John D. Goldsmith
Barnabas Horton
Jonas Hulse Jr.

Eleazer Hudson
John W. Hines
Daniel T. Jackson
Paul Jagger
Robert Kirk
John C. Kortright
Nathan Kerr
David Kirk
Elihu C. Keen
James Knox
Elijah Knapp
Artemas Long
Jared Lockwood
Isaac W. Loder
Samuel Millspaugh
Joshua McNish
Spicer McNish

| | | |
|---|---|---|
| Henry McNish | Adam Puff | Bezalell Smith |
| James McCarter | James Puff | Jonathan Thompson |
| Allen McCarter | John Robbins | Charles Tredwell |
| James McVey | Peter Robbins | Morrison Taylor |
| John Mires Jr. | James Ray | Richard Uptegrove |
| Joseph Monnel | John Rodgers | John VanBenschoten |
| Loderwick Moore | Isaac Selleck | David Warren |
| John C. Miller | Alva Slauson | Solomon Warren |
| John McVey | William Sayer | Eliphalet Warren |
| Arden McVey | Samuel Sands | Jonathan White |
| William McCarter | Jacob Stingham | James Watson |
| George Miller | Isaiah W. Smith | William Wilkin |
| Allen Nicolls | Elijah Screder | John Wood |
| Gilbert Ogden | Grant Smith | Virgil W. Youngs |
| Stephen Prescott | Silas W. Smith | |

Orange County was represented in the Navy by Silas H. Stringham, Charles Ludlow, Augustus C. Ludlow and Robert C. Ludlow, among others.

After the British captured Washington in 1814, a public meeting was held in Goshen, Aug. 30, to consider the propriety of repairing the fortifications at West Point or erecting new ones for public defense. General James W. Wilson was chairman of the meeting, and a committee to devise and report plans was composed of John Duer, Jonathan Fisk, William Ross, John W. Wilkin, George D. Wickham, James Finch Jr., and Nathan H. White. They reported at an adjourned meeting and recommended the following committee of defense, which was appointed.

For Minisink, John Bradner, Nathan Arnot; Deer Park, John Finch Jr., Joseph Baird; Wallkill, Henry B. Wisner, Benjamin Woodward; Goshen, John Duer, Freegift Tuthill; Warwick, Dr. Samuel S. Seward, Jeffrey Wisner; Monroe, James D. Secor, Benjamin Cunningham; Cornwall, William A. Clark, Joseph Chandler Jr.; Blooming Grove, Col. Selah Strong, Jeremiah Horton; Montgomery, John Blake Jr., Johannes Miller; Newburgh, John D. Lawson, Jacob Powell; New Windsor, Joseph Morton, David Hill.

# CIVIL WAR

## 56th NY Regiment

From the first there were 2,176 men & boys enlisted and assigned to this regiment. The incomplete record shows the names of 41 killed in battle, 23 d. of wounds; 216 d. of disease; 170 wounded & recovered; 415 discharged for disability & wounds; 67 transferred to other commands; 5 captured & paroled.

### Regimental & Company Officers
### Colonels

Charles H. Van Wyck, & Brig. Gen. U. S. V.

Rockwell Tyler, not mustered.

### Lieutenant-Colonels

James Jordan, to Aug. 5, 1862
John J. Wheeler, to Feb. 11, 1864
Eliphas Smith, not mustered

Frederick Decker, not mustered
Rockwell Tyler, to muster out & Brevet Col.

### Majors

Jacob Sharpe, to Aug. 5, 1862
Rockwell Tyler, to Feb. 27, 1864
James DuBois, not mustered

John J. Wheeler, to Dec. 15, 1862
Eliphas Smith, to Oct. 17, 1865

### Adjutants

Eli H. Evans, to Oct. 25, 1863

Henri B. Loomis, to muster out of regiment

### Quartermasters

John B. Gerard, to Sept. 5, 1862
Addison J. Clements, to muster out of regiment, from Co. F

Jesse F. Schafer, to Oct. 15, 1864, from Co. K

### Surgeons

Solomon VanEtten, to Sept. 28, 1864
Ira S. Bradner, Sept. 19, 1865; not mustered

George H. Fossard, Oct. 7, 1864 to July 5, 1865

### Assistant Surgeons

O. A. Carroll, Sept. 2, 1861 to May 13, 1863
Daniel S. Hardenburgh, Nov. 11, 1863, to April 1, 1865
George K. Saver, Brevet 1st Lt. & Asst. Surgeon

Albert S. Turner, Aug. 9, 1862, to Nov. 18, 1863
Ira S. Bradner, April 25, 1863, to muster out of regiment.

### Hospital Steward

George K. Sayer, from Oct. 20, 1861, to muster out of regiment.

### Chaplains

Charles Shelling, to Dec. 23, 1862

George P. VanWyck, Dec. 30, 1862 to muster out of regiment.

### Sergant Majors

William N. Phillips, to Jan. 18, 1862
Francis Hines, Co. E, to Aug. 8, 1862
Francis Might, Co. G, to July 1, 1864
James Gowdy, Co. C to May 18, 1865

Demmon S. Decker, Co. F, to Feb. 9, 1862
John Metcalf, Co. A, to Dec. 23, 1863
Robert C. Roper, Co. H, to Jan. 1, 1865
Frank Hotchkin, Co. F, to muster out of regiment.

Jesse F. Schafer, original, to Feb. 27, 1862          Noah D. Smith, Co. H, to muster out of regiment.

## Commissary Sergeants

Isaac Rosa, original, to April 12, 1862          William H. Merphy, Co. K, to Nov. 20, 1864
William H. D. Blake, Co. C, Nov. 22, 1864 to muster out of regiment.

## Regimental Band

| | | |
|---|---|---|
| Albert B. Berger | Charles Cromwell | William N. Frost |
| Hiram T. King | William H. Stewart | Richard D. Way |
| John Biddle | Elias Depuy | Elisha C. Harding |
| Joseph Kirkpatrick | Joshua B. Turner | Theodore H. Welch |
| George Canfield | George Depuy | George J. King |
| James Little Jr. | Charles Tuthill | Robert A. Wheat |
| Thomas H. Count | Calvin Depuy | |
| Cornelius J. Sloat | Theodore H. VanCleft | |

## Musicians--Drum & Fife Corps

| | | |
|---|---|---|
| David Aber, Co. B | Edward Nixon, Co. G | Westley Howe, Co. H |
| Timothy Lamoreux, Co. F | Dwight DeSylvia, Co. F | Cornelius Smith, Co. F |
| George Aber, Co. B | Charles V.L. Pitts, Co. H | Lewis E. Kennedy, Co. G |
| John Mead, Col. L | Nathaniel Graham, Co. L | William T. Smith, Co. I |
| Charles Baird, Co. H | Newell F. Reynolds, Co. D | Henry King, Co. D |
| Harman B. Miller, Co. A | John H. Grannis, Co. H | Charles Weightman, Co. E |
| Conrad Bender, Co. D | John T. Robinson, Co. A | George Kinsler, Co. K |
| Thomas Miller, Co. G | William Hamilton, Co. B | William Young, Co. F |
| Fred H. Bradner, Co. F | Henry Robinson, Co. C | |

## 124th REGIMENT

A distinctively Orange County regiment, as all companies were recruited in the county under President Lincoln's call of 1 July 1862. For the district of Orange & Sullivan Counties the military committee was: Hon. Robert Denniston, Blooming Grove; Hon. Andrew S. Murray, Goshen; Hugh S. Bull, Montgomery; Albert Post, Newburgh; James M. Barrett, Cornwall; Alexander Moore, Washingtonville; Morgan Shint, Monore. Later added to the committee were: E. A. Brewster & William Fullerton, Newburgh; C. H. Winfield, Thomas Edsall & Silas Horton, Goshen; James Cromwell & William Avery, Cornwall; C. C. McQuoid, Halstead Sweet, John G. Walkin & John Cummings, Wallkill; Charles J. St. John, John Conkling, Orville J. Brown & C. M. Lawrence, Port Jervis; C.B. Newkirk, Monroe; A. S. Dodge, Mount Hope; Dorastus Brown, Greenville; A. F. Schofield, Montgomery; A. G. Owen, Blooming Grove; John Cowdrey & Thomas Welling, Warwick.

Col. A. Van Horne Ellis of New Windsor was put in charge of recruiting. The regimental officers: A. Van Horne Ellis, col.; F. M. Cummins, lt. col.; James Cromwell, major; John H. Thompson, surgeon; T. Scott Bradner, chaplain; Augustus Denniston, quartermaster; De Peyster Arden, adjutant; Edward Marshall, asst. surgeon; R. V. K. Monfort, 2d asst. surgeon.

Members of the regimental band: Drum Major, --- Hart; buglers, William B. Wood, Moses P. Ross; fifes, John G. Buckley, Charles Whitehead, Arthur Haigh, George W. Dimick, Henry C. Payne; drums, Robert L. Travis, A. J. Millspaugh, George W. Camfield, John N. Cole, R. D. Stephens, Charles W. Bodle, Henry M. Cannon, William Hamilton, Henry Hoofman, C. Van Gordon, Jehue Price, J. M. Merritt, W. Johnston, James McElroy, Samuel W. Weeden.

Captains of companies were: A, Charles H. Weygant; B, Henry S. Murray; C, William Silliman; D, James W. Benedict; E, William A. McBirney; F, Ira S. Bush; G, Isaac Nicoll; H, David Crist; I, Leander Clark, K, William A. Jackson. Those below marked + indicate promotions, so one man's name may appear on more than one list.

Regimental & Company Officers
124th NY

## Colonels

A. Van Horn Ellis; killed in action at Gattysburg, PA, 2 July 1863
Francis M. Cummins

Charles H. Weygant

## Lieutenant Colonels

Francis M. Cummins +
Charles H. Weygant, mustered out with Henry S. Murray regiment 3 June 1865, Brevet Col.

## Majors

Charles H. Weygant+
James W. Benedict

Henry S. Murry
James Cromwell, killed in action at Gettysburg, PA, 2 July 1863

## Adjutants

William Silliman+
William Brownson
Wines E. Weygant

C. Depeyster Arden
William B. VanHouten

## Quartermasters

Augustus Denniston
Ellis Post

Henry F. Travis+

## Surgeons

John H. Thompson

Robert V. K. Monfort

## Assistant Surgeons

Edward G. Marshall
Edward C. Fox

Robert V. K. Monfort+

## Chaplain

Thomas Scott Bradner

## Captains

| | | |
|---|---|---|
| Charles H. Weygant+ | James W. Benedict | Ira S. Bush |
| Charles B. Wood | John C. Wood | Lander Clark |
| Thomas Taft | William A. McBurney | Henry F. Travis |
| Henry S. Murray+ | Daniel Sayer | William A. Jackson |
| Wiliam E. Mapes | Isaac Nicoll** | Lewis M. Wisner |
| Robert J. Malone | James O. Denniston | Thomas Bradley |
| James Cromwell+ | Henry P. Ramsdell | David Crist# |
| William Silliman+ | Thomas J. Quick | Theodore M. Roberson |
| James Finnegan* | Edward J. Cormick*** | |
| James A. Grier | John W. Houston | |

*Died of wounds, 28 Oct. 1864
***Killed in action near Petersburg, VA 1 April 1865

**Killed in action at Gettysburg, PA, 2 July 1863
#Killed in action 30 May 1864

## First Lieutenants

Charles B. Wood+
Charles T. Cressy
Thomas Taft+
David U. Quick
Wines E. Weygant
William F. Mapes+
Edward J. Cormick+
Abram F. Francisco
William Brownson+
Henry P. Ramsdell
Daniel Sayer+

John W. Houston
Ebenezer Holbert
Wm. A. Verplanck
Theodore M. Robertson+
Woodward T. Ogden
James O. Denniston
William H. Benjamin
Thomas J. Quick+
James A. Grier
John R. Stanbrough
Isaac M. Martin

Wm. B. VanHouten+
Charles Stuart
James H. Roosa
James Finnegan+
Lewis M. Wisner
John C. Wood+
Thomas Hart
Henry Gowdy*
John R. Hayes
Thomas Bradley+
John S. King

*Died of wounds 11 May 1864

## Second Lieutants

Charles T. Cressy+
Jonathan Birdsall*
Gabrial Tuthill
Henry P. Ramsdell+
James A. Grier+
Thomas Hart+
John W. Houston+
Ebenezer Holbert+
Thomas G. Mabie

Adolphus Wittenbeecher
Theodore M. Robertson+
Woodward T. Ogden
Sylvester Lawson
David Gibbs
William H. Benjamin+
Joshua V. Cole
Samuel W. Hotckiss
David U. Quick+

Lewis T. Schultz
Isaac M. Martin+
Milnor Brown**
Charles Stuart+
William W. Smith
James Finnegan+
Jacob Denton***
Lewis M. Wisner+
John R. Hayes

*Killed in action near Petersburg, VA 22 Oct. 1864
**Killed in action at Gettysburg, PA 2 July 1863
***Killed in action 3 May 1863

## Other Civil War Military Organizations
## from Orange County, NY

Company I, 71st Regt., N.G.S.N.Y., recruited in Newburgh, mostly from Co. L, 19th Regiment, May 20-31, 1861, by Capt. A. Van Horne Ellis. Mustered out 30 July 1861. Officers:

A. VanHorne Ellis, Captain
George W. Hawkins, 2d Lt.
William H. Garrison, 2d Sgt.

John McMeekin, 3d Sgt.
James D. Hamilton, 4th Sgt.
Charles Decker, 1st Corp.

Marshal M. VanZile, 2d Corp.
Henry T. Travis, 3d Sgt.
Thomas Riley, 4th Sgt.

May 28, 1862, within 7 hours the above company was again recruited for 3 months. Officers:

A. VanHorne Ellis, Captain
William H. Garrison, 1st Lt.
James C. Taggart, 2d Lt.
John W. Forsyth, 1st Sgt.

Henry F. Travis, 2d Sgt.
John McMeekin, 3d Sgt.
James B. Montgomery, 4th Sgt.
Thomas Riley, 5th Sgt.

Robert Acheson, Corp.
David M. DeWitt, Corp.
William M. Verplanck, Corp.
Edward J. Hall, Corp.

In May 1862, 19th regiment of militia, commanded by Col. William R. Brown, ordered to Washington. Officers:

William R. Brown, Col.
James Low, Lt. Col.

David Jagger, Major
George Weller, Qtm.

William J. Hathaway, Adj.

Col. Brown's 168th Regiment in Feb. 1863 served at Yorktown for its whole term of service.  Mustered out Oct. 31st.
Officers:

| | | |
|---|---|---|
| William R. Brown, Col. | Bennett Gilbert, Capt. | Marshal VanTile, 1st Lt. |
| James Low, Lt. Col. | George McCleary, Capt. | George R. Brainsted, 1st Lt. |
| James C. Rennison, Lt. Col. | Samuel Hunter, Capt. | Thomas P. Terwilliger, 2d Lt. |
| George Waller, Major | John D. Wood, Capt. | Isaac N. Morehouse, 2d Lt. |
| James C. Rennison, Major | James C. Rennison, Capt. | James H. Anderson, 2d Lt. |
| Daniel Torbush, Major | Myron A. Tappan, Capt. | George C. Marvin, 2d Lt. |
| William R. Hathway, Adjutant | Marshal VanZile, Capt. | Andrew J. Gilbert, 2d Lt. |
| James H. Anderson, Qtm. | Nathan Hubbard, 1st Lt. | Samuel C. Wilson, 2d Lt. |
| George C. Spencer, Qtm. | Oliver Taylor, 1st Lt. | Paul Terwilliger, 2d Lt. |
| Jacob M. Leighton, Surgeon | Jacob K. R. Oakley, 1st Lt. | George W. Hennion, 2d Lt. |
| Edward B. Root, Asst. Surgeon | Archibald Ferguson, 1st Lt. | Daniel Low Jr., 2d Lt. |
| R. Howard Wallace, Chaplain | James H. Searles, 1st Lt. | George R. Brainsted, 2d Lt. |
| William H. Terwilliger, Capt. | Lawrence Brennan, 1st Lt. | Bartley Brown, 2d Lt. |
| Daniel Torbush, Capt. | James T. Chase, 1st Lt. | Lester Genung, 2d Lt. |
| James H. Anderson, Capt. | DeWitt C. Wilkin, 1st Lt. | |
| Isaac Jenkinson, Capt. | William D. Dickey, 1st Lt. | |

A company of cavalry recruited in the fall of 1861 by Morris I. McCormal as part of Col. VanWyck's "Tenth Legion," when detatched from this regiment was mustered in as Co. C, 1st Mounted Rifles, had 95 men & served 3 years.  Officers:

| | | |
|---|---|---|
| Morris I. McCormal, Capt. | Charles F. Allen, 1st Lt. | Arthur Hagen, 2d Lt. |
| Ardice Robbins, Orderly Sgt. | | C. R. Smith, Qtm. Sgt. |

Orange Co. was represented in the 7th, afterward 2d regiment of cavalry; also known as the Harris Light Cavalry.  Volunteers mostly in Co. B, under Capt. Charles E. Morton of New Windsor.  Alanson Randall, native of Newburgh, was col. 1864-5.

15th Cavalry, Co. M recruited in Orange Co. in 1863-4.  Officers:

| | | |
|---|---|---|
| William D. Dickey of Newburgh | Alfred Newbatt, 1st Lt. | Captain |
| Julius Niebergall, 1st Lt. | John Ritchie, 2d Lt. | Robert B. Keeler, 2d Lt. |

17th Independent Battery was recruited in Orange Co.  Officers:

| | | |
|---|---|---|
| Peter C. Regan, Capt. | Eugene Scheibner, 1st Lt. | Abram Kniffin, 1st Lt. |
| Martin V. McIntyre, 1st Lt. | John S. Bennett, 1st Lt. | Abram Kniffin, 2d Lt. |
| Charles S. Harvell, 2d Lt. | Abraham Smith, 2d Lt. | William H. Lee, 2d Lt. |
| Edward Kelly, 2d Lt. | | John B. Brosen, Jr., 2d Lt. |

The 1st Regiment of Engineers, known as Serrell's, had in its ranks 3-400 men from Orange Co.
Company C of the 98th NYSV was mostly recruited in Newburgh 1863-4 by Capt. James H. Anderson & Lt. J. K. R. Oakley.

# PORTRAITS OF NEWBURGH LEADING CITIZENS

Below is a list of persons whose portraits appear in *Newburgh, Her Institutuions, Industries & Leading Citizens, Historical, Descriptive & Biographical*, published by Ritchie & Hull, Proprietors of the Newburgh Journal in 1891. This old volume does not include much in the way of genealogical data on their families. Not only portraits can be found in this volume, but so are illustrations of landmarks and local businesses. This volume, and many used in this compilation, are available on microfilm from the Church of the Latter Day Saints through their Family History Libraries and is available on microfiche from the Michigan Microform Co.

George B. Adams
John C. Adams
John P. Andrews
Rev. Octavus Applegate
Thomas F. Balfe
Hugh S. Banks
Edgar C. Barnes
George Barnes (store of)
Rev. Robert H. Barr
Lewis J. Bazzoni
Rev. Robert H. Beattie
Horatio B. Beckman
George Beggs
Moses C. Belknap
James Bigler
Edward T. Bogardus
Maj. Edward C. Boynton
Capt. Ambrose Bradley
Eugene A. Brewster
Alfred Bridgeman (residence)
Jacob S. Brill
William B. Brokaw
Henry Kirke Brown
Rev. John D. Brown
John W. Brown
William R. Brown
J. B. B. Brundage
Stephen M. Bull
Ephraim Bullis
William F. Burke
Ira Caldwell (store of)
Daniel G. Cameron
Col. George A. Cantine
Rev. John W. F. Carlisle
Rev. Samuel Carlisle
Enoch Carter
Henry Carter
Abram S. Cassedy
William F. Cassedy
James Chadwick
Joseph Chadwick
Albert N. Chambers
William Chambers
Isaac C. Chapman
Joseph H. H. Chapman
Edson H. Clark
George Clark
George H. Clark
Leander Clark

Leander Clark Jr.
E. Y. Clarke
O. M. Cleveland
Gov. George Clinton
Isaac Cochran (residence)
James Cochrane
Thomas Coldwell
John Corwin
James M. Crane
C. Emmet Crawford
Mark Crawshaw
Samuel Crawshaw
James C. Cubit
W. A. M. Culbert, M.D.
James Cunningham
John Dales
Patrick Delany
Augustus Denniston
Nathaniel Deyo, M.D.
Col. William D. Dickey
James A. Donoghue
Joseph F. Donoghue
Timothy Donoghue Sr.
Charles H. Doughty
John W. Doughty
Andrew J. Downing
Charles Downing
Michael Doyle
Henry Dudley
James G. Dunphy
Frank S. Eager (store)
Grant E. Edgar
John Ellison (house)
Smith Ely, M.D.
Rev. Rufus Emery
Charles Estabrook
Enoch L. Fancher
Rev. J. G. D. Findley
Rev. John Forsyth
Nehemiah Fowler
Thomas Powell Fowler
John Galt
Walter W. Gearn
Cornelius S. Gibb
W. S. Gleason, M.D.
James H. Goodale
Charles T. Goodrich
James Gordon, M.D.
R. H. Gorrie (store)

Francis Gouldy (residence)
James G. Graham
James G. Graham Jr.
Rev. William K. Hall
Charles H. Halstead
James Hamilton
Abner J. Harper (residence)
William Harrison
William R. Harrison
James Hastings
Glen A. H. Havemeyer (residence)
Col. Edward D. Hayt
Joel T. Headley
Rev. John C. Henry
John Hilton
William Hilton
M. H. Hirschberg
Rensselaer Howell
Frank S. Hull
Ezra I. Hunter
Daniel Irwin
Rev. Alexander Jack
Gilbert E. Jacobs
Charles C. Jacobus
Charles S. Jenkins
Mrs. E. R. Johnes (residence)
Beverly K. Johnston
Rev. John Johnston
Rev. Arthur Jones
Charles F. June
William H. Kelly
George W. Kerr
Samuel G. Kimball
William G. Kimball
Rev. James B. King
R. J. Kingston, M.D. (residence)
Henry B. Lawson
William K. Leech
Chancey M. Leonard
James J. Leonard
S. J. Leslie (store of)
James J. Logan
Rev. Andrew Longacre
Francis Lynch (residence)
Thomas M. McCann
Rev. Joseph McCarrell
Rev. Robert McCartee
Henry T. McCoun
L. W. Y. McCroskery

John W. McCullough
William McMeekin
Jeremiah D. Mabie
Benjamin J. Macdonald
William K. Mailler
J. D. Malone, M.D.
Rev. Carl C. Manz
William H. Mapes
Cyrus B. Martin
John H. Martin
Thomas S. Marvel
Albert D. Marvin
Elmer E. Matthews
John W. Matthews
Theodore Merritt
Arthur M. Meyer
Rev. Emil F. Meyer
George S. Meyer
J. Blackburn Miller
James W. Miller
S. C. Mills (residence)
George R. Mitchell (store)
John J. Mitchell, M.D.
Almet S. Moffat
R. V. K. Monfort, M.D.
James B. Montgomery
John J. Monell
Bartholomew B. Moore
David A. Morrison
Charles E. Moscow
George Moshier
Munson Muir (residence)
Rev. H. V. S. Myers
Benjamin B. Odell
Benjamin B. Odell Jr.
Hiram B. Odell
James Orr
Rev. E. S. Osbon
David A. Osborn
James J. Owen
James Patten

Elias Peck, M.D.
George Peck (store)
Rev. William L. Penny
Charles Plumsted
Alfred Post
E. R. Post
Maj. James Clarence Post
Rev. Arthur Potts
Homer Ramsdell
H. Stockbridge Ramsdell (res.)
A. B. E. Remillard
Nathan H. Richardson
Samuel Ritchie
Henry Rudolph
Edward M. Ruttenber
J. W. F. Ruttenber
George A. Sanford
James H. Sarvis
Rev. F. B. Savage
Samuel Sayer
Wilmer W. Schermerhorn
John Schoonmaker (residence)
William Schram
John L. Schultz
George W. Seaman (store)
Rev. Jeremiah Searle
Augustus Senior (store)
Charles B. Shaw
E. Kane Shaw
George W. Shaw
G. H. Sheldon (residence)
Samuel E. Shipp
Henry W. Siglar
Edwin T. Smith
Lewis M. Smith
Joseph A. Sneed
Charles E. Snyder
Rev. William T. Sprole
Daniel B. St. John
Robert Sterling
Halsey R. Stevens

Edward Stocker
Dr. L. S. Straw
Clayton E. Sweet
William G. Taggart
Grant B. Taylor
James F. Templeton
William L. Theall
Rev. DeWitt B. Thompson
Rev. J. R. Thompson
Howard Thornton
Rev. William H. Tole
William D. Traphagen
John F. Tucker
John H. Valentine
Joseph VanCleft
E. A. Walsh (residence)
William S. Wands
Peter Ward
Cornelius L. Waring
Daniel S. Waring
Jonathan N. Weed
A. Y. Weller (residence)
George Weller
George C. Wenzel
John I. Westervelt
Wilbur H. Weston
Col. Charles H. Weygant
Samuel Whitaker
Robert Whitehill
L. Y. Wiggins, M.D.
John G. Wilkinson (store)
Francis A. Willard
Charles E. Williams (residence)
N. P. Willis
Arthur Wilson
Jonathan D. Wilson
Tilden H. Wilson
William Wright
Charles N. Woolley, M.D.

*Birthplace of De Witt Clinton, New Windsor.*

# ORANGE COUNTY FAMILIES
## ADDENDUM

The below families were found too late to be included in the main text.

## AMERMAN FAMILY E-163

Albert Amerman, b. Holland, settled on L.I. & later removed to NY City.

His son, Derick, b. NY City, removed to Newburgh. Derick served in the Rev. War & after the war was in business with Abel Belknap, miller at Chambers' Creek, later known as Niven's Mill. Derick was a captain & ran the sloop *Siren* between Newburgh & New York City for 40 years. He was a member of the First Presbyterian Church of Newburgh until 1796, when he joined the Associated Reformed Church at Little Britain. Derick d. 4 March 1826, aged 67. His descendants still res. in the village & vicinity.

## ROGERS FAMILY E-168

Jason Rogers was an early settler of Newburgh, of English Puritan descent. He removed from New London to Newburgh 1785/6, served in the Revolutionary War & d. aged 78 on 9 May 1836.

His son Jason was of Louisville, KY. Served as a lt. in the 1st KY Volunteers at Monterey, Mexico. He was a graduate of the military academy at West Point. This 2d Jason m. a niece of Col. Preston of SC.

## HUGH SPIER E-169

Hugh Spier was b. Glasgow, Scotland; to Newburgh, NY 1788. He was a cabinet maker & member & elder of the Associated Reformed Church. He d. 1826, aged 69. He is described as a man of strong mind and great originality of character, he possessed more ready wit and repartee than most men.

## CAPT. MACHEN OF NEWBURGH E-204-5

Capt. Machen was an English officer who came to NY before the Rev.; during the war entered service on the side of the Americans. He established a fort at the Highlands in 1777. After the war he located at Machen's Pond, now known as Orange Lake, once called Big Pond. He manufactured copper for 'change & circulation.' His son, also designated as only 'Capt. Machen,' fought in the War of 1812. Nothing further of his family is given here.

## BOOKSTAVER FAMILY E-258-9

Jacob Bookstaver (Boch Staver) in 1735 purchased land in the present Town of Montgomery. His home was a mile or two to the north of the Dutch Church, now owned by David Bookstaver, a desc. Jacob emigrated from Germany along with Frederick Sinsabaugh & Johannes Youngblood (Jong Bloet).

Jacob was the first deacon of the German Reformed church in this town.

## EAGER FAMILY ADDITIONS E-302-3, 309

This family is documented here in the families portion, but additional information is here added. William Eager the emigrant's wife was Elsa McGrada. They m. in Ireland & had two children before emigration & one b. on passage (William). The McGrada family was originally of Scotland. Their children:

Mary, m. William Monell.
Elizabeth, m. James McMunn.
Thomas, m. Martha McNeil.
Ann, m. John Davis.
WILLIAM, m. (1) Miriam Butler (no surviving issue) & (2) Ann Bull.
Jane, m. John Harlow.

WILLIAM EAGER, s/o the emigrant, is described as tall & spare; of fair complexion, with a fine Roman nose which gave character to his whole face; in temper quick & self willed, like a flash of gunpowder & all was over. He was grave & thoughtful "and we never heard him laugh." William's son Thomas m. Margaret, d/o John Blake of Neelytown.

In 1813 the Eager family suffered a malignant fever & it is recorded that the following died:

Henry, a black man aged 40, d. April 3, 1813
Thomas Eager (s/o Wm.), aged 48, d. April 11, 1813
Ann Eager, aged 73, d. April 13, 1813
William Eager, aged 85, d. April 13, 1813

## DANIEL BURT FAMILY RECORD E-425

This family is recorded on page 22 here without the children of Daniel, originally of CT, which are:

Extract from Family Record of Daniel Burt

Phebe, b. 15 July 1738, m. Daniel Lobdell.
Daniel, b. 20 Oct. 1740, m. Martha Bradner.
Martha, b. 3 April 1743, m. Daniel Whitney.
Hannah, b. 24 May 1745, m. James Benjamin.
Ruth, b. 3 July 1747, m. Edy Newbury.
Lydia, b. 1 May 1750, m. Daniel Jayne.
Sarah, b. 15 Dec. 1752, m. Joshua Carpenter.
Esther, b. 17 May 1755, m. Benjamin Coleman.
Ann, b. 27 Jan. 1758, m. Gideon Scott.
James, b. 25 Oct. 1760, m. Abigail Coe.

There is also in this source the mention of a Benjamin Bert, no relationship given to any of the above. Benjamin came to the town of Warwick c. 1760 & settled on a farm, now owned by Belden Burt, probably a desc.

## ARMSTRONG FAMILY E-426-8

The name of the first emigrant was William. [NOTE: In this copy the name of William is struck out & 'Francis' is handwritten in.] The family is Scotch, but emigrated from Ireland. The emigrant, William (or Francis), had several children, among them:
ROBERT, b. 1754.
William.
John.
Archibald.
Elizabeth Borland, still living.
Polly Jackson.

The emigrant settled early in the town & most of his children were grown up before the Revolution.

ROBERT ARMSTRONG, s/o the emigrant, m. Rachel Smith, b. 1768; their children:
Julia, b. 1 Aug. 1788, m. John Roe.
Jasper, b. 20 April 1790, m. Sarah Coe.
Robert G., b. 18 July 1793, m. Sarah A. L. Lewis.
George W., b. 7 March 1796, m. Fanny Wheeler.
Maria, b. 18 Sept. 1798, not married.
Harriet, b. 12 July 1801, m. (1) John Smith & (2) Calvin Sawyer.
John C., b. 15 April 18032, never married.
Rachel, b. 15 July 1805, m. Polladore Seward.
Sally S., m. Ira Brown.

ROBERT fought in the Battle of Minisink, was one of the first members of assembly of Orange Co. He d. at his residence in Florida, Orange Co., 30 May 1834, aged 81. His obituary is reprinted in this source.

# INDEX

256

257

Braffett, Sarah 186
Brainsted, George R. 248
Brander, John 203
Brant, Antho. Beetal 235
  Joseph 15
Brase, John 240
Breck, Benoni 239
Breed, Phoebe M. 122
Brennan, Lawrence 248
Brett, Augustus 165
  Robert 49
  Roger 49
  William 165
Brewster, --- 28
  --- (Elder) 15
  Charles A. 191
  E. A. 245
  Edward 211
  Eugene 15
  Eugene A. 15, 16, 136, 167,
    249
  Francis 15, 229, 239
  George Richard 15
  Hannah 168
  Henry 15, 211, 214, 225,
    239, 240
  Henry S. 15
  Isaac 239
  Jesse 240
  Jno. 211
  John 210, 211, 220, 229,
    238, 239
  John E. 11
  John W. A. 191
  Mary 184
  Nathan 238
  Nathaniel 15
  Nathaniel R. 15
  Ruth 76
  Ruty 76
  Samuel 15, 91, 209, 214,
    233, 234, 241
  Timothy 210, 211, 224, 238
  Walter H. 15
  William 15
  William C. 15
Briarly, Sarah 113
Brickerhoff, Susan Jane 63
Bridgeman, Alfred 249
Bridges, R. 14
Bridgum, Mary 9
Brill, Jacob S. 249
Brinckerhoff, Abraham
  Cortright 161
  Cornelia 161
  David H. 161
  Hendrick 161
  Jane 161
  Maria 161

Brinckerhoff, Martha 161
  Peter 161
  Roeloff 161
Brink, George E. 15
  Hendrikjen 159
  Hiram 15
  Ignatius 119
  Leander 15
  Solomon 175
Brinson, Maria 15, 20
  Samuel 15, 211
  Thomas 15
Bristol, Maria B. 174
  Nathan 174
Britain, James H. 102
  Sarah S. 102
Broadhead, Charles 48
  Wessel 48, 49
Brock, Robert 225, 240
  T. Hunt 15
Brockway, Robert 207
Broderick, Patrick 227, 228
Brodhead, Charles B. 44
  Harvey 181
  John 44
  Mary 44
  Wyntje 44
Brokaw, William B. 249
Bronson, --- (Mrs.) 183
  Esee 235
  Henry O. 82
  John 229
  Susan 14
Brooks, Alida W. 15
  Charles W. 15
  Chauncy 15
  Clarence 16
  Cuppe 235
  Dora L. 16
  Elsie 16
  F. B. 183
  George H. 16
  Hannah 165
  Helen 16
  John 225, 234, 239
  Jonathan 212, 224, 234, 238,
    241
  Lena C. 16
  Malcom 15
  Merry 16
  Michael 237
  Minnie M. 15
  Phoebe J. 16
Brophy, Ellen 54
Brosen, John B. 248
Bross, Hannah J. 125
Brovort, John 97
Brower, Adolphus 122
  Catharine 199
  John 111

Brown, Achsah 16
  Amelia 17
  Ann 17, 168
  Ann Eliza 16
  Anna Jane 16, 61
  Anna W. 15, 16
  Annie C. 16
  Augusta P. 16
  Bartley 248
  Betsey 146
  Bruce B. 16
  C. Frank 16
  Charles 17
  Charles F. 27
  Charles L. 16
  Chichester 16
  Daniel 242
  Daniel T. 17
  David 7, 16
  Dorastus 245
  E. A. 101
  Eber L. 16
  Edna 17
  Edward 16, 17
  Edward Allen 16
  Effa 140
  Elisha 242
  Eliza Jane 175
  Elliot 17
  Esther 17
  Eve 45
  Frank 17
  Genevieve 16
  George 16
  George Ogden 17
  Hannah 127
  Hannah Jane 16
  Hannah M. 17
  Harriet F. 17
  Hedges 17
  Helen 16, 17
  Henry 17
  Henry Kirke 249
  Hezekiah P. 17
  Ira 252
  Isaac 208, 212, 230, 232,
    233, 238
  Isabella 16
  Jacob 30, 240
  James 16, 17, 93
  James M. 51
  James P. 215
  James S. 16
  John 15, 16, 17, 31, 61, 92,
    229, 236
  John A. 149
  John C. 16
  John D. 249
  John Hobart 16
  John J. 16

Brown, John James 16
  John K. 16
  John Ross 17
  John Taylor 16
  John W. 16, 130, 249
  Josephine 17
  Joshua 229, 235
  Laura V. 16
  Leonard Wilson 16
  Linus W. 17
  Louisa 17
  Louisa Ann 17
  Lucretia 17
  Manson R. 83
  Margaret 8, 149
  Margaret T. L. 16, 92
  Martha 199
  Mary 16, 180
  Mary Frances 63
  Mary J. 74
  Mercy 93
  Milnor 247
  Minnie A. 101
  Nathaniel 17, 93
  Neal 242
  Orville J. 245
  Peter J. 137
  R. T. 17, 187
  S. C. 123
  Samuel 82, 242
  Sarah 16
  Silas C. 79
  Susie L. 16
  Thomas 17
  Thornton Knox 16
  U. Grant 17
  William 17, 238
  William R. 247, 248, 249
  William S. 17
Browne, Joseph 235
  Robert 215
Brownson, Abraham 91
  William 246, 247
Bruce, George 16
  Jeanet 16
  Robert 3
Bruen, Evelina 21
  Mary Evelina 21
Brundage, Abijah 242
  George C. 101
  J. B. B. 249
  Jonathan 207
Brunel, Jeanne Masic 46
Brush, Joshua 207
  Margaret 178
  Polly 120
  Samuel C. (Mrs.) 164
  William 18
  Zophar 120
Bruyn, Catharine 72

Carpenter, Hannah 25, 196
Hester D. 4
Isaac L. 25
Isaac R. 24
Jacob 24
James 25, 196, 235
Jane Belknap 24
Jemmy 25
Jesse 24, 105
Jesse C. 25
Joel 24
John 25, 93, 203, 219, 220,
   223, 239, 240, 242
John C. 25
John D. 37
John W. 25
Joseph 14, 63, 188, 200,
   233, 239
Joshua 251
Julia 38
Julia Ann 25
Keziah 156
L. S. 4
Lawrence F. 25
Leonard 7, 24, 25, 163
Lewis R. 26
Lillie Dale 25
Lizzie 25
Maggie Jane 25
Margaret 37
Mary 93, 222
Mary C. 25
Mary F. 25
Mary Ida 25
Mary S. 25
Michael 196, 236
Moses 210, 235
Mowbray 111
Nathaniel 25, 31
Nathaniel Bradner 25
Nehemiah 25, 231, 232
Noah 212
Oliver R. 25
Phebe 24
Rhoda 128
Richard 223
Ruth 195, 200
S. G. 25
Samuel 14, 25, 236
Sarah 14, 24
Sarah L. 25
Sarah Lydia Stearns 25
Sol. 228
Solomon 25, 195, 203, 228,
   236
Solomon G. 25
Susan 195
Timothy 239
Virgil K. 112
Warren 25

Carpenter, William 24, 26,
   38, 171, 231, 236, 240
William (Mrs.) 85
William H. 25
Carr, Anna 81
B. Seward 180
George 81, 219
John 240
Lewis C. 123
Carrel, Anna 134
Carroll, O. A. 244
Vernon B. (Mrs.) 23
William 222
Carscadden, Arthur 233
Martha 6
Carscaling, Robert 207
Carskadan, Catharine 124
Robert 124
Carson, Matilda 157
Thomas 157
Carter, Adolph 26
Ann 26
Bridget 66
Caleb 90
Catharine 26
Charles 26
Elizabeth 26, 66
Enoch 26, 40, 41, 249
George 26
Henry 249
Henry W. 26
Jonathan 26, 66, 154
Joseph 26
Margaret 26
Mary 26, 40
Rebecca 26
Richard 26
Sarah 26
Carvey, John 236
Matthias 236
Walter 147
Case, Absalom 233
Adelbert L. 26
Amelia 26
Anson 26
Bethia 123
Caleb 232
Daniel 183
David 164
Dell 26
E. Inman 26
Eliza 16
Elizabeth 21
Flora 26
George Whitfield 191
Hephzibah 162
Howard L. 26
Ira L. 26
James M. 26
Jefferson 26

Case, Jennie 55
John 26, 93, 235
John B. 26
John E. 26
Joseph 26, 236
Joseph M. 26
Joshua 183, 208
Joshua L. 26
Mary 172
Mary H. 2
Phebe 171
Phineas 229, 238
Ruth Ann 171
Sarah 8, 26
Sarah J. 26
Sarah Jane 53
Stephen 26, 208, 241
Stephen J. 26
Tisdale 26
Walter 27, 72
Walter Everett 171
Wheeler 27, 191
Casen, David 238
Cash, --- 109
Betsey 27
Daniel 27
Fanny 27
Hannah 27
Isaac 27
James M. 140
John M. 27
Mehitable 27
Meritt H. 27
Merrit H. 140
Merritt H. 171
Millicent 27
Nathan 27
Phebe M. 27
Polly 27
Reuben 27, 83, 109, 171
Sally 27, 171
Selah J. 27
Solomon V. R. 27
Stephen 242
Ziphorah 27
Cashaday, P. 225
Cashman, --- (Mrs.) 161
Casrkadan, Robert 209
Cassaday, Patrick 238
Cassedy, A. S. 27, 45
Abram S. 27, 249
Arichibald 27
J. Townsend 27
William F. 27, 249
Cassidy, P. 225
Casteel, Irma Josephine 90
Casterlin, Charles E. 27
Fred 27
Harold M. 27
Richard 27

Casterline, Jonathan 222
Caulfield, Julia 61
Causter, David 240
Cavanaugh, Catharine A. 148
Caywood, Chauncey C. 95
Elizabeth 95
Hannah M. 95
John 95
Nicholas H. 95
Celly, John 241
Chadeayne, Henry F. 27
John 27
Chadwick, James 249
Joseph 27, 249
Chamberlain, Abigail 95
Roswell W. 51
Ruby 95
Chambers, Abraham
   Goasbeck 78
Albert N. 249
Catharine 78
Daniel 212
John 92
Mark 237
Rachel 105
Susanna 44
William 204, 249
Champion, Mary 1
Chandle, Joseph 211
Chandler, --- 34
A. K. 182
Abigail 28
Abraham 236
Enos 8, 28
Experience 28
Hannah 28
John 23, 24, 28, 34, 220
Joseph 27, 28, 210, 212,
   224, 240, 243
Lydia 25, 28
Maria 23, 24
Mary 20, 28
Nath'l. 211
Nathaniel 27, 195
Phebe 28
Samuel 237
Sarah 28
Chapman, Caroline J. 78
Catharine 78
Charles F. 78
Deborah A. 78
Isaac C. 78, 249
Joseph H. H. 78, 249
Louisa 78
Mary E. 78, 174
Paddock 78
Silas 174
Susan A. 78
Thomas P. 78
William G. 78

Earll, Samuel 241
Easton, Ada 56
  Harriet 79
  Harriet D. 56
  James 56
  Nellie R. 56
  Nellie W. 56
  Sylvia E. 56
  Thomas Horton 56
Eaton, Alexander 56
  Daniel H. 56
  Gabriel 56
  James 56
  John 56, 149
  Robert 56
  Rosella 51
  Samuel 56
  Thomas 56
  William 56
Ebina, George 204
Ecker, Charles 57
  Clara 57
  Cornelius 56
  Deborah 56
  George 57
  Isaac 56
  Jan 56
  Magdalentje 56
  Phebe 56, 57
  Sarah 56, 57
  Stephen 56
  Susan 56, 57
  Sybout 56
  Theodore 57
  William 56, 57
  Wolfert 56, 57
  Wolvert 56
Edgar, Grant E. 249
Edison, Thomas 14
Edmeston, James 227
Edmiston, William 209
Edmonds, Gilbert 207
Edmonston, Cornelia Mitchell
  57
  DeWitt Clinton 57
  Harris 57
  James 57
  John Decker 57
  Sally 57
  Samuel 57
  Thomas 57
  William 57
  William Henry 57
Edsall, Almeda 92
  Alva Wisner 57
  Burt 175
  Hilah 146
  Marian 57
  Maurice 57
  Richard 33, 146

Edsall, Thomas 245
  Thomas A. 57
Egars, Elijah 237
Egbertsen, Jannetje 43
Egger, Daniel 238
  William 238
Eggers, Daniel 222
  Landrine 237
  William 222
Eldoris, John 228
Eldridge, Elisha 223
Eliot, Thomas 233
Elliot, Archibald 208
  John 235
  Joseph 235
  Margaret 121
  William Drummond 121
Elliott, Clyde 57
  Edward R. 57
  Joseph 57
Ellis, --- 42
  A. Van Horn 246
  A. Van Horne 245, 247
  Joseph G. 191
Ellison, --- (Col.) 42, 59
  John 209, 249
  Thomas 204, 209, 227, 228
  William 209
Ellsworth, Benjamin 204
  Henry 234
  James 204, 227
  Josiah 227
  William 204
Elmendorf, Anna 47
  Conrad 47
  Jenneke 44
  Margaret 44
  Margret 47
  Petrus 43
Elmendorph, Lucas 44
Elmer, --- 57, 58
  Jesse 57, 166
  Jonathan 58, 219
  Mary 57, 58
  Nathaniel 57, 58, 166, 219,
    229
  Richard A. 3
  William 57, 166
Elston, --- 33
  Erastus 95
  Esther Eliza 33
  Jacob 33, 141
  Jane 28
  Jayne 75
  Joseph S. 141
  Lemuel Ellsworth 33
  Margaret 33
  Margaret Cole 141
  Margaret Corwin 33, 141
  Mary Elizabeth 118

Elston, Sarah 33, 94
Elsworth, Moses 227
Elting, Ann Bevier 37
  Eliza Ann 59
  Elizabeth 132
  Jan 47
  Jemima 37
  Josiah 48
  Peter 49
  Roelof 48
Eltinge, Abraham 48
  Jacobus 44
  Jannetje 44
  Noah 48
  Philip 73
  Roelof 47
Ely, Caroline A. 71
  Edward 184
  Moses 12, 16
  Smith 249
Embler, Adam 242
Emerson, --- 88
  Phebe 86
Emery, Rufus 249
Emmons, Thomas J. (Mrs.)
  99
Emsley, Mary A. 71
Engles, Thomas 236
Ensign, James 220
Erlcs, John 210
Ervin, William 230
Erwin, Robert 230
  William 124, 216
Estabrook, Charles 249
Etting, Peter 64
  Sarah 64
Eustace, --- (Dr.) 24
Eustice, J. J. 24
Evans, --- 58
  Austin 58
  Charles A. 58
  Eli H. 244
  Emeline C. 141
  Frances 58
  George W. 58
  James 58, 75
  James Sidney 58
  John 58, 216, 217, 224
  John A. 58
  Sidney 58
  Thomas Grier 58
  Thomas Grubb 58
  William 58
Evens, Henery 1
  Henry 207
Everet, --- 23
  Annie 104
Everett, Abigail 58
  Addison 58, 59
  Alonson 58

Everett, Ann Eliza Adelaide
  59
  Azubah 58
  Benjamin 58
  Daniel 124, 229, 231, 241
  Darwin 59
  David 58, 59, 109
  Deborah Ann 59
  Edward Wheeler 140
  Ephraim 58, 59
  Freelove 58
  G. S. 163
  Gabriel 58
  Genevieve 59
  George 58
  George Whitfield 59
  Harriet 20
  Harvey 20, 58, 59
  Henry L. 59
  Hephzibah 58
  Hudson 86
  Isaac B. 116
  Israel 58
  J. M. 223
  John 203, 219
  Julia 58
  Lewis 58
  Lydia 58
  Oliver 58
  Phoebe C. 106
  Sarah A. 59
  Schuyler 59
  Walter 20, 58, 59
Everitt, George 241
Everson, Phebe 86
  Tho. 211
Everston, George 240
  Thomas 240
Ewen, --- (Dr.) 217

Fairchild, A. 215
  Aaron 154, 208
Fairfield, Jeremiah 22
  Paulina 22
Falconier, Justus 212, 215
Falld, William 130
Falls, --- 59
  Alexander 59, 209, 227
  Edward 59, 209, 230
  Francis 227
  Samuel 59
Fancher, Clinton W. 59
  Darius 59, 141

Fancher, Edwin 59
Elias 59
Enoch L. 249
Frank 59
Hannah 195
Julia 59
Lewis 128
Lillie 59
Margaret Lord 128
Sayer 59
Fanning, Samuel 242
Sarah Louise 128
Faren, John 239
Fargeson, Samuel 155
Farman, Abigail 33
Farnham, Stephen 95
Farnum, Diana 59
Elisha 103
Henry H. 59
John 34
Mary 195
Peter E. 59
Preston 103
Farrar, Constance 182
J. A. 182
Farrell, --- (Miss) 71
Edward F. 71
Farrington, Daniel 28
Farver, Anna 137
Faulkender, Sarah 82
Faulkener, --- (Capt.) 205
Faulkner, --- (Col.) 109
Achsah 11
James 18, 45, 209
John 11, 230
Luther Winthrop 113
Prudence 187
William 11, 116, 206, 227,
230
Faulknor, James 233
Faurot, James D. 110
Lucetta 156
Theodore 156
Fay, Helen 139
Feagles, Anna 60, 128
Anna D. 140
Caroline 59
Charles 59, 60
Clariss 59
David 59
David R. 128
Elizabeth 60
Emma 59
George W. 59
Henry 60
Henry B. 59
Henry Barney 59
Jacob 25, 60, 133, 153
Jacob H. 59
Jacob R. 59

Feagles, John 220
Mary 59, 60, 182
Mary Elizabeth 59
Mary S. 25
Nathaniel 59
Nathaniel R. 59, 60
Robert 59
Susan 59, 60, 128, 153
William 59
Fear, Thomas 227
Feber, Abram 60, 215
Catharine 60, 215
Isaac 60, 215
Margretta 78
Feef, Robert 227
Fegate, Jacob 236
Feigler, John 237
Feller, Tobias 119
Felter, Cronamus 227
Matice 205
Matthew 230
Fenton, Hugh 237
Ferger, Jeremiah 236
John 236
Ferguson, Aaron 222
Archibald 248
Elizabeth 92
Ephraim 242
James 222
John (Mrs.) 103
Julia Ann 130
Lawrence 240
Melicent 80
Richard 39
Russell S. 151
Samuel 222
Ferrier, Elmira 98
John M. 31
Ferries, Richard M. 176
Ferris, Elizabeth 123
Ferry, Frances Emily 65
Sylvester 45
Ffrench, --- (Rev. Dr.) 213
Field, Charles 240
William 36
Fields, --- 4
Fiere, Andrew 60, 215
Anna 215
Anna Maria 60
Daniel 60, 215
Johannes 60, 215
Fillmore, --- 216
Fince, John 218
Finch, Catharine 60
Clara 87
Coe 60
Daniel 223, 229
Isaac 203, 223
Jabez 237
Jacob 236

Finch, James 60, 167, 243
Jesse 60
John 60, 108, 218, 222, 236,
243
John L. 87
Julia 60, 87
Margaret 60
Mary 108
P. G. 60
Samuel 237
Sarah 60
Solomon 229, 237
William M. 108
Zophar 60
Findley, J. G. D. 249
Fine, Mary 158
Finley, Elisabeth 60
John 60, 107
Mary E. 46
Finn, Anthony 210, 229
Cornelia Seward 146
Mary Josephine 33, 142
Matthew James 142
Sarah Ann 146
Finnegan, James 246, 247
Finney, Eura E. 46
Loanna F. 46
Moses D. 46
Robert 46
Robert D. 46
Fintze, James 112
Fires, Philip 47
Fischer, Andries 60, 214
Johannes 60, 214
Maria Barbara 60, 214
Fish, Thomas 232
Fisher, Jane 43
John 204
Mary 124
Fisk, --- 60
Delaphine R. E. 60
James L. 60
John 60
Jonathan 175, 243
Mary M. 60
Moses 60
Theodore S. 60
William 60
Fiske, Jonathan 60
Robert 60
Fitch, --- (Mrs.) 65, 161
Ebenezer 118
Nathaniel 242
Susannah 118
Fitzgerald, Edward 84
Jeremiah 206
Mary 135
Thomas 220
William 225, 229
Fitzjare, William 211

Fitzpatrick, John 208
Flagg, Abigail 7
Elizabeth 10
Hannah 6
Mary 6, 10
Thomas 10
Flanagan, John H. 60
Flanigan, Hugh 228
Flavelling, Abel 235
John 235
Flemming, Elizabeth 5
Elizabeth Martin 5
William 5
Flewelling, James 242
Flewwalling, Morris 110
Flewwelling, Abel 61, 62,
127
Abigail 61
Charlotte 61, 127
Clarissa 61
Elizabeth 61
Gulford 61
Hannah 61
Jane 61
John 61
Mary 61
Morris 61
Samuel 61
Sarah 61
Flint, Isaac (Mrs.) 103
Florence, Gideon 241
John 241
Floyd, Jennie A. 26
John 197
Focken, Gerrit 48
Fogges, John (Mrs.) 103
Fondy, Elizabeth 64
Foote, Nathaniel 10
Patience 10
Forbes, Amy 29
Emeline 29
Ephraim 29
William 215, 236
Ford, --- 61
Benjamin 61
Bertha 61
Charles F. (Mrs.) 181
Charles T. 61
David 23
David J. 61
Davis 61
Harriet 23
Harriet Louise 61
Henry 61
Henry T. 61
J. Barlow 61
John 61
John M. 184
Katy 184
Patrick 61, 241

274

Gillies, Frank 67
  Frederick 67
  Homer 67
  Jacob 67
  James 67
  John 67
  John W. 67
  Martha 67
  Milton 67
  Sarah W. 67
  Wright 67
Gillis, Anna Catharine 69
  Daniel 207
  Jacob 227, 232
  Joseph 227
  Margaret 69
  Melchior 69
Gilston, Samuel 203
Gimar, Peter 223
Given, Samuel 233
Givens, May Jane 128
  Samuel 68
Glascow, Martha 109
Glass, James 67
Glatia, James 206
Gleason, W. S. 249
Glover, Andrew S. 119
Goaldsmith, Thomas 67, 68
Goble, Clarissa 172
  Mary A. 176
Godfrey, David 11, 236
  Esther 36
  Joseph 129
  M. L. 9
Goetchius, John E. 91
Goff, Elizabeth 67
  John 67
  Michael 67
Gold, Joseph 240
  Syvil 60
Goldsmith, --- 11
  --- (Capt.) 230
  Abigail 67, 68, 69, 169
  Adaline 68
  Alden 67, 68
  Ann Eliza 68, 86
  Anna 81
  Annie S. 68
  Benj. 211
  Benjamin 241
  Bethia 185
  Caleb 25, 236
  Catharine 68
  Charles 68
  Charles H. 68
  Daniel 233
  David 68
  Deborah 68
  Dicia 68
  Elisha 67, 68

Goldsmith, Elizabeth 25
  Hannah 183
  Hannah Leagh 68
  Henry 67, 68
  Henry M. 68
  I. R. 92
  James H. 68
  Jeremiah 207
  John 67, 68, 183, 184
  John Alden 68
  John D. 242
  Joseph 149
  Joshua 67, 68
  Leah 68
  Louis 69
  Martha 185
  Mary 7, 68, 141
  Mary L. 68
  Matilda 68
  Moses 242
  Phebe 68
  R. 211
  Richard 67, 195, 210, 211, 220
  Salem 242
  Sally Ann 68
  Sarah 68
  Stephen 68
  Susanna 195
  Thomas 67, 68, 211, 220, 221, 235
  Walter 68
Golow, John 17
Gomar, Peter 204
Goodale, James H. 249
Goodell, Orinda 186
Goodliffe, Hannah Anne 38
  James Yarrow 38
Goodman, Alpheus 179
Goodrich, Charles T. 249
  Giles E. 31
Goodsell, John 111
Goodyear, Wiilam 230
Gordiner, Elizabeth 159
Gordon, James 249
  John 242
Gore, --- 71
Gorrie, R. H. 249
Gott, --- 68
  Annei 68
  J. W. 173, 174
  Joseph W. 68
  Reeve Vanduzer 68
  Storey 68
Goude, George 197
Gouge, George 13
Gould, Hannah 118
  Hubbard 118
Gouldy, Francis 249
  Sarah E. 140

Gowdy, Henry 247
  James 244
  William G. 187
Graham, --- 24
  Adam 86
  Andrew 206, 227
  Catherine 16
  Florence 195
  George 16, 79
  James 206
  James G. 68, 249
  John 206, 207
  John J. 230
  Matthew 153
  Mittie 12
  Nathaniel 245
Grannis, John H. 245
Grant, Betsy 80
  Joseph 80
  William 139
Gray, James 211
  John A. C. 115
  Maggie 77
  Margaret 95
  Mary 29
  Minerva 2
  Sarah 70
Grazer, Schuyler D. 56
Greag, --- 28
Greake, William 176
Green, --- 54, 68
  Adaline 74
  Cynthia 153
  Daniel 68, 218
  David 232
  Elijah 212, 225, 239
  Emeline 68
  Hattie E. 103
  Helen A. 199
  Israel 68, 218
  James (Mrs.) 97
  John 74, 133, 217
  Jonathan 68
  Maria 113
  Mary 68
  Mary Jane 65
  Mehitable 68
  Nathaniel 68, 113
  Orange 68
  Osmer B. 68, 103, 199
  Samuel 95
  Sarah 68
Greene, Henry 194
  Mary 194
Greenleaf, John 29
Greenman, Amey 48
  Jeremiah 48
Greer, James 233
  Levi 96
Greery, Margaret 30

Greff, William 220
Gregg, Anne 115
  Catherine 115
  Hugh 211, 220, 239
  James 20
  Melissa 20
  Phebe E. 64
  Robert 220, 239
  Sylvester M. 64
  Thomas 240
  William 239
  William P. 106
Gregory, Benj. 211
  Benjamin 68, 210, 220, 239
  Catherine E. 69
  Elizabeth 164
  Elmer 69
  George 69
  George Elmer 69
  Goldsmith 69, 150
  Hannah 68
  Harvey 69
  Hiram 68
  James 68
  John 9, 69
  John Budd 75
  John H. 69
  Katy 68
  Lyman 242
  Mabel 74
  Margaret 8
  Mary 8
  Mary Jane 69
  Mary Louise 158
  Noah 68, 69
  Phoebe 9
  Samuel 68, 69
  Samuel O. 8, 74
  Sarah 9
  Sarah A. 69
  Seth 74
  Stephen S. 69
  Sylvester 68
  William H. 69
Grier, --- (Rev.) 69
  Frances Tuthill 69
  George 69
  George M. 69
  James A. 246, 247
  Jane 69
  John D. 69
  Mary Elizabeth 69
  Smith 69
  Thomas 69
  Thomas Evans 69
  Washington Decatur 69
  William 69
Griffin, David 36
  Edward 38
  John 36

278

Hudson, Ethel 86
Grace 86
Harrie 41
Henry 224
Huldah 12
John 210, 211, 220
Mittie 164
Richard 207
William 12, 211
William J. 85
William Reeves 86
Hue, Anne 48
Huff, James 240
Solomon 222
William 222, 237
Zephaniah 236
Hughey, James 86
John 86
Reobert 86
Robert 227
Hulbert, Eleazer (Mrs.) 103
Hulet, Sutherland 211
Hulett, Cyrus B. 86
J. Leslie 86
Joseph B. 86
Hull, A. Gerald 37
Benjamin 137
Frank S. 249
John 139
Rhoda 137
Hulse, Abigail 86
Addie B. 87
Ann 87
Barney H. 86
Benjamin 86
Charles J. 86
Clarissa 113
Edward 86
Edwin 68, 86
Elbert L. 87
Elisha 222, 236
Elizabeth 55, 86, 115
Elmendore R. 86
Eugenia C. 86
Everett B. 87
Fanny 86
Frances A. 86
George E. 86
Gilbert 86
Gilbert O. 143
Gilbert W. 86
Harriet A. 86, 152
Harriet Amelia 86
Henry L. 86
Hephzibah 180
Hudson E. 86, 166
Hudson K. 166
Jacob 238
James 86, 222, 237
James W. 86

Hulse, Janet P. 87
John B. 86, 152
John Edgar 86
John H. 87
Jonas 117, 129, 180, 181, 242
Julia 86
Julia A. 86
Justus 211, 239
LaGrange W. 86
Lottie B. 86
Maira 86
Martin 86
Mary 86, 87
Mary A. 86
Miriam 171
Oliver 86
Permelia A. 86
Phineas 86
Robert Emmet 87
Sarah 86, 196
Silas 86, 181, 222
Stephen 211, 240
Susan 86
Theodore 86
Thomas 86, 239
Thomas E. 86
Thomas N. 68, 86
Wilas 236
William 86
William A. 87
Hummell, Lillian C. 157
Humphrey, Ann 135
Charles 87
David 209
Hugh 241
James 209, 214, 230, 233
John 87, 214
Humphries, Sarah 49
Hunn, Catharine 87
Cornelia V. E. 186
Freneau 87
John S. 87, 186
John T. 87
Margaret 87
Mary 87
Peter F. 87
Thomas 87
Hunt, --- 87
Aaron 36
Charlotte 36
Clara R. 14
Hannah 108
Moses 232
Robert 87
Robert O. 87
Sarah Frances 139
Stephen 143
Hunter, --- 77, 87
--- (Dr.) 164

Hunter, Ann 82, 87
Archibald 228
Catharine 130
Catherine A. 164
David 112
Dermeda 70
Emily A. 87
Ezra I. 249
Fannie R. 52
Fanny 51
Frances 87
George 87
James 87, 206, 228
Jane 82
Jane Frances 54
Johanis M. 20
John 87, 230
Lorinda 165
Mary 28, 68
Mary E. 87, 164
Mary Ellen 114
Matthew 87, 155, 216, 230
Robert 82, 87, 206, 228, 230
Robert D. 165
Samuel 87, 248
Sarah 87
Stephen 87
William 212, 238
Huntley, --- 121
Hurd, Josiah 146
Hurlbut, F. (Mrs.) 103
Hurley, Thomas 212
Hurtin, William D. (Mrs.) 15
Hussey, Anna 142
Frederick 142
Margaret 142
Hutchins, --- 87
John Nathan 87
Huzzy, Polly 45
Hyatt, Belle 59
Mary 9
Sarah 9
Thomas 9
Hyberts, Ariaen 159
Hynard, Mary E. 64
Hyndman, Robert 87
William Hugh 87
Hyte, Ida Bronk 100

Ingersoll, --- (Mr.) 199
Catherine 130
Inkhoorn, Sarah 118

Innis, --- 88
Aaron 88
Benjamin 88
Elsie 88
James 88
Jane 88
Keziah 88
Lydia 88
Peter 88
Rebecca 88
Ross 88
Sally 88
Sarah 88
Sygant 88
William 88
Ireland, Stephen 207
Thomas 207, 235
Irwin, Daniel 249
Mary 188
Robert 124
William 88
Isaacs, Harriet M. 5
Iseman, Catherine 88
Charles Wesley 88
Christine 88
George H. 88
John E. 88
Isham, Lucy 10
Ivers, Alfred E. 75

Jack, Alexander 249
Jackson, --- 88, 188, 220
--- (Capt.) 210
Abel 237
Benjamin 237
Charles T. 88
Charles T. (Mrs.) 70
Clara 90
Daniel 88
Daniel T. 242
Elizabeth 11, 75
Ezra T. 88
Fanny 88
George 80
Hamilton 88
Henrietta 80
Henry 88
James 203, 206, 209, 234
John 88, 229, 235, 241
John C. 88
John C. (Mrs.) 88
Keturah Conkling 3
Melvina 113

Morris, William 236
Morrison, --- (Col.) 149
--- (Doct.) 207
David A. 116, 250
Hamilton 116
James 116
James W. 116
Jane H. 116
John 116, 233, 237
John H. 116
Maria 108
Martha B. 101
Mary A. 116
Rob. 233
William J. 116
William P. 116
Morrow, Nancy E. 22
Morse, --- 4
Annie 162
Mortimer, Emily 36
Morton, Charles E. 248
Charles F. 214
Edmund 172
Joseph 243
Margaret 172
Mory, John 238
Moscow, Charles E. 250
Mosher, James 242
Theophilus 207
Moshier, Anna 116
George 116, 250
Henry S. 186
Mabel 116
Mosier, James 237
Mouis, Johannes 205
Moul, Christoffel 204
Johannis 66
Philip 206
Mould, --- 117
Abraham 217
Anna 117
Anna Mary 117
Annie 44
Catharine 117
Christoffel 116
Christopher 117
Christopher J. 117
Daniel 117
Elenore 117
Elizabeth 71, 116
Emily 17
Emma F. 17
Eve 112, 117
Hamilton Morrison 71
Herman 117
Jessie 117
John 17, 117
John C. 117
John D. 117
Jonathan 116

Mould, Lemma 117
Magdelena B. 196
Maria 116
Martha 117
Mary 15, 117, 176, 177
Mary Esther 117
Moses 117
Philip 117
Ruamer 117
Stuffel 228
Thomas 143
William 117
Mowrey, Clarissa 192
Ebenezer 192
Mozer, Mary Josephine 160
Muir, Munson 250
Munson G. 131
Mulford, Lynden 79
Mulinder, Peter 227
Muliner, William 209
Mullenix, Priscilla 155
Mullicks, William 242
Mullinder, Peter 214
Mulliner, Alexander 130
Sarah 21
William 209, 234
Mullock, Mary Leverick 93
Munn, Hannah 10
Sally D. 8
Munnel, William 205
Munnell, George 205
Munson, Elizabeth 34
Murphy, John 234
Marguerite I. 107
Murray, --- 24, 117
Abby M. 117
Alexander 117
Amanda 117
Ambrose 117
Ambrose S. 117
Ambrose Spencer 194
Andrew S. 245
Archibald Y. 117, 242
Brewster 118
Charles 117
Cynthia 117
David 117, 180
Edmund B. 117
Ellen 117
Ezra 118
George 117
George W. 117
Henry B. 117
Henry S. 245, 246
Henry Spencer 117
Hugh 239
Jacob 117
James 117
Jeanette 187
Jehiel 118

Murray, John 117
Jonathan 118
Lucretia 118
Mary Ann 117
Reuben 118
Robert R. 117
Roswell 118
Roswell Gould 118
Sally 117
Viliate 118
William 117
William E. 118
Wisner 117
Murry, Henry S. 246
Murtfeldt, Edward 118
Henry W. 118
Mussey, Alfa 2
Mvanjoy, Francis 236
Myer, John 148
Martin 236
Myers, Christopher 237
Daniel 118, 222, 237
Daniel C. 118
Daniel VanAuker 118
Frank D. 118
H. V. S. 250
Henry 239
Jacob 232
John 222, 237
Phoebe 135
Samuel S. 118
Sarah 162
Mynderse, Burger 204
Myndetsen, Burger 204
Myres, Andrew 9

Nanny, David 210
Frances M. 118
Gardner K. 118
Johnson G. 118
Joseph 118
Maria 118
Sadie O. 118
Thomas S. 31
Ncafie, Alfred 118
Cornelius 118
Neail, Frank 40
Neal, --- (Mr.) 205
Nealy, James 227
Nearpass, Anna W. 119
Baltus 118
Benjamin 118

Nearpass, Catharine 118
Charles H. 119
Charlotte A. 119
Elizabeth 118
Emma E 119
Horace S. 119
Jacob 118
John 118
Mary 118
Michael 118, 119
Rachel 118
Sarah Temperance 119
William 118
William H. 118, 119
Neeley, Adam 119
Andrew 230
David 119
Isabel 119
Isabella 119
John 119
Mary 119
Matthew 119
Robert 119
William 119
Neels, Peter (Mrs.) 113
Neely, Abraham 45
Alexander 204
Edward 209
Grandy John 206
Henry 206
Henry Man 209
James 209
John 204, 222
Little John 206
Margaret B. 83
Matthew 234
Samuel 204
Thomas 205, 206
William 206
Neils, John 228
Matthew 228
Robert 228
Thomas 228
Neily, John 228
Nellis, Andrew J. 4
Nelson, --- 119
Cornelius 119
Elisha 119
Jacob 66, 119
John 214
Justus 119
Miphiboseth 119
Moses F. 119
Nestell, Harriet E. 201
Newbatt, Alfred 248
Newbold, Charles (Mrs.) 138
Newbury, Edy 251
Newkerk, Catharine 44
Conrad 44
Cornelius 44

297

Rose, Henry Elkanah 135
Israel 211
Johanna 135, 215
John 17
John B. 4
John C. 135
Joseph H. 135
Julietta 2
Leah 143
Lyman O. 135
Martha 17
Nellie E. 135
Peter 111, 135, 215
Silas 135
Stephen 190
William 44, 234
William C. 135
Rosegrout, Daniel 237
Rosekrans, Daniel 229
Rosencrants, Phoebe 199
Rosenkrans, Alexander 142
Dirck 142
Lydia 142
Maria 142
Ross, --- 136
Agnes 135
Alexander 124, 135
D. C. Houston 135
E. C. (Mrs.) 30
Edward 136
Edward C. 135
Emeline 92, 135
George H. 136
Henry 135
James 124, 135
Mary 135
Mary McClean 136
Moses P. 245
Robert 124, 135, 136, 207,
   208, 215, 230, 232
Sybil 88
Theo 135
William 124, 135, 136, 243
Round, John Wesley 136
Seward U. 136
Rouse, Peter 222
Rowe, Elizabeth 182
Matthew 182
Sarah E. 194
Rowell, Bessie 4
Warren 4
Rowland, Joseph 136
Joseph W. 136
Royce, Alpheus B. 136
Ann E. 136
Anna 103
Charles B. 136
Edith C. 136
Edward G. 136
Herbert B. 136

Royce, Isaac B. 136
James F. 136
Margaret A. 136
Nathaniel A. 136
Nellie B. 136
Solomon 136
Stephen W. 136
Thomas T. 136
William B. 136
William F. 136
Rudolph, Henry 136, 250
Rudyard, Ruth 114
Ruggles, Archibald E. 136
Edgar 136
Emma S. 136
Ruhl, Maia Catherine 72
Rump, Christian 155
John 207
Rumsey, --- 136
Abbie A. 190
Charles 136
Daniel 240
David 235
Earl 136
Eliza 136
Nathan 136
Nathan D. 136
Phebe 81
Phineas 81, 136, 220, 235
Phoneas 136
Royal S. 136
Samuel 190
Rundle, --- 199
Joel 199
Russel, William 207, 232
Russell, --- 137
Edward C. 137
Humphrey 137
John W. 137
Margaret 8
Phebe A. 137
William T. 137
Rutan, Hannah Maria 96
Robert 96
Ruttenber, Charles B. 137
E. M. 99
Edward M. 137, 250
J. W. F. 250
Walker F. 137
Ryan, John 242
Ryder, Henry 26
Ryerson, --- 96, 137
Abraham 138
Abram 137
Amos 137
Ann 137, 186
Anna 137
Annie 137
Blanding 137
Catherine 137, 138

Ryerson, Daniel B. 137
David 137
Della 137
Dolly 138
Elizabeth 31, 60, 137
Emma 137
Francis 137
George 137
Hannah 137
Hassel 138
Henry Ogden 137
Jacob M. 32
Jane 137, 138, 139
Jesse 137
John 137, 138
John B. 137
John N 137
John William 137
Joris 137
Lucas 137
Luykas 137
Martin 32, 137, 186
Mary 137
Nicholas 96, 137, 138
Nicholas N. 137
Peter 138
Peter N. 60, 96, 137
Richard 31
Ryer 137
Thomas 137
Thomas C. 137
William A. 137
Ryneck, Maria 81
Rysdyk, Elizabeth 133, 138
William M. 138
William T. 138
Rysdyke, Garret 104

Sacket, Samuel 238
Sackett, Charlotte 185
J. 210, 211
Joseph 2, 214
Justus 225
William W. 215
Sadlier, J. E. 114
Sagendorph, Frank 176
Sailbolt, John 147
Katarena 147
Salisbury, Abraham 72
Abram 72
Anna S. 189
Phoebe 73

Salmon, Gideon 236
Phineas 236
Samis, Henry 237
Sammis, James A. 98
Sammons, Gustavis 143
Rachel 143
Sampeon, Gershom 222
Sample, Sarah C. 18
Samson, John 241
Sanders, Rachel 59
William 204
Sandford, Ann 139
Charles 186
David 139
Dorcas 139
Ephraim 139
Esther 139
Ezra 139
Hannah 139
John 139
Mary 139
Matthew 139
Olive 139
Patience 139
Thomas Heigh 138
Sands, --- 138
Anna P. 132
Cornwall 240
David 132, 138, 224
Eleazer 138
Elizabeth 138
Esther 147
James 203
Levinah 138
Marietta 138
Mersey 138
Nathaniel 138, 211, 224
Phebe 138
Samuel 138, 207, 232, 241,
   243
Sandstar, Joshua 239
Sanford, --- 140
Abigail 139
Abram 139
Adaline 140
Addie 140
Alfred Harris 139
Anna 139
Bertha Elizabeth 140
Bessie 140
Catherine 139
Charles 140
Clara 139
David 138
Dolly 139
Ebenezer 138
Edward Burt 140
Eliza 139
Ella 139
Emily 139, 140

306

Swim, John 161
  Margaret (Mrs.) 66
  Samuel 161
  William 161
Swits, Cornelis 43
  Jacob 43
Symes, Lancaster 32
Symons, Adrientje 159
Sypher, --- (Mrs.) 163
  O. L. 163

Taber, Reuben 240
Tackling, James 222
Taft, Daniel 110
  Elizabeth G. 199
  Mary E. 110
  Robert 162
  Royal M. 162
  Thomas 162, 246, 247
  Thomas Knapp 162
Taggart, James C. 247
  William G. 250
Talbot, Robert S. 17
Talcott, Abigail 8
  David 8
  Jeffery 8
  Jonathan 8
  Josiah 8
  Lydia 8
  Olive 8
  Samuel 8
  Selden H. 162
Tallman, Phebe 194
  Samuel 194
  Sarah 194
Talmadge, --- 242
Talman, Frances M. 137
  Samuel 137
  Sarah 117
Tansdell, Gamaliel 236
Tappan, Myron A. 248
Tappen, Cornelia 30
  Johannes 49
  Peter 44
  Petres 30
  Rebecca 49
  Teunis 49
  Tyante 30
Tate, Esther A. 4
  John 205
  N. 126
Taylor, --- 54

Taylor, Alexander 233
  Angus 102
  Ann 162
  Anne 162
  Archibald 162
  Archibald R. 162
  Augusta 102
  Caleb 210
  Daniel 162
  E. 240
  Eleazer 240
  Emily 162
  Grant B. 250
  Hamilton R. 162
  Isaac 172
  James 233
  James W. 156
  John 76, 162
  John (Mrs.) 128
  John C. 162
  John C. R. 190
  Maria 102
  Mary Ann 62
  Morrison 243
  Nehemiah 207
  Oliver 162, 248
  Rachel 162
  Sarah A. 172
  Sarha 183
  Thomas J. 3
  William 162
  William E. 195
Teasdale, --- (Judge) 98
  Experience 98
Teed, Jesse 238
  Zepher 212
Telford, Alexander 233
  William 233
Teller, Helena 43
Templeton, James F. 250
TenBroeck, Jacob 43, 44
  Maria 43, 48
  Rachel 72
  Wessel Jacobse 43
TenBroock, Maria 44
TenEyck, Abraham 44
  Andrew 162
  Blandina 44
  Catharine 44
  Coe H. 162
  David 162
  George 162
  George W. 162
  Grietje 44
  Grietjen 47
  Hutson G. 162
  Mary L. 162
Tenhout, Severgn 203
Tennent, Gilbert 92
  William 92

Tennyck, David F. 162
  Elizabeth 162
  Francis 162
  Francis W. 162
  Harry P. 162
  Hattie 162
  Thomas 162
ter Willige, Evert 204
  John 204
Terhune, Adam 137
  Robert 110
Terry, --- 23, 162, 163
  Adeline 139
  Austin 162, 163
  Constant 162
  Dorothy 162
  Fannie E. 163
  Flora Bell 163
  Haven 162
  Havens 162
  Hephzibah 162
  Iravine 183
  Jemima 123
  John 162
  Lille Gertrude 163
  Mary 162
  Mary E. 147
  Nicholas 162
  Noah 222
  Sarah 163
  Tuttle 162
  VanRensselaer 162
  William A. 163
  Wilmot A. 163
  Wilmot C. 162, 163
  Youngs 162
Tervelger, Evert 49
Terwillager, Maria 79
Terwillege, Evert 203
  Johannes 203
Terwilliger, Cornelius 208
  Henrick 206
  Henrycon 205
  Matthew 234
  Nathaniel 242
  Paul 248
  Thomas P. 248
  William H. 248
Tery, Azuba 163
Tether, Beatrice M. 163
  Clifford F. 163
  Edward J. 163
  Eva J. 163
  Floyd E. 163
  Hannah 163
  Harry L. 163
  James E. 163
  Russell K. 163
  Sarah A. 163
Teunis, Maria 43

Thatcher, Caroline Knox 154
Thayer, Anna B. 25, 163
  Caroline M. 25, 163
  Charles F. 25, 163
  Elijah 163
  Elijah Carpenter 116
  Elizabeth C. 25, 163
  George A. 25, 163
  John 25, 163
  John S. 25, 163
  William 25, 163
  William L. 25, 163
Theal, Joseph 228
  Polly 13
Theall, Charles 62
  Margaret 62
  William L. 250
Thew, --- 168
  Abigail 163
  Daniel 163
  Elizabeth T. 163
  Garret 163, 168
  Gilbert 163
  James 163
  John 163
  Tunis 163
Thomas, Abigail 179
  Eph. 234
  John 139, 207
  Joseph 234
  Michael 211
  Moses 242
  Sally Ann 139
Thompason, Julia 82
Thompson, --- 57, 164, 166
  Abijah W. 164
  Albert 164
  Alexander 35, 164, 165
  Alexaner 20
  Alfred 165
  Andrew 84, 164, 206
  Ann 86
  Ann Eliza 89
  Ann Joline 171
  Anna 58, 164, 166
  Anna May 166
  Augustus 164
  Benjamin 165, 166
  Benjamin F. 165
  Caroline Augusta 165
  Carrie 165
  Catharine Ann 165
  Catharine G. 122
  Catherine 64
  Charles 165
  Charles F. 122
  Charles Hudson 166
  Charles M. 165, 166
  Christian 14
  Cornelia A. 165

Other Heritage Books by Martha and Bill Reamy:

*Erie County, New York Obituaries as Found in the Files of*
*The Buffalo and Erie County Historical Society*

*Genealogical Abstracts from Biographical and*
*Genealogical History of the State of Delaware*

*History and Roster of Maryland Volunteers, War of 1861-1865, Index*

*Immigrant Ancestors of Marylanders, as Found in Local Histories*

*Pioneer Families of Orange County, New York*

*Records of St. Paul's Parish, [Baltimore, Maryland], Volume 1*

*Records of St. Paul's Parish, [Baltimore, Maryland], Volume 2*

*St. George's Parish Register [Harford County, Maryland], 1689-1793*

*St. James' Parish Registers, 1787-1815*

*St. Thomas' Parish Register, 1732-1850*

*The Index of Scharf's History of Baltimore City and County [Maryland]*


Other Heritage Books by Martha Reamy

*1860 Census Baltimore City: Volume 1, 1st and 2nd Wards*
*(Fells Point and Canton Waterfront Areas)*

*Abstracts of South Central Pennsylvania Newspapers*
*Volume 2, 1791-1795*

*Early Families of Otsego County, New York, Volume 1*

*Early Church Records of Chester County, Pennsylvania, Volume 2*
Martha Reamy and Charlotte Meldrum

*Abstracts of Carroll County Newspapers, 1831-1846*
Martha Reamy and Marlene Bates

2466021

Made in the USA